Christology of the Old Testament
Volume 1 - Primary Source Edition

Reuel Keith, Ernst Wilhelm Hegstenberg

Nabu Public Domain Reprints:

You are holding a reproduction of an original work published before 1923 that is in the public domain in the United States of America, and possibly other countries. You may freely copy and distribute this work as no entity (individual or corporate) has a copyright on the body of the work. This book may contain prior copyright references, and library stamps (as most of these works were scanned from library copies). These have been scanned and retained as part of the historical artifact.

This book may have occasional imperfections such as missing or blurred pages, poor pictures, errant marks, etc. that were either part of the original artifact, or were introduced by the scanning process. We believe this work is culturally important, and despite the imperfections, have elected to bring it back into print as part of our continuing commitment to the preservation of printed works worldwide. We appreciate your understanding of the imperfections in the preservation process, and hope you enjoy this valuable book.

CHRISTOLOGY

OF THE

OLD TESTAMENT,

AND A

COMMENTARY

ON THE

REDICTIONS OF THE MESSIAH BY THE PROPHETS.

BY

E. W. HENGSTENBERG,

Doctor of Phil. and Theol. and Professor of the latter in the University of Berlin.

TRANSLATED FROM THE GERMAN,

BY REUEL KEITH, D. D.

Professor in the Protestant Episcopal Theological Seminary of Virginia.

VOL. I.

CONTAINING THE GENERAL INTRODUCTION AND THE
MESSIANIC PROPHECIES OF ISAIAH.

ALEXANDRIA, D. C.:
PUBLISHED BY WILLIAM M. MORRISON.
ANDOVER: PRINTED BY GOULD AND NEWMAN.
1836.

Entered according to Act of Congress, in the year 1836,
BY REUEL KEITH,
in the Clerk's Office of the District Court for the District of Columbia.

AUTHOR'S PREFACE.

The basis of the present work is formed of prelections respecting the subject of which it treats. The author held them with peculiar pleasure, and with the conviction, how necessary it is, and how salutary it would be to Christianity and Theology, for the Old Testament to regain its ancient and well grounded rights; and the wish to contribute something to this in a wider circle also, induced him to revise and enlarge his work; without intending however that all traces of the mode in which it originated should be effaced.

Although the author is conscious of having labored with honest and persevering diligence, yet he is very far from not perceiving the imperfections of his work. It was the object here, where old and new theological prejudices stand in opposition to each other, to strike out a new path, and in the very outset always to find the right course, and satisfy all requisitions, was a task difficult in itself, and impossible for him to perform. Yet he believes that the work, even in its present form, can serve in some manner to relieve the pressing necessity, and at the same time prepare the way for the appearance of one more complete. He proceeds upon the principle, that before the erection of the new edifice, the rubbish must be thoroughly removed and the ground cleansed; hence his work receives an irregular form and a temporal character; but perhaps the author of the more complete one, will give him some thanks, when he finds he can now commence the new structure without hindrance.

At the same time, however, he entertains a firm and unshaken conviction, that the principles he has followed are the only true ones, and that the essential doctrine of his work, not indeed by the force of his arguments (for the most specious refutation of these would leave the former untouched) but by its intrinsic truth must prevail, as it has done in all ages of the church. All assaults directed against that, will leave him entirely uninjured, as not affecting what is properly his own. On the other hand, he will gratefully receive every correction relating to particulars, and adopt it, if after deliberate examination, he finds it well founded. That this instruction should always be imparted in the proper tone, judging from what himself and others have often experienced he dares not expect, indeed he would contradict his own fundamental views in theology if he only greatly desired it. As his concern is with the subject alone, it will not be difficult for him to separate what relates to that, from what relates to the person. It is only the former that he will notice, either in the way of acknowledgment, or refutation. May the Lord of the church bless a work begun and completed in dependance on him, and make it the means of confirming the faith of at least some individuals.

TRANSLATOR'S PREFACE.

It would be superfluous for the translator to speak in commendation of this work, since he has given the highest expression of his estimation of its value, by bestowing upon it the labor requisite to make it accessible to those who are unacquainted with the language of the original.

It may however be satisfactory and useful to the reader to be informed, that it has been my object to present him with (what the work professes indeed to be) a *translation*; to put him fairly in possession, not of my own thoughts, but those of the author, so that the translation shall be to the English reader, what the original is to the German. I am very sensible, that I have not been able to reach the standard of *perfection* at which I aimed; but trust that I have not altogether failed in the accomplishment of my object. This hope, I may add, is strengthened by the opinion expressed by more competent judges than myself, who have done me the favor to examine portions of the work.

The translator feels himself greatly indebted for the general correctness of the typography, to the gentlemen at Andover, to whom, in his absence, the supervision of the press was entrusted. Some errata, however, of considerable importance, have escaped their vigilance. These, at least so far as they have fallen under my notice, are printed at the close of the volume. I can only commend them to the notice and the candor of the reader. From those who are at all acquainted with the difficulty of attaining entire correctness in the printing of books, a censorious judgment is certainly not to be feared.

Hoping that this translation may serve to promote the great object for which, I am persuaded, the original was composed by its highly gifted author, the glory of Christ and the salvation of mankind, and with an earnest prayer that it may be attended with His blessing, I present as an humble contribution to the theological literature of my country, and bespeak for it the indulgence of the critical reader towards its many imperfections.

THE TRANSLATOR.

Theol Sem near Alexandria, D C.
July 15, 1836

CONTENTS.

GENERAL INTRODUCTION.

Chapter First.—Preliminary Observations, ... 9
Chap. Second.—History of the Messianic Prediction among the Hebrews.
  1. Messianic Predictions in the Pentateuch, . 25
    a In Genesis: 26
      The Protevangelium. Gen. 3. 14, 15, . 26
      Gen 9 26, 27, ... 41
      Promises to the Patriarchs, . . . 46
      Gen. 49 10, ... 50
    b. In the remaining Books of the Pentateuch, . 63
      Num. 24· 17, ... 63
      Deut. 18. 15—18, ... 67
  2 The Messianic Psalms, ... 73
    a. Psalms in which the Messiah in his glory is described, ... 76
      Psalm II, ... 76
      Psalm XLV, ... 86
      Psalm LXXII, ... 98
      Psalm CX, ... 107
    b. Psalms in which the suffering Messiah is described, ... 121
      Psalm XVI, ... 121
      Psalm XXII, ... 130
      Psalm XL, ... 148
  3. Predictions of the Messiah in the Prophets, . . 152
Chapter Third.—The Deity of the Messiah in the Old Testament, ... 161
Chap. Fourth.—A suffering and atoning Messiah in the Old Testament, ... 187

CONTENTS.

Chap Fifth.—The nature of Prophecy, . . . 217
Chap. Sixth.—The means of proving the reference of particular prophecies to the Messiah, . . . 245
Chap Seventh.—Literature of the Messianic Predictions, . 259

THE MESSIANIC PROPHECIES OF ISAIAH.

Introductory Remarks, ... 276
   Chap II—IV, ... 287
   Chap VII, ... 307
   Chap. 8 23—9 6, ... 343
   Chap XI, XII, ... 366
General Preliminary Remarks on Isa. XL—LXVI, . . 395
Genuineness of Isa. XL—LXVI, ... 398
Contents of Isa XL—LXVI, ... 424
   Chap 42 1—9, ... 444
   Chap. 49. 1—9 461
   Chap. 50· 4—11, ... 477
   Chap 52· 12—LIII, ... 484—560

GENERAL INTRODUCTION.

CHAPTER I.

PRELIMINARY OBSERVATIONS

The fall of man rendered necessary divine institutions for his salvation. Having thereby broken off his vital connexion with God, and lost the favor bestowed upon him in his creation, man still retained indeed faint traces of the Divine image, consisting in an obscure remembrance of his original happy condition, and an earnest desire to regain it; yet this was insufficient of itself to effect the great end of his being, a reunion with his Maker. It was of value only as it made him capable of receiving the aid afforded from above; it rendered his return to God possible, but could not be its efficient cause. The need of a Divine interposition for the restoration of fallen man, who was no more able of himself to regain his lost communion with God than to establish this communion at first, is evident from experience and observation, which show that he is averse to good, inclined to evil, and incapable of fulfilling by his own strength the demands of the holiness and justice of God. But with respect to the way in which God should interpose, we could determine nothing without experience. No speculative reason could have decided before the establishment of the Divine Institutions for man's salvation, that they must be precisely what they are; nor can it prove by a priori arguments that the method adopted was the only one that was possible, was necessary, and founded in the nature of God. We learn its necessity rather from the fact of its having been adopted, for God does nothing which is unnecessary and has not its foundation in His nature. We are moreover taught it in Scripture, which represents the method revealed as necessary, and the only one that was possible. And this testimony is confirmed by our own experience, since in proportion as we appropriate to ourselves the means of salvation which God has provided, we learn, not merely from human reason, but from the witness of the Spirit, that these means, and these only, are efficacious to heal the diseases of our souls.

The revelation contained in Holy Scripture teaches us, that the centre of all divine institutions for our salvation, is a manifestation of God in the flesh, the mission of a divine Redeemer, who by his perfectly innocent life, his undeserved sufferings and his expiatory death, delivered from original sin and the actual sins which flow from it, (the consequences of the transgression of Adam, with whom all his descendants are mysteriously connected,) and justified before God all those, who through faith in Him are made partakers of all the blessings which He procured, and become one with Him; a Redeemer who vanquished the prince of this world, and despoiled Him of that right which He had gained by their voluntary submission to His sway, who presented to them in their own nature an image of the divine holiness, which they might affectionately embrace, and attain a growing conformity to it in the present life, to be perfected in that which is to come; and supplied them with strength for this through the Holy Spirit, procured again for mankind by His death, who as a new source of life implanted in man reunited him to God in the bonds of life and love and became the mediating principle between them both, a Redeemer who in opposition to that kingdom of darkness established on earth with the fall of man, of which Satan was the head and all natural men the subjects, founded an extensive kingdom of God, of which He was himself the Head, and whose subjects should be all those who should suffer themselves to be delivered by Him from their former bondage, and become incorporated with Him, united with their Head and with one another by the bond of the Holy Spirit, as the members of the kingdom of darkness are connected with their head and with each other by the bond of the spirit of the world, which their own strength cannot break; who finally when the present course of the world shall have ended, will abolish even the outward consequences of the fall, the evil which sin has occasioned, and, after the utter extinction of the kingdom of darkness, glorify his divine kingdom on the renovated earth.

Why the sending of this Divine Redeemer and Restorer, which had been purposed from eternity,[*] did not immediately succeed the fall—why four thousand years must first elapse, and in the mean time diseased humanity seek in vain to heal itself, in the absence of the

---

[*] See Knapp Dogm. II p 120

divine Physician who alone could give relief, is a question too profound for human wisdom, which in this life is imperfect, and even when it has humbled itself under the mighty hand of God, receives from Him only the light it needs for sanctification. From the lateness of his advent we can only with certainty conclude, that He could not have been sent at an earlier period, if the results of his mission were to be, in all respects, the same as at present. We can however with great probability assign the reason existing in the human race for this delay, if we consider the nature and condition of fallen man, and God's dispensations towards him, from the time of his apostasy to the coming of the Redeemer. We perceive that God could send his Son into the world, only when the way was first sufficiently prepared for his advent. The design of this preparation could be none other than to produce among an important portion of the human race, such a state of things as is requisite in order to the acceptance of the divine aid when proffered. For although man has nothing positively good to present to God, when he returns to him, but must receive all at his hands, yet he must have a susceptibility for the divine blessings, before he can enjoy them. With the heathen and the Jews God pursued very different methods, in order to qualify them for the reception of his mercy.

The heathen were in general left to themselves. God suffered the disease, which had poisoned their whole nature, to put forth all its power, that when the Physician should appear, they might not deceive themselves respecting their true condition. The fundamental evil of fallen man is pride—the feeling that he possesses powers and advantages, which, even before his apostasy, he enjoyed only in consequence of his fellowship with God. Pride, however, is never more effectually humbled, made to feel its weakness, and look beyond itself for aid, than when left to make a trial of its strength. At the time of the Messiah's advent this trial had been fully made by the most distinguished people of the heathen world. They had already wearied themselves sufficiently long in their own ways, and had learned by degrees that they could lead to nothing firm and sure. Their religions, the offspring of human invention, had outlived their influence; and the illusion which once blinded the eyes of their votaries had passed away. In vain were the efforts to restore their ancient authority by new embellishments. The true religion only carries within itself the principle of a perpetual renovation. The self-made systems of the Philosophers had run their course, one had supplanted another, until at last, just in consequence of their multiplicity, men had become distrustful of their truth, and of all human science, and longed, though often perhaps unconsciously, for higher certainty They had seen the transient nature of all human greatness and glory, that the bloom of nations as well as of individuals faded away, and that even what was most exalted and seemed established for thousands of years was hastening to its overthrow;—they beheld Greece and Rome themselves assailed by domestic and foreign foes, and on the brink of ruin Hence arose in the minds of men, an earnest, though indistinct desire to obtain some sure resting-place, some haven of security amidst the storms of time; to fasten themselves to something not subject to this constant alternation of growth and decay; to be able to labor for objects which did not contain within themselves the germ of their destruction —And in a moral point of view also, how easily would history dissipate the proud dreams of the natural man, did he not entirely avoid its light. The attractive garb, which vice had assumed in former times, was laid aside, and it now appeared in its native and hideous deformity. Pretended virtues also were stripped of their disguise. "Certatur ingenti quodam nequitiae certamine." Seneca, de Ira. II 8 And thus an undefinable anxiety was awakened to be rescued by a higher hand from the power of natural corruption, to be delivered from the monstrous embrace of the reigning wickedness. This longing after something stable in theory and practice, after redemption from sin and evil, was enlightened and satisfied by the preaching of the gospel of Jesus Christ *

We have already said that a different method was adopted to prepare the Jews for the Redeemer's advent. Among them the preparation was made by a direct influence. It was in the first place the *conditio sine qua non* of the appearing of the messenger that the knowledge of Him by whom He was sent should not be entirely lost, at least among those to whom He should manifest himself at the appointed time. This, however, required an immediate divine interposition; so prone is man, when left to himself, to the senseless worship of idols. God therefore separated from his kingdom, Abraham, the father of that people among whom the Saviour was to appear, allured him to his service by blessings and promises, and by conde-

---

* See Neander, Kirchengesch Bd 1. Tholuck, über das Wesen und den sittlichen Einfluss des Heidenthums mit hinsicht auf das Christenth in Neander's Denkwürdigkeiten, Bd. I.

scending to his weakness raised him by degrees to himself He afterwards pursued the same course, not only towards the immediate descendants of the patriarch, but the whole people who derived their origin from him Besides his general relation to all mankind, He sustained toward them the peculiar relation of King. He established all their institutions, of which he made himself the centre; He sought, in a manner suited to affect their senses, to bind them to Himself, and ensure their fidelity by the law of visible retribution manifest in all the events of their history, according to which, faithful devotion to His service was rewarded by prosperity, revolt and perfidy punished by adversity He strengthened their faith by a visible sign of His presence, and by many wonderful works, and made known to them his will, exhorted, warned and threatened them by sending continually new ambassadors clothed with his own authority and power —Further, the promulgation of the law especially contributed to prepare the way for the coming of the Redeemer The moral law is, indeed, imprinted on the heart of fallen man, and ennobles his corrupt nature But then he possesses no living principle to bring his sinful inclinations under subjection to this law The law is dead, while the inclinations to evil are full of life The conflict between conscience and the love of sin is insupportable; and as man finds it to be impossible by his own power to subdue the latter and secure to himself true peace of mind, he seeks a false and unsubstantial peace by suppressing the voice of the former. In order to effect this purpose he brings down to his own standard the attributes of God and the demands of His holy law. But that it might not be in the power of the Hebrews to pursue this course, God gave them an outward revelation of his law. And now the opposition between the will of God and the will of man was too obvious to be concealed; and as mere semblance of peace could no longer be maintained, it became necessary, that true peace should be sought. "By the law is the knowledge of sin," and where this knowledge truly exists, there also will be found the desire to be freed from sin, or in other words, the feeling of the need of redemption

But though God, in his wisdom and holiness, had purposed that many centuries should elapse between the fall and the redemption of man, yet immediately after the former and at subsequent periods he was pleased to make known that great salvation and deliverance from the consequences of the first transgression, which should be accomplished in future times.

The knowledge of this original Revelation is not entirely lost even among heathen nations. As, on the one hand, the doctrine of a happy primeval condition of mankind is diffused through all antiquity, so that even Voltaire himself in his "Philosophy of History" is obliged to confess, "that the fall of degenerate man is the foundation of theology among nearly all ancient nations," so, on the other we meet with hopes more or less definite of a time of restoration.* It is true that several of the Fathers, and especially Clement of Alexandria, have considerably exaggerated this fact, from a mistaken desire to render the christian religion acceptable to the heathen;† and indeed these expectations are often so general, as to seem not so much the remains of an original revelation, as the aspirations of a mind dissatisfied with the present, and hoping that its conceptions would be realized at some future period,—expecting in the progress of time the return of that happy condition, which according to the obscure indwelling consciousness of man, existed at the origin of the human race. Much however remains of so definite a character, that in all probability it was derived from an ancient revelation; especially when we consider this doctrine in connexion with those of the creation, the fall, and the curse which sin has brought upon the world, and which undeniably owe their origin to tradition. This is particularly the case with the doctrine of the Persians on this subject, whose religion is in general distinguished from that of other nations of antiquity by more worthy conceptions of God, and loftier representations of a future life. The Persians expected the present course of the world, in which a conflict is carried on between the kingdoms of Ormuzd and Ahriman, which produces that strange mixture of physical and moral good and evil, which we witness, to be succeeded by a time of restoration, in which Ahriman is to be entirely destroyed, and men are to be purified from sin, and enjoy a perfectly happy and peaceful life on the glorified earth. An important passage on this subject is found in Plutarch, (*De Iside et Osiride*, c. 47. ed. Hutten, t. 9, p. 168): "Ormuzd, born of the purest

---

* Vgl. die Sammelungen bei Stolberg, Religionsgesch. 1 Beilage 4 "über die Quellen der morgenländischen Ueberlieferungen." Rosenmüller, Altes und Neues Morgenl. 1 p. 13 sq. Tholuck, von der Sünde und vom Versohner p. 271 sq. Schmitt, Grundidee des Mythus Frank 1826. (An uncritical compilation.)

† Vgl. Eckhardi, non Christianorum de Christo testimonia. Quedlinb. 1725, p. 63 seq.

light, and Ahriman, the offspring of darkness, fight against each other. But a predestinated time will come, when Ahriman, after having filled the earth with famine and pestilence, shall thereby be entirely destroyed and extirpated. Then shall the earth be smooth and level; all men shall be happy, speak but one language, and be united in the same mode of life and the same political condition. But Theopompus says, that according to the doctrine of the Magi these two gods are alternately to triumph and to be subdued, each for three thousand years, and that during the next three thousand years they will mutually contend, and the one will make war upon the other and destroy what he had accomplished. But finally, the god of the lower world, Ahriman, shall be entirely vanquished. Men will then be happy; they will need no more nourishment, and cast no more shadows." See the Commentary on this passage by Anquetil du Perron, in Kleuker's Zendavesta, Anh. I. p. 127—144. We find in the Zend books and the Bundehesch a similar representation of the happiness of mankind after the renovation of the earth, which is to take place when the world shall have existed twelve thousand years. "Then there will be no night, no cold nor hot wind, no corruption, no fear of death, no evil caused by Dews,* and then the fiend, the ambitious prince, shall exalt him no more." Anq. du Perron, l. c. p. 138. If, however, such passages only as these existed, it might appear probable that this expectation was of human origin; but we see it in other instances connected with the appearance of a person of more than human power and dignity. We will not here appeal to the doubtful testimony of Abulfaradsch, who, (in his historia dynastiarum p. 54,) asserts that Zoroaster taught, that in the last times a virgin should miraculously conceive, and at the birth of her child a star should appear in the day-time with the sign of the virgin in the centre, and at its appearance the disciples should go to worship the child and offer him their gifts. It is the word which established the heavens." It is easy to see that this relation is not strictly true. It may, however, be shown by other and unexceptionable testimony that it is not a mere fabrication, but rests on historical grounds. We introduce here in the first place a passage from the Schahristan, (see Hyde: De Relig. Vet. Pers. p. 388, ed. II.) "Zoroaster relates in the book of Zendavesta that in the last time a man shall appear named Oschanderbega, that is, Man of the World. He will adorn

---

* Evil Spirits.

the world with religion and righteousness. During his time Peetiarch also will appear and greatly injure the interests of his kingdom for twenty years. Afterwards Osiderbega will manifest himself to the inhabitants of the world, promote righteousness, destroy iniquity, and restore the ancient order of things. Kings shall obey him and all his undertakings shall prosper. He will give the victory to true religion. In his times, rest and peace shall prevail, all dissensions cease, and all grievancy be done away." Here, therefore, we find two persons united in the restoration, Oschanderbega and Osiderbega. Similar to this is the statement which Tavernier received from a Persian priest, mentioned in his Travels. (See Reisebeschreibung IV. 8. t. 1 p. 181 of the Germ. Trans., and also in the Appendix to Hyde l. c.)

According to this statement the restoration is to be effected by three miraculously begotten persons, the last of whom, Sennorethotius, will be the most illustrious and will convert all. Under him the General Resurrection and the Judgment will take place. Then the kingdom of darkness shall be entirely subverted, the hills shall be made low, etc. We find also a threefold person even in the Zendavesta and Bundehesch. The three prophets were named Oschederbami, Oschedermah, and Sosiosch, and their origin is derived in a wonderful manner immediately from Zoroaster. In the last times, after the earth shall have been afflicted with evil of every kind, plague, pestilence, hail, famine, and war, Oschederbami and Oschedermah first appear with great and supernatural powers and effect the conversion of a large portion of mankind. At last Sosiosch, the greatest of the three, makes his appearance. Under him follows the Resurrection. He will judge the living and the dead, give new glory to the earth, and remove from a world of sorrows the germ of evil. (Zendav. vendidad, 19 II 375.) "Paris and all her plots shall be defeated by him whose origin is the fountain, by the victorious hero Sosiosch, who shall be born of the water of Kanse; by Oschederbami and Oschedermah, who shall come forth from the ground." (Bundehesch, 31, Th III p 111.) "After that Sosiosch will restore the dead to life, by that which comes forth from a bull and a white *hom*. Sosiosch will give all men this liquor to drink, they shall be great and incorruptible as long as being endures. All the dead as they had died, great or small, shall drink thereof and live again. And finally, at the command of the righteous judge Ormuzd, Sosiosch will, from an elevated place, render to all men what their deeds deserve. The

PRELIMINARY OBSERVATIONS.

dwelling of the pure will be the splendid Gorotmann. Ormuzd himself will take their bodies to his presence on high." (See Kleuker's Zendavesta, Th III p 30; Angh. Th. I. p. 281, seq.) If we leave out of view the division of that among three persons which belongs only to one, analogous to which is the notion of two Messiahs among the later Jews and the Samaritans, we shall not fail to perceive the coincidence of this expectation with the prophecies of the Old Testament, and the fulfilment, and shall not be disposed to ascribe it to any mere human origin. Among the Greeks such expectations were far more rare, indefinite, and general It is, however, erroneous to assert, as has been done, that they were strangers to these hopes, and possessed only the tradition of an *ancient* golden age.* Hesiod expected the return of a better time, (Works and Days, v. 174, Elton's Version) ·

> " Oh, would that Nature had denied me birth
> 'Midst this fifth race, this iron age of earth ;
> That long before within the grave I lay,
> Or long hereafter would behold the day ·
> Corrupt the race, with toils and grief opprest,
> Nor day nor night can yield a pause of rest "

Among the Platonic and Stoic philosophers this expectation afterwards gave rise to the doctrine concerning the great year of the world, or that period when, with the same position of the stars and planets in the heavens, all things will return to their original condition, and to the same course of events † (See Heyne's Virgil, T I p 96, ed. a. 1800; Voss zu Virgil's landlichen, Ged. I. p. 185) More definite expectations seem to have existed among the Romans, but upon a close examination it becomes exceedingly doubtful whether they were derived from an original revelation No evidence of this is afforded by the two well known passages, viz. that of Suetonius, Vita Vespasiani, c. 4 : " Percrebuerat oriente toto vetus et constans opinio esse in fatis, ut eo tempore Judaea profecti rerum potirentur ," and that of Tacitus, Hist 5 13: " Pluribus persuasio inerat, antiquis sacerdotum literis contineri, eo ipso tempore fore ut valesceret oriens " It is true that Kaiser (Psalmen, p. 335) has recently asserted, that the ideas of the Messiah, which, according to these passages, were current among the Romans, were derived from the East and from the Sybilline books; appealing, in support

---
* Tholuck, l c p 274 † Works and Days (Elton's Version)

of his opinion with regard to the first, to the expression, "oriente toto vetus et constans opinio," and with regard to the second, to the expression, "antiquis sacerdotum literis contineri." But still the Jewish origin of these ideas which is obvious, and confirmed by a passage in Josephus, (De B Jud. VII 5 4) is not by any means excluded by these expressions With respect to the first, the dispersion of the Jews after the Babylonish exile must have made their religious opinions in general, and especially their hopes respecting the Messiah known beyond the boundaries of Judea, and have secured for them an unobserved entrance; and as to the second, it is well known, that not Christians, but Jews first put into the mouths of the Sybils expectations of a Messiah in spurious predictions after the true Sybilline prophecies were lost

An appeal is also made in favor of the existence of the Messianic predictions in the Sybilline books of the Romans to another apparently important testimony, the Fourth Eclogue of Virgil, composed in honor of the consul Pollio. Virgil here announces the near approach of that era celebrated in Cumaean song, "Ultima Cumaei venit jam carminis aetas," and that during the consulship of Pollio, with the birth of the expected child, the golden age will return. The Emperor Constantine it is true supposed, that this eclogue might express an expection of a Messiah, derived from the prophecies of the Cumaean Sybil. (See Eusebius, Vit Const. V. 19, 20) The same is asserted by Augustin in several passages, (especially de civit dei 10,27, and Epist 155 (Bened 258.) ad Martianum) "Nam omnino non est, cui alteri praeter dominum Christum dicat genus humanum:

> Te duce si qua manent sceleris vestigia nostri
> Irrita perpetua solvent formidine terras

Quod ex Cumae, i. e ex Sibyllino carmine se fassus est transtulisse Virgilius, quoniam fortassis illa vates aliquid de unico salvatore in spiritu audierat, quod necesse habuit confiteri." So also many later writers. Compare the references of Heyne, l. c p. 94. But 1 It is nevertheless very uncertain whether Virgil really alluded to a prediction of the Cumaean Sybil Boecler, (Dissert. in h ecl dissert acad T II. diss 11.) Fabricius, (Bibl. Graeca, l. 1, c. 3, § 14) and Eckhard (l c p 44 sqq) have suggested, that Virgil refers to the poem of Hesiod, who was born at Cumae, and whose poem therefore might as well be called Cumaean, as Ascraean from the place of his later abode Perhaps the poet might have intentionally employed the former name to indicate, that, like a Sybil, Hesiod had prophesied of future times. The supposition, that Virgil alludes to Hesiod, is confirmed by the close resemblance of their imagery, when the former describes the golden age to come, and the latter that which was past, and may the more readily be allowed, since Hesiod, as we have seen, expected this period to return.

2. But granting that Virgil referred to the Cumaean Sybil, he could not have had in view the ancient and genuine Sybilline predictions. These had long before been burnt with the Capitol. (See Voss, l. c. p. 182 seq.) The writings, which passed in the time of Virgil under the name of Sybilline prophecies, were in a great measure spurious. (See Servat Gallaeus de Sybillis earumque Oracc. Amst. 1688, p. 363 seq.) It might easily have happened, that the Jewish expectations of a future restitution should have been clothed in the Roman costume, and ascribed to the Sybil. But even this supposition is unnecessary, since in the Eclogue of Virgil there is no expectation indulged beyond the return of the golden age, the same which we find among the Greeks.

But now when we turn to the Hebrews, an entirely different prospect is presented. We could not have expected to find among the Heathen nations any thing more than vague and distorted anticipations of a happier future. Their hopes were circumscribed by the revelations on this subject, which were early imparted to mankind, and which were necessarily indefinite and general in consequence of the character and condition of those who received them. Moreover, these revelations must have been greatly corrupted in the course of time, since they were opposed to the sentiments of the Heathen, left to themselves and having no participation in the farther revelations from above. But among the Hebrews, on the contrary, these hopes, instead of standing by themselves, appear in the most intimate connexion with the whole system of the Theocracy. The early predictions were secured from every species of corruption by being committed to writing. Frequent new revelations kept the expectation of the people alive, and rendered it continually more and more definite. And thus the doctrine of a coming Redeemer, even when partially misunderstood, became the soul and centre of all theocratic expectations; and the more so, since, as the people of the old covenant were left in as much darkness respecting the time of his first coming as Christians are respecting that of his second, their hopes were not weakened by the great distance of the period of their accomplishment. Since, therefore, the disclosures respecting the coming of a Redeemer, made to the Hebrews, alone have the seal of Divine authority; since they only have come to us pure and free from all human additions, we are very properly accustomed to give to them exclusively the name of Messianic predictions. This appellation is derived from Ps ii. and Dan 9 24—27. There the great Redeemer bears the name of משיח, *anointed*, which is elsewhere peculiar to the leaders of the *visible* Theocracy, but is here given to the head of the *spiritual*, whom the Prophets describe by images taken from those leaders, and designate by their names.

We now proceed to consider the various purposes which these predictions promoted in the Theocracy, a task which is the more necessary, the oftener it is brought as an *a priori* objection against the existence of real prophecies of the Messiah in the Old Testament, that the prediction of events so remote must be useless, and therefore unworthy of God

1. If their views had been limited to the present, the covenant people would have been in danger of becoming extremely contracted and selfish This state of mind could not fail to be attended with most injurious consequences It would lead them to unworthy and degrading thoughts of God, to limit either his omnipotence or his love, and to the most pernicious ideas of their own excellence, since the preference of them to the Heathen, were it to be permanent, would hardly be regarded as founded on anything else than superior natural qualifications, which rendered them, above all other people, worthy of the favor of God. It was therefore highly necessary, that the means should be perceived as such, and that the view should be directed beyond the preparatory arrangements to the great end to be attained. Hence it was announced, even before the establishment of the Theocracy, and afterwards continually kept in view, that the special relation of God to Israel was only temporary, and that in future times a great Deliverer should appear, in whose kingdom all the nations of the earth, Heathen as well as Jews, should be embraced. The necessity of this is manifest from the fact, that, notwithstanding such plain predictions, the greater part of the Jews, blinded by their worldliness, gave themselves up to the most destructive belief in God's special regard for their own nation. How difficult would it have been even for the truly pious, without these predictions, to preserve themselves from the prevailing error !

2. The promise of the Messiah was a means of retaining the peo-

ple in their allegiance to the Lord, in times of calamity. On him, as the great Restorer and Enlarger of the Theocracy, the prophets grounded their consoling declarations. Thus, for example, Isaiah, 7. 14, shows the unreasonableness of the fear that the state would be entirely destroyed by the Assyrians, from the fact, that the people from whom the Messiah was to spring could not be thus destroyed; and Jeremiah, 23. 6, and Ezekiel, 34. 23, present to the view of the despairing people their future illustrious King. Although the prophets often refer for consolation to nearer and joyful events of less importance, yet they never fail to return to this as the greatest of blessings and the pledge of all the others. Compare Isa. 10. 11. (See Calvin's Institutes, II. 6.) This design of the predictions of the Messiah, which respected the whole people, could be accomplished even when they were erroneously apprehended from misunderstanding the imagery in which they were clothed. And thus even those who through their own fault indulged for the most part worldly expectations of the Messiah would be preserved in outward allegiance. Nor was this of small importance, since the continuation of the external Theocracy was indispensable to the manifestation of Christ. The kernel was preserved by means of the shell.

3. The prediction of the Messiah was a means of promoting genuine piety and true devotion to God. The Prophets distinguish between the pious and the ungodly. They proclaim that the Messiah will bestow rich blessings upon the former, but by his righteous punishment destroy the latter. What could have presented to the pious a stronger motive for perseverance, and to the wicked for conversion, than the lively representation of these rewards and punishments? Compare Isa. ii.—iv. Mal. 3. 19, etc.

4. In the Old Testament, moreover, the Gospel, which proclaims forgiveness of sins through the mercy of God, accompanies the law. How must those, in whom the law had accomplished its end, have been consoled by the hope of pardon, when he, who *was to take* upon himself their sins as he *has taken* ours, set before them the condition of their salvation in predictions like those recorded in Isa. liii.

5. But the chief object of prophecy was, so to prepare the way for Christ, that when he should come he might be identified by a comparison of the prediction with its fulfilment. How necessary it was is shown by the fact that notwithstanding this preparation the greater portion of the people misapprehended the Messiah. This however was the case only with those, whose worldly views prevent-

ed an impartial comparison of the prediction with its fulfilment. Had he not been particularly described before his coming, it would have been extremely difficult for even the spiritually-minded to identify him.* The importance of the Messianic predictions in this respect is manifest from the testimony of Christ and his Apostles. Christ, indeed, declares, that a disposition of mind, which qualifies to receive the outward proofs of his divine mission, is indispensable to the knowledge of himself, John 7: 17, and ascribes the unbelief of the Jews to the want of this disposition, John 5. 44. But he also represents the evidence from prophecy as perfectly sufficient in itself, and reproves the Jews because they did not acknowledge it as such, John 5. 39—47. He was pointed out by God himself, through John the Baptist, as the *promised* Messiah, John 1. 19—41. He declared himself to be such, John 4· 25, 26. Matt 26. 63, 64. 11: 3, etc. And lest the coincidence between the prediction and its fulfilment might be thought fortuitous, he repeatedly says, " The prophecy must needs have been fulfilled," Luke 24: 25, 44, etc. Matt 26. 54. Matthew 5. 17, he gives, as an end of his being sent, the fulfilment of the prophecies. How important for the establishment of his claims he regarded the agreement between the prophecy and its fufilment, we learn from the fact, that at his last entrance into Jerusalem he so ordered all the circumstances as to make them harmonize with the predictions concerning him, Matt. 21. 1. John 12. 12. That Jesus was the Christ, constituted an important part of what the Apostles announced, not only to the Jews but also to the Heathen, Acts 10: 43. 1 Cor. 15. 3. 2 Cor. 1. 20.

The importance of these predictions, under the old dispensation, cannot then be doubted. The question may however arise, whether they are still important to the Christian Church. This has recently been denied by Schleiermacher, (Dogm I. p 116). See in reply Steudel, de Messianorum vaticc. momento in nostrae etiam aetatis pios Christi cultores vi sua nequaquam destituto prolusio Tub. 1823.

1. A previous question here arises, whether genuine prophecies of the Messiah really exist in the Old Testament. This Schleiermacher denies. He finds there only indistinct longings, expressions of the feeling of the need of redemption, such as we meet with among the Heathen, and asserts that the contrary opinion cannot be satisfacto-

---

* Twesten, Dogm I p 323 " Es bedurfte am Ende nur des frohen $εὑρή\-καμεν$ Joh 1 42, 46, um die Israeliten ohne Falsch zu ihm hinzuführen "

rily maintained. This assertion will be sufficiently refuted in the sequel. We only remark here, that with its truth or falsehood the authority of Christ and his Apostles must stand or fall. That *they* believed the Scripture to contain genuine predictions, is evident from the passages in their writings already referred to, as well as a great number of others to be hereafter quoted in the proper place

2 The authority of Christ and his Apostles is equally subverted by the assertion, that an accurate and particular agreement between the event and the prophecy is of no importance. If this be the case, why is the coincidence of the prophecy with its fulfilment shown in the minutest circumstances of the life of Christ? Wherefore did he, when risen from the dead, explain to his Apostles those passages in the Old Testament which treated of his life, his sufferings, and his death? Wherefore did he so order every thing in his last visit to Jerusalem, that the prophecies and their accomplishment should accurately coincide? If it was important for that age to show this agreement, it is no less so for ours, since the Apostles pursued this course with Heathen as well as Jews. The majority of the people of Christian countries are in the same condition as the Jews at the appearance of Christ, they know him not and have yet, for the first time, to become acquainted with him This result, it is true, can no more be effected in their case than in that of the Jews, by the Messianic predictions alone, nor indeed can all the external proofs of the truth of Christianity combined, however conclusive in themselves, produce conviction, so long as the mind is not susceptible of the impression they are designed to make.* But where the mind is open to receive this evidence, the fulfilment of prophecy exerts the happiest influence. This is too clearly proved by history to be denied † In how many instances have men been first drawn to the Saviour by reading the fifty-third chapter of Isaiah! How many disciples have been strengthened in the beginning of their course by this and similar predictions! That such is not the effect in our day, as frequently as in past times, must be ascribed to an infidel exegesis, which has darkened the true import of these predictions. The time however

---

* Herder justly says—Briefe p 244 .—" No man will be actually compelled to embrace the Christian faith by citations from the Old Testament, because their fulfilment still depends on the spirit of many occurrences which must be gathered from them all and felt in its oneness "

† Vgl Twesten Dogm I p 323

must surely come, when this proof of the truth of Christianity, which must not indeed be considered by itself, but in intimate connexion with all the rest, will be restored to its just importance and authority.

3. Nor are these prophecies of value to those only who are just commencing the Christian life they are no less beneficial to more advanced believers. The faith of no one is so strong and constant, that he need despise the means of strengthening it, vouchsafed by God himself. and the Christian will be the less inclined to do this, the more intimately and spiritually he has become united to the Redeemer. The farther he has advanced, the more earnestly does he desire to comprehend the divine institutions for his salvation in all their relations, and follow the plan which the wisdom of God saw fit to devise. Here nothing is unimportant. The smallest trace has meaning, because it is connected with the whole. All is mutual; as the completion sheds light on the preparation, so does the preparation illustrate the completion.

Finally, when Schleiermacher farther objects, that we cannot rest our strong faith in Christianity on Judaism, since our confidence in that is unquestionably far weaker, Steudel has already well replied, that we do not rely on the predictions, in themselves considered, but on that evidence which results from comparing them with the fulfilment. Besides, the idea of a weaker faith in the Old, and a stronger one in the New Testament, cannot be admitted by him whose conviction is consistent, for whoever truly believes Christ and the Apostles, must acknowledge the divine authority of the Old Testament, to which they give so clear and definite testimony.

If now we trace the progress of the Messianic prediction in general among the Hebrews, we shall see, that the reign of David forms an important era in its history It is true, indeed, that this prophecy is not the work of men, but the inspiration of that Spirit, who, under the Old Testament, glorified the Redeemer who was to come, as among us he glorifies him now that he has come. But as we shall hereafter see, the representations of prophecy were necessarily figurative. The Messiah, therefore, could not be fully exhibited until history had given to the Prophets materials, from which their metaphorical representations could be formed The earlier Theocracy supplied no sufficient ground-work for a complete delineation of him. His character and offices, therefore, first appear fully unfolded in the time of David, to whom the Messiah was promised as a descendant. As the visible Theocracy then furnished the materials for the representation of the Messiah's kingdom, so the typical head of the former served as the model of all that should be said for the glory of his antetype, the head of the latter

CHAPTER II.

HISTORY OF THE MESSIANIC PREDICTION AMONG THE HEBREWS.

1. *Messianic Predictions in the Pentateuch.*

a In Genesis.

If we leave out of view the revelations, which, during the period of history comprized in Genesis, may have been imparted, in moments of high and divine excitement, to individual believers for their own benefit, (see John 8 56,) and examine the prophecies of the Messiah as recorded in this book, we shall perceive them continually increasing in precision and clearness.

The promise of the Messiah, given immediately after the fall, as it is the first, is also the most indefinite. Opposed to the fearful threatening stands the consoling promise, that the reign of sin and its consequent evils should not last for ever; that the posterity of the woman should one day gain the victory over their dreaded conqueror Here all except the victory itself is left undetermined, we are not informed how it is to be achieved, nor whether by some peculiarly gifted race, or by a single individual, among the descendants of the woman

After the destruction of a sinful world, when Noah with his three sons alone remained, the *general* promise was so far circumscribed, that deliverance was to be accomplished through the posterity of Shem The prediction became still more definite, when God began to prepare the way for this salvation by separating a single individual, Abraham, from the corrupt mass, to make him the depository of his revelations, and by afterwards specifying which of his descendants should inherit this honor with all its attendant blessings, to the exclusion of all the rest, according to his own free purpose. From among the descendants of Shem, God selected, first, the family of Abraham, next that of Isaac, and lastly that of Jacob; as the one from which the promised salvation should proceed. But even these annunciations, though more distinct than those of an earlier period, are still very indefinite, when compared with those which were subsequently given, and with the fulfilment. In them the blessing, indeed, was foretold, but not its author. It remained still uncertain, whether by means of a single individual, or a whole race, descended from the patriarch, salvation should be extended to the remaining people of the earth. The method, also, by which this blessing should be imparted, was not clearly revealed.

A part of this obscurity was removed by the last Messianic prediction of Genesis, 49 10 After what had taken place, it was indeed to be expected, that it would not be left undetermined, which of the twelve sons of Jacob should be the source of salvation to the whole world ; and that, when the patriarch, just before his death, delivered over to his sons, in the spirit of prophecy, the promises imparted to himself and his forefathers, he would not omit that which was more important than all the rest. Here, however, not only does the Messianic prediction receive its usual limitation, by the selection of Judah as the one to whom the promise belonged, but becomes unexpectedly much more definite and clear Here, for the first time, the *Person* of the Messiah comes before us, and the nature of his kingdom is defined; for he is represented as a *peaceful* Prince, who should unite under his mild sceptre all the nations of the earth.

We proceed now from these preparatory remarks to an exposition of the particular passages

THE PROTEVANGELIUM, OR THE FIRST ANNUNCIATION OF THE GOSPEL.

As the mission of the Messiah was rendered necessary by the fall, so the first obscure intimation of him was given immediately after that event It is found in the sentence denounced against the tempter, Gen. 3 14, 15, the true import of which we shall only understand, when we have ascertained who the tempter was.

It is in the first place beyond all doubt, that a real serpent was engaged in the temptation, and, consequently, the opinion of those must be rejected, who regard the serpent as merely a symbolical designation of the evil spirit * This opinion would make it necessary, in order to be consistent, that we should adopt the allegorical mode

---

* Its most skilful defender is Cramer in den Nebenarbeiten zur theologischen Literatur St 2

of interpretation throughout the whole narrative. For in a connected paragraph like this, uniformity of interpretation must prevail ; and we are not at liberty, in the same historical relation, to adopt at one time the allegorical or symbolical, and at another the simple and literal method. Against the allegorical interpretation of the whole there are many objections, as the connexion with what follows, where the history of the same human pair, which are brought into view, is carried forward,—the accurate geographical description of Paradise, —the fact, that the condition of mankind, threatened in this narrative as a punishment, actually exists,—the absence of every indication, from which it might be inferred that the author designed to write an allegory and not a history,—the passages in the New Testament, where the account of the fall is referred to as a real history, 2 Cor. 11 3 1 Tim. 2 13, 14. Rom 5 12,— the embarrassment, uncertainty, and capriciousness of the allegorical interpreters, when they attempt to exhibit the truth intended to be conveyed, which, if the author had designed his composition for an allegory, must have been so obvious as to be easily discovered *

The presence of a real serpent is proved, moreover, not only by the remark, chap 3 1 "Now the serpent was more subtile than any beast of the field," but by the punishment denounced, which must necessarily refer, in the first instance, to the serpent These last reasons may also serve to refute the idea of others, that Satan assumed merely the *semblance* of a serpent

But if it is certain, that what Eve saw was a real serpent, it is no less so that he was not the principal tempter, but only an instrument, employed by an evil spirit with which she was unacquainted † In favor of this we advance the following reasons 1 Although the writer intentionally related the history as it had been handed down to their descendants from the parents of mankind, who could judge of things only as they appeared to the eye, and has employed no word to point out the invisible author of the temptation, yet, that he designed to lead his reflecting reader to the knowledge of him, is manifest from the whole character of the narrative, while, at the same

---

* Vgl Zachariä bibl Theol II p 229 ff. Lüderwald, die allegorische Erklärung der drei ersten Cap Mosis, insonderheit des Sündenfalls in ihrem Ungrunde vorgestellt Helmst 1781

† This has been acknowledged among recent critics by Rosenmüller Comm 1. p. 109. Schott, Theolog dogm p. 128, ed. 2 Hahn, Dogmatik p. 345 f

time, he had his own sufficient reasons for confining the great mass of the people to the outward appearance, and not explaining its cause, the knowledge of which might so readily give rise to that destructive superstition, which was so widely spread among the other nations of the East. What deserves peculiar regard is, that the serpent speaks and exhibits, in general, all the marks of a rational being. This need not have appeared surprising to Eve. She was so little acquainted with the nature of animals, their characteristic difference from men, and the powers with which God had endowed them, that the speaking of the serpent could have awakened in her mind at most only an obscure suspicion of the agency of some higher and invisible power. But what reflecting reader of later times would not be led to the knowledge of this invisible cause, as soon as he connected the certainty that here was something beyond the power of an ordinary serpent, with the probability, that he, known from other sources to be the author of all evil, performed an active part at its first entrance into the world? True indeed, after Abarbanel, Le Clerc, Eichhorn, Doederlein, Dathe, Less, and especially Gabler, (zu Eichhorn's Urgeschichte, II. 1 p 154 seq) have sought to show, that the account of the conversation of Eve with the serpent must be explained by a well known Orientalism, according to which, external objects, even though inanimate, that give rise to thought, are personified and introduced as speaking. The serpent, by his harmless use of the fruit, awakened many thoughts in the mind of Eve, and suggested a doubt with respect to the prohibition. This rising doubt, with the accompanying desire, is expressed in accordance with the genius of the Orientals, in the form of a dialogue between the serpent and Eve. Even Hahn l c has of late strangely advocated this opinion, and endeavoured to establish it, as the result of a grammatico-historical interpretation. But it is liable to these objections: it ascribes to a simple historical relation that which can have place only in poetry; it rests entirely upon caprice, since, against all the rules of sound exposition, it understands one part of the narrative literally, and allegorizes the other; it is sustained by no analogous place in the writings of the Old Testament, since even with respect to the history of Balaam there is no good reason for rejecting the literal interpretation, which even Herder (see his Briefe das Studium der Theologie betreffend, Th. 1 p. 26 seq) has defended; it rests upon no other foundation, than the alleged absurdity of supposing a literal conversation to have taken place between the serpent and Eve,—a foundation which of itself gives way the moment the agency of an evil spirit is supposed. Storr, therefore, has well observed against this supposition (De Protevangelio Opusc. t II p 422), "Haec opinio a natura rerum priscaeque vetustatis simplicitate sic abhorret, ut tam artificiose affectatum tumorem narrationi vetustae tribuere nequeamus, nisi indubiis auctoritatibus coacti, quas vero penitus desideramus." Besides, there are many other things which suggest the idea of an invisible author of the temptation, concealed under the visible,—the declaration, chap. 3. 1, so remarkably suited to awaken attention, and the curse itself, which plainly relates in a higher sense to an invisible tempter, as it does in a lower to the visible agent which he employed.

2 We draw another argument from the tradition of the fall of our first parents, preserved in the sacred books of the Persians. According to the Zendavesta (Th. 3 p. 84, 85), the parents of the human race, Meschia and Meschianeh, were created by God pure and good, and destined for happiness on condition of humility, obedience to the requirements of the law, and purity in their thoughts, words, and deeds. But betrayed by the cruel "Ahriman, who from the beginning sought only to deceive," they fell from God, and forfeited their happiness by eating fruit. According to the same book (III. p 62), Ahriman springs from heaven to earth in the form of a serpent, and another distinguished evil spirit is called (Th 2. p. 217) the serpent Dhu. (See Rhode, die heil Sage d. Zenvolkes, p 392.)

3 Among the Jews, also, there is a tradition, that Satan was concerned in the temptation of our first parents. By the envy of the devil, says the book of Wisdom, 2· 24, came death into the world. In later Jewish writings, Sammael, the head of the evil spirits, because he tempted Eve in the form of a serpent, is called נחש הקדמני, *old serpent*, or simply נחש, *serpent*. (See Eisenmenger entd Judenth I p 822.)

4. But what gives indubitable certainty to the agency of Satan in this transaction is the testimony of the New Testament. Apoc. 12 9, the leader of the evil spirits is named $\dot{o}$ $\delta\varrho\acute{a}\chi\omega\nu$ $\dot{o}$ $\mu\acute{e}\gamma\alpha\varsigma$, $\dot{o}$ $\ddot{o}\varphi\iota\varsigma$ $\dot{o}$ $\dot{a}\varrho\chi\alpha\tilde{i}o\varsigma$ (נחש קדמני) $\dot{o}$ $\varkappa\alpha\lambda o\acute{u}\mu\varepsilon\nu o\varsigma$ $\delta\iota\acute{a}\beta o\lambda\iota\varsigma$ Likewise 20 2. Paul, indeed, 2 Cor. 11. 3, ($\dot{\omega}\varsigma$ $\dot{o}$ $\ddot{o}\varphi\iota\varsigma$ $E\ddot{u}\alpha\nu$ $\dot{\varepsilon}\xi\eta\pi\acute{a}\tau\eta\sigma\varepsilon\nu$ $\dot{\varepsilon}\nu$ $\tau\tilde{\eta}$ $\pi\alpha\nu o\upsilon\varrho\gamma\acute{\iota}\alpha$,) after the example of the narrative itself, suffers the unseen cause of the temptation to remain concealed, and speaks only of that which was visible, but that the former was not unknown to him is evident from Rom. 15 20, ($\dot{o}$ $\delta\grave{\varepsilon}$ $\vartheta\varepsilon\acute{o}\varsigma$ $\tau\tilde{\eta}\varsigma$ $\varepsilon\dot{\iota}\varrho\acute{\eta}\nu\eta\varsigma$ $\sigma\upsilon\nu\tau\varrho\acute{\iota}\psi\varepsilon\iota$ $\tau\grave{o}\nu$

σατανᾶν ὑπὸ τοὺς πόδας ὑμῶν ἐν τάχει,) where the allusion to Gen. 3. 15, is not to be mistaken. Finally, that Christ himself, John 8. 44, calls Satan, with reference to his having brought death into the world by sin, ἀνθρωποκτόνον ἀπ' ἀρχῆς, we must maintain, after the example of the generality of the old interpreters, namely, Origen, Chrysostom, Augustin, Theophylact, and in harmony with most of the modern, as Kuinoel and Tholuck, even though the opinion first advanced by Cyril of Alexandria, that the Saviour rather alluded to the murder committed by Cain, has found an acute defender in Nitzsch, (see his Abhandlung uber den Menschenmorder von Anfang in der theol. Zeitsch. v. de Wette, Schleiermacher und Lucke III. p. 52 seq.) and is also preferred by Lucke. Our reasons are the following: That the phrase ἀπ' ἀρχῆς must be taken in its strictest sense, is shown by the parallel passages already referred to in the Apocalypse, as well as in the Jewish writings; and that Christ, when he called Satan ἀνθρωποκτόνος, had in view the fall of our first parents, is shown by the passage quoted from Wisdom, 2. 24, as well as that to which Tholuck has appealed in the Sohar Chadasch, where the ungodly are called " the children of the old serpent, who has slain Adam and all his descendants." Besides, how could Jesus expect his words to be understood by his hearers, except as referring to the moral and indirect physical murder also, which Satan commenced with the parents of mankind, since his agency in the fall was the prevailing belief of the people, while the idea, that he tempted Cain, to which there is no allusion in the Mosaic narrative, cannot be supposed to have been so generally received, that Christ would have alluded to it in such vague and indefinite terms? True it is alleged, that also in 1 John 3. 12, the murder committed by Cain is referred to Satan; but there this reference is not only plainly pointed out, but the reason of it is manifest in what goes before. Finally, that Christ alluded to the fall is confirmed by the fact, that the murder committed by Satan is placed in the nearest connexion with his lying disposition, as manifested in the seduction of our first parents. The force of their arguments will not surely be destroyed by the single consideration, which has been urged in favor of the reference to the deed of Cain, viz., that Christ had just before charged the Jews with a murderous disposition in the strict and literal sense, and with hatred of the truth, and therefore called them the children of the devil, and that consequently, in order to justify this language, Satan must be represented as a literal murderer. It is here erroneously taken for granted, that in the temptation of our first parents, he was a murderer only in a spiritual sense. He was so in the simplest and most literal sense of the term, since the transgression, caused by him, involved the loss of immortality. Compare with the relation in Genesis, Wisd 2. 24. Rom 5. 12. Hence the assertion, that allusion to the fall would have been a mere playing upon words, is seen to be groundless.

5. To these particular testimonies from the New Testament, we lastly add another of considerable weight, lately advanced by Hahn, drawn from the parallel between the history of the first and second Adam. Compare Rom 5 14, etc 1 Cor. 15 45 That Christ must be tempted by the prince of this world, in order that, by his persevering resistance, he might despoil him of his dominion over it, shows that Adam also, was assailed by the same tempter, and by being overcome laid the foundation of this dominion.

But before we proceed further, and make use of the results we have gained, we must first examine the grounds on which the agency of Satan, in the fall of man, has been controverted. These have been most fully stated by Eichhorn, (Urgeschichte, Th III p 114 seq) and Gabler (Th II. p. 137, seq) These critics have been followed by Dathe on the Pentateuch, Kuinoel (Mess Weiss. p. 2), Jahn (Vacticinia Messianna, p 216, 222, and Nachtrage zu seinen theol Werken p. 148), and lastly, Baumgarten-Crusius (Grundyuge der bibl. Dogm p. 348). Their principal objections, the insufficiency of which may be seen from what has already been advanced, are the following

1. "The author calls the serpent, in reference to the history of the fall, and the deception which he practised upon Eve, the most subtile of all the beasts of the field. Had he been thinking of a supernatural cause, he would not have made this assertion, since the devil could just as well have employed the most stupid animal " To this we reply, that the author related the circumstances as they appeared to our first parents, and, ignorant as they were of the invisible cause, they must have ascribed a high degree of cunning to the serpent from the part which he acted. Moses states this fact with the design of leading his more intelligent readers to a right solution of the problem.

2 "The devil cannot speak by means of a serpent, since the serpent has no organs of speech." We answer here with Calvin, " Si incredibile videtur locutas esse deo jubente bestias, unde homini ser-

mo, nisi quia ejus linguam deus formavit? Editas sine lingua in aere fuisse voces ad illustrandam Christi gloriam, Evangelium praedicat; minus hoc rationi carnis probabile quam ex brutorum animalium ore elici sermonen. Quid igitur hic impiorum petulantia insectatione dignum inveniet?" That speech should appear to proceed from the mouth of a serpent is just as conceivable as the influence of the soul on the body, and many other things of the kind.

3. "How can it be reconciled with the goodness and wisdom of God, that a powerful spirit should have been permitted to tempt the parents of mankind to apostasy? God must have foreseen the fall which would be the consequence of this permission; and did he, nevertheless, permit this diabolical deception? Who can justify this proceeding? We should have no need to acknowledge the validity of this objection, did we know of nothing further to oppose to it than the words of Calvin. "Utinam se a deo judicari potius sinerent homines, quam sibi in eum judicium sacrilega temeritate sumerent! verum haec carnis arrogantia est examini suo deum subjicere." For where we are assured on sufficient grounds, that any thing has been done by God, we are not to have our confidence overthrown by the inability of our short-sighted reason to justify his proceedings. "Canst thou draw out Leviathan with a hook?" But in this instance we are not obliged to appeal solely to the infinite distance between God and man, for we can give at least a probable justification of this dispensation of Providence. This would indeed be impossible, if we held the opinion of the old divines, which so magnifies the divine image as to ascribe to Adam the *actual exercise* of the highest wisdom and holiness. But this opinion is contrary to the Mosaic relation. The assertion, that man was made in the image of God, implies rather that he possessed the capacity of these attributes, and was free from that moral depravity which we bring with us into the world as an inheritance derived from him. The narrative moreover shows, that his condition was analogous to that of childhood. This low condition of unconscious innocence was to be changed into one of intelligent piety and devotion to God; and to effect this change probation was necessary. For this purpose God gave the command, and at the same time permitted the temptation to transgress. Had man endured the trial, he would have been carried forward, without the necessity of a painful course of discipline, from one degree of improvement to another. The foresight of man's disobedience could not move God to guard him from temptation. It was better for man, if he

would not persevere in goodness, to be brought to perfection by suffering the effects of his sin, than to remain in his former imperfect condition. We must not consider the fall apart from the redemption. God, who foresaw the fall, had already purposed, by a method of salvation of his own appointment, not only to remove its consequences, but also thereby to bring man to that perfection, which he would indeed have attained by firmly resisting the tempter, but did not possess at his creation, and could not have acquired without a trial. (See the excellent remarks by Krummacher, Paragraphen zu der heil. Geschichte, p. 46 seq.)

4. "The curse is directed only against an irrational creature." It must, we admit, have fallen in the first place upon the serpent, and the punishment of the only author of the temptation that was known to man was well fitted to inspire an abhorrence of sin. But a double reference of the curse is not hereby excluded, and we are justified in making it, when Satan is proved to have been engaged in the temptation.

5. "It cannot have been the opinion of the writer, that an evil spirit was concerned in the fall of man, since in the whole of the Old Testament until the period of the Babylonish exile, there is to be found no trace of such a spirit. The idea of Satan was borrowed from the Chaldeans, and, after their example, the Jews made him play the part of a tempter with our first parents." But that the doctrine concerning Satan prevailed among the Jews before the Babylonian exile is evident, in the first place, from the very ancient book of Job, which only a very few critics venture to assign to as late a period as the exile. It is true, that, after Herder, Eichhorn, Ilgen, and Jahn, Baumgarten-Crusius, (bibl. Theol p. 295) has lately endeavoured to give currency to the opinion, that the Satan of the book of Job is not the Satan of the later books of the Old Testament, but rather a good and pure angel, who sustained only the office of a complainant, informer, or attorney-general. In proof of this he alleges, that the writer numbers him among the sons of God, and that the odiousness of his office ought not to be transferred to his person. But not to mention that the new derivation given to the word שטן cannot be justified on grammatical principles, this hypothesis has nothing in its favor. When the writer makes Satan to appear before the throne of God, he employs a poetic fiction. He no more intended this for a real transaction, than he actually believed that Jehovah, whose infinite power and wisdom he has so gloriously exhibited, needed to de-

liver up a man to Satan to be proved, in order to ascertain the genuineness of his virtue. When it is said that Satan appeared in the midst of the angels before God, we cannot infer, as some have done, that the writer regarded him as one of the good angels. In fine, Satan is here entirely consistent with himself. His nature is craft, hatred, and envy. (See Gesenius l. c. Storr opusc. II p. 426.) Nor is it by any means true, that the existence of evil spirits is not taught in the Pentateuch as even Schott (epit. theol. dogm. p. 113) has lately acknowledged. The opinion of those who think Satan to be intended by Azazel, to whom the goat, Lev. 16: 8, is sent away into the wilderness, is the only one that agrees with the context. (See Spencer leg. rit. l. III diss. 8, cap. I, § 2. Gesenius Handworterb. s. v. Rosenmuller, Winer lex. s. v.) Baumgarten-Crusius (l. c. p. 294) has indeed objected, after the example of Deyling (obss. sacr. I. p 51) that the bringing of an offering to an evil spirit would not only be inconsistent with the import of this particular ceremony of atonement, but in opposition to the whole system of the Mosaic religion. There is however no ground for the supposition, that one of the goats was brought as a sacrifice to Azazel. So far as he was regarded in this light, he was consecrated, as well as the other to Jehovah. Compare verse 10. His being sent forth was only a symbolical transaction. By this act the kingdom of darkness and its prince were renounced, and symbolically the sins to which he had tempted, and by which he had sought to enslave either the people or individuals, were sent back to him again, and the truth was expressed, that he to whom God grants forgiveness is freed from the power of evil. The correctness of this explanation must be evident to every attentive and unprejudiced reader of the whole passage. The contrast between ליהוה and לעזאזל verse 8, as well as the tradition of the later Jews, that Azazel is a name of Samuel, speaks in its favor. See passages quoted by Spencer, Rosenmuller, and Winer. The passage in Deut. 32: 17, is less explicit. The word שֵׁדִים which there occurs, is rendered by the Seventy δαιμόνια, and by the Vulgate daemonia, and in favor of the opinion, that it signifies invisible wicked spirits we have also the Syriac, ܦ݁ܺܐܪܳܐ, *evil demon*. It is very true, that Moses says but little concerning the kingdom of darkness, and speaks with a degree of obscurity, which only the more intelligent could penetrate, but for this, he had, as we have already seen, his own sufficient reasons. He observed a similar conduct with respect to other doctrines also, for example, that of immortality, of which he gave only brief hints, intelligible to those alone to whom the knowledge of it would be beneficial. Against the supposition that the Hebrews derived the doctrine concerning Satan from Chaldea, we may urge not only the passage referred to, but also the fact, that the Ahriman of the Persians, and the Satan of the Hebrews, are entirely different beings. The Ahriman of the Persians is the fundamental principle of evil, coeternal with that of good, and if not entirely equal with it in power, at least so nearly equal as to carry on against it a long and arduous warfare. The Satan of the Hebrews is, on the contrary, entirely subject to Jehovah; without his permission he dares to injure no one, to tempt no one to evil.

Thus, it has been sufficiently shown, 1st, that a real serpent was present at the temptation, and 2d, that it was the mere instrument of the actual seducer, Satan. Hence arises the necessity of giving a double meaning to the curse denounced against the tempter. It must refer, in the first place, to the instrument, for otherwise it would have been entirely unintelligible to the first human pair, and without an immediate aim; but in its chief import it must relate to the real tempter, since he alone had properly done what deserved the punishment and curse. Let us now upon these principles proceed to interpret the passage. "Because thou hast done this," (it is said verse 14) "thou art cursed above all cattle, and above every beast of the field: upon thy belly shalt thou go, and dust shalt thou eat all the days of thy life."

So far as these words relate to the serpent, there are two opinions respecting their meaning. Some suppose, that after the fall a change took place in the nature of the serpent, others, that he retained the same nature as before; but after the fall, that which was his nature became his curse. The most able defender of the latter opinion is Calvin: "Nihil erit absurdi, si fateamur pristinae conditioni iterum addici serpentem, cui naturaliter jam subjectus erat, ac si dictum esset · tu ausus es miserum et putidum animal in hominem insurgere, quem praefeceram totius mundi dominio ! quasi vero tuum esset, quum terrae esses affixus in coelum penetrare. Ergo unde emergere tentasti, jam te retraho, ut sorte tua contentus esse discas, nec amplius insolescas in hominis contumeliam." But we must, nevertheless, decide in favor of the former opinion, since, as Le Clerc and Rosenmuller have well remarked, it accords far better with the context, and no man would ever have thought of another interpretation had it not been for the influence of doctrinal views. The difficulty however which led to the second exposition is of no real importance. It is in itself probable, and consistent with his well known character, that Satan should have chosen a pleasing and attractive instrument of temptation. Since, in the view of the author, the fall not only deranged the whole constitution of man, but extended its baleful and accursed influence through the whole system of nature (Gen. 3:17), since, before the fall, the whole world of animals bore the image of the innocence, and the peacefulness of man, and the law of mutual destruction had not yet begun to operate among them (chap. 1:30);* how can it appear strange, that the instrument of the temptation was itself made to suffer in a peculiar degree the consequences of the first transgression?

These words doom the serpent to exhibit the loathsomeness of sin by means of that disgusting form, which, as well as every thing evil and hateful, was the consequence of the first transgression. He must, as it were, serve as a visible representative of the kingdom of darkness, and Satan its head, who had employed him as his instrument. But here we meet with the objection, that it was absurd to inflict a curse upon the serpent, since the poor animal was not to blame for being abused by a higher power. (See Gabler, zu Eichhorn's Urgesch. II. 1, p. 174.) In reply to this, we may well be satisfied with what Calvin has long since said: "Si cui absurdum videtur poenam de bruto animali exigi alienae fraudis, in promtu est solutio: quum esset in hominis gratiam creatus non temere maledici, ex quo versus est in ejus perniciem. Hac ultione probare deus voluit, quanti aestimet hominis salutem: quemadmodum si pater gladium, quo filius occisus fuerit, execrationi habeat." The punishment of the serpent is neither more or less unjust than the suffering condition into which the fall has brought the whole creation, (comp. Rom. 8:20, etc.) than the Mosaic direction, that a beast which had been abused, should be burnt with the guilty author of the crime, or than the bringing of animals to the altar to be slain as sin offerings.

If now we refer this verse to the spiritual author of the temptation, omitting what belongs only to the instrument, it declares: extreme

---

* That the whole animal world cannot possibly have come from the Creator's hand in its present condition has been strikingly shown by Krummacher Paragrapha 2 heil Gesch p. 63 seq. But he has also in opposition to the Holy Scriptures derived the *imperfect* and *evil* from the want of control over matter in the creation and has therefore maintained a dualism.

contempt, shame, and humiliation shall overtake thee. Thus Calmet on the passage. "This enemy of mankind crawls as it were on his belly through the shame and disgrace to which he is reduced"

Satan believed that he should enlarge his kingdom and his power by the seduction of man, but God, who viewed the fall in connection with redemption, saw this transaction in a far different light The eating of dust or ashes occurs also elsewhere as the symbol of the deepest humiliation and grief.

Verse 15 And I will put enmity between thee and the woman, and between thy seed and her seed it shall strike thy head, and thou shalt strike his heel *

As it respects the serpent, the meaning is, thy posterity shall inflict upon that of the woman curable wounds, but hers upon thine incurable The serpent is killed when its head is crushed, while injuries on other parts of the body are not fatal; his bite is no where so harmless as on the heel.†

Such was the only meaning which our first parents at least attached to the divine threatening. But imperfectly as it was understood, it must have inspired them with abhorence of sin as well as strong consolation They regarded the serpent as the sole author of that misery the full burden of which they felt How consoling then must have been the assurance, that he by whom they had been overcome, who had seemed the more to be dreaded from their ignorance of the presence of an invisible and higher power, should not perpetually enjoy his triumph, but suffer defeat and overthrow from their posterity. Far more consoling must have been this assurance to them, or at least to their descendants, when, by becoming acquainted with the natural

---

* We give to the verb שׁוּף with Gabler zu Eichhorn. Urgeschichte II 1 p 190 f, Jahn and others the meaning to strike It has in its favor not only that it is here equally appropriate in both members, but suits also the only two other places where it occurs besides Job 9 17 and Ps 139 11 Every other interpretation requires more meanings than are to be given to the word.

† That by the head and heel a *majus* and *minus*, a victory over the serpent race should be signified, was seen by Calvin Interea videmus, ut se clementer in homine castigando gerat dominus, in quem serpenti non ultra permittit, quam ut calcaneum attingat, quum illi subjiciat vulnerandum serpentis caput Nam in nominibus capitis et calcanei distinctio est inter superius et inferius That it was not designed to represent merely the natural antipathy of men and serpents is evident, from the fact that then no peculiar punishment would be announced to the serpent, which nevertheless the connexion shows to have been the design of the writer (See Gabler zu Eichhorn Urgeschichte II 1, p 189)

powers of the serpent, they were led to distinguish between the visible and invisible cause of their temptation.

Our own experience bears testimony to the truth of the divine threatening, that enmity should henceforth exist between the serpent and the human race. Abhorrence of the serpent is natural to man. Thus Calvin: "Fit arcano naturae sensu, ut ab ipsis abhorreat homo, ac quoties nobis horrorem incutit serpentum aspectus, renovatur defectionis nostrae memoria."

As it respects the chief import of the threatening, its relation to Satan, the greater part of the earlier Christian interpreters think that the Messiah is directly pointed out by the seed of the woman who should bruise the serpent's head.* But to this it may be objected that it does violence to the language to understand, by the seed of the woman, any particular individual, and the more so since we are compelled to understand by the seed of the serpent, a plurality, the spiritual children of Satan, the head and members of the kingdom of darkness, called in the New Testament, ὄφεις, γεννήματα ἐχιδνῶν, and τέκνα τοῦ διαβόλου. This difficulty is avoided, when, by the seed of the woman we understand her posterity in general. According to this explanation the sense is as follows: "True thou hast now inflicted on the woman a severe wound, and thy associates shall continue to assault her posterity. But, notwithstanding all thy malice, thou and thy associates shall be able to inflict on mankind only curable wounds; while, on the contrary, the posterity of the woman shall one day triumph over thee and make thee feel all thy weakness."

This interpretation is given even in the Targum of Jonathan, and that of Jerusalem, which, by the seed of the woman, understand the Jews, who at the coming of the Messiah shall triumph over Sammael. That Paul so understood the passage appears from his allusion to it, Rom. 16. 20, where the promise is regarded as relating to Christians as a body. It is afterwards found in Calvin a very skilful defender.†

---

* So at last Dr Broix, Ursprung and allmählige Entwickelung des Messianismus, p. 26 seq.

† He says, "Quare sensus erit, humanum genus, quod apprimere conatus est Satan, fore tandem superius. Interim tenendus est vincendi modus, quem scriptura discribit. Filios hominum captivos saeculis omnibus duxit Satan pro sua libidine et hodie luctuosum illum triumphum continuat. Sed quia fortior emersit e coelo, qui illum subjugaret, hinc fit, ut illi similiter tota dei ecclesia sub capite suo magnifice insultet."

Among the moderns it has been adopted by Herder,* Storr in his Protevangelium, and Krummacher paragraphen, p. 100, who thus gives the meaning of the passage: "That which is of God must prevail—a redemption must succeed the fall—the closed gates of paradise open again."

According to this interpretation the passage justly bears the name of the Protevangelium, which has been given it by the church. But still the future triumph of the kingdom of light over the kingdom of darkness is announced only in general forms. The person of the Redeemer, who is the leader in the conflict and supplies his people with all their strength to maintain it is not here revealed. More however we should not expect in the very beginning of the human race. A gradual progress and development are as observable in the kingdom of grace as in the kingdom of nature. The prediction contains much that coincides with the tradition of the other nations of Asia, who possessed only the original revelation which was comparatively obscure, while among the Hebrews new revelations were continually shedding fresh light, and rendering more and more complete the glorious image of the Redeemer

Let us now briefly examine the objections which have been brought against the existence of the protevangelium in this passage, at least so far as they concern the interpretation we have given. We can spare ourselves the trouble of collecting them from the numerous writers by whom they have been advanced, since Eichhorn, (Urgesch Th II 2. p. 292) and Gabler have already performed this task.

1 "Why do Christ and the Apostles, who refer so many passages of the Old Testament to Jesus, make no use of this? It must

---

* Briefe, das Studium der Theologie bet. II S 225 (Tub. 1808.) "The serpent had injured them; it became to them an image of evil and temptation, at the same time also of the curse, contempt and punishment To men the encouraging prospect was given, that they, the seed of the woman, should be stronger and nobler than the serpent and all evil They should tread upon and crush his head, while he could avenge himself only by a slight wound upon the heel; briefly the good shall gain the upper hand of the evil This was the prospect. How clear or how obscure it appeared to the first human pair it is not our present purpose to inquire. It is enough that the noblest opposer of evil, and he who most effectually bruised the head of the serpent among the descendants of Eve, stood in this prospect and indeed preeminently belonged to it Thus then was given at that period only an outline of natural and sensible images which was filled up and completed in future times."

have been of all others the most important and most worthy of their attention. Why then do we not find so much as an allusion to it?" The answer is easy. The writers of the New Testament did not distinctly refer this prophecy to Jesus, because it is not sufficiently definite, since it contains no direct reference to the person of the Messiah. It was natural that the writers of the New Testament should quote the many more obvious passages. It is not however true that the New Testament contains no allusion to this passage. See the place already referred to in the epistle to the Romans, in which Rosenmueller himself, on Gen 3· 15, acknowledges the allusion. But that Christ and his Apostles here found the Protevangelium in our sense of the term is plainly proved by those passages in the New Testament from which we have shown that they believed Satan to have been concerned in the apostasy.

2 "By the seed of the serpent, neither bad men nor fallen angels can well be intended, for in what sense can they be called the posterity of the devil? Bad men must be excluded because they belong to the descendants of Eve and consequently cannot be put in opposition to them." We remark in reply that nothing is more common in the Scripture than for the natural relation between father and son to be transferred to spiritual subjects. In this same book men of a godly disposition are called the sons of God. The scholars of the Prophets bear the name of their sons, and that it is no uncommon thing to transfer this relation to Satan and his associates is shown by the appellation of the ungodly in the New Testament to which we have referred. In the passage also of the Sohar already quoted they are named the "children of the old serpent." With respect to the second part of the objection it by no means shows that ungodly men cannot belong to the seed of the serpent, although the import of this term is not limited to them but embraces all the subjects of Satan. "Facile videmus," says Storr, (I c p 431) "etiam serpentis progeniem esse progeniem mulieris, sed indignam hoc nomine ex quo desciverit ad communem sui generis hostem. See also Calvin on the passage.

3 "The gospel would have been entirely unintelligible to our first parents, for they felt no need of a Redeemer and had no idea of the design of his appointment." This assertion is contradicted by the narrative. That Adam and Eve after eating the forbidden fruit were seized with a deep sense of guilt is evinced by the shame they felt, the common offspring of those sinful desires and of conscience,

as well as by their tormenting fear of God, with whom they had hitherto enjoyed affectionate communion. This feeling of guilt must have been greatly increased when the curse, which God had denounced against the earth, began to be executed, and man was driven out from paradise. Nature before in subjection, but now risen up in rebellion against him, his frail body, which from the moment of the fall had begun to die, and especially the disquietude of his own breast, all reminded him of his guilt. But the conviction of his guilt must have made him feel his need of a redemption, and thus have prepared him to welcome the promise of a future victory over the kingdom of darkness. Nor was this promise important to Adam and Eve alone, but to all their posterity. And it is from this and similar predictions, imparted to mankind in the earliest times, that the doctrine of a future and glorious redemption was derived, which, as we have seen, existed among heathen nations.

Genesis 9 : 26, 27.

This passage contains the blessing of Noah upon his two sons, Shem and Japheth. Even v. 26, "Praised be Jehovah the God of Shem," intimates the preservation of the true religion among the descendants of Shem. The patriarch, whose expressions are not to be regarded as mere wishes of his own, but as predictions also, beholds a degree of prosperity destined for his son Shem, so great, that instead of announcing it to him in direct terms, he is moved to break forth in praise to God, by whom it was to be conferred.*

The nature of this prosperity was indicated in two ways. 1. God is not called by the name Elohim, expressive of his general relation to the world, but by the name Jehovah, which refers to his revelation and to his institutions for man's redemption.† 2. Jehovah is styled the "God of Shem." Both imply that God would sustain to the posterity of Shem a relation entirely peculiar, favor them with

---

* Bochart Phaleg II 1 c 65 seq ed IV "Reo in propria persona maledixerat propter admissum scelus, quia mali fomes et scaturigo est in ipso homine. At Semi pietate delectatus, deo maluit benedicere, quia deum noverat esse auctorem hujus boni."

† See the inquiries respecting both names by Sack, "Commentationes theol." Bonnae 1821, p 1—24, and by "Ewald, die composition der Genesis kritisch untersucht," Braunschw. 1823, p 7 seq.

revelations of his will, and make them partakers of his temporal and spiritual blessings.

V 27 goes still further. Its immediate object indeed is only to pronounce the blessing of Japheth; but at the same time it includes a far greater blessing destined for Shem, and thus completes the declaration respecting him in the foregoing verse. "May God enlarge Japheth, may he dwell in the tents of Shem." But as this passage has received various interpretations, we must justify the one we have now given

The first difference among interpreters is occasioned by the words יַפְתְּ אֱלֹהִים לְיֶפֶת. The verb יַפְתְּ which forms a paronomasia with the noun יֶפֶת is future apoc. Hiphal of פָּתָה. This verb in the Hebrew commonly means. *to persuade*, or *enable one to do any thing*. Giving it this meaning here, interpreters (see Calvin on the passage) translate it thus "Alliciat Deus Japhetum, ut habitet in tentoriis Semi." The objection urged against this interpretation by several expositors, after the example of Bochart in his admirable examination of this passage, (Phaleg. III. l. c 147 seq) that only Piel not Hiphil occurs in this sense, is inconclusive, since an unusual conjugation may have been chosen for the sake of the paronomasia. Nor is the other objection of more weight, that פָּתָה nearly always means *to persuade* in a bad sense, since there are passages as Jer 20 7, where it is used in a good one. It is however decisive against this interpretation that פָּתָה in such a sense is never construed with לְ, but always with the Acc. case. Kelle (die heil. Schriften in ihrer Urgestalt II p 122) has, it is true, attempted to remove the difficulty by translating. 'May God intercede for Japheth.' May God be Japheth's intercessor with his elder brother, that he may grant him equal privileges with himself But besides that this translation is extremely forced, such a modification of the meaning of the word פָּתָה cannot be justified. We must therefore agree with those interpreters who give to the verb פָּתָה the meaning *to be broad*; which indeed occurs but once in the Hebrew, Prov 20 19, but is the prevailing one in Chaldee For this interpretation we have not only the authority of most of the ancient versions; (the LXX render πλατύναι ὁ θεὸς τῷ Ἰαφεθ. The Vulg *dilatet Deus Japheth* Onkel Ar) but it is confirmed also by the consideration that verbs of a similar import are elsewhere construed with לְ. (See chap. 26. 22.) חַרְחִיב יהוה לָנוּ. Ps 4. 2, בַּצָּר הִרְחַבְתָּ לִּי, 'In time of trouble, thou hast enlarged for me,' i e the place Prov. 18 16, יַרְחִיב לוֹ,

'The gift of a man maketh wide for him,' i. e. his way or access. The sense of the first member of the parallelism therefore is: God shall give Japheth a numerous posterity, who shall possess widely extended territories. The accomplishment of this prediction has been happily pointed out by Bochart and Fuller, Miscel Sacra, II 4 p 165 seq. The descendants of Japheth have not only gained possession of all Europe, but likewise a large portion of Asia.

Another difference of opinion arises in the second member, with respect to the subject of the verb וישכן. According to a very ancient interpretation אלהים is to be supplied. ו will then be adversative, and the meaning, "God will indeed enlarge Japheth, but he will dwell in the tents of Shem." The inferior condition of Japheth would then be contrasted with the exalted privilege of Shem, with whose descendants God should glorify himself first in the tabernacle, afterwards in the temple by the symbol of his gracious presence, and lastly and in the highest sense should dwell by the incarnation of his Son. So Onkelos: "dilatet deus Semo, et habitet, שכינתו (the symbol of his presence), in tentoriis Semi." The ancient book Bieschith Rabba on this place in Schottgen de Mess p 141 has אין שכינה שורה אלא באהלי שם, 'the Shekinah dwells only in the tents of Shem.' Theodoret also brings forward this interpretation, and well explains the passage, Interrog 58 in Genesin: τοῦ μὲν Ἰαφεθ τὴν πολυγονίαν προείρηκε, τοῦ δὲ Ζὴμ τὴν εὐσέβειαν. Τὸν γὰρ θεὸν ἐν τοῖς σκηνώμασι τοῦ Ζὴμ κατοικήσειν προείρηκε, κατῴκησε δὲ ἐν τοῖς ἐκ τοῦ Ζὴμ πατριάρχαις καὶ ἐν τοῖς ἐκ τούτων βεβλαστηκόσι προφήταις. Καὶ ἐν τῇ σκηνῇ πρότερον καὶ ἐν Ἱεροσολύμοις ὕστερον. Ἀκριβὲς δὲ τέλος ἔσχεν ἡ προφητεία τὸ τῆς οἰκονομίας μυστήριον, ὅτε αὐτὸς ὁ θεὸς λόγος ἐσαρκώθη καὶ ἐνηνθρώπησε. Also Fuller l c Dathe on this passage and others also adopt this exposition. And certainly there are numerous parallel passages where God is represented as dwelling among the Israelites, the posterity of Shem, Ps 132 13, 14. "For the Lord hath chosen Zion, he hath desired it for his habitation. This is my rest forever, here will I dwell, for I have desired it." To this interpretation it has been objected, after Bochart, by Le Clerc, Rosenmuller and others, that, 1st, as the foregoing verse relates entirely to Shem, so must this relate entirely to Japheth and 2d, that the reference to Shem is inadmissible, because the last words of the verse, "and Canaan shall be his servant," must of necessity be referred to Japheth and his descendants, since otherwise there would be a useless repetition of what had already been said in the preceding verse in relation to Shem. But the objections are not conclusive. With respect to the former it may be said that the mind of Noah was so full of the great salvation in reserve for the descendants of Shem, that, in announcing the inferior blessings destined for Japheth, he might naturally have returned again to the former, and more clearly expressed what was only intimated in the preceding verse, and to the latter, the charge of useless repetition is obviated if למו is referred, as in accordance with our interpretation it must be, not to Shem alone, but to both Shem and Japheth, thus. "God will enlarge Japheth, but dwell in the tents of Shem, and Canaan shall be the servant of both." Such an aggravation of the punishment announced against Ham and his descendants well accords with Noah's state of mind. But there is another objection which cannot be so easily answered. It is plain that Noah intentionally used the name Jehovah in speaking of Shem, and Elohim in speaking of Japheth.* It is still more improbable that if Jehovah was intended to be the subject of the verb ישכון this name would have been left to be supplied by the reader. We are therefore compelled to regard Japheth as the subject. But still there are two different interpretations of this second member of the sentence.

Following Michaelis, Vater takes Japheth indeed to be the subject, but regards שם not as a proper name but as an appellation. *Name—illustrious name—renown*, "May God give to Japheth an extended country: may he dwell in renowned habitations." This is sustained by Gesenius, Hdwb. s. v and also by Winer. But it is in the highest degree unnatural to suppose that שם is here suddenly employed in a totally different meaning from that which it has in the verse before, and no one would resort to such an interpretation except from extreme necessity.

The translation "may Japheth dwell in the tents of Shem" is therefore the true one. But with respect to its import there is again a difference of opinion. Many interpreters, as Bochart, Calmet, Le Clerc, and others, understand the passage literally, or at least they regard the literal as the principal meaning. It is here foretold that the posterity of Japheth should one day gain possession of the country belonging to the posterity of Shem and reduce them to subjection. They compare the passage with the prediction of Balaam,

* This was perceived by Vater Comm p 89 Sack I c p 13 Kelle has allowed himself to be led by it to the unfortunate hypothesis that v 26 is an interpolation of a transcriber or reviser

Num. 24: 24, according to which the Chittim, a people descended from Japheth, should oppress Ashur and Eber, and find it fulfilled in the conquest of Palestine by the Greeks and Romans. But this interpretation is certainly inadmissible. Bochart himself remarks that the blessings of Japheth should be regarded only in a manner supplementary to the blessing of Shem. How then can we suppose that Noah, to favor Japheth, should here by predicting evil diminish the value of the splendid promises made to Shem, who was plainly to be exalted above both his brothers?

We must then adopt the figurative interpretation, according to which, by the dwelling of Japheth in the tents of Shem, it is to be intimated that the true religion was to be preserved among the posterity of Shem, and imparted by them to the descendants of Japheth, who were to be received among the true worshippers of God. So Jonathan: condecorabit dominus terminum Japheti et proselyti fient filii ejus et habitabunt in schola Semi. So also Jerome, though he perceived not its full import, in Quaestiones Gen. Opp. T III. p. 134 Fr.: Quod autem ait: et habitet in tabernaculis Sem, de nobis prophetatur, qui in eruditione et scientia scripturarum ejecto Israele versamur. Better Augustin: Hoc prorsus, hoc praenuntiabatur cum diceretur: latificet deus Japheth et habitet in tentoriis Sem, id est in ecclesiis, quas filii prophetarum apostoli construxerunt. But most happily Calvin. Sensus est, temporale fore dissidium inter Sem et Japhet; deinde venturum tempus, quo rursus coalescant in unum corpus et commune habeant domicilium — Certo vero certius est vaticinium hic de rebus secundum hominem incognitis proferri, cujus non alium fuisse autorem, quam deum eventus demum ostendit. Duo annorum millia et aliquot secula fluxerunt antequam gentes et Judaei in unam fidem aggregarentur. Tunc filii Sem, quorum major pars diffluxerat et se absciderat a sancta dei familia, simul collecti sunt, ut sub eodem tabernaculo agerent. Gentes etiam ex Japhet progenitae, quae diu palantes ac vagae fuerant, in idem tabernaculum receptae sunt. Deus enim nova adoptione unum populum ex diversis effecit et fraternam unitatem sancivit inter alienos (Comp. Eph. 2: 14, 19. John 10: 16.) Atque id factum est suavi et blanda dei voce, quam in Evangelio protulit: et quotidie adhuc impletur vaticinium hoc, quum dispersas oves invitat deus ad suum gregem, et hinc inde colligit, qui recumbant cum Abraham, Isaac et Jacob in regno coelorum.

The figurative mode of expression found in this passage has its parallel in various places of Scripture. Zech. 12 7, 'the tents of Judah,' and Mal. 2 12, 'the tents of Jacob' are the designation of the Theocracy. Luke 16 9, ' reception into everlasting habitations' is reception into the everlasting kingdom of God. This interpretation is also confirmed by a comparison with the promises to Abraham, Isaac, and Jacob As it is there foretold, that through the descendants of the Patriarchs all nations should be blessed, so here it is predicted that the institutions to be established among the posterity of Shem should afterwards be extended to the posterity of Japheth. The only objection to this interpretation advanced by Mercer and others, that many of Ham's descendants have participated in the salvation that originated with the posterity of Shem, is refuted by the remark that here the object being to punish Ham for his crime, only the future adversity, and not prosperity of his descendants was foretold; while, on the contrary, only prosperity was announced to Shem and Japheth, higher to the former, inferior to the latter.

PROMISES TO THE PATRIARCHS

The first promise which here comes under consideration was made to Abraham before he emigrated from his native land to Canaan. Gen 12 3, it is said " In thee shall all the families of the earth be blessed " The same promise is repeated Gen 18: 18, only instead of (מִשְׁפְּחוֹת) we read nations, (גּוֹיִם). Chap 22 18, this promise is repeated to Abraham as a reward for his ready compliance with the command to offer up his son Isaac There the indefinite expression " through thee," (בְּךָ) is explained by " through thy seed," (בְזַרְעֶךָ) Chap 26 4, the same promise is confirmed to Isaac Chap 28 14, it is delivered to Jacob In the former two places, it is "through thee," in the two latter " through thy seed;" but here it is instead, "through thee and thy seed," the ו being exegetical It has been attempted, by two different and equally inadmissible modes of interpretation, to reject the true import of these promises After Jarchi and other Jewish interpreters, Le Clerc translates ' by thee, or by thy posterity, shall all the families of the earth bless themselves ' " Hoc nomine exemplove prolato benedictiones apud plurimos Orientis populos concipientur his aut similibus verbis: benedicat tibi Deus, ut benedixit Abrahamo." So likewise Eckermann theol Beitr. II 3 p 40. But this forced interpretation is in total opposition to the usage of the language. The conj. Niph. of the verb בָּרֵךְ which occurs in three of these places, cannot possibly have the meaning which this interpretation supposes and even the conj. Hithpael which is found in chap. xxii and xxvi, and upon which the chief reliance is placed, has never the sense "to wish one another prosperity," but it means in all the other places where it is used, (Deut. 29. 19. Is. 66. 16. Ps. 72. 17), "to regard one's self as blessed, or happy, to promise one's self prosperity." If we adopt this latter meaning, the reason of the alternate use of Niphal and Hithpael will be easily explained. They both convey the same idea. "Through thee, or through thy descendants, the nations shall regard themselves as blessed," that is, "they shall thereby be blessed." But this is not all. The interpretation of which we are speaking renders the promise so utterly insignificant, that no imaginable reason can be assigned for the frequent verbal repetition and renewal of it. And finally, it would be a singular hyperbole, to say that all the people of the whole earth should wish one another prosperity, appealing to the instance of Abraham.

Another way of setting aside the reference of this promise to the Messiah has been taken by Bertholdt (de ortu theologiae vet.) after the example of Ammon (Christologie). He says, "Abrahamo, Isaaco et Jacobo facta erat a deo spes, fore ut reliquae gentes terrae Canaanis מִשְׁפָּחוֹת גּוֹיֵי הָאָרֶץ — הָאֲדָמָה — posterorum suorum potestati se subjicerent atque sic honores et beneficia populis foedere cum aliis junctis ex vulgari consuetudine concessa in se conferrent.* But this exposition betrays its origin still more clearly than the foregoing. Besides the manifest insipidity of such a meaning, so little in accordance with the circumstances in which the promise was given, we urge chiefly the following objections. 1. The restriction of אֶרֶץ and אֲדָמָה solely to the land of Canaan, and of מִשְׁפָּחוֹת and גּוֹיִם to its inhabitants is entirely arbitrary, since in no one of the places cited, does the context warrant this: but every thing tends to show that these comprehensive expressions are employed in their unrestricted signification.

2. That they have always been understood by the Jewish people in this unlimited sense, is manifest from the passages of Scripture where the extension of the Messiah's salvation to all the heathen na-

---

* In like manner also Baumgarten-Crusius, (bibl. theol. p. 368,) only that he supposes the descendants of Abraham should possess the whole earth, and its inhabitants so far be blessed by them as to enjoy the favor of being ruled by them. A very remarkable blessing!

tions is announced with special reference to this promise. See Ps. 72 17, etc. Bertholdt himself confesses, (l c p 104,) that these passages show that the Israelites, in the time of David and Solomon, understood that the promised salvation was not to be confined to the inhabitants of Palestine, but extended to all the heathen nations through the descendants of Abraham. He seeks however to evade the obvious inference by the difficult assumption, that such an interpretation could have proceeded only from ignorance of the laws of "historical hermeneutics."

3. It is not easy to see how God can have promised to Abraham, that, through his posterity, temporal blessings should be conferred upon the inhabitants of Canaan. In direct opposition to this is the promise made to him, Gen 15 18, that his posterity should possess the whole land of Palestine, and have dominion over all the tribes of its inhabitants, who are there mentioned by name V. 16. The sentence of extermination to be executed by the Israelites in after days, is plainly alluded to in the observation that the iniquity of the Amorites, here put as a part for the whole, was not yet full. These and similar passages forbid us to think that the heathen inhabitants of Canaan had a right to expect from the posterity of Abraham *honores et beneficia.*

The undeniable meaning of the promises made to the Patriarchs is, that through their posterity salvation should be conferred upon all the nations of the earth The nature of this blessing, however, is not accurately defined. But even the Patriarchs themselves could have inferred from sure indications that temporal blessings could have been intended only so far as they are the necessary consequences of spiritual blessings, and as true religion never fails to improve the outward condition of man They could not have supposed that the promise referred to mere *temporal blessings,* because they could have perceived no method by which such blessings were to be conferred upon the heathen through their posterity Farther, how could they think that all the nations of the earth were to obtain temporal blessings through them, when it had been foretold that their posterity would be the source of temporal *calamities* to many of the heathen nations, by reducing them to subjection? See Gen. 15: 16, etc. Finally, since the object of the blessings partly given and partly promised to the Patriarchs and their descendants was to promote the knowledge and practice of the true religion, and since they were imparted on this very condition, (see Gen. 17: 1. 18 17—19 22. 16—18.

26 5) the Patriarchs must have expected their posterity to be the source of blessings to the heathen only by introducing them to the privileges of this religion

This much they could easily have inferred from the language of this promise. As to the mode in which this blessing was to be extended to the heathen, it gives no information. In order to a further development of this mystery, a more particular revelation from God was necessary.* That this was vouchsafed to Abraham, although no where expressly mentioned in his history, is not only probable from the near relation in which he stood to God, Gen 18 17, but is rendered certain by the testimony of the Lord himself, John 8 56, where he affirms that Abraham had been favored with a prophetic view of his future manifestation

The prediction we have been examining is often quoted in the New Testament, and its fulfilment assigned to the time of the Messiah, Acts 3 25, 26 Rom 4 13—16. Gal 3 8 and 16 A difficulty occurs in the last place, from the circumstance that Paul lays a peculiar stress upon the singular זַרְעֲ, which is so often used in a collective sense, and seems desirous of showing from it that Christ alone could have been intended by the seed of Abraham, through whom the heathen should be blessed But this difficulty is removed by the remark, that Paul by no means asserts the necessity of this interpretation, (which, judging merely from his knowledge of Hebrew, could not have been the case, and which we see from Rom. 4. 13, he was far from intending) but only its *possibility* The fulfilment shows that the heathen were not to be blessed by the descendants of Abraham in general, but by one of them in particular, and Paul draws our attention to the fact that the Lord, who when he made the promise, had its fulfilment, which he Himself had to accomplish, already in view, intentionally selected an expression, which, besides the more comprehensive meaning that would naturally be given it by the Patriarchs, admitted also the more restricted one which was es-

---

* Herder very justly remarks, Briefe das Stud d Theol. betr II 273. Since all the nations of the whole earth were to be blessed in the seed of Abraham, we could and ought to regard this blessing in all its universality, and include in it every thing whereby his people should benefit mankind As Christ therefore belongs to those noble benefactors of the human race, the blessing refers to him, not *indirecte* but *directe*, and, since he is preeminent, *directissime* before all others. Abraham however did not clearly see his form in this germ, the whole edifice of his merit in this bud, nor could he see it without a special revelation

tablished by the accomplishment. Who can reasonably deny that such may have been the motive for choosing this expression? We have a case analogous to this in the Protevangelium, and the old interpreters have erred in regarding them both as necessarily referring directly and solely to the person of the Messiah. See also on Deut xviii. and on 2 Sam vii

---

Genesis 49 10.

We here premise that we decidedly hold the genuineness of Jacob's blessing contained in chap XLIX On a careful examination of the grounds which its opposers, Heinrichs (de Auct. atque. Aet. h. c Gott 1790), Vater, De Wette, Friedrich, Justi and Bleek have taken, their chief objection seems to be the doctrinal and therefore inadmissible one, that the passage cannot be genuine because it contains manifest references to future events, the knowledge of which Jacob could have had no natural means of possessing That it does indeed contain such references cannot be denied Granting that, with respect to some of the predictions of Jacob, human causes might be pointed out, which might have given him an anticipation of the future, and rejecting several distinct references arbitrarily assumed by the opposers of its genuineness, still it contains many annunciations of many events too definite and too strikingly confirmed by history to be ascribed to natural causes; unless indeed we are willing to resort to extremely forced expedients, like Hensler, (Bemerkungen uber Stellen in den Psalmen und der Genesis p. 417 seq) and Stahelin (Animadversiones quaedam in Jacobi Vatic Basel 1827, comp vs. 7, 10, 13. Fritsche, achtheit der Bucher Mosis, p. 138). But there is, we believe, no occasion for this. Unless we are prepared to deny the historical truth of the whole book of Genesis, and thus involve ourselves in inextricable difficulties, and likewise disregard the authority of the New Testament, we must acknowledge that Jacob, as well as Isaac his father, and Abraham, also received immediate revelations from God. Why then may not this have been the case in the present instance, especially as it is so easy to assign an end which is worthy of God in this last revelation of his purposes to Jacob. The remaining objections are manifestly sought in order to conceal the fact that the opinion of their authors rest entirely on doctrinal grounds. When it is asserted that a strain of poetry so lofty, animated and rich in imagery could not have proceeded from a superannuated old man, (comp Justi Nationalges. der Heb. II. p 2) on the brink of the grave, it is not necessary to refer to the help of God, which forced the soul of the patriarch from the depressing influence of the body It may suffice to remark, on the one hand, that the discourse does not possess the high poetical character ascribed to it, and on the other, that we must not judge of it by the present condition of society, when, with the predominance of the understanding, poetry has become a work of art, but we must transport ourselves back to the remotest antiquity, when the liveliness and vigor of the imagination made poetry the work of nature, and objects were presented in connexion with poetical expression and imagery Much light is thrown on this subject by the history of the old Arabian poetry. The poets of that country, before the time of Mohammed often recited long poems extempore. (See Tharaphae Moall ed. Reiske p. 40. Antarae Moallakah ed. Menil, p. 18). The poet Lebid, who reached the great age of 157 years, (see Reiske Prolegg ad Tharaphae Moall. p 30. De Sacy, Memoires de l'Acad des Inscript. t. I. 403 seq) composed a poem while dying. (See Herbelot Bibl. Or p 513)

The poet Hareth, when he recited extempore his Moallakah, which is still extant, was already 135 years old. (See Reiske l. c) Of just as little consequence is the alleged difficulty of conceiving how the blessing promised by Jacob could have been handed down *verbatim* to Moses. Here also the history of the Arabian poetry furnishes the best refutation The art of writing was introduced among the Arabians but a short time before Mohammed (See De Sacy l. c. p. 306, 348 Amrulkeisi Moall ed. Hengstenberg, p 3) Until then their longest poems, some of which consisted of more than a hundred verses, were preserved by mere oral tradition,* and those which still remain bear literal evidence of the fidelity with which they were handed down It has been often remarked, that before the invention of writing, the power of memory was much greater than at present

As it would therefore have been an easy task for the descendants of Jacob to have retained the comparatively brief expressions of the founder of the race; so must the importance attached to them have furnished a powerful motive to transmit them with the greatest fidel-

---

* See Nuweiri by Rosenmüller, Zoheiri Moal p 11

ity from generation to generation. Such was the length of human life, that the tradition needed to pass through but few hands in descending to Moses. and who can assure us after all that Moses did not find this passage already committed to writing?

We should digress too far from our purpose, were we to give any thing more than some brief hints of the positive arguments for the genuineness of this portion of Scripture All is natural and too exactly in harmony with the circumstances of Jacob, to have been the work of a later author. See especially verse 18, where the Patriarch breaks forth in an ejaculation and prays to God that his happy dissolution may soon take place A later writer would have put into the mouth of Jacob far more of the events that had already happened, and have introduced something exactly suited to the existing condition of each tribe How little characteristic, for example, is what is said of Ashur, Naphtali, Gad and Benjamin. On the contrary, that such mere hints should have been given by Jacob is sufficiently probable; for his weakness compelled him to be brief, and he could express only what was given to him. Had the writer lived after Moses, he could never have spoken of the distribution of the Levites in such terms as are here employed for the purpose of humbling their ancestor, and least of all could he have done this had he been contemporary with David, when the lot of the children of Levi, so commended by Moses, had become still more honorable See Teller (ubersetzung des Segens Jakob's und Mosis u. s w Halle 1766. Einleitung), who is the ablest defender of the genuineness of the passage. and see Hensler and Stahelin ll cc. Mossler (Dissert h c Wittemb 1808), Jahn (Vatic Mess. II. p 169), Rosenmuller (Comm. in Pent ed 3 t. I. p 684 seq), Hug (Zeitschrift fur die Geistlichkeit des Erzbisthums Freiburg I. p. 113 seq) and others

If it is then evident that we have here before us, in Gen. XLIX, the words of the dying Jacob, instead of being surprised we naturally expect to find in them an allusion to the times of the Messiah The promises which were first made to his fathers and were afterwards delivered to Jacob himself embraced two objects—first, a numerous posterity, and their settlement in the land of Canaan, and second, the blessings which, through them, should be conferred upon all nations How then can it well be supposed that Jacob, when delivering over these promises to his *sons*, should stop short at their first object—that, beholding them in spirit already in possession of the promised land, he should describe the dwelling places they should receive, and many circumstances of their history, and neglect to mention the second object which was incomparably more important, and had been so often repeated? Is it not far more likely that, as before among the sons of Abraham and Isaac, as here also among the sons of Jacob, the individual should be pointed out, who according to the will of God was to be the inheritor of this promise which was continually assuming a more definite form?

The probability of the supposition is not a little strengthened by the singular unanimity of exegetical tradition in its favor. The Jews, in the first place, as far back as this tradition can be traced, regard v 10 as predicting the Messiah. Thus it was interpreted by the Chaldaic paraphrases; the Targum of Onkelos, of Jerusalem, and of Jonathan; the Talmud, the Sohar, and the old book Bereshith Rabba, and even by several of the more modern commentators, as Jarchi, though they were tempted by that strong prejudice to which others yielded to give the passage which holds so important a place in the controversy with Christians another interpretation. See the passages cited by Raym Martini Pug Fid. ed. Carpzov pass. Jac. Alting Schilo, Franck. 1660. 4, also in the Opp. t V Schottgen Hor Hebr II. p 146, and most fully in the Jac patriarch, de Schiloh Vatic a Depravatione Clerici assertum op Seb Edzardi, Londin. 1698. 8. p 103 seq The unanimity of the older Jewish writers, notwithstanding all their difference of opinion as to the import of this prophecy, in regarding the Messiah as the subject of it, shows how firm and sure and of course how ancient was the tradition they followed. The Samaritans also explain the passage of this Messiah. See Samarit. Briefwechsel mitgetheilt in Schnurrer, von Eichhorn's Repert 9. p. 27. True, it seems from other passages, (Epist Samaritan. ad Job. Ludolfum in Eichh Rep. 13 p 281. 89, compared with De Sacy, de vers Sam Arab. Pentateuchi in Eichhorn's Bibliothik 10 p 54), that a part of them holding the doctrine of two Messiahs, one who had already appeared, and another who was yet to come, referred the passage solely to the former, and denied its relation to the true Messiah; but this proves nothing, since, as Gesenius also has remarked, (Carmina Samaritana, p 75) that the notion of two Messiahs is of modern origin among the Samaritans as well as among the Jews, and in all probability the reference to the true Messiah, which, as we learn from the former of the writings mentioned above, was never entirely given up, was at the earlier period generally adopted.

Finally, in the Christian church, the Messianic interpretation has from the earliest times (as we find it mentioned even by Justin Martyr) been generally approved. Even Grotius himself is here obliged to find the Messiah, and Le Clerc appears as the only critic of his time who opposes this interpretation. This remarkable unanimity justifies us in adopting the principle, that the reference to the Messiah must not be rejected, unless it is proved to be erroneous by other and better arguments. until then, it deserves the preference to all other interpretations, even allowing them to be in other respects equally well founded.

We examine first, the justness of the Messianic interpretation. Every thing depends upon the meaning which we give to the word Shiloh. Among the interpretations of this word which are consistent with the reference to the Messiah, there are three which deserve particular examination.

According to some expositors שִׁילֹה is compounded of the noun שִׁיל and the suffix ה for ו. The noun signifies child "until his, i. e Judah's, son or descendant, the Messias, shall come" Thus Jonathan, עד זמן די ייתי מלכא משיחא זעיר כנוי, 'usque ad tempus, quando veniet rex Messias, parvulus filiorum ejus.' Calvin also approves this interpretation. Also Knapp, Dogm II p 138. But this meaning of the word is incapable of proof. The comparison with the noun שִׁלְיָה, Deut 28 57, is not to the purpose. It is an unnatural supposition that שִׁלְיָה, *membrana foetum involvens*, here stands *pro ipso foetu*. Equally inadmissible is the comparison with the Rabbinic שׁלִיל, *embryo*, allowing it to be also an old Hebrew word; or the Arabic سَلِيل, because it does not mean *son* in general, but 'foetus mas recens natus, quasi ex matre extractus;' because the forms of the two words are different, and because the comparison of the Arabic is proper only when the Hebrew can give us no adequate assistance. But the greatest objection to this interpretation as well as to the one which follows is, that they ascribe a different etymology to the word שׁילה in this passage from that of Shiloh, the name of a place which is written in precisely the same manner.

2. According to others, the word is erroneously pointed. They propose to read שׁלה compounded of the prep שׁ for אֲשֶׁר and suf. ה for ו. They suppose the language to be elliptical; "until he comes to whom it is, or belongs," that is, the dominion, or the sceptre. This interpretation is very skilfully defended by Jahn, Einleit. in A T. I p. 507 seq and Vatic Mess. II. p. 179

seq. It is approved also by Hess, De Wette, Krummacher and others. The principal argument of its advocates, is, that most of the old translators adopted this punctuation. And at all events this must be conceded. True Buxtorf, (Anticrit p. 714), with whom Rosenmuller agrees (l. c p. 702) has denied it with respect to Onkelos, and the Targum of Jerusalem, which translate: donec veniet Messias, cujus est regnum, while he asserts that שילֹה is translated simply by משיחא, and that what follows is an addition similar to those which often occur in the Targums. But this opinion, which would appear not altogether improbable, if we consulted only the Chaldee paraphrasts themselves, is seen to be erroneous by a comparison of the other ancient versions. If, and such is indeed the fact, it cannot be denied that this was the punctuation which they adopted: we are driven to the supposition which would otherwise be the most obvious, that it was adopted also by the authors of the Targums. In the Septuagint a very ancient variety of readings is found, and $\tau\grave{a}\ \grave{a}\pi o$-$\kappa\varepsilon i\mu\varepsilon\nu a\ a\grave{v}\tau\tilde{\omega}$ and $\tilde{\tilde{\omega}}\ \grave{a}\pi\acute{o}\kappa\varepsilon\iota\tau a\iota$. Both readings, "that which is appointed for him," and "he to whom it is appointed," of which in all probability the first is the original, presuppose the punctuation שֶׁלֹה. So also Ag. and Symm. who translate, $\tilde{\tilde{\omega}}\ \grave{a}\pi o\nu\varepsilon\tilde{\iota}\tau a\iota$, as well as the Syriac and R. Saadias Haggaon: 'ille cujus est.' But the defenders of this interpretation fall into an error, when they conclude, from the fact that the old translators adopted this pointing, that it was the received one in their time. Were this the case, how can it have happened that it no longer exists in any of our manuscripts? For the circumstance that forty Mss collated by De Rossi have שלה without *yod* is of no importance. It is merely a defective way of writing which often occurs in words of a similar kind. If we reflect, what history proves, that the Jews watched with the most anxious solicitude over the uncorrupted preservation of the received text of the Holy Scriptures, according to its consonants and pronunciation, and did not venture to adopt an emendation of that text, though recommended by the strongest probability, while, on the other hand, the old Jewish and Christian translators allowed themselves great freedom in this respect, it will appear most likely that they found the present pointing of the word as the received one, but felt obliged to depart from it, because, according to it, they could give to the word no suitable derivation, while on the contrary the pointing which they adopted agreed with the traditional reference of the passage to the Messiah. But if this were so, the authority of the ancient translators is of no more value than that of any modern interpreter, and all objections here exist, which may in general be urged against changing the punctuation, without the strongest reasons.

Another argument for this interpretation has been taken from Ezek. 21. 32 (27). The words עַד־בֹּא אֲשֶׁר לוֹ הַמִּשְׁפָּט, "until he come whose is the dominion"—are regarded as a manifest paraphrase of שִׁילֹה. It cannot indeed be denied that Ezekiel here had in view the passage under consideration; and, upon this, we derive an argument of no small weight against all opposers of its reference to the Messiah. But still there is no objection to understand the words, "he whose is the dominion," as a paraphrase of Shiloh, regarded as a name of the Messiah, according to the interpretation next to be considered. Against that now under consideration, we urge not only that the prefix שׁ for אֲשֶׁר occurs no where else in the Pentateuch—an objection which is not of itself sufficient, since it does occur in the song of Deborah, Judg 5. 7, but also that the supposed ellipsis is so unnatural that scarcely an analogous example can be found. See Stanger, theol. Symm. II. p 238 seq.

3. And lastly, others have interpreted Shiloh as a kind of proper name of the Messiah derived from the verb שָׁלָה quievit, the pacificator, the author of peace. It has been thus explained, after the example of many of the older interpreters (Luther: Held. Castalio: Sospitator. Vers. Tigur in marg. felicitator), by Brentano, Muhlert (uber Schiloh in des sterbenden Jakob's Segen, in den Analekten von Keil und Tschirner II 3.) Kanne, (Christus im A. T. 1. p. 210 seq.) Rosenm. (3d Ed.) Winer (Lex s. v.) Baumgarten-Crus (Bibl. Theol p 368.)* This interpretation is liable to no objection, and has every thing in its favor. With respect to the form of the noun, it is fully sustained by analogy. Thus כִּידוֹר *tumult of war*, from כָּדַר *to be troubled*, כִּיבוֹר from כָּבַר, שִׁיהוּר from שָׁהַר, שִׁלֹה from שָׁלָה, צִיּוּק from צָעַק, קִיטוֹר from קָטַר. We had an example of a similar formation of a word ending in ה in the name of a place, גִּלֹה from גָּלָה, Jos. 15. 51. Jahn has indeed objected to translating it *pacificator*, that no certain examples can be produced when

---

* It would therefore, after these defenders of the Messianic interpretation, be too late for any one with Justi 1 c p 56, to reject it without further arguments, with the simple remark: Allegory and mysticism found the Messiah in this passage and ascribed to it a meaning, which must have been unknown as well to the dying Jacob as the collector of the Mosaic records, or a poet of the time of David. See, finally, Ammon Christol. p 28.

a noun of this form has an active signification. Allowing this to be the fact, we need only suppose that שילה originally had the abstract meaning *rest*, which is favored by the use of Shiloh as the name of a place; but that here however, as in numberless other cases, the abstract is used for the concrete. Thus the word שָׁלוֹם *peace*, of similar import, is not only, in general, used in a concrete sense, he who is *prosperous, peaceful, secure*, (comp. Gesen. u Winer s. v.) but also precisely in the same way as שילה as *nomen agentis*, and as a designation of the Messiah, Micah 5. 4. וְזֶה הָיָה שָׁלוֹם, *and this man shall be peace*, i. e. the author of peace, see Ephes. 2. 14. So in Isa. 42: 6, the Messiah is called the "covenant of the people and the light of the heathen," i e the author of the covenant of the people, and of the light of the heathen. 2 No name is more consonant to the other Messianic expectations of the Hebrews, than that of Peacemaker, which, according to the more comprehensive meaning given by the Hebrews to words which signify *rest* and *peace*, includes also, the idea of one who brings salvation. See שלה e. g Ps 122: 7. Not only is peace said to be in general characteristic of the times of the Messiah, (Ps. LXXII. Zech 9 10. Jer. 23 6. Isa XI, etc); but he himself bears the name, Isa 9 5, of שַׂר הַשָּׁלוֹם, *Prince of Peace*, of the same import as the word Shiloh, most probably given in reference to that name in the passage before us. See also the similar appellation in Micah 5 4. Similar also is the name commonly given to the Messiah by the Samaritans, השהב or ההתב, as participle of the verb תוב or שוב, *restitutor*, not as Gesenius (Carm Samarit. p. 76) supposes *conversor*, since the verb שוב, when transitive does not mean *to convert*, but *to restore*, comp Isa 52 8 Nah. 2: 3; and since the Samaritans (see Samarit. Briefwechsel in Eichh Repert. 9 p. 27), grounded their views of the Messiah entirely on the Pentateuch, it is probable that the prevailing name of the Messiah among them, was no other than the Shiloh of the passage before us.

Having thus settled the meaning of the word Shiloh, we proceed to give the translation of the whole verse

"The sceptre* shall not depart from Judah, nor the lawgiver†

---

* שבט, *staff, sceptre*, the insignia of dominion, which, however, was worn not merely by kings, but also by generals, and other high officers. The old translators reject the trope, and render—*ruler*, or *dominion*.

† מחקק, *lawgiver, commander, ruler*, LXX ἡγούμενος. Many interpreters. *the staff of command*, which will agree with שבט in the parallelism

from between his feet,* until the Peacemaker comes, and him shall the nations obey."†

The meaning of this language according to most of the interpret-

---

Moreover מִבֵּין רַגְלָיו, *out of the place between his feet*, might then easily admit of a liberal sense. But this interpretation is without proof.

* After the LXX, Jerome, Onkelos, the Targ. Hieros. and Jonathan, many interpreters (as Jahn, Rosenm. and others) take מִבֵּין רַגְלָיו as *euphemismum generationis*, and as standing elliptically for אֲשֶׁר יֵצֵא מִבֵּין רַגְלָיו. They appeal especially to Deut. 28: 57, (the after birth, הַיּוֹצֵאת מִבֵּין רַגְלֶיהָ.) This passage, as Gesenius also remarks, is not conclusive. They appeal also to the somewhat similar forms of expression which often occur: 'de femore or de visceribus alicujus exire,' for *to be begotten*. But in all the places where these forms occur, the verb יָצָא is inserted, see for example Gen. 35: 11. Ex. 1. 4. 2 Sam. 7: 12, and we would not here assume so harsh an ellipsis, unless no other suitable interpretation could be found. This interpretation moreover destroys the parallelism which seems to require that מִבֵּין רַגְלָיו should answer to מִיהוּדָה. This difficulty vanishes when we assume with some interpreters that the figure of *a lion* which occurs in v. 9, is here carried forward—"Exprimuntur mores ac habitus leonis, dum incubat praedae suae, quam accubando inter pedes suos ita servat ac tenet, ut nemo eam ipsi facile eripiat." But another interpretation established by Ernesti (Opus philol. crit. p. 173 seq.) has yet more to recommend it. According to this מִבֵּין רַגְלָיו is synonymous with the simple מִמֶּנּוּ. As the Hebrews not unfrequently place the special in all cases instead of the general, so do they often employ the members of the body for the whole man. Thus especially is יָד *the hand*, often used. In the Arabic بَيْنَ يَدَيْ, *between the hands*, is often put for *with*, Alcoran Sur. 60, v. 12, بَيْنَ أَيْدِيهِنَّ وَأَرْجُلِهِنَّ, *between her hands and feet*, stands for: *in herself, with herself*. In Greek we find the corresponding forms ἐκ τῶν ποδῶν ἀποχωρεῖν and ἐκ ποδῶν ἀπέρχεσθαι, for *to go away*. In Latin also, *pes* occurs redundant in the same manner. Thus Cic. pro rege Deiot. 1, § 2, uses the expression, *servum abducere a legatorum pedibus*, for *a legatis*.

† The noun יְקָהָה is to be derived from the verb יָקַה which does not it is true occur again in Hebrew; its meaning however is ascertained by means of the corresponding Arabic وَقِهَ *to obey*. The noun in Prov. 30: 17, as well as here, has the meaning *obedience*. Some interpreters, after the example of the LXX, (αὐτὸς προσδοκία τῶν ἐθνῶν.) The Syr. and Jerome erroneously translate *expectation*. That by עַמִּים we are not to understand, as Hug l. c. p. 122 supposes, the tribes, but the heathen nations, is evident, since this prophecy refers back to the former ones, according to which all nations were to be blessed in the seed of Abraham, Isaac, and Jacob. See Isa. 11: 10, etc.

ers, (see many of the moderns, Muhlert and De Broix ll. cc. Kleuker in his elegant remarks on this prophecy who regards it as predicting the Messiah) is, that the tribe of Judah should not cease to subsist as a people, and have a government of their own, until the Messiah come, then however it should lose its dominion, which was fulfilled, soon after the coming of Christ, by the destruction of Jerusalem

We however believe the following to be its true meaning: Judah shall not cease to exist as a tribe, nor lose its superiority, until it shall be exalted to higher honor and glory through the great Redeemer who shall spring from it, and whom not only the Jews, but all the nations of the earth shall obey. This exposition of the passage is, in the first place, liable to no philological difficulty. For that עד כי not unfrequently means *usque ad—et etiam postea* is well known. This usage is happily explained by Abenezra, see Pentaphyllum Rabbinicum in Gen. xlix stud Loscani p 22: "Non est sensus verborum sceptrum esse recessurum cum venerit Schiloh; sed haec locutio similis est illi: non deerit huic panis, donec veniat tempus, quo ei erunt agri vineaeque multae (i e quando veniet tempus ejusmodi, multo minus ei panis deerit), item Gen 28· 15 Non deseram te, usque dum fecero, quod locutus sum tibi, quod nempe velim te reducere in hanc terram, i e multo minus te reductum in terram deseram. similiter dicitur: non auferetur sceptrum de Jehudah, donec veniat Schiloh, i. e nunquam auferetur sceptrum de Jehudah, multo minus, quum venerit Schiloh"

The objection of Deyling (Obss s. II p 83) against the interpretation is unfounded "Patriarcha loquitur de sceptro temporali· Messiae autem sceptrum et regnum, quod in terrarum orbe constitutum habet, est spirituale et mysticum" The kingdom of the Messiah, in the Old Testament, is not placed in opposition to the theocracy, but appears as a continuation of it. Comp 1 Sam. 7: 12, etc As according to Isaiah 9 6, the Prince of peace sits upon the throne of David, and prolongs the duration of David's kingdom forever; and Amos 9 11, the fallen tabernacle of David is to be rebuilt by him, so here the Redeemer, who shall spring from Judah, appears as the Enlarger of his dominion, hitherto limited to a single people, over all nations.

What especially determines us to prefer the above explanation to the other, which is generally received, is, that the future termination of the dominion of his tribe, which, according to the latter explanation, is here foretold, does not at all accord with the joyful nature of the remaining part of this address to Judah. Besides, it is here too early to announce the future rejection of Judah; and such an interpretation can be admitted, only, when no other one can on good ground, be established. And, lastly, it supposes Jacob to have left the promise of the Messiah indefinite, instead of restricting it to one of his sons, according to the custom of the Patriarchs

Let us now turn our attention to the fulfilment of this prophecy. Two things are foretold That the tribe of Judah should not cease to exist as a people, and have a government of its own, until the Redeemer should appear. And here we must bear in mind, that the prophecy relates to its permanent condition before the coming of the Messiah Thus Calvin· "Si quis excipiat aliter sonare verba Jacob, solutio in promtu est, quidquid unquam deus de externo ecclesiae statu promisit, ita fuisse restringendum, ut judicia sua interim exerceret puniendis hominum peccatis fidemque suorum probaret." The temporary cessation of the national subsistence, therefore, as for example, during the Babylonian exile—granting that the tradition of the Jews, that they still existed as a people, and had governors of their own (ראשי הגלות) during that period, is not to be believed—can as little disprove the truth of this prediction, as the period of unbelief and apostasy which is passing away destroys the truth of the promise which Christ gave to his New Testament church. If we take this into consideration, we shall see that history most strikingly confirms this part of the prediction; while the ten tribes have never had a *national* existence, since they were carried away into captivity, the tribe of Judah returned, and continued to subsist, till the appearance of the Messiah, while *the other* tribes, with their institutions and privileges, had long before passed away If any one is disposed, with many interpreters, to go further, for which however there is properly no sufficient reason, and find in this verse a prediction, not only of the continuance of the national self-subsistence of the tribe of Judah until the coming of the Shiloh, but also of its superiority over the other tribes, history will supply him with the evidence of its fulfilment. Even during the journey through the wilderness, and afterwards in the time of the Judges, this tribe maintained a certain preeminence; with the elevation of the house of David it obtained the regal dominion After the division of the kingdom, it had the advantage of possessing Jerusalem, the legal capital, and the temple; after the return from the captivity, it gave the name to the whole nation; and the high council was established within its limits, which decided in temporal and spiritual affairs. Even under the dominion of the Romans it retained no inconsiderable power. See Deyling l. c. p. 99 seq. Buddeus Hist. Ecclesiast V. T. I. p. 342 seq. Muhlert l. c. p 54 seq.

2. It was also predicted, that, through the Messiah, the tribe of Judah should extend its dominion over many nations. The fulfilment is shown in Matt. 1: 1—16. It is in allusion to this prophecy that Christ is called, Rev. 5: 5, the lion of the tribe of Judah.

We now take a view of some of the most important of those expositions of this passage which exclude the Messiah: whose origin, after what has been said, can scarcely be conceived to have been any thing else than doctrinal prejudice. The Jews felt themselves compelled to drop the Messianic interpretation, since, were it retained, they would have nothing to reply to the inference of the Christians, that the Messiah must long since have come, because the tribe of Judah, since the destruction of the temple, had lost its national self-subsistence. The interpreters have been governed by their general hostility to Messianic predictions in the Old Testament. Some others, as Michaelis, have hesitated from the supposed difficulty of showing its fulfilment.

1. Not a few interpreters have defended the opinion that Shiloh is the name of a town in the tribe of Ephraim. Thus, after the example of several Jewish expositors, especially Teller (Notae crit. et exeg. in Gen. 49 etc. Halle 1766 p. 130 seq.) also Mendelssohn, Eichhorn, Ammon, Rosenmuller in the two earliest editions, Kelle (die heil Schriften in ihrer Urgestalt II p 436) and others. The sense is as follows: Judah shall be the leader of the tribes during the whole journey to Canaan, until they come to Shiloh. Then, in consequence of the distribution of the tribes according to the boundaries assigned to them, it shall lose its preeminence. We bring forward but a few of the difficulties with which this interpretation is encumbered. It is, in the first place, highly probable that the town of Shiloh had no existence in the time of Jacob. It is no where mentioned in the Pentateuch. We meet with it first in Joshua 18: 1, where Joshua conducts the people from their station at Gilgal to Shiloh, and there erects the tabernacle. It was probably originally nothing more than a mere resting place, like Gilgal, which gradually became a town. The idea is favored by the name Shiloh, *rest*. In the passage referred to, after the assembling of the people at Shiloh is mentioned, it is expressly added, and "the land was subject to them," and chap. 21. 44 (comp. 22. 4) it is said that at that time the "Lord gave the

people rest from all their enemies round about." See Bachiene Palastina II 3 p 409 seq. But further, granting the town of Shiloh to have existed in the time of Jacob, yet there would be something very strange in the abrupt mention of a place so little known. The prophecy, moreover, is by far too splendid to relate merely to the inconsiderable preeminence enjoyed by the tribe of Judah during the journey: which consisted merely in its marching in front of the others. Moses who belonged to another tribe, was solemnly called of God to the chief command. Joshua also, was not of the tribe of Judah. The bare fact that this tribe marched in front in the journey would surely have been no adequate fulfilment of the promise; indeed it did not agree with it in any respect. Lastly, this interpretation requires that an adverb of place, as *there*, be arbitrarily supplied in the last member of the verse.

2. After the example of Gulcher, Explic. nova Loc Gen 49, Lips 1774, also in Barkey mus. Hag II. 2 Dathe explains it thus 'quam diu prolem habebit ei gentes obedient.' In the same way Ilgen. 'As long as his posterity endures, nations shall obey him.' In opposition to this we remark that the meaning, *son, descendant*, cannot be correct, that עַד כִּי never signifies *so long as*, but always *until*, that the sense becomes extremely flat and insipid, and ו before the last member is entirely disregarded. Moreover, according to this explanation, all connexion between the name of a place שִׁילֹה and שִׁילֹה in the passage, is destroyed.

3. Some (as Vater—Justi) translate: 'until rest comes, and the people obey him.' "Judah is represented as a warrior who shall not lay aside his arms nor sceptre of command, until he shall have vanquished all his enemies, and quieted all his opposers." This interpretation is also approved by Gesenius, in the last edition of his small lexicon, with this modification, however, that we have here the notion of a Messiah, though no prediction of any particular person as such. This interpretation, as modified by Gesenius, is not so much refuted by negative objections, as by all the positive arguments which have been adduced to prove that the Messiah is here personally foretold. Still, it is unnatural to make the last member refer back to Judah, and כבט and מְחֹקֵק, contrary to their meaning, are restricted to leaders in war. But even this interpretation will not answer its purpose of preventing the reference of the prediction to a particular person as the Messiah, since, it is impossible to conceive, how the author could regard the voluntary submission of the nations to the tribe

of Judah, in the time of the Messiah, as possible, unless he expected the Messiah to spring from that tribe. And thus, even according to this interpretation, the passage, though indirectly, foretels the promised Messiah.

4. After the LXX, (ἕως ἂν ἔλθῃ τὰ ἀποκείμενα αὐτῷ) Stahelin l. c. p. 12: translated, 'donec veniat, quod ei debitum est.' But this interpretation is founded on the supposition already shown to be false, that instead of שִׁילֹה, the pointing should be שֶׁלֹּה.

Other interpretations which have still less in their favor, we believe, we may pass by without notice, and hope that enough has been said to vindicate the ancient and well founded reference of this prophecy to the Messiah.

b. MESSIANIC PREDICTIONS IN THE REMAINING BOOKS OF THE PENTATEUCH.

The materials of the last four books of the Pentateuch are such, that prophecies of the Messiah could not occur in them so frequently as in Genesis. Having in that book opened the prospect into futurity, and, at the same time, prepared the way, by the law respecting the prophets, for clear discoveries, and for showing the connexion of the new preparatory arrangements, with the great end to be attained, Moses could now the more content himself with the actual preparation for the coming of the Messiah, by the firm establishment of the theocratical institutions. Under these, it was necessary the people should live before the hope of the Messiah could be rightly conceived, and exert its proper influence, and it was well that their views at present should not be too far diverted from them.

The first passage, commonly referred to the Messiah, is contained in the prophecy of Balaam.

NUMBERS 24. 17, SQQ.

"I see him, but not now; I behold him; but not near. A star goes forth from Jacob; a sceptre arises out of Israel. He smites the borders of Moab, and destroys all the sons of Seth, and Edom shall be a possession, Seir also shall be a possession for his enemies. Out of Jacob shall come forth a Ruler, and shall destroy the last remnant out of the city." A powerful ruler of the Israelites, who shall arise at a future time, and gain a signal triumph over their enemies, the Moabites and Idumeans, here presents himself to the spiritual eyes of the prophet. By the Prince, the Jews from the earliest times have understood the Messiah, either exclusively, or else principally, with a secondary reference to David. Onkelos translates, "Quando surget rex ex Jacob et ungetur Messias ex Israel." Jonathan: "Cum surget rex fortis ex domo Jacob et ungetur Messias et sceptrum forte ex Israel." In the Sohar, on the words "I see him, but not now," it is remarked: 'This was in part fulfilled at that time. It will be completely fulfilled in the days of the Messiah.' See the passages quoted by Jos de Voisin in dem Prooem. on R. Mart. Pug. Fid. p. 68. R. Mart III. 3. cap 11. Schottgen, Jesus Messias p. 151. It is evident how widely this interpretation prevailed among the Jews, from the circumstance that the famous Pseudo-Messiah, who appeared in the time of Adrian, borrowed from it the surname Bar Chochab, son of the star. From the Jews, this exposition passed to the Christians. Cyril of Jerusalem defended it against Julian. See Jul. ed. Spanh. p. 263 c. Either its exclusive relation to the Messiah was maintained, or it was allowed to refer indeed in the first instance to David; but then both himself and his temporal victories were regarded as typical of Christ, and his spiritual triumphs, which the prophet had clearly in view. The most skilful defenders of this interpretation, are Calvin, Le Clerc, Mieg (de Stella et Sceptro Bileamitico, in dem Thesaur. theol. phil. nov. p. 423 seq.) Boullier (Dissert. syll. Amst. 1750 Diss. 1) in some manner also Rutg. Schutte (Comment. in h. l. in der bibl. Hagana 1, 1 p. 48 ff. On the contrary it has found an ingenious and able opposer in Verschuir (Biblioth. Brem. nova class. III. 1. p. 1—80, reprinted in s. Opuss. cc.) He denies its relation to the Messiah in any sense, and regards it as applicable alike to David, John Hyrcanus and Alex. Jannaus. He refers the 17th verse to the first two, the 19th to the last: an unnatural supposition, since the same ruler is obviously described in both verses. After him, Michaelis and Dathe have opposed the Messianic interpretation, and asserted the exclusive reference of the prophecy to David. So also has De Wette (Kritik der Isr. Gesch. p. 364) among the more modern critics, who wishes to prove from it the fictitious character of the whole history, and the spuriousness of the Pentateuch, unjustly, however, since Balaam, who is represented in the narrative as a real prophet of the true God (see Boullier l. c. p. 2 seq.), might very well have received a disclosure of future events for the benefit of the theocracy. On the other hand, Rosenmuller (3d Edit.) and B. Crusius (Bibl Theol. p. 369), have defended the Messianic interpretation, only however in the Jewish sense.

In itself considered, the supposition of an inferior reference to David, and a higher one to Christ, is liable to no objection. In this case, neither David, nor Christ as an individual, but the royal race, who should hereafter arise among the people of Israel, would have been represented to the prophet as personified; and, guided by the fulfilment, we should then have had to decide what might belong to the one, or the other member of this race. Thus the promise to David, 2 Sam. vii, relates to the whole royal race, and the fulfilment enables us to judge what refers to Solomon, what to other leaders of the visible theocracy, and what to Christ. And there are very frequent instances besides, when whole races are beheld by the prophets as individuals. But it is not enough that there is no *a priori* objection to this supposition; in order to establish it here, as in 2 Sam vii, positive proof is required. But proof sufficiently strong scarcely appears to exist, as the following examination will show.

1. It has, it is true, in its favor the argument from tradition. But as this is never conclusive alone, so it loses nearly all its force from the fact that the passage furnishes the Jews with a welcome support of their worldly expectations concerning the Messiah. A single ancient testimony in favor of the reference of Isa. liii to the Messiah, is of more weight than all their Messianic interpretations of this passage combined.

2. No evidence can be drawn from the New Testament. An appeal has been made to the account of the star which announced the birth of the Redeemer. Thus Origen c Cels 1, 12 § 2. Mosh. But the two cases have nothing in common, as is evident even from the total silence of Matthew, who makes a point of showing the agreement between prophecy and its fulfilment. Besides, it is not a literal star that is meant by Balaam. He uses the "star" metaphorically, as is customary among all nations, to designate a great and illustrious ruler.

3. It is equally impossible to bring forward internal evidence of its application to Christ in any sense. The prophecy is completely fulfilled in David. This king destroyed many of the Moabites, and made the remainder tributary. Comp. 2 Sam. 8: 2 and Ps. 60. 10,

where the first fulfilment is described in language at least equally strong as that of the prediction. He also subdued the Idumeans, 2 Sam. 8. 14. 1 Chron. 18. 12, 13, as well as the neighboring enemies of the theocracy, 2 Sam. 8. 11, 12.

But we must not leave unexplained the internal evidences which the advocates for the reference to the Messiah have here brought forward. Their chief argument is taken from the words, "he shall destroy all the sons of Seth." By the "sons of Seth," we are to understand the whole human race, since all men are descended from Seth the son of Adam. So Onkelos who translates בְּנֵי אֲנָשׁ. Were the opinion correct, there would be, at all events, one feature of the prophecy which would not suit David. But to this, Michaelis has well replied, that men might aptly enough be called after their first and last common ancestors, sons of Adam, or sons of Noah, but it would be very strange were they to be named after the eight patriarchs who came between. Besides, the context does not allow of this exposition. Balaam speaks first, v. 17, of Moab; v. 18, of Edom; and shall he here between them abruptly make the whole human race the subject of his prophecy? The parallel, moreover, between Edom and Seir, v. 18, leads us to think that the sons of Seth are nearly, if not entirely, identical with Moab. Several interpreters suppose them to be the same, and that among the descendants of Moab, one particularly distinguished bore the name of Seth. But the opinion of Verschuir (l. c. p. 40 seq.) is the more probable, who regards שת as an appellation for שֵׁאת from שָׁאָה, *fragorem edidit*. This interpretation is confirmed by an appeal to Jer. 48. 45, where the prophet imitates this passage, and instead of בְּנֵי שֵׁת, he places in parallelism with Moab בְּנֵי שָׁאוֹן *filii tumultus*, 'sons of tumult,' an appropriate designation either for the Moabites above, or the neighboring tribes also, who were always restless and inclined for war. In a similar way are these people, 2 Sam. 7. 10, called בְּנֵי עַוְלָה, and Macc. 2. 47 οἱ υἱοὶ ὑπερηφανίας. Our appeal is also made to Balaam's exordium, which would lead us to suspect something far more important. But then, it is forgotten, that in v. 3, he makes one equally pompous, without afterwards announcing any thing more than the temporal prosperity of Israel, and lastly, much stress is laid on the declaration of Balaam to the king of Moab, that he would foretell what should happen to his people בְּאַחֲרִית הַיָּמִים. This expression, it is thought, can be understood only of the times of the Messiah. It is true that the later prophets are accustomed to use it with this specific meaning. It is, however, equally certain, that, at an earlier period, it was used indefinitely, meaning simply the future, the time to come. Deut. 4. 30. Gen. xlix.

There is then no sufficient reason for referring this prophecy to the Messiah. But on the other hand, the objections to this reference are strong. It is indeed true, that the increase of the extent and glory of the divine kingdom by the Messiah, is often represented under the image, borrowed from the relation of the earthly theocracy, of the conquest of those who were to be received into it. See Ps. 110. 3. But then the context always enables us to perceive that the representation is figurative. It is not so, however, in the present case. It appears rather from v. 14 " I will show thee what this people shall do to thy people," that it is misfortune and not prosperity, that Balaam announces to the king. This difficulty would indeed vanish, were we with other interpreters to understand the prediction as announcing not the conversion, but the destruction of the enemies of Christ, as in Ps. ii, and cx. But this opinion is not sufficiently sustained by the remark, although correct in itself, that the prophets frequently designate the enemies of the Messiah's kingdom by the name of some nation peculiarly hostile to the visible theocracy, since it is manifest, that the mention of the Moabites is not here figurative, and as a part for the whole, from the circumstance that Balaam had the king of the Moabites before him, and declared it to be his purpose to speak concerning the future destinies of *his* people. Further, although the Messiah in other places is exhibited as a strict judge of his enemies, yet this character is never given to him as his *only* character, while the blessings he will confer on those who submit to his authority are entirely overlooked. The person described by Balaam cannot possibly be the same, who, according to the promises made to the patriarchs, was to confer blessings upon all nations, and according to Gen. xlix, was to be the author of peace to whom the nations were to yield a willing obedience.

Deuteronomy 18 · 15—18.

"The Lord thy God will raise up unto thee a prophet, from the midst of thee, of thy brethren like unto me; unto him ye shall hearken: according to all thou desirest of the Lord thy God in Horeb in the day of the assembly, saying, Let me not hear again the voice of the Lord my God, neither let me see this great fire any more, that I die not. And the Lord said unto me, They have well spoken that which they have spoken. I will raise them up a Prophet from among their brethren, like unto thee, and I will put my words into his mouth, and he shall speak unto them all that I shall command him."

If we leave out of view the unfortunate attempts at interpretation of those, who, as Abenezra, Bechai and Ammon (Christol. p. 29) understand Joshua to be intended by the prophet here promised, though neither the name, nor the characteristic marks of a prophet are any where ascribed to him, or Jeremiah, as is the case of Baal Hatturim and Jalkut out of the book Pesikta, and as Abarbanel supposes, we may divide the explanations of this passage into three classes 1. Some take נביא collectively, and understand by it the prophets of all periods. So Origen (c Cels 1. 9, § 5 Mosh.), the Arabic translators, and most of the later Jewish expositors as Kimchi, Alschech, and Lipmann (Nizachon 137). Also Abenezra and Bechai prefer this interpretation, next to that which makes Jeremiah the subject of the prediction Several recent critics, likewise, among others, Rosenm, Vater, Baumgarten-Crus (Bibl. Theol. p. 369), take this view of the prophecy. 2. The exclusive reference to Christ has been from the earliest times maintained by most interpreters in the Christian church. It was adopted by Justin Martyr, Tertullian, Athanasius, Eusebius (Demons Evang. 3, 2 9, 11), Lactantius (4, 17), Augustine (c. Faustum 16, c. 15. 18. 19), Isidore of Pelusium (1 3 op. 49). It was maintained by Luther (t 3. Jen Lat f 123) and became the prevailing one in the Lutheran church It was also approved by the reformed interpreters. Among its earliest defenders, the most eminent are Deyling (Misce Sac II 175), G Frischmuth (Diss de propheta, Mosi pari, printed in the Thesaur theol phil I. p. 384), and Hasaeus (de propheta promisso Deut 18 15 in dem Thes theol. phil nov. I. 439). In recent times it has been advocated by Doderlein (Instit theol II § 228), Kocher (Mess Briefe, p 165 seq), De Broix (Ursprung und Entwickelung des Messianismus p. 64), Pareau (Instit. Interpret V. T p 506), Knapp (Dogm II. p 138), and others 3. Others have taken a middle course, understanding נביא indeed collectively, but, at the same time, regarding the promise as completely fulfilled only by the mission of Christ, in whom the idea of the prophetic order was completely realized. So Nic de Lyra, Calvin, several Rom Catholic expositors, Grotius, Le Clerc, Dathe, and others.

We here in the first place bring together the arguments which favor the reference to Christ. 1. It is authorized by tradition. The later Jewish expositors have indeed, as we have seen, relinquished it But then this has arisen entirely from polemic views. It can be satisfactorily proved, that the Messianic interpretation was, throughout, the prevailing one among the older Jews.* In evidence of this an appeal has been made sometimes to 1 Macc 14. 41: καὶ ὅτι οἱ Ἰουδαῖοι καὶ οἱ ἱερεῖς εὐδόκησαν τοῦ εἶναι αὐτῶν Σίμωνα ἡγούμενον καὶ ἀρχιερέα εἰς τὸν αἰῶνα, ἕως τοῦ ἀναστῆναι προφήτην πιστόν. This however is incorrect. For that we are not here to understand by the credible prophet, i. e. one sanctioned by miracles or fulfilled predictions—the Messiah—the prophet promised by Moses, as after Luther many of the older expositors have done, is evident from the absence of the article, and also from the adjective πιστός. The sense is rather: 'Simon and his family shall hold the highest dignity in the State, until God himself by a future prophet, (there being none at that time) should make another appointment.' See Michaelis on the passage Sufficient evidence is, however, supplied by the New Testament. The manner in which Peter and Stephen quote this passage shows that it was usually referred to the Messiah. They deem it superfluous to prove this, but consider it as universally acknowledged. It is highly probable that Philip had this passage especially in view when he said to Nathanael, John 1 46: ὃν ἔγραψε Μωϋσῆς ἐν τῷ νόμῳ—εὑρήκαμεν Ἰησοῦν John 6 14, the people at the feeding of the five thousand exclaim· ὅτι οὗτός ἐστιν ἀληθῶς ὁ προφήτης ὁ ἐρχόμενος εἰς τὸν κόσμον The Messianic interpretation therefore was not that of a few learned men, but of the whole people The appeal, as a probable evidence, to John 1. 21 and 7. 40, is on the contrary groundless, since the prophet is there distinguished from Christ. See Kuinol on the passage This interpretation prevailed also among the Samaritans. The woman of Samaria says, John 4. 25. οἶδα ὅτι Μεσσίας ἔρχεται, ὁ λεγόμενος Χριστός· ὅταν ἔλθῃ ἐκεῖνος, ἀναγγελεῖ ἡμῖν πάντα As the Samaritans received only the Pentateuch, the idea which is here expressed of the Messiah, as a divinely enlightened instructor, could have been derived from no other source than the passage before us. The last words agree almost verbatim with those in v. 18 of the prophecy, "and he shall speak unto them all that I shall

---

* That the Messianic hopes of the Jews at a very early period, were already fastened upon the passage, is acknowledged by Bertholdt (de Ortu Theol Jud p 109

command him." Traces of this interpretation are also found in the Midrasch Koheleth, quoted by R. Martini Pug. Fid II 15, where it is said "Dixit R Barachia nom R Isaaci: qualis liberator prior, talis liberator posterior."

2. It rests on the sure evidence of the New Testament. It is not improbable that Christ himself, as some have supposed, particularly referred to this place, John 5. 46, when he says that Moses wrote of Him; since the expression of Christ relates rather to that part of the Pentateuch, where Moses acts in his own person, than where he appears as a mere reporter. Christ, also, might sooner expect the Jews to acknowledge that this prophecy was fulfilled in Himself, than that in Gen. XLIX, which presents the Messiah in his glory. Further according to Luke 24. 44, he explained to his disciples the prophecies relating to himself in the Pentateuch. And it cannot be supposed, that the very passage, Acts 3 22 and 23, which was brought forward by Peter as the most conclusive of all, should not have been so represented by Christ. The manner in which the citation is made, excludes the idea that Moses speaks of Christ only as included among the Prophets, taken collectively. Peter says expressly, Moses and the later prophets have foretold τὰς ἡμέρας ταύτας, and it appears from τοῦ προφήτου ἐκείνου, that he did not understand the singular in a collective sense. That Stephen, Acts 7. 36, also referred the passage to Christ would not of itself be conclusive, for the authority of Stephen ought not to have so much weight as that of the Apostles. But we must not overlook Matt. 17. 5, according to which a voice was heard from heaven in attestation of Christ, οὗτός ἐστιν ὁ υἱός μου ὁ ἀγαπητός, ἐν ᾧ εὐδόκησα· αὐτοῦ ἀκούετε. As the first part of this declaration is taken from the Messianic prediction in Isa. XLII, so is the second part from the passage under consideration, and by the use of its words its meaning is clearly shown.

3. There is also internal evidence of its relation to the Messiah. That Moses designed by the word נָבִיא to designate an individual and not the collective body of the prophets, appears from the constant use of the suffixes connected with it, while in the case of the collective nouns, it is usual to interchange the singular and plural. The force of this argument is evident from the fact, that not a few non-Messianic interpreters have been compelled by it, to make some particular individual the subject. We hesitate the more to allow, till better reasons are offered, that נָבִיא here stands as the singular for the plural, since the word does not elsewhere occur as a collective noun, nor are

the prophets any where spoken of in the manner alleged. The doctrine concerning the Messiah was already current among the people. How then could they understand the promise, in which only one person was mentioned, in any other way than as referring at least chiefly to the one expected? The word כָּמֹנִי v. 15, and כָּמוֹךָ v. 18 corresponds, to say the least, better with the Messianic interpretation than with any other. It is true that the elder interpreters improperly chose to extend the conformity to every particular, and thus fell into the inconsistency on the one hand of arguing therefrom that, according to Deut. 34. 10, no later prophet may have been like Moses, comp also Num 12. 6 7, while on the other hand they assert however a dissimilitude between Moses and Christ, and must take the comparison only in the way of reference But still the difficulty of making the prophets collectively the subject remains, though we limit the resemblance to the words of Moses himself. The *tertium comparationis*, according to v 18, consists in the office of Mediator Because the Israelites are unable to endure the terrors of the Divine majesty, God will communicate with them in future times through a Mediator, as he had hitherto done through Moses. This can be true of the prophetic order only in a certain sense, and is properly accomplished only in Christ, who is the one Mediator of the New Covenant, as Moses was of the Old

There are however some arguments which seem to oppose the exclusive reference of the prophecy to Christ, as an individual 1 The connexion. This is twofold Moses, v. 15, first utters the promise in his own name Here it refers to what had gone before Moses had forbidden the people of Israel the use of all those means, whereby the idolatrous nations sought to go beyond the boundaries of human knowledge Thou shalt not do so, is his language. For what they seek in vain by these unlawful expedients shall be really imparted to you from God. Not only was it entirely proper on such an occasion to remind them of the Messiah, since his manifestation, being the most perfect of God's revelations, best satisfies the desire for higher degrees of knowledge, but it would have been strange indeed if the founder of the old dispensation, when so suitable an opportunity presented, had neglected to direct the attention of the people to the author of the new one, and had spoken only of the intervening and inferior communications from God But on the other hand, it would not be less remarkable, if Moses had taken no notice of these, if having in chap xiii laid down the distinctive marks of the true and false prophets, he had here referred merely to the divine revelations to be expected at a far distant period, and overlooked those to be vouchsafed in the meantime, and had thus neglected to employ a method peculiarly suited to prepare the way for his exhortations. In v. 18 the promise stands in a different connexion. V. 15, Moses had delivered it in his own person. In order to give to it the higher authority, he relates in the following verses when and in what manner he had received it from God. It was delivered to him on Sinai, where God in the promulgation of the law had communicated directly with the people, in order to give them a deeper impression of the holiness of the law, strengthen their confidence in the mediation of Moses, and show them the folly of desiring any other method of divine communication. But the people, struck with consternation before the dreadful majesty of God, had prayed that he would no longer speak to them directly, but through a mediator, as he had done in times past, see Ex. xx. In consequence of this request, God said to Moses: "They have well spoken, I will raise them up a prophet from among their brethren, like unto thee, and I will put my words in his mouth; and he shall speak unto them all that I shall command him." We cannot fail to perceive that here, if ever, a divine revelation of the coming of Christ, who, as Mediator between God and man, veiled his Godhead and brought the divinity in human form near to men, would have been appropriate. But at the same time we should expect on the other hand an allusion to the inferior messengers of God who were to precede him.

2. But the exclusive reference to the Messiah as an individual seems most inconsistent with the 20—22 verses. There the marks of a false prophet are given. If the foregoing had no relation to the true prophets, it will be difficult to perceive any just connexion of ideas in the passage. How then can the two suppositions, that Moses had the Messiah undeniably in view, and yet that the prediction relates also to the prophets in general, be reconciled? Most naturally in the following manner. Moses had Christ here in view, though not merely in reference to his visible manifestation, but also his previous invisible influence likewise; comp. 1 Pet 1: 11, where the spirit of Christ is said to have spoken through the prophets. Moses does not indeed speak of the prophets as a collective body, to which Christ also in the end incidentally belonged, as Calvin and other commentators quoted above supposed; but the prophetical order appeared to him personified in Christ, in whom his idea of it was completely real-

ized. There is then here a reference to the other prophets also, not however as individuals, but in relation to that spirit by which, though in an inferior degree, they were influenced and made one with their head. They were contemplated in Christ, because they were merely his organs. His spirit gave them their being.

2. The Messianic Psalms.

The Messianic prediction, as we have already seen, extends back far beyond the time of David. We find it even in the book of Genesis assuming continually a more definite form. First, there is the promise in general terms, that the posterity of the woman should gain the victory over the kingdom of Satan; then we are taught that salvation should come through the descendants of Shem; from these again, Abraham is selected; from his sons, Isaac; from the sons of Isaac, Jacob; and lastly, from the twelve sons of Jacob, Judah, to be the ancestor of the great Redeemer and Pacificator, whose peaceful dominion should be extended over all the people of the earth.

Henceforth the Messianic prediction received no considerable enlargement, nor a more specific determination until the reign of David. But as heretofore only the tribe had been designated from which the Redeemer was to spring, so now the particular family was selected. This was done in the prediction which God by the prophet Nathan delivered to David at a time when penetrated with gratitude for victory over all his foes, and his elevation from the deepest obscurity to the highest honor, he had resolved to erect for God a permanent temple, instead of the moveable tabernacle in which he had hitherto vouchsafed to dwell, 2 Sam. vii. Some interpreters as Calovius, have erroneously referred this promise exclusively to the Messiah. It contains too many things which can relate only either to Solomon or the other natural descendants of David, to allow of this interpretation. For example, v. 13, the descendant of David builds a temple for God; language which taken in connexion with the previous mention of David's desire to build a temple, can be understood only of the earthly temple to be erected by Solomon; according to v. 15, when the descendants of David should commit iniquity, God would not cast them entirely away, but visit them with gentle chastisement; here, also, the reference to a mere human and therefore sinful posterity is plain. Moreover, in 1 Chron. 22: 9, etc. this promise is said by David himself to relate in the first instance to Solomon, and that Solomon so understood it is manifest from 1 Kings 5 5. 8 17, etc. 2 Chron 6 7. But on the other hand, we would just as little venture with Grotius and others, to refer it to Solomon alone, or with others, to Solomon and the rest of the earthly kings of the house of David. When we reflect that the promise of the great Redeemer, who should spring from the tribe of Judah, could not be unknown to David, we feel certain, that in the words, " And thy house and thy kingdom shall be established forever before thee: thy throne shall be established forever,"* he must have seen something far more than could ever be fulfilled in his son Solomon, or any of his mere human descendants, who like every thing earthly and mortal must one day come to an end.

That he certainly did so is plain from the powerful emotion which according to v. 18 the communication awakened in his bosom. Just views of it have been taken by those who as Augustine, de Civ. Dei 17. 8, 9, give it a double reference, first to Solomon and his successors, and also to Christ. It is very frequently the case in the prophetic annunciations that whole families and races are viewed as an individual, and then, whatever belongs to their different members is ascribed to him. See for example the blessing of Jacob, Gen XLIX. So is it also in the passage before us. Many things relate only to David's natural posterity, as the building of the temple and the mild chastisement others exclusively to the Messiah, as the repeated assurance of the endless duration of his dominion; and, finally, others are fulfilled in an inferior sense in Solomon and his descendants, and in a higher one in Christ, as the promise, " I will be his Father and he shall be my Son."†

---

* That עַד עוֹלָם does not as Grotius supposes, here indicate merely a comparatively long period is evident from the parallel passages, Ps LXXXIX where the promise is repeated, and where, v 30 the phrase is explained by לָעַד and כִּימֵי שָׁמַיִם, v 37 by כַּשֶּׁמֶשׁ, v 38 by כְיָרֵחַ and from Ps LXXII where there is likewise a reference to this promise, and the expression לִפְנֵי שֶׁמֶשׁ is employed. Nor can an appeal be made in favor of the opposite opinion to Ps 21 5 For the reference of the Psalm to David as an individual is certainly as inadmissible as its reference to the Messiah.

† Comp Mich Crit colleg p 461 seq Hess Gesch David's I. S 423 seq Anton de Vatic Mess Muntinghe on Ps II The Messianic interpretation is also established by the testimony of the New Testament, comp Luke 1 32, 33 Hebr 1 5

Thus therefore an important advance was made. Relying upon this prediction the prophets not only announced the derivation of the Messiah from David, and borrowed from his life the lineaments with which when ennobled and perfected they might describe his illustrious descendants; but David also himself and other holy men who composed the Psalms, were led by the Divine Spirit into a deeper understanding of this promise, and received further illumination respecting its object.*

The Psalms which are justly regarded as prophetic of the Messiah may be divided into two classes:

I. *Psalms in which the Messiah in his glory is celebrated and his dominion described by images drawn from the earthly theocracy.*

Here belong Psalms II., XLV., LXXII. and CX. These have much in common, and so plainly refer to the same subject, that if the Messianic character of one be established, that of all the rest will follow. When we compare these predictions with those of an earlier period, we at once discover an important difference. Heretofore they had been more brief, more in the form of allusions; but now the foundation being provided, the prophecies could become finished descriptions. To David the Messiah was announced as a king, as his successor on his throne. And thus in his own contemplation, and in that of the other holy authors of the Psalms, the earthly head of the Theocracy formed the substratum of its future illustrious Renovator and Restorer. This mode of contemplation has been misrepresented by recent critics, and, with entire disregard of the manifold indications of a king of a far higher character, they have come to the conclusion that all the Psalms of this class relate only to an earthly head of the Theocracy. The fact was in part erroneously interpreted even by those among the older critics, who as Calvin, Grotius, and Bochart (see his Epist. ad Morlejum, p. 42) felt themselves con-

---

* That David in particular was excited by the Divine promise, and afterwards received further illumination from the prophetic spirit which dwelt within him, is asserted by Peter, Acts 2:30, 31. The latter rests moreover on the testimony of the Lord himself Matt 22:43, where he says, "David spake ἐν πνεύματι, moved by the Holy Spirit. That true Messianic predictions are contained in the Psalms is evident from the fact that the Lord after his resurrection proved to his disciples that all that had happened to him had been foretold not only in the other books of the Old Testament, but also in the Psalms.

strained by it to adopt the notion of a double reference; an inferior one to David, and a higher one to the Messiah. We proceed now to an examination of the individual Psalms of this class.

Psalm II.

The name of the author of this Psalm is not given in the superscription. But tradition ascertained by its being classed among the Psalms of David, the fact that events of his time form the ground work of its representations, comp. Pareau Instit. interpr. V. T. p. 511, and its resemblance of his acknowledged Psalms, especially to the cx., and the testimony of the New Testament, Acts 4. 25, all combine to prove it to have been composed by David. Its contents are as follows. The holy Psalmist in prophetic vision beholds a multitude of nations with their kings in mad rebellion against God and his anointed, their rightful sovereign, v. 1—3, while v. 4, 5 he raises his eyes from the wild tumult on earth to God enthroned in the exalted rest of heaven, and declares that he will easily quell the powerless rebellion; he hears, v. 6, the voice of Jehovah proclaiming that he had established his anointed as king, and consequently, all resistance to his authority being likewise directed against himself the Omnipotent must be fruitless. Immediately after, the Psalmist, v. 7—9, hears another voice, that of the anointed, declaring that Jehovah has given to him as His Son, whom he demonstrates to be such by powerful proofs, the people of the whole earth for his possession, with the right and the power to inflict the severe punishment upon all who should resist his lawful dominion. He now, v. 10—12, addresses the kings as if they were actually present, and exhorts them ere the fearful vengeance threatened against the despisers of the Son should burst upon their heads, to seek forgiveness by humble submission to their king, the Son of God, who is no less merciful to his friends than terrible to his enemies.

This Psalm, according to the view we have taken of its contents, possesses, like many of the predictions of the prophets, a dramatic character. Different persons one after another, as the author himself, the rebellious kings, Jehovah, his Son and anointed, make their appearance and speak or act without the change of person being expressly mentioned.

The question now arises, who is meant by the anointed and son of God? That the Messiah is intended appears from all those arguments in general by which he can be shown to be the subject of any passage of the Old Testament

1. The testimony of tradition. It is an undoubted fact and unanimously admitted even by the recent opposers of its reference to him, that the Psalm was universally regarded by the ancient Jews as foretelling the Messiah. Matt 26 63, the high priest asks Jesus whether he were the Christ, the Son of God, and thus borrows from it two appellations of the expected Redeemer, and also in John 1 49 Nathanael says, with reference to this Psalm, to Christ, "Thou art the son of God, thou art the king of Israel." In the older Jewish writings also, as the Sohar, the Talmud, etc., there is a variety of passages in which the Messianic interpretation is given to this Psalm. See the collections by Raym Martini, Pug Fid. ed. Carpzov, in several places, and by Schottgen, de Messiah p. 227 seq. Even Kimchi and Jarchi confess that it was the prevailing one among their forefathers, and the latter very honestly gives his reason for departing from it, when he says, he preferred to explain it of David for the refutation of the Heretics, לתשובת המינים, that is, in order to destroy the force of the arguments drawn from it by the Christians. The words "for the refutation of the Heretics" are indeed omitted in many Jewish and Christian editions, probably from fear of the censors of the press, and because this confession was found to be too candid. But Pococke in his notes miscel ad Portam Mosis, p 308 seq ed Lips. has restored them from a manuscript, and they are found also in an Erfurt Ms The Christians sought to prove his eternal generation from the Father. To deprive them of this proof, the more modern Jews thought best to refer it to another subject

2. Here if any where, plain references of the New Testament speak in favor of the Messianic interpretation Acts 4: 25, 26, the whole company of the Apostles quote the first verses of this Psalm, and refer it to Christ. It is true that, after Eckermann (Beit. 1, 2, 133 seq), Ammon (Christol. p. 38) has asserted that they made use of these verses merely that they might offer their prayers to God in a more emphatic language by adopting the words of the Old Testament; but the incorrectness of this opinion is easily shown. The form of the quotation itself, $\dot{o}$ $\delta\iota\grave{\alpha}$ $\sigma\tau\acute{o}\mu\alpha\tau o\varsigma$ $\varDelta\alpha\beta\grave{\iota}\delta$ $\tau o\tilde{v}$ $\pi\alpha\iota\delta\acute{o}\varsigma$ $\sigma o\upsilon$ $\epsilon\grave{\iota}\pi\acute{\omega}\nu$, proves that the Apostles believed the Psalm to contain a direct prediction of Christ. It is usual on other occasions, when a Messianic

prediction is quoted from the Psalms, to refer to a Divine revelation as to its source. Matt 22 43. Acts 2: 30, 31. To this we may add that the Apostles found the Messianic interpretation handed down by tradition, and confirmed it, as appears from other passages also, by their own authority. Acts 13 33, Paul quotes v 7 of this Psalm, and explains it of the resurrection of Christ. That this is not a mere allusion, as Eckermann (l. c p 174 seq) and Ammon assert, is evident from the fact that the Apostle advances this and other passages as a proof that the promise made to the fathers was fulfilled in the resurrection of Christ. Heb. 1. 5, v. 7 is quoted as evidence of the exaltation of Christ above all angels, and Heb. 5. 5 it is said that God spake the words of this verse to Him.

3 A no less striking proof in favor of this interpretation is afforded by the Psalm itself. It plainly possesses features which correspond to no earthly king, and can belong to the Messiah alone. In the first place, the king anointed appears as a being of a nature more than human We here first appeal to v. 7. " Thou art my son , this day have I begotten thee." We concede to the modern critics, that from the appellation *son of God* abstractedly considered no conclusion can be drawn. It is not unfrequently given to the earthly leaders of the Theocracy But then, in such instances the appellation results from the idea, not of generation, but of representation and subordination; it is not the natural, but the moral relation of father and son which is transferred to the relation between God and his earthly representative The name *son of God* in such cases is entirely synonymous with that of servant of God. But that here the name of *son of God* must be taken in a different sense, and indicate a proper sonship is shown by the other member of the parallelism, This day have I begotten thee It has often been thought that the eternal generation of the Son from the Father is asserted in these words The word היום *day*, has been taken as the designation of eternity, in which there is neither past nor future, and which may therefore most fitly be expressed by the image of the present So among the Church Fathers, Athanasius, and Augustine, who says : " In aeternitate nec praeteritum quidquam est, quasi esse desierit , nec futurum, quasi nondum sit, sed praesens tantum, quia quidquid aeternum est, semper est." Notwithstanding this interpretation was opposed by Theodoret in ancient, and Calvin in modern times, it became very generally prevalent; and among recent writers, it has been defended by Muntinghe, who nevertheless speaks doubtfully, and Ringeltaube in

his remarks on the passage, and Michael Weber (Progr generatio filii dei aeterna, nova l Ps 2 7, explicatione illustr. Witt 1786) It is however untenable, since writers of the Psalms never represent eternity by the present, although this is often done by the later theologians and philosophers.* But equally unfounded is the explanation of many modern interpreters, who, in order to give the verse an earthly subject, translate יָלַד either to adopt or to make son in the sense of subordination and representation The first of these translations, which is especially defended by Ilgen (de notione tituli filii dei, Jena 1794, copied in Paulus Memorabilien St. 7. s. 162) is liable to this objection, that not a single instance can be found where יָלַד occurs in the sense supposed This De Wette himself confesses, Comm p 111. We cannot say, he remarks, with Ilgen that יָלַד here means to adopt, nor has it this meaning Ps. 87 4—6, to which he appeals for proof Equally unsustained is the other interpretation. We give to the verb יָלַד here the declarative meaning sufficiently established and correct.† See the examples in Glassius philol. s 3. No 15.‡ It is not uncommon in the language of Scripture to say of a person or thing, that it *becomes*, when it is made known to be what it is. See Rom. 1. 4, where from a disregard of this usage ὁρισθέντος has been falsely rendered *who was proved*, in which sense the verb does not occur. But יָלַד in the declarative sense can mean nothing else, than to declare to have been begotten. I have this day begotten thee—I have this day declared that thou art begotten by me. This, then, is in all respects the same as, I have declared thee as my son · so also Jer. 2 27, " Thou art my Father,"

---

* Compare upon B Philo de Profug p 458, ed Francof. · σήμερον ἐστὶν ὁ ἀπέρατος καὶ ἀδιεξίτητος αἰών· μηνῶν γὰρ καὶ ἐνιαυτῶν, καὶ συνόλως χρόνων περίοδοι δόγματα ἀνθρώπων εἰσὶν, ἀριθμὸν ἐκτετιμηκότων, τὸ δὲ ἀψευδὲς ὄνομα αἰῶνος, ἡ σήμερον.

† In this sense Paul also understood the expression, Acts 13 33, where he explains the verse of the resurrection as the fact whereby Christ was eminently declared to be the Son of God The declaration of Jehovah must be regarded as being made at the time when by clear proofs He had made known his son as such then הַיּוֹם may preserve its suitable interpretation.

‡ Comp Calvin on this passage Non genitus dicitur nisi quatenus pater filium suum esse testatus est—non ut filius dei esse quoad se inciperet, sed ut talis patefieret mundo Haec genitura non de mutuo patris et filii respectu intelligi debet, sed tantum significat ab initio absconditum in arcano patris sinu obscure deinde sub lege adumbratum, ex quo prodiit cum claris insignibus cognitum fuisse dei filium

and " thou hast begotten me," are also used as synonymous. But this can be the case only when the literal meaning of the word *son* is retained, and not when it is used in a mere moral sense. The parallelism then requires that the words " thou art my son," should be taken literally. That kings, however, are not called the sons of God in this sense, but only metaphorically is generally acknowledged by interpreters. See Rosenmuller and De Wette on the passage. The latter says, "the predicate *son of God* expresses either the special love of God towards the subject, and the moral resemblance to Him, or that the regal dignity is conferred by God, or both." Not a single example has been adduced, where *to beget*, means to make a son in the metaphorical sense. In 1 Cor. 4 15, the discourse is concerning a total regeneration by the communication of the Holy Ghost, analogous to a physical one. We add to these considerations, that in v. 12 the subject of the Psalm is called simply *the son*, which indicates a sonship of a peculiar and exclusive character, that renders any more accurate definition unnecessary, and if we compare Ps 45: 7, and Ps 110· 5, where the same subject receives the names אֲדֹנָי and אֱלֹהִים, there can no doubt remain that the language before us relates to one who is the son of God in a literal and proper sense. Besides, there are other traits that indicate his superhuman character, see particularly v. 12. There the rebels are exhorted to submit with humility and reverence to their king, because his wrath would soon be kindled, while, at the same time, he would confer blessings upon those who put their trust in him. If what is here said of *wrath* will not as De Wette remarks agree with an earthly king, much less will the exhortation to seek the favor of this king and trust in his protection. The people of Israel were at all times exhorted by the sacred writers not to trust in feeble mortals, but to put their confidence in their mighty God and flee to him alone for succor. Comp Ps. 118. 9 146 13 Mich. 7· 5. The difficulty of reconciling this passage with the non-Messianic character of the Psalm was seen long ago by Abenezra, who sought to remove it by the supposition of a sudden change of the subject. Kiss the Son, lest he, that is, Jehovah, be angry. This supposition is approved also by Rosenm. and De Wette. But it is entirely arbitrary. Where no strong reason for an exception exists in the context, the pronoun must refer to the noun immediately preceding. Here this noun is Son, and so far from there being any reason for an exception to the rule, we have mentioned, it is said of him in v. 9 that He shall break the nations in pieces, with an iron sceptre, Comp also Ps. 110 6, 7

Further, the people and kings of the earth seek to cast off the yoke of Jehovah and the king whom he had established over them, v. 1—3. From one end of the earth to the other they are given to him by Jehovah for his possession, v. 8. The utmost extravagance could not make these declarations respecting any earthly head of the Theocracy. On the other hand, it is the standing description of the kingdom of the Messiah that it should extend to the ends of the earth and embrace all nations within its limits. Comp. Zech. 9: 9. Isa. 2: 2. Mich. 4: 1. Here several recent opposers of the Messianic interpretation, as Ammon (Christol. s. 36) have extricated themselves from the difficulty by maintaining that אַפְסֵי אָרֶץ signifies the utmost bounds of the kingdom of Judea. But Rosenm. and De Wette on v. 8 have already shown that אֶפֶס does not like גְבוּל mean boundary, but extremity; and that the phrase אַפְסֵי אָרֶץ is never used for the bounds of Palestine, but always in its widest signification. Equally arbitrary is the limitation of the comprehensive word גוים either to the surrounding tribes, or to the descendants of Israel. The parallel passages Ps. 72: 8—11, are decisive in favor of the most extensive meaning.

Further, the idea moreover of an earthly king is inconsistent with the fact that rebellion against the Anointed and Son of Jehovah, is represented as rebellion against Jehovah himself, and the nations are exhorted to submit to him with humility and reverence. It would have been a totally different case had the enemies here described been those who were meditating the subversion of the Theocracy, but instead of that they have no other object in view than to free themselves from the yoke of this king, and it is impossible to find an instance where aiming at such an object is treated as rebellion against Jehovah himself.

Finally, that the non-Messianic interpretation is entirely arbitrary, is manifest from the total disagreement of its defenders respecting the subject and occasion of the Psalm, as well as from the peculiar difficulties which attend every decision on these points except that which has been generally adopted. Before this interpretation can be in any measure probable, it must at least be shown that this Psalm may refer either to David or to Solomon. But even the possibility of this, is contested by Rosenmüller and De Wette, after the example of Hensler (Bemerkungen zu Stellen in den Psalmen und der Genesis S. 4.) with arguments which cannot be easily refuted. The opinion of those who, after the Jewish expositors, maintain that the Psalm was composed by David concerning himself, when the Philistines came up against him (2 Sam. 5: 17) is seen to be erroneous not only because the hill of Zion, v 6, is called holy, an appellation which could not be given to it till after the Tabernacle had been erected upon it, which was subsequent to the Philistine war, but also because the people and kings are here spoken of as striving to release themselves from a dominion to which they had before been subject, while neither the Philistines, nor any other foreign nation was at that time subject to the Israelites.* Against the supposition that it refers to the contest with Ishbosheth, or the rebellion of Absalom, there is the objection not only that the Psalm speaks of *foreign* foes, but also of several kings with their people. As little can the Psalm, as others suppose, relate to the war mentioned in 2 Sam VIII, for David had not then to contend with people, who, having before been reduced to subjection, had risen up in rebellion against his authority. Those who, notwithstanding these reasons, assert the reference of the Psalm to David must with Justi (Nationalges. der Heber. III. p. 89,) confess that they can point out no condition in the history of David with which it harmonizes, which is in fact to confess that he is not its subject, when we consider the comparative fullness of our accounts of his life.—Still less can this Psalm relate to Solomon; There is no mention of any rebellion against him, but we need not rely on this, for from the remark (1 Kings 4. 5. and 1 Chron. 22. 9) that constant peace prevailed during his reign, it is evident that there could have been no such resistance to his authority as is here described. Since then the reference of the Psalm to either David or Solomon is impossible, nothing remains for us but to adopt the Messianic interpretation. For should we concede to De Wette, as we are by no means disposed to do, that the expressions must not be too strictly interpreted, since a flattering court poet (!) may have indulged himself in much extravagance, yet even the grossest flatterer could not have used such language of any of the later kings. The extravagance of the poet could not then have appeared in the description of the present, but only in the promises of the future. Not only however are the people and kings of the whole earth prom-

---

* The additional argument advanced by Rosenmüller and De Wette, that David was not anointed on the hill of Zion, but first at Bethlehem, and afterwards at Hebron is not valid, because the preposition על can be very well rendered *over*, and then the chief seat of the Theocracy, as is often the case, designates the Theocracy itself.

ised to this king for a possession, but they are also represented as already in subjection to his dominion, and on the point of freeing themselves from it. This would be an historical fact, and it rests upon the non-Messianic interpreter by an appeal to history to show its existence, or at least its possibility. That this however cannot be done is evident from the fact that De Wette has not once ventured to offer a conjecture on the subject.

These reasons for the Messianic interpretation and against every other are so clear, that some of those whose doctrinal views must have strongly biassed them against it, have been compelled to decide in its favor. Thus Eichhorn (Biblioth. der Bibl Literat. 1 534) "The fact cannot be denied that if we suppose the Psalm to relate to the Messiah, every description retains its most natural meaning, every expression stands in its proper place, every word in a clear light What more can be required in order to establish this reference? No Jew therefore had ever thought of another person than the Messiah as its subject before hostility towards Christians in the 11th century chanced to recommend the reference to David And when discerning men even among Christian expositors concur with them in this, it is owing rather to rashness of decision, than to the absence of traits in the Psalm, which declare the Messiah to be its subject." Bertholdt is equally decided (De Ortu Theologiae Hebr. p 123) · "quae hic de rege dicuntur tam ampla et magnifica sunt, ut qualemcunque sive Davidem, sive Salomonem, sive alium celebrari statuere velis, parum apte et congruenter dici videantur." Rosenmüller, who in his first edition had defended its reference to Solomon, has in the second adopted the Messianic interpretation. Besides these we may mention among its defenders Dathe, Hufnagel (Diss. in h Ps.), Anton, Kuinoel (Mess. Weis. p 12 seq), who nevertheless has since changed his opinion and asserts its reference to David (Comm in Act Ap. p. 156), Knapp, Reinhard, Brentano, Dereser, Muntinghe, and many others.

It now only remains briefly to refute the objections which have been urged against this interpretation

1. " According to the doctrine of Christianity the Messiah is no conqueror of nations, bearing an iron sceptre; his kingdom is not of this world." So De Wette. For the refutation of this objection it is not necessary to adopt the explanation of Augustine and Theodoret, who understand the 9th verse metaphorically, and make it refer not

to the destruction of sinners, but of sins.* Although such a figurative representation is not entirely without example, yet here it is by no means allowed by the context. According to this, the Psalm speaks of severe punishment, which the Son of God will inflict upon his foes, if they obstinately persist in their rebellion against his rightful authority, while at the same time forgiveness is promised on condition of repentance and submission. But this is by no means in opposition to the doctrine of either the Old Testament or the New concerning the Messiah. In the Old Testament it is said of him, Isa. 11. 4, "He shall smite the earth with the rod of his mouth, and with the breath of his lips shall he slay the wicked," according to Ps. 72. 4, "He shall break in pieces the oppressor," and Ps. 110. 6, "He shall judge among the heathen, and destroy the enemies of his kingdom." In the New Testament the same Christ, who, when he came in the form of a servant, judged no man, shall hereafter appear in glory to inflict fearful vengeance on his foes. Comp. Matt. xxiv. and many other places. Even temporal judgments are ascribed to Christ, which are inflicted as an earnest of the great and final judgment of the enemies of the divine kingdom. Thus did he come to the destruction of Jerusalem, Matt. 10: 23. It is the more difficult to conceive how any one can here find a contradiction to the christian conceptions of the Messiah, since the New Testament from which these conceptions are derived, describes the punishment that Christ shall inflict upon his enemies, in the very words of this Psalm. See Apoc. 2. 27. 12. 5. 19. 15. The whole objection arises from not discriminating between the first and second coming of Christ, whereby men have been led to regard as general what is peculiar to the former. This objection was long since happily answered by Calvin. "Mirum videri posset, quum prophetae alibi Christi mansuetudinem, clementiam et facilitatem celebrent, hic rigidum et austerum plenumque terroris describi. Sed quia severa haec et formidabilis dominatio nonnisi ad incutiendum hostibus metum posita est: humanitati, qua suos Christus blande et suaviter fovet, minime contraria est. Nam ut se placidis ovibus amabilem pastorem exhibet, ita feras bestias necesse

---

* The former gives the sense thus "Contere in iis terrenas cupiditates et veteris hominis lutulenta negotia et quidquid de peccatore limo contractum atque inolitum est." The latter says συντρίψει αὐτοὺς ὡς σκεύη κεραμέως, ἀναλύων καὶ ἀναπλάττων διὰ τῆς τοῦ λουτροῦ παλιγγενεσίας, καὶ τῷ πυρὶ τοῦ πνεύματος στερεμνίους ἀπεργαζόμενος.

est ab eo durius tractari, ut eorum truculentiam vel corrigat vel compescat.—Et certe utrumque illi apte tribuitur, quia a patre missus est, ut pauperes ac miseros salutis nuntio exhilaret, captivos solvat, aegrotos sanet, tristes et afflictos ex mortis tenebris educat in lucem vitae Is. 61: 1. Rursum, quia multi sua ingratitudine ejus in se vindictam provocant, ad subigendam eorum duritiam, quodammodo novam personam induit."

2 "The Messiah is first to subdue the nations and bring them under his sway, but in this Psalm those who are already his subjects rise up in rebellion against him. It is also difficult to show the fulfilment of this. There have been people who for a long time declared themselves hostile to the doctrine of Jesus; but where is the nation which having received his religion, afterwards assailed and endeavored to extirpate it?" So De Wette and Hensler l c p. 4. The first part of this objection is done away by the remark, that in a prophetical view of coming events, every thing depends on the position which the inspired seer occupies He places himself either in the present and then extends his view over the future, or else, in the nearer future, and overlooks that which is more remote Thus, for example, Isaiah chap. LIII, takes his stand between the passion and glorification of Christ, so that the former appears to him as past, the latter as future So also here, the prophet feels himself, in spirit, placed in the time when the Messiah has already appeared and subjected many nations to his dominion He beholds them rising up in rebellion against their rightful Lord, and predicts that their efforts shall be all in vain, that the Father shall continually confer new glory upon the Son, and destroy those who despise him It will not appear strange that David should predict the future rebellion of people and kings against the Messiah, even if we leave out of view his supernatural illumination. He had learned enough of the corruption of mankind to anticipate that when his great descendant should appear, all would not cheerfully submit to him, or persevere in obedience to his authority. For the most striking refutation of the second part of the objection, we refer to the history of the last century God grant that it may not also be refuted by that of the present ! Rebellion against Christ may exist, while the christian name is retained, and we have one memorable example in recent times, where even this was no longer done.

3 "The whole character of the Psalm, the lively and progressive description, the vivid representation of the enemies, all lead to the conclusion that the aim of this poem was local, and its object a pre-

sent one." So Herder, Hebr. Poesie 2 p. 402, Moller, in Eichhorn's Bibl. 6. p. 207. But were this argument just, it would disprove all predictions of the Messiah; for, since the prophecies were given in a vision, every thing in them must appear as present, and the representations are always full of life, and not unfrequently assume a dramatic character.

Psalm XLV.

After a brief introduction, the sacred poet celebrates the praises of an illustrious king, who is distinguished by beauty of person, sweetness of speech, heroism and righteousness, v. 3 — 6. In his kingdom which is everlasting, and in which he appears with the highest comeliness and dignity; the most remarkable joys and honors are conferred upon him as the reward of his distinguished merit, v. 7—9. This splendor is heightened by his women, the daughters of kings, among whom one is particularly distinguished, who shines on his right hand in gold of Ophir, v. 10. To her the poet, v. 11—13, addresses himself. He exhorts her to devote herself, with all her affections, to her Lord and king, and sacrifice every thing else for him; since she will thus enjoy his tenderest love, and with it the highest reverence of the most flourishing nations. He next, in v. 14—16, describes the splendors of the bride, when introduced to the king, with other virgins, her intimate companions. Lastly, he again turns to the king, v. 17, 18, and promises him an illustrious progeny, who, under his auspices should rule the whole earth, at the same time expressing the hope that his poem in future ages would contribute to advance his glory among many nations.

There is a great diversity of views among interpreters in relation to the subject of this Psalm. Nearly all the older Christian interpreters ascribe it without hesitation to the Messiah. Among the moderns, this interpretation is held by Runge, (Comment in h. Ps. Dresd 1781), Michaelis, Lowth (de Sacr. Poes. Hebr. p. 611), Dathe, Anton (de Rat Proph. Mess p. 29), Kuinol (Mess Weiss p 56 seq.), Ringeltaube, Muntinghe, Pareau (Instit. Interp. V I. p. 511, 12), and others Rosenmuller also in the second edition of his Comm. has adopted it, with the remark that the non-messianic interpreters can have no claim to the merit of a correct exposition of the

Psalm. On the other hand, a large number of recent critics have defended the opposite interpretation. Among them, however, there is found a great diversity of opinion. Some regard it as a bridal ode, and as Grotius, Dereser and Kaiser (Ps. p 194), suppose it to have been sung at the marriage of Solomon with a foreign bride, probably the daughter of the king of Egypt—or as Augusti (praktische Einleitung in die Psalm s 30)—at the nuptials of a Persian king. Others on the contrary assert that what is said of the women, and especially of the queen, is only of secondary importance, intended to advance the main design of the poem, which is to display the glory of the king These again are so far divided that some, as Doderlein, who at an earlier period, in the Auctar. ad Grotium, had defended the Messianic interpretation (theol Bibl. 1. p. 183 seq.) suppose the king whose praises are celebrated to be an Israelite, while in the opinion of others, as Rosenmuller in his first edition, and De Wette, he is a Persian.

We feel compelled to refer the Psalm to the Messiah, for the following reasons:

1. The testimony of tradition. Not only does the Chaldee paraphrast explain the Psalm of the Messiah, but the same interpretation is found in many passages of other ancient Jewish writings. See the collection by Schottgen 1 c. p. 234 Even several later Jewish expositors, as Abenezra and Kimchi, relying upon tradition explain it in this manner. But we can trace this tradition much further back. It is utterly inconceivable that the collectors of the Psalms should have placed this in their collection had it been a bridal ode, intended for the marriage of an Israelitish king, or one composed by some miserable flatterer in honor of a Persian monarch.* The weight of this objection falls with peculiar force on those who make a Persian king the object of those praises which, according to their view, are squandered away in this Psalm. For were its subject a king of Israel, as David or Solomon, it might with some plausibility be said, see Stark, Carmina Dav. 1 p 462, that, in the time of those who collected the Psalms, its true interpretation was lost, and it was adopted by them, and consecrated to the worship of God, because they ascribed to it a mystical meaning, which, though erroneous, was already prevalent. But if the subject is a Persian king, he must have lived after the Jews and Persians had begun to have frequent intercourse with each

---

* De Wette upon v 17 "over all the earth," an extravagant flattery, which could have been offered only to a Persian king.

other, and consequently, after the Babylonian exile. The collectors of the Psalms therefore must have been nearly contemporary with the author of this poem, and they are chargeable with the guilt of having knowingly received among the Psalms of praise to God, a poem which, if it refer to a mere mortal, contains, as we shall soon see, blasphemous expressions. This supposition can surely have no weight with those who know how carefully the Jews after they had been taught by misfortune during the captivity, avoided whatever might tend to dishonor their God, and how strong their national pride and their hatred and contempt of whatever did not belong to their own people, became, precisely at this period.

2. The Messianic interpretation is sustained by the authority of the New Testament. The author of the Epistle to the Hebrews, chap. 1: 8, 9, quotes this Psalm to prove the exaltation of Christ above the angels. This cannot be merely an allusion, since according to the non-Messianic interpretation, his argument would lose all its force, and his appeal would be entirely useless.

3. Not less strong is the internal evidence. We will here, following the order of the Psalm, and produce those characteristics which are applicable to the Messiah alone. From the superscription, v 1, itself we derive a twofold argument. If this Psalm is a poem upon any worldly subject, how could it have been committed to the sons of Korah to be used in the service of God? Who can suppose that a nuptial poem, dedicated to Solomon, or an ode composed by some flatterer in praise of a Persian king, could have been sung in the public worship, and of course introduced into the sanctuary? Stark (1 c p. 453) perceived the force of this objection, and felt compelled by it to deny the genuineness of the superscription; though for this he had not the slightest reason. Further, the Psalm in the title is called מַשְׂכִּיל. Were the interpretation which De Wette gives to this word the true one, it would indeed afford us no argument. He supposes (Einl z d. Ps. s 38) the word signifies nothing more than *poem*, since, as he justly remarks, the meaning *didactic poem*, which was that of the greater part of the older interpreters, does not suit all the Psalms to which it is prefixed. But still the proof in favor of his explanation of the word is extremely feeble. He says; "according to Hebrew usage מַשְׂכִּיל, *intelligentia, doctrina*, can mean in general *poem*, just as the Arabic شعر properly *intelligentia*, and secondarily *poetry*. To this we object, that the part. Hiphil מַשְׂכִּיל never

occurs as a noun with the meaning *scientia, doctrina* And it can surely be shown by no analogous example, that a participle which means *being wise*, can stand absolutely for *a poem* Another objection is, that the Psalms designated by the epithet מַשְׂכִּיל are distinguished by some peculiarity common to all which is expressed by this appellation But the general meaning *poem* is by no means rendered certain by Ps. 47·8, as Gesenius has asserted. Another explanation, the result of a comparison with the Arabic ݣَاشَ, *similis, comparata fuit res*, which gives to the word the meaning *metaphorical, figurative language*, is not only inconsistent with the contents of these Psalms, but is liable to the further objection of departing from established Hebrew usage in the explanation of a word of such frequent occurrence We give to the word the meaning, *a devout poem*, and justify it by the usage of the language. The verb הִשְׂכִּיל has, it is true, the original meaning *to be intelligent, wise, prudent*. But another sense arises, namely, *to be pious, religious*, from the views of the Hebrews impressed on their language respecting the intimate connexion and mutual influence of the theoretical and the practical. Thus for example Ps. 14. 2, precisely in a Psalm, which occurring again as the LIII is entitled מַשְׂכִּיל, this word is put in apposition to נָבָל *a fool* in a moral sense, and as synonymous with דֹּרֵשׁ אֶת אֱלֹהִים, *one who seeks God, a pious man*. See besides, Gesenius and Winer.
2. This interpretation has in its favor the contents of the thirteen* Psalms to which מַשְׂכִּיל is prefixed. They have all a direct reference to God, and either express gratitude for his benefits, or supplications for his aid. This meaning agrees also with Psalm 47: 8, "God is king over all the earth, sing to him מַשְׂכִּיל, a devout song."
3. It is also supported by the adjunct תְּפִלָּה in Ps. CXLII The general expression מַשְׂכִּיל, which comprehends *a thankful*, as well as, *a supplicatory ode*, is rendered definite by this addition. But if this meaning of the word מַשְׂכִּיל be the only one that can be proved, it furnishes a strong argument for the Messianic interpretation of the Psalm This Calvin long since perceived, who remarks: "Ideo carmen simul vocatur מַשְׂכִּיל, ut sciamus non agi de obscoenis, vel minus pudicis amoribus, sed sub Salomonis figura sanctam et divinam Christi cum ecclesia conjunctionem nobis proponi" V 3 and 4 contain plain indications that they are not to be literally, but figuratively understood In the former the words "thou. art fairer than the

---

* Ps XXXII. XLII XLIV LII LV. LXXIV. LXXVIII. LXXXVIII LXXXIX CXLII.

sons of men," are by De Wette and others referred to personal beauty, which in ancient times was highly esteemed. But, that this was employed by the poet merely as an image to represent the high moral perfection of the king, is evident from the declaration, "therefore hath God blessed thee forever," since mere beauty of form cannot possibly be the ground of God's blessing.* De Wette and Rosenm., it is true, seek to evade the difficulty by translating עַל־כֵּן *while*, after the example of Calvin, instead of *therefore*. But this expedient is inadmissible, because this meaning of עַל־כֵּן is in general incapable of proof, see Winer s. v. כִּי, and is not necessarily required in any of the places quoted by De Wette on Ps. 42: 7; and because לְעוֹלָם would then be entirely unsuitable and superfluous; and lastly, because עַל־כֵּן can have no other meaning than that which it has in v. 8: "thou lovest righteousness and hatest iniquity, *therefore* he hath anointed thee," etc., in a similar connexion. V. 4, the king is summoned to gird his sword upon his thigh, but at the same time the writer intimates the metaphorical nature of the language by the exegetical phrase הוֹדְךָ וַהֲדָרֶךָ, 'thy glory and thy majesty.' What earthly monarchs effect by the sword shall this exalted Godlike king accomplish by his glory and majesty, whereby he shall vanquish his foes without the aid of any of those means employed by men. Altogether similar is the language of Isa. 11: 4: "He shall slay the wicked with the rod of his mouth;" that is, what other kings effect by instruments of punishment, he shall effect by his bare words. The words הוֹד and הָדָר are commonly employed in connexion, to designate the majesty and glory of Jehovah, see Ps. 96: 6. 104: 1. 111: 3. Rosenmuller and De Wette suppose that the sword of the king is called glory and majesty, *qui est decus tuum et splendor*. But the insipidity of this interpretation is obvious at first sight, and that it is erroneous is still more evident from the beginning of v. 5. The repetition of הָדָר which there occurs, "and in this thy glory," shows that the word is used in its full and literal import. The true interpretation was long ago perceived by Theodoret: τὴν ὥραν διαγράψας καὶ τὴν σοφίαν ἀποδείκνυσι καὶ τὴν δύναμιν καὶ τὴν πανοπλίαν, ᾗ χρησάμενος τοὺς ἐναντίους κατέλυσε. Καὶ τὸ πάντων ἡμᾶς παραδοξότατον πρᾶγμα διδάσκει. Αὐτὴν γὰρ αὐτοῦ τὴν ὥραν, καὶ πανοπλίαν λέγει καὶ δύναμιν. Περίζωσαι γάρ φησι τὴν ῥομφαίαν σου ἐπὶ τὸν μηρόν σου, δυνατέ, τῇ

---

* Theodoret: ὁ δὲ ψαλμὸς κάλλος αὐτοῦ καλεῖ οὐ τὸ τοῦ σώματος, ἀλλὰ τῆς ἀρετῆς καὶ πάσης δικαιοσύνης, τὸ ἁμαρτίας οὐ δεξάμενον σπῖλον, τὸ πάσης κηλῖδος ἐλεύθερον.

ὡραιότητι σου καὶ τῷ κάλλει σου. — The characteristics also given in v. 5, that the king whom the poet celebrates goes forth for the establishment and promotion of truth and righteousness joined with mildness, suggest the idea of a conflict which is not to be fought with fleshly weapons, and they cannot be taken in their natural import when referred to any other subject so well as when referred to the Messiah, of whom it is also said in Isa 11· 5, "that righteousness shall be the girdle of his loins, and faithfulness the girdle of his reigns' When in v. 6, the king is described as a mighty warrior, who subdues many nations, this does not at all suit Solomon who was engaged in no war, but agrees well with the Messiah, who likewise in Isa 53 12. Ps 110 5, and elsewhere, is represented under the image of a powerful and victorious warrior. But the strongest argument for the Messianic interpretation is found in v. 7. There the king is addressed as God The non-Messianic interpreters have here resorted to various expedients. Several of them take אֱלֹהִים not as the vocative, but as the genitive. How unnatural this interpretation is, and how plainly the mere result of necessity, appears from the fact that no one of the ancient translators, among whom the Jewish certainly cannot be charged with doctrinal prejudice, ever thought of it. All translate in the vocative The LXX ὁ θρόνος σου ὁ θεὸς εἰς αἰῶνα αἰῶνος. Aquila. ὁ θρόνος σου θεὲ εἰς αἰῶνα καὶ ἔτι. Symmachus: ὁ θρόνος σου ὁ θεὸς αἰώνιος καὶ ἔτι. Theodotion : ὁ θρόνος σου ὁ θεὸς εἰς τὸν αἰῶνα τοῦ αἰῶνος. The Chaldee . 'thronus gloriae tuae, domine, stabilis in sempiternum.' In favor of the vocative also is the foregoing voc. גִּבּוֹר v 4. Calvin has already justly said : "Quod Judaei locum hunc depravant, quasi ad deum fieret sermo, nimis putidum est ; quod etiam alii אֱלֹהִים in Genitivo casu legunt, ratione caret ac prodit eorum impudentiam, dum scripturam turpiter lacerare non dubitant, ne Messiae divinitatem cogantur fateri." But that this interpretation is inadmissible will be yet more clearly seen, if we carefully examine the different modifications with which it has been advanced. De Wette on the passage, and Gesenius on Is. 9 5, translate " Thy God's throne endures forever and ever ;" that is, thy throne entrusted to thee by God. They suppose that we have here a *stat. constr.* interpreted by a suffix, as in Levit. 26· 42, בְּרִיתִי יַעֲקֹב, *my Jacob's covenant*, that is, my covenant established with Jacob. But here an essential difference has been overlooked between the passage before us and the only alleged parallel passage, which serves apparently to confirm this interpretation. The exception to the rule, that the suffix belonging to two nouns in the construct state, can be attached only to the latter, (Ewald Gramm. p. 580) is justified in the passage quoted, only by the circumstance, that the second noun is a proper name, which cannot receive a suffix; here however there is no reason whatever why the suffix should not be attached to the second noun, and the supposition that the rule is here departed from, is entirely arbitrary. 2. After the example of Abenezra (Clavis s 123), Paulus, and Ewald (Gramm. p 627), translate, "thy throne is God's throne," supplying כִּסֵּא again before אֱלֹהִים. But no one of the advocates of this interpretation has produced a single example in favor of so harsh an ellipsis. Ewald says it occurs very seldom, and appeals to this passage alone.—Still more unjustifiable is the explanation of those, who, after R. Saadias Haggaon as cited by Kimchi, take אֱלֹהִים in the nom case: "Thy throne is God forever and ever," i. e. He will forever sustain thy throne. This has not even the semblance of support in the usage of the language; and it is manifest from the parallel passages in 2 Sam 7: 13, and Ps 89 29, that *forever and ever* must be an attribute of the kingdom and not of God. The demonstration that אֱלֹהִים cannot be understood otherwise than as the vocative, sufficiently refutes one class of our opponents. Not a few among them acknowledge this, but assert that the name אֱלֹהִים may be given to judges, kings, etc. So, after the example of Jarchi, Knapp, Ammon (Christologie, p. 45), Dereser (Psalmen p. 129), and others. But against this interpretation there are the following objections. 1. We will not with Winer and others deny that אֱלֹהִים is ever used for the magistracy among men. Thus it is said in Ex. 21: 6 and 22. 7, 8, that a man shall go with his cause before God, אֶל־אֱלֹהִים, i e as we learn from Deut. 19. 7, before the divinely appointed tribunal, which decided causes in God's name. This usage certainly occurs also Ps. 82 1, where, to awaken the consciences of the Theocratic judges, God is represented as appearing in their assembly, in which the Presidency belongs to Him, and which dispenses justice in his name, בַּעֲדַת אֵל and בְּקֶרֶב אֱלֹהִים. It is true that De Wette has attempted another interpretation. He supposes God to be represented as holding His court in heaven, in an assembly of the inferior gods, the angels. But this interpretation must be rejected, partly because the supposition that by אֱלֹהִים the angels are designated is unsupported by usage, and partly because it is unnatural to suppose that by אֱלֹהִים and עֲדַת אֵל in this verse the angels are intended, and on the contrary by אֱלֹהִים and בְּנֵי אֶלְיוֹן, v. 6, the earthly magistracy, since v 6 manifestly refers back to v. 1. But these passages nevertheless do not prove the point to be maintained. No where is any single magistrate called אֱלֹהִים, but always only the magistracy as such, representing the tribunal of God. Since therefore a Theocratic conqueror was never so called, certainly much less could the name be given to a king at the celebration of his nuptials, and least of all to a Persian king, who could not even be called son of God, since this title belonged exclusively to the leader of the Theocracy. 2 To understand *king* by אֱלֹהִים in this place is attended with the greater difficulty, since in the Psalms for the sons of Korah, this is the prevailing and almost exclusive name for the Deity instead of Jehovah. See Gesenius on Is 9. 5. 3 "Hoc nomen omni sua vi accipiendum esse, liquet ex ipsa contexta oratione, nam eodem dei nomine vates Messiam compellat v. seq., quod non diversum ab eo est, quo ipsum deum ibidem significat, quodque adeo, ut non diverso, sed eodem plane sensu intelligatur, suadet interpretandi simplicitas" Pareau Inst Interpr V. T. p 194. If now we moreover consider that Ps ii and cx ascribe to the Messiah names, attributes, and actions, which belong exclusively to God, we shall feel less hesitation to take אֱלֹהִים here in its full and natural meaning, and acknowledge the Messiah as the subject of the Psalm The promise of the eternal duration of his throne in the same verse leads us also to the Messiah. Allowing that עוֹלָם וָעֶד may in itself considered be capable of a limited meaning, yet that such is not the case here is evident from the context, the connexion with אֱלֹהִים and a comparison with the parallel passages, 2 Sam. vii and Ps. lxxxix., cited on our remarks on Ps. ii and especially with Ps lxxii. where v 5, we find as synonymous עִם שֶׁמֶשׁ and לִפְנֵי יָרֵחַ, and v 8, the subject of the Psalm is again called God. True, De Wette takes אֱלֹהִים as subject and a repetition "Thy God shall show that God is especially favorable to the king" But as it has been shown that אֱלֹהִים in the foregoing verse is the vocative and object of address, no other interpretation is admissible here An important argument for the necessity of the figurative interpretation is furnished by v. 11 "Hearken, O daughter, and consider and incline thine ear" How unsuitable the appellation *daughter* would be in an address to an earthly queen is manifest from the efforts of several non-Messianic interpreters to exchange it for another Thus Mendelssohn translates. "Princess, hearken, give me thine ear." Its offensiveness and incompatibility with the manners of the East has been fully shown by Doederlein, theol. Bibl 1 p 193 Teachers employ the epithet *son* when addressing their pupils Ps 34. 12. Prov. 1 8: "my son" etc. But a poet would have found but little favor had he been disposed to treat a daughter of Pharaoh or a Persian princess as his pupil But if we follow the Messianic interpretation all incongruity disappears. It is a frequent custom of the Hebrew poets and phrophets to personify lands, people and cities as young women or matrons See Isa. 4·4, "Daughters of Zion," for the cities of Judah, and 23 12. "Daughters of Zion," for Zion. But we need seek no farther for examples, since even in v. 13 the "Daughters of Tyre" stands for Tyre. So here the psalmist personifies the covenant people and represents them as a bride, who shall be brought in costly array to the illustrious king, who will take her as his beloved, on condition that she renounces for him all that she had loved before. This figurative representation need the less surprise us, since the same image is so often employed, in both the Old and New Testaments, to represent the revelation of God or of Christ to his people Thus, throughout the whole of the Song of Solomom, God appears as the lover, and the people of Israel as the beloved or bride See Rosenmuller, "uber des hohen Liedes Sinn und Auslegung," in den Analekten von Keil and Tschirner 1, 3, und den Aufsatz: "uber das hohe Lied," Evangel K. Z I. S 177 seq. Isaiah predicted 54 5, "Thy maker shall then be thy husband His name is Jehovah of hosts. And thy Redeemer the Holy one of Israel the God of the whole earth shall he be called" In Isa 62. 5, he says, 'For as a young man marrieth a virgin, so shall thy sons marry thee, and as a bridegroom rejoiceth over the bride, so shall thy God rejoice over thee' In chap. 50 1, the decree of rejection, which God pronounced against the people of Israel, is styled a bill of divorcement. Comp. further Jer. 3: 1. Hos i—iii Ez 16 23. In the New Testament also Christ calls himself a bridegroom, Matt 9 15 John regards himself as only the friend of the bridegroom, and points out Christ as the bridegroom who should possess the bride, John 3 29 See also Rom 7:4. Eph. 5 27. 1 Cor xi The necessity of the metaphorical interpretation may also be shown by v 15 There it is said, 'she shall be brought unto the king in raiment of needle-work, the virgins her companions that follow her shall be brought unto thee.' These virgins are the same who in v 10 are called kings' daughters We must not even on this account suppose with some interpreters that they are merely conductors and attendants of the bride. The words moreover, 'her companions,' and 'they shall be brought unto thee,' show that these virgins also, no less than the bride are to be united with the king in love. Here then an insuperable difficulty arises in the way of those, who regard this psalm as a nuptial ode since it was not the custom to take more than one wife at the same time.* But the Messianic interpretation entirely removes this difficulty The companions of the Queen, who though inferior in rank, are still to be united with the king, are then the heathen nations over whom indeed the people of Israel, as the ancient covenant people of God, enjoy a certain outward preeminence, but who according to the standing prediction of the prophets and the authors of the Psalms, were to have an equal share in the blessing of the Messiah's kingdom. Thus of old the Chaldee paraphrase and Kimchi, " filiae regum sunt gentes, quae omnes ad obsequium regis Messiae redigentur." A metaphorical representation altogether similar is found in Cant 6 7, 8. "There are threescore queens, and fourscore concubines, and virgins without number, but my dove is but one." Here therefore we are taught in the usual figurative language, what in other Messianic Psalms is simply expressed, as in Ps. 2 8, 'That the Messias shall take for his possession all the people of the earth,' Ps 72 8, 'That he shall reign from sea to sea, and from the Euphrates to the ends of the earth,' etc.—V 17, it is said, the king will make his sons princes in all the earth That the words בְּכָל־הָאָרֶץ can have only the meaning we have given and cannot be translated ' in all the land,' De Wette himself confesses He says, also, that it is only by the extravagance of flattery that such language could be addressed to a Persian king But besides the arguments already adduced against the supposition that the subject is a Persian king we may add the close resemblance between this psalm, and LXXII. which De Wette himself explains of a king of Israel The Messianic interpretation gives a sense as natural, as it is suitable. The poet derives his figurative representation from the circumstances of the time in which he lived. Solomon had divided Palestine into twelve departments, see 1 Kings 4 7, and 2 Sam 8 18 it would seem that David had already established his sons as agents under himself. The same

---

* That the psalm, unless it be referred to the Messiah, can be taken for nothing else, than a song of praise to a king on occasion of his marriage, appears from the exhortation v 11, which can properly relate only to a bride and not to a wife of the king. The same is true also of the promise v 17.

thing was done by Rehoboam 2 Chron. 11· 23. And as the earthly heads of the Theocracy divided their kingdom which was confined to the bounds of Palestine among their sons, so shall the Messiah divide among his offspring his far wider dominion, which extends over the whole earth. It follows, however, from the character of the union from which they spring, that these are not natural, but spiritual children. This metaphorical representation can moreover be sustained by analogous examples. See Is. 53. 10. Finally, the prediction in v. 18, that many nations shall praise him is to say the least, more applicable to the Messiah than to any earthly king.

Having thus brought forward the positive proofs for the Messianic character of the Psalm, it now remains to remove the objections which have been urged against it, at least so far as they have not been refuted by what has already been advanced. Of this character is the general charge, so often repeated by several non-Messianic interpreters, of capricious allegorizing. But this objection is valid only when the interpreter fails to show, either from internal or external evidence, that the literal meaning cannot be the true one, and that the author designed to represent spiritual objects by sensible images. See Anton l. c. p. 27. We take the objections principally from Paulus—Clavis S. 119, who has made a tolerably complete collection of what others, as Teller, zu Turretin de interpret S. Script. p 165 seq, Schulz, Critik der Messianisch Psalmen, Jacobi, Psalmen ubers, and lastly Kaiser have brought forward repeatedly.

1. "True there are frequently metaphorical representations in the Hebrew writers, but it is not the practice of a good writer to carry out the allegory so far." Thus Teller l c. p 185. But, in answer to this, we have a sufficient number of examples. even though we should not choose to appeal to the splendid example of the 'Song of Songs.' We need only compare the allegorical representations of the fall of Babylon, Is. XLVII. where Babylon is personified and described as a rich delicate lady, who is now bereaved of her husband, and overwhelmed in the deepest misery; the similar representations, extended to the minutest particulars, in Ez. XVI. and XXIII. and the figurative description continued through to the first three chapters of Hosea, and we shall be obliged to confess that the author of this psalm has confined himself within very narrow limits.

2. "The Psalmist, who could borrow his colouring from all the royal splendor of a Jewish monarch, in order to describe his Messiah, has nevertheless chosen very unskilfully, and given him a costume

which does not belong to him. The kingdom of the Jewish Messiah can indeed be presented to him as a bride clothed in all the splendor of the East, and attended by maidens and companions; but then he has but one bride, one spouse, the people of Israel "—One can scarcely conceive what is meant by this objection. Do they intend to assert that the sacred poets and prophets of the Old Testament regarded their Messiah as destined for the Jews alone ? This has already been sufficiently refuted by the passages quoted from the Psalm. But if it was expected that the kingdom of the Messiah should embrace the heathen as well as the Jews, since it is conceded that the Jewish people can be personified as his bride, what reason can be given why the heathen nations should not be represented in the same manner, especially as the circumstances of an Oriental court, where many wives of inferior rank stand by the side of one peculiarly distinguished, gives so much occasion to carry out the allegory to such an extent? Finally, the author, in ascribing to the people of Israel such an outward distinction, wisely followed the mode of representing the Messiah's kingdom which prevails throughout the Old Testament, where the Jewish people are always regarded as the original stock, and the heathen nations, who were only to be engrafted upon it, sustain a relation somewhat subordinate, a view of the subject afterwards confirmed by Christ, and his apostles, Rom. xi

3 "Figures like v 12, 'so shall the king greatly desire thy beauty' are improper, and not usual with the sacred writers" But then we must allow it to be equally objectionable, when Isaiah compares the delight of God in his people with that of the bridegroom in his bride; or when Paul styles the church a bride, not having spot, or wrinkle, or any such thing, and, therefore, enjoying the perfect love of her exalted bridegroom. To say nothing of other passages, is not spiritual beauty here also represented by the figure of personal beauty?

4. "How shall this bride of the Messiah forget her own people? She is herself this people personified" But precisely because the representation is figurative, and the covenant people appear personified as a bride, must the thought, that, after their union with this exalted king, they should render to him their exclusive love, and renounce every previous inclination, not directed to him, be expressed in a manner consistent with this figurative representation, and not with the event described; therefore in accordance with the relation between a bride and a bridegroom. The passage in Gen 2: 24.

"Therefore shall a man leave his father and mother," supplied the Psalmist with a beautiful ground work; he seems also to have had in view Gen. 21: 1: "And the Lord spake to Abraham, get thee out of thy country, and from thy kindred and thy father's house." The Chaldee well explains it on the whole, though the figure is too literally understood "et obliviscere opera mala impiorum populi tui et domum idolorum, quae coluisti in domo patris tui Abrahami."

5 "How came Tyre alone to be mentioned, instead of all the heathen nations?" The Messianic interpretation does not require us to suppose this; but that Tyre, as the richest city of the ancient world is here by synecdoche put for the richest nations, is, in itself considered, liable to no objection, and is moreover confirmed by the addition עֲשִׁירֵי־עָם, the richest of the people, i. e. the richest among all nations. Nothing, finally, is more common in the Old Testament than single names to be mentioned, while the writer has in view the whole, and not preeminently that particular part. There is a parallel passage in Ps. 72: 10: "The king of Tarshish and of the isles shall bring presents; the kings of Sheba and Seba shall offer gifts." Further, Isaiah 60 6: "All they from Sheba shall come; they shall bring gold and incense and declare the praise of the Lord." As in both these places Tarshish, Sheba, and Seba; so here, Tyre is used to designate the richest of the heathen nations.

The Messianic interpretation therefore is sufficiently justified. We only further remark that we must be on our guard against that caprice which would require something literal corresponding to each single line, which often serves only to complete the picture. Thus in v 8, 9, we must look for nothing more than the thought that God will confer upon the Messiah the highest exaltation and glory, which is represented by imagery borrowed from the splendor of an eastern court. So also the description of the royal bride v. 13—15, means only that the richest blessings and greatest glory shall be conferred upon the covenant people, if with sincere love, they devote themselves to their Lord and King

---

Psalm LXXII.

This Psalm, like the XLV, celebrates an exalted and illustrious king, who is distinguished for righteousness, and with benevolent concern takes under his care the miserable and the oppressed, v. 1, 2, 4, 12—15. Under his reign universal peace will prevail; and in consequence of the righteousness introduced by him, a rich abundance of blessings be poured forth, v 3, 6, 7, 16 These blessings are not like those conferred by distinguished earthly kings to endure only for a time and then be interrupted by his death; but like himself, they are eternal, and consequently the gratitude and reverence of his subjects towards him will be eternal also, v. 5, 7, 17. His kingdom is by no means confined to the limits of Palestine, but is coextensive with the whole earth All nations, even the most powerful, the most uncivilized, and the most remote, shall reverently obey Him, not indeed subdued by the power of his arms, but freely choosing his service under the influence of his righteousness alone, v. 8—11. Through him will be fulfilled the great promise made to Abraham, that in his seed all the nations of the earth should be blessed. Many interpreters regard David as the author of the Psalm. They suppose that he delivered it to Solomon just before his death. Thus the old Syriac version. "Davidis cum Salomonem regem constituisset;" the Arabic: "Salomoni filio Davidis." This also is the opinion of several later Jewish expositors, as Kimchi and Jarchi, and, among Christian interpreters, Geier and lastly Pareau l. c p 511. But this opinion is opposed not only by the ל in the superscription, which indeed often designates the person or persons to whom a Psalm is delivered over for musical performance, but never the person to whom it is dedicated; but still more strongly by the fact that the imagery of this Psalm is furnished by the reign of Solomon, which of course excludes David from being its author This is too evident to be mistaken, for example, in the representation of the permanent peace, which shall prevail under the reign of this illustrious king. The representations also in v. 10 and 11 remind us of 1 Kings 10 23—25: "So king Solomon exceeded all the kings of the earth for riches and wisdom; and they brought every man his present, vessels of silver, and vessels of gold, etc " V. 16 reminds us of 1 Kings 4 20 · " Judah and Israel were (under Solomon) many, as the sand which is by the sea in multitude, eating and drinking, and making merry " Others, as Bertholdt, Einl p. 1949 et al. understand the ל after the example of the LXX ($\varepsilon\dot{\iota}\varsigma\ \Sigma\alpha\lambda\omega\mu\dot{\omega}\nu$) in the sense of *de* in Latin—concerning; as designating Solomon as the subject of the Psalm. But this is impossible, unless it is intended, with several of the older interpreters, to understand by Solomon only him of whom Solomon was the type, the Peacemaker, Gen. 49 10, the שַׂר הַשָּׁלוֹם Isa ix, just as the Messiah is often by the Prophets called expressly by the name of David—and moreover ל never occurs in a superscription with the alleged meaning. We therefore take ל in its usual acceptation and regard Solomon as the author of the Psalm, after the example of the Chaldee interpreters in former and Kaiser in recent times. As David in Ps. ii. and cx makes the disturbed and warlike condition of his own kingdom the groundwork of his representation of that of the Messiah, so does Solomon employ the peaceful, flourishing and happy condition of his kingdom to represent that of his great descendant.

Let us now examine the reasons which make it necessary to refer this Psalm to the Messiah.

1. The clear testimony of tradition. The Chaldee paraphrasts render the first verse: "Deus scientiam judiciorum tuorum da regi Messiae, et justitiam tuam filio Davidis regis." Comp the numerous passages from the older Jewish writers by Schottgen c. I. p 238 seq. Jarchi's remarks exemplify that the forefathers explained the whole Psalm of the Messiah

2. The proof from parallel passages is here peculiarly strong. On the one hand, this Psalm contains the most distinct reference to an old Messianic prediction, the words of which it employs, and on the other, in a later prediction, the Messiah's kingdom is described in words taken from it. We cannot (for example) in v. 17, "and men shall be blessed in him, all nations shall call him blessed," mistake the allusion to Gen. 12 3. 22· 18. The author appears as the interpreter of the promise to Abraham. Thus of old, Theodoret: ἐνταῦθα τῆς περὶ τὸν Ἀβραὰμ καὶ τὸν Ἰσαὰκ καὶ τὸν Ἰακὼβ ἐπαγγελίας ἐμνημόνευσε. The second place is Zechariah 9 10. There the extension of the Messiah's kingdom is described in words taken from v. 8 of this Psalm: "and his dominion shall be from sea to sea, and from the river even to the ends of the earth." To this we may add its close resemblance to other Messianic predictions, namely besides Psalms ii, xlv, cx, with Isa ix and xi

3. There is nothing in this Psalm unsuitable to the Messiah, provided we distinguish the figures from that which they represent. But, on the contrary, many of its features can belong to no other subject. We will now go over the Psalm with reference to this point. De Wette finds even in v. 1 an objection to the Messianic interpretation. The prayer that God would give righteousness to the king is incon-

sistent with it, because the Messiah is regarded as the most righteous. We remark in reply that the discourse is not here concerning righteousness in general, but righteousness as God possesses and employs it in the government of the world, and as it was needed by this king in the administration of his kingdom. The imperative תֵּן however, as is evident from what follows, is not used in the optative sense, but is to be taken as the future, see Ps 110. 2. The weakness of this objection of De Wette is manifest from Isa xi, where the Messiah, before he enters upon his kingly office, and begins his reign, is endowed by God with all the requisite qualifications Isa 42 1, the Messiah first receives the Spirit of God, and then establishes righteousness among the heathen Comp. 49. 2. 61: 1. The fulfilment also shows that Christ, although with regard to his divine nature he combined in himself all perfections, yet as to his human nature, was endowed by the Holy Ghost with the requisite qualifications for discharging the duties of his office. The appellation *king* is justified not only by Ps 2· 6 45 8, but also by Jer. 33: 17. "David shall never want a man to sit upon the throne of the house of Israel"— Ex. 37. 24 . " and David my servant shall be king over them." The title *king's son* belongs to the Messiah as son of David, and is of similar import with the metaphorical title elsewhere used, צֶמַח דָּוִיד *sprout of David*. The traits of character given in v. 2 and 4, rectitude in governing and peculiar concern for oppressed innocence, one of the most illustrious virtues of a ruler, are of very frequent occurrence in the prediction of the Messiah See Isa. 11 4· " But with righteousness shall he judge the poor and reprove with equity for the meek of the earth " Peace also, which according to v 3 shall reign throughout his kingdom as the consequence of the prevalence of righteousness, is not unfrequently given as a characteristic sign of the times of the Messiah Comp Isa 9 6 : " Of the increase of his government and his peace there shall be no end." As in Isaiah 11. 9 the knowledge of the Lord, so here righteousness is given as the cause of that peace which distinguishes the kingdom of the Messiah. V. 5 furnishes a strong proof in favor of our interpretation : "They shall fear thee as long as the sun and the moon endure, throughout all generations " The evidence of this passage would indeed be greatly weakened were we to suppose with Calvin, Doederlein, Michaelis, and Dathe, that the object of this address is God But then, as Michaelis justly remarks, only the grossest flatterer could have made such a declaration in behalf of Solomon, since no king who does not himself reign eternally, can cause his people to fear God so long as the sun and moon endure. But there are sufficient reasons to suppose with most interpreters, and at least De Wette, that the author here directly addresses the king of whom he had spoken before in the third person. This opinion is favoured by a comparison with v 7, where the expression, 'as long as the moon endureth,' as well as the corresponding word לְעוֹלָם in v. 12, must relate to the king and not to God; and by 2 Sam 7: 15, which lies at the foundation of this as well as of all other Messianic predictions in the Psalms, where the phrase עַד עוֹלָם is likewise spoken of David's posterity. Comp. also Ps. 89 37, 38 and 45 7. Grotius, in order to show that such language may be spoken of a man, compares the passage in Ovid. "cum sole et luna semper Aratus erit." But there it is living forever in the memory of others which is spoken of; here on the contrary reverence is to be paid to one who himself lives, as appears from the verse itself, and a comparison with verses 7 and 17. But as eternity of dominion can be ascribed to no earthly king, so does it constitute one of the essential characteristics of the Messiah Isa. 9. 5, he is styled the Father of eternity, and according to v 6, he shall establish his kingdom from henceforth even forever.—V. 6, the image of a rain, which falls soft and lovely upon a new mown meadow, covering it with fresh green, while if drought prevail, the sun burns it, the roots and every thing withers, is very expressive of the Messiah. Calvin: "hoc praecipue in Christo videmus impleri, qui arcanam gratiam stillando facit ecclesiam suam pullulare." David in his last Psalm, 2 Sam. 23. 5, when he speaks with deep emotions of the promise made to himself respecting the Messiah, employs the same image to describe the blessings of his reign. That this passage refers to the Messiah is obvious, for David extols his great descendant, not as the sovereign of any one people, but as the Lord of the human race (מוֹשֵׁל בָּאָדָם), comp Pareau l c p. 499.—V. 7, we again have the characteristic marks of the Messiah's reign, righteousness, peace and endless duration.—V 8, the kingdom of this illustrious monarch extends over the whole world. "He reigns from sea to sea, and from the Euphrates to the extremity of the earth" There is here a very remarkable reference to the passage where the boundaries of the earthly Theocracy are given, viz, Exod 23. 31 · "And I will set thy bounds from the Red Sea even unto the sea of the Philistines, (the Mediterranean) and from the desert unto the Euphrates," and Deut. 11 24: "from the wilderness to Lebanon and from the Euphrates to the Mediterranean sea. The author of the Psalm takes two of the boundaries here given, and then instead of the corresponding ones, subjoins others which are far wider and coincide with the ends of the earth. It is true that after Sal Jarchi, and Michaelis, some interpreters would give to this verse a more restricted meaning. They would make "from sea to sea," mean nothing more than "from the Red Sea to the Mediterranean," and אַפְסֵי אָרֶץ not *the ends of the earth*, but merely *the extremities of Palestine*. But this interpretation has no philological support. There is no example to justify us in giving the alleged restricted meaning to the expression "from sea to sea," the same as Latin "per totam terram, quatenus maribus cincta est, (Chald. ab angulo maris magni usque ad oppositum angulum maris magni) unless it were limited by an additional epithet, as in the passage of the Pentateuch, to which we have referred. Nor does אַפְסֵי אָרֶץ ever mean the bounds of Palestine, but always those of the whole earth. Moreover, according to what follows not only Palestine, but the whole earth, with all lands and rulers shall be subject to this king. But extension over the whole earth is a usual characteristic of the Messiah's kingdom. See besides Ps. 2 8 22 28. Zech 9 10, among other places, Micah 5· 4: "He shall be great even unto the ends of the earth." v. 9—11 afford a strong proof of the correctness of the Messianic interpretation. Here, in the first place, merely as a part for the whole, several far distant nations, some of them rude and uncivilized, others rich and powerful, are named, who shall submit themselves to the king, and do homage to him with presents. Next, lest it might be supposed that none but the people mentioned by way of example, were to obey him, it is said, "all nations shall fall down before him, all kings shall serve him." The non-Messianic interpreters, as Dereser, seek to show the fulfilment in passages as 1 K. 10· 10, according to which the queen of Sheba, and v. 25, according to which others also, brought costly presents to Solomon. But though we would not wish to deny that this writer in his figurative representation, had these transactions in view, we must, nevertheless, assert that they are by no means a fulfilment of the prophetic language of the Psalm. What is said is far too great for Solomon, since several people are named, with whom he had no connexion; and every limitation is afterwards removed by the word "all." The gifts, moreover, which are here spoken of, are not, as Dereser has erroneously supposed, those of friendship, such as men brought to Solomon; but they are the signs of obedience, subjection and reverence, as Calvin has long since remarked "Quodvis tributum aut vectigal intellige, non autem voluntarias oblationes, quia loquitur de hostibus devictis et de subjectione eorum." Over all these people this king shall reign, and they shall serve him with the deepest humility. Every difficulty is removed by the reference to the Messiah. The bringing of gifts, is, then, merely a metaphorical representation of homage and reverence, just as in v. 15, the admiring gratitude of the delivered towards his deliverer, is represented by the figure of the bringing of gold from Sheba. The representation in v. 12, etc. of the method by which the king whose praises are celebrated, has gained so wide a dominion, suits no earthly king, but agrees well with the Messiah. He has not, like worldly conquerors, triumphed by the power of his arms; but by his illustrious attributes, by his righteousness and love, he has now the hearts of men, and made them yield a willing submission to his sway. Feeling the difficulty with which the non-Messianic interpretation is here attended, De Wette seeks in some measure to obviate it, by supposing with Pfeiffer, in Rosenmuller on the passage, that merely the external political relations of the king, are here mentioned. He would, it was hoped, afford protection to oppressed nations. But the mode of expression itself is decisive against this supposition. It is manifest, as in v. 2 and 4, individuals, and not nations, are spoken of. How could an oppressed people, for example, be called אֶבְיוֹן? The expression, also, v. 13, "He shall spare the poor and needy," shows that the subject of discourse is the conduct of the king towards his own subjects. And lastly, were De Wette's opinion just, still the passage, in any event, would only furnish a reason why some small, oppressed nations, in the neighborhood of Palestine, should become the subjects of the king. But this is altogether against the scope of the passage. It designs expressly to give the reason, why the wildest, and most distant, the richest and most powerful nations, yea, even the people and kings of the whole earth, will yield submission to this king. But the extension of the Messiah's kingdom, is in other passages, also, represented in a manner precisely similar. Thus, for example, according to Zech. 9. 10, the Messiah shall establish his reign over the whole earth, not by the force of his arms, but because he, the righteous one, will speak peace unto the heathen. According to Isaiah 9. 6, the increase of his dominion, and his power, go hand in hand. Comp. also, Is. xi. With respect to v. 15, we must first establish the true interpretation. We translate: " that he may live and give to him of the gold of Sheba, and pray for him continually, and bless him daily." We take "the poor," as the subject throughout, and understand "to live," as it frequently means elsewhere, to be sustained in life. Others, as De Wette at last, (2d Ed.) translate: "He (the king) lives, and they give him of the gold of Sheba." But against this interpretation we urge, that such a change of the subject is unnatural, that the future apoc יִיחִי, though sometimes used as the fut. apoc. indicative, is yet most naturally taken in its usual conjunctive sense, and that יִיחִי plainly stands in contrast with the phrase, "precious is the blood of the poor in his sight," in the foregoing verse, and therefore must, in like manner, be referred to the "poor." The argument of De Wette, that all which follows relates to the prosperity of the king, is of little weight, since, according to our interpretation also, the verse serves only to augment his glory. As now we understand the verse, the bringing of the gold of Sheba, which was regarded as the most precious, (Is 60 6) can be nothing else than a representation of the cordial and devoted gratitude of the ransomed towards their deliverer. An incongruity arises if we overlook the figurative character of the expression, since the poor man has no gold whereby he can show his gratitude to the king who delivers him. The expression, "and pray for him," borrowed from the intercession of faithful subjects for their beloved king, and therefore in a manner figurative, so far agrees with the Messiah, as the gratitude and love of his people are expressed in prayers for the advancement of his glory, and the continual increase of his kingdom. In a similar manner expressions, which in a literal sense can be used only of men, are not unfrequently transferred to God, and must be understood θεοπρεπῶς. Thus for example, the customary phrase ברך יהוה and אלהים, and still more that in Ps. 18· 47 "live Jehovah," where an expression common in acclamations to kings, is transferred to God.

The meaning of v 16, also, must be ascertained. Every thing depends on the translation of the ἅπ. λεγ פִּסָּה. Rosenm. and De Wette translate "abundance," there is an abundance of corn. But the philological grounds for this translation are extremely weak. On the contrary, we are justified in translating it by *minutum frumenti*, or a handful. The Masc. פַּס occurs Gen. 37: 3, 23, and 2 Sam. 13 18, 19, in the sense of *particula, pars minuta*. In the Chaldee portion of Daniel it is found with the additional word יְדָא in the sense of *vola manus*, Chap 5. 5 The Chaldee paraphrast, 1 Kings 18· 44, translates כְּכַף אִישׁ by כְּפִסַּת יָד. Rightly therefore has

Kimchi rendered פִסָה in this place, by מְלֹא כַף. It is, therefore, to be translated: "Though there were only a handful of corn in the land, yet on the summit of the hills its fruit will rustle like Lebanon;" i. e. though, before the reign of this king, there was such a scarcity that only a handful of grain remained for seed, yet this little will be so blessed, that even in the most barren places, as on the summits of the hills, the harvest, moved by the wind, rustles like the trees of the lofty Lebanon. And thus the superabundant blessings of the Messiah's kingdom are here characterised by a most expressive image. In the second part of the verse, "and out of the city," either out of Jerusalem, under whose image the theocracy, of which it was then the seat, presented itself, a sense which is rendered probable by the parallel passages soon to be cited, or out of every city in subjection to the great. out of the cities "men blossom as grass of the earth," the great populousness of the new kingdom of God to be founded by the Messiah, is described, by a metaphor signifying large population, taken from the condition of the earthly theocracy under Solomon, 1 Kings 4. 20. Similar is the description of the times of the Messiah, Zech. 2. 8: "Jerusalem shall be inhabited as towns without walls, for the multitude of men and cattle therein," with which comp. v. 15: "and many nations shall be joined to the Lord in that day, and shall be my people." Also Is. 49. 20. "The children, which thou shalt have after thou hast lost the other, shall say again in thine ears, 'the place is too strait for me, give place to me that I may dwell.'" V. 17 the words לִפְנֵי שֶׁמֶשׁ יִנּוֹן שְׁמוֹ we translate with Luther "his name shall be continued among his posterity as long as the sun endures;" on which he has made in the margin the appropriate remark "they shall honor his name forever and ever; although the aged die, yet their posterity shall do it." The word יִנּוֹן Fut Niph of the ἅπ λεγ. נוּן, but whose meaning is rendered certain by the noun נִין *soboles*, is properly *filiatur, sobolescit*. Rejecting the trope the LXX correctly render. διαμένει. Vulg. *permanet*. If *this* prediction is fulfilled in its highest sense only in the Messiah, much more is that contained in the second part of the verse: "And men shall regard themselves as blessed through him, all nations shall praise him." While the remembrance of a distinguished leader of the earthly Theocracy lives only within the narrow bounds of Palestine, endless praise and glory shall be ascribed to this exalted king for his never ceasing benefits, by all people of the whole earth. The language indeed would be greatly weakened, were we to translate וְיִתְבָּרְכוּ בוֹ with

Rosenmüller and De Wette: " by him will they bless themselves," i. e. they will use his name as a form of benediction. But the translation has no philological support. It cannot be shown that Hithp. ever occurs in this sense. On the contrary, since in the promises to the patriarchs to which this passage refers, Hithp. is used interchangeably with Niphal. We are compelled to believe that they are nearly synonymous. And in accordance with this is the translation, "they (it accords with the sense, though not with the grammar to supply the following כָּל־גּוֹיִם) shall regard themselves as blessed through him." a meaning which not only agrees with the Hithp. conj. but is also the prevailing one, Deut. 29. 18. Jer. 4. 2. And thus may the Messianic interpretation here also, to which, among the moderns, Dathe, Michaelis, Kuinoel (Mess W p. 77), Anton, Muntinghe, Pareau (1. c. p. 499), Rosenmüller (2d Ed.), Kaiser (Psalmen p. 221) and others adhere, have a well grounded claim to the general approbation it received in the earlier times of the church.

Psalm CX

An illustrious king is celebrated in this Psalm, whom God has exalted to sit with him on his throne, and to whom he has promised a wide extension of his kingdom and the dominion over numerous enemies notwithstanding all their efforts to resist, v 1, 2. He is surrounded by a host of warriors, who freely and joyfully devote themselves to his service, and clothed in sacred garments go forth to battle, v. 3. Nor does he enjoy merely the *regal* dignity, but, according to an unchangeable Divine decree, he shall unite with it the priesthood, as Melchisedec had done before, and not merely a short and transitory, but an everlasting priesthood, v. 4.—Those who refuse submission to his decree, however great may be their power, shall be "stricken through in the day of his wrath," v 5, 6.—He is ever engaged with untiring zeal in promoting the enlargement of his kingdom, v. 7.

The style of this Psalm, like that of the second, is somewhat dramatic V 1 the author addresses his hearers; v 2—4 the king; and v. 5—7 Jehovah. The grounds of the Messianic interpretation are here as strong as in any prediction of the Old Testament, so that this Psalm greatly confirms the interpretation we have given of the three preceding. For it is manifest, and ought never to have been overlooked, that when the Messianic character of one of the Psalms of this class is established, so also is that of all the others.* Especially is the resemblance between this and the 2d Psalm self-evident. The arguments for the Messianic interpretation are the following

1. The testimony of tradition. The prevalence of this interpretation in the time of Christ is evident, as is generally allowed from Matt. 22: 41—46. Christ then takes it for granted that the Psalm relates to the Messiah, and it did not occur to the Pharisees to question this fact, in order to escape from the difficulty in which they found themselves involved, though their interest must have led them to do so had there been any diversity of opinion on the subject. It is true that soon after the coming of Christ, the polemic prejudices of the Jews prevailed over their previous attachment to tradition, when the Christians derived from this Psalm one of the strongest proofs of the Deity of the Messiah, which they denied. Justin Martyr, in the dialogue c. Tryph p 86, Wurzb. and Tertullian, adv. Marc. 5, 9, mentions the explanation which makes Hezekiah the subject as common among them. and Chrysostom found them to entertain a great diversity of opinions. It was supposed to relate to Abraham—to Zerubbabel—to the Jewish people. But still the weight of the internal evidence and the authority of tradition induced many of the older Jews to adhere to the Messianic interpretation See the passages collected in Schottgen l. c p 246, by Michaelis Annot. uber. in Hagiogr 1 p 842, and by Wetstein on Matt. 22. 44

2. The evidence from the New Testament is scarcely more conclusive in any instance than in the present, so that all those interpreters who do not entirely reject the authority of Christ and the Apostles, though not inclined, in other respects, to acknowledge the

---

* See this subject pursued by Michaelis The three most important Psalms relating to the Christ, p 470, 471 " It is yet undeniable, that the same character there prevails, which we meet with, only more strongly and plainly drawn, in this Psalm In both we behold a king of Zion in the greatest splendor, his dominion widely extended, and his enemies subdued The eternity here attributed to him, and even the days of heaven and of the moon, likewise occur in the 72d Psalm In the 2d Psalm, he is the Son of God with the addition: God has begotten him, etc " Herder, Briefe I p 221 (Tub 1808) " The second Psalm accurately corresponds with this, and carries out the same subject almost to its issue, though in a more mild and quiet manner. The former is the threatening prelude to this bloody song of triumph, the distant magnificent thunder, before the dashing to pieces, which is itself described in the latter

Messianic interpretation, are yet compelled to adopt it here. Christ himself declares, Matt. 22. 44, comp. with Mark 12. 36, and Luke 20. 42, that David composed the Psalm ἐν πνεύματι, or, according to Mark ἐν πνεύματι ἁγίῳ, ברוח הקדש, under the influence of the prophetic inspiration, when futurity was disclosed to his view by the Spirit of God, and assuming its unquestionable reference to the Messiah, he proved from it the erroneousness of the representation of him at that time very current among the Jews, which did not recognize his superhuman dignity and Godhead. It is true, indeed, that some modern critics (Stolz in den Anm. zum N. T. — Borhek in Eichhorn's Bibl. für Bibl. Lit VI. p. 315 seq. —Paulus, Comm. on N. T. III. p. 325 seq.) have endeavored to set aside this testimony of Christ, by a new exposition of these passages, according to which, he, on the contrary, represented the Messianic interpretation of the Psalm as inadmissible. But although this interpretation has been briefly repeated by Paulus, in his "life of Jesus," we deem it sufficient, without further refutation, to notice it with a mere *recepisse*.* This Psalm is also quoted and explained as referring to Christ by Peter, Acts 2. 35, 36, in his discourse immediately after the effusion of the Holy Spirit. See 1 Cor. 15. 25 etc., Heb. 7. 17. There are besides very many allusions to it, see Eph. 1. 20. Acts 5. 31, and all those passages where Christ is represented as sitting at the right hand of God.

3. Let us now see how far the result obtained from external testimony is confirmed by internal evidence. In the first place, the Messianic interpretation is confirmed by the superscription, which ascribes the composition of the Psalm to David. For, if David was its author, neither himself nor any other person but the Messiah can be its subject. For what man could David consistently call his Lord? After the example of our Saviour himself, Theodoret already remarked, that if David, who stood on the highest eminence of human greatness, called another his Lord, that person must of necessity possess more than human dignity: Εἰ Δαβὶδ ὁ βασιλεὺς καὶ εὐσεβὴς βασιλεύς, ὁ καὶ προφητικῆς χάριτος ἠξιωμένος, κύριον ἑαυτοῦ καλεῖ τὸν δεσπότην Χριστόν, οὐκ ἄρα μόνον ἄνθρωπος κατὰ τὴν Ἰουδαίων ἄνοιαν, ἀλλὰ καὶ θεός, ὡς τοῦ Δαβὶδ δημιουργός τε καὶ κύριος. Similar is the language of Lactantius. "Qui propheta quum rex esset, quem appellare dominum suum posset, qui sederet ad dextram dei, nisi Christum filium dei, qui est rex regum et dominus domino-

---

* See on the contrary, Steudel Weihnachtsprogr. von 1823. p. 8 seq.

rum." Attempts have been made to set aside this argument in different ways. 1. Jarchi, Abenezra, Kimchi, etc. interpret: *de Davide*. 2 Paulus, Bertholdt (Eml. s. 1952), and others: *Davidi dicatus*. But both these explanations are inconsistent with the fact, that ל, in the superscriptions of the Psalms, never occurs in this sense 3. De Wette confesses that the superscription which ascribes the Psalm to David as the author, and of course excludes him as the subject, presupposes the Messianic interpretation, but then he denies its genuineness. This, however, is an arbitrary assumption, for which, as Paulus justly remarks, there is no reason. The reference to the Messiah is also proved by the words in the 1st verse, "sit thou on my right hand." This expression is figurative. Worldly kings place on their right hand not merely those whom they wish in a special manner to honor, as Solomon did Bathsheba, 1 K. xix, but those likewise, whom they associate with themselves in the government. Thus Salome, expecting that Christ was to found an earthly kingdom, Matt. 20 21 prayed for her two sons, James and John, that he would allow them to sit, the one on his right hand, and the other on his left. Passages from the Greek writers likewise in which a participation in the government is signified by sitting on the right hand, may be found collected by Knapp (De Christo ad dextram Dei sedente, in d. Opusc.) Sitting on the right hand of God is not however expressive of complete Divine majesty * And according to the Messianic interpretation the expression relates, as it does throughout the New Testament, not to the Divine nature of Christ, in which he is equal in dignity with the Father, but to his human nature, in which he has obtained a participation in the Divine government as a reward for the work of redemption. Chrysostom therefore errs when he says: εἶδες τὸ ὁμότιμον; ὅπου γὰρ θρόνος, βασιλείας σύμβολον· ὅπου θρόνος εἷς, τῆς αὐτῆς βασιλείας ἰσοτιμία † But still this language implies a

---

* Neque tamen id sic est intelligendum, ut qui regi dexter assideat, propterea ei per omnia aequalis habeatur, et par honore loco atque auctoritate, sed tantum ille habet, quantum regis arbitrio illi conceditur, tametsi socius est et comes imperii Knapp l c p 50.

† The truth on the other hand was seen by Theodoret μέγα μὲν οὖν καὶ τοῦτο—καὶ οὐ μόνον ὑπὲρ τὴν ἀνθρωπείαν φύσιν, ἀλλὰ καὶ ὑπὲρ ἅπασαν τὴν κτίσιν πλὴν ἀνθρωπίνως καὶ αὐτὸ εἴρηται· ὡς γὰρ θεὸς ὁ υἱὸς αἰώνιον ἔχει τὸν θρόνον, ἀλλ' ἔλαβεν ὡς ἄνθρωπος, ὅπερ εἶχεν ὡς θεός—ὡς ἄνθρωπος τοίνυν ἀκούει κάθου ἐκ δεξιῶν μου· ὡς γὰρ θεὸς αἰώνιον ἔχει τὸ κράτος

participation in the Divine glory and dominion; it is never spoken of earthly kings, who reign indeed as the servants of God and by his authority, but are not, on that account, co-regents with him *

V 3 The non-Messianic interpreters find themselves involved in great embarrassment by the expression בְּהַדְרֵי קֹדֶשׁ, *in holy ornaments*. De Wette attempts two ways of escape. The first makes the supposition, that the warriors appear clothed in sacred garments, on account of the religious ceremonies, the sacrifices, etc. which preceded their warlike expedition. But not only he himself confesses there can no proof be brought of such a practice, but it is highly improbable that it existed. For, since the sacred dress was peculiar to the priests, granting what cannot be proved from 1 Sam vii, that religious solemnities may have preceded the going forth to war, it cannot be supposed that, during their performance, the host of warriors were clothed in sacred garments. Still more improbable is the second supposition of De Wette, viz. that arming for war is intended, because קדש is spoken also of the arming of the war hosts. For קָדַשׁ alone never has this meaning. קַדֵּשׁ מִלְחָמָה, *to sanctify a war*, is rather the same as to prepare a *sacred* war, or to arm one's self for such a war, just as קַדֵּשׁ צוֹם, *to sanctify a fast*, or קַדֵּשׁ עֲצָרָה, *to sanctify a feast*, implies to appoint a sacred fast or feast. But the difficulty is entirely done away by the Messianic interpretation. The expression is then designed to mark the difference between this conflict and earthly wars. As the leader is at the same time king and priest, so shall the people whom he conducts to war, be an army of priests, arrayed in sacred garments, and not in the bloody clothing of the warrior, which according to Isaiah 9 4, shall be consumed in the flames together with all the instruments of war, at the appearing of the Messiah, whose kingdom does not, like the former theocracy stand in need of human weapons † V 4 furnish-

---

* Steudel (Weihnachtsprogr von 1823 p 17) "Quae similes citantur phrases, ut principem esse populi dei, 1 Sam 13 14. 2 Sam 6 21, antistitis munere fungi in dei familia ejusque regno, 1 Chron 17 14; in Jovae regni solio, in Jovae solio sedere, 1 Chron 28 5 29 23, id sibi volunt, nonnisi demandato a Jova imperio fungi, cum haec phrasis secundum a deo locum tenere, in imperii cum eo consortium iniisse, edisserat id quod in plures cadere haud potest, ut demandatio imperii"

† Calvin "Deinde ut iterum confirmet regnum hoc deo sacrum esse prae aliis, addit : pulchritudines vel decora sanctitatis, ac si diceret, non venturos, qui se Christo subjicient, quasi in conspectum profani regis, sed dei ipsius atque hunc scopum omnibus fore, ut deo cultum exhibeant"

es a strong proof in favor of this interpretation. There God confirms it by an oath, that this king shall be also a priest forever after the order of Melchesidec, who, according to Gen. 15 10, united in his own person the regal and the priestly dignity In this declaration a total change in the previous condition of things is implied. For, according to the Mosaic constitution, the priesthood was exclusively confined to the family of Levi, during the existence of the old covenant; and how carefully God watched over the preservation of this arrangement was shown in earlier times by the fate of the company of Korah, Dathan, and Abiram, and afterwards by that of king Uzziah, who, according to 2 Chron. 26 16, was smitten with an incurable leprosy, while intruding upon the priestly office by burning incense in the temple. Theodoret εἰ τοίνυν ἐκ Δαβὶδ ὁ Χριστὸς κατὰ σάρκα, ὁ δὲ Δαβὶδ ἐκ Ἰούδα· τήνδε κατὰ τὴν τάξιν Μελχισεδὲκ ἀρχιερωσύνην ἔλαβεν ὁ Χριστός, πέπαυται μὲν ἡ Λευιτικὴ ἱερωσύνη, εἰς δὲ τὴν Ἰούδα φυλὴν ἡ τῆς μείζονος ἱερωσύνης εὐλογία μετέβη Here again different methods have been devised to evade the difficulty. Several Jewish interpreters suppose, that כֹּהֵן *priest*, here, as in 2 Sam. 8 18, where it is said of the sons of David that they were כֹּהֲנִים *priests*, is used in a civil sense But then, in answer to this, Michaelis has well remarked that this king as כֹּהֵן is compared with Melchisedec, and consequently the word must be understood here in the same sense as in the history of Melchisedec,* where it undeniably means a priest, and further, that, since כֹּהֵן taken in a civil sense, would imply only an inferior dignity, it would be in the highest degree incongruous, after a preamble suited to awaken so great expectation, to ascribe it to the illustrious king Paulus and De Wette have taken another way They think, since the kings possessed the highest power in theocratical affairs, that the regal priesthood might be predicated of every king of Israel. That David may be declared a priest only so far as he could be one according to the fundamental principles of the Mosaic Institute, is self-evident; and that לְעוֹלָם, being limited by the subject, means merely, "during thy life time" But this supposition is untenable. If every king of Israel might have been called כֹּהֵן, how has it happened that not one of them ever received this title? Even though we were willing to concede that the appellation כֹּהֵן in a metaphorical sense, could have

---

* That Melchisedec was a priest, in the proper and full sense of the term, is evinced by the fact, that Abraham acknowledged his superiority, although he himself performed the functions of a household priest

been given to Kings, because they exercised the *jus circa sacra*, yet this figurative sense cannot possibly be the true one in the present instance. For the declaration of Jehovah is introduced with such solemnity—" he hath sworn," strengthened by the addition of " and will not repent," as leads us to expect not a mere matter of course,* but something very uncommon, and widely different from the existing state of things. Besides the word לְעוֹלָם can be taken in this connexion only in its most comprehensive meaning, as contrasted with the limited period for which the earthly priests exercised their office. The comparison with Melchisedec also, who was a priest in the full sense of the term, shows that a real and perfect priesthood, and an order of things, the reverse of that which then existed, are intended. In this comparison, the priesthood promised to the king is manifestly contrasted with that of Aaron. As in Ps LXXII, so also here, the Messianic interpretation is confirmed by the prophet Zechariah. In chap. 6. 13, plainly referring to this Psalm, he announces that the Messiah should hereafter unite the regal and the priestly dignity in his own person, and represents this as an occurrence altogether novel and extraordinary.

We come now to v 5. As in Ps 45. 7, 8, the king is called אֱלֹהִים, in Mal. 3: 1 הָאָדוֹן, and Isa. 9 5 אֵל, so here he receives the name אֲדֹנָי, which is peculiar to God alone, and is never ascribed to any created being. The non-Messianic interpreters have attempted to escape from this difficulty in three different ways ; either they have asserted without the semblance of proof, that אֲדֹנָי may be used in speaking of men,—as Rosenmuller 1st Ed —or they have capriciously changed the text so as to read אֲדֹנִי, or אָדֹן † instead of אֲדֹנָי — or lastly, they have supposed that not Jehovah, but the king is addressed, which is the opinion of De Wette. The " Lord on thy right hand," will then mean, " the Lord is thy support." But this opinion is erroneous. For first, although it cannot be denied that the expression, to be at the right hand of any one, may import the same, as to sustain him ; yet this sense is here inadmissible because it is not to be supposed that the Psalmist would in so brief a space employ

---

* Paulus. " David shall be *as* a priest" On the contrary Schnurrer· " formula· decretum Jehovae est, quod nunquam immutabit, ita comparata, ut quod proximis verbis dicitur, non possit non esse grande aliquid, eximium, singulare"

† This is opposed by all the old versions, LXX, Vulg, Syr, Ar, which translate *The Lord,* and the Chaldee· *The Shechinah of the Lord.*

the same expression in both a literal and a figurative sense; and would say in the beginning of his Psalm, that the king is on the right hand of Jehovah, and here, that Jehovah is on the right hand of the king. 2. But few surely will be disposed with Dereser to refer the 7th verse also, "he shall drink of the brook in the way, therefore shall he lift up the head," to Jehovah. Calvin has well remarked on this verse: "Similitudo est a strenuis et robustis ducibus sumta, qui dum festinant ad hostes persequendos, non indulgent delitiis, sed ad potum contenti sunt obviis quibusque fluminibus, et quidem in transcursu, ut stantes sitim e flumine restinguant. Nam et hoc modo Gideon cordatos et bellicosos milites expertus est, quia ignavos esse colligens, qui bibendi causa se curvabant, domum remisit." That this reference is inadmissible was seen by De Wette, who supposes "a very natural and customary change of person." But however common the change of persons may be, it will surely not readily appear to any one to be *natural* in the present instance. For it is obviously one and the same warrior, who in v. 5, 6 with resistless power overthrows the people and their kings, and in v. 7 is engaged in eager pursuit of the remnant of the host of his enemies, and suffers nothing to stay his course. Still De Wette has labored to adduce reasons against supposing Jehovah to be the object of address. He says 1. "It is incongruous that Jehovah should be here addressed and not the king, to whom the discourse had before been directed." But when the dramatic character which this Psalm has in common with Ps. II is considered, it is not easy to perceive wherein this incongruity consists. The opinion that the king is addressed Ps. 72. 5 is defended by De Wette himself, although he is not elsewhere addressed in the whole Psalm, but is always spoken of in the third person, and a direct address to Jehovah, immediately precedes! The change of the address is in general so frequent, that it is useless to bring forward examples. 2. "Besides, the king enthroned on the right hand of Jehovah i. e in a state of rest, cannot be conceived as engaging in war." This objection is founded on a misunderstanding of the words, "sit thou on my right hand until I make thy foes thy footstool." The sense is, although numerous and powerful enemies rise up against thee, they cannot prevent me from making thee a partaker of my dominion, until thou shalt have entirely subdued them by the power which I will impart. That sitting on the right hand does not imply a state of inaction is evident from v. 8, where the king appears at the head of a countless host, and where De Wette himself translates:

"thy people willingly follow thee to battle," and on v 7 which he agrees with us in referring to the king, in direct contradiction to his own interpretation, he remarks: "The poet in a lively manner places himself on the scene of conflict, where his king appears as a triumphant warrior." 3 "The expression 'in the day of his wrath,' agrees better with Jehovah." This is indeed the case if we make the Psalm refer to an earthly king; but not if its subject is Jehovah's exalted co-regent, the Messiah, of whom it is said also in Ps 2· 9, that "he will break his enemies with a rod of iron and dash them in pieces like a potter's vessel," and in v. 12 that "his wrath shall soon be kindled;" "but blessed are all they that put their trust in Him"

Relying upon the strength of these reasons the Christian church has always firmly held the Messianic interpretation. Chrysostom says that those who reject it are $\kappa\alpha\vartheta\acute{\alpha}\pi\epsilon\varrho$ $o\acute{\iota}$ $\mu\epsilon\vartheta\acute{\upsilon}o\nu\tau\epsilon\varsigma$ $\kappa\alpha\grave{\iota}$ $\mu\eta\delta\grave{\epsilon}\nu$ $\sigma\acute{\upsilon}\mu\varphi\omega\nu o\nu$ $\varphi\vartheta\epsilon\gamma\gamma\acute{o}\mu\epsilon\nu o\iota$, $\mu\tilde{\alpha}\lambda\lambda o\nu$ $\delta\grave{\epsilon}$ $\varkappa\alpha\vartheta\acute{\alpha}\pi\epsilon\varrho$ $o\acute{\iota}$ $\grave{\epsilon}\nu$ $\sigma\varkappa\acute{o}\tau\omega$ $\beta\alpha\delta\acute{\iota}\zeta o\nu\tau\epsilon\varsigma$ $\varkappa\alpha\grave{\iota}$ $\pi\varrho o\sigma\alpha\varrho\acute{\alpha}\sigma\sigma o\nu\tau\epsilon\varsigma$ $\grave{\alpha}\lambda\lambda\acute{\eta}\lambda o\upsilon\varsigma$. Not less strong is the language of Calvin, who must be allowed in this instance to be free from prejudice, since he regards all the remaining Psalms of this class as having a lower reference to an earthly king, although in this he is inconsistent, for the subject of them all is manifestly the same. "Quum de se hunc Psalmum compositum fuisse testetur Christus, non aliunde quidem nobis, quam ex ejus ore petenda est certitudo, verum ut cesset ejus auctoritas atque etiam apostoli testimonium, Psalmus ipse clamat se non aliam expositionem admittere. Nam ut nobis certamen sit cum pervicacissimis quibusque Judaeis, firmis rationibus extorquebimus, neque in Davidem, neque in alium quempiam, excepto solo Mediatore, competere, quae hic dicuntur" Among the modern interpreters, Dathe, Lowth, Michaelis, Kuinol, Muntinghe, v. d. Palm (Einige Liederen von David vertaald en opgehelderd), Knapp, Anton (l c p. 18), Schnurrer (Bibl Arab. II p 40), Velthusen (in a peculiar treatise in den "Materialien f. d Synode"), Steudel, Pareau (l. c. p. 510), Kaiser and others have adhered to the Messianic interpretation. Rosenmuller also in his second Edition has adopted it, after having in the first defended the reference to David.

It might now be expected that those who reject the interpretation would justify their disregard of the authority of Christ and his Apostles, as well as the internal proofs, by at least the semblance of reason; but here, as in so many other instances, we must content ourselves with a bare "stat pro ratione voluntas." They only occasionally remark, in passing, that the image of a warlike king destroying his foes, which is presented in this Psalm, contains few features that can agree with Christ. But here we reply, 1. That we must carefully distinguish the figure from that which it represents, and not disregard the fact that the features, which form the portrait of this great and more than human king, are taken as usual from an earthly head of the theocracy. Thus the expression, "God shall send forth the rod of thy strength out of Zion," means in simple language: God under thy reign will greatly enlarge the boundaries of thy theocracy, hitherto confined to Palestine. Comp. Is. 2· 3. Mich 4· 2 " From Zion shall go forth the law, and the word of Jehovah from Jerusalem " Ps. 72· 8 So v. 3 The spiritual triumph which Christ gains over the world by his friends and servants, is represented as is often the case, under the image of a victory in war. The king appears at the head of a host as numerous as splendid,* and entirely and cheerfully devoted to his service,† and at the same time however the figurative character of the representation is suggested by the expression " in sacred ornaments " In v. 5—7, the punishment which the king inflicts upon his enemies is represented by the figure of the fearful ruin which an earthly conqueror brings upon his vanquished foes. Comp. the similar representation in Isaiah LXIII. 2. It is however true that this king, even after the description is divested of its metaphorical character, appears as a severe judge and avenger of his enemies. But here is nothing inconsistent with the fulfilment, when we consider the point of view taken by the Psalmist. It is not the Messiah in his humiliation, which here, as well as in all the other Psalms of this class, presents himself, but the Messiah in his glory The author here, as in Ps. II, takes his station in that period of time when the Messiah, after having finished his work, has been exalted by God to a participation in his government, and endowed with power to subdue his enemies. But, that what Christ says of himself in reference to

---

* Both are included in the words "Out of the womb of the early dawn shall be to thee, the dew of thy youth," i e. thy war-host shall be like the dew, the son of the morning Thereby the increase of the people of Christ, which is as great as unperceived and sudden, and at the same time their amiableness and freshness are designated

† The noun נְדָבָה often occurs in the sense *voluntariae oblationes*. Com. e g Exod 35 29, and indeed not merely in the proper, but also in the spiritual sense, as Ps 119 108 This sense is here also more suitable than the one usually assigned to the word willingness, as *abstractum pro concreto*, for willing. The people present themselves as a free-will offering to their divine king

his lowly condition must not be transferred to him in his state of exaltation, we have already seen on Ps. II. Comp also Luke 20 27. Calvin strikingly observes· "Si quis roget . ubi igitur ille clementiae et mansuetudinis spiritus, quo praeditum fore alibi docet scriptura? respondeo sicuti erga oves mansuetus est pastor, lupis autem et furibus asper et formidabilis, ita Christum suaviter et placide fovere, qui se ejus custodiae committunt, sed qui obstinata malitia excutiunt ejus jugum, sensuros quam terribili potentia instructus sit"

As to the date of the Psalm, Palm and Muntinghe have not without reason assigned it to about the same time as the second. This idea is favored by their great resemblance. In both Psalms numerous enemies, who rise up against the king are easily vanquished and destroyed. In both, we hear Jehovah assuring the king of dominion and victory over his enemies. The supposition of Pareau, that the union of the priestly and regal dignity in the person of the Messiah was made clear to David, at the bringing up of the ark of the covenant, related in 2 Sam. 6 12—19, where he himself performed, in a measure, sacerdotal functions, is inconsistent with the fact, that he had not yet received the Divine promise which proved the ground work of all his Messianic hopes and prophecies.

II. PSALMS IN WHICH THE SUFFERING MESSIAH IS DESCRIBED.

From the Psalms already examined, we learn to know the Messiah as a divine and glorious king, whom all the nations of the earth shall obey, and also as a priest of a far higher and more illustrious order than the priests of the first covenant; who was, consequently, to make an atonement for the sins of his people; for this was the peculiar duty of the sacerdotal order. But the Psalms are silent both concerning the method, by which, as a king, he should gain his widely extended dominion, and, as a priest accomplish the work of expiation. Their authors contemplate him as having been already exalted to glory. But in another class of Psalms, those previous sufferings of the Messiah by which the atonement was made and which were rewarded by his subsequent glorification constitute the chief object of prophetic vision. This ought not to awaken surprise, as we shall hereafter more fully show, in the chapter concerning the idea of the suffering Messiah in the Old Testament. Already in Ps. II and cx, innumerable enemies array themselves against the Messiah. David himself and all other true believers of the Old Testament had so deeply experienced the corruption and wickedness of men, that they could have expected nothing else than the sufferings of their own lives should have their counterpart in the life of the Messiah; they were therefore sufficiently prepared for the Divine revelation on this subject with which they were favored.

To this class belong especially Psalms XVI, XXII, XL It is a peculiarity of those Psalms that the subject of them is himself introduced as speaking, while the subject of the foregoing Psalms is usually spoken of in the third person. Comp. however Ps. II. The interpreters who refer these Psalms to the Messiah are divided into two classes.

1. The larger number suppose that the Psalmist made the condition and the sentiments of the suffering Messiah his own, that he might introduce him as speaking, or rather speak himself in his person. This idea considered in itself is not objectionable Nothing is more frequent in poetry of all kinds, than for persons to be thus introduced, and in prophetic poetry this is the more natural, because the nature of the prophetic vision, in which every thing appears as present, necessarily gives to the representation a dramatic character. Thus for example in Ps. II the poet at one time speaks in his own person, at another in that of Jehovah, and lastly in the person of his exalted king; and this too without particularly designating who it is that speaks Thus also in Ps CX, Jehovah appears as the speaker. Thus the prophets in perpetual alternation, speak, now in their own person and now in the person of Jehovah They represent in their symbolical transactions at one time Jehovah, at another the Jewish people, and then again some other subject A remarkable illustration of this fact is found in Isaiah XLIX As the prophet in chap. XLII had in his own person directed the discourse to the Messiah, as if present, so here he speaks in the person of the Messiah to the Gentiles.*

2 After Calvin and Grotius, other expositors as Dathe and Steudel (Disquisitio in Ps XVI, Tub 1821), suppose that there is in these Psalms a sort of double sense, that the subject of them, in the literal and lower sense, is in each case the author himself, and that when thus interpreted, every thing that is said proposes a natural and consistent meaning. Nevertheless the Holy Spirit so influenced the minds of the writers that they uttered many things, applicable to themselves

---

* See the remarks of Pareau l c p 519

only in a metaphorical sense, but which were literally and completely fulfilled in the history of the Messiah. In support of this method of interpretation, they appeal to the typical character of the Old Testament in general; the persons and events of which obscurely represented and prefigured the Church of the New Testament, and especially to the circumstance that David in his sufferings and his exaltation was a type of the Messiah. They remark that in common life a man often utters expressions which he did not at the moment fully comprehend, but which subsequently appear to him of the greatest importance

It is easy to perceive the causes which gave rise to this method of interpretation There are in the Psalms of this class, besides those special descriptions which are fulfilled only in the history of Christ, general representations, which seem better to suit a pious and suffering Israelite, than the Messiah. Thus Ps 16 : 3, 4, the speaker numbers himself with the pious worshippers of God on earth with whom he contrasts the ungodly And the whole representation, v. 1—8, contains scarcely a peculiar circumstance which can be found in the history of the Messiah alone, unless indeed, as many interpreters have done, we supply by a forced interpretation what is wanting in the text. So in Ps. 22: 5, 6, the speaker appeals to the example of his forefathers, whose prayers God had heard when they were in distress, and grounds upon it his supplication for similar deliverance. Ps. 40 14—18, the description is so general that these verses occur again in Ps LXX, a Psalm of complaint and supplication suited to any suffering servant of God. And, in general, we find in the Psalms of prayer and complaint, which have no relations to the Messiah, passages entirely parallel with those in the Psalms of this class. These facts persuaded several interpreters to give up, as untenable, the opinion that the Messiah speaks in them throughout and exclusively. But, on the other hand, they had too much regard for truth, to deny the special references to the Messiah which they contain, and too much reverence for the testimony of the New Testament to resolve with the rationalists entirely to reject the Messianic interpretation They sought therefore to find a middle course.

It is scarcely necessary to remark that .this mode of exposition must be rejected, as soon as the difficulty in which it obviously originated is in some other way removed. But this is done, at least as we believe, by the two following considerations 1. Christ in his state of humiliation was entirely like us in every thing, except sin; like us, he placed his confidence in God, he lamented, complained, prayed. Much therefore which is said of him must be capable of a more general application. 2. It has been unjustly taken for granted, that, if we regard the Messiah as the speaker, we must suppose the authors of the Psalms to have been deprived of all agency and consciousness. Whether the Messiah be introduced as speaking himself, or be spoken of in the third person can here, however, occasion no difference; since the sacred poets would, just as much in one case as in the other, be hurried away beyond the circle of their own conceptions. With respect to those Psalms in which the suffering Messiah appears as the speaker, the writers not only received within a general impression of his severe sufferings, but special traits were revealed to them, which were peculiar to him, and could be affirmed of no other person. In describing this general impression, the ideas already in their minds were employed as the ground work. As, in their description of the glorified Messiah, an illustrious earthly king serves as the substratum: so here the image in general of a pious man in affliction presented itself to their minds, from their own experience and that of others. And, like the author of those Psalms which describe him in his glory, they gave to this image those special features, which suit only the Messiah. And thus all is made clear, and we need not with the older interpreters, who overlooked the human features in these Psalms, find special references to the Messiah when none exist, nor with recent interpreters, who perceive not the Divine features, deny such references when they are known to exist, both by internal evidence, and the clearest declarations of the New Testament.

The necessity therefore which alone could justify this second method of interpretation does not exist. On the contrary it is liable to several serious objections. 1. One of the most weighty is that in these psalms special traits occur, which in no sense can be applicable to David, or any other pious sufferer of the Old Testament. This mode of explanation therefore is attended with the same difficulties as that which the rationalists have adopted. See on Ps. xxii. 2. To this it must be added that it cannot be reconciled with the manner in which these Psalms are regarded in the New Testament, which, without any intimation of a double sense explains them simply of the Messiah. It even expressly denies the reference of Ps. xvi to any other object. 3. Ps. xvi, as well as Ps. xl, plainly shows how little this mode of interpretation is applicable to *all* the Psalms of this class. If we refer them to the Messiah they contain passages which can agree with him only and in no respect with a saint of the Old Testament under suffering; as his resurrection in the former, and his sacrificial death in the latter; if on the contrary we adopt the views of the Rationalists, who make the former speak only of deliverance from great danger, and the latter of willing obedience to the commands of God, the sense is completed in David or any other pious man in affliction, and the reasons for a higher reference to the Messiah disappear.

Two of the Psalms belonging to this class have been explained at large by Michaelis in his treatise, entitled " Critisches Collegium uber die drei wichtigsten Psalmen von Christo, den 16, 40 und 110. Frankf und Gott. 1759, 8," which while it contains much that is useful must yet, on account of its capriciousness, be used with caution

---

Psalm XVI.

The contents of this Psalm are as follows. The speaker commences with a prayer to God for his aid, founded on the assurance that he is his God, and his highest good, v 1, 2. He delights in the society of the faithful worshippers of Jehovah, while he avoids all companionship with those unhappy men, who seek their happiness from other sources and not from God, v 3, 4. He felicitates himself on account of his intimate relation to God, which is better than all the good things of earth, and expresses his gratitude for being made a partaker of this blessedness, v 7 Confiding in his relation to God, he need never be disheartened, on the contrary, even now, in the near prospect of death, he is consoled and joyful from the conviction that the Lord will not leave him forever in its power, but conduct him through it to a new life of happiness and glory, v 8—11

The portion of the Psalm, v. 1—8, is of a general character; those who affirm and those who deny its reference to the Messiah are in the main agreed as to its meaning. A difference of interpretation, however, arises at v. 9—11 According to the Messianic interpretation, the Messiah here expresses the hope of his resurrection and glorification V. 10 will then read, " thou wilt not abandon my soul to Sheol, nor suffer thy holy one to see corruption " עָזַב with לְ, *to abandon*, שַׁחַת *corruption*. The Rationalist interpreters, on the contrary, understand v. 9, 10 as referring to nothing more than the hope expressed by David, or some other pious man, that God would bestow upon him rich blessings even in the present life. They translate v. 10, "Thou dost not deliver over my soul to the realm of Hades, nor suffer thy darling to see the pit." שַׁחַת in the sense of *pit*.

The reasons for referring the Psalm to the Messiah are the following. 1. By far the most important proof is that which is derived from the New Testament. But no where is the testimony more complete than in the present instance; so that the Divine illumination of the Apostles and even of Christ himself depends upon the Messianic character of this Psalm since he promised them this illumination, and in their interpretation of those passages of the Old Testament which related to him, they followed his guidance. Peter, in his discourse immediately after the out-pouring of the Holy Spirit, explains the Psalm of Christ, and indeed of him only, in such a manner that he controverts its reference to David, and assigns the reasons why he could not here have spoken of himself, Acts 2 25—31. Paul also, Acts 13 35—37, not only refers it to Christ, but opposes the opinion that it was written concerning David. That the Apostles do not here speak in the way of accommodation, as Rosenmuller and De Wette in reply to Eckermann (Theolog Beitr. 1. 1. p. 98) remark, is evident, not to mention that such an accommodation is as utterly unworthy of the Apostles as incapable of proof, even from the fact that they find it necessary to vindicate the reference to the Messiah, and oppose the reference to David, whence it follows that the former was usual, and the latter prevalent among those whom they addressed. The assertion of De Wette, in direct contradiction to what he had just before remarked in reply to Eckermann, that the Apostles designed to declare nothing more than that, the *full, entire, deep* truth of the Psalmist's hope was first fulfilled and verified in Christ, fails to redeem their authority, because according to the interpretation of the Rationalists, nothing remains which has not been completely fulfilled in the history of the Psalmist, and of course the Apostles could have had no reason to oppose the correct and literal explanation, which refers the Psalm to David. Michaelis has justly remarked, l c p 3 · " if what Le Clerc and others allege respecting the literal sense of this Psalm be correct, Peter would have deserved to be told : with all thine apparent candour, thou art a deceiver, seeking to delude the ignorant multitude. Thou pretendest, that the Psalm speaks of a resurrection from the dead, and is incapable of any other interpretation; whereas it relates, if literally understood, merely to a deliverance from great danger of this life to which David, its author, was more than once exposed "—Again several defenders of the Messianic interpretation have, not without reason, assumed that, in addition to the testimony of the Apostles, we have also that of Christ himself. For as Christ, according to Luke 24. 27 and 44. 46, after his resurrection explained to his disciples the predictions concerning himself in the Old Testament, we should surely expect that a passage to which they give a degree of importance so entirely peculiar, and of which they speak with a conviction so strong and free from doubt, would be one of those which he had interpreted. And as, according to the latter passage, his resurrection also was predicted in the prophecies of the Old Testament, where could he more naturally have pointed it out to them, than in the Psalm before us? 2. Granting therefore, that we believed the contents of the Psalm to present many difficulties in the way of the Messianic interpretation, still, with the modesty which becomes a Christian expositor, we must rather accuse our own ignorance than impute an error to the authors of the New Testament. This however is by no means the case. The Messianic interpretation needs no peculiar and forced explanation, in opposition to the laws of the language. On the contrary, although we concede that the older interpreters, particularly Michaelis, have brought forward many reasons for the reference to the Messiah which will not bear examination, and acknowledge also that the method can be philologically justified, by which recent interpreters have set aside the references to Christ, which his church has always found in this Psalm; we must, nevertheless, assert, that every impartial critic must regard the Messianic interpretation of v. 9—11, as the easiest and most natural, and that it would be universally adopted were it not for the influence of doctrinal views. And in fact it appears that in ancient times no one ever supposed that these verses could contain any thing else, than the hope of a proper resurrection. Paul and Peter presuppose this as an established truth, and they speak with a confidence, which shows that they could not have expected from any of their hearers the objection that the Psalm spake merely of deliverance from great danger. That it was believed, that the words, " my flesh shall rest securely," could be explained only of incorruptibility, is shown by the Jewish fable founded upon it, that the body of David did not putrify. See Lightfoot on Acts 2. 29, and the remarkable passage from Jalkut Schimoni fol. 95 ed. Franc. by Michaelis l. c. p. 12. Kimchi also cites as the current explanation of these words, "post mortem sibi non esse dominaturum vermem," and interprets

v. 10 and 11, not of deliverance from danger, but of a happy resurrection.

It must, indeed, be conceded, that the true import of this Messianic prediction was difficult to be understood before its fulfilment. This is manifest from the fact, that as early as the time of Christ, it was pretty generally explained of David. But still it was surely by no means impossible, for an attentive student of the prophecies to understand it correctly. Whoever had learned from Isaiah LIII to know the servant of God, who after having died for us, should be exalted to the highest glory and enjoy a never ending life; or from Ps. XXII had become familiar with the thought of a Messiah, who should pass through suffering to glory, and at the same time had perceived that the speaker in a Psalm was not always of course its subject—might easily come to the conclusion, that not David, but the Messiah, in the expectation of whose advent the whole spiritual life of the people centered, here appears as speaker, and foretels his own resurrection. And even granting that no one under the Old Testament attained to this knowledge, it is yet so obvious to us, who can institute a far more extensive comparison of the prophecies illustrated by the fulfilment, that we must regard the Messianic interpretation as at least the most probable, even without the evidence of the New Testament. That the Psalm, according to the Messianic interpretation, contains things beyond the mere human knowledge of the Psalmist, need the less prejudice us against it, since Peter, Acts 2: 30, expressly remarks, that David as a prophet, i. e. by Divine revelation, here foresaw the resurrection of Christ.

We must now proceed to refute the objections which have been brought against the reference of the Psalm to the Messiah.

1. "V. 3, where the speaker expresses his longing after the pious worshippers of God, who dwelt in the land, i. e. in Palestine, does not suit the Messiah, but David, who, fleeing from the presence of Saul, was compelled to take up his abode among the heathenish Philistines." Thus Jahn Vatic. Mess II. p. 250. We here, in the first place, offer an explanation of this difficult verse. After many had despaired of interpreting the received text, and tried a variety of conjectural emendations, its genuineness has been acknowledged by the recent interpreters. They translate "As to the saints which are in the land, and the excellent, all my delight is in them." Thus also Jahn, Rosenmüller, and De Wette (2d Ed.), after the example of Luther and Storr, among the moderns (obs p. 295), whose interpre-

tation, however, does not *entirely* agree with that which we have quoted. It is truly said, that the appellation קדשים does not mean perfect moral holiness, which, according to the deep knowledge of man's sinfulness among the Hebrews, could be ascribed to no one, but rather imports, "dedicated to God," corresponding to the ἅγιοι of the New Testament. In this sense it occurs as a designation of the people of Israel, the Priests and the Nazarites. But then, we need not, with De Wette, take אַדִּיר, *illustrious*, in the sense "noble in disposition," in which it never occurs, since according to the parallelism it must likewise signify a *character dignitatis*, which to be sure presupposes nobleness of disposition. It rather imports as in 2 Chron. 23, 20, *the honorable*, with only the difference that, there, the honor comes from men, while here it is conferred by God.—But this interpretation is objectionable, not so much on account of the assumed connexion of the Nomin. absol. with the preposition ל, which, although it seldom occurs is not without example, as because the supposition is groundless, that the Stat. constr. אַדִּירֵי stands here for the Stat. absol. The Stat constr. can properly be placed instead of the Stat. absol., only when an intimate connexion exists, besides that of a genitive case. So before prepositions, before *vav* copulative, and the relative. The only example in which, without such intimate connexion, the Stat. constr. is put for the Stat. absol. are 2 Kings 9, 17, and Ps. 74: 19. But the forms שֹׁפֵעַת and הָיַת, which there occur, are to be taken as unusual forms of the Stat absol. and as such they are not without analogy. Comp. Gesenius Lehrg. p. 680 and 467. Ewald Gramm. p. 348 and 579. On the other hand, every difficulty will be obviated, if we take ל in its usual signification *to*—to the saints, i. e. associating with them, belonging to them—or in the sense, *instar*, *tanquam*, arising from this, and which, though less frequent, is equally certain, see Job 39, 16. Thus Winer. "As to the saints who are on the earth, and the excellent, all my delight is in them; for: in them I have all my delight." The former interpretation, "associating with them" appears to be preferable from a comparison with the following verse, where the speaker expresses his abhorrence of all connexion with the despisers of God. It was followed by Calvin: "Sanctis me adjungam socium,—nempe quod se applicabit ad pios dei cultores et illorum socius erit vel comes, sicuti omnes dei filios fraternae conjunctionis nexu inter se devinctos esse oportet, ut eodem affectu et studio patrem suum colant." If now we proceed to an examination of the objection of Jahn drawn from this verse, we shall perceive that it rests solely from laying a stress on the words אֲשֶׁר בָּאָרֶץ הֵמָּה. But that there is no reason for this, is evident from the pleonastic use of אֶרֶץ in the other instances, as for example in Ps. 76 19, עֲנְוֵי אֶרֶץ, where it occurs in a manner entirely similar. But if a peculiar stress must be laid upon these words, we could much sooner suppose, that the saints on earth are here contrasted with the angels who bear the title קְדוֹשִׁים κατ' ἐξοχήν, and almost as a proper name See Ps. 89 8 Job 5 1, etc

2. "V 4 also favors the reference of the Psalm to David. The abhorrence of idolatry, there expressed, does not suit the Messiah, whose chief enemies were not idolaters, but Jews; it agrees well however with David, who, during his residence among the heathenish Philistines, probably experienced strong temptation to idolatry, and at any rate, suffered much from its adherents." Thus Knapp and Jahn l. c. But granting that idolatry is in reality the special subject of this verse, as these interpreters suppose, it would nevertheless furnish no proof against the Messianic interpretation. For in any event it cannot, as Knapp assumes, be inferred from the contents of the verse, that the speaker had been tempted to idolatry, nor as Jahn supposes, that idolaters were his enemies The speaker would rather merely declare in v. 4 his entire separation from idolaters, as he does in v 3 his fellowship with the pious worshippers of God. The idolaters would then be mentioned as *species pro genere*, for all the despisers of the true God, because these were the chief, at the time of the composition of the Psalm; in accordance with the custom of putting a part for the whole, of which there are examples without number. It is, however, in the highest degree probable, that the supposition that idolatry is particularly mentioned depends entirely on a false interpretation. Reliance is placed in the first place, on the words יִרְבּוּ עַצְּבוֹתָם אַחֵר מָהָרוּ, which are translated "many are the idols of those who hasten after other, i e gods" But there are many philological difficulties in the way of this interpretation The noun עַצְּבוֹת has never like its cognate עֲצַבִּים the meaning *idols;* but always, that of *pains*. אַחֵר never stands alone for other gods, but only where Jehovah appears as the speaker, and contrasts himself with them, as in Isaiah 42· 8 The passage then should rather be translated as it has been by Storr, Rosenmuller, and De Wette, "many are the pains of those who hasten elsewhere" אַחֵר as Accus of the Neutr. in answer to the question *whither*, in the sense *ahorsum*, elsewhere. But that *elsewhere* is the same as, "after other

PSALM XVI.   127

gods," which De Wette asserts, is an arbitrary supposition. It signifies any departure whatever from God, any confidence, either in our own strength, or that of other created beings, or of idols.—Nor can it any more be proved from the words, "I will not pour out their drink offerings of blood," that idolaters are spoken of in this sense. The best interpreters agree that these words must not be literally understood, and made to refer to the common practice among the heathen of using blood instead of wine in their libations, or of mingling wine with blood, (See Michaelis l. c. p. 107), but that they are rather to be taken in a figurative sense. Drink offerings of blood, that is, those which God as much abhors as if they consisted of blood instead of wine, in accordance with his prescription. But God so regards not merely the offerings of idolaters, but those also of the outward members of the theocracy presented from mere selfish motives, and without that true theocratic disposition which was necessary to render the sacrifice acceptable See Isa 63: 3 : "He that (with such a wrong disposition) offereth an oblation is as if he offereth swine's blood." Prov. 21. 22 : "The sacrifice of the wicked is an abomination" The sense therefore is : I detest the sacrifices of the wicked which are displeasing to God Consequently there is no trace of any special reference to idolatry

3 "The plural חֲסִידֶיךָ in verse 10 is opposed to the Messianic interpretation. It is true that the marginal reading has, instead of this, the singular חֲסִידְךָ, and in favor of this reading there are very numerous important and critical authorities But the reading of the text is the more difficult, and therefore to be preferred According to this, however, the subject of discourse cannot be the resurrection, which is peculiar to the Messiah, but merely a deliverance from dangers which the Psalmist claims for all the pious in general as well as for himself" Thus Rosenmüller and De Wette But the marginal reading is certainly the true one. In favor of the singular we have not only the greatest number of manuscripts and the best, (156 codd. Ken 80 codd. Rossi), but still earlier testimony It is confirmed by all the old translations and by the Apostles, Peter and Paul For when they prove the resurrection of Christ from this Psalm, with the strongest conviction that their proof could not be invalidated, they make it manifest that in their time the reading *thy holy ones*, by which their whole interpretation could so easily be refuted, did not exist—and this is confirmed by the silence of the Jews. These reasons are so striking that even the most skilful defenders of the reading חֲסִידֶיךָ

Fischer (Proluss. de vit. lexic N. T. p. 184 seq) and Stange (Anticrit. in Psalm. p 101), undertake its defence only on the supposition that the plural here stands for the singular, and they declare that the idea of its being a proper plural is altogether inadmissible. The argument that the more difficult reading is to be preferred here, as well as every where else, which is urged in favor of the plural, is only specious, for it is in general absurd to extend this rule of criticism so far as to disregard the whole weight of external evidence. Besides, the authority of this rule depends entirely on the circumstance, that the origin of the easier reading can be more readily explained than that of the more difficult. But here the case is exactly the opposite. The plural must have been extremely welcome to the Jews, because it furnished them with the best means of refuting the Messianic interpretation of the Psalm, by which they were embarrassed even by the Apostles. That this reading was used for such a purpose is shown by the Perusch Tillim des Jacob de Mercado Amsterd. 1653. "Scriptum חֲסִידֶיךָ plene duobus Jod ut complectatur etiam sanctos alios praeter eum. Per חֲסִידֶיךָ igitur dicere voluit, etiam ego horum comprehendor numero et ero sicut unus ex illis." See other passages in Aurivillius, de vera Lectione voc. חֲסִידֶיךָ מן d dissert ed Michaelis p 136. If now, the reading חֲסִידֶיךָ may at first, as Michaelis (Crit Coll. p. 217), supposes, have originated by accident, which could so easily happen, or, as Aurivillius, l c p. 138, thinks, have been substituted for the reading of the text from polemic zeal against the Christians, in either case it was natural for later transcribers to prefer a reading, which so greatly favored the opinions of the Jews, and that nevertheless this was done only by comparatively few must be ascribed to the entire preponderance of external arguments.

4. "The construction of the verb עָזַב with the preposition לְ designates the *terminus ad quem*. If the Messianic interpretation were the true one, instead of לִשְׁאוֹל we should have בִּשְׁאוֹל." Thus Hufnagel (dissert in h Ps p 14). But the verb עָזַב with לְ, אֶל, and עַל signifies: *to give up one to another*, whether to be received or retained the connexion must in every case decide. Michaelis has justly remarked that Sheol is here personified, and represented as an insatiable animal, which will not surrender the prey, which it has once overpowered. See Prov 30 16 Ps 49. 15. Is. 5 14.

5 "The noun שַׁחַת never signifies *corruption*, as it must according to this interpretation, but always *grave*. And this meaning

of the word is here also sustained by the parallelism." Thus Rosenmuller, Jahn, De Wette. It is indeed true that the noun שַׁחַת commonly derived from שׁוּחַ *to subside,* as נַחַת from נוּחַ means *a pit, a grave.* But that another שַׁחַת derived from שָׁחַת *corrupit, perdidit,* with the meaning *corruptio, putredo,* was in use in the living language, appears from the testimony of the old translators, who, with the exception of the Chaldee, the latest among them, not only with Peter and Paul, render the word *corruption* in this passage, but also in others, where the connexion requires it to be translated *pit.* It is even capable of proof that the word occurs in this sense in the Hebrew text. Allowing it to be doubtful in other passages to which an appeal has been made, it undoubtedly occurs as Winer also confesses, in Job 17: 14, where שַׁחַת *corruption,* stands in the parallelism with רִמָּה, *worm,* Ps 55: 24, the meaning *corruption* is at least altogether the most probable, and approved even by Rosenmuller in contradiction to himself—and as to parallelism, that is certainly not destroyed by the Messianic interpretation. For the expression "thou wilt not give up my soul to Sheol,' is the same in other words as "thou wilt not suffer thy Holy One to see corruption," with only the difference perhaps, that according to the contrast which already occurs in the foregoing verse, the former as Dathe* rightly remarks relates to the soul, the latter to the body.

6. "This Psalm coincides so entirely in style, expressions and sentiments with the LVI, LVII, and LIX, which have the same appellation מִכְתָּם in the superscription and appear from external and internal evidence to relate to David's exile during the persecution of Saul, that it must necessarily refer, like them, to David and to the same circumstances of his life." Thus Rosenmuller. But on the other hand, even De Wette remarks, that he is unable to find this alleged resemblance, and surely every one will agree with him after a careful comparison. It is by no means so great as that which it bears to other supplicatory Psalms; its resemblance to them, however, according to our introductory remarks can be no objection to its reference to the Messiah.

7. "This interpretation is in opposition to all the notions of the Jews respecting the Messiah. They expected Him to be a hero, a conqueror, a mighty king; a suffering Messiah was unknown to

---

* "Utrumque negat vates sibi eventurum esse, neque animae in שְׁאוֹל apud inferos, neque corporis in sepulchro diuturnum fore domicilium."

them." Thus Ruperti (Ps 16 illustr in den Commentt. theol. ed. Velthusen etc t. I.) In answer to this objection we would refer to the chapter concerning the suffering Messiah in the Old Testament.

8. "The Jews by no means expected a resurrection of the Messiah, as appears from a passage of Maimonides, quoted by Pococke" (porta Mosis p 159. 60 ed Ox.) Thus Rosenmuller. But if this assertion were correct, still it would furnish no proof, for we can by no means infer with certainty, that a doctrine is not contained in the Old Testament, because the Jews, who were not favored with the light afforded by the fulfilment, and were moreover blinded by manifold prejudices, did not find it there. The assertion, however, is entirely erroneous. The unimportant testimony of the philosopher Maimonides, is more than overbalanced by the passages which Schottgen (de Messia p. 565 seq.), has adduced from the Sohar, the Talmud and Jalkut Shimoni. See Heinrichs on Acts 11· 24.

Among the recent defenders of the Messianic interpretation are to be mentioned: Michaelis, Dathe, Anton (l. c. p 19), Schnurrer (dissertt. p. 119 ff.), Ringeltaube, Dereser, Pareau (l c. p. 499, 509, 519), Steudel—who nevertheless supposes that the speaker is properly David who, v. 8, assumes the person of the Messiah—Kaiser, who sets up the strange hypothesis that David here speaks in the name of the high priest, in *abstracto*, but yet intermingles special traits which suit only his antitype, who was to be at the same time both king and high priest—and others

Psalm XXII

This Psalm consists of two parts, v 1—22 and 23—32. A worshipper of God in extreme distress presents before him his anxious complaint. He reminds him, that, since He had always delivered his pious forefathers from their affliction, he would appear to act inconsistently should he on the contrary abandon him to his unparalleled sufferings, to the contempt of the whole people, to the bitter mockery and scorn of his enemies, v. 1—8. He prays that God who had watched over him with such tender love from the commencement of his being, would not now forsake him, v. 10—12. But the feeling of misery is still too strong to be overcome; he is not yet consoled by the inward assurance that his prayer is heard. Again therefore does he give utterance to his emotions and bewail his still increasing wretchedness. He is encompassed by numerous blood thirsty foes. The most dreadful sufferings have consumed all his strength, intense thirst torments him; they have pierced his hands and his feet; every member is made to feel its peculiar anguish. His enemies feast their eyes with malicious joy upon the spectacle which he presents. They part his garments among them and cast lots upon his vesture, v. 13—19. This repetition of his complaint is then followed, v. 20—22, by a repetition of his prayer, now accompanied by the assurance of a favorable hearing.

In the second part, the speaker declares the method in which he will manifest his thankfulness for the promised deliverance, and also the consequences which shall flow from it. When freed from his distress, he will highly extol the goodness of God and exhort the believing Israelites to praise him and put their trust in Him, v. 23—25. And what is of still higher importance he will celebrate a sacrificial feast in honor of his Lord in accordance with his vow. This sacrificial feast shall be of a kind altogether unusual. Not merely the poor shall be partakers of it; but those also who enjoy the greatest abundance shall be invited along with the most needy. It shall not be too simple for the latter, and the former shall not be excluded from it by their wretchedness. And not only shall the believing Israelites in great numbers come to this feast, but the heathen likewise from one end of the earth to the other after they shall be converted to God in consequence of the deliverance of his devout worshipper, who is henceforth to be acknowledged as Lord and king in all the world. The nourishment which this feast will supply is not merely transient and corporeal, calling for nothing more than momentary gratitude. It is spiritual and everlasting, v. 26—30. Nor are the consequences of this memorable transaction to be limited to the present time. The heathen, who consecrate themselves to Jehovah, are henceforth to be numbered forever among his people hitherto limited to Israel alone,* and the mercy of God in the deliverance

---

* We explain the second member from v. 31 with Dathe and Jahn "deo erunt ut nova generatio ascripti i. e. in catalogum membrorum novae ecclesiae referentur." The verb ספר in the sense denied by Rosenmüller *numerare*, Ps 40 6 Job 38 37. The forced interpretation, it shall be related by the Lord in future generations, owes its origin solely to the effort to set aside a Messianic feature. The translation of לאדני by *by the Lord*, is as harsh as that of לדור by *in future generations*, and is unauthorized.

of his servant shall be celebrated with joyful thanksgiving from generation to generation, v. 31, 32.

Interpreters have taken three different views of this Psalm

1. The modern Jews and the Rationalists These are unanimous only in their opposition to the Messianic interpretation; in all other respects the greatest difference prevails among them. Many of them proceeding upon the supposition that David is named as the author in the superscription, make him also the subject But they differ widely when they attempt to fix on the period in the life of David to which the Psalm relates Some refer it to the time of Saul's persecution; others, of David's flight from Absalom, and others still of the Syrian war On the other hand, some interpreters of this class confess that no corresponding condition can be found in the life of David, and seek for another subject in Jewish history. So Jahn (Vaticinia Messiana II p 267 seq.), who regards Hezekiah as such. And lastly others seeing the difficulties which attend the reference of it to any individual subject besides the Messiah, resort to a supposed personification So Kimchi* and Jarchi,† who make the subject of the Psalm the suffering of the Jewish people in their present dispersion, and De Wette who seems inclined to the opinion that it describes the sufferings in the Babylonian exile.

2. A second class suppose that it contains many things which must be referred only to David, and others which are peculiar to Christ. They seek to reconcile this, by the supposition that David himself was the sufferer and composed the Psalm about the time of Saul's persecution, or Absalom's rebellion; but that under the guidance of the Holy Spirit, he uttered many things which are applicable to him only in an inferior, or a metaphorical sense, but are literally and completely fulfilled in the history of the Messiah. Thus Calvin, Melancthon, Musculus, Rüdinger, Grotius, Venema, Dathe, Seiler, Kuinoel and others

3. And lastly, by far the greatest number of interpreters acknowledge the Messiah as the exclusive subject of the Psalm. This inter-

---

* "Majores nostri dicunt, hunc Psalmum de Esthere esse compositum, et de Israelitis, qui tunc temporis versabantur in exilio.—Rectius videtur si dicatur, per cervam aurorae designari congregationem Israelitarum in praesenti exilio positorum —Singulari numero utitur, de toto populo Israelitico simul loquens, ipsi enim omnes sunt quasi homo unus in exilio"

† "Itura est (congregatio Isr) in exilium dixitque David orationem istam de tempore futuro"

pretation was followed by a portion of the older Jews. It has always been the prevailing one in the Christian church.

It has been held in recent times by Michaelis, Knapp, Ringeltaube,—who has given us several important remarks,—Less (von der Religion u s w p. 668 seq), Muntinghe, Hensler (Bemerkungen zu Stellen in den Psalmen und der Genesis p 42 seq), Uhland (animadd. exeg in Ps. XXII Tub 1800), Dereser, Pareau (l. c p. 509), Kaiser and others.

We feel compelled by the weight of evidence to decide in favor of the last interpretation. The principal arguments are the following:

1. It is sustained by the testimony of tradition. It is true that De Wette asserts p. 238, that the Psalm was never understood by the Jews of the suffering Messiah.* But this groundless assertion is sufficiently refuted by the clear testimony drawn from the Jewish writers by Jo H. Michaelis Comm in Ps p 138, and Schottgen de Messia p 232 etc These passages are the more conclusive, because the Jews must have been extremely desirous to find out some other mode of explaining the Psalm, both on account of their opposition to the idea of a suffering Messiah in general, and of the embarrassment in which they were involved by its close agreement, according to the Messianic interpretation, with the history of Jesus Christ. Hence we cannot explain why this interpretation was not entirely and universally rejected in any other way than by supposing that the doctrinal interest of the Jews was counteracted by the authority of tradition.

2 We urge in the next place the testimony of the New Testament. That Christ according to Matt. 27. 46. Mark 15 34, uttered the first words of this Psalm on the cross, would not of itself be conclusive, because he may have used them merely in the way of accommodation It is however a fact well worthy of attention. But on the other hand nothing can be more unnatural than the supposition, that the quotations in John 19 24 and Heb. 2 11, 12 are mere allusions.

---

* Jahn endeavors in vain to prove from Matt 27 43, that in the time of Christ, the Psalm was not understood of the Messiah. It cannot even be inferred from that passage, though it is probable for other reasons, that the Jews who mocked Jesus and who surely did not belong to the better portion, who were capable of receiving the idea of a suffering Messiah, did not adopt the Messianic interpretation.

3. But the most conclusive evidence is that drawn from internal sources. Numerous traits are here combined, which either singly or at least in this combination are not to be found in the history of David, or of any other person, than the Messiah. And here before we proceed to particulars we must premise a general remark. The opposers of the Messianic interpretation, as Hufnagel and Rosenmuller have made the task easy for themselves, by considering separately and not in their mutual connexion those features which are appropriate to the Messiah. But it is this latter consideration which is of peculiar force; for nothing but doctrinal prejudice can suppose that all the circumstances which have so literally concurred in the history of Jesus, can be met with in the same combination in the life of any other person. It is on this account that those facts become significant, which, as the piercing of the hands and feet are not in themselves considered peculiar to Christ, and may be often repeated. Let us here present in one view the principal characteristics of the Messiah. V. 8 it is said: "All that see me laugh me to scorn, they shoot out the lip, they shake the head." Matt. 27:39. οἱ δὲ παραπορευόμενοι ἐβλασφήμουν αὐτὸν, κινοῦντες τὰς κεφαλὰς αὐτῶν. V. 9, the scoffers are introduced saying: "He trusted on the Lord, that he would deliver him: let him deliver him, seeing he delighted in him." On the other hand in Matt 27:43 they say· πέποιθεν ἐπὶ τὸν θεόν· ῥυσάσθω νῦν αὐτὸν, εἰ θέλει αὐτόν. Both passages so literally correspond, that the resemblance cannot possibly be regarded as the result of accident. Michaelis has very properly remarked. "They quoted from this Psalm as people are accustomed to do, who are much conversant with the Bible, because its language harmonized with their sentiments without being aware of its character, and how unhappily for themselves they were fulfilling its predictions." But even were we to suppose that the revilers of Christ used these words independently of the Psalm, still the coincidence would not be at all the less remarkable. It is also manifest that Matthew selected, from among the many words that were uttered, these especially, for the purpose of pointing out the agreement between the prophecy and its fulfilment. Nor is there any doubt that in bringing forward the remaining circumstances in which this agreement consists, he designed to lead the reader of himself to the conviction, that in the sufferings of Christ, the most remarkable predictions of the Old Testament respecting the Messiah's sufferings, were completely fulfilled. And hence the opinion of those, who maintain that the dis-

tinct citations from this Psalm are mere allusions, appears still more erroneous. V. 15, 16 we read: "I am poured out like water, and all my bones are out of joint; my heart is like wax: it is melted in the midst of my bowels. My strength is dried up like a potsherd; and my tongue cleaveth to my jaws; and thou hast brought me into the dust of death." These words were literally fulfilled in the inexpressible anguish attending the crucifixion of Christ.* The exact fulfilment of the circumstance, "my tongue cleaveth to my jaws," which indicates extreme thirst (Lam. 4. 4) is expressly mentioned by John 19. 28.† But one of the most remarkable traits is that in v. 17, כָּאֲרִי יָדַי וְרַגְלָי. But here a more thorough investigation is requisite, in order to show, that these words must necessarily refer to Christ, since attempts have been made in various ways to disprove it. The form כָּאֲרִי occurs besides in Isaiah 38. 13, where it means, *as a lion*. Some interpreters after the example of the Jews, as Paulus and Ewald (Hebr. Gramm. p. 296) have adopted this meaning in the passage before us. But this interpretation is liable to the following objections, which have induced Rosenmüller, Jahn, De Wette, Gesenius and Winer decidedly to reject it. It by no means gives a consistent meaning. The verb הִקִּיפוּנִי can mean only *surrounded*, on account of the parallelism with סְבָבוּנִי, by which the interpretation also attempted by some "they have crushed," (in other respects also inadmissible, since in Hiphil it never occurs in this sense) is entirely excluded. If now, with Abenezra and Ewald, we take כָּאֲרִי as nominative in the sense of "as a lion," it is impossible to see how a lion can surround the hands and feet. At all events the figure would have been very unsuitable. Or if with Paulus we take the כָּאֲרִי in the accusative, "as a lion" the meaning is still more incongruous; since the sufferer, who in v. 7, under a deep sense of his misery, calls himself a worm, cannot possibly here compare himself with a lion. 2. Exegetical tradition also decides against this interpretation. The *Masora parva* remarks on this place, that כָּאֲרִי occurs here in a different sense from that which it has in Isa. 38. 13, where it plainly means "as a lion." All the old translators, although

---

* Hufnagel, diss. in h. Ps. "Acerbissimos dolores his verbis graviter describit, summosque cruciatus ita hominem afficere docet, ac si ipsa corporis compages firmis nexibus superstructa iis omnino destituatur."

† So also v. 19. "I can number my bones," which Jahn rightly explains "in singulis meis ossibus tremorem singularem sentio, ut ea dinumerare possim."

they differ in other respects, agree in regarding it as a verb. 3. If this interpretation be adopted, it is impossible to account for the origin of the various readings כָּאֲרִי — כָּאֲרוּ and כָּרוּ.*

We must therefore adopt the explanation of this difficult word, which after the example of Pococke (notae miscell. ad port. Mosis p. 57), Gesenius (Hebr. Wtb. II. 1339. Lehrgb. p 526), De Wette and Winci have approved

They take the form כָּאֲרִי as the irregular plural for כָּאֲרִים. It is true after Verbrugge, Ewald has objected, that this irregular plural form is only an arbitrary supposition, but the single example of מִנִּי Ps 45: 9 is insufficient to justify the assumption of this plural form. It is self-evident that the rendering "more than I" adopted by Ewald is extremely forced; and it has already been criticised by Winer. Not less unnatural are most of the remaining explanations, by which Ewald has endeavored to set aside the examples adduced by Gesenius. This form will consequently then be the plural participle of כוּר. Although this participle is properly כָּר, yet the *scriptio plena* is not in other instances without example. Thus Hos. 10: 14 קָאִם v Ez. 23 24, 26 שָׁאטִים (despisers) ; see Ges Lehrg. p. 401. The readings found in some manuscripts and editions כָּאֲרִי — כָּאֲרוּ and כָּרוּ give the same sense as that of the text, which to say nothing of its being found in all the manuscripts, deserves the preference, because it is the more difficult, and it is easy to explain, how the others originated from it. The first mentioned, which arose from ignorance of the irregular form of the plural, is likewise the participle, according to the *scriptio plena* The only difference is that כָּאֲרִי as the plural absolute would govern the following nouns in the accusative, to which Rosenmuller very unreasonably objects, while on the other hand כָּאֲרִי as the plural construct would be connected with the genitive The second, arising from the same effort to avoid the irregular plural, is the *scriptio plena* of the preterite of the verb כּוֹר, entirely synonymous with the reading of the text, according to which also the participle is put for the finite verb, as is often the case. The third is also the praeter of the verb כוּר, with the rejection of the inserted א contrary to the general rule.

The question now arises, What meaning shall be given to the verb כוּר, which does not again occur in Hebrew? The interpre-

---

* See on the other hand Bochart Hieroz. c 780. Michaelis Or. Bibl. XI. 209 etc

ters have here compared 1. The Arabic verb كَالَمَ for كَمَرَ. To this they give the meaning: *valide constrinxit, arcte colligavit:* "they have bound my hands and feet." Thus Rosenmüller, Gesenius, De Wette, Winer. But it is scarcely conceivable how an interpretation, which has so little philological support, could be so well received. This sense of the word is entirely without proof, it is not once given by Golius, nor the Camus, from which he drew his materials. For when it is said in the Camus كَوَّرَ ٱلْمَتَاعَ جَمَعَهُ وَشَكَّهُ *Kavvara lmataa,* "to collect and bind things," it by no means follows that the verb كَامَ can have only the meaning *to bind,* which is not given to it either in the first or any of the derivative conjugations. Plainly, its chief import is rather that of *collecting,* and the idea of *binding* is only mentioned incidentally as something belonging to that. It is also expressly remarked that even in the sense, *to collect,* the verb is used only of things, on the contrary the expression كَوَّمَ ٱلرَّجُلَ has an entirely different meaning, as we shall soon more clearly see.

2. Others (Fuller, Jahn) give to the verb כּוּר the meaning, *foedare.* Thus of old Aquila, who translates . ἤσχυναν *Foedare* would then mean, according to a mode of speech which often occurs —see the examples by Fuller (Miscell. III 12), and by Bochart (Hieroz. c. 780 ed. IV.)—*to stain with blood,* and as to the sense this interpretation would be about the same as the following. But for this meaning there is no sufficient philological support. It is founded chiefly on the fact that in the Mischna כָּאוּר occurs in the sense, *turpe, foedum;* see Buxtorf. But then כָּאוּר stands for the usual כָּעוּר according to a-permutation of א and ע, which is frequent in the late usage of the language. The Syriac has also been appealed to where the verb ܟܐܒ has the meaning: *reprehendit, incusavit, pudefecit,* but this meaning is very far-fetched. Lastly, the Arabic مَكْوُمٌ seems, *per consequens,* to mean · *ugly, offensive to the sight.* The original meaning appears to be that given in the Camus, ٱلْقَصِيرُ ٱلْعَرِيضُ, *short, broad,* derived from the verb كَامَ in the sense, *to collect.*

3. On the other hand there is every thing in favor of giving the verb כור the sense, *to pierce through*. This interpretation is sustained 1. by the Hebrew usage. כור is then synonymous with the verb כָּרָה *to bore through*, which often occurs. Such a permutation of the verbs עֹ and כֹּה is very common. Thus דום and דָּמָה *to be silent,* דוּךְ and דָּכָה *to bruise,* בוז and בָּזָה *to despise,* and many others 2 The testimony of the Seventy, who translate ὤρυξαν χεῖράς μου καὶ πόδας μου as well as the Syriac version, which has ܒܙܥܘ perforarunt, transfixerunt, and the Vulgate, *foderunt* This coincidence of the three most important direct translations deserves great regard 3. And lastly the comparison with the Arabic is decisive. There the agreement of כיר with כרה which we have assumed, really exists. In the Camus it is said : التكوير حفر الارض.

"The verb كَارَ in the II signifies *to dig in the earth*; further, وكَوَّرَهُ صَرَعَهُ وتَكَوَّرَ واكتَنَارَ in the II with Accus of the person the verb كَارَ means *to cut to the ground*, and is passive in the V and VIII." Then: كَوَّرَ الرجلَ اي طَعَنَهُ "كَارَ in the II with the Accus of the person, is synonymous with طَعَنَ *to bore through*"

And thus it appears that the translation, "they have pierced through my hands and my feet," is the only one sustained by philological and sufficient arguments These words, however can refer neither to David, nor to any other sufferer except the Messiah; since as Gesenius remarks, See p 1340, "men pierced indeed the body of their enemy, but not his hands and feet" They rather refer to Christ who, as in consequence of the punishment of the cross, endured this suffering.

But here we meet with yet another difficulty After it had been from the earliest time, received by the church as an unquestionable fact, that when Christ was crucified not merely his hands, but also his feet were pierced through with nails, an attempt has been made after the example of Dathe, by Paulus (Memorab IV p 36 seq u. Comment z. N T. III. p 751 seq.), to prove that this was not the case. He has been followed by Rosenmuller, Kuinoel, Fritsche and many others, no one of whom has thought of examining his proofs, which may be so easily refuted, and clearly manifest the existence of doctrinal prejudice, and the desire of setting aside a Messianic prediction,* that has clearly been fulfilled. We cannot here enter into a full examination, but shall endeavor to offer such remarks as may suffice to refute it. We observe, in the first place, that not a single reason can be adduced for the opinion that the feet were not nailed; since the passages in which the feet are said to have been bound with cords plainly prove nothing; for the hands also were bound, yet they were afterwards nailed. On the contrary, it can be proved by the surest historical testimony, that the nailing of the feet actually took place. An important proof passage is found in Plautus (Mostellaria act. 2. sc 1 v. 13.) There a slave who expected the worst consequences from the return of his master exclaims, "Ego dabo ei talentum primus qui in crucem excucurrerit, sed ea lege, ut offigantur, bis pedes, bis brachia." The word *offigantur* stands here as Bothe IV. p 514, remarks, in the sense of *affigantur*, which is the reading in several editions as the Bipont, and that of Gronovius. Paulus seeks to evade the force of this passage on two grounds. He remarks, 1. "It is manifest here from the tenor of this discourse, that the slave expected something *uncommonly* severe and cruel, and of course that *offigi pedes* was not usual in the punishment of the cross." But all that is extraordinary here, is manifestly what is implied in the word *bis;* usually the hands and feet were nailed but once; the slave dreaded a double nailing. The *offigi pedes* stands moreover in the same relation as the *offigi brachia*, and can be regarded as extraordinary no more than that. 2. "The text is uncertain. More correctly may be read with Pareus, *ut obfringantur bis pedes, bis brachia*, and then the subject of discourse will be the breaking of the arms and legs, as in the case of malefactors." But this reading is absurd, since the breaking of the legs shortened and alleviated the punishment instead of aggravating it. It is to be rejected on other grounds also. Pareus, upon whom Paulus relies, has it indeed in his edition of 1610; but on the other side, in the edition of 1619, and in the *analectis Plautinis*, he gives the reading *offigantur*, which is confirmed by manuscripts and which nothing but doctrinal prejudice can reject, in opposition to all critical authority (v Bothe l c.) The second important passage is taken from Tertullian (adv Marcionem III. 19. ed. Wurz I p 403.) "Si adhuc quaeris dominicae crucis

---

* There is also the further difficulty, that if the feet of Christ were pierced, it cannot be explained from natural causes, how at his resurrection he could leave the grave and walk about.

praedicationem, satis jam potest tibi facere vigesimus primus Psalmus, totam Christi continens passionem, canentis jam tunc gloriam suam: foderunt, inquit, manus meas et pedes, *quae propria* (al. edd. proprie) *est atrocia crucis*." The testimony of this writer is of the highest authority, because he lived at a time when crucifixion, which was first abolished under the christian emperors, was still practised, and he here declares, that the nailing of the feet as well as the hands belonged to the peculiar severity of this punishment. Paulus has here also invented a way of escape. He remarks, l. c. p. 755: Tertullian means to assert that the crucifixion of Jesus was attended with uncommon cruelty. But this extremely forced interpretation cannot be admitted, because in that case instead of *est* we should have had *erat*; and because the words " quae propria est atrocia crucis," relate not merely to the piercing of the feet, but likewise, of the hands; which therefore must also be regarded according to Paulus as a degree of cruelty peculiar to the crucifixion of Christ.

It is therefore sufficiently evident that in the punishment of the cross, not merely the hands but also the feet were pierced through. This is established also by the fact, that the Fathers in the numerous instances where they refer to the piercing of the feet of Christ, never so much as intimate that this was any thing uncommon, but always speak of it as the inevitable attendant of crucifixion. But even if it were not capable of proof, as it clearly is, that the nailing of the feet was customary in the punishment of the cross, we should still have evidence that it was done at the crucifixion of Christ, though it might have been unusual. We will not here appeal to the testimony of the Fathers among whom Justin says "As they crucified Him, they pierced through his hands and feet by driving in nails." Since it may be objected with some plausibility, as it has been by Paulus, that the reference of this Psalm to his crucifixion gave rise to the idea that the feet of Christ were nailed. We rely only on the passage in Luke 24: 39: ἴδετε τὰς χεῖράς μου καὶ τοὺς πόδας μου, ὅτι αὐτὸς ἐγώ εἰμι. The way in which Paulus endeavors to evade this testimony is indeed ingenious, but not on that account the less unsatisfactory. He supposes that Christ showed to his disciples, his hands and his feet, not as those parts of his body in which the marks of the crucifixion were visible, but as those, which, being naked, would give them an opportunity of seeing that he possessed flesh and bones. In opposition to this we have not only the corresponding passage in John 20. 27, where Christ convinced Thomas of the identity of his person by showing the *wounds* in his hands and side, but the expression itself shows that the disciples were first to identify his person (ὅτι αὐτὸς ἐγώ εἰμι) by seeing the wounds in his hands and feet, and then convince themselves by the sense of touch, that his body was real and not a mere apparition. Paulus also objects that Christ is said in John to have shown only his hands and side, but not his feet. But with equal propriety it might be inferred from Luke 24. 39, where he shows only his hands and feet that the wounds in his side never existed. The truth is that Christ pointed as he pleased, sometimes to these, sometimes to those marks of his identity. To have appealed to them all on every occasion, would have been superfluous. Another way of evading the force of this passage has been chosen by Kuinoel and others. They suppose, indeed, that Christ pointed out his hands and feet as the parts in which the marks of his crucifixion were visible, but contend that these marks in the feet were not made by nails, but the cords with which they had been bound. But then it would be impossible to conceive why he did not much oftener appeal to the far stronger evidence of the wound in his side, since some remaining traces of the cords on his feet, could not surely prove the identity of his person.

And thus it has been fully shown that notwithstanding all the objections and difficulties that have been invented and urged, the reference of v. 17 to the death of Christ on the cross, stands sufficiently confirmed. The stronger objection advanced by Hufnagel and repeated by Rosenmuller, that had the author intended to predict the sufferings of Christ on the cross, he must have given a far more accurate and detailed description, is scarcely deserving of refutation. For there are traits which, to say the least, do not so fully agree with the sufferings of any other person, as those of the Messiah. See. v. 15, 16 and 18, and it is unreasonable to require that prophecy should be as clear and circumstantial as history.

We now proceed with our purpose of noticing those traits which point out Christ as the subject of the Psalm. V. 19, is said, "they part my garments among them and cast lots upon my vesture." John 19. 23, 24. οἱ οὖν στρατιῶται, ὅτε ἐσταύρωσαν τὸν Ἰησοῦν, ἔλαβον τὰ ἱμάτια αὐτοῦ καὶ ἐποίησαν τέσσαρα μέρη, ἑκάστῳ στρατιώτῃ μέρος, καὶ τὸν χιτῶνα. Ἦν δὲ ὁ χιτὼν ἄῤῥαφος—εἶπον οὖν πρὸς ἀλλήλους· μὴ σχίσωμεν αὐτόν, ἀλλὰ λάχωμεν περὶ αὐτοῦ, τίνος ἔσται. Rosenmuller and Jahn (Vat. Mess II. p. 260), suppose that these words of the Psalm indicate merely the *purpose*, as if he had said, "they are already so sure of my destruction, that they determine how they will divide my clothes among themselves." This opinion manifestly owes its origin to the difficulty of finding in the life of David any thing corresponding to the language of the verse when taken in its natural and obvious meaning. But if it could be admitted, when we consider the verse by itself, yet it must be seen to be erroneous when we connect this trait with many others which were literally fulfilled in the history of Christ.

We now come to the second part of this Psalm. In v. 26—30 especially, the Messianic interpretation finds a strong support. The representation here is figurative. It was customary for the Jews in great distress to make vows, which chiefly related to the bringing of thank offerings Comp. Ps. 61. 9. 116. 14—18. Only the fat pieces of these offerings were burnt upon the altar, the rest after the portion designed for the priest had been cut off, was consumed in sacrificial meals, to which the offerers invited the stranger, the widow, the orphan and the poor, and made them partakers of their prosperity and joy. See Michaelis (Mos. R. II § 143.) Jahn (Archaol. III. § 103.) So here the blessings, which should flow to others from the deliverance of the sufferer, are represented under the image of a great sacrificial feast* to be prepared by him, of which not merely the pious Israelites should partake, but all the heathen likewise from one end of the earth to the other, who are now to be converted to the true God. Here the reference to the Messiah is so obvious that even Jarchi on the words of the 27th v. *comedent pauperes*, etc. remarks: "tempore redemptionis nostrae diebus Messiae." In the old Testament the hope of a general conversion of the heathen is always connected with the time of the Messiah, and constitutes one of its distinctive marks. Altogether similar to the passage before us is Is. XLII, XLIX, LIII, where the prophet describes the distinguished servant of God as one who should convert and bless the heathen. An exact parallel to these words in v. 29. "For the kingdom shall then be the Lord's and He shall reign among the nations," is found in the Messianic predictions of the prophets. Obadiah XXI, "and the kingdom shall be the Lord's." Zech. 14. 9, "And the Lord shall be king over all the earth, in that day there shall be one Lord and his name one.' V. 28 brings to remembrance the promises made to the Patriarch, and

---

* In the New Testament also, the blessings of the Messiah's reign are very often represented, under the image of a feast Matt. 8. 11. 22. 2. Luke 13. 29. 11. 16 Rev. 19. 9

announces their fulfilment. The non-Messianic interpreters are here involved in no little difficulty.* Several of them, as Mendelssohn and Hufnagel, seek to escape by giving to the future verbs in v. 26—30, an optative sense. But in opposition to this, Hensler l. c. p. 44, has already well replied, that, admitting what is contradicted by the whole tenor of the discourse and the perfect אָכְלוּ v. 30, that the speaker uttered only his wishes, still nothing will be gained by this, since no man could hope for what is not only entirely destitute of probability, but altogether impossible.

Having thus brought forward the positive arguments for the reference of this Psalm to the Messiah, let us now see to what objections each of the non-Messianic interpretations, that have been suggested, are liable. To those who make David the subject of the Psalm we reply, 1 that he was never in such distress as is here described. In the war with the Syrians, 2 Sam. x, to which Paulus conjectures the Psalm refers, he was throughout successful. With as little propriety can we fix upon the rebellion of Absalom. In this Psalm the sufferer appears alone, the object of universal scorn, forsaken of every helper, v. 12, given up to the violence of blood thirsty enemies and at the point of death; there David was in the midst of a brave and numerous host, and in no danger of his life. Nor in the persecution of Saul did the danger and distress of David rise to such a height. See a further examination of this point in Jahn l. c p. 266. 2 To this it must be added, that while this description of suffering contains much which does not suit David, there is on the other hand among so many particulars nothing which gives intimation of the event or the time to which this lamentation of David belongs. In other Psalms which are less circumstantial we can often tell whether they were composed in the flight before Saul, or Absalom, and can readily decide with precision concerning them. But this Psalm which so abounds in particulars does not afford us a single trace to lead us to the words in the history of David's misfortunes to which it relates. Michaelis. 3. David's sufferings were inflicted upon him by his own

---

* This also is plain enough from other attempts. Thus Paulus e. g. translates אַפְסֵי אֶרֶץ *border lands*, wholly against the *usus loquendi*. Jahn subjoins to the words "all nations shall fall down before thee," the limitation "nempe quae audient hanc gloriosam liberationem," which is refuted by the parallelism alone, "all the ends of the earth." De Wette explains v. 29 unnaturally, and in opposition to the parallel passages cited, "then all people shall pray to Jehovah as he is king of the world."

countrymen: the remembrance of his deliverance therefore must also be confined to the bounds of Palestine. How then could he possibly hope that his deliverance in the time of Saul's persecution, or Absalom's rebellion could make an impression on the heathen? How could he expect it to produce a result, which all the previous miraculous manifestations of God in the history of the whole nation, though made before the eyes of the heathen, had failed to effect?

The hypothesis of Jahn, which makes Hezekiah the subject of the Psalm has neither more nor less in its favor than a hundred others, which may be easily suggested, if we are willing to rest satisfied with certain general resemblances and overlook the rest, or evade them by a forced interpretation. It is refuted by the superscription itself, which can be rejected only by caprice, and which ascribes the Psalm to David as its author. Jahn erroneously supposes that according to this hypothesis the portion of the Psalm, v 26, etc will have its suitable meaning; since according to 2 Chron. 32· 23, the Divine aid vouchsafed to Hezekiah made such an impression on the nations that many of them brought offerings to the Lord at Jerusalem But this fact by no means proves, that they were led by Hezekiah's deliverance, to regard the God of Israel, as the only true God; they rather inferred from it in accordance with their polytheistic notions, that He also was one among many, and that it would therefore be well to secure his favor But that something far different is spoken of in this Psalm is self evident. Here the heathen shall be partakers with the person delivered in his prosperity and joy, here his deliverance shall exert a lasting influence on all the people of the whole earth, and produce the most beneficial of all changes; here they shall all be united in one kingdom and one great family under God as their only head.

The interpretation, which makes the Jewish people the subject, is liable to most of the objections which are urged against the same method of explaining Isaiah LIII, (see our remarks on the same place) It is even more untenable in the present instance, because the distinctive marks of an individual are more numerous, and we no where find the smallest trace to justify the idea of a personification. On the contrary the mother of the sufferer is mentioned, a tongue, jaws, hands and feet, bones and garments are ascribed to him, nay in v. 7 he is distinguished from the ungodly, and v. 23 from his brethren. But the most conclusive objection against this interpretation is that the subject of the Psalm is an *innocent* sufferer, whose sufferings are to promote the welfare of his own people, as well as that of the heathen, while on the contrary, the sufferings of the Jewish people were never undeserved, but according to the theocratical law of a visible retribution, were always the consequences of forsaking God, and as such they were represented by the prophets and sacred poets

The opinion that the Psalm relates in a lower sense to David, and in a higher to Christ, rests on two suppositions; 1 That it can be shown to be entirely fulfilled in a lower sense in the history of David; and 2. That it contains many things which cannot refer to Christ. That the former supposition is erroneous has been already sufficiently shown That the latter is equally so will be proved in the refutation of the objections against the Messianic interpretation, to which we now proceed.

1 "What seems most inconsistent is that not suffering itself, but deliverance from it is represented as the means of promoting the worship of the true God. Christ founded the kingdom of God by his sufferings which he freely endured, of course his chief peculiar work of redemption is rather mistaken than taught by the Psalmist. Of what use then to Christians is the Messianic interpretation of a Psalm, in which the notion of the Messiah is not to be found?" Thus De Wette But we meet even in the New Testament with a mode of representation altogether the same. Although Christ accomplished our redemption not by his resurrection but by his humiliation, not by his glorification but by his death, yet notwithstanding in numerous passages, his resurrection and glorification are given as the causes of man's salvation, because without these the import of his humiliation and death would have remained concealed. See Knapp opuscc. p. 343 In Isaiah LIII the persons speaking conclude from the deep humiliation of the Messiah, that he is smitten of God on account of his own sins, and they first come to the knowledge that he was wounded for their transgressions by seeing him exalted to glory. So also the subject of this Psalm, as long as his sufferings endure, is the scorn of men and despised by the people, v. 8; and with his deliverance commences as a consequence of his sufferings his influence on mankind which is so rich in blessings. Whether the Psalmist saw with entire clearness the efficacy of the Messiah's sufferings in advancing the work of salvation, we may leave undetermined, it is sufficient that the Psalm contains nothing in opposition to the Christian notion of the Messiah.

2 "The lamentations of this sufferer are unworthy of the Messiah. Christ did not like him pray for longer life from God, nor that

God would preserve him from the hands of his enemies; but he reckoned upon his death as a part of his plan." Thus Hufnagel (diss. II. in h Ps. p 6), Schulze (Critik der Mess. Ps) Here every thing depends on forming in our minds that image of Christ, which the New Testament presents, and not an arbitrary one of our own invention. Then shall we find those complaints not unworthy of him It is said of him, Heb. 5 7, that in "the days of his flesh he offered up prayers and supplications with strong crying and tears, unto him that was able to save him from death." We read in Matt. 26 36 Mark 14. 32, that Christ in Gethsemane said to his disciples just before his crucifixion, "my soul is exceeding sorrowful even unto death," and prayed to his Father, "if it be possible let this cup pass from me" Nor is this all. Christ himself when burdened with the sins of the whole world, uttered on the cross the first words of this Psalm, which express the strongest feelings of complaint.* As to the prayer for deliverance from the power of his enemies and from death, that actually can occasion no difficulty, since Christ as man actually offered the same prayer to God (comp the quoted passage) and it was completely answered in his resurrection from the grave Calvin · "Si roget quispiam, quo modo hoc Christo aptari possit, quem pater non eripuit a morte, respondeo uno verbo . fuisse potentius ereptum, quam si periculo occursum foret Quare mors non obstitit, quominus testata sit demum resurrectio, Christum fuisse exauditum."

3 "The sufferer, v. 5, 6, hopes for such a deliverance as his forefathers had experienced This agrees well with any ordinary Israelite in affliction, but not with Christ" Thus Dathe, De Wette. This objection has been already answered in the introduction to the Psalms of this class; comp Rom. 9 5

4. "Jesus could not have been predicted as praying for deliverance from the sword." Paulus, De Wette But here as in Zech 13 7, the *sword* is a figurative designation of a violent death. To insist on the literal interpretation would be to require that the paral-

---

* The cause of this deep distress and these complaints is strikingly given by Calvin "Certe suscepta nostra persona nostroque reatu necesse habuit ad dei tribunal se instar peccatoris sistere Hinc horror ille et pavor, qui ad deprecandam mortem eum coegit, non quia tam acerbum illi foret e vita migrare, sed quia ante oculos erat dei maledictio, quae peccatoribus incumbit Quodsi primo conflictu elicitae fuerunt sanguinis guttae, ut opus fuerit consolatore angelo, Luc 22 43, non mirum est si in ultimo agone confessus est tantum dolorem "

lel expressions, "the power of the dog," "the lion's mouth," and "the horns of the unicorn," be interpreted in the same manner. Calvin "Per gladium, per manum canis, per os leonis et cornua unicornium intelligitur praesens mortis periculum et quidem multiplex."

5 "Jesus never made vows for the preservation of his life like the subject of this Psalm." Paulus, De Wette. But if this single feature of the representation is to be taken literally, so must the whole. Then must we adopt the supposition, that the sufferer obliged himself to prepare a literal feast, of which all the inhabitants of the earth, Jews and Heathen, rich and poor, might partake, and thereby come to the knowledge and worship of the true God.*

6. "The sufferer in the Psalm is not yet in the power of his enemies, but only in imminent danger," (v. 12, 13, 21, 22). De Wette, Dathe But this supposition is not justified by the passages quoted. In v. 12 " be not *far* from me; for trouble is *near;*" *near*, as Abenezra long since remarked, is intentionally contrasted with *far*, and we cannot hence infer that the speaker was then merely in *expectation* of distress In the remaining verses the sufferer is represented as surrounded by blood-thirsty enemies. But this does not determine, whether he were already in their power, or in fear that he should be. But from other passages it is manifest that the former was the case For he whose hands and feet are pierced through, v. 17, whose clothes are divided, v. 19, must surely be already in the power of his enemies. But suppose it proved by the passage referred to that he was not yet in the power of his enemies, it would then only be necessary to give to the Psalm a wider scope, so as to make it include the sufferings of Christ both before and during his crucifixion.

7. "He laments a longer time than Jesus continued on the cross, or enduring the pains of death," v. 3 Dathe, Paulus, De Wette. But the crucifixion was not the commencement, but only the climax, of the sufferings of Christ. The passage already cited, Heb. 5: 7, is entirely parallel.

We know of no other objections which have been urged against the Messianic interpretation of this Psalm In conclusion we adopt the words of Theodoret. Ἐγὼ δὲ τὴν Ἰουδαίων ἐμβροντησίαν θρηνῶ, ὅτι τοῖς θείοις λογίοις διηνεκῶς ἐντυγχάνοντες, τὴν ἐν τούτοις

---

* Rightly Uhland l c "Persolutio votorum ponitur pro voluntaria gratitudinis demonstratione, cujus typus olim erat in votis post exauditas preces et liberationem ex angustia solvendis"

διαλάμπουσαν οὐ συνορῶσιν ἀλήθειαν, ἀλλ' εἰς τὸν Δαβὶδ εἰρῆσθαι τὸν ψαλμὸν ἀποφαίνονται — Τούτων γὰρ οὐδὲν ἐπὶ τοῦ Δαβὶδ ὁρῶμεν γεγενημένον, οὐδὲ ἐπί τινος τῶν ἐκ Δαβὶδ. Μόνος δὲ ὁ Δεσπότης Χριστός, ὁ ἐκ Δαβὶδ κατὰ σάρκα, ὁ ἐνανθρωπήσας Θεὸς λόγος, ὁ ἐκ Δαβὶδ λαβὼν τὴν τοῦ δούλου μορφήν. Πᾶσαν γὰρ γῆν καὶ θάλασσαν τῆς θεογνωσίας ἐπλήρωσε, καὶ πέπεικε τοὺς πάλαι πλανωμένους, καὶ τοῖς εἰδώλοις προσφέροντας τὴν προσκύνησιν, ἀντὶ τῶν οὐκ ὄντων, τὸν ὄντα προσκυνῆσαι θεόν.

Psalm XL.

We first give the contents of this Psalm according to the non-Messianic interpretation. David or some other suffering Israelite, thanks the Lord for a deliverance, which has been granted him, v. 1—6. He promises, from gratitude to God, to honor him, not by occasional sacrifices, but by devoting himself to his service and by complying with the moral requisites of the law, which would be far more acceptable in his sight, v. 7—9. He promises moreover zealously to proclaim the aid, which Jehovah had vouchsafed to him, and thus to glorify his name, v. 10, 11. But although the sufferer has happily escaped from one calamity, he is still surrounded by far greater sufferings and dangers. He therefore renews, v. 12—18, his supplication to his Lord, and prays that he would deliver him from the manifold evils which his sins have brought upon him, and put his enemies to shame; thus giving all true worshippers, as well as himself occasion to rejoice and confirm their faith.

If on the other hand, as many modern interpreters suppose, among whom are Michaelis (Crit. Collegium u. s. w. p. 455 sqq.), Ringeltaube, Knapp, Anton (l. c. p. 40), Dereser and others, the Messiah is throughout the subject of the Psalm. its contents are as follows. The Messiah, who is here, as in Isaiah XLIX. Ps. XVI and XXII introduced as speaking in the first place, anticipates the time, when, having finished his work and endured his sufferings, he will have been glorified by Jehovah. He renders him thanksgiving and praise for his deliverance. V. 1—5, he praises God for the wonderful mercies in general which he bestows upon men, and since it is impossible to mention all his benefits, he extols, only the greatest of all, the redemption accomplished by himself. Since no legal sacrifices of whatever kind could please and satisfy God, the Messiah having been taught by Him their inefficacy and made obedient to His will, presents himself as the true sacrifice of whom Moses had already written in the sacred books, resolved with joyful zeal to fulfil the will of God, v. 6—9. He again, v. 10, 11, praises the righteousness, faithfulness and love of God, which he had experienced in his deliverance. As the speaker, v. 1—11, had placed himself in the future, and contemplated his sufferings as already endured, v. 12—18 he returns to the present. Oppressed by the thought of the severe distress which he must undergo in making expiation for sin, he prays to God for his merciful support.

These two different views of the Psalm are occasioned chiefly by the different explanations of v. 7—9, especially of v. 8. According to the non-Messianic interpreters, the words בְּמִגְלַת סֵפֶר כָּתוּב עָלַי have the sense, "in the volume of the book—in the Pentateuch it is *prescribed to me,*" namely what I have to do, comp כָּתַב with עַל in this sense, 2 Kings 22. 13. According to the Messianic interpretation, the sense is as follows: "in the volume of the book it is written of me," both directly in the prophecies of the Messiah, and indirectly in all that is said of sacrifices and offerings, as these prefigured Christ. Comp. John 5: 39, 46.

There can be no doubt that those who acknowledge the Divine authority of the Epistle to the Hebrews, must decide in favor of the Messianic interpretation. The Psalm is there, chap. 10. 5 etc. quoted and explained of the vicarious sacrifice of Christ, in such a way as entirely to exclude the idea of a mere accommodation. Several interpreters have indeed sought, though with little success, to find a middle path. Those who, as Calvin and Muntinghe, refer the Psalm in a lower sense to David and in a higher one to Christ, fail in their purpose of sustaining the authority of the Epistle to the Hebrews. For granting the correctness of the explanation given in this Epistle of v. 7—9, the Psalm, as we have already seen, cannot in a lower sense be referred to David, for he could not represent himself as the true offering in opposition to those which were typical, nor say, that it was written of him in the Pentateuch. We can no more concur with Venema, Seiler, and Dathe, who assert that in v. 1—6 and 12—18, David speaks; but in v. 7—11, or as Kaiser thinks,* v. 7, 8,

---

* This is contradicted by the relation of v. 12 to v. 10, Calvin "Diligenter notanda est relatio, ubi David se labia non clausisse dicit, ut vicissim deus suas misericordias non obseret, vel cohibeat."

the Messiah; for the supposition of this unnatural change of persons has nothing to support it. The only objections which have been urged against the Messianic interpretation are not conclusive. 1. De Wette remarks, that the reference of the Psalm to the Messiah in the Epistle to the Hebrews, is grounded on the erroneous interpretation of v, 7 by the Seventy. But it can be shown that the Seventy have here given the sense, though not a literal translation of the Hebrew text. Unless we are to suppose their translation entirely unmeaning, the words σῶμα δὲ κατηρτίσω μοι can only mean " thou requirest nothing outward, but myself for sacrifice, and that I will freely offer to thee." The use of σῶμα need not surprise us here, since Paul, Rom. 12 1, exhorts Christians to present their bodies (τὰ σώματα), a living sacrifice, holy and acceptable to God. The corresponding Hebrew also אָזְנַיִם כָּרִיתָ לִּי is of the same import: " thou hast bored mine ears." To bore the ears is a figurative expression for the imparting of certain precepts, and rendering others willing to follow them.* This is shown, not only by the corresponding expression כָּתַה אֹזֶן which occurs in Is. 50 5 in the sense, to give a command and make one willing to execute it; but also by the practice of boring the ears as a sign of obedience, which, as it were, embodies the expression. Thus according to Ex 21 5, 6, the right ear of the servant who chose to remain with his master was bored. So also the Turkish monks are accustomed to bore their ears, as a sign of their attention to the Divine revelation and their obedience to the Divine commands; comp. Iken dissertt. p 226.† The same custom exists also among the Persians and the Tartars, ib p 227. Among the Turks, those who transgress any precept of their religion, are nailed by the ears, that they may learn to esteem and obey it; ib p 231. "Thou hast bored mine ears," is then the same as "thou hast taught me that not the bringing of outward offerings, but the offering of myself is well pleasing to thee, and hast made me willing to act in conformity with thy instructions." The LXX completely expressed this

---

* Vitringa "aperta auris est mens prompta et prona, tum ad recipiendas, intelligendas ac discernendas doctrinas, quae cui instillantur, tum ad obsequium mandati, quod per aures ad animum fertur"

† Septem Castrensis Mon de Turc. morib c 13 "Illi qui inaures portant in auribus, significant se obedientes esse in spiritu, propter raptuum frequentium." Another author "Il y en a aussi, qui porte quelque chose a l' oreille, pour marquer leur obeissance et leur soumission à l' esprit, qui les transporte dans des ravissemens"

sentiment. They only changed the phraseology, as the metaphor was not in use among the Greeks nor does the author of the Epistle to the Hebrews use the phrase σῶμα δὲ κατηρτίσω μοι in any other sense than that which according to the context belongs to the Hebrew words, if the Psalm relates the Messiah

2. Dathe objects, that it seems incongruous that the Messiah in the former part should speak of his sufferings as already endured, and thank God for his deliverance, while in the latter on the contrary he should pray for the Divine support in distress But this is not a decisive objection, since all depends on the station in which the sacred poet places the Messiah; whom he introduces as speaking There is nothing against the supposition that he first contemplates him after he had endured his sufferings and finished his work, and then in his state of humiliation In a similar manner in Isaiah LIII, the passion of the Messiah appears at one time as already past, at another as still future See on this passage.

3 Hensler (Bemerkungen zu den Ps und z. d Gen. p 63), urges particularly the words: "mine iniquities have taken hold upon me," v 13. This objection is certainly very plausible It does not however decide the question For the parallelism with רָעוֹת shows that עֲוֹנֹתַי is not here to be translated. *mine iniquities*, but the *punishment of mine iniquities*—a sense in which it often occurs and which is given by Abenezra and Rosenmuller But that in a Psalm, which treats of the vicarious satisfaction of the Messiah, and when this is contrasted with the offering of victims which suffered the punishment properly due to sinners, the sufferings inflicted upon him for sins not his own, might be called the punishment of his sins, is evident from the similar expressions in Isaiah LIII "he hath borne our griefs and carried our sorrows," "he was wounded for our transgressions; he was bruised for our iniquities; the chastisement of our peace was upon him" "The Lord hath laid upon him the iniquity of us all." This objection would be entirely removed were we to suppose with Pareau l c p 330, that the Psalm originally consisted of but 12 verses, the remainder having been afterwards added This opinion is favored by the entirely different character of the latter portion of the Psalm; the fact that it occurs again as the 70th Psalm, and that we have other examples of such additions. Still, however, we hesitate to adopt it.

III. Predictions of the Messiah in the Prophets

We have already seen, that the predictions of the Messiah in the Psalms were much more definite than those of an earlier date. Several points of high importance, as his deity, his sufferings, and his eternal priesthood, were here first disclosed; others, as the extension of the blessings of his salvation to the heathen, and his triumph over all his enemies, were rendered more definite and clear. The authors of the Psalms were succeeded by the prophets in the work of predicting the Messiah. Were the word prophet to be taken in its broader meaning, a designation of all those to whom extraordinary divine revelation were made; as in the Old Testament itself the patriarchs and several composers of Psalms are in this sense called prophets or seers, then indeed the Psalms which relate to the Messiah might be classed with the Messianic predictions of the prophets. Here, however, we use the word in its more ordinary and restricted signification, to designate those who possessed not merely the *donum*, but also the *munus propheticum*, men sent immediately from God, to the covenant people, appointed to guard his rights, and in his name to teach, counsel, exhort, rebuke, and reveal the future. We here offer, in the first place, some general remarks respecting the predictions of the Messiah by these ambassadors of God.

1. Though prophecy began to flourish in the time of Samuel, we possess none of the predictions of that early period. Our earliest written prophecies belong to the reigns of Uzziah, Jotham, Ahaz, and Hezekiah. We cannot with certainty determine how far the predictions of the older prophets, which have not come down to us, made important disclosures respecting the Redeemer. There are, however, reasons which make it probable that it was not until this later period, that the prediction of the Messiah became the grand subject of all the annunciations of the prophets. In them it does not stand unconnected with passing events; nor in the case of those who are called to act in public, does it proceed merely from their own necessities; but has almost always a distinct reference to the condition of the people, and is designed to aid the prophets in exerting a present influence upon them. The more the State declined, and the more powerful the enemies which rose up against it and threatened its destruction, the more did the desponding people, if they were to be preserved in allegiance to the Lord, need the assurance of the fu-

ture glory of the theocracy, and its preeminence over the heathen nations   The more corruption prevailed, the more necessity there was to alarm the ungodly, and comfort the pious, by pointing to the time when the Messiah should make a separation between them, and impart to the latter all the blessings of his kingdom. It was therefore in this later period, that the revelation of the Messiah was first entrusted chiefly to the prophets; as hitherto, when it had no reference to the condition of public affairs, it had been committed more especially to the holy Psalmists

2. Neither the authors of the Messianic Psalms, nor the prophets give at any one time a full description of the Messiah; they rather confine themselves to certain features of his character. And here an important difference is found between them   The writers of the Messianic Psalms, in accordance with the nature of this species of poetry, generally take such views of Him, as were suggested by their own lives, circumstances and experience. Thus David represents the Messiah as a sufferer, surrounded by powerful enemies, and at last after a severe conflict attaining to victory and glory   Solomon beholds him, as the sovereign of a vast, peaceful and prosperous kingdom , and sees the most distant nations paying their reverential homage by bringing Him presents   But the prophets, on the contrary, were not governed in their representations of the Messiah so much by their own experience and circumstances, as by the necessities of those to whom they spake, and the effect which they wished to produce on their minds. Hence it has happened that in their writings He is presented to us on the whole more in his state of exaltation, than as suffering and making expiation for us   It was one great object in revealing his future advent to the prophets to influence the great body of the people, who were not prepared for the doctrine of a suffering and atoning Messiah   How much the Messianic predictions of the prophets were modified by the necessities of the times, is especially evident from a comparison of the first part of Isaiah and Zechariah, with the second   The first part of Isaiah consists of a number of separate pieces, which were made public at the time they were composed. Here the appearance of the Messiah in his humiliation is only alluded to; while on the contrary he is constantly exhibited in his glory with a view to encourage the people under their outward calamities. The second part, on the other hand, which forms one connected whole, was probably not made known to the public; it was designed rather for posterity than the existing generation, and not so

much for the people at large, as for the pious individuals among them. Here therefore the prophet might exhibit the character of the Messiah in its full extent; and give prominence to those important features which in the first part were kept more in the back ground And thus we find in the second part, the idea of the teaching, suffering, and atoning Messiah every where prevalent.* So also in the prophet Zechariah In the first part, the discourses all relate to existing circumstances. It was here the main object of the prophet to tranquilize and console the minds of the people, who were disquieted and cast down, by a comparison of the present depressed condition of the theocracy, with its former prosperity and splendor In this part, therefore, we behold the Messiah only in his glory, and prepared to raise the now fallen theocracy to great honor, and extend its sway over the heathen nations Whatever might damp this joyful hope is kept out of view. In the second part, on the contrary, which was probably not published, the prophet is more at liberty. Here he announces the appearing of the Messiah in an humble condition, describes his death, the rejection of the greater part of the people, their restoration after having been purified by severe chastisement With these considerations before us we shall not be surprised, if we meet with the Messiah only in His exalted state in those prophets whose predictions were delivered as a whole in public, and related to the existing condition of the people, as was the case with Ezekiel, Jeremiah, Micah, Hosea and Amos,† and we shall not be disposed to regard as essential a discrepancy, which is owing entirely to a difference of circumstances. To each prophet such a revelation of the future was always made as accorded with the times in which he lived.

3. We cannot perceive in the Messianic predictions of the pro-

---

* It is evident from this, with what justice Bertholdt Einl s 1383, infers from the difference of the Messianic prediction in the first, from that in the second part, that they cannot be the work of the same author. That the Messiah in lowliness was not unknown to the writer of the first part, but that he carefully avoided rendering him prominent, appears from the slight notice chap xi, where the Messiah, as well as in chap liii, is compared with a sprout which shoots up from the roots of a tree, which has been cut down

† Pareau l c p 512 "Cum eorundem, quibus mala vel ingruebant, vel jam aderant gravissima temporum indole, conveniebat, ut promissus Davidis filius eo plerumque informaretur modo, qui istorum malorum metum sensumve leniret eorumque gravitatem compensaret"

phets, as we do in the Pentateuch,* a gradual advancement in clearness and precision. Isaiah sees the Messiah as distinctly as Malachi, and his prophecies, and those of Micah contain more special characteristics of him, than are to be found in Jeremiah and Ezekiel. This is explained by the circumstance, that each prophet always received his predictions directly from above, adapted to his own capacity which may have been greater in the case of the earlier, than the later prophets, and also to the necessities and the comprehension of those for whose benefit they were intended. But still the Messianic prediction, on the whole, continued to be more and more fully developed. Special traits were revealed to individuals along with such as were common to all. Some particulars, as for example, that the Messiah should honor the second temple with his presence, could, from the nature of the case, be made known only to the later prophets.

We here present a brief summary of the predictions of the Messiah by the prophets, following the chronological order.

1. *Prophets under Uzziah, Jotham, Ahaz, and Hezekiah, from 811—699 before Christ.*

1. Hosea. Principal passages: chap. 2 1—3 16—25. 3 5. 14 2 etc. The coming of the Messiah stands in contrast with the threatening that the people should be carried away captive by the Assyrians. This calamity shall be followed by a time of mercy and blessing. The Israelites shall return to Jehovah, and to the great and godlike descendant of David. Jehovah will then grant them forgiveness of sins, and again bestow upon them his ancient love. All strife shall cease. They shall enjoy peace and prosperity, who are reconciled to God.

---

* De Wette, Dogm 1 § 139, asserts the contrary, but without sufficient reason. His assertion that at first there was only the general hope of better times, unconnected with a person, rests on the groundless hypothesis, that Joel is the oldest of all the prophets, and is contradicted by the predictions of the Messiah as a person in the Pentateuch and in the Psalms. Hosea by no means connects, as is essential, his Messianic hopes with the house of David in a general way, but he expects a particular descendant of David, as a Restorer. How little reason there is to infer, from the fact that many chief points were left unnoticed by Hosea and Micah, a gradual progress of the Messianic hope, is evident from the circumstance that this is the case also with several of the later prophets, as Jeremiah and Ezekiel, who must nevertheless have been acquainted with the earlier and more definite predictions of Isaiah.

2 Amos. The threatening relates to the carrying away of the Israelites and Jews into captivity, and their dispersion into all lands; the prediction of prosperity, chap. ix, both to the return from captivity, and the introduction of the Messiah's reign. A great king shall arise from the fallen family of David, and restore it to its ancient splendor. Through him the theocracy shall be extended over the heathen who had heretofore been enemies, or strangers to it. Rich blessings shall be granted; even the inanimate creation shall assume new glory. The only special characteristic, is the appearing of the Messiah, when the family of David had fallen into obscurity.

3 Isaiah. Of all the prophets he is the richest in specific predictions of the Messiah. The principal passages are chap. 2. 4. 7. 14. 9. 11. 32. 42. 49. 50. 52. 13 etc. 53. 55. 1—5. 59. 20. 21. 61. Besides, there are many representations of the times of the Messiah, where he is not personally introduced. The prophet's view of the Messiah is for the most part connected with the prospect of deliverance from the Assyrians and also from the Babylonian exile. But still he is so full of the hope of the Redeemer, that he often makes a transition to it from other subjects. See for example, the prophecy against Egypt, chap. xix, and that against Tyre, chap. xxiii. In both instances the prophet concludes the representation of the calamities which were soon to fall upon these countries, with the prediction of their future prosperity when blessed with true religion. It is characteristic of Isaiah, on the one hand, that he discriminates so severely between the pious and the ungodly part of the nation, and so repeatedly excludes the latter from all the blessings expected in future times,—and on the other, that he dwells with such delight on the future enlargement of the theocracy by the accession of the heathen. His predictions plainly show, that he clearly perceived the connexion of the preparatory arrangements of Divine providence, with the great end to be accomplished, and that the former never usurped the place of the latter in his estimation. The Messianic predictions of Isaiah may be divided into two classes; those in which the glorified Messiah filled the whole vision of the prophet, and those in which he beheld him in his lowly condition, although at the same time he saw the glorious result of his humiliation. To the former class belong all that are found in the first part, and the LV and LIX chapters in the second part, besides many general descriptions of the Messiah's kingdom. The contents of these prophecies are as follows; after the people shall have been severely punished by the

hand of God, and long involved in the darkness of sin, and the calamities which result from it, the great Restorer shall be born of a virgin; he shall be truly God, and at the same time a descendant of the family of David, which before his advent will have fallen into obscurity. This king, who shall be great, wise, and righteous, and filled with the Spirit of God, shall dispel the darkness of those who receive him, free them from the Divine displeasure to which they stand exposed, and make them happy. The region of Galilee shall especially experience his blessings. The theocracy hitherto confined to a single people, shall become coextensive with the globe itself. Its holy members shall be blessed with perfect inward and outward peace; even external nature shall be freed from evil, after the destruction of sin which caused it, and restored to its original condition. The latter class consists of the remaining predictions of the second part. Here Isaiah represents the Messiah as an illustrious prophet and teacher, who, endowed by God with rich gifts, humbles himself and comes in meekness and lowliness to seek those who are lost. He announces the severe sufferings, the scorn and contempt of the people which await him, as well as his subsequent exaltation by the hand of God, the extension of his religion over the people of the earth, who shall humbly submit to his authority. The LIII chapter differs in one respect from the remaining portions of this class; his vicarious satisfaction is here brought distinctly forward as the *end to be accomplished* by the Messiah's sufferings. The special characteristics are: besides the descent of the Messiah from David, his Deity, his atonement, his death, his birth of a virgin, 7: 14, at a time when the royal family of David had already sunk into total obscurity, 11: 1, 53. 2, his being endowed with the fulness of the Divine Spirit, 11. 2. 42. 1, the peculiar blessing conferred on the region of Galilee, 8. 23, the opposition and unbelief of the covenant people, XLIX, his burial with a rich man, 53: 9.

4. Micah. Principal passages: chap. 4. 1—8. 5. 7. 7, etc. The promise is connected with the threatening of an entire desolation of Jerusalem by the Chaldeans. In the little town of Bethlehem, where the family of David originated, an illustrious Ruler shall be born, whose origin is eternal, and his majesty and his glory Divine. He shall make the theocracy glorious, and extend it over the heathen from one end of the earth to the other. The subjects of the Divine kingdom shall dwell in peace and prosperity under his reign. All that was opposed to the revealed will of God in former times shall be

done away, and all enemies of the theocracy be destroyed. The chief features of his prophecy are the divine and human nature of the Messiah, and what is peculiar to this prophet, his birth in Bethlehem.

5. Joel, who probably belongs to this period. Object of the threatening—the desolation of the land by the Chaldeans. Messianic passage, chap III. No representation of the Messiah as a person As a characteristic mark of the times of the Messiah, the description of which is connected with that of the deliverance from captivity, the outpouring of the Holy Spirit upon all men without distinction is particularly set forth. With this is connected the description of the heavy punishment, which shall be inflicted upon all the enemies of the kingdom of God.

2. *Prophets, shortly before and during the Babylonish captivity.*

1 Zephaniah. Object of the threatening: the carrying away of all the inhabitants of the kingdom of Judah, and the desolation of the land by the Chaldeans. The predicted salvation, chap 3 9—20, relates at the same time to the deliverance from captivity, and the times of the Messiah. The covenant people shall become as righteous and pure from all former defilement as prosperous and happy. The heathen also, as the prophet had already declared, chap 2 11, after having been severely chastised, shall embrace the true religion, and give themselves with one accord to the service of God.

2 Jeremiah. The return from the Babylonian exile, and the times of the Messiah are not always accurately distinguished by this prophet. The chief passages are chap. 3 16—18. 23. 1—8. 31: 31 etc. 33 14—26 After severe sufferings of the people, Jehovah will raise up a great descendant of David, through whom they shall obtain remission of their sins, and be delivered and blessed. Through his medium the old and imperfect covenant shall be succeeded by a new and better one What the law as an outward institution could not accomplish under the former dispensation, God shall effect under the new by writing his law in the hearts of his people. Chief characteristics: the cessation of the Levitical worship, chap. 3 16, the extirpation of sin, the writing of the law on the hearts of the people, and the establishment of a new covenant, 31. 31 etc. 23· 6. 33· 16

3 Ezekiel. Principal passages, chap 11. 17, etc. 17. 22—24. 21: 29—32. 34: 22—30. 36 25, etc. 37· 21—28. chap. 40—48. Object of the threatening; the Babylonish exile; the Messianic

prediction connected with the promise of deliverance from captivity. From the fallen family of David, deprived of its dominion on account of the crimes of the people, and after the Israelites shall have returned from exile, an exalted king shall arise, by the wonderful interposition of Jehovah, in whose sovereignty and protection the nations of the earth shall put their trust, and learn to know the true God as the supreme disposer of all things. Jehovah will then cleanse the people of Israel from sin and give them a new heart and a new spirit, he will take away the stony heart out of their flesh, and give them an heart of flesh, and free them from impurity. The theocracy shall be far more illustrious than ever before. The Spirit of God shall go forth from it like a living stream and quicken into life a world dead in sin. The characteristic representation of the agency of the Holy Spirit under the new dispensation is worthy of special notice.

4. Daniel. Principal places, chap. 2 44. 7 13. 14. 26. 27. 9. 25—27. After the overthrow of the four great kingdoms of the world, the Messiah shall establish his kingdom, which shall extend over all people and endure forever. The deliverance from exile shall not synchronize with the times of the Messiah; Jerusalem shall first be built again, but in troublous times; then at a future period the Messiah's kingdom shall come and with it the fulfilment of the prophecies, the forgiving of sins, and the giving of the Holy Ghost. The Messiah shall indeed suffer a violent death; but his death shall be avenged by a severe judgment upon the faithless people, by the ruin of the state and the sanctuary. But on the other hand, he will renew the covenant with those who acknowledge his dignity. Chief traits: the union of the divine and human natures in the Messiah, indicated by his appearing at the same time in the clouds of heaven, and in the form of a man, 7 13, the specification of the time which should elapse before his coming, the clear distinction between the deliverance from captivity and the times of the Messiah, the characteristic designation of the nature of the New Testament economy, the Messiah's violent death, the destruction of Jerusalem.

3 *Prophets after the captivity.*

It is peculiar to these prophets, that in them the intimate connexion disappears between the prospect of deliverance from the exile and that of the redemption by the Messiah, which we find in most of the earlier prophets, and thus the latter becomes more plain and definite.

1 Haggai, chap 2· 6—9 In him the Messianic prediction is suited to the occasion on which it was uttered He aims to console those who had seen the glory of the former temple. After a great political revolution shall have taken place, the glory of the second temple shall surpass that of the first. All the heathen nations shall seek admission into the theocracy Chief trait: the commencement of the Messianic times during the existence of the second temple.

2 Zechariah. His predictions of the Messiah are next to those of Isaiah, the most marked and definite. Chief places chap 2 3 8—10 6 9—15 8 18 etc 9 9 10· 11—14 The predictions of the first part, in accordance with their design to console those who were distressed at beholding the small beginning of the new State, are of a more general character and leave many weighty points untouched. The Messiah shall unite the priestly and the regal dignity Through him the sins of the land shall be blotted out, rich blessings be introduced, and the theocracy immeasurably enlarged, and extended over the heathen nations Collecting the features scattered over the second part, they form the following image · Jehovah at some future period shall interpose once more in favor of his poor people in a remarkable manner He will cause the great and promised king of Israel, who is united with himself by oneness of nature, to appear in humiliation and obscurity But deceived by their corrupt leaders, the greater portion of the people shall despise the mild guidance of this good Shepherd; they shall even pierce him through His flock, though scattered at first, shall be collected and guarded by Jehovah, and his death shall be followed by a divine judgment which shall sweep away by far the greatest portion of the Jewish people. The kingdom of this illustrious messenger of God shall be extended over all nations. The small remnant of the Jews, after being purified by manifold sufferings, shall finally be reconciled to Jehovah He will pour out his spirit upon them in after times. This shall move them to devote themselves to him whom they had pierced, with the deepest grief for their sins. Then shall they obtain the pardon of their transgressions Every thing shall be put away which under the former theocracy was contrary to the revealed will of God Finally the enemies of the theocracy shall once more assault it with united strength, and greatly afflict it But the Lord will defend his people, confer new glory upon his church, and annihilate its obstinate enemies. Chief traits the mysterious oneness of the Messiah with Jehovah, chap. 13 7, the union of the regal dignity with that of

the high priest, chap 3: 8—10 6: 9—15, the entrance of the Messiah into Jerusalem upon an ass, 9: 9, his being betrayed for thirty pieces of silver, 11: 12, his death, 12. 10. 13: 7, the unbelief of the greater portion of the Jews, their rejection and punishment, 11. 13 8, their final restoration, 12. 10, etc. 13: 9.

3. Malachi, chap. 1: 11. 2: 17—3: 6. 13—24. The Messiah, who is a partaker of the Divine nature, will not appear, as the Jews expected, to inflict vengeance on the heathen, but to institute a strict examination among the covenant people themselves. His appearance shall bring destruction to the ungodly, but blessings to the righteous. He will send a prophet like Elias before his coming. Should the end of his advent not be attained, the inevitable ruin of the land must be the consequence. The Lord will then collect for himself true worshippers from among all the heathen. The Messianic prediction in Malachi is intended not to console, but threaten and chastise: and thus the prominence given to certain points, and the passing over of others is explained. Chief traits · the Divine nature of the Messiah exhibited by the prophet, with peculiar clearness, his coming while the second temple remains, the punishment to be inflicted by him on the Jewish people. Entirely peculiar to Malachi is the sending of a forerunner of the Messiah.

CHAPTER III

THE DEITY OF THE MESSIAH IN THE OLD TESTAMENT.

That the Messiah according to the predictions of the prophets, would fully possess the human nature, is doubted by no one. He was not to make himself known like Jehovah and the angels in the Old Testament by a transient manifestation, but he was to be born, Is 7: 14. Mich. 5. 3, and grow up by degrees, Is. xi and liii. In reference to his human nature and origin, he is called a sprout of David, Is 7: 23. 5: 33, 15, the sprout of the root of Jesse, Is. 11. 1, and the fruit of the land, Is. 4: 2.

But as to the question, whether the Deity of the Messiah is taught in the prophecies of the Old Testament, there is less agreement.

The negative is pretty generally maintained by the recent critics. Thus Hufnagel (Bibl. Theol I. p 373, seq.), Bretschneider (Dogm. 1 p 429), Ammon (Bibl. Theol. und Einheit der evang Kirche II. 2. p. 51), De Wette (Dogm. 1. § 188 200), Gesenius (zu Jes 9 5), though the two last acknowledge the Divine nature of the Messiah in Dan. 7. 13, 14, Baumgarten-Crusius (Bibl. Theol p. 379 seq) and others On the other hand the existence of this doctrine in the Old Testament is maintained in accordance with the ancient church, by Michaelis (Dogm. Tub. 1785), Jahn (Vaticc. Mess. II, p. 235), Rosenmuller (zu Jes 7 14. 9. 5 Micah 5. 1), Knapp (Dogm 1. p. 226, seq) Pareau (instit. interpr. V. T. p. 194), Hahn (Dogm. p. 215, seq) etc

It ought not in the first place to be doubted, that Christ himself found this doctrine in the writings of the Old Testament He proved, Matt 22. 41, etc, the Deity of the Messiah from Ps cx, in opposition to the Pharisees, who expected him to possess merely the human nature. It is obvious that, unless we make this supposition, his whole argument is without meaning; and assertions, such as that he designed merely to excite to a more careful examination of the scriptural basis of faith in the Messiah, or only to exhibit the firmness of a higher Messianic view and hope, (words which convey no clear and definite thought) are sufficiently refuted by an unprejudiced inspection of the passage.

But independently of this testimony of Christ, an unbiassed examination of the passages of the Old Testament shows that this view of the ancient critics has originated in doctrinal prejudice. There are distinct passages, which prove that the sacred writers regarded the Divine nature, as united with the human nature of the Messiah, since either names, attributes, or works, which belong exclusively to God, are ascribed to him, and sometimes with a distinct contrast between his divinity and his humanity. We here present these passages in one view, while we refer to the critical examination of them in the preceding or ensuing pages of this work.

Ps. 2. 7, the Messiah is called the Son of God, not in a figurative, but proper sense. V. 12 the punishment of his foes is ascribed to him, and the rebellious are admonished to seek his protection Ps. 45 7, 8, the Messiah is called God Ps 110 1, David calls him his Lord V. 5 he receives the name אֲדֹנָי which belongs to God alone, and the punishment of his enemies is allotted to him.

Isa. 4 2 he is called צֶמַח יְהוָה *sprout of Jehovah*, that is, son of

Jehovah. In contradistinction to this definition of his Divinity, he is called in reference to his human nature פְּרִי הָאָרֶץ, the fruit of the land, he who should be born in Judah, or come forth from the house of Judah. Chap 7 14, as the humanity of the Messiah is indicated by his being born of a virgin, so is his Divine nature by the appellation Immanuel, *deus in terra*, God become man. The distinctive marks of his Divine nature are especially accumulated in Isa. 9· 5. He there receives first the name פֶּלֶא, *wonderful*, to indicate that he was exalted above the ordinary course of nature in his being and his works; next אֵל גבור, the mighty God, and then Father of eternity, that is, eternal. On the other hand his human nature and origin are designated by the words · "unto us a child is born." In v. 6 in the same manner as in the LXXII Ps eternity is ascribed to him and his dominion Chap 11: 4, Divine omnipotence in exercising the right of punishing his enemies is ascribed to him. As God, he inflicts punishment by his almighty word alone. According to v 10 the heathen shall devoutly seek him as an object of worship.

Micah 5 1, in opposition to his temporal origin from Bethlehem and his birth of a woman, his eternal preexistence is declared. "And thou Bethlehem—out of thee shall he come forth unto me, whose goings forth have been of old, from everlasting." V 3, the power and majesty of Jehovah are ascribed to him Hos. 3 5 it is said, "after that shall the children of Israel return and seek the Lord their God and David their king, i. e seek the Messiah." This must be a religious seeking, since the Israelites are to seek the Messiah in the same manner as Jehovah. Besides the word בִּקֵּשׁ often means "to strive to obtain communion with God and become the object of his favor." It is probable that the Messiah in the same verse is called טוב יְהוָה, "the goodness of Jehovah, or the revealer of his glory" The passage, Mal. 3 1, is especially clear. There Jehovah says he will send a Messenger, who shall prepare the way before him; and immediately after it is said, that when this has taken place, the Messiah will appear. The appearing of the Messiah therefore is identified with that of Jehovah. The Messiah receives the name הָאָדוֹן, which it is confessed is otherwise given only to the Most High God. To this Most High God, the head of the theocracy, and the king of Israel, the temple is otherwise always appropriated as his own possession, but according to Malachi it belongs to the Messiah He must then be truly God, united to Jehovah by an eternal oneness of being V. 2, a divine work, the judgment of the ungodly, is attributed to him, which is ascribed to no one but Jehovah.

Daniel also, chap. 7 13, 14, perceived the union of a human and a superhuman nature in the Messiah. He possesses indeed the form of man, but appears in the clouds of heaven.

Many declarations of the participation of the Messiah in the Divine essence, and of a mysterious union with Jehovah are found in Zechariah. Thus chap 12 v. 10, Jehovah speaks of himself as pierced, because this was done to the Messiah. Chap. 13 v. 7, Jehovah calls the Shepherd, who according to chap. 11 13 and 12. 10, is one with himself· "the man that was his fellow," and therefore describes the Messiah, who is associated with himself in an incomprehensible manner by a unity of essence, as likewise distinct from himself, in a manner equally incomprehensible

But the inquiry here arises, how can the doctrine of the Deity of the Messiah be reconciled with the fundamental doctrine of the religion of the Old Testament, the unity of God As a contradiction to this doctrine cannot be admitted, so does every passage, which ascribes to the Messiah Divine names, attributes, and works, at the same time virtually assert his essential oneness with Jehovah, while in the passages quoted from Malachi and Zechariah, it is expressly declared But would we more thoroughly understand the relation of Jehovah to the Messiah, as it was conceived by the Old Testament writers, we must institute a more extensive investigation respecting the character of the Messenger or Angel of God, (מַלְאַךְ הָאֱלֹהִים־ מַלְאַךְ אֱלֹהִים־מַלְאַךְ יְהוָֹה.) The New Testament makes us acquainted with God, the Father of Jesus Christ, as a spirit, who, being every where equally present, never manifests himself in a sensible form. But besides this concealed God, it makes known to us also a revealed God, associated with him by the oneness of their nature, the Son or λόγος, who has constantly filled up the infinite distance between the Creator and the creation, and been the Mediator in all the relations of God to the world and the human race; who, even before he became man in the person of Christ, was in all ages the light of the world, and to whom especially the whole direction of the visible theocracy belonged. Although this doctrine was first unfolded with perfect clearness in the New Testament, yet we find an essential distinction between the unrevealed and the revealed God, or the revealer of God even in the writings of the Old Testament We will here, in the first place, present in one view the principal passages, which speak of the messenger or angel of God; and then bring forward the proof, that they really contain the doctrine of a distinction between the concealed and the revealed God.*

Gen 16. 7, the angel of Jehovah is said to have found Hagar. V. 10, a work of God, the vast increase of Hagar's posterity is ascribed to him. V 11, he says that Jehovah had heard her distress, and thus predicates of Jehovah, what he had before said of himself. Moreover in V 13, Hagar expresses her astonishment that she had seen God and yet lived. Chap xviii, three men visit Abraham, who are afterwards, chap. 19. 1, called מַלְאָכִים. Abraham, who, as appears from the whole account, did not yet know his guests, (v. 3 instead of אֲדֹנָי should be read אֲדֹנִי) addresses himself chiefly to the one, whom he supposed, probably on account of the dignity of his person, to be superior to the rest. This angel afterwards, v. 14, 17 etc makes himself known as Jehovah. Having finished his discourse with Abraham he vanishes, and the two angels proceed alone towards Sodom, chap 19 1. V 24, this Jehovah, who is without doubt the same who elsewhere appears as מַלְאַךְ יְהוָה, is distinguished from Jehovah. "Then Jehovah rained upon Sodom and upon Gomorrah brimstone and fire from Jehovah out of heaven." It is true that after Calvin recent interpreters seek to explain away all that is extraordinary in this passage, by the remark, that in Hebrew the noun is often used in place of the pronoun. See Gesen. Lehrg p. 741. But then we cannot see the propriety of the phrase, *a semet ipso*, followed as it is by one of the same import, viz.. *out of heaven*. Others, as Bauer, Rosenmüller, Baumgarten-Crusius, connect, in opposition to the accents, *from Jehovah* with *fire and brimstone*, and regard the phrase as a designation of *lightning*, which in other places also, as '2 Kings 1. 12 and Job 1 16, is called *God's fire*. But this explanation also is unsatisfactory, because the rendering of גָּפְרִית וָאֵשׁ by *lightning*, rests on uncertain grounds, and does not correspond with the verb הִמְטִיר *to rain*, and even assuming the correctness of this interpretation, still the lightning had been already sufficiently characterized and distinguished from every fire arising from natural causes, by the expressions, "Jehovah rained," and "from heaven." At all events these explanations could not be admitted, unless the distinction between Jehovah, i. e., the *Messenger* of Jehovah who bears

---

* On the passages in Genesis see the treatise, Christus Deus in V T. libris histor p 1. sc Steinwender Königsb 1828

his name, because he possesses his nature, and Jehovah, did not elsewhere occur. Chap 21 17, the angel of God (מַלְאַךְ אֱלֹהִים) speaks to Hagar V. 18, he ascribes to himself a divine work, the increase of Hagar's posterity till they become a great people. Chap. 22 1, Abraham receives from God (הָאֱלֹהִים) the command to offer up his son. V. 11, when in the act of doing it, he is forbidden by the angel of Jehovah (מַלְאַךְ יְהוָה). This angel identifies himself with God, v. 13, in the words "Now I know that thou fearest God, since thou hast not withheld thy son, thine only son from *me.*" From the name, which Abraham gave to the place, v. 14, it is evident that he believed Jehovah himself appeared to him Chap. 31. 11, the angel of God (מַלְאַךְ הָאֱלֹהִים) appeared to Jacob in a dream. V. 13, the same person calls himself the God of Bethel, to whom Jacob had there made a vow, in reference to the event recorded in chap 28. 11 —22, where, in a night vision, a ladder had appeared to Jacob, on which the angels of God ascended and descended, and on the top of which stood Jehovah, who called himself the God of Abraham and Isaac, etc. The angel of God therefore here, identifies himself with Jehovah Gen. 32. 25, Jacob wrestles with one unknown, who afterwards makes himself known as God, by the name he gives to Jacob: Israel, one who wrestles with God, and the explanation of it · "thou hast wrestled with God," by the refusal to mention his own name, and lastly, by bestowing his blessing. Jacob names the place: Penuel, *face of God,* because he had there seen God face to face, and wonders that he is still alive.—The answer which אֱלֹהִים here gives to Jacob's inquiry after his name, corresponds entirely with that which was given, Judges 13 17, by the מַלְאַךְ יְהוָה to the same question. Hos. 12· 4, the same with whom Jacob wrestled, is called v 4 אֱלֹהִים, v. 5 מַלְאָךְ, v. 6 יְהוָה אֱלֹהֵי צְבָאוֹת. The angel therefore, is again identified with אֱלֹהִים and יְהוָה.— Gen. 48. 16, Jacob desires a blessing for the sons of Joseph from the God before whom his fathers had walked, who had taken care of his family, and from the *angel* who had been his protector (הַמַּלְאָךְ הַגֹּאֵל אֹתִי).

Exodus 3· 2 the angel of Jehovah appears to Moses in a flame of fire out of the midst of the bush V 4, it is said Jehovah saw that he drew near to see, and Elohim called to him out of the bush. V. 6 14—16 the angel of Jehovah ascribes to himself all the attributes of the true God, calls himself everlasting, the God of the patriarchs, Abraham, Isaac, and Jacob, and promises to deliver the Israelites from Egypt and inflict heavy punishment on their opposers. V. 5 Moses is commanded to put off his shoes from his feet, because the ground on which he stands is holy. V. 6 Moses covers his face because he is afraid to look upon God. From chap. 14. 19 it appears that the angel of God (מַלְאַךְ הָאֱלֹהִים) accompanied the Israelites on their march from Egypt, and that the pillar of cloud was the symbol of his presence. Chap. 23. 20 God says to the people, that he will send an angel before them, who shall guide them on their journey to the promised land. He admonishes them, carefully to obey him, because he was not an ordinary angel, but his name was in him (כִּי שְׁמִי בְּקִרְבּוֹ).* Chap. 32. 34, after the Israelites have sinned by worshipping the golden calf, Jehovah, i. e. the angel of Jehovah who has hitherto been their guide, refuses to conduct them any further himself, but says he will send his angel (מַלְאָכִי) before them, "for I will not go up in the midst of thee, for thou art a stiffnecked people lest I consume thee in the way," chap. 33. 3 At this sad intelligence the people are entirely inconsolable, v. 4. In consequence of their genuine repentance and the intercession of Moses Jehovah retracts the threatening, and says "my presence shall go with you;" i. e. I will myself be your conductor; (see Rosenm. on v. 14), unless we suppose, that he who is sent, as is often the case, speaks in the name of him who sends him, and then, *my presence* will mean, he who reveals me, the angel in whom my name is, chap. 23. 20 The latter opinion appears to be justified by Isaiah 63· 9, where he who is sent is called, as it seems, with distinct reference to this place, the angel of Jehovah's presence †

Num 20 16. The Israelites say, Jehovah had heard their prayers, and led them out of Egypt by an angel. (מַלְאָךְ)—the word is here entirely undefined, since there was no occasion to be precise. Chap. 22. 22, etc we meet with the angel of Jehovah in the history of Balaam.

Joshua 5: 14 As Joshua stands with his host before Jericho,

---

* Le Clerc remarks on this passage "Qui volunt τὴν δευτέραν τῆς τριαδὸς ὑπόστασιν e jugo Sinais montis loquutam (see Exod 3 with 20 3) angelum saltem creatum promitti hic fateantur oportet. Neque enim una eademque hypostasis sui nuntia esse potest" But this difficulty is only apparent, and is removed by the remark, that he who is sent here speaks in the person of him who sends him

† Com R Bechai on this passage · "Deus respondit Mosi facies meae ibunt Intelligit autem hac voce angelum illum, de quo scriptum est Jes LXIII. Angelus facierum ipsius juvit ipsos, h e angelus, qui est ipsa facies dei"

one unknown appears to him, with a drawn sword. To Joshua's question, whether he was friend or foe, he answered: "neither; but I am captain of the host of Jehovah," (שַׂר צְבָא יהוָה) that is, according to the constant usage of the language: not the leader—the protecting angel of Israel merely: but the Prince and commander of the angels, who are every where called the host of Jehovah. This Prince of angels claims for himself divine honor, precisely in the same way as the angel of Jehovah, (מַלְאַךְ יְהוָה) Ex. iii, by commanding Joshua to put off his shoes because the ground on which he stands is holy. Chap 6 2 he is called by the author of the narrative Jehovah For that we are not there to think of a Divine revelation imparted in another way to Joshua, as some interpreters suppose, is evident, since the appearance of this Prince of angels, who now for the first time gives directions to Joshua, would then be without an object.

Judges 2 1—4, the angel of Jehovah appears to the Israelites assembled in the place, which was afterwards called Bochim. He makes himself known as the person who brought them out of Egypt and led them into the land promised to their fathers, and says that in consequence of their disobedience, he will not drive out the heathen nations Chap 6· 11, the angel of Jehovah comes to Gideon V 14, he is called Jehovah At first being recognized by Gideon, he makes himself known by the words, "thou shalt deliver Israel, I send thee." Henceforth Gideon treats with him as if he were a Divine person, although for greater certainty he asks of him a sign that he was what he desired, and took him to be He addresses him, v. 15, by the name אֲדֹנִי, he begs permission, v. 18, to bring him an offering,* v. 21. The angel touches the offering with the end of

---

* Le Clerc, the author of the ex Hdb. on this passage, Winer on the word מנחה through a misapprehension of the following words. "and Gideon saw," etc suppose that Gideon did not desire to present an offering to the known angel of Jehovah, but to prepare a repast for him who was unknown. We will not urge against this the אֲדֹנִי v. 15, since it is possible, apart from the rest, that here, as Genesis 18, the original reading was אֲדֹנָי. The Seventy in some manuscripts have κύριέ μου, in others on the contrary, ἐν ἐμοί κύριε But how could Gideon regard the one who addressed him as a mere man, or at least, how could he suppose, that he wished to be regarded as such, as he had said to him, v 14 "I send thee," v 16 "I will be with thee and thou shalt smite the Midianites" On this supposition v 17 is entirely inexplicable, where Gideon desires him who had appeared to give a sign that he speaks with him Le Clerc here supplies בשם יהוה entirely without au-

his staff, when fire bursts forth from the rock and consumes it. In the mean time the angel suddenly disappears. V. 22, "and Gideon saw that it was the angel of Jehovah," that is, he was confirmed by the giving of the desired sign, and the sudden disappearance of the angel, in the conviction that a superhuman person had been discoursing with him. He now expresses his fear that he must die, since he had seen the angel of Jehovah face to face, but being in this respect pacified by Jehovah, he builds an altar, to which he gives the name, *Jehovah's peace*. Chap. 13. 3, the angel of Jehovah appears to the wife of Manoah. She indeed knows him not, but supposes him to be Divine from his majestic deportment. V 6, at his second appearance also he is not recognized at first by Manoah and his wife, as is expressly remarked v. 16 But he afterwards makes himself known, by refusing to give his name, because it is wonderful, by miraculously consuming the offering,* and disappearing in its flame. "Then Manoah was convinced that he was the angel of Jehovah." V 21, he now says to his wife, "we shall surely die, because we have seen God."

2 Kings 19 35 The angel of Jehovah destroys the Assyrian host, which threatened destruction to the theocracy.

Is. 63 9 it is said, "Jehovah was their helper, from every affliction he delivered them,† and the angel of his presence saved them In his love and in his pity he redeemed them; and he bare them, and carried them all the days of old." Here the angel of Jehovah is called the angel of his face, that is, the angel by which he makes himself known, as the human soul is expressed in the countenance. Compare the corresponding declarations concerning Christ ἀπαύγασμα τῆς δόξης καὶ χαρακτὴρ τῆς ὑποστάσεως τοῦ θεοῦ Heb. 1: 3; εἰκὼν τοῦ θεοῦ τοῦ ἀοράτου Col 1· 15. 2 Cor. 4· 4 and Ex. 23 20. Every thing is ascribed to Him which is elsewhere ascribed to Jehovah. He redeemed the Israelites, and watched over and cherished them as a tender mother does her child

We meet with מַלְאַךְ יְהֹוָה unusually often in Zechariah. From

---

thority. The relation, chap 13 15, where Manoah offers to prepare a repast for the angel of Jehovah, cannot here be compared, since there, v. 16, it is expressly remarked, that Manoah knew not that it was the angel of Jehovah

* This is only briefly intimated by the words וּמַפְלִא לַעֲשׂוֹת v 19 "he acted wonderfully" because the author took it for granted, that the reader would supply the rest from the similar relation, chap. 6

† "In omni angustia eorum non angustum fuit " Kocher.

him the prophet received all his revelations. He distinguishes him, chap. 2 12—15, from Jehovah of hosts, and says he is sent by him to the heathen to punish them for what they had done to the covenant people, and yet the prophet gives to him the name of Jehovah of hosts; comp 6 15 Chap. 3: 2, the same is called יְהוָה who, v. 1, had been named מַלְאַךְ יְהוָה. Chap. 12. 9 מַלְאַךְ יְהוָה is spoken of in connexion with אֱלֹהִים as if equal with him in dignity and glory

Ps 34 8, and 35 5 we find that ascribed to the angel of Jehovah, which is elsewhere ascribed to Jehovah himself, viz. the protection of the pious and the punishment of the ungodly.

Having made this simple representation of the fact, we now proceed to examine the different explanations which have been given of it. 1. The opinion most widely prevalent is that, which makes the angel of Jehovah, not a person united with God by oneness of nature, but an inferior angel through whom God executes his commands, speaks and acts. That divine names, works and predicates are ascribed to these inferior angels, and divine worship rendered to them is explained by the supposition, that they kept their own personality out of view; and while executing God's commissions, spoke and acted in his person, and that those to whom they were sent, as well as the sacred writers, looked beyond the mere agents to Him by whom they were employed It is highly probable that this was the opinion of Origen He says, Opp t III f. 229, ed. Ruaei, in reference to Ex III: ἦν δὲ ὁ θεὸς ἐκεῖ ἐν τῷ ἀγγέλῳ θεωρούμενος. It was defended with peculiar zeal and ability by Augustin The principal passage is, de trinitate l. III. c. 11 "Proinde illa omnia, quae patribus visa sunt, cum deus illis secundum suam dispensationem temporibus congruam praesentaretur, per creaturam facta esse, manifestum est Et si nos latet, quomoda ea ministris angelis fecerit, per angelos tamen esse facta non ex nostro sensu dicimus, ne cuiquam videamus plus sapere, sed sapimus ad temperantiam, sicut deus nobis partitus est mensuram fidei, et credimus, propter quod et loquimur. Exstat enim auctoritas divinarum scripturarum," etc (He appeals to Heb 2 1, where the law given by the ministry of angels is contrasted with the Gospel published by the Lord himself)—" Sed ait aliquis cur ergo scriptum est dixit dominus ad Moysen, et non potius: dixit angelus ad Moysen? Quia cum verba judicis praeco pronuntiat, non scribitur in Gestis · ille praeco dixit, sed ille judex, sic etiam loquente propheta sancto, etsi dicamus propheta dixit, nihil aliud quam dominum, dixisse intelligi volumus. Et si dicamus Dominus dixit, prophetam non subtrahimus, sed quis per eum dixerit admonemus. — — Sed jam satis quantum existimo demonstratum est, quod antiquis patribus nostris ante incarnationem Salvatoris, cum deus apparere dicebatur, voces illae ac species corporales per angelos factae sunt, sive ipsis loquentibus vel agentibus aliquid ex persona dei, sicut etiam prophetas solere ostendimus; sive assumentibus ex creatura, quod ipsi non essent, ubi deus figurate demonstraretur hominibus, quod genus significationum, nec prophetas omisisse, multis exemplis docet scriptura."—See tract. 3 in Jo 17. 18 de civ. d. 16, 29.—Similar to this is the language of Jerome on Gal. 3· 19 (Opp ed. Frft t. 9 p 138): "Quod autem ait lex ordinata per angelos, hoc vult intelligi, quod in omni V. T., ubi angelus primum visus refertur et postea quasi deus loquens inducitur, angelus quidem vere ex ministris pluribus quicunque sit visus, sed in illo mediator loquatur, qui dicat: ego sum deus Abraham, deus Isaac, deus Jacob Nec mirum si deus loquatur in angelis, cum etiam per angelos, qui in hominibus sunt, loquatur deus in prophetis, dicente Aggeo et ait angelus, qui loquebatur in me, ac deinceps inferente: haec dicit dominus omnipotens.* Neque enim angelus, qui esse dictus fuerat in propheta ex sua-persona audebat loqui: haec dicit dominus omnipotens" The same view is briefly and forcibly expressed by Gregory (M mor l 28 c 1): "Modo angeli, modo dominus vocantur, quia angelorum vocabulo exprimuntur, qui exterius ministrabant, et appellatione domini ostenditur, qui eis interius praeerat." At a later period this opinion was defended by several Jewish interpreters, as Abenezra, who remarks on Ex. 3· 2. השלוח ידבר בלשון שולחו, "He who is sent speaks in the name of him, that sent him." It was afterwards gladly embraced by many Romish interpreters, as well as by the Socinians and Arminians. See Grotius, zu Ex 20. Clericus, zu Gen. 16. 13 18. 1. Ex. 20: 1. 23. 20 † Nor has it been without defenders in recent

---

* Jerome had in view the passages of Zechariah chaps 1 9 13 14. 2 7 (comp v 12) where after the example of the Seventy (ὁ λαλῶν ἐν ἐμοί) he translates the words הַמַּלְאָךְ הַדֹּבֵר בִּי by "Qui loquebatur in me"

† "Nomen Jehovae si proprie loquamur, non tribuitur angelis, sed deo in iis apparenti, quemadmodum nulla ratione instrumenti habita, ei, qui instrumento utitur actio tribui solet —Nec periculum fuit, ne Israelitae pro deo angelum propterea colerent, obversabatur enim eorum animis deus deorum, coeli et terrae creator, seu ipse loqueretur, seu per interpretem angelum, nihil intererat, recte ad eum ferebatur eorum cultus."

times Among others, Vater on Gen. 16: 7, Gesenius on the word מַלְאָךְ and on Isaiah 63. 9, Bretschneider Dogm. 1 p 429, who however hesitates between this and the hypothesis to be brought forward under No. III, Baumgarten-Crusius Bibl Dogm p 307, Schmieder in his acute dissertation: Nova interpretatio l. Gal. 3· 19, p. 28 seq.

The advocates of this hypothesis were influenced by very different motives The Fathers, to whom we have referred, believed themselves compelled to adopt it by certain passages in the New Testament The Romanists were actuated by the desire to find some scriptural authority for the worship of angels the Socinians were influenced by their dislike of the orthodox doctrine concerning the trinity, Grotius and his followers by their low esteem for the Old Testament, and also by their views of God which were derived rather from reason than Scripture; and the rationalists by the dread of here encountering a mystery, and a preparation for the Christian doctrine of the trinity.

We now proceed to examine this hypothesis We cannot here agree with all its earlier opposers,* and with its latest assailant, in maintaining, that the supposition is in itself considered inadmissible, that the angels might speak and act in God's name, and be addressed and regarded as God The passages, however, by which Le Clerc on Gen. 16. 13 would show, that it was not unusual for those who are sent to speak in the person of him who sent them,† are not conclusive, since in them the mention of him who sends always precedes, and the persons sent give notice that they speak not in their own name, but in that of Him who sent them The examples would be analogous only in case the angel of Jehovah had on every occasion, when about to speak and act in His person, declared . " God has sent me to speak or to do this " But the defenders of this hypothesis have no occasion to go so far for their reply to the objection Le Clerc here combats. It is furnished more completely by the Scripture itself. Gen chap 19. 18, Lot addresses both angels with the name אֲדֹנָי which belongs to God alone, and the following words : " Behold now, thy servant hath found grace in thy sight, and thou hast magnified

---

* The most important among them are. Deyling (Obss zu Gen 48 15, 16, obss miscc II 74 seq und zu Ex III, l c V 1 seq), Vitringa (zu Isa. 63. 9), Vitringa fil (de lucta Jacobi, bibl Brem cl 1 fasc 6 p 773 seq), Jahn (hermeneut p 112), Stier (Christus der Engel Jehovah s, in den Andeutungen l p 222 seq), Steinwender l c

† 1 Kings 3 2, 3 Luke 7· 6 Quinctil instit or IV 1

thy mercy, which thou hast shewed unto me in saving my life" etc., show that he beheld and addressed in the person of the messengers Him who sent them. In like manner, v. 21, the angels also answer not in their own person, but in the person of Jehovah "see I have accepted thee concerning this thing also" etc.* It is true that the latest defender of this hypothesis,† has endeavored, like Justin Martyr in his dialogue with Trypho, to avoid the difficulty by the supposition, that Jehovah may have suddenly returned, after the two angels had discoursed alone with Lot. But there is not in the text the smallest foundation for this supposition, it is rather shown to be erroneous by v. 18, where it is expressly said, "and Lot spake to them" (אֲלֵהֶם), evidently to the same who, v. 17, had led him out of the city and commanded him to flee to the mountains.—Another argument is supplied by the passages in which the prophets are said to do what they foretell. Thus, for example, Jacob says of Simeon and Levi: "I will divide them in Jacob, and scatter them in Israel."‡ Jer. 1. 10, God says to the prophet: "See I have this day set thee over the nations and over the kingdoms, to root out, and to pull down and to destroy and to throw down, to build and to plant." Comp. Gen. 27. 37. Ez. 13. 19. 32. 18. 43. 2. It is true indeed that most interpreters explain these passages, by ascribing to the active verbs a declarative meaning; but since the same power of God which gave the prediction accomplishes also its fulfilment, it is far more natural to suppose that to be ascribed to the prophets, which the power of God that works in them as instruments would perform, and these passages can be adduced with more propriety in confirmation of this hypothesis, since the personality of the angels might be more easily kept out of view, than that of the prophets, inasmuch as the appearance of the former was in general so indistinct and transient.

Nevertheless there are other reasons, which are conclusive against it

---

* Calvin on this passage: "Quum duos videat, sermonem ad unum direxit unde colligitur Lot non substitisse in angelis, quin satis persuasus erat, neque proprium illis esse imperium, nec salutem suam in eorum manibus esse positam. Eorum vero conspectu non secus ac speculo ad contemplandam dei faciem utitur."

† Steinwender l. c. p. 22.

‡ The objection of Steinwender l. c. p. 13, against the application of this analogy is unjust, that the prophets never attribute to themselves as an action what they announce as future.

1. There is a grammatical objection which is of itself decisive This hypothesis presupposes that without any angel in particular being specified, sometimes one, and sometimes another is the subject of the discourse. But instead of this it is always, *the* angel of God, one distinguished from all the rest, who makes his appearance. Even the words מַלְאַךְ אֱלֹהִים cannot be translated *an* angel of God. It is true that the name אֱלֹהִים as originally an appellative, often retains the article, but it is not therefore the less treated as a *nomen proprium* * In addition to this appellation מַלְאַךְ הָאֱלֹהִים with the article and מַלְאַךְ יְהוָה. the latter of which can never be otherwise translated than the "angel of Jehovah;" see Ewald Gramm. § 305, 308, are used interchangeably with it. The neglect of this rule of grammar by Augustin is not surprising, since he was confined to the Latin version whose ambiguous *angelus Jehovae* allowed his interpretation, but it is strange that it should have been disregarded by so many recent critics,† and that even Gesenius himself on Isaiah 63 9 should speak of *an* angel who had conducted the Israelites through the desert Isaiah 63. 9 also refers to a definite angel. When Jehovah there says, "the angel of my presence saved them," we cannot explain this language, as Gesenius has done, by *an* angel of Jehovah without doing violence to grammar. For the *suff.* belongs not to the *terminus consequens* of the *construct state*, but to the complex idea, Ewald § 306

2 But it may be further shown, that this definite angel of God is by no means one of an ordinary kind, but one exalted above all created angels. We here leave out of sight every thing that can possibly be explained by the hypothesis that the angel may have spoken in the name of Jehovah, although this hypothesis, is rendered less probable by the fact, that wherever the angel of Jehovah appears, this change so constantly occurs, but never in the case of any other angel. There is sufficient evidence besides to prove the truth of our position The angel who represents Jehovah is accurately distinguished from all others in the relation in Gen. xviii. The two an-

---

* See Ewald Gramm p. 569: but when these words, (the *appellativa* which have passed over into *nomina propria*) lose the article, they still constantly retain in the language partly from their origin, partly from their meaning, the same power and value, as the *nomina* with the article

† Thus e g Schnurrer (spec. comm. Arab. R. Tanchum p. 49), understands Judges 2 1—4 by the מַלְאַךְ יְהוָה a prophet, which explanation is already refuted, to mention no other, by this grammatical objection alone.

gels who accompany him always appear in the back ground, and are manifestly his inferiors. So also chap. 28: 11—22, Jehovah, or as he is called, chap. 31. 11, the angel of God, stands on the top of the ladder, and the angels descend and ascend upon it. This distinction is very manifest in Ex. 23. 20, where Jehovah gives to the Israelites, as a leader, the angel in whom his name is, i. e. who is a partaker of his nature,* compared with chap xxxiii, where the people were deeply afflicted by the declaration of this their Divine leader, that he would no longer conduct them himself, but would give them over to an angel, one who did not like himself possess the omnipotence of God. How much Le Clerc was embarrassed by this passage, is evident from his remark upon it. Jehovah's angel also in Joshua v, represents himself as higher than all created angels, where he first names himself the prince of angels, and then claims Divine honor. We are led to the same conclusion by the appellation "the angel of the Lord's face," Is. LXIII, which can relate to nothing else, than the perfect revelation of the Divine being. To this evidence must be added the passages, where those, to whom the angel of God appeared, express the conviction, that they had seen God "face to face," and at the same time the fear that they must die. These passages incontestibly prove that men perceived in the angel of Jehovah something more than a created angel. For we no where find the slightest reason to suppose that the sight of such an angel was thought to endanger life.

II. Still easier of refutation is another hypothesis advanced by Herder (Heb Poesie II. 47), and approved by Rosenmuller, although the latter varies in his explanation of the different passages. According to this the angel of Jehovah is nothing more than a designation of a natural cause, or of a visible sign, by which Jehovah makes known his presence. Thus, Ex III, the burning bush, and on the journey through the desert the pillar of cloud, was this angel. We here mention only some of the numerous objections, to which this hypothesis is liable.

1. Were it true, then, wherever an appearance of the angel of Jehovah was mentioned, it would be connected with an operation of nature. But this is the case only in the two instances of the burning bush, and the pillar of cloud. And in both these the angel

---

* See the corresponding expression concerning Christ $\dot{\epsilon}\nu$ $\alpha\dot{\upsilon}\tau\tilde{\omega}$ $\varkappa\alpha\tau o\iota\varkappa\epsilon\tilde{\iota}$ $\pi\tilde{\alpha}\nu$ $\tau\dot{o}$ $\pi\lambda\acute{\eta}\varrho\omega\mu\alpha$ $\tau\tilde{\eta}\varsigma$ $\vartheta\epsilon\acute{o}\tau\eta\tau o\varsigma$ $\sigma\omega\mu\alpha\tau\iota\varkappa\tilde{\omega}\varsigma$. Col 2 9. Calvin: "In ipso residebit gloria ac majestas mea."

of Jehovah is clearly distinguished from the visible sign. Ex. 3: 2 it is said, "and the angel of Jehovah appeared to him *in* a flame of fire, out of the midst of a bush," and v. 4, "God called to him out of the midst of the bush," but according to the hypothesis of Herder, it should have been simply, Jehovah appeared to him, and Jehovah called to him. Chap. 14: 19, it is first related that the angel of God, and then that the pillar of the cloud, went behind the camp of Israel. But how much more irreconcileable is this hypothesis, with those places, where, without any visible manifestation, merely the voice of the angel of God is heard from heaven, as Gen. 21: 22.

2. That the angel of Jehovah is not a mere transient appearance, but a being whose existence is permanent, appears from Gen. 48: 15, where Jacob supplicates his blessing upon the sons of Joseph.

But we refrain from further consideration of an hypothesis, which is refuted by every passage, where the appearance of the angel is mentioned.

III. Others regard the מַלְאַךְ יְהֹוָה as identical with Jehovah, not a different person from him, but only the form in which he manifests himself. Thus Sack (commentatt. theoll. Bon. 1821 p. 19) who prefers to translate מַלְאָךְ *mission*, rather than *messenger*,* and Pustkuchen (Untersuchung der Bibl. Urgeschichte, Halle 1823 p. 61), who asserts that מַלְאַךְ יְהֹוָה wherever it occurs, is equivalent to the Greek θεοφανία. Rosenmuller also, though not consistent with himself, appears inclined to this opinion on Gen 16: 7. Since he there explains מַלְאַךְ יְהֹוָה by "symbolum illud visibile, quo deus sese hominibus conspiciendum praebuit."† To this view accedes De Wette (Dogm. 1. § 108. 83), "the angels are originally personifications of the powers of nature, or the extraordinary operations and providence of God, hence the angel of Jehovah, as having no personality of his own, is interchanged with Jehovah or Elohim." Ewald also seems inclined to it. he (Gramm. p 245) lays peculiar stress upon the circumstance that according to its form the name מַלְאָךְ has properly, not a personal, but only a neuter or indefinite sense, and signifies *mission*. So also Koster (Meletamata critica et exeg. in Zachariae partem posteriorem p. 68). This hypothesis is certainly plausible, and

---

* — — "ita ut מלאך יהוה non tam personam a Jehova distinctam, sed naturalem illam apparitionem, qua Jehova loqui et se manifestare voluit, indicare videatur. Persona, quae agnoscitur in nuntio Jehovae, semper Jehova ipse est, ac nobis fortasse מלאך potius *mission*, quam *messenger* vertendum esset."

† Comp. against on Zech. 3: 2 "Vocatur legatus de nomine principis sui."

would be quite sufficient to explain some passages. But a careful examination of them all, shows it to be groundless, and the fact on which it rests, and which seems to require it, is fully explained by the remark that the Divine wisdom under the old dispensation rather concealed the difference between the person who sent and him who was sent; because the preservation of Monotheism was then of more practical importance than the knowledge of the different persons in the Godhead, and therefore every thing was carefully avoided, which might in the least endanger the doctrine of the Divine unity, through the strong inclination of the people to polytheism. Hence it is obvious, why the oneness of מַלְאַךְ יְהוָה with Jehovah, rather than the distinction between them is made prominent. The principal arguments which compel us to believe that by מַלְאַךְ יְהוָה, a being is designated who, while he is united with Jehovah by oneness of essence, is yet personally distinct from him, and that מַלְאָךְ is not to be translated *mission,* but *messenger,* are the following.

Gen 48. 15, the angel who had been Jacob's protector is expressly distinguished from Jehovah. Were he not a being who had a personal subsistence, how could Jacob implore blessings from the God of his father, and then from him? A personal distinction is plainly made in Ex 23: 20, where Jehovah promises the Israelites to send the angel before them, in whom his name should be. Jehovah speaks of him constantly in the third person, ascribes to him personal attributes, etc. Yet more definite does this distinction appear in Joshua 5. 13. The מַלְאַךְ יְהוָה there names himself the captain of the Lord's host, and therefore implies his subordination, although immediately after he again ascribes to himself Divine honor. The translation "mission of Jehovah" is entirely excluded by Isaiah 63. 9; since it would be absurd to translate מַלְאַךְ פָּנָיו the "mission of his face." But this hypothesis, besides being refuted by these passages, is certainly not one which naturally and at first view presents itself to every one; for as Vitringa, on Isaiah 63: 9. "*omnis relatio ex certo logicae canone distinguit.*"

There are however weighty arguments, which furnish a common refutation of all these hypotheses.

1. It should the less surprise us to find in the Old Testament, a revealer of God equal with, and yet distinct from him, a mediator between God and the world, and we have the less occasion to endeavor to blot out the marks of it, by inadmissible hypotheses, since it exists among all the ancient nations of the world. We shall here content

ourselves with pointing it out among the Persians. As their religion is the most nearly related to that of the Old Testament, we have the stronger reason to believe, that they derived this doctrine also from the original revelations. The Zendavesta distinguishes between Zervane Akerene, the unrevealed God and the original source of all things, and Ormuzd, the chief of the Amshaspands ("Jehovah's prince of angels"), who as the first of creatures is the maker of all other creatures, possesses equal majesty with God, is the mediator in all his relations to the world, and communicated to Zoroaster all his revelations. Comp. Rhode (die heilige Sage des Zendvolkes p. 317). Ormuzd, this chief of the Amshaspands—this being enveloped in splendor, appears in the Zend writings under two very different aspects. First, as a creature possessing his own body and soul, who was produced by the Zervane Akerene, like the other Amshaspands. And thus he belongs to them and is himself one, although the first and greatest. Secondly, he is represented as the Almighty creator of heaven and earth, as the creator and God of the six other Amshaspands, and infinitely exalted above them. How can we fail to perceive the resemblance between the מַלְאַךְ יְהוָה and Ormuzd! Here is a passage especially deserving attention in the Zendavesta Bd. 1. p. 169: "I draw near to thee, O fire (Orvazeschte), powerfully working since the origin of things, the cause of the union, which I am content not to explain, between Ormuzd and the being enveloped in splendor (Zervane Akerene)." Here a mysterious union is asserted between the unrevealed God and the revealer of him, by means of fire (Orvazeschte), to which the Zend books ascribe what in the Old Testament is attributed to the רוּחַ אֱלֹהִים, the source of all life in the physical and moral creation. See Rhode p 182, 345.

2. Secondly, all these hypotheses are contradicted by the tradition of the Jews. The ancient Jews regarded the angel of God, in every instance, not as an ordinary angel, nor an operation of nature, nor the unrevealed God himself, but as the only Mediator between God and the world, the author of all revelations, to whom they give the name of *Metatron*. This was originally an appellative, and therefore could be given to different beings* and we must carefully

---

* Respecting the etymology of this name very different opinions have been advanced. By far the most probable is the derivation defended by Danz l. c. p 727, etc and Buxtorf s v from the Latin *metator*, which is translated by Suidas ὁ προαποστελλόμενος ἄγγελος πρὸ τοῦ ἄρχοντος. The source of the appellation seems to be Is 63 9, where the revealer of God is called the an-

distinguish, as is done in many passages of the Jewish writings them-

gel of Jehovah's countenance. Comp Elias Levita, Tischbi f 53 b Eisenmenger p 396: "the Metatron is the prince of the countenance (שר הפנים) and it is said of him, that he is that angel who always looks upon the face of God." It is in favor of this derivation, that Metator in the sense, legatus, as a synon of שליח is used in the Rabbinical dialect, (comp Buxtorf c 1191, Danz p 725); that the *metatron* as an *appellativum* demonstrably occurs in the same sense, comp. Breschit Rabba in Buxtorf c 1193, that the Rabbins with tolerable unanimity give the meaning of ὁδηγὸς as the proper import of the words, although they differ from one another as to its derivation, and finally that several Rabbins distinctly give this etymology Comp the passages in Danz l c p 724, seq Next to this the most probable is that from the Latin *mediator*. The Metatron bears in the Sohar the name עמודא האמצעיתא *columna medietatis* Comp Sommer Theol. Sohar p 36. Still the word *mediator* does not elsewhere occur in the Rabbinic language, and moreover this derivation is supported by none of the arguments which favor the former Another has still less to support it, which was given by Majus, (Theol Jud p 72), and last by Meyer (Blätter f. hohere Wahrh IV. 188) from μετά and θρόνος i q. ὁ μέτοχος τοῦ θρόνου, ὁ σύνθρονος. But μεταθρονος is not even a Greek word, and still less can it be shown that it has been naturalized in the Rabbinic dialect Further, the Rabbins founded the whole doctrine of the Metatron on passages of the Old Testament, and in all probability they derived the same also from this source But there is no passage, where the name *sharer of the throne*, ὁ μέτοχος τοῦ θρόνου, is attributed to the angel of God. Finally, it is in itself decisive, that the name was originally not peculiar to the angel of Jehovah We introduce here only a single passage, where it occurs in this more general sense Jalkut Rubeni in Daz. p 731. "Si non fuerit justus in hoc mundo, tunc Schechina vestit sese in quodam Metatron" Compare all the passages where the inferior Metatron is spoken of But least of all can we give our approbation to the more recent hypothesis, that of Schmieder He derives the word (l. c. p 41 seq. Excursus de Mitatrone), from the Persian *Mithras* There is nothing in favor of this derivation but a slight similarity of sound The similarity of nature, particularly urged by Schmieder is only apparent The Metatron of the Jews is the highest revealer of the concealed God, as a partaker of his nature, and his majesty, as we have already seen; like Ormuzd from whom all revelations are derived On the contrary the Mithras is an inferior being, created by Ormuzd, a valiant combatant indeed in his host, but far subordinate to the great Bahman, the king of the Amshaspands There is only an apparent foundation for a relationship between Mithras and Metatron in the passages of Plutarch (de Is et Os. c. 46), and the Zend books, where Mithras is called a mediator. For the Metatron of the Hebrews mediates the relations of the concealed God to the creation On the contrary, Mithras is called mediator, only inasmuch as "during the struggle between Ormuzd and Ahriman, he *mediates* the influence of the latter to render it harmless" The doctrine concerning him has also more of a physical than a moral import, comp Rhode (das Religionssys-

selves,* between the higher and the inferior Metatron, the latter of whom stands in the same relation to the former, as the former does to the most high God. The doctrine concerning the inferior Metatron, who is supposed by some to be Enoch, is probably founded on Ex. 32. 34. The higher Metatron is often identified with the Shechina, the residence of God in the world. Thus it is said for example in the book Tikkune Sohar, in Glaesener Theol Soharica p 37 · "Metatron est ipsissima Schechina et Schechina Metatron Jehovae vocatur, quia corona est decem Sephirarum." See the full proof of this in Danz, in Meuschen. N. T. ex Talm illustr p. 733 seq Edzardi Tract Berach p 232. Other passages however show, that in another respect, they distinguish between the two, and only so far identified the Metatron with the Shechina as the former concentrated and personally manifested himself in the latter. Thus, for example, it is said in the book Eschel, Abraham, in Danz l. c. p 735: "Columna medietatis est Metatron, in quo apparet sanctus ille benedictus in Schechina sua." And in another passage in Sommer l. c p. 36 · "Deus O. M ejusque Schechina sunt intra Metatronem, quippe qui vocatur Schaddai" Still more clearly is this view expressed in a passage of R. Moses Corduero l c p 736: "Angelus hic vestimentum est Schechinae et Schechina occultat sese in ejus medio, suasque ipse ostendit operationes per eundem Non tamen Schechina ipsa—sed si dicere fas esset Schechinae vocarem exilium" See other passages in Knorr a Rosenroth, Kabbala denudata 1 p. 528.

---

tem des Zendvolkes p 264 seq) In fine, as the original appellative meaning of the name, decides against its derivation from the Persians, so is there no analogy in favor of it, while it can be proved that names were often borrowed from the Greek and Latin Comp e. g. Armillus, the Greek ἐρημολαος, and *Matrona*, which occurs so frequently in the Cabbalistic writings

* By not distinguishing between the two, great confusion has been occasioned in Eisenmenger We cite here only a few passages "Schechina longe excelsior est Henocho convenienter cum illo quod per traditionem accepi, fore metatorem magnum et metatorem parvum, quorum magnus est ipsissima Schechina, e qua ille emanat et de nomine ejus Schechina vocatur Metatron" In another place "Invenimus in Sohar, quod duo sint metatores, Metatron maximus et Metatron parvus creatus." Comp others in Danz p 730, 735 That the assertion of several Rabbins, that מיטטרון with *Yodh* denotes the superior, and without *Yodh* the inferior metatron, is incorrect, is shown by Schnieder, l c p 28, from the paraphrase of Jonathan on Gen 5 24, where the orthography with *Yodh* occurs, although the inferior Metatron, is the subject of remark

Sommer p. 37, where R. Moses Corduero says שכינה חתומה בתוך מטטרון "the Shechina is enclosed in the Metatron." From this and other passages it appears, that the relation of the Shechina to the Metatron was regarded in about the same light, as that of fire Orvazeschte to Ormuzd among the Persians. The Metatron is not a created being, but an emanation. See R. Mose ben Hoschke in Danz p. 737: "Manifestum hinc est, quod sit Metatron emanationis et Metatron creationis, qui est nuntius. Metatron autem emanationis est ille, qui Mosi apparuit in rubo." He is united with the most high God by oneness of nature. R. Bechai in Edzardi Tract. Talm Berachoth p. 231: "Rabbini p. m. verba אל תמר בו explicarunt ne permutes me in illo (ut alium me, alium illum esse putes) dicitque hoc ideo deus ad Mosem, ut intelligeret, utrumque unum esse et arctissime unitum, absque separatione. ... Est ille dominus ipse et legatus, domini." He is called in the Talmud (comp. passages in Sommer l. c. p. 45) שר העולם, *the prince of the world.* He is the visible revealer of God. See the Sohar in Sommer p. 38. "Indumentum τοῦ שדי est Metatron." He is called the angel "cujus nomen sicut nomen domini sui," Talm. Tract. Sanhedrin in Sommer l. c. He holds dominion over all created things; Sohar in Sommer l. c. p. 35. "Metatron servus Jehovae, senior domus ejus, qui est principium creaturarum ejus, dominium exercens super omnia, quae ipsi sunt tradita. Tradidit vero ipsi dominium deus O. M. super omnes exercitus suos." Othioth Rabbi Akkiva in Eisenmenger, II p. 396, says: "The Metatron is the angel, the prince of the face, the angel the prince of the law, the prince of wisdom, the prince of strength, the prince of glory, the prince of the temple, the prince of the kings, the prince of the rulers, the prince of the high, exalted, many and glorious chiefs in heaven and on earth." All the splendid predicates, which are separately attributed to him in other places, are combined in a remarkable passage of the Cabbalistic book Rasiel in Edzard l. c. p. 234.

That this doctrine is of Jewish origin, and could by no means have been borrowed from the Persians, is plain from the fact, that its development from the Old Testament is manifest in all the places where it is found. In every instance, there is either a distinct quotation of the passages where the מַלְאַךְ יהוה occurs, or a plain reference to them. In favor of its high antiquity many reasons can be given. That it already existed in the time of the LXX, appears from Isa. 9. 5, where the אל יועץ פלא is translated. μεγάλης βουλῆς ἄγγελος, probably, as Gesenius rightly remarks, on theological grounds, to indicate that in the Messiah, not the most high God, but the Revealer of Him, would appear. R. Alschech on Gen. 18. 2 in Danz l. c. p. 734, characterizes this doctrine as traditional: "Omnis angelus absolute dictus in scriptura est princeps facierum Metator, cujus nomen est sicut nomen domini ejus, secundum sermonem doctorum nostrorum p. m. ad textum biblicum: ecce ego missurus sum angelum ante facies tuas etc., et ecce angelus meus ibit etc." Further, if this doctrine were of later origin, it would be difficult to conceive how it could have been so widely diffused; it is found not merely in the cabbalistic writings, but in those of the most diverse character. We meet with it, not only in the Talmud, but already completely developed even in the book Sohar. There is strong proof of the great antiquity of the principal portions of this book; though, like nearly all the old Jewish writings, it must have been subject to numerous interpolations. See Tholuck, Stellen aus dem Sohar. Berl. 1824. Vorr. But Schmieder justly remarks, l. c. p. 25: "Cabbalistica de Mitatrone doctrina in libro Sohar ita exculta est, ut nec illa aetate recens inventa, sed variis multorum meditationibus versata et aucta jam fuisse videatur." The antiquity of this doctrine, is confirmed also by many passages in the New Testament, especially in the Epistles of Paul; which leave little room to doubt, that the expressions which were current among the Jews concerning the Metatron were transferred to Christ, and justly, as we shall see hereafter, inasmuch as the מַלְאַךְ יְהוָה, or Metatron, was to be manifested in the Messiah.* The resemblance between these passages of the New Testament, and those in the Rabbinical writings, is too great to have been accidental. And lastly, the existence of this doctrine even in the writings of Philo argues in favor of its antiquity (quis rerum divinarum haeres p. 50) τῷ δὲ ἀρχαγγέλῳ καὶ πρεσβυτάτῳ λόγῳ δι' ἀρετὴν ἐξαίρετον ἔδωκεν ὁ τὰ ὅλα γεννήσας πατὴρ, ἵνα μεθόριον στὰς τὸ γενόμενον διακρίνῃ τοῦ πεποιηκότος· ὁ δὲ αὐτὸς ἱκέτης μέν ἐστι

---

* Comp. for example, the quotations from Othoth R. Akkiva with Eph. 1. 21 etc. Sohar f. 77 Sulzb. in Sommer l. c. p. 35, the Metatron is called תחלת בריותיו של מקום, "the beginning of the creatures of God." Comp. πρωτότοκος πάσης κτίσεως Col. 1. 15. The Metatron is the glory, the veil of God, by whom God is revealed, who is his image, and in whose likeness man is made. R. Bechai in Edzard l. c. p. 232. Jalkut chadasch p. 237. Sohar l. c. and p. 111 f. 91. Sulz. Sommer p. 36.—Comp. εἰκὼν τοῦ θεοῦ τοῦ ἀοράτου, Col. 1. 15; ἀπαύγασμα τῆς δόξης καὶ χαρακτὴρ τῆς ὑποστάσεως τοῦ θεοῦ, Heb. 1. 3. 2 Cor. 4. 4.

τοῦ θνητοῦ κηραίνοντος ἀεὶ πρὸς τὸ ἄφθαρτον, πρεσβευτὴς δὲ τοῦ ἡγεμόνος πρὸς τὸ ὑπήκοον. But the antiquity of this doctrine does not prove the antiquity of the *name* Metatron also, as the exclusive designation of the archangel. It rather appears from a remarkable passage of Rabbi Menachem of Rekanat, in Eisenmenger l. c. p 374, that this prince of angels originally received a great variety of appellative designations, until at length one of them, viz. Metatron became his standing title, and a sort of *proper name*. In Jonathan on Ex. III, the angel of Jehovah bears the name of Segansagel; in Jalkut Schimoni, in Eisenmenger p. 375, and in many other places, see Danz l. c. p. 733, 34, he is called Michael

We believe then, that we have satisfactorily shown that by the angel of Jehovah is to be understood the Revealer of God, who being a partaker of his Godhead, and united with him in the same nature, was the Mediator in all his relations, first with the patriarchs, and, afterwards with the visible theocracy This Revealer of Jehovah then was expected as a great Restorer in future times This is evident from those places in the Old Testament, which ascribe to the Messiah divine names, attributes, and works; for if the Messiah were God, he could stand according to the whole system of the religion of the Old Testament in no other relation to the most high God, than that which the angel of Jehovah was thought to sustain Further, the passage in Malachi 3 1 affords the most distinct testimony in favor of the identity of both. There the Messiah bears the name of מַלְאַךְ הַבְּרִית, the angel of the covenant, either according to the general import of בְּרִית, the angel, who is the mediator in every engagement between God and men, or, according to its special meaning, the angel who established the covenant of Sinai with the people of Israel From this appellation therefore, it appears, that the Messiah is the same as the מַלְאַךְ יְהוָֹה, whose agency in giving the law at Sinai, is not indeed expressly mentioned in the Mosaic account, but is rendered sufficiently certain by analogy, and by the positive testimony of the prophet As the מַלְאַךְ יהוה in those passages, where he is expressly named, bears interchangeably the names יְהוָֹה and אֱלֹהִים, so must we often suppose him to be intended, where Jehovah only is spoken of throughout. Comp Gen. 32 24 etc. with Hos. 12. 4—6, also Ex. chap. III, where the angel of Jehovah makes himself known, as the God of Abraham, Isaac and Jacob, and the deliverer out of Egypt, and Ex. 20· 3 where the angel is not mentioned, and Jehovah says. "I am the Lord thy God, who brought thee up out of the land of Egypt." Allowing it to have been the office of the מַלְאַךְ יְהוָֹה in general, to act as Mediator in the transactions between the invisible God and men, his mediation must be assumed in many instances, where it is not expressly mentioned.—That the identity of the מַלְאַךְ יְהוָֹה and the Messiah was known under the Old Testament, is favored also perhaps by the two passages Hos. 3. 5 if we regard טוּב יְהוָֹה as synonymous with כְּבוֹד יְהוָֹה, the visible manifestation of the Shechina of God, which was concentrated in the מַלְאַךְ יְהוָֹה, and Mic. 5: 1, if we translate the word מוֹצָאוֹת, *goings forth:* "Whose goings forth have been from eternity," i. e. he who from eternity goes forth from the invisible God and reveals him. The identity of the two is also intimated Isa. 9. 5, where the same title is given to the Messiah, which the angel of Jehovah, Judges 13. 18, assumes himself.

This identity of the angel of Jehovah, or the Metatron and the Messiah was acknowledged also by the later Jews, as appears by the passage already quoted from the Alexandrine version. That it was presupposed by the writers of the New Testament as generally received, appears from the passages to be cited below. We here introduce but one remarkable passage from the Sohar (Sommer l. c p. 35). "Cum dicitur servus ejus, intelligitur servus Jehovae, senior domus ejus, paratus ad ministerium ejus. Quis vero ille est? Metatron hic est, sicuti diximus, futurus ut conjungatur corpori (i. e. corpus humanum adsumat) in utero materno." See other passages by Edzardi Cod. Talm. Berachoth p. 230. But, what renders this identity indubitably certain is, the evidence of the New Testament, in which Christ appears as the Mediator of the old covenant, and every thing is attributed to Him, which in the Old Testament is spoken of Jehovah, and his Revealer. John 1. 11, it is said, that he come εἰς τὰ ἴδια, but the ἴδιοι received him not. In the Old Testament the people of Israel are always represented, as the נַחֲלַת יְהוָֹה, *inheritance* or *possession of Jehovah.* According to John 12: 41, Isaiah saw the glory of Christ and spake of him; on the other hand, in the passage referred to chap. vi, Isaiah saw the glory of Jehovah. 1 Cor 10: 9, it is said Μηδὲ ἐκπειράζωμεν τὸν Χριστόν, καθὼς καί τινες αὐτῶν ἐπείρασαν, καὶ ὑπὸ τῶν ὄφεων ἀπώλοντο. According to this passage, therefore, Christ was the leader of the Israelites through the wilderness, and was tempted by them. On the other hand, the Pentateuch relates that they were led by the מַלְאַךְ יְהוָֹה, and in Numbers 21. 5—7, that they tempted Jehovah. 1 Pet. 1. 10, declares that the spirit of Christ spake by the prophets; but the prophets themselves always refer to Jehovah, as the source of their predictions. According to Heb. 11. 26, Moses preferred reproach for the sake of Christ, τὸν ὀνειδισμὸν τοῦ Χριστοῦ, to the treasures of Egypt; the narrative in Exodus informs us, that he sacrificed every thing to the service of Jehovah. According to Heb. 12. 26, at the giving of the law, the voice of Christ shook the earth, in Exodus, this was done by Jehovah. The disagreement is only in appearance between these and certain other passages, urged by Augustine in support of the opinion that by מַלְאַךְ יְהוָה we must not understand Christ, but some one of the created angels. The least difficult of all is Acts 7. 53, where Stephen says, the Jews received the law εἰς διαταγὰς ἀγγέλων. When Stephen after the example of the Old Testament, Deut. 33. 2. Ps. 68. 18, speaks in the plural number of angels who were concerned in giving the law, he does not intend to deny, that one among them infinitely exalted in power above the rest took the lead as the highest revealer of God.* That such an exalted ἄγγελος κυρίου was well known to him, appears from v. 30, where he says, the angel of the Lord appeared to Moses in the bush, and calls his voice, immediately after, the voice of the Lord. Comp. 35. 36. Indeed in v. 34 it is expressly asserted that this angel spake to Moses and the people on Mount Sinai. But the appellation ἄγγελος should the less surprise us, since Christ likewise, Heb. 3. 1, bears the corresponding name ἀπόστολος. The same explanation may serve for Gal. 3: 19, where the law is said to be διαταγεὶς δι' ἀγγέλων. The passage in Heb. 2. 2 is more difficult, where the law appears to be placed below the gospel, because the former was made known by the ministry of angels, the latter by the Lord himself. The expressions δι' ἀγγέλων and διὰ τοῦ κυρίου stand here in manifest contrast. But that it cannot be the object of the writer to ascribe the giving of the law merely to ordinary angels, and to exclude the Revealer of God from the transaction, appears from chap. 12. 26, where he affirms that the voice of the Lord at the giving of the law shook the earth. He can therefore intend to assert the superiority of the gospel to the law, only so far as the revelation made by the Lord as מַלְאַךְ יְהוָה was imperfect compared with that which he made by becoming man. We must then in a certain respect distinguish between the מַלְאַךְ

---

* Comp. Sohar f. 96 ed. Solisb. (Edzardi tract. Talm. Berachoth p. 227). "Quando divina majestas habitat circa hominem, tum innumeri alii exercitus sancti adsunt ibi simul."

יְהוָה and the Son of God, and not with the fathers and most of the old theologians, venture to say that they are perfectly identical.* That the Mediator of the New Testament was also as מַלְאַךְ יְהוָה the Mediator in all the relations of God to the people of the Old Testament, was, with the exception of the above-named fathers, the unanimous opinion of the ancient church. The fathers of the first synod of Antioch declare in a letter to Paul of Samosata, before his deposition (Colet. conc. coll. Venet. 1 p. 866. 70), that ὁ ἄγγελος τοῦ πατρὸς αὐτὸς κύριος καὶ θεὸς ὤν, μεγάλης βουλῆς ἄγγελος, appeared to Abraham and Jacob, and to Moses in the burning bush. Justin Martyr shows in the dial c. Tryphone f 265 ed. Thirlb. that Christ spake to Moses from the bush, and says he was called the angel of the Lord, ἐκ τοῦ διαγγέλλειν τοῖς ἀνθρώποις τὰ παρὰ τοῦ πατρός, καὶ ποιητοῦ τῶν ἁπάντων, comp Apol 1 p 91. Constitutt. apost. V. 20 b. Coteler. 1 p. 325. Irenaeus c. haeres. IV. 7. § 4. Theophilus II. 31. Clem. Alex. Paed 1, 7. Tertull. c. Prax. 7, 16. Cyprian. c. Jud II. 6. Hilar. de trin. IV § 32. Eusebius, demonstr evang 5, 10 séq. Cyrill. Hieros. p. 322 ed. Ox. Cyr. Al. in Exod. 1 1 opp 1, 262. Chrysost hom 48 in Gen Ambros. de fide ad Grat. Opp. t. II p. 460 Bened u A. Theodoret says: interr 5 in Ex. opp t. 1 ed. Hal. p. 121 on Ex. III: καὶ ὅλον δὲ τὸ χωρίον δείκνυσι θεὸν ὄντα τὸν ὀφθέντα. Κέκληκε δὲ αὐτὸν καὶ ἄγγελον, ἵνα γνῶμεν ὡς ὁ ὀφθεὶς οὐκ ἔστιν ὁ θεὸς καὶ πατήρ· τίνος γὰρ ἄγγελος ὁ πατήρ; ἀλλ' ὁ μονογενὴς υἱός, ὁ μεγάλης βουλῆς ἄγγελος.

Let us now briefly sum up the result of the preceding investigation. In the prophetic Scriptures, a divine as well as human nature is attributed to the Messiah, and yet every polytheistic idea is excluded by the assumption of his essential unity with the most high God. It was expected that the angel, or revealer of Jehovah, who had often before made himself occasionally visible, and acted as the Mediator between God and the people in all their transactions, would assume human nature in the person of the Messiah, and redeem and bless both Jews and Gentiles.

Here the question yet arises. If the distinction between the revealed and the unrevealed God was already made known under the

---

* With this agrees the remark of Grotius on Ex xx 'Errant graviter, qui hic per angelum intelligunt secundam dei hypostasin. Variis enim multiplicibusque modis deus locutus est patribus, at per filium ultimis demum temporibus Heb 1 1"

Old Testament, wherein is the New Testament in this respect superior to the Old? The preference consisted in this under the Old Testament, the distinction was necessarily kept more out of view, and hence might easily appear to be founded, not so much on a relation in the Godhead itself, as on a relation to those, to whom the revelation was made. In the Old Testament, the Mediator commonly spake and acted in the name of God, whom he revealed. Nor could it be otherwise before the λόγος had become flesh. Hence the revealer, and he who was revealed, in a manner lost themselves in each other, and notions similar to those of Sabellius might easily arise. But under the New Testament, on the contrary, they appeared distinguished from each other, as father and son. Religion thus gained a twofold advantage. It became more spiritual, and at the same time more an object of sense; more *spiritual*, by the exclusion of those limited conceptions of the spirituality, the omniscience, and the omnipresence of God, which arose from confounding the Revealer with him who was revealed; more an object of sense, because the Son of God, in his life, sufferings and death, brought the Divine Being nearer to man, than was possible in the transient appearances of his angel under the Old Testament. But such a condescension of the Deity to fallen man is indispensable to his becoming like God. See Hess, Jehovah der Gott Israels in d. Bibliothek f. heil. Geschichte Bd. 2.

CHAPTER IV.

A SUFFERING AND ATONING MESSIAH IN THE OLD TESTAMENT.

THE majority of recent theologians do not hesitate to deny that the idea of a suffering and dying Messiah in general, and that of the vicarious nature of his sufferings and death in particular, is to be found in the prophecies of the Old Testament.* See our remarks on

---

* After Kuinoel (Mess. Weissag. Vorr. and on Isaiah 53), Umbreit acknowledges, indeed, the existence of the idea of a suffering and atoning Messiah in the Scriptures of the Old Testament, but asserts that it could not have originated before the times of the Babylonian exile. He says (Theol. Studien

Isaiah chap. LIII; but especially De Wette de morte J. C. expiatoria. They assert that the Israelites expected in the Messiah merely a powerful earthly king, who should easily bring all their enemies

---

und Critiken 1, 2 p 225) "Thus the transformation of the Messiah, as an expected king of kings, into a teaching and suffering prophet, is readily explained by such a spiritual revolution. This Lord, whom the prophets of a former period announce, as a redeemer of the people and author of everlasting peace on earth, becomes a servant in the mouth of our Seer (the alleged author of the second part of Isaiah who lived at the time of the exile), when the people themselves having gained from oppression and suffering the spirit of humility, which sanctifies and makes happy, now behold in the mirror of such an acquired disposition, the image of the expected Redeemer." In reply we offer the following remarks. 1 This opinion is founded on the false assertion, to be more fully refuted hereafter, that the second part of Isaiah was not composed before the exile. 2 It is indeed true, that the idea of a Saviour in the form of a servant, can be entertained only by him, who has himself become truly humble. But can this be denied of a David, or an Isaiah? The idea of the Messiah by no means originated with the whole people, but with individuals, to whom God revealed it, as they were prepared for its reception. But those means which God employed to effect this preparation, and which will be more fully explained below, were already in existence before the time of the exile. It could then, at most, be merely asserted, that at this period, such a disposition became *general* among the people, as made them ready to receive the prophetic annunciation respecting the suffering of the Messiah. But this position would be no proof of the notion of which we are speaking, and though *a priori* probable, it would yet be refuted by history, which shows, that the people by no means acquired true humility of heart by their sufferings in the captivity. The exile had indeed the effect of eradicating their former inclination to idolatry, but that the root of bitterness in the heart, from which this sprung, still remained, is plain, from the fact, that with the exile, self-righteousness and the merit of works, which are both the offspring of pride, first became prevalent among almost the whole people. But how irreconcilable this state of mind is with a susceptibility for the idea of a suffering and atoning Redeemer, is still shown by daily experience. How little, in general, suffering, which does not of itself produce the good, but only in connexion with Divine grace, and an ardent desire to obtain it, tends, in its own nature, to cause this susceptibility, is clearly shown by the disposition of the Jewish people in their present exile. The severer their sufferings, which cannot be compared with those in the Babylonian exile, the more crude and carnal do their expectations become. 3 Were the assertion of the author correct, we should expect the most numerous predictions of a Messiah in the form of a servant, in those prophets, who lived during the captivity, as Ezekiel and particularly Jeremiah, whose humble mind, and broken heart, would have urged them chiefly to this. But it is precisely in these prophets, that we find the contrary. As the distress of the people increased, their descriptions of the Messiah became the more splendid

under subjection And certainly could they show that this was the only view entertained of him, they might with far more ease give some plausibility to their assertion, that the notion of a Messiah was of purely human origin; and in this manner remove the difficulty arising from the wonderful coincidence of prophecy and its fulfilment, and prepare the way for the opinion that it was only, either by his own mistake, or on the principle of accommodation that Christ appropriated to himself declarations of the Old Testament, which originally related to totally different subjects.

But to this view, those only can accede, who disregard the authority of our Lord, whose holy lips could neither lie, nor err, and that of his Apostles, who were taught by himself the true import of the predictions of the Old Testament, and guided into all truth by the same spirit, which spake by the prophets. From their own clear and explicit declarations we can prove that in the prophecies of the the Old Testament, they beheld the Messiah, not only in his exaltation and glory, but also in his humiliation and suffering Omitting for the present their numerous citations of particular passages of the Old Testament, relating to the suffering of Christ, which have been, or will be noticed in the proper place,* we here direct our attention only to some passages of a general character. Matt 26:24, the Lord says. "the son of man goeth as it is written of him," that is, be not offended that the son of man suffers and dies, you see that this is his destination, for you find it foretold long ago in the prophecies of the Old Testament. Matt. 26 54, the Lord shows Peter the folly of his vain attempt to resist on the ground that he might, if he pleased, summon far different defenders to his aid, but chooses to dispense with their assistance, because what the Scriptures had foretold concerning his sufferings and death must be fulfilled· $\pi\tilde{\omega}\varsigma$ $o\tilde{v}\nu$ $\pi\lambda\eta\rho\omega\vartheta\tilde{\omega}\sigma\iota$ $\alpha\acute{\iota}$ $\gamma\rho\alpha\varphi\alpha\acute{\iota}$, $\ddot{o}\tau\iota$ $o\ddot{v}\tau\omega$ $\delta\epsilon\tilde{\iota}$ $\gamma\epsilon\nu\acute{\epsilon}\sigma\vartheta\alpha\iota$. And v. 56, he meets the prejudice, which his enemies might raise against him in consequence of his deep humiliation, by the frequent remark, that he could easily defeat their designs, but freely gives himself up to their will, in order that the prophecies of Scripture respecting his sufferings and death might be fulfilled.† Luke 18. 31, Christ informs the

---

* Comp on Isa 42 49 50. 53 Zechariah 11 12. 13. Ps 16 22 40

† That the words $\tau o\tilde{v}\tau o$ $\delta\grave{\epsilon}$ $o\lambda o\nu$ $\gamma\acute{\epsilon}\gamma o\nu\epsilon\nu$, $\ddot{\iota}\nu\alpha$ $\pi\lambda\eta\rho\omega\vartheta\tilde{\omega}\sigma\iota\nu$ $\alpha\acute{\iota}$ $\gamma\rho\alpha\varphi\alpha\grave{\iota}$ $\tau\tilde{\omega}\nu$ $\pi\rho o\varphi\eta\tau\tilde{\omega}\nu$ were spoken by Christ, and not by the Evangelist, as some interpreters have supposed, appears from the $\dot{\alpha}\lambda\lambda'$ $\ddot{\iota}\nu\alpha$ $\pi\lambda\eta\rho\omega\vartheta\tilde{\omega}\sigma\iota\nu$ $\alpha\acute{\iota}$ $\gamma\rho\alpha\varphi\alpha\grave{\iota}$ of Mark 14 49.

Apostles, on his last journey to Jerusalem, that now all was about to be accomplished, which had been written by the prophets concerning his sufferings and death Luke 24 25, etc. to the two disciples on the way to Emmaus, who lamented his death, and were offended at it, he says "O fools and slow of heart to believe all that the prophets have spoken; ought not Christ to have suffered these things, and to enter into his glory?" He then expounded to them, as he had done before his death to the Apostles,* the chief predictions in all the writings of the Old Testament, which concerned himself, and especially those which related to his sufferings. Luke 24 44—46, after his resurrection, he says to the Apostles, that what he had told them before his death had now come to pass; viz that all the prophecies of the Old Testament in relation to himself must be fulfilled. He then explained to them the true import of Scripture, especially of those predictions of the sufferings and death of the Messiah, which they had heretofore misunderstood, and said unto them, "thus it is written, and thus it behoved Christ to suffer, and to rise from the dead the third day." Acts 3· 18, Peter says, in his sermon immediately after the effusion of the Holy Spirit, that God had now caused the fulfilment of all that he had spoken by the mouth of his holy prophets, "that Christ should suffer." The same Apostle teaches, 1 Pet 1 11, that the spirit of Christ in the prophets had foretold his future sufferings, and the glory that should follow. Acts 17: 3, Paul in the synagogue at Thessalonica proves from the Scriptures of the Old Testament, that Christ must suffer, and rise from the dead, and it appears from Acts 26 22, 23, that this was his usual method of teaching 1 Cor. 15 3, he mentions as the chief point on which he had insisted in his instruction of the Corinthians, that Christ had died for our sins *according to the Scriptures.*

But this plain testimony of Christ and his Apostles, is by no means all with which our modern critics have to contend, there is sufficient proof besides of the unsoundness of their views.

---

* Matt 16 21 ἀπὸ τότε ἤρξατο ὁ Ἰησοῦς δεικνύειν τοῖς μαθηταῖς αὐτοῦ, ὅτι δεῖ αὐτὸν ἀπελθεῖν εἰς Ἱεροσόλυμα, καὶ πολλὰ παθεῖν κ. τ. λ. καὶ ἀποκταν-θῆναι Christ shows the necessity of his suffering and death from the prophecies of the Old Testament, which could not remain unaccomplished without endangering the honor of the God of truth That the δεῖ refers to this, appears from the parallel passages 26 54, 56. Luke 24 25, etc Equally erroneous therefore is Paulus "necessary from duty," and Fritsche "*fatale, in fatis esse, ut abiret*"

It is in the first place manifest, that various natural causes, although not of themselves sufficient to lead the prophets, who derived their wisdom only from above, to the doctrine of a suffering and atoning Messiah, must yet have prepared them for a willing reception of it, when revealed. This doctrine need not have appeared to them as something entirely foreign, which they could only receive as a revelation, and with which they could have no further concern. Both as men and as members of the theocracy,* they must have found in their own minds many ideas, with which it might be connected

---

* Lücke Comm Z Joh I p 470 "The tragic idea of a suffering Messiah, who should bear the sin and guilt of the people, and make atonement for them, is in our judgment a necessary element of the Messianic belief It belongs to the tragic character of Judaism from the beginning, it has its secular historical root in the fundamental relation between joy and hope in the world, and its national type, in the symbolic sacrifices of the Messianic dispensation Men of deep reflection, like John the Baptist, having turned their thoughts away from the world, had an obsure anticipation, in the idea of a Messiah, of a new bond of union between heaven and earth, and regarding in a moral point of view the delay of its fulfilment as well as the general increase of sin and guilt, could not dispense with the tragic thought of a suffering, and through suffering triumphant Messiah, and must make him the firmest support and the author of their spiritual faith and hope." How far we agree with this representation will be seen from the following remarks In the first place, the idea of a Messiah in this passage is regarded as of purely human origin. "Men of deep reflection," according to their own necessities, and anticipations and without a Divine revelation, have added new features to the image; a view which is refuted with equal ease, by the writings of the prophets, and the declarations of Christ and his Apostles, who assert, that the spirit of Christ spake by the prophets (1 Pet 1 11) and that no prophecy was given by the will of man, but that holy men of God prophesied as they were moved by the Holy Ghost (2 Pet 1 21) Accordingly causes, like those assigned by Lucke, could never produce a peculiar modification of the notion of the Messiah, but only the susceptibility for it, in the case of the ancient prophets, as well as of John the Baptist, who by a like vocation, was as far removed as they from all human caprice Then, it is remarkable, that while the author asserts, that profound thinkers like John must of *necessity*, conceive the idea of a suffering and atoning Messiah, he nevertheless denies, that it was entertained by any of the prophets of the Old Testament and only makes John attribute it to their predictions Is then Isaiah inferior to John in depth of thought? But this commentary, in many respects excellent, exhibits in general, the inconsistency of the new theological faith, arising from the neglect of unbiassed study of the New Testament How, e g except from dependence on the explanation of the Old Testament by the rationalists, could the author, in opposition to the authority of Christ and the Apostles which he has defended, deny the reference of Isaiah LIII to the Messiah, which without their testimony,

Let us consider first those sentiments on this subject, which they must have possessed as men. Every person of deep reflection will be led, both by his own experience, and his observation of others, to the knowledge of that sinful corruption, whose poison has pervaded the germ of every thing earthly. And how can he perceive that enemies both within and without, are continually rising up against all that is good and divine, and striving to destroy it, how behold the unceasing activity of the powers of darkness, and not anticipate, that should the Divinity personally appear on earth, in order to destroy ungodliness and sin, the end could be attained only through conflict and suffering? How should not sin rise up in all its strength, where that which is divine appears in its purity, since it never rests, even in this world, where holiness in its feeble struggles, and even in alliance with sin, yet begins the combat against it? And on the other hand, it is equally natural to anticipate, that what is thus purely divine, cannot always be kept in subjection. Our own experience teaches, that it is overcome in us, only, because evil and its temptations have their seat within us. And thus the doctrine concerning the appearance of the Divinity in the person of the Messiah, was accompanied by the anticipation, that he must pass through suffering to glory, and it needed only an intimation from above, to render this anticipation certain, and impress it with the seal of divine authority. How deeply the idea of a Divine sufferer and conqueror is grounded in human nature is manifest from the expressions of it, which are met with even among heathen nations—Indians, Persians, Greeks and people of the North. Comp Tholuck (die Lehre von der Sunde und vom Versohner p 290 seq.), Buttmann (uber den Mythos des Herakles), Creuzers (Symbolik Th 2 S. 270).

But, it is no less true, that the doctrine also of the expiatory sufferings, and vicarious satisfaction of the Messiah, possesses an original adaptation to the nature of man. Man is made for Christ, the atoning Saviour, were it not so, were there not some secret attraction, some obscure presentiment in his soul, how can it be explained, that

---

must be clear to every unprejudiced mind. Surely this inconsistency, which gives so many advantages to the opposers of truth, so much occasion of perplexity to the honest, but doubtful inquirer and pain to believers, will disappear in the further and freer advancement of the more recent theology, since the error is not as in the case of the adversaries, grounded in the heart, but in science, which continually advancing, must by the rejection of what is foreign, be developed and consolidated on all sides

that this doctrine alone, as history shows, has power to restore that peace and tranquillity which he has lost, and which he labours in vain to find in any other way, and that it should produce this effect not upon men of any particular organization, or degree of improvement, but upon all without distinction from the most rude to the most cultivated? But the original adaptation of the spirit of man to the vicarious satisfaction of the Divine Redeemer, shows itself, not merely in his acceptance of it when made known to him by revelation, but also in the various means, which he previously employs, in order to satisfy his obscure presentiment and earnest desire. The idea of substitution pervades all the religious systems of the heathen, arising from the same necessity, which was real, though not well understood, and which all these systems, though in widely different ways, sought in vain to realize Comp. Krummacher, Paragraphen z. heil. Gesch. p 103. But among the Jews the influence of these natural causes, which every where operated to prepare the way for the doctrine of the sufferings, and the substitution of the Messiah, was strengthened by others, which were peculiar to the theocracy. As the ancient theocracy was the foundation of the new, so the principal persons described in the Old Testament form the basis of the representations of the author of the new covenant, the Messiah was to unite in his own person the three chief offices of the theocracy, viz. the regal, the prophetic and the sacerdotal. See the further discussion of this subject in chap v. What was more natural, than that the Jews should have been disposed to combine the essential properties of them all, in their conception of him, and to acknowledge any feature already exhibited in the type, when enabled by revelation to perceive it in the image of the Messiah? And thus we see, how they were prepared to receive without hesitation, the doctrine concerning his sufferings and satisfaction.

The Messiah appears in the prophets first as king, here however David, whose name itself is transferred to him, is the perpetual groundwork of the representation " But who—we use the words of Eichhorn—suffered more, in a greater variety of ways, and more innocently than David? From a shepherd he rose to be a king, through what hosts of rivals and enemies, was he compelled to force his way to this eminence? Repeatedly must he flee with his harp in his hand before the javelin of Saul; how often, both alone and attended, must he roam through the desert, pursued by him, who should have loved and honored him, as a member of his house, and successor to his throne? Ishbosheth contended with him as a rival; and he never knew repose until the royal house was entirely destroyed. Then he engaged with various success in wars with the neighboring States, from Egypt to the Euphrates, and after so many victories he at last found his most dangerous enemy in his own son, the rebellious Absalom."—What now was more natural, than that David, who knew himself to be a type of his great descendant, should be disposed to find the principal events in the life of his Lord, prefigured by those of his own? and that the later prophets should only have been waiting for a higher sanction of their anticipation, that the illustrious king expected in future times, would pass through suffering to joy, through humiliation to glory, and through ignominy to honor, like the celebrated king in former times, the vicissitudes of whose life had been strikingly represented in his own Psalms.*

The Messiah appears, secondly, as a Divine teacher, and here the prophetic order is the ground-work. See on Is 42. 49. 50 The prophets went forth, clothed in poor and coarse garments, not seeking their own prosperity, nor their own honor, but the honor of him who sent them, and whose word was a burning fire within them, so that they could not if they would, withdraw from his service They neither sought nor found the good things of this world; but lived in poverty and want For devoting their lives to God, they were rewarded with mockery and persecution, imprisonment and death. They were obliged to conceal themselves in deserts and caves, and often they had not where to lay their heads. The author of the Epistle to the Hebrews, chap. 11 37, says of them: "they were stoned, they were sawn asunder, were tempted, were slain with the sword. they wandered about in sheep skins and goat skins: being destitute, afflicted, tormented (of whom the world was not worthy) they wandered in deserts and in mountains and in dens and in caves of the earth " With this should be compared the discourse of Christ,

---

* Herder, Geist der Hebr Poesie II p 441, well observes· "Once more they unfold in him, even the fortunes of David and the seed which was promised to him. The former had much to suffer before he could found his extensive kingdom; the latter must be chastised with the rod of men, 2 Sam xiv, though the favor of Jehovah his father should not depart from him Both were applied in all the troubles, of which the prophets were witnesses, to the future king and the introduction of his kingdom This is the key to the representations of the prophets, which are so wonderful and in appearance so contradictory "

Matt 23: 29, etc. 2 Chron. 24: 17 2 Kings 21: 16 Neh 9 26 A lively image of the life of the prophets, in its worldly debasement and divine exaltation, is furnished by the history of Elijah and Elisha. In the book of the Kings, this is well represented in the predictions of Jeremiah He says, chap 2 30, "your own sword has devoured your prophets like a destroying lion." "I was," he declares, chap 11· 19, "like a lamb, or an ox that is brought to the slaughter; and I knew not that they had devised devices against me, *saying*, let us destroy the tree with the fruit thereof, and let us cut him off from the land of the living, that his name may be no more remembered." "Woe is me," he says chap 15 10, "my mother, that thou hast borne me a man of strife and a man of contention to the whole earth!" V. 15, 18, "O Lord, thou knowest; remember and visit me, and revenge me of my persecutors; take me not away in thy long suffering; know, that for thy sake, I have suffered rebuke. Why is my pain perpetual, and my wound incurable which refuseth to be healed? Wilt thou be unto me altogether as a liar, and as waters that fail?" Further, 20. 7, "O, Lord thou hast persuaded me, and I was persuaded; thou art stronger than I, and hast prevailed; I am in derision daily, every one mocketh me" V. 10, "I hear, how many upbraid and terrify me every where; accuse him! Yea, we will accuse him, say all my friends and companions, if we may overreach him and come near to him and avenge ourselves on him" V. 14—18, his distress rises so high that he suffers himself to be hurried on by his passion, to curse the day of his birth * But yet in all these sufferings, the prophets often had occasion to experience also, that the Lord, their helper, was more powerful than men, their foes The Lord acknowledged them, gave testimony in their favor by the fulfilment of their predictions, often proved them to be his messengers by miracles, and avenged them of their enemies Since then, they alternately experienced through life the extreme corruption of men, and the resistless power of God, which was *infinitely superior to evil*, why should they not have been easily led to anticipate that their great successor in whom the *ideal* of their order, which was only imperfectly exhibited in themselves, was to be realized, should in like manner pass through ignominy and suffering, to glory and joy? On the one hand, he was to appear among the same people, whose depravity was the

---

* Comp Rosenmüller, Leiden und Hoffnungen der Propheten, in Gabler's neueste theol Journ II 4. 1799. Dess Comment zum Jes t III p 324 sqq ed II

source of their sufferings, and whose sinfulness must be the more excited to oppose him, because in him it encountered that which was purely divine, and without any mixture of sin. And, on the other hand, how could God abandon him to suffer without assistance and exaltation to glory, whom he highly esteemed, and who was a partaker of his nature, since he had so faithfully interposed in favor of his servants, who, though sincere indeed, were always imperfect and sinful. The third principal office which God established in the theocracy was the sacerdotal; and as this consequently became a ground-work of the idea of the Messiah, the prophets must have been led at once to the doctrine of his sacrificial death. Men expected from the Messiah, what the priests could indeed well represent, but not impart by their sacrifices, viz. the abolishing of sin, which must precede the reunion with God—that purity which was necessary for inward communion with him; just as the priests procured for them again, that which was requisite to restore them to the privileges of the outward theocracy. The blotting out of sins is mentioned in many places as the characteristic mark of the times of the Messiah. But how shall he accomplish this? By the offering of men and animals? Even Moses, of old, was far from ascribing to them this power,* and the views of the prophets on this subject are placed beyond a doubt by their own plain declarations.† Or shall he effect it by exciting a zeal for virtue, by means of his doctrine? The prophets were too well acquainted with the corruption of the human heart in general, and of that of the people of Israel in particular, to expect so great a result from the inculcation of a new doctrine. They were moreover already familiar with the idea of substitution; since the legal sacrifices, though merely symbolical in reference to acceptance with God, were strictly vicarious and possessed a real efficacy with

---

* This De Wette also confesses, De morte expiat p 20 not. "Neque alio nisi sensu symbolico victimarum substitutio in locum offerentis sumi potest, licet postea sicut omnia symbola, in superstitionem verterit." Comp Süskind in Flatt's Magazin III p 204 seq.

† Comp e g Is 66 1—3 1 11, 12 Am 5 25 26 Jer 3 22, 23 Ps 51. In order to recall to the memory of the people the true import of sacrifices, the prophets impress upon them in this and other passages, the doctrine, that sacrifices were pleasing to God, only when brought with a believing disposition, and that whoever should present them without this, far from appeasing God, would only the more provoke his displeasure

respect to the outward theocracy.* If now it was anticipated that the Messiah would procure remission of sins by a far greater and more excellent offering, which like the animal sacrifices should be vicarious, though in reference to a far higher end; what other victim than himself should he, who was at the same time both priest and sacrifice, present to God?

The doctrine then of a suffering and atoning Messiah could easily be associated with many ideas already in the mind. But still the prophets could not announce this doctrine to mankind, without a special revelation from God. How many opinions were there, with which the doctrine of immortality might easily have been connected, how many natural reasons in its favor, how many intimations of it, and yet we do not find it expressly declared, in the writings of either Moses or the prophets; for God delayed to reveal it on grounds arising from the nature of the theocracy; and the sacred writers carefully guarded against blending that which appeared probable to men,

---

* From not distinguishing between the two, great confusion has arisen in the investigation of the design and import of the sacrifices under the Mosaic dispensation. So great was the multiplicity of the laws, as to render it impossible, even for him who was conscientious in their observance, exactly to fulfil them. It was, therefore, necessary, that a method should be provided, which would at once preserve the sanctity of the law, and lessen its pressure. This was effected by allowing him, who had exposed himself to punishment by transgressing the theocratic laws, to obtain redemption by the offering of sacrifices. In this respect, however, they were expiatory only for transgressions, which did not spring from a wicked contempt of the law, but rather from ignorance, or carelessness. Great and wilful offences were punished with expulsion from the theocracy, or with death. Sacrifices only could procure theocratical purity in certain cases, and this purity was connected with the outward conduct alone, and not with the accompanying disposition. But the sin-offerings affected not merely the relation of the sinner to the outward theocracy, but also to the holy and righteous God; in this respect, however, they were not efficacious, but only symbolical. (In reference to the former relation it is said, Heb. 9:13, of sacrifices, they sanctify $\pi\rho\grave{o}\varsigma\ \tau\grave{\eta}\nu\ \tau\tilde{\eta}\varsigma\ \sigma\alpha\rho\varkappa\grave{o}\varsigma\ \varkappa\alpha\vartheta\alpha\rho\acute{o}\tau\eta\tau\alpha$, in reference to the latter they are called, v. 9, $\mu\grave{\eta}\ \delta\upsilon\nu\acute{\alpha}\mu\varepsilon\nu\alpha\iota\ \varkappa\alpha\tau\grave{\alpha}\ \sigma\upsilon\nu\varepsilon\acute{\iota}\delta\eta\sigma\iota\nu\ \tau\varepsilon\lambda\varepsilon\iota\tilde{\omega}\sigma\alpha\iota\ \tau\grave{o}\nu\ \lambda\alpha\tau\rho\varepsilon\acute{\upsilon}o\nu\tau\alpha$, and it is said, 10:3, that they effected only the $\dot{\alpha}\nu\acute{\alpha}\mu\nu\eta\sigma\iota\varsigma\ \dot{\alpha}\mu\alpha\rho\tau\iota\tilde{\omega}\nu$, since it is impossible that the blood of bulls and goats should take away sins; with which comp. Philo de vita Mos. l. III. p. 669 $o\grave{\upsilon}\ \lambda\acute{\upsilon}\sigma\iota\nu\ \dot{\alpha}\mu\alpha\rho\tau\eta\mu\acute{\alpha}\tau\omega\nu,\ \dot{\alpha}\lambda\lambda'\ \dot{\upsilon}\tau\acute{o}\mu\nu\eta\sigma\iota\nu\ \dot{\epsilon}\rho\gamma\acute{\alpha}\zeta o\nu\tau\alpha\iota$.) When the sinner caused the blood of the animal to be poured out, he declared, that he had deserved death, if God were disposed to deal with him according to his justice, instead of his mercy. The efficacy of the sacrifices, in this respect, depended entirely on the disposition with which they were presented.

with what was made certain by the inspiration of God. But in the case before us the revelation from God was not withheld. This is evident from the passages, which relate to the sufferings and death of the Messiah. We here collect them together, that they may be seen at a single view. The demonstration of their true import is intentionally postponed, until we come to examine them separately. They consist of three classes.

1. Places which treat of the humiliation and sufferings of the Messiah in general. That the Messiah should at first be small and of no reputation, is indicated by Isaiah chap. 11. 1, where he compares him with a feeble twig or shoot, which springs up from the root of a tree, that has been cut down. A similar figure is employed by Ezekiel, 17. 22. He represents the Messiah as a weak and tender shoot, which, planted on a high mountain, continues to grow until it becomes a stately tree, beneath which all the fowls of heaven dwell. Zechariah also, 9. 9, treats of the Messiah in his state of humiliation. He predicts that he shall come lowly (עָנִי) and riding upon an ass, that is, he shall not appear as a powerful worldly Ruler, but in a lowly condition, and in the form of a servant, and in humility lead a wearisome life. But the most striking picture of the Messiah in his humble condition, as he goes forth meek and lowly to seek that which was lost, is given in Isaiah XLII and XLIX. In the last mentioned chapter, the idea of suffering is subjoined to that of humiliation; the people of Israel, whom this servant, the Messiah, must bring back to God, resist; he is called, v. 7: he whom all despise, whom the nation abhorreth, the servant of tyrants. The idea of suffering is predominant in chap. L. V. 6, where he is introduced as speaking, he says "I gave my back to the smiters, and my cheeks to them that plucked off the hair; I hid not my face from shame and spitting." That the suffering Messiah is set before us in Ps. XVI, XXII and XL., we have already seen. According to Ps. 22. 7—19, his hands and feet were pierced, and his garments divided among his enemies.

2. Passages in which his death was foretold. All the passages which speak of the humiliation and sufferings of the Messiah do not mention the death, in which they were to terminate, and which was to be his pathway to glory. There are however besides the passage in Isaiah LIII, which will soon be examined, distinct references to his death in Psalm 16. 9—11, where the Messiah expresses the hope, that Jehovah will not leave him in the grave, but restore him to life;

in Zech. 12. 9, where it is predicted that the Jews at some future period should return to the Messiah, whom they had previously pierced; also in 13 7, where the sword is drawn against the Shepherd of Jehovah, or in other words, death is inflicted upon him, and in Dan. 9 26, where the Messiah is cut off for the sins of the people; and for this, they are to be punished by the destruction of their city

3. Passages in which the end to be obtained by the suffering and death of the Messiah is declared. The prophets in many places mention the remission and extirpation of sin, as the characteristic mark of the times of the Messiah, and as the object of his mission See Dan. 9 24 "To finish the transgression, and to make an end of sins, and to make reconciliation for iniquity, and to bring in everlasting righteousness." Zech 13. 1 "In that day there shall be a fountain opened to the house of David, and to the inhabitants of Jerusalem for sin and for uncleanness." But as in most of these places, they do not explain the method by which sins should be forgiven and done away; so on the other hand when they predict the sufferings and death of the Messiah, they for the most part speak only of the fact, without assigning the reasons for it. But yet there are passages, in which the sufferings of the Messiah are represented as being the cause of the forgiveness of sins, which should be granted in his time Ps. xxii, the extension of true religion is to be the consequence of his sufferings This passage leaves no doubt that these sufferings are the cause of the extirpation of sin; but still it remains uncertain how this cause is to produce its effect. This uncertainty is removed by the passage in Isa LIII, where it is declared that he suffers and dies in our stead, that he bears the sufferings due to us as the punishment of our sins, and by this means justifies us before God.*

We find then the assertion of our opponents entirely groundless, whether we examine it by the Old Testament or the New. This much however is correct, that the prophets do not so often discourse of the suffering and atoning, as of the glorified Messiah. But this circumstance can be satisfactorily explained † Had they fashioned their predictions according to their own inclination and choice, without respect to those, whom they addressed, they would doubtless

---

* See Part II on the chapter, where it will be proved that the passages cited teach the doctrine of a vicarious satisfaction

† See the full development in Seiler die Weissagungen und ihre Erfullung, p 146. etc.

have presented us far more frequently with the image of the Messiah in his humiliation, which would have been the most consoling and joyful to their humble minds. But they could communicate only what they received, and this was always suited to the circumstances of those who heard them. Their influence was not confined to the few pious servants of God, but extended to the whole mass of the people, and the design of the theocracy was greatly promoted by retaining them even in outward allegiance to God. But this was not to be effected by the doctrine of a suffering Messiah;, for before this doctrine can strengthen and elevate the soul and bind it, much preparation is necessary to fit the ground for the reception of the seed. This doctrine is unintelligible and offensive to men who are rude, sensual, and unconscious of their sins. Upon such persons, the representation of a triumphant Messiah would exert a far more powerful influence, and the lower the State declined the more did they need such a representation for their encouragement. And thus we perceive why this view of the Messiah is so constantly given, particularly by Ezekiel and Jeremiah, prophets who lived at the time of the captivity. Here, where the temptation to apostasy was so strong with the great body of the people, it was peculiarly important to oppose to it a powerful motive to allegiance.—The divine wisdom then had respect to all the necessities of the people. On the one hand, it caused the humble and suffering Messiah to be announced, that believers under the old covenant might put their trust in him, as their future Saviour, and the efficient cause of the forgiveness of their sins, and that when he should appear, the honest inquirer need not be perplexed by a want of correspondence between the prophecies of his condition, especially as the divinity in the form of a servant is in itself considered offensive to the natural man, as such, and becomes a temptation to unbelief. On the other hand, it caused the Messiah in lowliness to be less prominent than the Messiah in glory, in order that he might be found by those only, who were placing their reliance on him, and remain unknown to those, to whom he must have been an offence.

But were the predictions concerning a suffering and atoning Redeemer sufficiently plain to be understood by those, who possessed the requisite preparation of mind? In order to answer this question, we are led to an investigation which has been often prosecuted in modern times, and with various results; viz., whether this doctrine of a suffering and atoning Messiah was known among the Jews in the time of Christ. After the example of all the older theologians, Kuinol, Corrodi, Schmidt, Staudlin, Politz, Hartmann, Bertholdt, and others, have in recent times decided in the affirmative. On the other hand, besides Döderlein, Ammon, Seiler, Bauer, Gabler, Eckermann, we find De Wette especially maintains the negative. The latter has devoted the whole of the first part of his treatise *De morte expiatoria* to this investigation. Of the same opinion also is Bretschneider (Dogm I. p. 134 seq), and Baumgarten-Crusius (Bibl. Theol p. 133).*

It is indeed undeniable, that in the time of Christ, by far the greater portion of the Jews neither knew nor desired to know any thing of a suffering, dying and atoning Messiah They expected only a Messiah, who should come in his glory. This, as a generally acknowledged fact, scarcely stands in need of proof The doctrine of the cross was to the Jews a stumbling block, 1 Cor. 1: 23. The Pharisees and doctors beheld in the sufferings and death of Jesus, a proof that he could not be the Messiah. "He delivered others; if he be the Christ, the chosen of God, let him deliver himself." According to John 12: 34, the belief generally prevailed among the people, that the Messiah was not to die. Even the Apostles themselves were far from entertaining the idea of a suffering and dying Redeemer. The clearest and most explicit declarations of Christ upon this subject, were either not understood, or soon expelled from their minds by their worldly hopes and forgotten. Comp Mark 9. 32. Luke 18. 34. Matt 16 22.

But this, instead of appearing strange, is what we should natural-

---

* In respect to the literature we refer to De Wette l c p 3—5 The different doctrinal interests which have governed the investigation, are strikingly exhibited by Stäudlin über den Zweck und die Wirkungen des Todes Jesu, in der Gotting Bibl f theol Litt I p 252 seq The rationalists were influenced by two opposite motives, either the fear, that if the Jews found predictions of the suffering and atoning Messiah in the Scriptures of the Old Testament, it must also be conceded that they really existed, or the hope, that if the existence of the doctrine of the vicarious satisfaction of the Messiah among the Jews could be proved, the assertion might be rendered plausible, that the authors of the New Testament had taught it only by way of accommodation, or from being embarrassed by the prevailing views of their day In the case of the supernaturalists, on the contrary, this hope and fear were exactly reversed With respect to the latter, Seiler, who plainly allows himself to be influenced by it, should have quieted himself by his own words. "Is a proposition therefore false, because the Jews regard it as a truth? Should a divine teacher be prevented from speaking the truth, because the Jews also acknowledge it?

ly expect, especially after what has just been remarked respecting the way, in which the doctrine of the sufferings and death of the Messiah was revealed in the writings of the Old Testament. Experience shows, that the doctrines of a religious document are acknowledged and believed by those who adopt it as the rule of judgment, only so long as they do not contradict their lives and sentiments. But when this is the case, the offensive doctrine is set aside, either because the attention is diverted from those passages in which it is taught, and which are declared to be dark and unintelligible, and fixed upon those which seem to be of an opposite character, and more agreeable to the inclination; or else their meaning is perverted by forced interpretations. Abundant evidence of this might be collected from the history of the true religion, as well as from that of all false religions; indeed it would be sufficient to refer merely to modern and recent times. But that the doctrine of a suffering and atoning Messiah was in direct opposition to the reigning disposition of the Jews at the time of Christ's appearance, scarcely needs to be proved. The state of mind which prepares the way for the reception of this doctrine is the knowledge of our sinfulness, and consequent need of redemption. But the Evangelists have left us the plainest proof that this preparation did not exist among the great body of the Jews in the time of Christ, that, in the pride of their hearts, they rather expected to be justified before God by their works: that unawakened by the Holy Spirit, ignorant alike of God and of themselves, they longed for a deliverer only from outward degradation and misery, and not from the far heavier inward bondage in which they were held.

We shall, however, be surprised, if it can be made to appear, as some maintain, that not only the greater part, but all the Jews in the time of Christ, were far from expecting a suffering and atoning Messiah. But still it would by no means follow from this, that no prophecies of such a Messiah are to be found in the Old Testament, but only that the whole people, influenced by their worldly views, had confined themselves to that portion of the Messianic predictions which best suited their inclinations, or at most, that the better disposed among them were too weak to resist the example of the multitude. We can, however, show from sure grounds, that the better portion of the Jewish people at the time of Christ's appearance, and, even at a later period, expected a suffering and atoning Messiah, and that the origin of the opposite opinion, can be explained only by ascribing it to doctrinal prejudice

We naturally look to the writings of the New Testament, as the chief sources of information on this subject. The apocryphal books of the Old Testament, as well as the writings of Josephus and Philo, are generally of little use in ascertaining the opinions of the Jews respecting the Messiah, and they say nothing of his sufferings and atonement. Comp. de Wette l c. p 34, 35 and the authors there quoted. The New Testament has the advantage over the remaining Jewish writings, both in point of time and of certainty.

Two passages which it contains, especially deserve attention. Luke 2. 35, the aged Simeon, ἄνθρωπος δίκαιος καὶ εὐλαβὴς, προσδεχόμενος παράκλησιν τοῦ Ἰσραήλ, foretels to Mary that a sword would pierce through her soul, (καὶ σοῦ δὲ αὐτῆς τὴν ψυχὴν διελεύσεται ῥομφαία), an expression too strong to be understood of any thing short of the most severe and bitter suffering. See Ps 42. 11 73· 21 De Wette l c p. 52, knows of no other way to set aside this passage than flatly to assume, that the first two chapters of Luke were written at a later period, notwithstanding the strong grounds, especially the internal, by which their genuineness has been recently defended. See d Rec in Bengel's Archiv. f d Theol I, 1 p 52. This much, however, must be conceded, that this passage proves only that the doctrine of a *suffering*, not an *atoning* Messiah, existed among the Jews, for Simeon refers merely to the human causes, not to the divine purposes of the Redeemer's suffering.

But the second passage, John 1: 29, goes further. It leads us to the conclusion, first, that not only the doctrine of the sufferings and death of the Messiah, but also that of their *vicarious* efficacy was known to the enlightened Israelites in the time of Christ, and secondly, that they had derived it from the writings of the Old Testament. John at the sight of Christ then exclaims· ἴδε ὁ ἀμνὸς τοῦ θεοῦ ὁ αἴρων τὴν ἁμαρτίαν τοῦ κόσμου. After these words had been explained as referring to the vicarious death of the Messiah, by all the older interpreters except the Socinians, and some of the followers of Arminius; Herder, Paulus, Ziegler, Gabler, Kuinoel in modern times attempted to set aside this unpleasant result by another interpretation; De Wette (l. c p. 52) on the other hand, by casting suspicion on the evangelist John, in reference to what he says concerning the Baptist. On the contrary, among the recent defenders of the right interpretation, are to be mentioned especially, Storr in his profound discussion: "Grammatische Bemerkungen über Joh. 1 29 in Flatt's Magazin, II. p 193 seq, Lücke and Tholuck in their commentaries.

We examine first the objections which have been urged against referring this declaration of John to the sacrificial death of Christ 1. "John, at the time, could have had no knowledge of this, for had he possessed it he would have imparted it to his disciples. That he did not impart it, however, appears from the inability of the Apostles of Jesus, among whom were some who had formerly been disciples of John, John 1: 37, to understand their Master, when he foretold his approaching sufferings and death. Further, that John taught the common opinions of a Messiah in glory, is manifest from the embassy which he sent to Jesus, Matt xi. Had he believed in the humiliation of the Messiah, how could he have been perplexed by the proceedings of Jesus? And lastly, how little acquaintance with the work of redemption he possessed, is evident from his being called by Christ himself, 'the least in the kingdom of heaven'" Comp Gabler Meletemata in h l. 1. p 10. De Wette l. c p. 53 Kuinol in Joh. p. 149. In reply to these objections, arising from that deficiency of psychological knowledge which belongs to rationalism, we offer the following remarks. First, as to the ignorance of those Apostles, who had formerly been the disciples of John, concerning the vicarious death of Christ. When the Baptist exclaims, "behold! this is he who by suffering and death atones for the sins of the world," it does not follow, either that he himself possessed a connected and particular view of this subject, or that he fully explained it to his disciples. Although John on the whole rightly understood the prediction of the suffering and atoning death of the Messiah, yet before the fulfilment much must have remained dark and ambiguous to him, as well as to all other enlightened Israelites. He could therefore have given only *intimations* to his disciples, and even these he might have withheld, under the guidance of that wisdom which induced our Lord so long to defer instructing his disciples respecting his sufferings and death, and especially the end they were designed to accomplish, and then to discourse with them on the subject, only comparatively seldom and briefly. But even granting that John gave these intimations, the same causes operated in this case which afterwards prevented the Apostles, either from understanding, or remembering the declarations of Christ, respecting his approaching death. Comp. Matt 16: 21 with Matt 20 20 seq. The conception of a suffering Messiah was foreign from the whole train of thought to which the worldly disciples of John were accustomed, and found in their minds nothing with which it could be associated; and even if it gained admittance at first it must have been soon expelled, by the prevailing notions of the people with whom they still harmonized in sentiment. Equally inconclusive is the evidence to be derived from the embassy of the Baptist. If we are unwilling to suppose that in an hour of weakness his knowledge of the suffering and atoning Messiah may have been obscured, a supposition by no means unnatural, still every thing is easily explained, when we call to mind that John who derived his knowledge from the prophecies of the Old Testament, expected a Messiah who was not merely to suffer and die, but likewise, through suffering and death, to be exalted to glory. If now John supposed, (as according to these predictions in which the feeble beginning and the subsequent glorious completion of the Messiah's kingdom are ultimately blended, it was almost unavoidable that he should), that Christ after having passed through suffering and death, would immediately establish the *regnum gloriae,* how must each moment of delay have appeared too long, while, in prison, he anxiously looked for that deliverance, of which the triumph of the Messiah was the only ground of hope!* And lastly in the passage in Matt. 11: 11, where Christ places John below the least member of the new covenant, he surely did not deny that he possessed the knowledge of his expiatory death. This passage does not refer, as De Wette asserts, either exclusively, or chiefly to the *intelligentia rei Messianae,* although in this respect the genuine members of the new covenant, who possessed the knowledge of the finished sacrifice of Christ, enjoyed far greater advantages than those of the old, who could only look to this sacrifice as still future. The characteristic difference between the members of the old covenant, and those of the new, to which Christ here directs the attention, rather consists, not indeed entirely, but principally, in the possession by the latter, of the $\pi\nu\epsilon\tilde{\nu}\mu\alpha$ $X\varrho\iota\sigma\tau o\tilde{\nu}$ *spirit of Christ,* which could not be imparted until his sacrificial death had

---

* De Wette is wrong in asserting a contradiction between this relation and the passages, John 1 20, etc. and John 3 28, etc. according to which, John had the firmest conviction of the Messianic dignity of Jesus. If it can, as is possible, be inferred from them, that John doubted, this only proves, what every Christian is acquainted with by his own experience, a momentary weakness of faith, occasioned by impatience in view of his unhappy condition, and his disappointed hope that Christ would hasten the completion of his work. That in the depths of his soul his faith was yet firm in the Messianic dignity of Jesus, appears from his seeking the resolution of his doubts from Christ himself. It is still easier to remove the remaining apparent contradictions, which De Wette is disposed to find in the history of John.

changed the relation between God and the world. 2. It is said that, "the allusion cannot be to a lamb, as a *sacrifice*, but only as a symbol of meekness, calmness, and patience, as in Isaiah 53 7. The figure cannot be taken from the paschal lamb, because that was not properly a sacrifice, nor from the sin and trespass offerings, because in them lambs were never used." This objection is any thing but well grounded In the first place there is no reason why the figure may not have been taken from the paschal lamb; for in the Old Testament, the paschal lambs are expressly called זבחים, Ex 12 27 23. 18, and by Josephus and Philo θυσίαι and θύματα, and the possibility of their being referred to in this instance is decidedly proved by the passage 1 Cor. 5 7 καὶ γὰρ τὸ πάσχα ἡμῶν ὑπὲρ ἡμῶν ἐτύθη Χριστός It is true indeed that the figure is not strictly accurate, inasmuch as this lamb was not an expiatory sacrifice, but if its inaccuracy did not prevent Paul, it surely may not have prevented John from employing it But for this reason it is nevertheless more probable that the figure was taken from the propitiatory sacrifice, where it is entirely appropriate. That sheep were used for trespass offerings as well as for proper sin offerings, appears from the passages quoted by Storr l c. p 196, particularly from Lev. 4 32.*
The objection, that in this passage of Leviticus, sheep and not lambs are mentioned, is obviated by the remark that the Greek ἀμνός is often used in a wider sense; and the LXX employ it in some passages as the translation of the Hebrew כבש, which indeed is the case in the present instance See Biel thes phil. s v ἀμνός Kircher conc. s. v. כבש. That John here uses ἀμνός in this more comprehensive sense, is evident from the fact that in the passage in Isaiah, which he had in view, the words כש and רחל are found, which latter the LXX elsewhere render πρόβατον, but here ἀμνός in the above mentioned sense Sheep indeed were not the only, nor the most usual offerings of this kind; John, however, had many inducements to borrow his figure from *them*. The comparison with any of the other animals offered in sacrifice would have been degrading; he wished to exhibit at once the resignation and patience with which Jesus would

---

* That the difference between expiatory and purifying sacrifices, by which it has been attempted to set aside several of the passages quoted, if not entirely groundless, is unimportant, might be easily shown, if this were the place for such an investigation Gabler himself confesses, that the Evangelist John paid no regard to it. Wherefore then may not this have been the case with John the Baptist in like manner?

present himself as a sacrifice, (comp. die Stellen des Festus bie Storr l. c. p. 194), and above all, he was influenced by the example of the prophet Isaiah.

3 "The word αἴρειν in the Alexandrian version never means: *to bear*, but always *to remove, take away*, and particularly in connexion with nouns, which signify sin, it never means, to take it upon oneself, or to atone for it by suffering its penalty." But were the first assertion correct, it would not be conclusive, since the word occurs in this sense, if not in the Septuagint, yet in the classic writings, and even in several passages of the New Testament also, as Matt. 27: 32 It is, however, by no means true, that the word is not used in this sense in the Septuagint. See Lam. 3. 27. (Comp. Storr l. c. p. 200 seq.) But if the meaning *to bear*, is sufficiently established, it is of no importance, that αἴρειν τὴν ἁμαρτίαν is not used by the LXX in the sense of atoning for sin by suffering its punishment, since it is not material whether αἴρειν, or another word of similar import be employed, as Isaiah 53: 4 τὰς ἁμαρτίας ἡμῶν φέρει, v 11, ἀνοίσει, v. 12, ἀνήνεγκε, Symmachus v. 11, καὶ τὰς ἀσεβείας αὐτῶν αὐτὸς ὑπενέγκει.

Those critics, who, as we have seen repeat the old interpretation on insufficient grounds, have substituted two new ones, in its place. 1. Gabler retains the sense "to bear," and makes ἁμαρτία signify . wickedness, and the sense of the passage Christ shall deeply experience the wickedness of men, but patiently endure it. In opposition to this, however, De Wette has already justly remarked, l. c. p. 54, that this interpretation violates the usage of the language, since ἁμαρτία cannot mean wickedness, which is always expressed by ἀνομία, πονηρία, κακία, or a similar word 2 Others, as Kuinoel, give to the word αἴρειν the meaning, *to put away, to remove;* they regard the lamb as merely an image of patience, and explain the passage thus "behold this innocent sufferer, who, by his doctrine and example, shall remove the sin of the world" But it is a decisive argument against this forced explanation, that it dismembers the expression of John, since the connexion between the figure of the lamb, and ὁ αἴρων τὴν ἁμαρτίαν τοῦ κόσμου, is destroyed

Against both these interpretations and in favor of that which has been generally received, we offer the following remarks

1 There is no reason to doubt, and it is generally conceded, that John had in view the passage in Isaiah LIII. As now the eminent servant of God, who, v 7, is compared to a lamb, on account of his

patience, is there represented as an expiatory victim, אשם, who should bear the sins of the world, or in other words take upon himself the punishment of them. See v. 4, τὰς ἁμαρτίας ἡμῶν φέρει. V. 5, ἐτραυματίσθη διὰ τὰς ἁμαρτίας ἡμῶν. V. 11, καὶ τὰς ἁμαρτίας αὐτῶν αὐτὸς ἀνοίσει V. 12, καὶ αὐτὸς ἁμαρτίας πολλῶν ἀνήνεγκε, so the expression, ὁ αἴρων, etc. in which we cannot fail to perceive that these passages are all comprized, can refer to nothing else than substitution and atonement,* and of course, unless we choose in an unnatural manner to dismember the passage, the lamb must be regarded as an expiatory victim.

2. That the lamb is not merely an image of resignation and patience, but a sacrifice for sin, is evident from numerous passages of the Apocalypse, where Christ is called an ἀρνίον ἐσφαγμένον, or when the αἷμα τοῦ ἀρνίου is spoken of, chap. 5: 6, 12. 7. 14. 12 11 13 8. In 1 Peter also, 1. 19, Christ is called a lamb without spot or blemish, by whose blood we were redeemed. The force of these parallel passages, Gabler himself acknowledges; and concedes, that the Evangelist John understood the expression of the Baptist in the sense for which we contend, but resorts to the unnatural supposition that he was mistaken.

It is proved then, that at the coming of Christ the doctrine of a suffering and atoning Messiah was not unknown to the more enlightened Jews. For that John the Baptist was by no means first taught it by an immediate divine revelation, as some have supposed, is evident; since he derived it from Isaiah LIII, and presupposed the relation of the passage to the Messiah as undeniable. The result, however, to which the New Testament has led us, is not a little confirmed by the more ancient writings of the Jews. The authors of the Talmud, as well as the Cabbalistic and other writings, looked for a suffering and atoning Messiah, though in respect to the way in which he should atone for sin, they differed widely from each other. We here omit the quotation of particular passages, especially as we shall have occasion to adduce several of the most remarkable, when we come to Isaiah LIII. We now merely refer to the collections by Schottgen, hor Heb. t. II on Isaiah LIII and Ps. XXII p. 551. Hulsius theol. Judaica p. 309. Corrodi Chiliasmus I p 284, etc. Schmidt Christol. Fragmente p. 18, etc. and p. 43, and De Wette l. c. p. 61.

---

* De Wette l. c. p. 55. "Ubi locutiones de Jesu munere Messiano adhibitas deprehendimus, quae ad illum locum referendae videntur, de expiatione cogitemus necesse est."

We must however, here examine the manner in which De Wette has sought to weaken the force of these passages. He takes the ground that all the Jewish writings, which contain the doctrine of a suffering and atoning Messiah, were composed long after the time of Christ, and in this he is doubtless correct, although the book Sohar as to its essential elements, certainly belongs to a much earlier period than he allows. He then endeavors to show, p 41 etc. that this doctrine, unknown to the ancient Jews, was received into the later Jewish system of religious doctrine from Christianity, and when this had been done, the doctrine was attributed to certain passages of the Old Testament, either in imitation of the Christians, or because the passages, though not properly relating to the Messiah, yet were of such a nature, as to invite to this false interpretation, so soon as the notion of a suffering Messiah was entertained See l c p. 70

But this assertion of De Wette's is already shown to be groundless, since it is certain from the evidence of the New Testament already adduced, that this doctrine existed among the Jews, as early as the time of Christ. The chief additional objections, to which it is liable are the following.

1. To him who is in any degree acquainted with the stand which the Jews have taken against Christians from the beginning, it is impossible for this reason alone to conceive that they should have borrowed this doctrine from them. It is true that De Wette appeals to other things, which must likewise have passed from the Christians to the Jews, viz. the baptism of proselytes, certain petitions in the Lord's prayer, and certain parables of the New Testament, which have their counterpart in the Talmud. But not to insist that it is disputed and improbable, that these things, except the last, really were borrowed from the Christians, there is a great and obvious difference, between borrowing a single usage, which might have happened altogether imperceptibly, because that which already existed needed only to receive a more definite and limited character, or a single sentence, stamped with the impress of the Old Testament, and therefore liable to be regarded as common property; and adopting a doctrine directly opposed to the carnal disposition, foreign from the received system, and moreover fundamental in that of adversaries. Here, if any where, the incontrovertible rule applies, which is laid down by Schmidt, Christol Fragm. p 6, for the examination of the old Jewish doctrines, viz " representations of the Messiah, as unlike the common opinions of the Jews, which make him a temporal king,

as they are analogous to those of the Christians—representations, which the later Jews could not without manifest difficulty have combined with their other ideas, are ancient, and were prevalent in the time of Christ."

2 In the whole christology of the Jews, there is nothing in the way of analogy to confirm, but every thing to refute this assertion. Their views of the Messiah, as will be evident to any one upon a careful examination, rest upon Old Testament grounds, though upon a perverted interpretation of the prophecies We would here direct the attention only to the doctrine of the sorrows of the Messiah חבלי המשיח, which as De Wette himself remarks, p. 61, is connected with that of a suffering and atoning Messiah, and the Old Testament origin of which, he likewise in the same place acknowledges. Even the most specific conceptions of the Messiah can be traced to the Old Testament prophecies, either rightly or erroneously understood; or at least to the effort to reconcile their apparently conflicting declarations. Thus e. g. the fable concerning the leprosy arose from a false interpretation of Isaiah 53 4, as plainly appears from the Talmud, as will be shown in our remarks on the passage

3. Had the Jews borrowed from the Christians the doctrine of the suffering, atoning and dying Messiah, it is impossible to see, why they did not also adopt the easy method of reconciling this doctrine with that of an exalted and glorified Messiah, which the Christian religion presented to them. The apparent contradiction in the passages of the Old Testament, which contain both doctrines, is removed in the Christian system in a manner the most easy and natural, by the doctrine of the Messiah's twofold appearance, in obscurity and in glory, and his twofold condition, of lowliness and of exaltation But instead of this the Jews resort to the strangest and most groundless hypothesis, in order to remove the difficulty; plainly showing, that without being influenced in the least by Christianity they develope the doctrine in question from the prophecies of the Old Testament, on which much darkness certainly existed, before it was dispelled by the light of their fulfilment. The principal hypotheses to which we allude are the following.

1. The doctrine concerning the Messiah Ben Joseph and the Messiah Ben David The former was to be slain in the war with Gog and Magog, the latter to complete the deliverance of the covenant people, and live and reign forever * The origin of this fiction

---

* That this doctrine was of later origin, Glaesener de gemino Judaeorum

is manifest. The Jews were unable to obviate the difficulty presented by those passages, which speak of the death of the Messiah, which is removed by the Christian doctrine of the two natures of Christ, and his resurrection from the dead, and they therefore believed themselves compelled to adopt the opinion, that there should be two Messiahs. This is manifest from the following reasons. That this doctrine is to be traced to Zech. 12. 10, is shown by a comparison of two passages in the Gemara of Jerusalem, (which probably belongs to the year 230, or 270 A. D.) and the Gemara of Babylon, (probably of the sixth century, see Wolf Bibl. Hebr. II. p. 674, 686). In the former passage it is said, in reference to Zech. 12. 10 · תרין אמורין חד אמר זה הספידו של משיח וחורנה אמר זה הספידו של יצר הרע, ("There are two opinions respecting this place, one that it speaks of a lamentation on account of the Messiah, the other, on account of innate sinful desires." In the second passage, in the tract, Succot. fol. 52, col. 1 in Glaesener de Gem. Jud. Messia p. 46, it is said, on Zech. 12. 12 ("And the land shall mourn, every family apart") האי הספידה מאי עבידתיה פליגי בה רבי דוסא ורבנן חד אמר על משיח בן יוסף שנהרג וחד אמר על יצר הרע שנהרג בשלמא למאן דאמר על משיח בן יוסף שנהרג היינו דכתיב והביטו אלי את אשר דקרו וספדו עליו כמספד על היחיד, ("But what shall be the cause of this lamentation? On this point R. Dusa, and the doctors disagree. According to the one opinion, it is for the Messiah Ben Joseph, who shall be slain; according to the other, it is for the inbred sinful desires, which shall be slain. But peace be to him, who understands it of the death of the Messiah Ben Joseph. To him particularly, does the passage in Zech. 12. 10 refer · And they shall mourn for him, as one mourneth for an only son, etc.") How little they knew what to do with Zech. 12. 10, before the notion of the Messiah Ben Joseph had been invented, is seen from its being explained of יצר הרע; the incongruity of which could not however induce the authors of the Gemara of Babylon entirely to reject it, because of the inconvenience of referring it to the Messiah. This difficulty was removed by the fiction of two Messiahs, and now in the second passage, i. e. that from the Gemara of Babylon, the interpre-

---

Messia, Helmst 1739, p. 145 seq., Schottgen l. c. p. 359, and De Wette who borrows from them, have proved, from the fact, that the oldest paraphrasts, Jonathan on the Prophets, and Onkelos on the Pentateuch, explain of the Messiah Ben David, all those passages, which the later writers refer to the Messiah Ben Joseph.

tation which makes the mourning to be for יצר הרע, was decidedly rejected. That this doctrine was suggested by the passage of Zechariah is further evident from its being constantly grounded upon it, by the Jewish writers, and expressed in the words of the prophet. See the places in Glaesener l. c. p. 56, 57, 147, app. p. 9. Finally, the doctrine concerning the Messiah Ben Joseph, bears precisely the character of one, which was invented merely to explain a difficult passage of Scripture, and laid aside as of no further use, when that purpose was answered. Nothing more is done with this Messiah than to suffer him to die, as soon as by the aid of another prophecy (Ezek. xxxvii) a possible occasion was found for his death; no further concern is felt for him afterwards, as Glaesener justly remarks, p. 41: "Altum nunc est in scriptis Judaeorum de Messia Ben Joseph silentium. Postquam enim cum reliquis a Messia Ben David et Elia a mortuis excitatus fuerit, nihil de eo ulterius deprehenditur. Nulla ei praerogativa prae reliquis Israelitis in regno Messiae Ben David conceditur, nullumque praemium pro clade perpessa imoque ipsa morte pro illis suscepta propositum."* We have still to examine the objections of De Wette to this explanation of the origin of the doctrine, l. c. p. 79. "Had this fable," he remarks, "been invented only to get rid of the notion of the suffering of the Messiah Ben David, why is it found among those also, who do not hesitate to make this Messiah suffer and atone for sin, as is the case with the author of the book Sohar, and the Babylonian Gemarists." This objection affects only those critics, who as several in former times, and Schmidt and Staudlin among the moderns, assert, that the doctrine of the Messiah Ben Joseph, was invented solely for the purpose of explaining all those passages which treat in general of a suffering and atoning Messiah. It does not apply to us, who attribute the origin of this doctrine to the difficulty of admitting the *death* of the Messiah Ben David. The assertion however is erroneous. There is nothing said concerning the sufferings and deep humiliation of the Messiah Ben Joseph before his death, and as far as we know there

---

* Glaesener, append. p. 11, has indeed retracted this statement, since he introduces two passages, according to which, the Messiah Ben Joseph is to be a kind of subordinate king in the Messiah's kingdom; but they both belong to entirely later authors, R. Meier Aldabi and Menasse Ben Israel. Glaesener in this instance, as well as throughout his treatise verifies the objection brought against him by Schottgen l. c. p. 366, of confounding the doctrine of the ancient and modern Jews.

is only a single passage quoted by Eisenmenger I. p 720, and De Wette p 76, in which an atoning efficacy is ascribed to his death. This passage however is taken from the book Schne Luchoth Haberit, written by R. Jeschaja Horwitz, who died 1610 (Wolf Bibl I p 703), and is therefore too recent to be of any importance. On the other hand in the older books, as the Sohar and Talmud, suffering and atonement are constantly ascribed to the Messiah Ben David, most probably because the possibility of his substitution was believed to be founded in his higher and more than human nature. But that the *death* of the Messiah was held to be irreconcilable, particularly with his higher nature, and therefore the doctrine of a second Messiah of an inferior nature was introduced, is evident from a passage of the Sohar, in Sommer Theolog Sohar p 91. "Illo ipso die proveniet Messias, proprietatibus vitalibus, perfectionibus et praerogativis convenientibus instructus. Quae tamen natura non relinquetur sola, sed adjungetur ipsi Messias alter, filius Josephi.—Quia vero iste erit collis inferior, destitutus proprietatibus vitalibus, morietur hic Messias et occisus in statu mortis permanebit ad tempus, donec recolliget iterum vitam hic collis et resurget." "If we adopt this opinion," says De Wette further, "we cannot explain, why the inferior Messiah should be named Ben Joseph or Ben Ephraim, and yet this name cannot have been given him without a cause.' But we must here distinguish between what may have been the origin of the doctrine, and of the name of a second Messiah. When the doctrine of a second Messiah had been invented for another purpose, an attempt was made to accomplish a secondary object by the name attributed to him. According to the predictions of the Old Testament, the reunion of the ten tribes with the Jews, was expected in the times of the Messiah, and this opportunity was taken to confer an honor upon them, by giving to them at least the inferior Messiah; since the superior, as a descendant of David, must derive his origin from the stock of Judah. The truth of this explanation of the origin of the name appears from the fact, that the inferior Messiah is called promiscuously Ben Joseph and Ben Ephraim, not only in the later writings, but in many passages of the Sohar also, (see for example Schottgen l. c p. 551) and in one place cited by Schottgen p 360, he is even descended from the tribe of Manasseh, while the Messiah Ben David bears also the name of the משיח בן יהודה. See Glaesener p 53. That the purpose to honor the ten tribes did not give rise to the doctrine itself (as Paulus asserts, Comment. zu N. T I. p 250), but merely influenced in the choice of the name, appears from the fact already noticed, that the Messiah Ben Joseph after his history is carried forward to his death, and his resurrection also mentioned is entirely forgotten

De Wette, after Gläsener, supposed that the Jews invented this doctrine to point out the collecting of the ten tribes by the Messiah from all regions of the earth, and their restoration to the land of Canaan. But independently of the positive arguments for the explanation which we have given, the improbability of this hypothesis is easily seen. In none of the places cited by Glasener p. 202, etc. and De Wette p. 81, with the exception of two from the book of Mikveh Israel, composed by R. Manasseh Ben Israel, of no authority, both because its origin is recent, (it first appeared 1650, see Wolf Bibl. 1. p 783), and because its contents were not derived from tradition, is the work of assembling the Israelites from the various countries of their dispersion and conducting them to the holy land, assigned to the Messiah Ben Joseph, on the contrary, after his resurrection, the Israelites return of themselves and assemble before him. But how could there have been any occasion to invent this doctrine; for would they assemble themselves together a second time before the Messiah Ben David, under whom also according to the Jewish doctrine, their final collection was soon to follow? Comp. Glasener p. 69. We have seen already, that the most essential part of the doctrine of the Messiah Ben Joseph, is his death. Should we follow De Wette's hypothesis, we could not so much as give a single reason why he should die. It is very clear that the reasons which De Wette adduces are inadmissible: "since only one Messiah is to reign, it would seem advisable that the other should be put out of the way." But here it is not sufficiently considered that even the Messiah Ben Joseph is to share in the general resurrection, effected by the Messiah Ben David and Elias. Were this a real difficulty, as it is not, since even the Messiah Ben Joseph could be appointed to a subordinate station in the kingdom of the Messiah Ben David, it would not be removed by his death. "The feeling of need of an atonement, might have given occasion to the invention of this doctrine of his death." But we have seen already, that they ascribed no atoning efficacy to the death of the Messiah Ben Joseph, but rather expected it from the vicarious sufferings of the Messiah Ben David. "The sin of Jeroboam seems to have required his death." This can only be proved from a single passage of the book Jalkut Chadasch, (see Wolf Bibl. II. p. 1308) which is of very recent times, and is held by the Jews in little respect. That the more ancient Jews did not admit this hypothesis is evident from the fact, that they attributed the atoning efficacy to the sufferings of the Messiah Ben Joseph. The guilt of the sin of Jeroboam would be washed away, even by the vicarious sufferings of the Messiah Ben David.

2. The second hypothesis which was invented to reconcile the passages which speak of a suffering and of a glorified Messiah, is the doctrine, that he, before his appearance upon earth, had atoned in Paradise for the sins of men, by unspeakable sufferings. This theory is found especially in the book Sohar, but occurs not unfrequently elsewhere. See the passages in Eisenmenger II. p 330. Glasener p. 28 seq. Bertholdt Christologia § 25. De Wette p. 65, and also the principal passages from the Sohar in our introduction to Isa. LIII. How could men have fallen upon this strange opinion, if they had borrowed the doctrine of a suffering and atoning Messiah from Christianity, where the sufferings and exaltation of the Messiah stand in so natural a connexion.

3. With the same view, the very prevalent opinion was invented, that the Messiah is already born, but until the time of his appearing expiates the sins of the people; an opinion, whose antiquity is manifest, from its occurrence in the *dialogus cum Tryphone Judaeo*. The existence of these two different hypotheses very clearly shows how much perplexity was occasioned by the doctrine of a suffering and atoning Messiah. That the latter owed its origin solely to the embarrassment arising from this doctrine, appears from the fact, that as often as the birth of the Messiah occurs, it stands in connexion with his sufferings and atonement. See passages by Glasener p 23 seq. Corrodi 1 p 284 f. De Wette p 66. De Wette indeed asserts, that the notion, that the Messiah was already born, was the result of sure calculation, according to which, he must have already come. But strange as it may seem, among all the passages quoted in support of his opinion, and which are borrowed from Glasener p 15, etc. who there adduces them for another purpose, there is not one which is conclusive, or which even relates to the subject. The question discussed in all these passages, is not, why the Messiah must have been already born, but why he had not yet appeared. The reason assigned was the want of repentance and good works among the Israelites. By this means, they relieved themselves from difficulty under every disappointment in their calculations, and we nowhere find them resorting

for aid to the unnecessary assertion, that the birth of the Messiah had already taken place. The explanation we have given of the origin of the notion of the birth of the Messiah, is confirmed by the time at which it was fixed. It is asserted with tolerable unanimity to have taken place at the time when the city was taken, and on the very day when the temple was destroyed. See the passages in Glasener p. 25. With the destruction of the temple, the offering of sacrifices necessarily ceased. Pained by the loss of their accustomed method of reconciliation with God, the Jews, in order to provide another, placed the birth of the Messiah, (which they supposed they must assume in order to obtain a time for his suffering) precisely at the time when the sacrificial service ceased, and made his suffering and atonement then commence.

And thus we have come to the conclusion, that the doctrine of a suffering and atoning Messiah very anciently existed among the Jews, and was not the result of Christian influence, but derived from the writings of the Old Testament. This much may however be conceded, that after the coming of Christ, it was more widely spread, and willingly received among them. This may perhaps have been owing in part, to their attention having been called to this point of their general doctrine concerning the Messiah, by the prominence which the Christians gave to it. But it is certainly to be attributed, far more to the circumstance, that the feeling of the need of atonement, when it could no longer find a specious satisfaction, in consequence of the destruction of the temple, was the more directed to the Messiah. In confirmation of this we refer to a passage of the Sohar in Sommer theol. Sohar p. 94. "While the Israelites were in the holy land, they removed all their wickedness and punishments by holy exercises and by offerings; but now, (since the Levitical service has ceased), must the Messiah take them away from men." From this passage De Wette rashly infers that the general doctrine concerning the sufferings and atonement of the Messiah, originated with the destruction of the temple. But does it follow, because that which had ceased, was so highly valued in after times, that it must have been during its existence? The Levitical offerings were never able to satisfy the need of redemption, which was felt by men of deep reflection, and we have already seen that they earnestly expected the higher satisfaction promised them in the Old Testament.

CHAPTER V.

THE NATURE OF PROPHECY.

On this subject, many erroneous views are current. The prophetic Scriptures are viewed in the same light as all the rest, or if a difference is made in the principles it is overlooked in the practice of interpretation. We must examine this subject the more thoroughly, since the true explanation, as also the defence of numerous Messianic passages, depends on a correct theory of prophecy. At present, however, we confine our researches entirely to the *method* in which revelations were made to the prophets; other analogous inquiries do not suit our purpose and belong to another place.

Our first inquiry relates to the condition of the prophets immediately before, and during the act of prophesying. Since the controversies with the Montanists, it has been the prevailing opinion of the Church, that the essential difference between the prophets of God and the heathen diviners, consists in the fact, that the latter spake in an ecstasy, but the former in full possession of reason and consciousness; and consequently with a clear knowledge of what they uttered. According to Eusebius, Miltiades wrote a book: περὶ τοῦ μὴ δεῖν προφήτην ἐν ἐκστάσει λαλεῖν (hist. eccl v 17.) Epiphanius (adv. haeres Montani c. 2) remarks: ὅσα γὰρ οἱ προφῆται εἰρήκασι μετὰ συνέσεως παρακολουθοῦντες ἐφθέγγοντο, and chap. iv seq he endeavors to show that the possession of intelligence and consciousness is the surest mark of true prophecy. Jerome (praef in Jes.) expresses himself to the same effect in several places. "Neque vero, ut Montanus cum insanis feminis somniat, prophetae in ecstasi loquuti sunt, ut nescirent quid loquerentur, et cum alios erudirent, ipsi ignorarent quid dicerent." Prooem. Nahum. "Non loquitur propheta ἐν ἐκστάσει, ut Montanus et Priscilla Maximillaque delirant, sed quod prophetat liber, intelligentis est quod loquitur." Praef in Habak. "Prophetae visio est, et adversum Montani dogma perversum intelligit, quod videt, nec ut amens loquitur, nec in morem insanientium feminarum, dat sine mente sonum." But Chrysostom (homil 29 in ep ad Cor.) speaks the most definitely respecting the difference between the heathen diviners and the prophets of Jehovah τοῦτο γὰρ μάντεως ἴδιον, τὸ ἐξεστηκέναι, τὸ ἀνάγκην ὑπομένειν, τὸ ὠθεῖσθαι, τὸ ἕλκεσθαι, τὸ σύρεσθαι, ὥσπερ μαινόμενον. Ὁ δὲ προφήτης οὐχ οὕτως, ἀλλὰ μετὰ διανοίας νηφούσης καὶ σωφρονούσης καταστάσεως, καὶ εἰδὼς ἃ φθέγγεται, φησὶν ἅπαντα· ὥστε καὶ πρὸ τῆς ἐκβάσεως κἀντεῦθεν γνώριζε τὸν μάντιν καὶ τὸν προφήτην. Later theologians have generally followed the fathers of the church.

This view of the subject arises from the correct feeling, that there must be an essential difference between the condition into which the true prophets were brought by the Spirit of God, and that of the false prophets, who were not subjected to its influence. Still a close examination of the passages of the Scriptures relating to the state of the former, shows that the nature of this difference has been misconceived, and that the true prophets, also, were in a state essentially unlike their ordinary condition; a state of ecstasy in which the use of their rational powers was suspended, their own agency ceased, and they became completely passive under an overpowering influence of the Spirit of God; so that as Philo says, the prophets were interpreters, whose organs God employed to impart his revelation.* Even the preparation usually made for it, shows the state of the prophets to have been an extraordinary one. They made use of music to lull their passions to repose, and inflame their love for that which was divine. See 2 Kings 3: 15. 1 Sam. x.† Then they were seized by the Spirit of God, and indeed in so powerful a manner, that their own agency was suppressed. This is evident from the expressions: "the hand of God, or the Spirit of God came upon him or fell upon him." Ez. 1: 3. 1 Sam. 19: 20 and 2 Kings 3: 15. 2 Chron. 15: 1. The irresistible nature of this seizure is indicated in Jer. 20: 7, by the words: "Lord, thou hast persuaded me, and I have suffered myself to be persuaded; thou hast been too strong for me, and hast prevailed." To the same purpose is the language of the New Testament: ὑπὸ πνεύματος ἁγίου φερόμενοι ἐλάλησαν ἅγιοι θεοῦ ἄνθρωποι, 2 Pet. 1: 21, with which Knapp compares the expressions of profane writers: κατέχεσθαι ἐκ θεοῦ, corripi deo, deum pati.‡

---

* Compare e. g. besides many other passages, de praem. et poen. p. 711 ed. Hoesch. ἑρμηνεὺς γάρ ἐστιν ὁ προφήτης, ἔνδοθεν ὑπηχοῦντος τὰ λεκτέα τοῦ θεοῦ.

† Cornelius a Lapide remarks, on the 1st chapter of Ezekiel, that the prophets took their station by the side of the river, that in the stillness and delightful scenery around them, they might, through the soft murmur of the water, be refreshed, enlivened, and prepared for the Divine ecstacies.

‡ Crusius justly regards the fact, that the condition of the prophets while

The suppression of their own agency, terror before the Divine Majesty, and the extraordinary nature of God's revelations, were attended with great perturbation and agony of spirit. When Abraham, Gen. 15: 12, had a vision, it is said: "Behold horror and great darkness fell upon him." When the Spirit seized Balaam, he falls to the ground, Num. 24: 4. Ezekiel likewise, 1: 28, and John, Rev. 1: 17. Daniel 10: 8—10, after beholding a vision is entirely deprived of his strength and sinks down with faintness, and chap. 8: 27, he was sick "certain days" in consequence of his struggle. The inward conflict was at times so great, that the prophets tore off their clothes, 1 Sam. 17: 24, where it is said of Saul that he also, no less than the other prophets has stripped off his clothes, fallen to the ground, and prophesied. That the prophets were in an extraordinary state, is evident from their having been declared insane by unbelievers. Thus the servants of the court, 2 Kings 9: 11, say to Jehu, after a prophet had been with him, "Wherefore came this mad fellow (מְשֻׁגָּע) unto thee?" See a passage perfectly similar, Jer. 29: 26. That there were external indications that this state was altogether of an unusual character, appears also from the relation, 1 Sam. chap. x. It is said to Saul, v. 6: "The Spirit of the Lord shall come upon thee, and thou shalt prophesy with them," and v. 11, as he prophesies with the prophets, all who had known him before exclaim with surprise: "What has happened to the son of Kish? Is Saul also among the prophets?" There must, therefore, have been something more observable in Saul than merely his joining with the disciples of the prophets in their songs.

There is, then, no reason to doubt, that the Hebrew prophets as well as the heathen Seers were in an ἔκστασις. The LXX, Gen. 15: 12, employ this very expression. We find in the New Testament, terms which are at least equivalent. Christ and the Apostles often declare, that the prophets spake ἐν πνεύματι, and John in like manner, Rev. 1: 10 and 4: 2, designates his ecstasy by the words: ἐγενόμην ἐν πνεύματι.

We may then apply to the true prophets also, what Plato has en-

uttering their prophecies was extraordinary, and not the usual, permanent one, as the occasion of their so frequently repeating the formula, "Thus saith the Lord;" while the Apostles, whose divine illumination was permanent, and connected with their own consciousness, use it but seldom, and only when they wish to distinguish their own advice from the commandments of the Lord, 1 Cor. 7: 10. Theol. proph. I. p. 94.

larged upon in his Ion and Phaedrus, viz that prophesying is necessarily accompanied by the suppression of human agency, intelligence and consciousness. But peculiarly appropriate is the view of the prophetic condition given by Philo (quis rerum div sit haeres, p 404 ed Hoesch.): ἕως μὲν ἔτι περιλάμπει καὶ περιπολεῖ ἡμῶν ὁ νοῦς, μεσημβρινὸν οἷα φέγγος εἰς πᾶσαν τὴν ψυχὴν ἀναχέων, ἐν ἑαυτοῖς ὄντες οὐ κατεχόμεθα ἐπειδὰν δὲ πρὸς δυσμὰς γένηται, κατὰ τὸ εἰκὸς ἔκστασις καὶ ἡ ἔνθεος ἐπιπίπτει κατοκωχή τε καὶ μανία. Ὅτε μὲν γὰρ φῶς ἐπιλάμψει τὸ θεῖον, δύεται τὸ ἀνθρώπινον· ὅτε δὲ ἐκεῖνο δύει, τοῦτ᾿ ἀνίσχει καὶ ἀνατέλλει· τῷ δὲ προφητικῷ γένει φιλεῖ τοῦτο συμβαίνειν. ἐξοικίζεται γὰρ ἐν ἡμῖν ὁ νοῦς κατὰ τὴν τοῦ θείου πνεύματος ἄφιξιν· κατὰ δὲ τὴν μετανάστασιν αὐτοῦ πάλιν εἰσοικίζεται. θέμις γὰρ οὐκ ἔστι θνητὸν ἀθανάτῳ συνοικῆσαι. διὰ τοῦτο ἡ δύσις τοῦ λογισμοῦ καὶ τὸ περὶ αὐτὸν σκότος, ἔκστασιν καὶ θεοφόρητον μανίαν ἐγέννησε. Since then we have found that the fathers did not accurately distinguish between true and false prophecy, the question arises in what did the difference between them consist? Tertullian long ago made a distinction between ἔκστασις and μανία, *furor*, and attributed the latter to the false prophets. This was correct. The true prophets were certainly elevated to a loftier region. The action of the inferior principles of the soul, as well as its consciousness and self-possession, was suspended; the capacity for contemplating the things of God was emancipated from its earthly fetters, and thus prepared, like a pure mirror, to receive the impressions of Divine truth. The unusual condition of the body which accompanied this ecstasy, was caused by the struggle of the prophet, resisting the Spirit of God, which, with the triumph of the latter, terminated in repose. The ecstasy of the heathen seers, on the contrary, consisted it is true in the suppression of reason and consciousness, but then this was owing to the inferior faculties of the soul being excited to opposition against the higher. This conflict did not tend to repose, but the more the excitement increased, the higher the tone to which the feelings were roused, and the more violent the storm of passion, the more complete the inspiration was supposed to be.* In the end, a variety of narcotic means were employed See v Dale, de

---

* ' Pseudopropheticus spiritus, cum evehi nequeat supra infimam et obscuram regionem sensus et materiae, aut adtolli in serenum visionis propheticae coelum, operam dat, ut magis atque magis confirmetur in phantasiae regione. Quamobrem vates et pseudoprophetae veteres et recentiores soliti sunt, quoad ejus fieri potuit, phantasiam suam evehere." Jo. Smith de proph.

oraculorum ethnicorum origine atque auctoribus, p 140 seq.— The state of the prophets was supernatural, that of the heathen diviners was unnatural, a momentary insanity, as the derivation of the Greek μάντις from μαίνω indicates. The Pythia is represented as insane by the Scholiasts in the Plutus of Aristophanes and by Lucan l. V.

> — Bacchatur demens aliena per antrum
> Colla ferens, vittasque dei, Phoebaeque serta
> Erectis discussa comis, per inania templi
> Ancipiti cervice rotat, spargitque vaganti
> Obstantes tripodas, magnoque exaestuat igne
> Iratum te, Phoebe, ferens

So the Cassandra of Lycophron. According to Lucian, the seers foamed at the mouth, their eyes rolled, their hair flew, their whole appearance was ferocious, and their motions those of a madman.

From the fact that the prophets, when uttering their predictions, were not in possession of reason and consciousness, but in an ecstasy, we deduce now an important consequence. They received all divine revelations by an immediate perception. While in the case of the Apostles, the illumination of the Holy Spirit equally pervaded all the powers of the soul, and by no means excluded the operation of the understanding, in that of the prophets the impressions were all made on the internal sense, which, when reflection and the external senses were at rest, received the revelations of the Spirit of God.

The evidence of this is indeed already included in that which established the reality of the prophetic ecstasy. It is however susceptible of independent proof. We make our first appeal to the important passage, Num 12 5—8. There the distinction is pointed out between the Divine revelation made to Moses, and that made to the prophets. The appointment of Moses to be the founder and lawgiver of a dispensation required perfect and intelligible proof. The Divine revelations were therefore imparted to him internally and externally, in plain and literal terms, οὐ δι' αἰνιγμάτων, as Philo has expressed it. On the contrary they were always imparted to the prophets in visions (בַּמַּרְאָה) or in dreams, and of course while reflection and outward sensation were suspended,* a method which

---

* In coincidence with this passage, the older Jewish interpreters determined the distinction between the divine revelation made to Moses, and that made to the prophets. "Statuunt phantasiam exhibere hac in re quasi scenam quandam, in qua visa et simulacra intellectui objiciantur, quemadmodum fit in somniis quotidianis—ut viderent in visis intelligibilia mysteria adeoque

sufficiently answered the design of their office. We are led to the same result by the appellations frequently given to the prophets, רֹאִים and חֹזִים, as well as to their predictions : — מַחֲזֶה — חִזָּיוֹן — חֲזִי — חָזוּת — חָזוֹת — חָזוֹן and מַרְאָה — מַרְאֶה.*

In these appellations the word *see* is used in a wider sense for every mode of immediate perception; as it sometimes is in other cases, as for example, Ex. 20: 18. The passage in Num. 24: 3, 4 deserves particular attention. Balaam there calls himself "the man whose eye is opened, who sees the visions of the Almighty, whose eyes are opened, when he falls to the ground."

Of the same description are the numerous passages, in which the prophets assert that they see and hear things imperceptible by the senses. "I see him," says Balaam, Num. 24: 17, "the illustrious king of Israel, but not now; I behold him, but not nigh." Isaiah sees the Lord sitting upon a lofty throne surrounded by seraphim. Micaiah, 1 Kings 22: 19, sees the Lord sitting upon his throne, and all the host of heaven standing by him on his right hand and left. Ezekiel, chap. xxxvii, sees a field covered with dry bones of the dead, which were reanimated by the breath of the Lord. The immediate connexion between the ecstasy and the activity of the internal sense is plain from Ez. chap. I. It is said v. 3: "The hand of the Lord was upon him there;" and directly after, v. 4: "and I saw, and behold it came." Habbakuk, 2: 1, placed himself upon the watch, to *see* what the Lord would say to him. Daniel hears a loud voice on the banks of the Ulai. See Ez. 17: 12. 40: 3, 4. Zech. 1: 14. Apoc. 4: 1. 21: 10. Am. 7: 13.—Finally, this view of the mode in which divine revelations were made to the prophets, is sustained by all those facts, which, as we are about to show, have necessarily resulted from it.

This characteristic of prophecy has not been entirely unknown to the great body of interpreters.† But they have usually confined it

---

in his typis et umbris, quae spiritualium rerum erant symbola, continerentur simul antitypa.—Verum si phantasia non sit propheticae illustrationis scena, sed impressio rerum fiat sine schematibus aut picturis in ipso intellectu, is tunc censetur gradus Mosaicus, in quo deus facie ad faciem conversa loquitur." Jo. Smith l. c. See Kimchi, Vorr. zu d. Psalmen.

* Maimonides Morch Neb. II, 36: Nomen מראה a ראה significat, quod ad facultatem imaginatricem tanta perveniet actionis perfectio, ut homini ita res apparcat ac videatur, aesi exterius sibi exhiberetur eamque sensibus externis perciperet."

† It has been most imperfectly understood by those who have written gen-

to those portions of the prophecies in which it is particularly obvious, as Isa. chap. vi, Ez. chap. i, the first part of Zechariah, and the second part of Daniel, which have therefore been exclusively denominated *visions*.* But as there is no real difference between these predictions and the rest, our arguments are equally applicable to all; and there is ample evidence that all possess sufficient characteristics of a vision,† if the facts are correctly apprehended.

We now proceed to unfold the peculiar properties which result from this nature of prophecy.

I. We have no right to expect that the prophets will always describe the events of which they speak in all their connexions and relations. "The prophet," says Herder, Letters p. 108, " was not a preacher according to our notions, still less an expositor of a doctrinal topic." Such a connected and comprehensive mode of representing a subject, can be expected only of one, who teaches in the possession of his understanding and consciousness. The prophets uttered on every occasion merely what was communicated to the internal perception, and that only was communicated, which was suited to the existing condition of things. This is especially the case with the Messianic predictions, and to these our present discussion has particular reference.

---

eral treatises on the hermeneutics of the prophetic writings; as Gulich, before whose Theologia Prophetica there is found a Hermeneutica Sacra, the second part of which treats de interpretandis prophetis;—Crusius, whose Hypomnemata ad theol. preph. Vol. I, contain some valuable remarks relative to this subject;—Meier, Hermeneutik des A. T. Bd. 2; and Pareau, Instit. Interpr. V. T. p. 476 seq. Anton also in the often quoted writing: de ratione prophet. Mess. interpret. affords little aid. The best treatises are found in Maimonides, Doctor perplexorum II. 36 seq.—in John Smith in the very valuable Dissertatio de prophetia et prophetis, a copy of which is inserted before Le Clerc's Commentary on the Prophets;—in Velthusen, in the estimable treatise: De optica rerum futurarum descriptione, ad illustr. l. Jes. 63, reprinted in Velthusen, Kuinoel and Ruperti Commentt. Theoll. VI. 75 seq. which has been mostly followed by Ewald, David II. 356 seq. and Jahn Einl. II. p. 368.

* The explanation, which usually follows the visions, belongs to the ecstasy, as much as does the vision itself. Maimonides, l. c. cap. 43, illustrates this by a comparison with a person dreaming, who in imagination, as if he were awake, relates his dream to another and explains its meaning.

† De Wette, after the example of several others, Einl. § 205, explains the visions in the stricter sense to be a mere arbitrary figurative dress. Gesenius, zu Jes. I. p. 253, maintains the contrary. We shall, nevertheless, hereafter have occasion to show, what a deleterious influence has been exerted upon this commentary also, by a misapprehension of the nature of prophecy.

The prophets never at any one time present the whole compass of the doctrine concerning the Messiah. In one place they are concerned chiefly with his person, in another they are exclusively employed in describing the nature of his kingdom. Often the Messiah in his glory is the object of their contemplation. Malachi leaves the first appearing of Christ in a state of humiliation unnoticed, and does not mention the interval between his forerunner, and the destruction of Jerusalem. Frequently the minutest circumstances are noticed, while those of far more importance are omitted. Often the most joyful events of the future are alone exhibited, at another time the prospect is chiefly filled with those of a gloomy character. Thus Jeremiah, for example, chap 23. 5, 6, connects the conversion of the first fruits of the Jews, with their general conversion expected in future times, and omits to mention the intermediate rejection of the greater part. So also Ez 34. 22—30. 37. 21—28. On the contrary, Malachi and Daniel exhibit chiefly the opposite side of the picture, the rejection of the people, the desolation of the land, and of the city. The prophets often overlook all the obstacles which oppose the progress of the Messiah's kingdom, and therefore exhibit in one view its feeble commencement and its glorious completion. To this peculiarity of prophecy Paul seems to refer, when he says, 1 Cor 13: 9 ἐκ μέρους γὰρ γινώσκομεν, καὶ ἐκ μέρους προφητεύομεν. We infer from it that all individual predictions must be regarded merely as fragments, and that we possess a complete picture only when we have collected and combined the several features. This may the more easily be accomplished, since history shows us in what order they must be arranged.

In recent times as the general nature of prophecy has been misunderstood, so also has this quality which results from it. The attempt has been made to show from it, that the prophets differed from each other in regard to the idea of a Messiah, and this has been urged as a proof that this idea was of human origin. Where Joel, for example, describes only the nature of the Messiah's kingdom, and not the Messiah himself, it is inferred, that his expectations were not connected with a *person*. Since Jeremiah speaks only of the Messiah in glory, he can have had no idea of a suffering Messiah. The incorrectness of this mode of considering the subject, may be easily shown even from the views of our opponents. It would prove not only that the prophets contradicted one another, but likewise themselves. Thus for example, Isaiah in chap. II, as also Joel, without mentioning the Messiah himself, gives a description of His times On the other hand, in the prophecy connected with this, chap. IV, and delivered at the same time, the Messiah is named So also in the second part of his prophecies, many Messianic representations of a general character are found, in connexion with those which relate to the Messiah as a person, see chap LIII, etc. Jer 31: 31 etc speaks only of the nature of the Messiah's kingdom, while, in chap. XXIII and other places, his person is the subject of discourse Isaiah, in many passages, describes only the glorified Messiah; but in chap. LIII, he draws a portrait of the Messiah in his humiliation, which he represents as the cause of his subsequent exaltation to glory.

If then we treat the prophets as we are accustomed to treat the classic writers, and if we should not determine the doctrine of Plato from any single passage, but from the whole of his works, it is plain, that, in order to understand the representations of the Messiah by any one prophet, we must combine into a single image the various features occurring in different places. If this be granted, it is likewise obvious that we are not to infer, because particular prophets have left unnoticed large portions of the great picture, that they were therefore unacquainted with them. Were more of the predictions of Joel extant, they would probably supply each other's deficiencies, as in the case of Isaiah Had Jeremiah prophesied under the same circumstances as Isaiah in his second part, he would not have omitted to describe the suffering Messiah. It appears moreover at once, that this view is erroneous, since it requires us to suppose, that the later prophets were ignorant of all former predictions, and even of the popular belief of the whole nation.

This error of recent critics arises from viewing the prophets too much as mere doctrinal teachers, and consequently expecting them to bring forward in each place the whole compass of their doctrine. Did we regard them as $J\overset{ov}{ews}$, which they really were, we should not be surprised to find, that they communicated only what they *saw*, without intermingling, what they had previously learned in the ordinary way from the revelations made to other men of God, and from the general belief of the people. The plausible objection to the view we have taken, which may be drawn from the alleged use of earlier predictions by subsequent prophets, will be answered, when we come to Isaiah chap II.

II If the medium through which the prophets received their revelations was the internal sense, all must have appeared to them in the present time. This explains many individual peculiarities. 1 It is not then surprising that the prophets should speak of events and persons which belong even to the most distant future, as if actually present, or even point to them. Thus, for example, in Isaiah 9. 5, it is said, "a child is given to us, a son is born to us." In like manner, chap. 7. 14. 42. 1, he points to the Messiah, "behold my servant whom I uphold, mine elect in whom my soul delighteth." Isa. 45. 1—8, Cyrus appears, and is addressed. Often a demonstrative pronoun is used instead of a noun. The misapprehension of this peculiarity of the prophetic writings has led some interpreters to think, that here, and in other places, the discourse related to persons and events actually present, and consequently their interpretations were entirely false. 2. Hence the want of precision in the use of the tenses by the prophets is explained. As they contemplated objects not in time, but in space, no accurate determination of time ought to be expected from them. They often employ either the *aorist*, or the *praeter* when speaking of the most distant future. The true reason of this was not generally perceived even by the older interpreters. On such places we usually find the remark, that the prophet employed the praeter to indicate the certainty of the fact. So even Vitringa on Isa. 7· 14. The truth however was seen by Iken on Isa LIII, in der Bibl. Hag. II, 238 seq. whose very significant words we cannot refrain from quoting : "Fundamentum talis styli dispositionis ex modo, quo prophetis futura revelabantur repetendum potius censeo. Non semper illud fiebat expressis verbis. Toti interdum corripiebantur spiritu , facultas mentis, cujus ope res nobis representamus, in iis acuebatur, ita ut recondita futuri temporis fata in imagine quasi ipsis exhibita non aliter contemplarentur, acsi oculis ea cernerent. Hinc non potuerunt non praesenti aut praeterito tempore uti, cum naturalis dicendi ordo id flagitaret," etc. 3. From the same cause must the distance of time generally have been unknown to the prophet, without a special revelation. They were not so much chronological historians as describers of pictures. When for example they saw the Messiah standing before them, by what means could they know how long a time should elapse before his advent. B. Crusius very justly observes. "Prophetae divina luce, qua illuminantur, ad futura plerumque prospexerunt, quemadmodum fit, quando coelum stelliferum intuemur. Videmus enim supra nos sidera; quanto a nobis intervallo absint, nec non quae propius, quae remotius distent, non item animadvertimus." Hence when they speak of the times of the Messiah their language is altogether indefinite: thus the common phrase בְּאַחֲרִית הַיָּמִים, which properly means only, *in future times*. Indeed they say expressly that the time is not known to them, but only to God. So Zech 14 7. Thus is explained the characteristic peculiarity of the prophecies, without the knowledge of which a large portion of them must be entirely misunderstood, viz. that events, which are separated by great distance of time from each other, appear as *continuous* The prophets in vision could contemplate objects only in juxtaposition, not in succession. Let us illustrate this by some examples. The city of Babylon received its first shock when it was taken by the Persians; but yet more than a thousand years elapsed before its utter downfall and total extinction Nevertheless Jeremiah, chap L and LI, connects the capture and its final destruction without mentioning that there was any interval between. In the predictions relating to the theocracy, where either blessings or judgments, as the spiritual eye of the prophet rested on the joyful or gloomy side of the picture, are foretold, those that are nearer and less important are connected in the representation, with those which are more distant and of greater moment, in such a manner that the vast space of time which intervenes is not intimated. Here the combination always depends on the internal relation of the nearer and the more distant events. So Isaiah XI, omitting all the intermediate occurrences, makes the redemption by the Messiah *immediately* follow the deliverance of Israel from the Assyrians. In the same manner Isaiah, Micah, Hosea, Amos, Ezekiel and Jeremiah very often connect the restoration from exile with the redemption through the Messiah, although no prophet represents him as the leader of the returning captives. With Zechariah, who lived after the exile, the scene had already changed He connects the more spiritual redemption of the Jews with their nearer temporal deliverance, partly under Alexander and partly in the time of the Maccabees Even in the description of the Messiah's kingdom, its gradual development is unnoticed and its beginning and glorious end are placed in immediate connexion So Zechariah, 9 9 and 10, describes the splendid completion of the Messiah's kingdom, immediately after having represented him in a state of humiliation Joel, chap III, does not distinguish between the first effusion of the Spirit on the day of Pentecost, and that which the church is always to enjoy Sometimes events, instead of being placed in juxtaposition, are blended together just as in a distant prospect objects flow into one another and appear mingled when in reality they are far apart. This remark throws much light, especially on the second part of Isaiah. There the deliverance from exile, and that through Christ, very often appear in juxtaposition, but in many representations they are presented to the eye of the prophet combined; sometimes the one, and sometimes the other being the more prominent. In like manner all the judgments of the future are frequently brought together in one view—the fore ground and the back ground are blended.* Ignorance of these properties of the prophetic representations, has been the cause of much misapprehension. Prophecies intimately connected have been torn asunder by critics, because it was not perceived that the prophets frequently place events in immediate succession, which are connected with each other by some internal relation, although they are far apart in point of time. See our remarks on Isa. xi. Others avail themselves of this juxtaposition and blending together of the most distant events, to disprove the divine origin of the prophecies; but very unjustly, because it does not imply, that the prophet's views were false, but only limited. Had a prophet foretold that Christ would appear after a definite number of years, and the event not correspond with the prediction, it could not have proceeded from God; but when, in accordance with the general nature of a vision, he refrains from all determination of time, to which he makes no pretension, we can no more object to the divine origin of prophecy on this ground, than we can because each individual prophet did not foresee every event of future time. Others, who acknowledge the divine origin of prophecy, have been led, by this blending of near and distant events, to form other erroneous opinions. As they take it for granted, that each representation must necessarily relate to the same time, or the same objects, they endeavor to remove by a forced interpretation whatever does not accord with the principle on which they proceed. Jahn especially has frequently fallen into this error. See his representations of the contents of the prophetical books in his Introduction to the Old Testament. Or, they suffer themselves to be led, by this and another peculiarity of the prophetic style hereafter to be developed arising from the prevalence of imagery in the visions of the prophets, to the unnatural assumption of a double sense, and thus give ample room for the indulgence of caprice.

---

* "Quemadmodum simili fallacia optica longissime distans turris domus propinquae tecto incumbere aut lunae discus montibus nemoribusque contiguus videtur." Velthusen l. c. p 89.

That the prophets were conscious of this characteristic of their predictions, appears from their comparing themselves so often with watchmen, who from some lofty tower overlook the surrounding region, and give notice of the approach of friends or foes. Comp. with 2 Sam. 13 34 18: 24—27. 2 Kings 9 17—20, the passages in Micah 7 4 Jer. 6· 17. Ez 3: 17. 33: 1—9. How essential this property is to the nature of prophecy, appears from its characterising even the predictions of Christ, and it is in a great measure owing to ignorance of it, that they have so often been falsely interpreted To him also the events of the future presented themselves, as in a large picture, and therefore in space, not in time. In describing its separate parts, as the destruction of Jerusalem, and the day of judgment, the designations of time, which he employs as εὐθέως Matt. 24. 29, relates to the succession of the objects, as they appeared to him in prophetic vision, and not as they were actually to take place On this subject the passage in 1 Pet 1 10—12 is replete with instruction There the Apostle asserts that true and divine revelations of the future, namely, concerning the suffering of the Lord and the glory that should follow, were imparted to the prophets by the Spirit of Christ Nevertheless they sought in vain to discover the time when the events they predicted should take place, and in this respect, they were far behind those who lived at the time of the fulfilment of their predictions See on this passage the treatise of Klenker (De nexu inter utrumque foedus prophetico. Helmst. 1791.)

It now remains to answer the question, how we can ascertain the chronological order of events predicted in this manner. The means of doing this, some of which were possessed by the prophets and their contemporaries, and others peculiar to those who were to come after them, were the following

1. The prophets were often divinely instructed respecting the order of time in which the events were to happen. Thus it was revealed to Jeremiah in an extraordinary manner, that the Babylonian exile would continue seventy years. Thus in Joel 3 1, the time of the Messiah is plainly represented by the phrase אַחֲרֵי כֵן as commencing after the deliverance from exile; Isaiah, 8 23, distinguishes two courses of time, one before and the other after the Messiah; and Daniel gives the time that should elapse between the deliverance from captivity and the commencement of the Messiah's kingdom, but yet, which deserves especial attention, in so obscure a manner, that his contemporaries could learn nothing further from his prophecy, than

that the former event should precede the latter, and the more definite knowledge was referred for those who lived after the fulfilment. So also Christ, in the gospel of Matthew, after having, throughout the whole of the foregoing representation spoken of the two future analogous events, without noticing their distance from each other in time; distinguishes between them in chap. 24 34, 36, where the contrast between πάντα ταῦτα and τῆς ἡμέρας ἐκείνης should be well considered, and says that the former, the destruction of Jerusalem, shall take place before the eyes of the present generation; the latter, the day of judgment, in some remote and unknown period Aided by such designations of time, we may without serious difficulty, in those prophetic representations also, where they are wanting, convert the juxtaposition of events into a succession, though the exact distance between them may remain undetermined.

2. The succession of events which are blended together may be easily ascertained by a comparison with other passages in which they occur separately Thus in the second part of Isaiah, it is only necessary to select the passages in which the deliverance by Cyrus, and that by Christ were separately presented to the mental vision of the prophet, and compare them with those in which the two events are intermingled and the separation of them will not be a difficult task.

3 The prophets sometimes indicate the mode in which events are to take place, not taking their station as is usually done in the actual present, and thence overlooking the future, but in the nearer future as if it were the present, and thence overlooking the more distant future Thus Isaiah in the second part of his prophecies generally places himself in the Babylonian exile; in chap LIII between the sufferings and the glorification of the Messiah, because the former were to be represented as the conditional ground of the latter His sufferings are expressed in the past tense, his exaltation in the future.

4 But by far the surest means was the fulfilment. Even before the Messiah's appearance, this afforded considerable aid in respect to the predictions concerning him. The deliverance from exile and the redemption by Christ are very often placed in juxtaposition, or blended together. Now when the former had taken place, it was easy to distinguish what related to each respectively. And thus we find the prediction of the Messiah becomes more pure and distinct in the prophets after the exile. But this means was rendered still more efficacious by the coming of Christ. We have already seen that

the appearance of Christ in a state of humiliation, and the final glorification of his kingdom are not in point of time separated from each other by the prophets. But after the first event had taken place, this separation could be easily made. So also Christ's own predictions necessarily became much more distinct after the first event to which they related, the destruction of Jerusalem, had taken place.

III. If all disclosures of the future were made to the prophets in mental vision, it must have been by figurative representations; since only images and not abstract notions could in this way be perceived. But the images in which the future was presented to the mind of the prophets must have been taken from objects and relations with which they were familiar. Since on the one hand, God does not operate as if by magic on the minds of those to whom he communicates himself, but in a manner adapted to their peculiar capacities and knowledge, and on the other the prophecies would not have answered their purpose, had they consisted of unknown images; for they must have been totally unintelligible.

If we apply this rule to the Messianic predictions, it necessarily results from the nature of prophecy, that the kingdom of the Messiah should be represented by metaphors taken from the Mosaic dispensation, and that the facts as well as the persons of the former should receive the names of those of the latter, which were connected with them by an internal resemblance. This mode of representation is founded in the fact that the Mosaic economy was ordered with distinct reference to the Christian dispensation and prefigures it. As it respects the three offices of prophet, high priest, and king, this was long ago noticed by Eusebius in a full discussion of the subject (Hist. Eccl 1, 3), the result of which is given in the following verses ὡς τούτους ἅπαντας τὴν ἐπὶ τὸν ἀληθῆ Χριστὸν, τὸν ἔνθεον καὶ οὐράνιον λόγον ἀναφορὰν ἔχειν μόνον ἀρχιερέα τῶν ὅλων, καὶ μόνον ἁπάσης τῆς κτίσεως βασιλέα, καὶ μόνον προφητῶν ἀρχιπροφήτην τοῦ πατρὸς τυγχάνοντα.

We will now illustrate these remarks by examples. In their representations of the Messiah the existing theocracy furnished the prophets with a threefold groundwork to which they might superadd, in each instance, the difference between the original and the type. The Messiah appeared to them as an exalted king, and all the traits peculiar to him they combined in the image of an illustrious leader of the earthly theocracy, whose glory was only a faint reflection of the glory of his great successor. Compare Mich v, Isa xi, Jer. XXIII.

And as the Messiah was most completely represented by David, he is called expressly by his name. See Hos 3 5, Jer. 30: 9, Ez. 34 23. He appeared to them also as a prophet endowed with all the fulness of the Holy Ghost, who, completely realizing the *ideal* of the prophetic office, should teach, admonish and rebuke, not merely within the narrow limits of Palestine, like the prophets by whom he had been prefigured, but among all the people of the earth Comp Is. 42. 49 and other passages And lastly he appeared to them as a high priest, who should actually procure that forgiveness of sins, which was only symbolically represented by the high priests of the old covenant. Ps. cx, Zech. vi, Isa liii. And as the Messiah was regarded as the most exalted prophet, high priest and king, so his kingdom appeared not as separate and different from the theocracy, but its fullest completion. Frequently Jerusalem or Zion, as the existing seat of the theocracy, served to designate it. Thus Joel 3: 5, expresses the thought, that only the members of the theocracy should escape in the heavy judgment which impended, by the words: "in Zion and in Jerusalem shall be deliverance." Isaiah, Micah and Ezekiel contemplate the future triumph of the theocracy over all the religions of the heathen, as an exaltation of the mountain, on which the temple stood, above the hills, and the future conversion of the heathen appeared to the two former, as their flowing to the hill of Zion, and to Jer. 23 8, as a vast enlargement of Jerusalem The same mode of representation extends to all the individual traits. The universality of the influence of the Holy Spirit in the times of the Messiah, appears to Joel as a general extension of the three forms of divine revelation existing under the old covenant. Zechariah expresses the idea that all nations shall worship the true God, by predicting their participation in the feast of tabernacles. The perfect love and faithfulness of the people towards their God appear to Hosea chap. ii and xiv, Mic. chap. v, and Zechariah xiii, as the putting away of whatever, under the former theocracy at any time, or especially in the days of the prophet, disturbed the relation to God, for example, the service of Baal, or idolatry in general, seeking help from Assyria and Egypt, and false prophecy. When the glory and felicity of the Messianic times are exhibited, the prosperous condition of the theocracy under David and Solomon becomes the basis of the redemption. Comp e g Hos. 2 20, Jer 23 6, Mic. 4 1 and Zech. 3 10 with 1 Kings 4 24. The general truth, that peace and love should prevail among the people when they had found reconciliation with God, was received by the prophets under the image of the termination of the most deplorable dispensation that occurred during the theocracy, the separation of the kingdom of Israel and Judah Comp. Hos 2 2 Isa. 11 13. The enemies of the Messiah's kingdom were not only designated by the general name of the enemies of the theocracy גוים, but they not unfrequently bore precisely the name of some one people at the time peculiarly hostile or powerful, which appeared in the vision of the prophets, as the representative of all the rest. Thus they are called in Isaiah xxv, Moab. Isa. LXIII and Amos 9. 12, Edom; and Ezekiel XXXVIII, Magog — These examples, which might with care be greatly increased, will be sufficient to illustrate our view of the subject.

This peculiarity of prophecy has been in many ways overlooked or misunderstood Two opposite errors may especially be observed. The first is that of the carnal Jewish interpreters, whose example the majority of the rationalists have followed, though influenced indeed by other motives These either entirely fail to perceive the metaphorical character of the prophecies, or without any governing principle of hermeneutics, they adhere to the literal interpretation, in all cases where it will serve to confirm their preconceived opinions. The leading interest of the Jews is positive, that of the modern critics negative. Those orthodox interpreters also, who insist upon a strictly literal interpretation of that portion of the prophecies which have not yet been fulfilled, are in some degree involved in the same error. This mode of interpretation has always been followed by some in England and has also many defenders in Germany, especially in Wurtemberg The second mistake is that of those who deprive the prophecies of all substance and meaning, by giving undue prominence to their figurative character This mode of interpretation is adopted by rationalists; and while those who followed the foregoing method, were influenced by the desire to point out a contradiction between the Old Testament and New, it is the prevailing motive with these, by generalizing as much as possible, to do away the coincidence between the prophecy rightly understood and its fulfilment. Comp for example, Meiers Hermeneutik des A T. Part. II It is not unusual to see the very same interpreter following either mode of explanation, as suits his convenience. This error is also partially committed by those orthodox interpreters who seek, often through unbelief of all that relates to the humiliation of Christ, to set aside the reality that lies at its foundation, and so explain all that the prophets reveal concerning the future glory of the kingdom of God, as to render it a mere shell without a kernel.*

Would we avoid these different paths of error, we must, after having proved the figurative character of prophecy in general, as necessarily resulting from its nature, establish sure rules by which to distinguish between the image and the fact it represents.

1 Where a comparison can be made with the fulfilment, it affords the surest guide in making the distinction. But here caution is necessary, since the prophets, as we have before shown, often represent events as successive, which are separated from each other by a long period of time, viz : the obscure beginning and the glorious termination of the Messiah's kingdom. It must therefore be accurately ascertained beforehand, whether a prediction has been in general and to what extent, already fulfilled In this respect the declarations of the New Testament concerning the future development of the kingdom of God, will be of the greatest service The Apocalypse particularly is important inasmuch as it again takes up the yet unfulfilled portion of the prophecies of the Old Testament, and represents their accomplishment as still future In relation however to that part of the prophecies which can be shown to have been already fulfilled, partly by a simple comparison of the prediction with history, and partly by the declarations of Christ and his Apostles, we may with perfect propriety avail ourselves of history in order to distinguish between what is figurative, and what is literal. We must however make a clear distinction between these two questions . In what sense did the *prophets* understand these predictions? and what meaning did *God* intend them to convey? These questions are shown to be different, as soon as it has been proved that the prophets spake in an ecstasy We cannot in the ways proposed find the answer to the first, nor is it of much importance to us. Since the prophets were only organs of the Holy Spirit, we may not inquire whether during their ecstasy and the suppression of reason and consciousness, they

---

* Crusius in his Theol Proph 1 p 632, remarks against such interpreters " Quanquam autem sic in dogmatibus fidei et morum orthodoxiam retinent, errore tamen exegetico decipiuntur, qui magni profecto momenti est Nam qui ita sentiunt, coguntur scripturas tam coacte interpretari, ut quando simili licentia Judaei utuntur, hos refutare non possint, sin duntaxat his eam non concedant, nec ipsi eam sibi arrogare debeant " But such interpreters are under still greater embarrassments in regard to rationalist critics, than they are in respect to the Jews Comp Gesenius z Jesaia III p 22.

understood correctly, or incorrectly; and they afterwards stood in the same relation to their predictions as their hearers or readers, so that their views of them cannot be decisive of their true import. But the second question may be answered by the fulfilment. The same God, who opened the prospect of futurity to the prophets, effected also the accomplishment of their predictions. The rule of interpretation, which requires us always to seek the sense intended by the author, is thus preserved inviolate. The difference between us and our opposers lies rather in the answer to the question, Who is to be considered as the real author of the prophecies. They look only at the human instruments, we elevate our thoughts to the Divine Author Several interpreters, as Seiler and Jahn (Einl. in's A. T. II p 373 seq), endeavor to find a middle course. They adopt the notion of a double sense of prophecy ; the one, that which the prophets conceived, the other, that which God designed But this assumption is entirely untenable, and arises from substituting for the sense which an author has in his own mind, that which others derive from his writings. In every composition, the former can be but one, the latter may be as various as its readers are numerous. It is only with the former that we are concerned, and we are fully justified in seeking it by a comparison with the fulfilment, as soon as we have become convinced that prophecy is from God, by a comparison of the prophecy with history, by the testimony of the New Testament, and the evidences by which the prophets demonstrated their divine mission to their contemporaries. While our opponents are unable as they always must be to show that this conviction of ours is unfounded, they ought not to question our right, to call history to our aid in determining the sense of prophecy. History, moreover, not only makes us to divest the prophecies of their metaphorical and theocratic dress, but also often serves as a guide where without its aid and confined to the prophecy alone, we might be inclined to extend that which is figurative too far. Thus in Ps xxii, for example, we should perhaps regard the parting of the garments, the piercing of the hands and feet, etc. as the mere filling up of the picture, if these particular circumstances were not repeated in the history of Christ; in Zech ix, the Messiah's riding upon an ass might have been thought a mere figurative description of his humble condition, his meekness, and pacific character, if history did not make it necessary to refer it to a transaction which symbolically represented these qualities ; and without its light, the reward of thirty pieces of silver, in Zech. xi, would have suggested only in general the idea of the little success which attended the efforts of the Messiah among the Jews. And so in many other instances

Besides, there are marks, by which to distinguish between the figurative and the literal, which are contained in the prophecies themselves, and of which therefore the prophets and their contemporaries might have availed themselves; although it must often have been difficult for them to make the distinction, for want of the surest guide—the fulfilment. These marks we have yet to exhibit.

2 Those descriptions are obviously figurative in which there is a distinct reference to earlier occurrences in the history of the Israelites. Here we are always to select only the general, fundamental idea which connects the future, with the past event. Thus when it is said, Isa 11: 15, 16. The Lord in effecting a new deliverance for the Israelites will dry up the Arabian Gulf, and divide the Nile into seven streams, so that we may pass over dry shod; the fact here foretold is only the redemption of the covenant people which is presented to the prophet under the image of the former deliverance from Egyptian bondage. So also Zech 10 11. When Hosea, in reference to the deliverance of the Israelites, says, chap. 2 14, 15· God will lead them into the desert, there he will speak kindly with them, then he will conduct them into the land of Canaan, and first indeed into the fruitful valley of Achor, it is generally acknowledged, that the prophet designs to express by this representation, taken from the earlier history of the Israelites, nothing further than the thought, that God would first deliver them from misery, and then comfort and abundantly bless them. See Isa. 4 5. 12 3.

3 In numerous other places we are compelled to have recourse to a metaphorical sense, or make the prophets directly contradict themselves Should we for example, as several cabbalists have done, comp Glasener (De gemino Jud Mess p. 52), understand those passages literally, in which the Messiah is called expressly King David, and give to them the meaning: David will arise from the dead, and take possession of the kingdom, we should make them contradict others, in which he is designated as the sprout or son of David Should Jer. 33 18 be taken in the literal sense, as predicting the continuation of the Levitical priesthood, and the sacrificial service, this passage contradicts chap. 31: 31, which declares that in the time of the Messiah all are to stand in an immediate relation to God, and chap 3. 16, according to which the Levitical worship shall cease,

not to mention the passages in the remaining prophets, and other arguments to be brought forward in their place in proof of its figurative meaning. This argument is especially valid against those, who give a literal construction to those passages, which speak of the wars and victories of the theocracy in the time of the Messiah. The prophets in many places give especial prominence to the fact, that the kingdom of the Messiah is to be a kingdom of peace, and all the heathen under a divine influence are voluntarily to become its subjects. If now the same prophets, who describe the kingdom of the Messiah as entirely peaceful, nevertheless speak of wars and triumphs of the theocracy, (comp. Isa. chap. ii with chap. ix, etc.), in the one case or the other their expressions must necessarily be figurative. In any such case the figure must always be sought on the side, where an occasion for it can be shown by considering the images usually employed by the prophets.

4. Other passages contain in themselves the evidence that they are not to be otherwise than figuratively interpreted. Thus, even independently of the distinct testimony of Christ, and of history, we need not with the older Jews,[*] and some recent critics, as Bauer, and Baumgarten-Crusius, understand by the prophet Elijah whose appearance Malachi announces, the real Elijah, but another prophet who should be like him. For we must not ascribe to the prophet a meaning so absurd, while such a figurative representation is sustained by the most certain analogies; for example, the metaphorical use of the name David, which is generally acknowledged. Thus the literal interpretation of Isa. 53. 12 appears at once to be inadmissible, because a worldly triumph is not to be won by the deepest humiliation, and worldly rulers do not impart forgiveness of sins, and justification to their subjects. At first sight there seems to be much in favor of understanding the last eight chapters of Ezekiel literally, but still they contain many passages, which are not capable throughout of any other than a figurative sense, and which therefore give us a clue to the right interpretation of the whole. This rule applies, especially, to the passage chap 47. 1—12. A great stream of water, of unfathomable depth, shall issue from the temple. This stream shall restore the waters of the Dead Sea, and diffuse life wherever it flows. Only the pools, and the miry places, which do not receive its waters, remain unhealed. Who that has even a slight acquaintance

---

[*] See the passages in Lightfoot on Matt 17 10. Eisenmenger II. p. 696 seq. Glaesener l c p. 67 seq.

with the figurative language of the Old Testament, can fail to perceive in this passage, a representation of the influence of the Holy Spirit, under the Christian dispensation. The same may be said of the similar figurative representation, Zech. 14: 10. That Edom, in Isa. xxxiv and lxiii, is only a metaphorical designation of the enemies of the theocracy, is indisputably evident from the context, as the threatened judgment is represented as extending to all the people of the earth.

5. In discriminating between the imagery and what it was designed to represent, we must have regard to the general character of each individual prophet. It is plain that although all the prophets behold the truth in images, yet with some of them, these images have far more reality, and the figurative dress is far more transparent than with others, just as in this respect, a considerable difference is observable in each particular prophet, according as his own agency was more suppressed at one time than another. This was perceived long ago by several learned Jews (comp on this place J. Smith, Maimonides l. c. cap. 45), who sought to make it the ground of a classification of the prophets. If for example a passage like that in Ez. xl—xlviii were found in Isaiah, there would be far stronger reasons than at present for giving it an interpretation as literal as possible.

6. In many instances the attention is expressly directed to the figurative character of a description, and an intimation given of the reality which lies at the foundation. Thus in Zech. 10 11. the metaphorical representation suggested by the deliverance from Egypt: "they shall go through the sea," the prophet himself explains by adding the word, "affliction." The wars in Ps 110 3, cannot be of this world, because the Psalmist sends forth the warriors in sacred garments. Ps. 45 3 cannot be understood of beauty of person, since the beauty there celebrated is the ground of God's blessing.

7. In the case of predictions yet unfulfilled, this discrimination is always to be made in accordance with the analogy of the faith. Since the same Spirit spake by the prophets and by the writers of the New Testament, there can be no contradiction between them. As Theodoret has aptly shown in his remarks on Ezekiel xlviii (Opp ed. Hal II p 1045 seq), and as we shall more fully prove in the proper place, this principle requires us to reject that explanation of the prophecies relating to events still future, which by understanding them in a literal sense, makes them foretel the future preeminence of the Jewish people, the rebuilding of the temple, and the restoration of

the Levitical service. But then this rule must be applied with caution, and be preceded by a careful examination of the system of doctrine contained in the New Testament. It has manifestly been misapplied in various ways. For instance, by those who, entirely mistaking the reality which lies at the foundation of the figure, wish to interpret spiritually all prophecies, which relate to the prosperous external condition of the kingdom of God, under the pretext, that the kingdom of Christ is spiritual; a pretext founded on overlooking the distinction between the kingdom of grace, and the kingdom of glory, which latter, according to the New Testament, as well as the Old, was to be established on earth

8 As the prophets and their contemporaries were not always able, by those marks which were given, to distinguish between the figure and the reality, so neither have we always the means of doing it with certainty, in the case of those prophecies which are yet to be fulfilled It is necessary here not to go beyond the evidence in our decisions. As, with respect to that part of the prophecies which have been already fulfilled, history has taught us to distinguish, contrary to appearances, between the figure and the reality, so must we wait for its light, before we can decide respecting much that yet remains to be accomplished.

IV A necessary result of the condition of the prophets, while delivering their predictions, as we have represented it, is their obscurity, considered in themselves, and before their fulfilment, which nevertheless is to be considered as only comparative This obscurity is the result of the three properties already mentioned 1. Clear views of only certain portions of the vast future were usually granted to the prophets Their prophecies must be joined together, and the fragments combined so as to form a whole, if prophecy and its fulfilment are to correspond This is not difficult for us, since history teaches where each particular feature must be arranged, nor were those who lived before the fulfilment entirely destitute, as we have already seen, of the means of making this combination. It must at all events have been far more difficult for them, and the prophets themselves may often have erred in this respect. That, for example, it was difficult for those who were without the light afforded by the fulfilment, to reconcile those passages in which a Messiah in glory, with those in which a Messiah in humiliation is foretold, is evident from the fact, that the Jews invented for that purpose the fiction of two Messiahs. 2. Still more was this obscurity produced by the circumstance, that the prophets contemplated the future in space, not in time, and that therefore near and distant events, which resembled each other, were often contemplated by them as connected, or blended together. It is true that here also, even before the fulfilment, a combination of various marks could afford much light, but then it must have been very difficult always to discover these marks, and it was easy to err. If, for example, the prophets themselves after their ecstasy was over, or their contemporaries, or their immediate successors, studied the predictions in which the deliverance from the Babylonian exile, and the redemption by Christ appear as continuous, they might easily have fallen upon the opinion, that both events were actually to take place in connexion. How easily this opinion could arise, we see from Malachi 2 17. From this passage it is evident that the idea had become firmly established among the Jews in the exile, that they should be delivered and exalted to great prosperity by the Messiah, and that the worldly-minded part of the people murmured at the disappointment of this hope. The intimate connexion of the feeble commencement, and the glorious end of the Messiah's kingdom in the prophetic representations caused even John the Baptist, and the Apostles to expect, that the appearance of Christ must be immediately followed by the erection of his visible kingdom 3 But a still greater cause of this obscurity was the figurative character of the prophecies. We have seen indeed that, independently of the fulfilment, marks for distinguishing between the figure and the reality are not wanting. But still it must be very difficult, and often impossible, to carry out this distinction into particulars The prophets, and the other members of the old covenant, stood in the same relation to the prophecies of that period, as we do to those which relate to the future development of the kingdom of God, viz., to those of the Apocalypse. We perceive their figurative character, and yet in particular it is often impossible to decide, what is real and what was designed merely to complete the picture. Still greater misapprehension must be caused by the figurative character of the prophecies, when the inherent difficulty is increased, by their being interpreted by those whose carnal disposition led them to desire to find expressed in them certain hopes which they fondly cherished. The carnal national pride of the Jews caused them to despise all the means of correct information which they already enjoyed, they collected from the prophecies, by a literal understanding of the theocratic images, their worldly conceptions of the Messiah and his kingdom.

That this comparative obscurity of their predictions was not unknown to the prophets themselves, appears from many of their own declarations. Isaiah, Jeremiah and Ezekiel often assert that their predictions are unintelligible to the worldly minded portion of the people, and would first be understood by them from being fulfilled to their injury. See Isa. 6: 9—13. 29. 10 etc., Jer. 23: 20. 30: 24. Ez. 33. 33. Daniel and Zechariah declare, in several places, that they do understand the meaning of their visions, and at a later period are first taught their import. This implies, that the meaning of those visions as Ez. chap. XL—XLVIII, which were followed by no explanation, must remain obscure to the prophets. Chap 12: 4. 9, Daniel is commanded to seal up a vision which was entirely unintelligible to him, until the last time, or the time of the fulfilment, when many should come and fully understand it. But this peculiarity of prophecy is described with peculiar distinctness in the remarkable passage of 2 Pet. 1: 19—21, which affords a confirmation of our whole view of the subject. See on this the excellent treatise of Knapp, the first of his Opuscula. Peter, in the preceding verses, had appealed in proof of the truth of Christianity to historical facts, confirmed by sufficient testimony. He next, in the passage before us, appeals as a second proof to the whole compass of the Messianic predictions of the Old Testament, which had now become clear and certain by the fulfilment, whereas before its shining light fell upon them, they resembled a faintly burning taper, which could imperfectly illuminate the surrounding darkness. He then assigns the cause, why prophecy does not acquire its full light, and with that the usefulness of which it is capable, until after the fulfilment. The prophets themselves had not a clear knowledge of the import of their predictions,*

---

* We take ἐπίλυσις with Knapp in the ordinary and established sense, *interpretation*. Steudel objects against this (in d. Weinachtsprogr von 1823 p. 26 seq.), that Peter could not justly found the proof, that the prophets did not understand the meaning of their own communications, upon the fact of their being given by divine inspiration. But in saying this the term, φερόμενοι seems to have escaped his notice. Peter grounds his proof, not upon divine inspiration in general, but upon the *ecstasy* of the prophets in which consciousness and the self control of their mental powers were suspended. Steudel as well as Ullmann (Aechtheit des zweiten Briefes Petri p 38) and indeed Oecumenius, wish to understand ἐπίλυσις as meaning *prophecy itself*, and they appeal to a passage in Philo, where the prophets are called θεοῦ ἑρμηνεῖς. But, supposing it to be proved that this word *might* bear such a sense in some cases, yet it could not in this, for the following reasons; first, because "inter-

because they did not speak of themselves, nor even in the possession of reason and consciousness, but in an ecstasy, and as the instruments of the Holy Ghost (ὑπὸ πνεύματος ἁγίου φερόμενοι.) This passage is important for us in two respects. 1 It confirms the right which we have already shown to be well founded, but which is denied by our opponents, of dispelling the darkness of the predictions of the Messiah by the light of their fulfilment. In harmony with this, is the passage already quoted, 1 Pet 1. 10—12, where it is said to have been revealed to the prophets themselves, that the perfect knowledge of what they foretold concerning the mysterious advent of the Messiah, belonged to the time of the fulfilment, and that the chief import of prophecy did not relate to them and their contemporaries, but to those who were to come after 2. The reason of the obscurity of the prophecies, and the consequent need of the light of history is ascribed to the fact, that the prophets spake in an ecstasy, and thus the ground of our whole representation is strengthened.

Recent interpreters, as they despise the comparison of the fulfilment with the prediction, go back to the position of those who lived before the fulfilment, and from the darkness which through their own fault continues to rest upon the prophecies, they draw an argument against their divine origin Thus for example Ammon (Christol p XII) declares: " The simple sentences expressed in cool historical prose Israel has no king to expect, but a teacher: this teacher will be born at Bethlehem in the reign of Herod, he will sacrifice his life for the truth of his religion, under Tiberius; through the destruction of Jerusalem, and the utter ruin of the Jewish State, he will propagate his doctrine in all parts of the world;—these few sentences would not only bear the character of true predictions, but could their genuineness be shown, they would be incomparably more valuable than all the oracles of the Old Testament put together." But without being permitted to fathom the depth of the divine counsels, we are able to prove those requisitions unwarrantable, and inconsistent with the

---

pretation" here must necessarily be referred back to προφητεία γραφῆς, secondly on account of the parallel passage in the first Epistle, where likewise he is speaking of the obscurity which attended prophecy even to the prophets themselves; and finally because a confirmation of the principal idea καὶ ἔχομεν βεβαιότερον τὸν προφητικὸν λόγον, as it is furnished in 20 21, by the first mode of explanation, is far more in place, than a confirmation of the subordinate idea ᾧ καλῶς ποιεῖτε προσέχοντες, as it would stand in the same verses, according to the second explanation.

design of prophecy, and to justify the method in which God has been pleased to reveal his purposes 1 It is contrary to the nature of God to force men to believe He conceals himself in his works and in his providence, in order that he may be found, only by those who seek him. And thus, on the one side, he made the prophecies so plain, that those who did not voluntarily deceive themselves, might understand all that was essential and important, and on the other he left them so obscure, that those who disliked the truth should not be compelled to see it We might with the same justice require God to perform daily miracles to convince the despisers of his name of their folly, as desire greater clearness in the prophecies. 2. Had they possessed the clearness of history, their accomplishment would have been impossible. Had God, for example, caused the sentences just quoted to be written down; had the life of Christ, his rejection by the Jews, and its mournful consequence, the destruction of Jerusalem been in every respect described as completely and as intelligibly even for the carnally minded, as in the New Testament, the purpose of redemption, which required the death of Christ, could not have been accomplished By the present character of the Messianic prophecies, on the contrary, the end of leading the pious to the manifested Messiah, was completely attained, without thereby defeating a higher and far more important plan 3 Besides, the obscurity spread over certain portions of prophecy rendered them far more beneficial to believers, than they otherwise could have been. If, for example, the believers who lived many centuries before Christ's appearance had known that it would be so long delayed, how much would their love have been cooled, and their hope enfeebled? How could the expectation of the Messiah have become the central point of their whole religious life? Had the primitive Christians foreseen that the second coming of Christ would be deferred at least eighteen hundred years, how much feebler would have been the influence of this doctrine, than when they expected his advent every hour and were directed to watch, since he would come as a thief in the night, in such an hour as they did not expect. 4. We have already had frequent occasion to remark, that a larger part of the Messianic predictions was designed to exert an immediate influence upon the mass of the people, and retain them, even though it were only in profession, faithful to the Lord. This object could not have been attained had they possessed the clearness of history. It was however well accomplished by so ordering the prophecies, that even their misapprehension, through the fault of those to whom they were given, was attended with beneficial results. The rude and carnal people took possession of the covering, and believed they had found the substance itself; and contributed to preserve the outward conditions required in order that the true contents of prophecy might be realized. 5. Should it be asked what end could be answered by that portion of prophecy which was obscure in itself, and not owing to a carnal disposition, we suggest that the prophets, as appears from the passages already quoted from the New Testament, uttered their predictions, not merely for their contemporaries, but for posterity. For the former the perspicuous part was entirely sufficient. We conclude with the words of the excellent Pascal (Pensées sur la religion. Amst 1734 p 95), which indeed refer to the whole of revelation, but admit of special application to the prophecies: "Il y a assez de lumière pour ceux, qui ne desirent, que de voir, et assez d'obscurité pour ceux, qui ont une disposition contraire.—Il y assez d'obscurité pour aveugler les reprouvez, et assez de clarté pour les condamner et les rendre inexcusables.—Le desein de dieu est plus de perfectionner la volonté, que l'esprit. Or la clarté parfaite ne serviroit qu'à l'esprit, et nuiroit à la volonté.—S'il n'y avoit point d'obscurité, l'homme ne sentiroit pas sa corruption. S'il n'y avoit point de lumière, l'homme n'espereroit point de remede.—Tout tourne en bien pour les elûs jusqu'aux obscuritez de l'ecriture, car ils les honorent à cause des clartez divines, qu'ils y voyent. et tout tourne en mal aux reprouvez jusqu'aux clartez; car ils les blasphêment à cause des obscuritez, qu'ils n'entendent pas."

V. The dramatic character of the prophecies is owing to the condition of the prophets while delivering them. Both persons and events presented themselves to their mental vision; this is as it were the theatre on which the former appeared, speaking and acting; comp Is. xiv and lxiii and Ps ii. Hence we can explain the frequent change of the speakers, sometimes as Isa 14. 3, 4 with previous notice, often without, and we are justified in supposing that the Messiah in particular is in many places introduced as speaking. Comp our remarks on Ps. ii, xvi, xxii, Isa. xlii, xlix.*

VI. Lastly, from the condition of the prophets, the opinion is pro-

---

* Gulich l. c p 92 "Prosopopoeiae istae apud prophetas ἀκέφαλοι sunt multae. Quia nempe ut, quum res geritur, tales sermones audiuntur vel saltem audiri possunt sine omni nomenclatore, qui indicet quis ille sit, qui loquitur, ita prophetae in visione sermones audiunt et renuntiant."

ved to be correct, that the symbolical transactions which they described, were for the most part, not real but only passed in vision, an opinion, which (as Maimonides long since perceived),* the nature of them obliges us to adopt. For since the sphere of the prophets, so long as they were in ecstasy, was not the external, but the internal world, every action performed by them in this state must of necessity be internal also. The cases where these symbolical actions can be shown to have really been performed are to be regarded as exceptions, in which the prophets departed from their proper sphere † See the further discussion on Hosea chap. I—III.

CHAPTER VI.

THE MEANS OF PROVING THE REFERENCE OF PARTICULAR PROPHECIES TO THE MESSIAH.

If the predictions of the Messiah are to accomplish the end for which they were given, the confirmation of our faith, their reception must not rest upon a mere opinion of our own, a feeling not to be relied on, which associates itself with a particular expression, often erroneously apprehended, but upon firm grounds, which, being in themselves perfectly valid, can be rejected only from doctrinal prejudice It is not to be denied that the fathers, and not a few of the older theologians, have here been much too easily satisfied, and have thereby given great advantage to the enemies of revelation It is the more incumbent on us to treat this subject thoroughly, since we dare not,

---

* Comp l c chap XLVI He says justly "Absit ut deus prophetas suos stultis vel ebriis similes reddat eosque stultorum aut furiosorum actiones facere jubeat "

† Comp Jo Smith l. c p 14 " Prophetica scena, intra quam omnes peragebantur apparitiones, fuit ipsius prophetae phantasia, omniaque, quae deus ei revelata volebat dramatice in phantasia gerebantur, ita ut plures interdum inducerentur in scenam personae, inter quas propheta partes etiam suas agebat. Itaque prout dramaticus ille apparatus postulabat, opportuit eum, ut ceteros actores partes suas agere, aliquando verbis et narratione rerum gestarum, aut propositione quaestionum, aliquando eas partes ferentem, quas jussus erat per alios agere, adeoque eum non tantum sermone, sed etiam gestibus et actionibus locum suum inter alios obtinere "

like those who undertake to prove what is generally acknowledged, and doubted only by some individuals, calculate upon a disposition in the larger portion of readers already inclined to believe, and prepared beforehand by the tradition of the church, but must rather suppose the existence of that mistrust which is ready to withhold assent, even after the strongest proofs have been produced. Indeed we hope even by such proofs to overcome this mistrust, only where it is not founded on total unbelief in divine revelation, the reality of which, must be in some measure taken for granted in proving the reference of prophecies to the Messiah, but arises merely from inability to free itself, by an independent examination, from the fetters imposed by the prevailing opinion of the day, which originally sprung from this unbelief, and which endeavors by all means to have its base descent forgotten. Still our aim will be fully accomplished, if, besides effecting this, we can oblige the opposer of the truth to confess that upon our principles we do not act capriciously, and that they are prevented only by theories from approving the conclusions at which we arrive.

The argument in support of the Messianic interpretation, must always be accompanied by a refutation of the objections that have been urged against it. It is self-evident that here nothing which is in itself plausible must be passed over. The defender of this interpretation does not confine himself to those objections which appear to him of this character, and which it would be dishonest to omit. He must also examine those, whose real weakness has been disguised by their continued and confident assertion. Interest or authority has here given great importance to what was in itself utterly insignificant. The examination of even weak objections is yet attended with the advantages of drawing the attention to the prejudice which has guided the inquiries of opponents, and shows that the chief difference is not scientific but practical. To this end it is also necessary that purely dogmatic arguments should not be passed over in silence. It is sufficient, however, merely to mention them: perpetual refutation is unnecessary.

The positive proofs that any particular prophecy relates to the Messiah are the following.

1. A prediction is properly referred to him, when it can be shown, that its most particular declarations are completely fulfilled in the history of Christ, while this is not only incapable of proof, but in the highest degree improbable, in the history of any other person; or, when it possesses traits, which from the nature of the case can be-

long to no other subject.* An instance of the first, occurs in Ps. xxii. All the marks given are found again in the history of Christ; that they should have occurred in the same connexion in the life of David is improbable, and several particulars, as the piercing of the hands and feet, and the division of the garments, can by no means be referred to him. Instances of the second kind occur in all those places where divine dignity is attributed to the subject of the prophecy. This argument is with perfect propriety applied also in the case of Isa. liii. When it has been proved that this passage contains the doctrine of vicarious satisfaction, its reference to the Messiah is at the same time established; since such a satisfaction effected by man may be shown to be in direct contradiction to the religious conception of the Old Testament, while on the contrary history testifies, that it was really accomplished by Christ. Of this means of proof the Apostles availed themselves, Acts 2. 31—35. 13:35. It has been urged as an objection against it, that the prophets are to be treated as poets, in whose productions each particular expression is not to be urged, but much is to be regarded as embellishment, and, that if a representation can then be shown to be applicable, either to the writer himself, or to some other person living in his time, it is unreasonable to explain literally one part of it, with which the history of the Messiah may agree, as for example, the piercing of the hands, Ps xxii, and the vicarious satisfaction, Isa. liii, and to regard the rest—on the contrary, the dogs, lions, bulls Ps. xxii, and the diseases and division of the spoil, Isa. liii, as metaphorical. See Meier, Hermeneut des A. T. II. p 479 seq. But the objection would be in some measure just, only when we were entirely without the means of distinguishing between the figure and the reality. If this, however, were the case, the interpretation, not merely of the Messianic, but of all prophecies, would be difficult indeed. But with what ease discrimination can be made, is manifest from the very example referred to. Since it surely needs no proof, that, in Ps. xxii, the dogs, lions and bulls cannot be taken literally, the piercing of the hands and the feet, on the contrary, cannot be figurative, since metaphors must be taken from prevailing usages, and it is not customary to pierce the hands and feet of enemies. That in Is. liii, the richness and division of the spoil must be understood in a figurative, and the vicarious satisfaction on the contrary in a literal sense we shall prove

---

* Even the superscriptions sometimes furnish a proof of the Messianic interpretation. Thus, e. g. Ps xiv and cx.

in our examination of the passage. This objection is indeed so far well grounded, that it can be required of us before we maintain on internal evidence the exclusive reference of a passage to the Messiah, to establish the proper meaning of the declarations which it contains.

2. An important proof for the Messianic interpretation may be derived from parallel passages. These are of two kinds. 1. There are frequently in later predictions on which the Messianic character is distinctly impressed plain references to those of an earlier date, in which the Messiah is described in more general terms Thus, for example, Ez 21 27, in a prediction which can be shown to relate to the Messiah, avails himself of the words of Gen. 49. 10. In like manner Ps. 72: 17 repeats the promise to the patriarchs and teachers, that they will be fulfilled through the Messiah. Zech. 6 13, has a plain reference to Ps cx. 2. In other instances it can be shown, that several passages must necessarily relate to one and the same subject, and, of course, all the marks which prove the Messianic character of one passage, are equally applicable to the rest Those which are indefinite may be shown to refer to the Messiah by a comparison with those which are definite; and thus we have in favor of the Messianic character of Isa XLII, XLIX, L, LXI, not only the evidence furnished by these passages themselves, but the far stronger proofs by which the undoubted Messianic character of chap. LIII can be demonstrated So also, if the reference of Ps. cx to the Messiah is proved, that of Ps II, XLVI, LXXII follows of course See other examples in Pareau l. c. p. 501 seq.

3. The force of both these proofs becomes still greater, when it can be shown that a prediction was explained of the Messiah by the older Jews, whose opinions respecting the interpretation of Scripture were not determined by controversy with Christians See Kleuker, über die Altonaer Bibel p 154 seq. In the case of a people of so uniform a character, and so tenacious of all that had been handed down from their forefathers, exegetical tradition is of no small importance In reference to other subjects this is indeed generally acknowledged in recent times. Jewish tradition is reckoned among the chief means of explaining the import of words, and we are in fact in many cases referred to it alone, since the authority of the old translation depends chiefly on their giving testimony concerning this tradition See Gesenius, Gesch der hebr. Sprache und Schr. s. 70 seq 93 seq. De Wette Einl in's A. T. § 35. In recent

times, the later origin of the system of vowels and accents in its present form, is generally asserted, and yet critics do not venture to depart from it without the most urgent reasons; merely, as is manifest, because the authority of the Jewish tradition is acknowledged, in favor of which a close examination gives the clearest testimony. How inconsistent then would it be, when so much importance is attached to it on the one side, to allow it to have no weight on the other! Its evidence becomes so much the more conclusive, when the sense which it gives is in opposition to the sentiments and wishes of the people. For then we can easily imagine a reason for the rejection of this sense, but not for its adoption, unless it were the true one originally intended. When, for example, the Jewish tradition acknowledges in Isa. LIII and Ps. xxii the suffering Messiah, it is of far greater weight than when it gives a Messianic character to other passages, which represent the Messiah in glory. The chief sources of this tradition, are the New Testament, the old Chaldee paraphrases, the Cabbalistic writings, especially the book Sohar, the Talmud, the collections of old Jewish explanations of Scriptures, known by the name Medraschim, the writings of the later Jewish commentators, which often quote the traditional explanation, even when they are led by doctrinal interest to depart from it, and lastly, the writings of the fathers, especially of Jerome. Collections of testimonies from Jewish writers may be found in the following works: Raymundi Martini pugio fidei adversus Mauros et Judaeos cum observatt. Jos. de Voisin ed. Jo. Bened. Carpzov Lips. 1687 fol.—Petr. Galatini opus de arcanis Catholicae veritatis. Basil. 1561 fol.—Christ. Schottgenii horae Hebr. et Talm., in theologiam Judaeorum—antiquam et orthodoxam de Messia impensae Tomus II. Dresd. 1742 4to, and in a German work of the same author: Jesus der wahre Messias aus der alten und reinen Judischen Theologie dargethan und erlautert. Leipz. 1748 8vo.

4. Among external arguments, the evidence of the New Testament holds the most important place. Here, however, it must first be determined, whether a passage of the Old Testament is explained properly and exclusively of Christ, either by himself or by the Apostles. In this respect the older theologians have greatly erred, since they concluded at once from the mere citation of a passage in the New Testament, that it was a prediction of a particular person, as the Messiah. This decision is often indeed not difficult, as for example, with respect to Ps. xvi, Isa. 7: 14; see our remarks on those pla-

ces The quotation of a passage from the Old Testament with merely the forms· καθὼς γέγραπται, καὶ ἐπληρώθη, τότε ἐπληρώθη, ἵνα πληρωθῇ or ὅπως πληρωθῇ affords little evidence that it relates to the Messiah. These forms are more comprehensive; besides being used where a proper fulfilment of a personal prediction is indicated, they occur in the following cases. 1. Sometimes when only the repetition of what occurred in the history of a type is to be pointed out in that of its antitype. Here indeed, there is in some measure a proper fulfilment, inasmuch as the similarity of the events which happened to both was caused by the providence of God. The plainest proof of this is furnished in Mark 9 13 ἀλλὰ λέγω ὑμῖν, ὅτι καὶ Ἡλίας ἐλήλυθε καὶ ἐποίησαν αὐτῷ ὅσα ἠθέλησαν, καθὼς γέγραπται ἐπ' αὐτόν. Christ there says that it was necessary that the history of Elias, a type of John, should be repeated in the history of the latter, he even considered the history of Elias as a prophecy of the history of John Olshausen* justly explains in the same manner the passages of John 19 35, where after he had related that the bones of Christ had not been broken, he adds· ἐγένετο γὰρ ταῦτα, ἵνα ἡ γραφὴ πληρωθῇ ὀστοῦν οὐ συντριβήσεται αὐτοῦ. These words are by no means, as Steudel (in der Beurtheilung der Schrift von Olshausen, Bengel's Archiv 7 p 427) supposes, taken from Ps 34 21, where only a similar, not a corresponding passage occurs, but from Ex. 12. 46 and Num. 9 12 There it is forbidden to break the bones of the paschal lamb, and it was only because John considered the paschal lamb as a type of Christ, that he could place this occurrence in connexion with the declaration there made. He was so convinced of the applicability of that which was said respecting the type to him whom it prefigured, that he places immediately after a proper Messianic prediction in connexion with it We ought perhaps to explain in the same way also Matt 2 15, where after having related the residence of Christ in Egypt, he says . ἵνα πληρωθῇ τὸ ῥηθὲν ὑπὸ τοῦ κυρίου διὰ τοῦ προφήτου λέγοντος ἐξ Αἰγύπτου ἐκάλεσα τὸν υἱόν μου It is impossible that the passages quoted from Hosea 11: 1, according to the context, can have any other reference than to the people of Israel, and Matthew surely was far from regarding it as a proper prediction relating to Christ. But he refers it to him so far as Israel on the one hand, viewed in respect to its election, or as Son of God, was a type of him, while on the other,

---

* Ein Wort üb tiefern Schriftsinn Konigsb 1824 p 65 Comp dess V Sendschreiben an Steudel ub die Bibl Schriftausl Hamb 1825 p 15

in reference to its conduct toward God, it represented the natural man. 2 These forms also sometimes occur when a declaration of the Old Testament is indeed properly of a more general character, so that it can be applied to all the particular relations which it comprehends. Yet, so that the ideal relation apprehended, first appears as fully realized in the history of Christ, that here the reality for the first time fully coincides with the idea. As an example, we may refer to the New Testament quotations of Ps LXIX. David in this Psalm, which in all probability was not called forth by his circumstances as an individual, represents the relation sustained to the ungodly by a pious man suffering for God's sake This ideal relation is most completely realized in that of Christ to Judas, his betrayer. With propriety, therefore, is verse 10 of this Psalm in John 2 17, John 15. 25, referred to Christ, and v 26, Acts 1.20, to Judas The sacred writers had the more right to regard such declarations as fulfilled in the history of Christ, as they proceeded upon the principle that the authors of the Psalm spake under the special influence of the Holy Ghost, whence it followed that the ideal description could very well have a designed reference to the real relation, although the authors of the Psalm were unconscious of it. Hence we can explain why even in respect to those particulars that are in the first instance to be understood figuratively, as the drinking of vinegar, (comp v 22 with John 19 28), the Evangelist points out the coincidence with the history of Christ The same may be said of the quotation from Ps. XLI; comp John 13 18, Acts 1· 16, where the supposition of a mere simile is excluded by the form of citation: ἔδει πληρωθῆναι τὴν γραφὴν ταύτην, ἣν προεῖπε τὸ πνεῦμα τὸ ἅγιον διὰ στόματος Δαβίδ. 3 The sacred writers sometimes use these forms where a declaration of the Old Testament well applies to persons and events of the New, not indeed because it distinctly refers to them individually, but according to the fundamental idea which it contains Thus Christ himself, Matt 13 14, introduces with the words · καὶ ἀναπληροῦται αὐτοῖς ἡ προφητεία Ἡσαίου, the passage of Isaiah 6 9 and 10 in reference to the unbelieving Jews of his time, which nevertheless in the first instance refers to the contemporaries of the prophet, as Paul expressly said, where, Acts 28· 25, he quotes the same passage with the same words. καλῶς τὸ πνεῦμα τὸ ἅγιον ἐλάλησε διὰ Ἡσαίου τοῦ προφήτου πρὸς τοὺς πατέρας ἡμῶν; comp Matt 15: 7. The same is true in reference to the quotation of Ps. LXVIII in Eph. 4 8—10; the internal relation between the two occurrences is evident. As Jehovah is represented in this Psalm as having come down to bestow temporal gifts upon the people of the Old Testament, and as having ascended again to heaven after he had done this, so has Christ, who is identified with the Jehovah of the old covenant, descended to bring spiritual gifts to the people of the new covenant and afterwards reascended to his lofty dwelling place. Here also the fulfilment must not be regarded as accidental, but designed by the Holy Ghost, as appears from the manner in which the passage of the Psalm is treated by Paul. 4. Sometimes these forms are employed where a declaration belongs indeed directly and properly to the person to whom it is referred, but nevertheless, in a more comprehensive and higher relation, of which the more limited and inferior, in reference to which it is quoted, is only a particular and entirely necessary consequence, or merely a copy. Thus it is said, Matt. 8:17, after Christ's healing the sick has been related: ὅπως πληρωθῇ τὸ ῥηθὲν διὰ Ἡσαΐου τοῦ προφήτου λέγοντος· αὐτὸς τὰς ἀσθενείας ἡμῶν ἔλαβε καὶ τὰς νόσους ἐβάστασε. While the same passage of Isa. LIII is elsewhere, as in 1 Pet. 2:24, justly referred to the removal of spiritual evils by Christ, of which his healing bodily diseases was a symbol. See our remarks on the passage. So John 18:9, after he has described the affectionate care of Christ for the temporal welfare of his disciples, subjoins: ἵνα πληρωθῇ ὁ λόγος, ὃν εἶπεν, ὅτι οὓς δέδωκάς μοι, οὐκ ἀπώλεσα ἐξ αὐτῶν οὐδένα, appealing to a declaration of Christ, which in the first instance marked his concern for their spiritual welfare and its happy effects which, however, sprung from the same source as his concern for their temporal welfare. 5. In some few places these forms occur where a mere *simile* is quoted. So at least it appears to us, when Matt. 2:17, in the account of the slaughter of the children of Bethlehem, the passage, Jer. 31:15, which relates to the carrying away of the Jews into exile, is quoted with the form: τότε ἐπληρώθη τὸ ῥηθὲν ὑπὸ Ἱερεμίου τοῦ προφήτου. We are not able to perceive an internal connexion designed by God, between these two events. We interpret the passage in Matt. 13:35 in the same way. After relating how Christ spake to the people in parables, Matthew then adds: ὅπως πληρωθῇ τὸ ῥηθὲν διὰ τοῦ προφήτου λέγοντος· ἀνοίξω ἐν παραβολαῖς τὸ στόμα μου. These words are the commencement of the 78th Psalm. The appropriateness of the quotation as a simile, is not to be mistaken. As Asaph there delivered his instructions in a historical dress, and in such a manner that the proper meaning of his discourse was clear only to him who reflected deeply, and was not satisfied with the historical facts as such, so Christ also exhibited in a similar dress the deepest truths, which remained concealed from the great mass of the people. On the contrary, it is scarcely conceivable how an internal connexion designed by God, between this Psalm and the occurrence, in reference to which it is quoted by Matthew, can be shown without the most unnatural and forced hypothesis. We therefore agree with Knapp (Opuscc. p. 609 und Dogm. II. p. 136) and Steudel (l c p. 444) in opposition to Olshausen, so far as to regard the forms in question, as sometimes indicating a mere resemblance. We freely concede to Olshausen, that a multitude of passages have been in this way explained, the quotation of which depends upon a far deeper reason, and yet we assert this principle of interpretation as being in general, and without reference to the particular places, derogatory to the honor of Christ and his Apostles. This result could in no case follow unless these forms of quotation implied that the sacred writers wished to indicate a deeper relation than that of mere resemblance. This must be decided by an appeal to the usage of the language; the particles ἵνα and ὅπως, of which only one, however, occurs in the latter place, can here prove no closer connexion, since in the loose phraseology of the New Testament they are manifestly used in a more comprehensive sense than in pure Greek. Comp. Fritsche (Excurs 1 ad Matth.), Winer (Grammatik des N. T. II. p 117 seq.) But in general such forms of citation are to be regarded in the same light as proverbs. We must not determine their meaning by the individual words, but must inquire in what sense the whole phrase is used. But here usage decides for the most comprehensive meaning in which also the corresponding phrases לקיים מה שנאמר, etc. occur in the Talmud and other writings.* Comp. Surenhus. βιβλ. καταλλαγ. p. 2 seq. Wahner Antiquitatt. Hebr. I p. 527 seq. Here, therefore, the question cannot be concerning a dishonest accommodation, and just as little concerning a practice which was useless and therefore unworthy of the Holy Scriptures, since every mode of appeal to the Old Testament was suited to bring the Gospel near to the Jews, for whom Matthew in particular, chiefly wrote. Since then, these forms of quotation are used for various

---

* How much the meaning of such forms can be generalized in the ordinary usage of a language, is shown among others by a passage of Jerome (ep 103 ad Paulin.) 'Caeterum Socraticum illud impletur in nobis, hoc tantulum scio, quod nescio.''

purposes, it must be decided on other grounds, whether the authors of the New Testament introduce a passage as a proper personal prediction, in some other of the abovementioned relations. In not a few instances this can be decided from the New Testament itself. When this is not the case, the proof from the New Testament is only additional evidence, which first becomes valid when the reference to the Messiah as a person has been shown from internal arguments.

But so soon as the proof can be produced, that a passage is explained by Christ or his Apostles as properly belonging to the Messiah, this is of itself sufficient, and we must assume beforehand that all difficulties, which are urged against this interpretation are only apparent. Here critics after having adopted a false interpretation of the Old Testament, in opposition to that of Christ and his Apostles, have employed various means to set aside their authority. Before they ventured to proceed to the last extremity, they resorted to two expedients. Either they asserted, after the example of Semler (apparat. ad liber. N T. interpret. p. 94, 95), that Christ and the Apostles themselves, far from finding in the Old Testament proper predictions of the Messiah, only wisely accommodated their mode of instruction to the prevailing prejudices, or they sought by the most forced interpretations, to prove that it is only by mistake that Christ and his Apostles have been supposed to explain passages of the Old Testament as really predictions of the Messiah. Thus Eckermann in his Essays, Vol I. Lastly, when all had been duly prepared, they cast away of their own accord supernatural expedients, and openly declared that Christ and his Apostles, in the explaining of the Old Testament were not guided by settled principles of interpretation, or a definite exegetical tradition, but only connected its prophecies in an arbitrary manner with the history of Christ.* And thus they have saved us the trouble of refuting the two former views. But the last assertion deserves no refutation, if its abettors carry it so far as to deny that Christ himself rightly interpreted the prophecies. It is the pure offspring of unbelief.† For is Christ truly God and was it his

---

* Comp for example, Gesenius Comm z Jesaias 111 p 160, 61

† It is, (and such being its origin it cannot be otherwise), any thing but new, although it has not been heretofore so openly and freely advanced. This appears, among others, from the remarkable passage of Franc Junius, Vorr zu d Schrift parallela sacra "De atheis non fuissem unquam ita crediturus, nisi me tenellum adhuc ipsorum agmina summo discrimine salutis meae sollicitassent ante triginta annos, cum literis humanioribus operam in Gallia darem Vidi enim puer, vidi eo tempore versutissimas illo-

Spirit which spake in the prophecies, how should he not have possessed a deeper knowledge of the Scriptures than we who cannot understand them without his guidance? We must, however, notice a view of this subject arising from another cause, from an unwilling dependence on the investigations of the rationalists respecting the Old Testament, entertained by those who bow indeed to the authority of Christ, but on the other hand so far agree with our opponents as to limit the infallibility of the Apostles to what concerns doctrines and morals, and assert their liability to err in their proofs in general, and particularly in their interpretation of the Old Testament.

The evidence appealed to in favor of this view is, that the infallibility of the Apostles, in the explanation of the Old Testament, is contradicted by an examination of the passages interpreted by them. But let the inquirer not take this for granted; and that it would be wrong to do so, will be made, in the course of this work, sufficiently evident to satisfy those who entertain the same general views of the faith as ourselves; let him, leaving for once all particulars out of sight, look only at the necessary consequences of his own principles and he will not accede to an opinion, which not only gives great advantages to opponents, but must have a pernicious influence on the firmness and consistency of his own belief. For the notion that faith would be confirmed by giving up subordinate points, rests entirely on self-deception. That it is contradicted by experience, is easily shown by referring to analogous cases. Is morality, for instance, strengthened, when we are careless in small matters, and seek to be right only in great ones? Is not rather faithfulness in small things the surest means of moral improvement? This assertion would be true only when the extension of faith to matters of least moment, would, necessarily, cause them to be overrated in comparison with those of chief importance. This may happen, with respect to particular individuals, but it is not therefore a necessary consequence, as may be shown by numerous examples of a different character.

---

rum technas et machinationes, quum animae imprudenti meae facerent insidias periculosissime. Illi enim non solum τα ἐναντιοφανῆ ὡς ἐνάντια gloriosissime obtrudebant, quae in script. sacr. affirmabant esse quam plurima, verum etiam ipsius Christi Evangelistarum Apostolorumque (at quorum hominum!) sermones fere singulos scriptaque carpebant τῆς ἑτεροφωνίας nomine, eamque ut probarent arbitratu suo acervatim proferebant ex V. T. locos, qui adducuntur in Novo. Garriebant res plane diversas eum in modum confusas esse, imperite ab illis factum clamabant, et fieri a nobis impie, qui autoribus et artificibus adeo imperitis fidem haberemus."

But how much this assertion contradicts the nature of faith, is evident from the fact that it will be universally condemned by uneducated Christians, to whom, in this case, the appeal may very properly be made. This is also confirmed by the many instances where the doubts of unsettled minds find support on this very ground, and thence extend themselves to other points of the Christian faith. And this is nothing more than might be naturally expected; since the assertion that the Apostles were fallible in argument, and fallible in doctrine and morals, is altogether arbitrary, and must appear to every one as only the result of embarrassment. The declarations of Christ, in which he attributes infallibility to the Apostles, and which need not here be cited, are altogether general, they are either conclusive, and then they exclude their liability to error in argument; or they are not conclusive, and then their fallibility in doctrine also must be conceded. But if the Apostles of Christ were fallible in argument and doctrine, then we must acknowledge the possibility of error even in the discourses of Christ, and since they have been delivered to us by the same Apostles, and were so frequently misunderstood by them before they were guided into all truth by the Holy Spirit. And thus doubt on this point, when carried out to its legitimate consequences, ends in universal scepticism. Further, this assertion would be altogether improbable, even on psychological principles; for the infallibility of the Apostles must have been owing to a divine power, which resided in them. But that were surely a strange power, which extended its assistance merely to the doctrine, but not to the proofs, especially as the difference between them is not distinctly marked. How unnatural this separation is, must appear to every one who seriously examines the subject. Who that should do this, and not guard against the danger by an abstraction—as is commonly done, though without preventing a secret germ of doubt from remaining in the soul—would not be led to question e. g. the infallibility of the Apostle Peter in doctrine, if the whole argument is unsound, by which, in his discourse after the outpouring of the Spirit, he not only refers Ps. xvi to Christ, but opposes its reference to David. To these considerations, we subjoin the following. It is said in the Gospel, that Christ himself explained to his disciples those passages which treated of him, namely, of his suffering and resurrection. Comp. 24 25—27 and 44—47. Is it not then in the highest degree probable, that those passages which the Apostles chiefly urge, are precisely the same which were explained to them by Christ? Must we not then fear, that if we re-

ject their authority, we shall at the same time endanger that of Christ? We appeal moreover to the testimony of the church of Christ in all ages. The interpretation, not only of Christ, but of his Apostles also, has ever been held as authentic and obligatory, and when individuals asserted the contrary, they were considered as having gone over to the ranks of unbelief. But what is so universal and prevalent must not be placed in an arbitrary connexion with thorough Christian knowledge, but of necessity proceed from it. And since even the earliest fathers in their citations of the Old Testament rely upon the authority of the Apostles, the Apostles must certainly have laid claims to this authority. But allowing them to have done this without sufficient reason, they would have committed an error in doctrine, the possibility of which is contested. That they claimed this authority can be proved also in another way. Were the Apostles left to themselves, and fallible only in reference to argument and the interpretation of Scripture, we should expect them to give us some intimation of so important a fact, especially, as they well knew in other respects how to distinguish what proceeded from their own minds, enlightened and sanctified by the ordinary operations of the Holy Spirit, from that which proceeded immediately from Him. Comp. 1 Cor 7: 6. 12: 40. Such an intimation however we nowhere find, on the contrary, they speak with the same firmness and assurance in their interpretation of Scripture, as in their doctrines.—Lastly, if we compare without prejudice the interpretation of Scripture by Christ and by the Apostles, we shall perceive that they are altogether similar; we can, therefore, scarcely question the correctness of the Apostles, without at the same time cherishing a secret doubt of that of the Lord himself. That it is no unimportant subject which is here discussed, will be rendered more evident to many by the following passage of Herder, whose testimony in this instance must be acknowledged to be impartial. He says (Briefe uber das Stud. d. Theol p 214 seq.)
" I hear it frequently asserted. Passages and predictions of the Old Testament are fulfilled in our Redeemer for the most part only by way of accommodation, not otherwise. In the Old Testament they had another sense, another connexion, another design. They are distorted and applied to Christ by popular error, by the false rules of Jewish exposition and hermeneutics, by the ignorance of those who cited them. Briefly, we have only by the *beneficium* of allusion and Jewish explanation, an accommodated Christ. I cannot jest over this, my friend, I pity. Did I know of no better method of interpre-

tation, I would always, though as the last resort, pity myself. For reflect with earnestness and impartiality on what must be the end of all this. I am ready to concede, that Paul as a scholar of the Rabbins, that the evangelists so far as they being Jews, wrote for Jews, may in unessential things have employed such allusions and favorite modes of interpretation, for the sake of explanation and illustration $\varkappa\alpha\tau'$ $\mathring{\alpha}\nu\vartheta\varrho\omega\pi o\nu$, the main point, if it rested on other and better proofs, would lose little or nothing, by this dangerous neighborhood. But suppose now, that in the main point also, they urged such proofs; that Christ himself in matters of chief importance relied on such accommodations as we are at present considering, and tell me where now remains, I will not say inspiration, but the sure word of the God of truth. Did he send his Son into the world, and could he not send him with infallible credentials? Could he not at least guard him and his ministers from producing false credentials? That Jesus was an honest man, the weak sceptic can readily concede; but could not this honest man deceive himself? Could he not the more easily do this, when he felt himself impelled towards good objects which were beyond his reach? And, if he deceived himself, even in the application of a single prophecy, which did not belong to him; but which he assumed to himself only by accommodation, why did God sanction him by miracles? By that greatest of miracles, his resurrection? Did he intend to build for us a trap-bridge between deceit in interpretation and honesty in conduct, between self-delusion and good intention? This would be the most dangerous trap-bridge that was ever built, not only for the Jewish people, but for all people in all ages of the world into whose hands the Old and the New Testament should ever come. What? A Christ sent for all times, for all nations, and demonstrated by Jewish accommodations all of which, perhaps, even his contemporaries did not adopt, for whom only and indeed for the weakest and most unlearned portion of whom they were designed? He comes from the God of truth, and has this God given evidence of his coming which is of mere temporary value? Has he so undeniably borne testimony to him by miracles, and so imperfectly and ambiguously by an application of the prophecies? Since what he and his disciples brought forward in his favor, we either adduce no more, or receive it merely from respect to them, and on the contrary, what we most rely upon they did not, and who knows whether we shall long continue to do so ourselves? The interpreter cares not for the dogma and cuts it away; the dogma seizes upon this and that straw for support; how when the border of the field is reached, and the last sickle strikes? What then? You see, my friend, every security is here doubtful, and is at the bottom unsound."

We have here only one remark to add. Since the promise of freedom from error was given to the Apostles alone, a difference must be made between their writings and those of all others. Were a passage, for example, explained of the Messiah only in the epistle to the Hebrews, this would be decisive only with those, who either acknowledge Paul to be the author of this epistle, or are convinced on other grounds of its divine authority.

CHAPTER VII

Literature of the Messianic Predictions

At a very early period, the interpretation of the prophecies of the Messiah was governed by interested motives. Making a wrong application of the correct principle, that Christ is the centre of the Old Testament, and especially of prophecy, (Origen in Mat ed. Rauer t III. p 472), commentators sought to find, even when the context and the usage of the language were decidedly against it, a direct reference to him, either by a literal or an allegorical explanation; they gave equal weight to all citations in the New Testament; they often expressed the conviction, that it were better to seek Christ ten times, where he was not, than to fail of doing it once, where he might be found; in passages which were really Messianic, they often allowed forced expositions in order to make them refer to Christ as an individual, or to multiply the objections against the non-Messianic interpreters. This was the prevailing method of interpretation with most of the fathers. It soon obtained the ascendency in the Evangelical church, although among the reformers Calvin at least went rather to the opposite extreme. The most thorough knowledge of this mode of interpretation can be obtained from the following works:

Abr. Gulichii (Prof. zu Nimmwegen, nachher zu Hamm, endlich zu Franeker) theologia prophetica. Acced. Hermeneutica sacra, praeceptiones, tum S Scripturam universe, tum speciatim prophetias summatim explicans. Amstelod. 1675 4to. 2te Ausg 1690. Dess, librorum prophet. V. et. N T. compendium et analysis. Opus posthumum. Amstel. 1683 4to

Nucleus prophetiae in duas partes distributus prima de vaticiniis, altera de typis illustrioribus V. T.—auct. Anton. Hulsio. (Prof. in Leiden). Lugd. Bat. 1683 4to.

Nicol Gurtleri (Prof. in Deventer) systema theologiae propheticae. Amstelod. 1702, ed. II Francof. 1724 4to

Die Kette theils der in den Büchern des A T. befindlichen buchst. Vorherverkundigungen von dem Heilande des menschlichen Geschlechtes untereinander theils des in den Opfern gestifteten Furbildes von Ihm mit der ersten Vorherverkundigung, durch Joach. Oporin. (Prof in Gottingen). Gott 1745 4to.

Among these works, that by Hulsius is without doubt the most important, and even now the most useful, especially on account of his diligence in collecting, and acuteness in refuting, Jewish interpretations. Far greater capriciousness prevails in the works of Gulich, who entirely follows Cocceius' method of interpretation, and has brought into one view what is found scattered throughout his commentaries on the prophetic Scriptures. The work of Gurtler also is liable to the charge of great capriciousness. It was the design of Oporin to show the connexion of all other Messianic predictions with the four celebrated promises Gen 3 15, 12 3, Deut 18 18 and 2 Sam. vii, and the constant reference of the later to the earlier. Pursuing this object with too much partiality, he has often asserted references without sufficient reason

It was manifestly not to be expected that this mode of interpretation could remain without opposition, and it was natural that this opposition should be carried to excess, as one extreme leads to another. In the ancient church, Eusebius of Emesa first sought to sift the passages referred to the Messiah, and distinguish what could be explained of him only by an allegorical, and what by a literal interpretation. See Hieronymus cat scr eccl c 119. Diodorus of Tarsus followed in his footsteps, who referred to Christ only in a higher sense, many prophecies which were explained exclusively of him by others, and asserted that there were but few which belonged to him μόνον καὶ κυρίως, κατὰ ῥητὸν and καθ' ἱστορίαν. The scholar of Diodorus, Theodore of Mopsueste, proceeded still further; he wrote a book especially against those who followed Origen's method of interpretation; his principles were declared heretical and condemned, they found therefore but few adherents who went as far as their author. Among them is to be mentioned Cosmas Indopleustes, who perverted even the plainest predictions of the Messiah, as Zech. 9: 9 10, which passage he made to refer in the first place and properly to Zerubbabel. Theodoret and Chrysostom endeavored to follow a middle course, which should combine all that was true in both methods. (See this subject treated at large by Ernesti in his learned narratio critica de interpretatione prophetiarum Messianarum in ecclesia Christiana in d opuscc p 495 seq) Grotius went far beyond all his predecessors in the ancient church In his preface to the Old Testament he disingenuously asserts, that he has referred only *locos nonnullos*, which have been commonly explained of Christ, to events which lay nearer the prophets, since he finds in scarcely six or seven places, namely, Gen. 49 10, Dan. 9. 24, Haggai 2. 7, 8, Mal 3. 1, direct and proper references to Christ. Not a single passage of Isaiah is explained by him as properly relating to the Messiah The opposition in which he is thus placed to the New Testament he seeks to conceal by the supposition, that many declarations, which directly and properly relate to nearer persons and occurrences, are to be referred in a higher sense to the times of the New Testament, a supposition which he plainly adopts to relieve himself from embarrassment, and one by which the authority of the New Testament is by no means sufficiently sustained. Grotius' mode of interpretation is adopted also by Hammond, Le Clerc, especially at an earlier period, Limborch and the Socinians. See especially Reuss, opuscula theoll. II p. 118 seq This whole method of interpretation was occasioned chiefly by the following reasons. 1 We have already mentioned the influence of opposition In the prevailing mode of interpretation, truth had been often sacrificed to the love of a theory Perceiving this, men were already prepared to distrust the current explanation, even where it rested on grounds which were sure, although not always clearly perceived by its defenders. They could not avoid perceiving that the authors of the New Testament often cited declarations of the Old Testament, even where they did not design to point out a proper and fulfilled prediction of the Messiah And thus, instead of inquiring with care in what sense and to what purpose each declaration is quoted in the New Testament, they were induced to reject alike all citations 2. A chief reason was deficiency in the knowledge of the manner in which the prophets perceived what they predicted. This knowledge was wanting also for the most part among the defenders of the Messianic reference of the prophe-

cies. While they were ignorant of the true reason of the mingling and juxtaposition of things in the prophetic vision, the prophecies of the Messiah appeared to them as disconnected, having no relation to what preceded and followed, or they must resolve by a forced interpretation to make that refer to the times of the Messiah, which manifestly belongs to an earlier period. Their opponents were the less capable of remedying this difficulty, since their minds were generally intelligent but not of a contemplative turn. Grotius himself remarks, that his method of interpretation was owing chiefly to this reason: "feci autem hoc, quod viderem male cohaerere verborum rerumque apud prophetas seriem, quae ceteroquin pulcherrima est."
3. As love to Christ, and firm faith in him, led the advocates of the opposite method of interpretation to many forced explanations, so the want of these qualities manifestly operated in favor of the method of which we are speaking. Those critics who had rather refer the plainest predictions of the Old Testament to any other subject than the Messiah, are accustomed to dilute and explain away what is said of him in the New Testament also, and we do them no injustice when we attribute their conduct in both instances to the same source. Nor is any evidence to the contrary furnished by the fact to which Ernesti l. c. p 529, appeals, that Grotius, the ablest of the interpreters, has himself written an admirable book in defence of the Christian religion. A wide distinction, it is true, must be made between these interpreters, and those of whom we are now to speak.

Hitherto theologians had been unanimous in holding the fundamental truth in general, that the Old Testament contained a true divine revelation, and special predictions of the Messiah, which were given by the inspiration of God; the only controversy was respecting particular passages. A totally different view, affecting the very foundation of faith, first appeared in the latter half of the last century. The opinion, which was then constantly becoming more and more prevalent, that nature constitutes a whole independent and complete in itself, upon which God neither will nor can operate, either internally by inspiration, or externally by miracle, necessarily caused the prophecies of the Messiah to be regarded in an entirely different light. For information on this subject, we refer especially to the following works. 1 Exegetical works in which the Messianic predictions are separately examined. Entwurf einer Christologie des A. T. von Chr. Fr. Ammon. Ein Beitrag zur endlichen Beilegung der Streitigkeiten uber Messianische Weissagungen und zur biblischen Theologie des Verf. Erl. 1794. This author, whose earlier opinions should be distinguished from his later belief, thus gives the design of his work in the preface. "It aims to establish the assertion, that providence it is true prepared the way for the appearance of Christ by the whole system of the Jewish worship, and by the patriotic wishes of the prophets; but that it is impossible to prove from the oracles of the Hebrew seers, that they were favored with a certain and definite view of the divine author of our religion, of his person, and his history." It is therefore only by a misnomer that the work can be called *a christology*. But the author has not taken too much pains in order to prove his assertions. But caprice is carried to a still greater height, in the complete explanation of all the prophecies of the Messiah in the Old Testament, Altenb. 1801 (von dem Pred. Scherer), a production of which it is hard to say whether the ignorance exceeds the arrogance, or the arrogance the ignorance. The opposite of a christology of the Psalms has been put forth by J. H. Schulze.(Kritik aller Messianichen Psalme. Stendal 1802.) An attempt which was acknowledged to be unsatisfactory even by the rationalists themselves. 2. Writings and treatises which attempt to explain by natural causes the origin and development of the hope of a Messiah among the Hebrews. The following are the most important. Meine Gedanken uber die Entstehung und Ausbildung der Idee von einem Messias; von Heinr. Stephani Numb. 1787. Stahl, von den M. W. in Eichh. Bibl. f. Bibl. Litt. Bd. 6. Prof. Ziegler, vernuft- und schriftmafsige (!) Erorterung, dafs der Beweis fur die Wahrheit und Gottlichkeit der christlichen Religion mehr aus der inneren Vortrefflichkeit der Lehre, als aus Wundern und Weissagungen zu fuhren ist, sammt einer Entwickelung des wahrscheinlichen Ursprungs der Ideen vom Messias, in Henke's Magazin I. 1. p. 20 ff. Konynenburg, Untersuchung uber die Natur der Alttest. Weiss. vom Messias, aus dem Holl. Lingen 1795. Sittig, die Messiasidee in ihrer Entwickelung. Bamberg 1816. 3. Works on biblical theology in general, or the theology of the Old Testament in particular, in which the doctrine concerning the Messiah is at the same time discussed. Here belong: die (fluchtige) Theologie des A. T. von Bauer. Leipz. 1796. p. 363 ff. Das Handbuch der Bibl. Theologie von Hufnagel. Erl. 1785—91. II, 1. Bertholdt, de ortu theologiae vett. Hebr. Erl. 1803. p. 100 ff. De Wette. Bibl. Theol. p. 111 ff, womit zu vergl. dess. Beitrag zur Charakteristik des Hebraismus in den Studien von Daub und Creuzer 1807. II. p. 241.

307 u d. Einl. z d. Psalm. Baumgarten-Crus Bibl. Theologie p. 366 ff Other treatises, in no respects important, we here omit; since even those we have cited repeat some few thoughts, with slight modifications, to the disgust of the most patient.

The main features of the view of the rationalists, as they are repeated in most of the above mentioned works, and of which the greatest part are found in them all, are the following. The hope of a Messiah is nothing more than a patriotic phantasy of the prophets. It originated in a natural way, without any immediate divine influence, and indeed in the following manner The nation in the time of David and Solomon had attained to the highest summit of power and prosperity, soon after it fell from this elevated condition; by the separation of the ten tribes, the power of the people was first broken, the invasion of the Assyrians and afterwards of the Babylonians brought them to the brink of ruin Idolatry and corruption of manners were continually gaining the ascendancy What now could be more natural, than that the prophets, rising above the present, should expect from the future, the return of the times of David and Solomon, and connect this with an illustrious future descendant of David, under whose righteous reign the people should be as happy, as devoted to God, and should gain the victory over their unjust opposers?

If we ask for the grounds of this view it is manifest, that this is a matter with which most of its defenders have given themselves no concern, and that what they advance can have no weight with any but those who agree with them in their doctrinal views, which in their consequences must necessarily lead to Atheism Ziegler l. c. p. 83 remarks as follows. 1 "The human origin of the idea of a Messiah is evident from this, it was changeable like the fate of the people It is, however, impossible that the changeable image of different times should ever be fully realized at any certain time in one unchangeable subject." But the divine origin of the idea of a Messiah is very clear from precisely the fact, that those views of him were always presented, which were at the time best suited to promote the design of the theocracy, and adapted to the necessities of those to whom the prophecy was imparted, and that nevertheless all these scattered traits were combined in the image of the manifested Messiah This objection would be valid only in case real contradictions existed. But who will undertake to point out such? All that was apparently contradictory was perfectly explained by the appearing of the Messiah But if on the other hand, the idea of a Messiah had been of human origin, how could we expect it to be encumbered with these apparent contradictions, which it was so difficult for the Jews to reconcile. 2 "There are many things, which have not been fulfilled in Christ The Messiah for example is represented as a king, which character the true Messiah did not sustain. He was to spring from Bethlehem, and yet Jesus was of Galilee; he was to remain on earth forever, and Christ left it after a short course of action " The first objection can have no weight with those, who know Christ not merely in his humiliation, but also in his glory. Christ, to whom, according to his own words, Matt. 28. 18, all power in heaven and on earth is given, is a king in the truest and most proper sense, and of his kingdom all earthly dominion is only a faint resemblance. That God himself is often called a king shows that an outward worldly dominion is not necessarily connected with the idea of a kingdom. The second is entirely unfounded, since Christ, if we do not utterly deny the credibility of the evangelists, although his parents resided in Galilee, sprung from Bethlehem, the seat of the house of David, where he was born by the special guidance of providence, that the prophecy might be accurately fulfilled. The third is of just as little moment, for that Christ should always remain on earth is no where asserted in the Old Testament, but only that he should reign forever, and this we expect with perfect certainty founded on the word of the Lord, Matt 16. 18. That the Jews in this way misunderstood the prophecies of the Old Testament, John 12: 34, can surely prove nothing Had they not been prevented by their carnal minds from rightly understanding the predictions of the suffering and dying Messiah, the words of Christ, v 32, would not have been unintelligible to them. It amounts to just as little, when Ammon and lately B Crusius wish to prove that we must entertain but a low idea of the divine illumination of the prophets from the circumstance that Christ, Luke 7. 28 and Matt. 11 11, says that John, although the greatest prophet under the old dispensation, is yet less than the least member of the new kingdom of God. Herein consists the great advantage of the members of the new covenant over the prophets, that while the latter were the mere instruments of the Holy Ghost, the former were in their whole nature made the subjects of his permanent influences; that the one only faithfully delivered what was communicated to them from God, often without any thing more than an obscure conjecture as to its meaning; that the other on the contrary obtained from the accomplishment a clear insight into the whole divine plan of salvation, together with far more powerful motives for growth in holiness. If the Lord here intended to deny the inspiration of the prophets, he has most expressly contradicted his other declarations, in which he represents them as the organs of the Divine Spirit. The assertion of Bauer l c. p 404 is founded on a misunderstanding of the prophecies. "The hope of the prophets has not been fulfilled Their state never reached the high summit of prosperity after the exile, and this religious and political kingdom with all its rites instead of enduring forever came to an end more than 1700 years ago." The promises of prosperity and of endless duration were given to the theocracy only in as far as it was the true kingdom of God. In this respect, the kingdom of God to be founded by Christ was only a continuation of the former, and he himself has confirmed the previous promises by the declaration that the gates of hell shall never prevail against his church. On the other hand, the prophets are so far from promising to the outward theocracy as such, prosperity and eternal duration in consequence of the coming of the Messiah, that they rather connect with it the rejection of the covenant people and the destruction of the city See the passages soon to be quoted These are the objections of opponents so far as we have met with them. As what they advance is of no validity, so have they no right to expel the ancient view of this subject from the place to which it is so justly entitled and to assert that the idea of a Messiah actually did originate in a way in which at all events it is only possible that it might have originated. But yet we will here bring forward the principal arguments not only against the reality, but the possibility of such an origin of this idea, as they allege. Knapp Dogm II, 21 seq. Pareau l c p 493 seq and especially Kleuker de nexu prophetico p. 72 seq. have already produced several well grounded replies.

1. The whole view of the prophetic order which lies at the foundation of this hypothesis is false, and can be easily refuted from the Old Testament itself and the authority of Christ and his Apostles. Herder (Briefe p 234) well remarks, that no man may venture, as this hypothesis does, to regard the prophets as dreamers and fanatics without at the same time giving up as a dream, or condemning as a deception, the history of the Jewish people, God's economy towards them, in short his whole existence in connexion with the Old Testament For the prophetic order necessarily belongs to the whole of the theocracy, in which the founder of it himself has appointed its

place This hypothesis, therefore, is contradicted by all the arguments which establish in general the divine origin, and the divine superintendence of the theocracy. Further it is refuted as often as the fulfilment of a single particular prophecy is pointed out, even if it does not relate to the Messiah. For if God, in other instances has acknowledged them as his ambassadors, we dare not regard the idea of the Messiah, as the offspring of their invention. Whoever, therefore, adopts this hypothesis, must at the same time approve all those violent measures, by which recent critics have sought to conceal, or do away the remarkable coincidence between the prophecies and their fulfilment. One single prediction, as Jer 50. 51, Zech. 9: 1—8, is sufficient to show the erroneousness of this view of the prophetic order and therefore the unsoundness of this hypothesis. It is generally opposed by all those proofs whereby the prophets established their divine mission. Further they were themselves most firmly persuaded that they did not speak according to the suggestion of their own minds, but by the influence of the Holy Spirit, (see for example Jer. 20· 7, etc.), and with this conviction they cheerfully bore the sufferings which their prophecies brought upon them. That they deceived themselves into this conviction has indeed been asserted, but never proved. Moreover no analogy can be adduced to show that the prophets gave themselves up to such sanguine hopes as are here supposed. On the contrary, when these hopes were universally indulged and the false prophets promoted them by fictitious predictions, they announced the threatening calamity, regardless of the danger they incurred See, for example, Jer. xxviii On the other hand, we no where find a trace, that the false prophets, who sought the favor of the people by disclosing agreeable prospects, ever prophesied of the Messiah. Lastly, as often as Christ and the Apostles mention the prophets, they speak of them as extraordinary messengers of God, under the influence of the Holy Spirit Thus to cite but one of numerous passages, it is said 2 Pet. 1: 21: ὑπὸ πνεύματος ἁγίου φερόμενοι ἐλάλησαν ἅγιοι θεοῦ ἄνθρωποι

2. In like manner this hypothesis stands in direct opposition to what Christ and the Apostles assert, respecting those prophecies especially which refer to the Messiah. According to it the agreement of the prophecies with the history of Christ was only accidental; on the contrary, Christ often declares it to be one object of the events of his life to fulfil the prophecies of the Old Testament, and thus establish their divine origin; see the passages in the chapter concerning

the suffering Messiah. He declares himself to be the person foretold by the prophets, he expresses the conviction that nothing could befal him, which had not been already predicted by them He upbraids the disciples, Luke 24. 25, for the weakness of their faith in the prophecies, when according to the hypothesis of recent critics this faith was only foolishness. He explained, Luke 24· 44, etc , to the Apostles, the prophecies concerning himself in the Pentateuch, the prophets, and the Psalms In numerous passages he and his Apostles show the coincidence between the prophecies and their fulfilment, which according to this hypothesis did not exist. It is therefore manifest that the reception of this hypothesis is inseparably connected with the total rejection of the authority of Christ and his Apostles; for it leaves only the alternative of charging them with dishonesty, or ignorance.

3 The opponents themselves only profess to explain how this hope might naturally have originated subsequently to the division of the kingdom If then it can be proved that the idea of a Messiah existed at an earlier period, their hypothesis is shown to be false. But this can easily be done; so that B. Crusius himself characterizes the assertion, that the idea of a Messiah was of so late an origin, as untenable and obsolete. All that is true in this assertion is only, as we have already remarked and proved, that the Messianic hope assumed a new form, with the introduction of royalty, because a new groundwork was now given for the contemplation of the prophets. But this hope existed substantially the same, long before. We meet with very distinct expectations of a Messiah even in the Pentateuch, not merely representations of the Messianic times, but also predictions of a particular person as the Messiah, Gen. XLIX and Deut. XVIII. The opponents have here resorted to various expedients. Some seek to set aside the passages which refer to the Messiah by other explanations, the erroneousness of which we have already shown Others, as Ziegler l. c. p. 61, etc. assert that the views in the Pentateuch cannot be called Messianic expectations, because they are not connected with the person of a king But it is impossible to perceive why the idea of a king should be regarded as the only and characteristic mark of a prophecy of the Messiah. We must then also deny that passages like Isaiah 42 49 and 53. where the Messiah is represented as a prophet and high priest (although every other explanation has been refuted) are properly called Messianic predictions. It is abundantly evident that in the passage, Gen. XLIX, which is refer-

red to the Messiah even by Rosenmuller, Winer, and B. Crusius, he appears as the person to whom all nations should become subject. Lastly, others, as De Wette, appeal to the later composition of the Pentateuch; but independently of the fact that this assertion rests upon insufficient grounds, the Messianic predictions of the Pentateuch contain even internal proof of their antiquity. Their becoming gradually more and more definite as we have shown, can be explained only by the supposition that we have here true history and not fiction. Further, this hypothesis is refuted by the existence of the Messianic prediction, 2 Sam. vii, and of the Messianic Psalms belonging to the time of David. That this circumstance can neither be reconciled with, nor explained by it, is expressly remarked by its defenders. Thus for example Ziegler l c. p 73, says: "But now in the time of David and Solomon there *was no occasion* to desire, or anticipate a greater benefactor of the nation, since they were the most successful kings the nation had ever had. The Psalms therefore in our collection which belong to this period contain in all probability no anticipation of any thing further, but the sacred poets found the materials for their songs before them, or took them from former times "* Ziegler therefore thus concludes: " since this hypothesis is true, there can be no Messianic predictions in the Psalms belonging to the time of David and Solomon." We on the contrary invert the argument; since, as we have sufficiently proved, these Psalms contain the plainest predictions of the Messiah, therefore must this hypothesis be false

4. The opponents themselves do not pretend to explain by their hypotheses any thing more than the origin of the idea of a mere human Messiah in glory, who would exalt the theocracy to great power and dominion. The nature of that hope of a Messiah which they attempt to explain, may be learned from the following passage of De Wette's Beitr p. 307: " He shall put an end in deed and in truth to those evils, which no philosophy, nor faith could abolish; he shall make those prosperous, who ought to be so; he shall humble the present grievous arrogance of the wicked, the ungodly and the barbarians; and cause the poor, suffering and oppressed Israelites to

---

* In like manner Bauer l c p 374 ' If this development of the gradual origin of the idea of a Messiah is correct, it could not have arisen before the period of the kings, and indeed the later kings." P 375 " What could have led to the idea of a deliverer of the nation under David and Solomon, as the kingdom was powerful and the nation extending itself in every direction ?"

triumph over them. They who have so long been a proverb and derision of the nations shall become their terror and scourge; they who have so long been the slaves of the nations shall become their rulers and kings" But this is the Messianic expectation of the later and carnal Jews, not that of the prophets. And the very fact that these critics are compelled to falsify the idea of the Messiah, is a confession that they cannot derive the true notion of him from mere natural causes. They must by a forced interpretation set aside all those passages which contain the doctrine of his Deity and sufferings, his death and vicarious satisfaction, and, in general, those which treat of him in his humiliation. For they do not themselves venture to assert that these doctrines can be accounted for on natural principles. And so long as the arguments remain unanswered by which we have shown the existence of these doctrines (see the chapters on the Deity of the Messiah and on a suffering and atoning Messiah), we are justified on this ground alone in rejecting this hypothesis —Further, if this hope is the offspring of the patriotism of the prophets, how can those passages be explained, which connect with the appearing of the Messiah a great and purifying divine chastisement of the covenant people themselves, the unbelief of the larger portion of them, their rejection and the destruction of the city of Jerusalem Is. XLIX. Dan. IX. Zech. XI, XIII. Mal III. See also Ziegler l. c. p 70, 71, who confesses all this, and the chapter on the Messianic predictions by the prophets. How can we account for the fact that the prophets are unanimous in not confining the prosperity of the times of the Messiah to the ancient covenant people, but extending it to all the heathen nations; that they delight to dwell so particularly on this very part of the Messianic prospect, and return to it so continually? This generally acknowledged fact (Ziegler l. c p. 69 seq De Wette, Bibl. Theol. p. 112) cannot be even plausibly explained according to this hypothesis What induced the Hebrews to think that salvation should be extended from them over the whole world? Whence is it, that even in the book of Genesis the declaration is continually repeated, that in the seed of Abraham all the nations of the earth should be blessed?* What made Isaiah, chap LXVI, suppose that the heathen

---

* Ziegler asserts, erroneously and without any proof, that the Messianic hopes were first ennobled by Isaiah In their very origin, they are equally comprehensive and free from national limitation, as in the latest prophets Thus we find them in Genesis throughout, and also in the psalms belonging to the age of David and Solomon. When Ziegler l. c p 67 says "The period

should not only in general belong to the people of God, but should also hold the sacerdotal office among them? While according to this hypothesis we should expect nothing else, than that the time of the Messiah would bring prosperity only to the Jews, and destruction and servitude on the contrary to all other nations. And whence is it, that history so perfectly corresponds with this hope of the prophets?

5. According to the hypothesis of our opponents, adversity must have been the source of the Messianic hopes. But it is strange that adversity should have had this effect only among the Jews, and that precisely among them also these hopes which had no foundation except in their own minds, should have been so strikingly fulfilled. There is no people mentioned in history, who have not fallen from the summit of greatness and renown and been subject to adversity, often far greater than that of the Israelites at the time of the supposed origin of these expectations. Whence does it arise then, that the eyes of other nations in time of adversity were painfully turned to past times of prosperity, but those of the Israelites, on the contrary, looked joyfully to the future? How did it happen, that with them this joy, with other nations distress and despair, steadily increased with the increase of their adversity? It cannot here be said in reply that, as we ourselves have before shown, expectations of a better period of the world existed among other nations also. For these expectations stand alone and disconnected and could have had no influence on the conduct of the people. But among the Hebrews on the contrary, the hope of the Messiah powerfully influenced the whole conduct of life, it remained always the same, and was believed and handed down at all times with equal strength of conviction. The opponents answer here, that the reason why adversity produced this special effect among the Jews, is to be found in the ancient promises. Abraham had already embraced the hope of better times, and transmitted it to his descendants. Moses indeed announced to the people the punishments which should follow the transgression of the divine laws, but he also declared, that God mindful of his ancient prom-

---

of Messiah's kingdom must be called an iron age for the remaining nations upon God's earth; it becomes continually more so, the more the Hebrews feel the people [*Leute*, probably for *Härte* severity] of other nations, the barbarians of the East, and learn to bow their necks," he describes the nature of the Messianic predictions exactly as it must be, if this hypothesis were true; so likewise De Wette l. c. The difficulty however is, that the description is entirely at variance with the fact.

ises to the fathers, and of his former benefits would not utterly reject this people, but be at all times ready to receive them again with kindness as his own. Nathan promised to David in the name of Jehovah that the government should always remain in his family. And thus the hope of better times in general and also its connexion with a descendant of David may be easily explained. (See Bauer l c. p. 366 seq. Bertholdt l. c. p. 111). But by this means the difficulty is not done away, it is only removed further off. The new question now arises, how came the patriarchs, Moses, Nathan, by these hopes and promises, which conflict so entirely with the ordinary course of history? To the first question, Bertholdt replies, that the origin of the expectations of the patriarchs may be traced partly to the whole mode of thinking among the ancient orientals, and partly to the solitary pastoral life of Abraham and his descendants: "originis causa ulterius quaerenda est cum in veteris Orientis incolarum ingenio omnino, tum inprimis in vita, quam Abrahamidae per longum tempus a reliquis gentibus sejuncti agere solebant solitaria." But this is really a strange deduction. That Abraham, a shepherd-prince who possessed no fixed property, that his immediate descendants, whose power was scarcely equal to that of a petty Canaanitish king, that the people living under hard bondage in Egypt, should have imagined that salvation should go forth from them to all the people of the earth, can this be explained in general by the mode of thinking of the ancient orientals, or especially by their secluded manner of life? How then did it happen, that none of the old Arabian emirs, who must have felt the influence of the same causes, ever embraced the same hopes? And wherefore are all these groundless hypotheses invented? Entirely, on account of the doctrinal prejudice, that the agency of a supernatural cause in the world of sense is impossible. For when this prejudice is laid aside, there is no necessity for an explanation of facts which history renders certain; since every thing explains itself; all appears in the most beautiful order, the earlier promises prepared the way for the later, the later refer back to the earlier, until at last he who gave them all caused their fulfilment

6. This hypothesis fails to explain how the most particular traits, for example, the birth of the Messiah of a virgin and in Bethlehem, at a time, when the royal family of David had fallen into the deepest obscurity, his agency, especially in Galilee, the appearance of his forerunner, etc., all which are verified by history, were inserted in

the prophecies of the Messiah * If any one chooses, as some have done, to suppose that God so ordered these historical circumstances that the prophecies which were the invention of men, should yet in a measure be fulfilled, he would gain nothing on the one side, since he would then assert that God exerts an influence on the world; and on the other he would substitute a forced and unnatural explanation of the fact for the simple and natural one, confirmed by the authority of Christ and his Apostles For if we are unable in general to deny the agency of God in the coincidence between the prophecy and history, which is the more natural supposition, that the Spirit of God wrought in the minds of the prophets, or that God afterwards so ordered the course of events, as to give his sanction to human error? Do we not thus make the Holy God the author of a delusion and the abettor of the arrogance of man?

7. According to the view of our opponents, the idea of the Messiah is of purely Jewish origin. See Bertholdt l. c. p 109 De Wette l. c. p. 138 How then will they explain the existence of this doctrine among the Samaritans also? John 4 25, the Samaritan woman says, that she knows the Messiah would come, and she expects from him the explanation of difficult points of religion; according to v. 42, the Samaritans expected in the Messiah $\sigma\omega\tau\grave{\eta}\rho\ \tau o\tilde{v}\ \varkappa \acute{o}\sigma\mu o v$, one who should redeem and bless the whole world. That the Samaritans cherish Messianic hopes, appears from their correspondence in the 17th century with some of the learned, and from the Samaritan fragments recently made known by Gesenius. See on Gen. XLIX and Deut. XVIII. It cannot be said in reply that the Samaritans at a later period derived this doctrine from the Jews We are forbidden to think this by the deep rooted hatred existing between them. Besides, the hope of the Messiah among the Samaritans rests solely on

---

* For this reason the incorrectness of this hypothesis may be made clear to every unprejudiced person, since we need to look no further than to the 53d chap of Isaiah This is pointed out in the following passages from the philosopher Bonnet, (Paling. philos. Werke Bd 16, p. 372, 73) "Je tombe sur un ecrit, qui me jette dans le plus profond etonnement Je crois y lire une histoire anticipée et circonstanciée de l'envoyé, j'y retrouve tous ses traits, son charactère, et les principales particularités de sa vie Il me semble en un mot, que je lis la deposition même des temoins. Je ne puis detacher mes yeux de ce surprenant tableau quels traits! quel colorit! quelle expression! quel accord avec les faits! que dis je? ce n'est point une peinture emblematique de l'avenir fort eloigne, c'est une representation fidèle du présent. et ce, qui n'est point encore, est peint comme ce, qui est."

the passages relating to him in the Pentateuch, and entirely wants that definiteness which was afterwards given to it by the prophets. The Samaritans, therefore, must have derived this hope from the kingdom of Israel. It cannot therefore have been of merely Jewish origin

8. The view of our opponents does not explain, how among other people also, disconnected expectations of a better age of the world, and Messianic representations, should be found. These, as we have already seen, point to an original revelation which was in various ways changed and distorted among the heathen, but was preserved in its purity, and constantly rendered more and more distinct among the Hebrews.

So much for the refutation of the view of recent critics. There are not wanting treatises on the prophecies of the Messiah, whose authors have been either entirely free from its influence, or only partially affected by it. Though the merit of several of them is undeniable, yet all are liable to the objection of not being founded on a clear and just conception of the nature of prophecy, on which indeed the discussion of the Messianic predictions so greatly depends. These treatises are the following

Messianische Briefe zur Ehre der christlichen Religion und des A. T. (von Prof. Kocher) Jena 1785, (written with good intention, but of little importance)

Rationem prophetias Messianas interpretandi certissimam nostraeque aetati accomodatissimam exponit C. G Anton (Prof. zu Wittenb.) Dessau 1786 4to. A very fundamental and learned treatise, embracing most of the Messianic passages, and is still worth reading

Messianische Weissagungen des A T. ubersetzt und erlautert zum Gebrauche fur angehende Theologen, (von Prof Kuinol) Leipz. 1792. Undecided and incomplete, a mere explanation of the individual passages, without a comprehensive and thorough introduction.

Appendix Hermeneuticae s exercitationes exegeticae, auct Jo Jahn. fascic I II Vaticinia de Messia Viennae 1813 Beyond a doubt the best modern work on the Messianic prophecies, distinguished by sound and thorough philology. Still, however, the so necessary general introduction is wanting, many important passages are omitted; in respect to others the esteemed author has been led by the difficulties, which a correct theory of the prophecies would have removed, to arbitrary references and to a rejection of the authority of the New Testament

Christus im A. T. Untersuchungen uber die Vorbilder und Mess. St. von J A. Kanne. Th 1 2. Nurnb. 1818. The excellent author in this work has followed an extremely arbitrary, allegorical mode of interpretation, and has therefore—we say it with pain—rather injured, than aided the cause for which he labored with so true a zeal. See in reply: Steudel, uber die Behandlung der Sprache der heil. Schrift als einer Sprache des Geistes Tub 1822.

Ueber den Ursprung und die allmahlige Entwickelung des Messianismus. Eine Abhandlung von Joh. Jac. Broix, Subdiacon der Diocese Aachen. Landsh 1822. Weak in philology; has otherwise many good remarks; its tendency is laudable.

THE MESSIANIC PROPHECIES OF ISAIAH.

INTRODUCTORY REMARKS.

The superscription, chap. 1: 1, places the prophet Isaiah under the reign of the kings, Uzziah, Jotham, Ahaz, and Hezekiah. The correctness of this testimony can also be shown with certainty from other sources. That the prophet first came forward under king Uzziah, is evident from the superscription of chap. vi. This chapter contains a representation of the vision, by which Isaiah, in the year that Uzziah died, received his call to the prophetic office. It is true that no one of the oracles found in our collection is assigned by a definite superscription to the reign of Jotham, but weighty reasons compel us to believe that the prophecies of chap. ii—v were composed under him. But several of the existing prophecies, from chap. vii onward, belong to the reign of Ahaz, and that he was actively employed under Hezekiah, we learn from chap. xxxvi—xxxix. We have certain accounts of his agency, only until the 15th year of this king, at the commencement of which the embassy of the king of Babylon came to Jerusalem. See chap. xxxix. He must therefore have exercised his office at least 47 years, from 759—713 before Christ, viz. one year under Uzziah, 16 under Jotham, 16 under Ahaz, and 14 under Hezekiah. It is however more than probable that Isaiah lived much longer. From the statement, 2 Chron. 32. 32, that he wrote the life of king Hezekiah, it appears that he survived him.* The account of the Talmud and the church fathers, that he died a violent death under Manasseh, the successor of Hezekiah, conducts us still further. This saying, which is alluded to even in the epistle to the Hebrews, (chap. 11: 37, where a comparison

---

* That Isaiah still lived for a time under Manasseh, is asserted, not only by Joh. H. Michaelis in the bibl. Hal. and the writers cited by him, but also in recent times by Jahn, Gesenius, Moller, Bertholdt (Einl. S. 1349), Staudlin (Neue Beiträge p. 12, 17 seq.)

with the tradition shows that ἐπρίσθησαν must be referred to Isaiah) has indeed been greatly corrupted by false additions; but it has been too widely spread, is related by writers too diverse from each other, and is moreover in itself too probable, to have no foundation in fact. See Staudlin in der Gotting. Biblioth. der theol. Litt Bd I. p 323 seq.* Even in the Talmud, the original tradition, which asserts only that Isaiah was slain by Manasseh, may be distinguished from the later embellishments. Comp Gesenius Einl p. 12. The silence of the historical books respecting so important an occurrence has indeed been urged, but considering the briefness of the narrative it is sufficient, that 2 Kings 21 16, it is related that "Manasseh shed much innocent blood in Jerusalem." The innocent persons, who were murdered, were doubtless those who abhorred the idolatry introduced by Manasseh, and therefore, especially the prophets; Isaiah may have been one of them, without being mentioned by name, particularly as on account of his advanced age, he had probably at that time in a great measure relinquished his public duties. See the introduction to chap XL—LXVI. The supposition, that Isaiah still lived for a time in the reign of Manasseh, is favored also by the character of the second part of his prophecies This contains many things, particularly the lamentations over gross idolatry, sacrifice of children and evil rulers, which do not suit either the times of the captivity or the reign of the pious Hezekiah, but correspond well with that of Manasseh This is so evident, that not only most of the advocates of the genuineness of the second part, suppose it to have been composed under Manasseh, e g Grotius on chap 43: 27 Jahn Einleit II. 1. §'104. Moller, de authentia orac Jesaiae c 40—66, p 118 seq. but even its opponents, as Eichhorn (Hebr Propheten Bd. 1. p. 415,) cannot forbear perceiving in many places (chap. LVI, LVII, LXVI) the age of Manasseh.†

---

* Justinus Martyr dialog c Tryphone p 349, ed Col ὃν πρίονι ξυλίνῳ ἐπρίσατε Tertullianus de patientia c. 14 His patientia viribus secatur Esaias Ej Scorp c. 8 Lactantius l IV c 11 Esaias, quem ipsi Judaei serra consectum crudelissime necaverunt Ambros in Luc c 20 Esaias, cujus facilius compagem corporis serra divisit, quam fidem inclinavit Augustin de civ dei l 18 c 24 Hieron zu Jes. c 1, 10 c 20, 27 These and other passages from the fathers, oriental writers, and the Talmud are to be found in Michaelis Praefatio in Jes c 5 in the bibl Hal Joh G Carpzov Critica sacra P II p 97.

† The proof is less certain which Gesenius adduces from chap XIX, that the prophet's life was prolonged until the first years of Manasseh. For his argu-

Nor does this supposition ascribe to Isaiah an extraordinary old age. Allowing him to have been twenty years old, when he entered upon his office, (that an earlier call to the prophetic office was not uncommon appears from Jer. 1· 6), at the death of Hezekiah, he would have been about 82, and there is no reason to suppose he might not have lived 7 or 8 years longer under Manasseh. Indeed the priest Jehoiada according to 2 Chron. 24. 15, reached the age of 130.* As Isaiah led the abstemious ascetic life of the prophets, we may suppose that the powers of his body and mind even in old age remained unimpaired.

Isaiah was therefore contemporary with Hosea and Micah. Of the circumstances of his life, little is known to us. He appears to have had his permanent residence at Jerusalem. Of his agency under Jotham, we know only what may be learned from the prophecy, chap. II—V. Probably, he lived at that period in greater seclusion on account of his youth. Under the ungodly Ahaz, he came forth in the full power of an ambassador of God, but his counsel and his warning were derided. Hezekiah, a worthy head of the theocracy, first acknowledged him and followed his counsels; under the ungodly Manasseh he probably retired and lived in the happier future, but still without entirely resigning, in the comfortless present, his office as a reprover, (see chap. LVI—LVIII) until at last, he sealed with his death, the truth, for which he had lived.

Great respect was paid to him after his death. The historical books, in general so very sparing in their accounts of those prophets, whose writings we possess, are comparatively full in their notices of him; Jeremiah imitated him, (comp. Jahn Einleit. p. 463 seq.) and marks of the diligent reading of his productions are found in other prophets. But at a later period, the fulfilment of his prophecies of far distant events, as the conquests of Cyrus, the return from captivity, the overthrow of the Babylonish monarchy, procured for the prophet a still higher reputation than those already fulfilled in his lifetime, respecting the overthrow of the Syrians and the Israelites, the invasion by the Assyrians, the deliverance accomplished by the help of God, and the extension of life for fifteen years vouchsafed to

---

ment rests on the erroneous assumption, that the prophets represented only events which lay near at hand, and could be foreknown by human caculation.

* The tradition of the great age of Isaiah has been preserved among the oriental Christians, who attribute to him an age of 120 years. See Herbelot biblioth. Orient. p. 501 s. v. Ischaia. Abul Pharagius hist. dynast. p. 67

Hezekiah, etc. Josephus relates (Antiq. Jud. XI, 1 § 12) that Cyrus was moved by reading the oracle of Isaiah, relating to himself, to the acknowledgement of the God of Israel, the deliverance of the Jews, and the rebuilding of the temple.* Jesus, the son of Sirach, says of him, chap. 48 22—25. Ἠσαΐας ὁ προφήτης ὁ μέγας καὶ πιστὸς ἐν ὁράσει αὐτοῦ—τι εὐματι μεγάλῳ εἶδε τὰ ἔσχατα, καὶ παρεκάλεσε τοὺς πενθοῦντας ἐν Σιών. Ἕως τοῦ αἰῶνος ὑπέδειξε τὰ ἐσόμενα καὶ τὰ ἀπόκρυφα πρὶν ἢ παραγενέσθαι αὐτά. Philo and Josephus speak of him with equal reverence. He must, however, have attained the highest degree of authority, when the most splendid portion of his predictions was fulfilled by the appearing of Christ, and the establishment of his kingdom. The whole New Testament is interwoven, sometimes with direct quotations, and sometimes with thoughts and expressions, undesignedly borrowed from his prophecies; rarely is the cardinal doctrine of Christianity, the doctrine of the vicarious satisfaction, delivered by the Apostles, without a manifest allusion to Isaiah. The writings of the fathers are full of his praise. Comp. the collections of J. H. Michaelis, praef. in Jes. p. 9 seq. Gesenius Einleit. p. 41. Jerome says: "Sic exponam Esaiam, ut illum non solum prophetam, sed Evangelistam et Apostolum doceam," and in another passage: "Non prophetiam mihi videtur texere Esaias, sed evangelium," and Augustin also, remarks, de civ. dei l. 18. c. 29, that in the opinion of several, his numerous predictions of Christ and the church, entitled him to the name of an evangelist, rather than a prophet. When Augustin after his conversion inquired of Ambrose, which of the sacred books he should chiefly read, Ambrose recommended Isaiah "quod prae ceteris evangelii vocationisque gentium sit praenuntiator apertior." Cf. Aug. conf. IX, 5.

---

* This account has been, it is true, rejected by several recent critics, as destitute of historical support; but Jahn, Archäologie II p. 231 seq. justly observes, that it furnishes the only explanation of the conduct of Cyrus towards the Jews. He especially draws the attention to the circumstance, that this relation is only the commentary on Ezra 1. 2, where Cyrus in his edict in favor of the Jews, says: "Jehovah the God of heaven has given me all the kingdoms of the earth, and commanded me to build him a house at Jerusalem in Judea." Now these words plainly presuppose, that Cyrus was acquainted with the prophecies, chap. 44. 28, and chap. XLV. Gesenius passes them over in entire silence. The account of Josephus compared with the passage of Ezra is so far of weight, as it gives an important testimony in favor of the genuineness of chap. XL—LXVI. For Cyrus would hardly have acted without examining into the alleged age of the prophecy laid before him, which, according to the opinion of the opponents, was not composed until a year before

Isaiah, like all the prophets, had a twofold calling; to exert an influence on the present, and to reveal the future. With respect to the former, called to be a minister of the old covenant, he pointed to its foundation, the law, and required above every thing else, that it should be maintained, chap. 8 16, 20 30 9, 10 But called also to be a minister of the Spirit, not of the letter, under the old covenant, his zeal was awakened against those who sought the substance in the observance of the outward form, who in their regard for that which was suited to the old covenant, and to the pupilage of mankind, forgot what was common both to the old and the new Comp e. g. chap. 1: 11, etc 29 13. 58 1, etc The fundamental idea, which pervades his prophecies, is, that the glory belongs to God alone, shame and humiliation to man, that all confidence must be placed in the Creator and not in the creature, that all help in temporal and spiritual concerns, comes from him alone, that every inclination, every effort, which is directed towards perishing objects, instead of him, is sinful. Hence the frequent annunciation of the ruin of all that is proud and lofty—hence his hostility against idolatry, as well as vice in general, which constantly appears to him as ingratitude to God, as treason against him—hence his resistance of those, who, when the State was oppressed by foreign enemies, expected aid from alliances with powerful and neighboring nations All help comes from God, he will not abandon his *faithful* covenant people, the *unfaithful* will only be plunged in still deeper distress by all their alliances and preparations for war. He constantly seeks to impress upon the minds of the people the fundamental law of the theocracy proclaimed by its author, the reciprocal relation between fidelity and heartfelt confidence towards God and prosperity, and between unfaithfulness and adversity; and shows that the people should blame themselves and not God, in all their calamities, and that he, being full of mercy, is ready to pardon their sins, and deliver them from their distress, if they will only return to Him

In exerting an influence on the present times, the prophet was sustained and aided by the second part of his office, that of disclosing the future, which nevertheless was designed to accomplish other and far more important objects The predicted destruction of the kingdom of Israel, the desolation of Judah by Sennacherib, the Babylonish captivity, and the total desolation of the land, must have served, by exemplifying the law of a visible retribution, to make his censures and admonitions the more impressive, while the prediction of the deliverance from the Assyrians, and the return from the exile, must have consoled the pious and encouraged them to be faithful. The predictions against foreign nations showed the Israelites the omnipotence of their God, and the feebleness of all that was human, and powerfully dissuaded them from trusting in the help of man, at the same time they clearly exhibited to them the retributive justice of God, which decided the fate, even of those nations to whom he had not revealed himself, and much more, that of his covenant people. But with Isaiah, the substance of the prophecies in a stricter sense, is the annunciation of the Messiah. A sprout of David, according to his human nature, but at the same time God from eternity, born of a virgin, at a period when the royal family of David had fallen into the deepest obscurity, will live, suffer, and die, to abolish the sins of mankind—after his glorification, his kingdom will be founded on earth, and extended over all the heathen nations, until the earth shall be full of the knowledge and the worship of the Lord, through the Spirit, which will be poured out upon all flesh. And as Isaiah, when acting upon his contemporaries, insisted on faith in general, despair of our own strength, and confidence in the power of God; so in his Messianic predictions, he appears as a herald of faith in its stricter sense.

The style of Isaiah is, in general, characterized by simplicity and sublimity; in the use of imagery, he holds an intermediate place between the poverty of Jeremiah, and the exuberance of Ezekiel. In other respects, the style is suited to the subject, and changes with it. In his denunciations and threatenings, he is earnest and vehement, as Luther strikingly remarks (Tom III Jen Lat. f 286 b.) · "Si quis penitus posset introspicere affectus prophetae, videret in singulis verbis caminos ignis et vehementissimos ardores esse;" also Moses Amyrald (praef ad paraphr. Psalm f. 3.): "tonat ille nonnunquam atque fulgurat et terribili verborum strepitu atque fragore, non Graeciam, ut de Pericle dictum est olim, non Judaeam et vicinas regiones, sed caelum et terram et elementa reliqua et universam mundi naturam, miscere et confundere videtur." In his consolations and instructions, on the contrary, he is mild and insinuating; in the strictly prophetic passages, full of impetuosity and fire. He so lives in the events he describes, that the future becomes to him, as the past and the present.

The arrangement of the collection is as follows · the whole may be divided into two parts, the first of which embraces chap. i—xxxix.

Chap. I—XII of this part contain prophecies against Judah and Jerusalem, these stand in the correct chronological order, except that chap VI, which contains the consecration of the prophet, and belongs to the year in which king Uzziah died, should have been placed first. Chap. II—V belong to the reign of Jotham; all the rest, as far as chap. 10. 4, to the time of Ahaz, the following, to the end of chap. XII, to that of Hezekiah. Chap XIII—XXIII contain a series of prophecies respecting foreign nations, interrupted only by chap XXII. Chap. XXIV—XXXV consist chiefly of predictions concerning Judah, which probably all belong to the reign of Hezekiah. Then follows chap. XXXVI—XXXIX, an historical appendix, containing accounts of the agency of Isaiah, during the same period. The second part, chap. XL—LXVI, was probably composed in the time of Manasseh, and constitutes one connected whole.

In recent times doctrinal views raised doubts respecting the *entire* genuineness of Isaiah; a fact, which, through all centuries, had been regarded as indisputable both in the Jewish synagogue, and the Christian church. As soon as the principle had been once established on *a priori* grounds, that miracles and prophecies were impossible, and that the course of nature could not be subjected to a higher influence; the genuineness of a large portion of Isaiah's prophecies could not be acknowledged, any more than that of the Pentateuch. A late defender of their entireness makes the striking remark, that the tradition of his having been sawn asunder, even allowing it to be false, may nevertheless be regarded as a type of the fate which Isaiah has experienced in our time. It will not be difficult for a future defender to refute the pretended arguments, by which men have sought to conceal their doctrinal prejudice, he will find materials already prepared not only in the writings of the advocates of the genuineness, but even those of its opposers, who are in the highest degree discordant among themselves, and what one defends another rejects. The examination of the genuineness of the second part, which we shall hereafter institute, is all that is of importance to our purpose.

Of the aids for the interpretation of Isaiah, we here adduce only the most valuable, and especially those most suited to our object. A more complete collection is given by Rosenmuller and Gesenius.

The Jewish commentators are of far less value, when they treat of the Messianic prophecies, than elsewhere, since doctrinal views here biassed their judgment, and led them to adopt the most forced interpretations. They follow the Messianic interpretation, only where, by a false, literal explanation, they can reconcile the prophecies with their carnal ideas of a worldly Messiah, who should come in glory See for example chap xi. Where, on the contrary, in chap. vii, the agreement with the history of Christ is too striking, or where, as in the prophecies of the second part, a Messiah in humiliation is announced, they contend, *pugnis et calcibus*, against the Messianic interpretation, and reject even the authority of their fathers, whom they every where else so highly revere.

The Greek fathers have commented, it is true, only on the Alexandrine version; but still, in their case, the knowledge of the original was in some measure supplied by comparing the Septuagint with the translations of Aquila, Symmachus and Theodotion What they contribute towards a more thorough understanding of Scripture is not to be despised The most important among them are Chrysostom, whose Ἑρμήνεια, nevertheless, extends only through the first eight chapters, (Tom III. ed. Francof) and especially Theodoret (Tom. II. ed. Hal.) Along with much useless matter, he gives many luminous remarks From the Latin church, only the commentary of Jerome has been preserved to us (Tom. V ed Bas et Francof.) He, indeed, surpassed Theodoret and Chrysostom in the knowledge of Hebrew, and his work contains many striking observations. But he enters far less into the spirit of the prophet, and gives many crude, allegorical observations

Of the commentaries, belonging to the time of the reformation, that of Calvin holds the first place, which originated from discourses committed to writing by another hand, and afterwards revised by himself. It appeared in four editions The first that of Geneva, fol. reprinted in the 4ten Bde opp ed Amstel Calvin's critical knowledge of the Hebrew was not great; but his intelligent and unprejudiced spirit, guided by his sound exegetical principles, often led him to the right interpretation of words. He is particularly valuable, as a practical commentator ; knowledge of the human heart, which he so eminently possessed, is as necessary to the interpreter of Isaiah, as philological learning. Although, at least in his commentary on Isaiah, he is far from being disposed to deny the references to Christ, where they exist, he yet knew how to distinguish the twilight of the Old Testament from the meridian splendor of the New. The recent interpreters have very generally left him unnoticed From Luther we possess nothing on Isaiah, but a very brief and unsatisfactory college prelection edited by one of his hearers, and published in the sixth part of the Halle edition of his works.—Among the critics of the 17th century, Grotius deserves especially to be named, though he cannot be with praise, so far as the Messianic predictions are concerned. He is generally wanting in depth; and in the interpretation of the Old Testament, he was not sustained by a thorough knowledge of language; and in explaining the Messianic prophecies he fails, even in what elsewhere distinguishes him, a certain exegetical tact, and an easy method of interpretation. A secret leaning to unbelief is manifest in his exposition of the Messianic passages of Isaiah, as well as of the other prophets, and he may be regarded, in many respects, as the precursor of the rationalist interpreters of Scripture. His commentary on Isaiah is found in the third volume of Vogel and Doederlein's edition of his Annotationes in V T. Several of the most important interpreters before the middle of the 17th century are found collected in the work Critici sacri Bd. 4. der Ausg. Lond 1660 und Bd 2. der Ausg Frankof 1695 fol and in the extract in Poli Synopsis criticorum Tom III. The chief work on Isaiah, however, was produced by Vitringa in the beginning of the 18th century, who died as professor of theology at Franecker 1722. This commentary first appeared at Leuwarden 1714 fol. and was afterwards several times reprinted. In this work Vitringa surpassed all, who had gone before him, and none of his successors has equalled him in spirit, learning and acuteness, though it must be confessed they have in some things improved his interpretation The allegorical explanations, which are every where intermingled, are the weakest part of his work. He would have accomplished more in the interpretation of the Messianic predictions had he known how to place himself more in the prophetic vision, and had he better understood the poetical and figurative character of the prophetic style. He would then have combined the various lineaments of the picture in one whole, and not have sought for something in history corresponding to each particular feature. He is not free from doctrinal prejudice, and proceeds too capriciously in searching for the historical fulfilment. The remarks on Isaiah by J H Michaelis in the Bibl Hal are valuable, particularly, for the very rich collection of parallel passages The commentary of Le Clerc (V. T prophetae etc. Amstelod. 1731 fol.) is not equal to his commentaries on the historical books, partly because, in general, he was not so well qualified to interpret the poetical and prophetical writings, (as his examination of the poetical parts of the Pentateuch shows), and partly because his mental powers had already suffered from age. He, nevertheless, exhibits in the exposition of several Messianic predictions, an impartiality, considering his former tendency to rationalism, scarcely to be expected. The work of the English lord bishop Lowth on Isaiah, London 1778 quarto, has indeed in other respects many deficiencies, and particularly indulges in great caprice in criticism, but in reference to the Messianic predictions, possesses decided merit. Of all the interpreters before and since his time, Lowth most clearly perceived the nature of the prophetic vision; his remarks on the blending together of the redemption from captivity and the redemption by Christ are excellent, and accustomed by a diligent study of the poets to understand the figurative character of the prophetic style, he shows himself equally free from credulity, and unbelief. He would have been the author of a new and just method of treating the prophetic writings and especially the predictions of the Messiah, if the suggestions given by him had been followed out and applied to particulars A German translation with notes and additions by Koppe, professor in Gottingen, appeared soon after the English original.

Towards the close of the last century, the revolution in theological opinions produced an entire change in the mode of explaining the prophet. The partial direction given to the understanding blinded its judgment; since it made it impossible for the critic to leave his own little sphere and place himself in the circumstances of another; to trace the connexion, which in Isaiah is rather internal than external, was thereby rendered impossible The deeper interpretation which can be practised only by one, who has within himself some affinity with the writer to be explained, no longer existed. Doctrinal prejudice so far prevailed, that among the Messianic predictions, those only were allowed to be such which were of a more general character, and might be explained, if necessary, as resulting from human conjecture. An attempt was made to set aside all more definite prophecies of Christ, by referring them to some other subject. These faults characterize nearly all the commentaries on Isaiah, that have appeared since that time, a praiseworthy exception, however, is that by v. d. Palm (Jesaias vertaald en opgehelderd door J. M. van der Palm Amsterd. 1805, 3 Tom 8vo) which though not properly designed for the learned, rests on thorough investigation; it were to be wished indeed that the author had regarded the prophet more in the character of a *seer*, the statements of the contents of the different prophecies is the happiest part of the work.—Among the recent commentaries on Isaiah, two are especially distinguished; that of Rosenmuller, and that of Gesenius. The former first appeared at Leipzic 1793, in three parts; afterwards in a completely revised edition, Leipz 1810—20, in three volumes. Great learning, cautious selection from the existing exegetical materials, and diligent collection of whatever had hitherto been done for the explanation of words, advantageously distinguish this commentary, the basis of which is that of Vitringa. The author is also less prejudiced than most interpreters of this period. In the second edition, he appears almost always in the first part, as an advocate for the Messianic interpretation; he even adopts it in chap. VII, where it had become the custom to regard it as entirely antiquated; in chap. IX he finds the true Deity of the Messiah declared, etc. He shows himself, however, less unprejudiced in the explanation of the predictions of the Messiah in the second part, which is indeed surprising, since the Messianic interpretation of chap. LIII, is certainly attended with less difficulty, than that of chap VII. It seems in part to be owing to the circumstance, that in the progress of his work, the authority of the Jewish expositors gained too much influence over him; an influence, which was strengthened by the prejudice, that the idea of a suffering and atoning Messiah was foreign from the Old Testament The commentary of Gesenius (Der Prophet Jesaia, ubersetzt und mit einem vollstandigen philologisch-kritischen und historischen Commentar begleitet. 3 Th Leipz. 1821), has not rendered superfluous the work of Rosenmuller. The author, especially in the second part, has paid far less attention to the different interpretations than Rosenmuller, and has, in other respects, omitted much which the latter had already sufficiently explained. Gesenius has certainly been more independent in ascertaining the meaning of words, and in this respect, has rendered a great service to the prophet. His diligence has considerably increased the materials of exegesis, by collecting a number of striking parallel passages, especially from Arabian and Syrian writers which though not indeed numerous, have been very accurately read. His historical illustrations, especially of the prophecies relating to foreign nations, are, for the most part, very valuable and fundamental, and his acuteness, which sometimes, alas! is led astray by his preconceived and false opinions, has made many new discoveries The translation is faithful, and not modernized. With respect to his general view of the prophetic order of the Messianic predictions, etc., the author is not original, but dependent on De Wette.—The remaining works, founded on the same principles, but not however written with the same depth of philological investigation, e g die Clavis uber den Jesaias von Paulus Jena 1793, der Commentar von Bauer in dem 8ten und 9ten Bande von Schulze's und Bauer's Scholien zum Alten Testamente, der Commentar in dem 5ten und 6ten Stucke des exegetischen Handbuches des Alten Testaments Leipzig 1799, (whose author would now comment in a very different manner), are, in comparison with these two commentaries, of little moment. Capriciousness in interpretation is carried to the highest extravagance in a work on the Hebrew prophets by Eichhorn. Gottingen 1816—19, 3 Bde. His exposition of Isaiah LIII, may justly be called monstrous.—Among the recent translations, the most distinguished are that of Dereser (in der 1sten Abth des 4ten Bandes des Brentanoschen Bibelwerkes), valuable especially for the observations subjoined, which, particularly on the Messianic prophecies, deserve all regard, and that of Augusti (in dem 4ten Bande der Schriften des Alten Testaments von De Wette und Augusti. Heidelb. 1810).

Isaiah II—IV.

These chapters form one connected discourse, which may however be divided into three parts.

Chap 2 2—4, the prophet describes the happy times of the Messiah, when the theocracy now limited to a single people, and greatly harassed and despised, should be extended over all mankind, true religion be propagated from Jerusalem, and after the submission of all nations to the authority of God, all dissension and strife should cease.

The second part of the discourse, chap. 2 5—4. 1 consists of admonitions, description of the prevailing corruptions and threatening of the divine chastisement. As the prophet had previously described the times of the Messiah in order to prepare the people for his admonition, so now, in order to arouse the ungodly from their security, and quicken the zeal of the pious, he discloses a different scene;—the divine chastisements, whereby, so far from the whole people having a part in the Messiah's kingdom, a large portion of them should be destroyed. This section is introduced by the exhortation to the people, contained in v. 5, to walk in the light of Jehovah, i. e. to make themselves worthy to share in this blessedness, by genuine piety. The prophet next describes, alternately, the reigning depravity, and the divine judgments thereby occasioned. The representation is in a great measure general; and as it is merely the application of the fundamental principles of the theocracy, that punishment necessarily follows sin, that all that is proud will be humbled, and all that is lofty abased by the Lord, it may, for the most part, with equal propriety be referred to all the various judgments inflicted upon the Jews, the carrying away into captivity, the capture of the city by the Romans, etc.; nay in the highest and fullest sense, the threatening will be accomplished by the last general divine judgment, to be inflicted upon those, who place their trust in the creature and not in the Lord. But as is usual in the representations of the divine judgments, there are here also some special features, which make it necessary to regard the prophet as threatening, not only the judgments of God in general, but especially the Babylonish exile. Of this sort, e. g. is the predicted carrying away of all the nobles, and handicraftsmen, chap. 3. 3, which was strikingly and literally fulfilled, when king Jehoiachim, was carried away by Nebuchadnezzar 2 Kings 24. 14, and the annunciation v. 9, that boys and children—i. e. inexperienced and unskilful rulers should receive the government of the state.

Chap. 4. 2—6, forms the third part of the discourse. That he might not too much discourage the pious, and at the same time might give his admonition the more effect with the ungodly, the prophet, before he concludes, takes another survey of that happier future, with the description of which he had commenced. After the divine chastisement, those who shall either have continued faithful to their God, or have again returned to him, shall be exalted to happiness and glory, through a Redeemer, who shall be both God and man. The whole church of God, which had heretofore consisted of a mixture of righteous, and wicked, shall then be holy. As of old, the people of Israel in their exodus from Egypt, were led by a visible symbol of the divine presence, so will the new church of God enjoy his gracious presence, and be defended by it from every danger.

The time, when the prophecy was composed, can be ascertained with considerable certainty. The state is represented as being in a flourishing, and warlike condition, and the luxury which had followed wealth is especially rebuked. See chap 2. 7, and the whole latter part of chap. III. Such, however, was the condition of the State, according to the accounts of the historical books, in the time of Uzziah and Jotham. The prophecy can scarcely have been composed under Uzziah, because Isaiah entered on his office in the year that Uzziah died; and also because it is probable, that in chap. II, Isaiah had before him the prophecy of Micah, who came forward first under Jotham. Nor is there any more reason to assign it to the time of Ahaz. Under him a great apostasy was followed by heavy calamities. At the very beginning of his reign, the land was invaded by the Assyrians and Ephraimites, who had already in the time of Jotham combined against Judah, and had been waiting only for the death of this king; the devastation they produced was so great, that the soil could not be cultivated for a long time afterwards, and the people were obliged to live solely on the produce of their herds, chap. 7: 15, 16. Afterwards the king became tributary to the Assyrians. It is true that Gesenius, Comm. p. 176, thinks the prophecy was probably composed in the first years of Ahaz, before the invasion of the Israelites and Assyrians, when the former prosperous condition still continued. But in striking contradiction to this, l. c. p. 268, he seeks to show, what is undoubtedly true, that this invasion took place in the very first year of Ahaz, and indeed immediately after he had ascended the throne. We are then compelled to assign the composition of the prophecy to the time of Jotham. The mention, chap. 3: 12, of the rule of children and women, forms no objection, since by נְעָרִים not precisely the kings are meant, but in general, the leaders of the people, nor the mention of idolatry, since that continued under Jotham, although he himself was devoted to the service of God.

Our purpose requires us here to examine only the first and third part of the prophecy.

Isaiah 2: 2—4

This section, with some unimportant changes, is found also in the prophet Micah, 4. 1—3, and in accounting for this circumstance the interpreters are not agreed. They suppose either, that Isaiah made use of Micah, or Micah, Isaiah, or both, an older and well known prophecy. The first opinion is by far the best sustained; for 1. The prediction in Isaiah is disconnected with what goes before, and yet begins with the copulative Vav; in Micah, on the contrary, it stands in connexion with what precedes and follows. Only in case it were found equally disconnected in Micah, as in Isaiah, might we suppose, that both had taken a more ancient oracle and prefixed it to their prophecies, as a sort of text, or motto. 2. In the discourses of the prophets, the promise usually follows the threatening; this order is observed by Micah, in Isaiah on the contrary, the promise contained in this passage precedes the threatening, and another promise follows. This of itself renders it probable, that Isaiah first described the view of futurity, which was disclosed to him, in the words of a prophecy, which perhaps at that time had attracted special attention in order, that afterwards, when following the usual course, he should return to the promise, he might give it in his own words.—The older theologians supposed in such cases, that the passages were communicated alike to both the sacred writers by the Holy Spirit. The truth here lies between this view of the subject, and that adopted in recent times. The same vision was granted to Micah and Isaiah, the substance could not have been borrowed, since all was disclosed to the prophets in vision, and therefore immediately. But they might have borrowed from each other, when clothing in words that which was given to them in vision. In the case before us, Isaiah, who uttered his predictions at a later period, may have remembered a prophecy of Micah, and availed himself in a great measure of its words, because they seemed to him best suited to express the views he had received. In accordance with this, are the sentiments of Abarbanel.

V. 2. "And it shall come to pass in the last time, that the mountain of the house of Jehovah shall be firmly established on the top of the mountains, exalted above the hills, and all nations shall flow to it, as a river."

The phrase אַחֲרִית הַיָּמִים originally signifies any period of future time, whether nearer or more distant. In this sense it occurs Gen. 49 1 Dan. 2 28. Commonly however the prophets used this expression, in a stricter sense, of the time of the Messiah, so that with proper limitation the saying of Kimchi is correct: עכל מקום שנאמר באחרית הימים דוא ימות המשיח. The prophets employed this general expression, because the definite time was unknown to them. 1 Pet 1 11. The LXX properly translate ἐν ταῖς ἐσχάταις ἡμέραις, and the Chald. בסוף יומיא. By "the mountain of the Lord's house," is to be understood, either the hill Moriah alone upon which the temple was built, or the whole mountain of Zion, of which Moriah was considered as a part, whence it is so often said, in Scripture, even after the ark of the covenant had been brought from Zion to Moriah, that God dwells in Zion. Comp. Bachiene Beschreib v. Palästina II, 1. § 75.—The word נָכוֹן *Part in Niphal* from כּוּן *firmare*, firmly established, signifies more than merely placed. The comparison of 1 Kings 2. 45, where the same word is used for the firm establishment of the throne of David, shows, that here also the meaning is, that the temple-mountain shall not be exalted perhaps for a moment, but forever, and that no power shall be able to bring it down. The words בְּרֹאשׁ הֶהָרִים on account of the connexion with the foregoing נָכוֹן can only mean : "on the summit of the mountains." The poetical representation may be either according to Michaelis, as if other great mountains, Sinai, Lebanon and Bashan should run together, place themselves one upon another beneath it and elevate it upon their snowy summit, so that it could be seen to the ends of the earth, or it may be supposed that the expression "it shall be established on the top of the mountains," implies that it will be so exalted as to be far above all other mountains, the loftiest of which shall appear to serve, as it were, for its foundation—מִן in מִגְּבָעוֹת is to be taken, comparatively. נִשָּׂא properly, *lifted up*, then, *elevated*. Here therefore it is said, that the small and inconsiderable temple-mountain shall hereafter be exalted and remain above all the mountains of the earth. The question now arises, in what sense is this to be taken. Some among the Jews understand it entirely according to the letter. They suppose, that in the days of the Messiah, God will bring down Mount Tabor, and Carmel, and place Jerusalem upon their summit. See the passage in Galatinus de arcanis Catholicae veritatis l. V c. 3. But the more intelligent, even of the Jews, have perceived, that this could not have been the sense intended by the writer. That the elevation of the mountain is moral and not physical, is acknowledged by all judicious interpreters. But it may still be asked, whether we are to look for the figure in the exaltation alone, or in the mountain also. The latter explanation is adopted by those among the fathers, as Jerome, Augustin, and Tertullian, who understand by the mountain, Christ. It is manifest however, that this interpretation is arbitrary, and does not result from any necessary relation, between the figure, and the reality. No less arbitrary is the explanation of several other Christian interpreters, who think that the church of Christ is particularly designated by the mountain of the Lord's house. Those come nearer the truth, who understand the theocracy to be intended by it, according to a *metonymia loci pro re locata*. The sense will then be, the theocracy, before limited to a single people, shall hereafter be enlarged and extended over all nations, the religion of the Israelites, which had its chief seat on mount Zion, shall from thence gain the victory over all false religions. Thus Michaelis and others. But the following verse, where Zion and Jerusalem must be taken literally, renders it more probable, that here also the figure is to be confined to the exaltation, and the mountain is to be taken literally. But in what way then shall the mountain of the Lord's house become more illustrious, than all other mountains of the earth? Because upon it, or at Jerusalem, the glory of the Lord shall be more clearly revealed, than in any other place. indeed from thence shall the true religion, to be founded by the Messiah, be extended over the whole world. Calvin: "Montes alii poterant altitudine superare, sed quia gloria dei praeeminet, montem etiam in quo patefit, eminere necesse est. Montem ergo Sion per se non praedicat, sed cum suo ornatu, quo etiam universus orbis illustrandus erat." Cocceius has well remarked, that the elevation does not consist in the accession of the heathen, since this is not its cause, but its consequence: "Gloria templum ita illustrans est praesentia Messiae et effusio spiritus sancti." Kimchi and Abarbanel find a reason for the placing of mount Zion in opposition to the other mountains in the circumstance שהאומות היו עבודים לאלהיהם על ההרים הרמים ועל הגבעות הנשאות, that the heathen worshipped their idols on lofty hills and mountains. They suppose the prophet to predict that in the time of the Messiah the hill of Zion—the seat of the true religion shall gain the victory over the other mountains where offerings were made to idols. But of this special allusion there is no proof. A parallel passage is found in Ezekiel 40.2: "In the visions of God brought he me into the land of Israel, and placed me on a very high mountain. upon it was as a built city." Here also the prophet beholds the comparatively insignificant hill of Zion exalted in the time of the Messiah. The passage is also illustrated by Ps. 68. 16, 17, where the neighboring loftier mountains are represented as envious of the preference given to mount Zion by Jehovah, in choosing it as his dwelling place. Jarchi strikingly remarks, that the predicted elevation of the mountain of the Lord's house, above all mountains, at the same time expresses the superiority of the revelation of the divine glory, about to be made upon it, over all its manifestations before the coming of the Messiah. "Majus erit signum, quod fiet in isto monte, quam signa quae facta sunt in montibus Sinai, Carmel et Tabor." "And all nations flow together to it as a river." The verb נהר, *to flow*, then, flow towards as a river. The praeter is determined to be the future by the preceding future. In the use of the tenses the prophets are very inaccurate, since they beheld all in the present. The reception of the heathen into the theocracy, glorified by the appearance of the Messiah is here figuratively represented, as if they were all journeying to mount Zion, exalted above all mountains, and serving them as it were for a banner. Then particularly shall be fulfilled the promise, constantly repeated even in Genesis, that the religion of Abraham should at a future period be extended to all the heathen nations.

V. 3 "And many nations go and say Come, let us repair to the mountain of Jehovah, and to the house of the God of Jacob, that he may teach us his ways, and we may walk in his paths. For from Zion shall go forth the law, and from Jerusalem the word of Jehovah." The representation in this verse is metaphorical. Cocceius has justly said "phrasis sumta est a consuetudine Israelitarum, qui solebant templum adire, ut sacerdotes ibi populum docentes et Mosen ac prophetarum oracula praelegentes audirent." All the Israelites were obliged to appear annually before the Lord in his temple, in order to show their reverence for him, and be instructed in his ways. The image is taken from these pilgrimages to Jerusalem. At that time, not merely one single people, but all nations of the earth shall go up to the seat of the true God or divested of the theocratic covering: all nations shall return to the worship of the true God and embrace his revealed religion, which shall be preached from Jerusalem to all mankind. The image has been explained by Cocceius "quemadmodum Israelitae domi et in synagogis legentes, audientes et meditantes legem et prophetas, censebantur in templo deum loquentem audire, ita qui evangelium in omnibus gentibus praedicatum audiunt, censentur templum adire." It is figuratively represented as if the nations who receive the annunciation of the true religion made from Jerusalem proceed thither in order to be instructed in its truths. The plural עמים רבים is by no means a limitation of כל הגוים in the preceding verse. The expression rather contains an implied antithesis. Formerly only one people journeyed to Jerusalem to show their reverence for Jehovah, but now many nations. The word לכו properly Imp of הָלַךְ formed from יָלַךְ, then again a summons like the Latin *age* or *agite*. To indicate the zeal with which the nations should press to the mountain of Jehovah, the prophet represents them as exhorting and urging each other onward. Altogether similar is the prophecy of Zechariah 8 21, 22: "The inhabitants of one city shall go to another and say · let us go to pray before the Lord, and to seek the Lord of Hosts, we will also go with you," etc. The word הורה is elsewhere construed with the Accus. and with בּ *of the subject*, and only here and in the parallel passage of Micah, with מן *of the subject*; properly to instruct one in any matter. There is no reason to suppose with Drusius, that the expression is emphatic "de viis suis, quia scil ex parte tantum cognoscimus" The way of Jehovah is the way, in which he wills that men should walk, the mode of life, which is pleasing in his sight. In Arabic, religion is called expressly سَبِيلُ اَللّٰهِ *the way of God*, in the New Testament ὁδός *way* To walk in the way of Jehovah, to regulate the life according to his revealed will, is put in opposition to walking in our own way, and ordering our life according to our own inclination Isa 53 6 The heathen will first obtain the knowledge of religion and then live in accordance with its dictates. On the words that he may teach us, etc. Kimchi well remarks, והמרה הוא מלך המשיח: "the teacher is the king Messiah" The true religion shall be extended to the heathen particularly through the Messiah, according to the constant predictions of the prophets. The last words, "for from Zion shall go forth the law, and the word of the Lord from Jerusalem," are not spoken by the people exhorting one another; but by the prophet. In them he gives the reason, why the nations journey with such zeal to Jerusalem According to several interpreters, Zion and Jerusalem are here an image of the theocracy. The sense would then be: the people shall seek access to the theocracy, because in it only is the true revelation of God to be found But it is much better to understand Zion and Jerusalem literally At Jerusalem the glorious revelation of God by the Messiah shall take place; from these shall the knowledge of it be extended to all the heathen nations; therefore are all their eyes directed thither. Theodoret: οὗτος ὁ εὐαγγελικὸς λόγος ἀπὸ τῆς Ἱερουσαλὴμ οἷον ἀπό τινος πηγῆς ἀρξάμενος πᾶσαν τὴν οἰκουμένην διέδραμε, τοῖς μετὰ πίστεως προσιοῦσι τὴν ἀρδείαν προσφέρων What the prophet here says literally, Ezekiel expresses in figurative language, chap 47. 1, etc. where the extension of the true religion from Jerusalem over the whole earth, is represented under the image of a river, which springs up in the temple, and then flows forth. See also Zech 14 8. The word תּוֹרָה properly *law*, stands here for religion in general, entirely synonymous with דְּבַר יְהוָֹה, *the word of Jehovah*. In like manner מִשְׁפָּט chap. 42. 1—4, and νόμος in the New Testament, Rom 3 27. The reason of this more extended meaning is, that the prophets in their representation of the Messiah's kingdom, employ the expression, which in their time designated the corresponding things in the theocracy. The religion under the old covenant was a תּוֹרָה *law*, hence the religion also to be founded by the Messiah bears this name. So Calvin "prophetico more loquitur: nam cum lex usitata esset, ejus nomine totam doctrinam dei comprehendere solebant." According to Vitringa, who is followed by Koppe, and v d Palm, a metaphorical idea here lies at the foundation, taken from the courts of princes, who give their authority to the commands, which go forth from their palaces; Zion is, as it were, the residence of Israel's king, whence he sends forth his commands to the ends of the earth. But as this interpretation is without support, so the comparison of the parallel passages, shows that if we must suppose a figure of some kind to lie at the foundation, it should much rather be that of a stream flowing forth from Jerusalem. But at all events, the word תֵּצֵא implies, that the religion of Jehovah, heretofore confined to a single people, shall break through these narrow limits and extend over all the heathen nations ,

V 4 "Then will Jehovah be a Judge between the people, and rebuke many nations, they shall beat their swords into ploughshares, and their spears into pruning hooks, no people shall lift up the sword against another; they shall learn war no more." In the first two members of the verse, the subject is not expressed, and is supplied in different ways by interpreters. Abarbanel and Jarchi, whom several Catholic interpreters follow, render *judicabit iste mons* Theodoret and Mark, *judicabit verbum dei*. Rosenmuller, after Kimchi and others · "the Messiah will judge" But there can be no doubt, that Jehovah should be taken as the subject, who shall accomplish, through the Messiah, indeed, what is here attributed to him. According to Calvin and Vitringa, "he will judge among the nations," is equivalent to he will reign, will have his throne among them. But although the verbs, which signify *to judge*, in the Shemitish languages have for the most part the secondary meaning *to reign*, because in ancient times, both functions were usually combined in one person; yet this cannot be the case in the instance before us. Since from what follows; "and they shall beat their swords," etc. which indicates the effect of this judging, it appears, that the word is to be limited to the settling of disputes, prevailing among them, which meaning also is required even by the construction of the verb with בין. שכט with בין *to judge between*, to act the part of an umpire between two contending parties. The verb הוכיח *to show, to prove*, then with ל *to convince any one of a fault, to instruct, to rebuke.* See Gesenius s. v. The sense the nations which have hitherto selfishly followed each one its own interest, and allowed themselves in manifold acts of injustice towards each other, shall then acknowledge Jehovah as their common judge. His spirit and word shall convince the aggressor of his misconduct, (as the umpire shows to each of the contending parties his injustice) settle every controversy and produce general quietness and peace. The images under which this peace is then exhibited, are not unusual in heathen poets also. Martial XIV, 34.

Pax me certa ducis placidos curvavit in usus
Agricolae nunc sum, militis ante fui

On the contrary, Joel 4: 10. Virg Georg. 1 506. Ovid fast. 1. 697, the change from peace to war is represented under the image of a conversion of the instruments of agriculture into swords and spears. The divine doctrine and the divine life shall prevail among all people, and unite them in the bonds of love and harmony. את an instrument of agriculture, which cannot be certainly determined; that it differed from מחרשת *a plough*, appears from 1 Sam 13 20, 21.

It now remains to make some remarks on the whole prophecy.

1. Even Theodoret had occasion to refute those who referred it to the condition of the Jews after their return from the Babylonish captivity. Among recent interpreters, this reference is approved by Dathe, Hensler and Vogel, while Grotius refers it entirely to the time, when the city was delivered from the siege of Rezin and Pekah. But how untenable this view is, appears from its requiring v. 3 to be referred to the peace, which should be granted to the Jews by the Persians and other nations; since that verse does not speak concerning the friendly conduct of the heathen nations towards the Jews, but that which God should cause these nations to show towards one another. In this prophecy, the characteristic marks are again given, which in the Messianic predictions of all the prophets, and especially of Isaiah, are attributed to the time of the Messiah. First, the extension of the religion of Jehovah over the whole earth. See

e. g. chap. 9. 6. 11. 10. 19. 18, etc. 42. 49. 53. 60. Ps. 22. 28. Then universal peace. See e. g. chap. 9. 4. 11. 6—9. Ps. 72. 3. Zech. 9. 10.

2. The prophecy belongs to that class in which the person of the Messiah is not described, but only the nature of his kingdom. But we have before shown in the general introduction, that it cannot thence be inferred, that the hopes of the prophet were not connected with a personal Messiah. Gesenius ascribes to him the idea, that the conversion of the heathen was to be effected by the prophets. But this is contradicted by the following reasons. 1. The notion, that the prophets were to be the mediators of the new covenant, which should embrace the heathen also, is found neither in Isaiah, nor in any other prophet. See the refutation of this hypothesis at chap. LIII. 2. Not only do precisely the same traits that are found in this portion occur in the other personal Messianic predictions of Isaiah, but the Messiah appears as a person, even in the prophecy, chap. IV, which is a continuation and completion of the same discourse, of which the passage before us forms a part. Gesenius himself says, I. s. 224: "Isaiah is accustomed to connect the hope of the better times with a king." 3. According to Gesenius' own opinion, this portion is a fragment from the larger prediction of Micah 4. 5. But in that, there is first a passing allusion to the person of the Messiah, chap. 4. 5, and afterwards he is fully described in his person and his office, chap. 5. 1 etc. Isaiah, therefore, could expect nothing else, than that his hearers and readers would connect the hopes here expressed with the same subject with which they had been connected in the well known prediction of Micah. Precisely for this reason it was superfluous to point out the person of the Messiah, as every one would of himself refer the prophecy to him.

3. The Jews urge against the fulfilment of this prophecy in Christ, that the peace here predicted did not follow the introduction of Christianity, but on the contrary, many and bloody wars have since been waged. This objection has caused much difficulty to Christian interpreters, because they erroneously supposed that we must look for the complete fulfilment in an early period of the Christian dispensation. Several of the fathers (Theodoret, Cyrill, Eusebius, Chrysostom) refer the prophecy to the external peace which prevailed in the Roman empire at the introduction of the Christian religion. But this is a very unfortunate hypothesis, since the peace here described is not to be the result of external causes, but an effect of the recep-

tion of the true religion The view of those is nearer the truth, who think that the prophet represents, not so much what would actually happen, as what the Gospel would be suited to effect, and would effect, in all those who should embrace it by a true faith Thus the author of the *dialogus cum Tryphone*, a beautiful passage, from which we must here quote· οἵτινες ἀπὸ τοῦ νόμου καὶ τοῦ λόγου τοῦ ἐπελθόντος ἀπὸ Ἱερουσαλὴμ διὰ τῶν τοῦ Ἰησοῦ ἀποστόλων τὴν θεοσέβειαν ἐπιγνόντες ἐπὶ τὸν θεὸν Ἰακὼβ καὶ θεὸν Ἰσραὴλ κατεφύγομεν καὶ οἱ πολέμου καὶ ἀλληλοφονίας καὶ πάσης κακίας μεμεστωμένοι, ἀπὸ πάσης τῆς γῆς τὰ πολεμικὰ ὄργανα ἕκαστος τὰς μαχαίρας εἰς ἄροτρα καὶ τὰς σιβύνας εἰς γεωργικὰ μετεβάλομεν, καὶ γεωργοῦμεν, εὐσέβειαν, δικαιοσύνην, φιλανθρωπίαν, πίστιν, ἐλπίδα κ. τ. λ But this explanation is also unsatisfactory. It is the uniform doctrine of the prophets, that, after every opposing enemy of the kingdom of God shall have been subdued, it will be exalted to a glorified condition, in which the peace, whereby its members had been inwardly blessed, shall also outwardly prevail in the whole conduct of the people, nay even in the irrational part of the creation, and all discord, which originated with the fall of man, and all destruction shall cease See, e g chap 11 6, 7 To this period this prediction also in its highest sense refers. It has already been fulfilled, in so far as every member of the Messianic kingdom has acquired a peaceful disposition, and Christianity has influenced the conduct of whole nations and softened their former cruelty into comparative mildness. The prophet here, as usual, overlooks the gradual development of the Messiah's kingdom, and embraces its commencement and its termination in the same description. This is true also in reference to the predicted conversion of all the heathen nations. Its fulfilment has already commenced, its completion will follow in future times. Still it must be observed, that the spiritual eye of the prophet is here attracted to the one prominent side of the picture ; the other therefore remains unnoticed in his description. It is the uniform doctrine of the prophets, and of the New Testament, that a large portion of mankind will persist in rejecting salvation, and consequently be destroyed by a divine judgment before the kingdom of God shall be glorified We can therefore infer from this prophecy only, that the saving power of the Gospel shall hereafter be extended to a much greater portion of mankind, than it has hitherto been

4. Michaelis and Palm, after the example of the Jews, refer this prophecy to a time, when Jehovah will establish his residence at Zi-

Isaiah 4.2.

on; and thence extend his reign over all nations united in one theocracy. This view originates here, as well as in other places, from not perceiving the figurative character of the prophetic discourse, the inconsistency of such an erroneous literal explanation, is manifest from the fact. that its defenders themselves are obliged to understand the exaltation of the mountain of the Lord's house figuratively.

Isaiah 4:2 seq.

After the prophet in the preceding part had sought to give effect to his admonition by announcing the divine judgment which threatened obstinate sinners, he now endeavors to accomplish the same purpose, by describing the happiness which those who remained faithful should enjoy, after the destruction of the wicked. Chrysostom: ἐπειδὴ σφόδρα κατέσεισε τὴν διάνοιαν αὐτῶν τῇ τῶν λυπηρῶν ἀπειλῇ καὶ τὴν συμφορὰν ἱκανῶς ἐτραγῴδησε καὶ μακρὸν ἀπέτεινε λόγον τὰ φοβερὰ διηγούμενος, μεταβάλλει λοιπὸν ἐπὶ τὰ χρησιότερα. Τοῦτα γὰρ ἰατρείας ἀρίστης τρόπος μὴ καίειν μηδὲ τέμνειν μόνον, ἀλλὰ καὶ τὰς ἐνεῖθεν γινομένας ὀδύνας προσηνέσι παραμυθεῖσθαι φαρμάκοις.

V. 2. "Then will the Sprout of Jehovah serve for decoration and for honor, the fruit of the land for exaltation and for ornament, to the escaped of Israel." The phrase ביום ההוא stands here, as it often does, in an entirely general sense, for *then* — after the judgments. See 10: 20 Zech. 14: 6. As the Messianic representation, in this passage as well as the foregoing, embraces the beginning and end of the Messiah's kingdom, so the determination of time by no means implies that the divine judgments threatened against the covenant people in the preceding part, will be inflicted before the commencement of the times of the Messiah. To the prophet, who beheld all in vision and therefore as present, the judgments in the foregoing portion were presented as combined in one picture, here on the contrary, he beholds in the same manner, the blessings of the Messiah's reign, so that the phrase ביום ההוא properly relates, not so much to the succession of events in reality, as in the vision of the prophet. We must not so much regard the determination of time, as the main thought which runs through all the Messianic predictions of Isaiah, and has been confirmed by history, viz, that not all the members of the visible theocracy, but only the pious part of them would share in the blessings of the Messiah's kingdom.—In this prophecy all depends on the interpretation of צֶמַח יהוה .

I After Grotius, Dathe, Vogel, Michaelis, Koppe and Augusti, Gesenius understands by it, the new increase of the people after their defeats He explains it thus "Then again will the Sprout of Jehovah be splendid and glorious, and the fruit of the land excellent and beautiful for the delivered of Israel. Fruit of the land is taken in a literal sense, and understood to mean the product of the land" This explanation is liable to the following objections. 1. This meaning of the expression צֶמַח יהוה can be proved by no parallel passage; as often as it occurs of persons it is never used collectively, but always of an individual. 2. "It cannot signify the people of Israel, since they are included in the epithet פליטה, and plainly distinguished from it" Thus Gesenius himself in his lexicon In his commentary, he endeavors to weaken the force of this objection by asserting that the לִפְלֵיטַת יִשְׂרָאֵל need not necessarily be referred to the first member of the verse also But this is a very improbable supposition We must then assume, that the particle ל before לִצְבִי and לְכָבוֹד serves merely as a periphrasis of adjectives *beautiful* and *glorious;* while on the contrary in connexion with the nouns לְגָאוֹן and לְתִפְאֶרֶת which immediately follow, and exactly correspond, it retains its usual import: "for decoration and for ornament" 3 It is by far the most natural supposition that צֶמַח יהוה and פְּרִי הָאָרֶץ correspond to each other, and designate one and the same subject, which is here only represented according to its different relations For as the *termini antecedentes* צמח and פרי signify one and the same, so do the *termini consequentes* יהוה and הארץ stand in a manifest antithesis. 4. It is an entirely unsuitable expression, that the fruits of the land should be for exaltation and ornament, to the deliverer of Israel, the splendid description of the gracious blessings of God, which follows, compels us to think, that the prophet had in view something of a higher import.

II The difficulty No 2. is avoided by the explanation of Schleusner (Analekten von Keil and Tschirner), who by צמח יהוה understands the divine mercies and blessings, and by פרי הארץ likewise the products of the land But this is supported neither by any established usage of the language nor by a single instance of a similar figure.

III The Chaldee paraphrasts, (בְּעִדָּנָא הַהוּא יְהִי מְשִׁיחָא דַיְיָ לְהֶדְוָה וְלִיקָר) Kimchi, Vitringa, Rosenmuller and others understand by the צמח יהוה the Messiah. This interpretation has everything in its favor. The representation of the Messiah under the image of a sprout or shoot is in general very common in the Scriptures. Chap. 11. 1 he is called חטר and נצר, *Branch* and *Shoot;* v. 10 of the same chapter, as well as chap. 53. 2 שרש and יונק; and in reference to the same image it is said of him, v. 8, נגזר *he was cut off*. Rev. 5. 5 the Messiah is called ῥίζα Δαβίδ. But especially was the figurative designation of the Messiah צמח so common, as to become a proper name. He is not only called צמח דויד, *branch of David* Jer. 23. 5. 33. 15, but Zech. 3. 8 Jehovah calls him expressly עבדי צמח, and chap. 6. 12 he is called איש צמח שמו—a man whose name is צמח. Gesenius supposes that if by צמח יהוה the Messiah is to be understood, it must in every case be taken in an entirely indefinite sense, since the hope of a Messiah in the time of Isaiah was in its incipient state and had not become fixed. But that Branch or Sprout of Jehovah is synonymous with Son of Jehovah, appears from the following reasons. 1. יהוה generally stands in contrast with the צמח דויד. If this means a son of David, so also must צמח יהוה designate a son of Jehovah in the proper sense. 2. צמח יהוה in this passage stands in opposition to פרי הארץ. Vitringa and others translate these words *fruit of the earth*, and understand by them the Messiah according to his human nature. But it would be far better to take הארץ here with the article for the land of Judea. And as now *the fruit of the land* designates him who was to be born in Judah, or spring from the house of Judah, so also Branch of Jehovah can refer only to this origin. 3. The only objection, which has been brought against this explanation is, that in the time of Isaiah there could have been no knowledge of the Divine and human nature of the Messiah. But this assertion is already sufficiently refuted by the prophecy of Micah alone, which Isaiah had before him when he composed this prophetical discourse. There, chap. 5. 1, in a manner altogether similar, the temporal birth of the Messiah at Bethlehem = fruit of the land; and his everlasting procession from the Father = Branch of Jehovah, are placed in intimate connexion. See Rosenmuller on the passage. If we refer to Isaiah himself, not only are the temporal birth of the Messiah, chap. 7. 14, and his Divine dignity contained in the name Immanuel, contrasted, but we find precisely the same antithesis as in the passage before us, chap. 9. 6. unto us a child is born = fruit of the land, unto us a Son of God is given = Branch of Jehovah. The Seventy who translate ἐπιλάμψει ὁ θεός, and the Syriac interpreters. *erit ortus domini*, have understood the word צמח of the rising of the sun, although it never has this meaning and is used only of the springing forth of plants. "The escaped of Israel," a designation of the pious portion of the people, who, spared in the threatened judgments of God, shall now participate in the blessings of the Messiah's reign. The sense of this verse then is: While the people shall be visited with a severe divine punishment, a small remnant shall remain faithful to Jehovah, whom a divine Redeemer shall bless, make happy, and glorify.

V. 3. "And he that remains in Zion, and is left in Jerusalem, shall be called holy, every one who is written among the living in Jerusalem." The collectives הַנִּשְׁאָר and הַנּוֹתָר are synonymous with פְּלֵיטַת יִשְׂרָאֵל in the preceding verse. In respect to the words *in Zion* and *in Jerusalem*, the idea of place is not to be urged. Zion and Jerusalem, as the seat of the theocracy, stand here for the covenant people, who, in the vision of the prophet, cannot be separated from their place of residence. That local limitation was not the purpose of the prophet, appears from the following verse, where in connexion with Jerusalem, the other cities are mentioned, and the idea of the covenant people in a comprehensive sense is thus expressed. According to the usual idiom of Isaiah, "shall be named," stands for "shall be." קָדוֹשׁ must neither be translated with Koppe, by *inviolable*, nor with Michaelis limited to the renunciation of idolatry, but be taken in its full import. It points out an essential difference between the kingdom of the Messiah, and the former theocracy; while in the theocracy the pious and the ungodly were mingled together; in the new kingdom of God, after the great separation between the righteous and the wicked, those only shall have a part, who represent in their lives the holiness of its Head, and thus fulfil the requisition, "Be ye holy for I am holy." This is the constant doctrine of the prophets. Chap 11: 9: "They shall not sin, nor destroy on all my holy mountain, for the land is full of the knowledge of the Lord, as the water covers the bottom of the sea." The ground of this holiness is assigned chap LIII; the eminent servant and son of God, who, chap. 4 2, shall be for decoration and for ornament to the members of his kingdom, will cleanse and justify by his vicarious sufferings the human race sunk in sin. Jeremiah and Ezekiel predict that in the times of the Messiah God will give a new heart of flesh in place of the heart of stone. In the last words "every one that is written among the living in Jerusalem," the figure is taken from the custom of enrolling the names of the citizens on a list. Ez. 13 9: "they shall not be written in the catalogue of the house of Israel," is identical with the parallel phrase, "they shall not remain in the assembly of my people." Such a book is here, and in other passages of Scripture, figuratively attributed also to Jehovah. To enter the name of any one in this book is to appoint him to life; to blot out the name of any one, is to appoint him to death. Exod 32. 32, Moses, after the Israelites had sinned by worshipping the golden calf, prays "now forgive their sin; if not, blot me also out of thy book, which thou hast written," i. e. "slay me." See Ps. 69. 29. 139. 16. In the first instance then, those who are written among the living, are no other than the *escaped*, those *who were left in Zion, and remained in Jerusalem*, of the preceding verse. Chrysostom· οἱ ἀφορισθέντες μηδὲν παθεῖν δεινόν, and the sense of the verse: "the faithful servants of Jehovah, who shall be spared during the heavy judgments to be inflicted by him, shall constitute a select and holy company." Still it appears that the expression החיים stands here at the same time in a certain pregnant sense· *life = happiness*. The ungodly shall indeed all perish by the divine judgments, but the godly shall be preserved, and participate in the blessedness of the Messiah's reign In this pregnant sense· to appoint to true life, to happiness, to a participation in all the privileges of the Messiah's kingdom, the expression occurs, among other places, Dan. 12 1. Apoc. 3· 5. 13 8 20 15 22 19 Phil. 4 3 Luke 10 20. So of old the Chaldee paraphrast "all those appointed to eternal life shall see the consolation of Jerusalem, i. e. the Messiah"

V. 4 This happy condition of the chosen will be introduced, "when Jehovah has washed away the filth of the daughters of Zion, and removed the blood-guiltiness of Jerusalem from the midst of her, by the spirit which will judge and burn." Several fathers explain the verse of a purification of the better portion of the people So Theodoret· κάθαρσιν δὲ τὴν διὰ λουτροῦ παλιγγενεσίας προλέγει. But this explanation is obviously unnatural. The prophet here returns to the punishments, which shall overtake the ungodly, while the pious partake in the blessings of the Messiah's kingdom. Daughters of Zion, and of Jerusalem, according to Gesenius, is a poetical enunciation, for all the inhabitants of Jerusalem But this explanation is inadmissible. 1. Because not the sons of Jerusalem, but Jerusalem itself is contrasted with the daughters of Zion; but there is surely no reason to understand by Jerusalem only its male inhabitants 2 The figure is also entirely unsuitable. It cannot be said of the sinful inhabitants who were devoted to destruction, that their sins should be washed away, this expression would be proper, only upon the supposition, that Jehovah still designed to grant them forgiveness and mercy It may however well be said of the city, to which also מִקִּרְבָּהּ leads us, that Jehovah purifies it from sin, when he destroys the sinners We must therefore, with Rosenmuller and others, understand by daughters of Zion, the remaining cities of Judea. It is a usual figure with the orientals, to regard the capital as the mother, and the other cities as her daughters. See Jos. 17. 16. 1 Chron 18 1. It is a strange remark of Gesenius, that this is indeed a geographical, but not a poetical expression, since manifestly it can only have passed over from the language of poetry into that of geography. The same image lies at the foundation, chap 40 9, where Zion, as the mother, is called upon to announce to the remaining cities of Judah, as her daughters, the joyful tidings of redemption Sins are here represented under the image, common among all nations, of physical impurities. דמים blood, or blood-guiltiness includes also, robbery, oppression, and in general all aggravated crimes. The word דוּחַ occurs in Ex 40· 38 2 Chion. 4 6 in the sense, *to wash off, purify*. The washing away of sin from Jerusalem, and the remaining cities, or without a figure, the putting an end to sins, is effected by the spirit of judgment and the spirit of burning, i e by a judging and burning spirit The spirit of God is the divine power by which he operates upon and fills the creation, the source of physical and moral life, which penetrates the dead mass, and gives it form and expression, the bond of union between the Creator and the creatures he has made. Gen. 1. 2. Ps 104. 30. Job 33 4 It is this spirit, by whom God upholds and rules the world 2 Kings 2· 16, the disciples of the prophet believed him to have taken away Elisha Hence the judgment upon the ungodly is here also represented as executed by him בָּעֵר is the Infin Nominasc. in Piel. Of the two senses of the verb in Piel, *to burn* and *to take away*, several interpreters here prefer the latter; but the former, which also occurs chap 40· 16 and 44: 15, and which the LXX adopt, πνεύματι καύσεως, gives a far better meaning. The image is taken from a fire, in which impure metal is melted; and as the fire separates the dross, so would the divine spirit of judgment separate the ungodly See Ez. 22 21. "Yea I will gather you and blow upon you the fire of my wrath, and ye shall be melted therein," or the figure may be from stubble, which is consumed by fire, Mal.

3. 19 In a manner altogether similar it is said, Matt. 3: 11, that Christ would baptize the ungodly with fire.

V. 5. " And Jehovah creates over the whole place of mount Zion, and over her assemblies, a cloud by day, and a column of smoke, and the splendor of a flaming fire by night. For around all that is glorious is a covering." The figure is here taken from the journey of the Israelites through the desert. During that journey they were guided, and at the same time, protected by a visible symbol of God's gracious presence, a Shekinah as the Jews call it. By night it resembled a pillar of smoke, which allowed the fiery splendor enclosed in the midst of it to shine through, (עָשָׁן וְנֹגַהּ אֵשׁ לֶהָבָה) by day it assumed more the form of a cloud, as it was then more spread out (עָנָן). This phenomenon was: 1. A sign of the divine presence suited to the necessities of an unrefined people, which afterwards settled over the ark of the covenant in the holy of holies, Ex. 40. 34 etc. 1 Kings 8 10. It was Jehovah's seat, whence his commands and answers to the inquiries of the Israelites were issued. Its varied aspect now pleasing, now terrific, revealed the corresponding intentions of God towards his people, Ex. 16 10. The ungodly were consumed by fire, which fell from this cloud, Lev. x. Num. xvi. 2. It served the Israelites for guidance, defence and protection. It pointed out the direction, which they should take in their journey through the desolate wilderness, Ex. 13. 21. During the passage through the Red Sea, it stood between them and their foes, and prevented them from coming near each other. Lightning darted down from it upon their enemies, and put them in confusion, Ex. 14. 19—24. By day, when it spread itself out, it afforded them protection from the heat of the sun, Num 10 34. Ps. 105. 39. Now a similar favor shall be vouchsafed to his purified and holy Church after the coming of the Messiah. The figure includes two things, the divine presence, and the divine protection; both have been experienced by his church in their commencement, since the coming of the Redeemer, as God in Christ was really present with men, and since his glorification is present with his church, and replenishes it by his Spirit, so does he defend it from every danger; but the prediction will be perfectly fulfilled at the completion of the Messiah's kingdom, in a way, which can now only be conjectured. Parallel is chap 60 1, where it is said כָּבוֹד יְהֹוָה, his gracious presence shall arise upon the church. See 19 20. Zech 2. 10 Theodoret says· ἡνίκα τὸν Ἰσραὴλ ὁ θεὸς ἠλευθέρωσε τῆς τῶν Αἰγυπτίων δουλείας, ἦγεν αὐτὸν νεφέλης ἐπικειμένης καὶ νύκτωρ μὲν δαδουχούσης καὶ τοῦ φωτὸς χωρηγούσης τὴν χρείαν, μεθ' ἡμέραν δὲ σκηνὴν καὶ ὄροφον μιμουμένης καὶ τῆς ἡλιακῆς ἀκτῖνος τὸ λυποῦν ἀπειργούσης. Τούτων ἀπολαύσειν νοητῶς μετὰ τὴν τοῦ σωτῆρος ἡμῶν ἐπιφάνειαν τοὺς εἰς αὐτὸν πεπιστευκότας ἡ προφητεία προλέγει καὶ διὰ τῆς νεφέλης ταύτης ἀπαλλαγήσεσθαι τοῦ ὑετοῦ σκληρότητος καὶ καύματος καταφλέγοντος. מקראים *festival assemblies, assemblies for the praise of God.* Others render, *places of assembling*, but the word never has this meaning. While heretofore the symbol of the Divine presence dwelt in the holy of holies, 1 Kings VIII, which no man except the high-priest, and he only once a year, might enter, in the time of the Messiah, the immediate presence of God will be experienced in every assembly of his saints. v. 3. The last words of this verse are best translated with the LXX (πάσῃ τῇ δόξῃ σκεπασθήσεται) Jerome (super omnem gloriam protectio) and Rosenmuller. "for around all that is glorious is a covering" The reason is here given, why God would cause his mercy to rule over the glorified church. As men are accustomed carefully to wrap up and guard costly articles, lest they should be injured, so God with his mercy surrounds his church adorned with illustrious virtues and guards it from every danger. חֻפָּה a noun, *covering, case*. A similar construction occurs Deut. 32. 39 יְהִי עָלֵיכֶם סִתְרָה. Gesenius translates it thus: "for all that is glorious is protected." He takes חֻפָּה not as a noun, but as the praeter in Pual. But the verb חפה never means *to protect*. Pual moreover is not elsewhere used; and the construction is not so natural. After the Chaldee, Kocher translates: "Nam supra omnem gloriam erit protectio," and explains: "talis חפה promittitur, quae omnem ante cognitam speratamve gloriam excedat exsuperetque." But then חפה would require the article, since it must be translated by, *this* protection. כי also would not then be appropriate. Other explanations, in which neither the accentuation, nor the division of the verse is regarded, we pass over.

V. 6. "And a tabernacle shall be for a shade by day from the heat, and for a protection and for a refuge from storm and rain." The simple meaning is God guards his church from every danger. Affliction and trouble can injure it no more, than the heat and rain can injure him, who is under the covering of a thick tent. That which affords this protection to the church will be the gracious presence of Jehovah, mentioned in the foregoing verse.

We have now only to add a few general remarks.

1. The opinion of those, who as Michaelis and v. d. Palm think

the prophecy was fulfilled in the latter half of Hezekiah's reign, refutes itself. By the צֶמַח יְהוָה can be intended neither according to Michaelis, the Jewish people, planted by God, nor according to v. d. Palm king Hezekiah, but only the Messiah. The error into which these interpreters have fallen is the more manifest, since they themselves adopt the Messianic interpretation of the 20th chapter, which obviously must refer to the same times.

2. The comparison of the prophecy of the Messiah, chap. II, with this shows very clearly, how necessary it is to consider the individual Messianic prophecies only as fragments, which supply each other's deficiencies, since commonly only partial views of the object were exhibited to the spiritual eye of the prophet. As an important deficiency in the representation, chap. II, is supplied by this, in the mention of a personal Messiah, so on the contrary a deficiency in this, is supplied by the predicted participation of the heathen in the blessings of the Messiah's kingdom which is found in that.

Isaiah VII.

The remarkable prophecy contained in this chapter is preceded by a historical introduction. Rezin, king of Damascene Syria, and Pekah, king of Israel, had already under the reign of Jotham combined against the kingdom of Judah, and, about the beginning of the reign of Ahaz, they invaded the land with a formidable army, See 2 Kings 16. 1—6. The unbelieving king Ahaz was greatly alarmed, instead of putting his trust in Jehovah, he believed he could obtain deliverance, only by an alliance with the Assyrians, and resolved to send an embassy to them with presents. Such an alliance threatened the theocracy with the greatest danger, partly because every sin against the theocracy, according to its law of visible retribution, must be expiated by a visible divine judgment, and such a sin would here be committed, since the confidence, which belonged to God alone, would be withdrawn from him, and reposed in men, and partly because in a political point of view, an alliance with a warlike power greatly superior, and intent only on its own aggrandizement, was much more dangerous to the Jewish state, than even the present war. The prophet Isaiah, called by his office to guard the divine rights, and to avert the danger which must spring from their violation, by warnings, admonitions, threatenings and promises, is sent to Ahaz to inspire him with courage and confidence in God, just as he is employed before the city in making the necessary arrangements to cut off the advancing hostile army from its supplies of water. The prophet first seeks to operate upon the mind of the king, who was probably surrounded by his nobles, and a multitude of the common people, by taking with him his son, whose symbolical name, which contained a prediction of the future destinies of the nation, indicated that the fear of the king for the entire ruin of the State was unfounded He then endeavors to make upon the king thus prepared a deeper impression, by the distinct prophecy relating to the present condition of the State, that his enemies would not only entirely fail in their plan of dividing the kingdom of Judah between them, but also that the kingdom of Ephraim was itself near that ruin, which it designed for others, and finally within 65 years would entirely lose its national existence, v 1—9. Ahaz makes no reply, but his whole deportment shows that he is unimpressed by the discourse of the prophet, and determined to persevere in his resolution, not to look to God, but to the Assyrians for deliverance The prophet, commissioned by Jehovah, now offers to confirm the certainty of his declaration by a miraculous sign, to be determined by the king, without any restriction, that there may be no suspicion of imposture. But the unbelieving Ahaz dreads communications from heaven, has already chosen his own mode of deliverance, prefers to rely on human aid alone, and declines the offer of the Lord with a courteous reply, which is even borrowed from the law, Deut. 6:16 : " I will not ask, neither will I tempt the Lord" A sign is then forced upon him, because, as king of Judah, he must see and hear for the whole people, how true and faithful the Lord is * The future appearing of the Messiah was at that time the general belief of the people, but fear, which always renders men inconsistent, caused them to forget this faith, and expect the total subversion of the State. The prophet now gives this wonderful event, as a sign, that the apprehensions of the king and the people are groundless. So certain, he declares, as the Messiah shall hereafter be born of a virgin among the covenant people, so impossible is it that the people, among whom according to former promises he is to be born, and the family from which he is to descend can be brought to ruin The prophet does still more;

---

* V Meyer, Blätter für höhere Wahrheit III. p 101.

he fixes the period, at which the land shall be entirely freed from its enemies. The overthrow of the two hostile kingdoms shall follow in the same space of time, as will elapse between the birth of the Messiah, whom in vision he beholds as present, and his arriving at an age to distinguish good from evil, consequently in about three years, v. 10—16. The prophet had thus far directed all his efforts to convince Ahaz, and the people, that on the side from which they expected danger, nothing was to be feared. he now, however, while the spirit of God disclosed to him the prospect of futurity, announces, that the danger would come from precisely the quarter, from which the unbelieving Ahaz expected deliverance, namely, from the Assyrians. They would invade the land, and lay it waste, v. 17—25. It appears from 2 Kings 16. 7, that the prophet's discourse made no impression upon Ahaz. He sent an embassy with large presents to the king of Assyria. Damascus also, 2 Chron. 28. 5, the capital of Syria, was taken by the king of Assyria, Tiglath Pilezer, after Ahaz had suffered a terrible overthrow from Rezin and Pekah, 2 Kings 16. 9. The land of Israel was laid waste, and a great part of its inhabitants were carried away into captivity, 2 Kings 15. 29. And thus the prediction of the prophet, respecting the destruction of the two allied kings, was fulfilled exactly at the appointed time. But the deliverance, which would have been wrought for Ahaz without further sacrifices, had he believed the prophet and followed his counsel, must be purchased at a heavy price. He was obliged, even at that time, to suffer severe distress from the Assyrians; see 2 Chron. 28. 1—20, and the dependence on Assyria, into which he was brought, formed the first link in that chain of misfortunes, which, partly by the Assyrians, partly by their successors, the Babylonians, fell upon the kingdom of Judah. And thus also was the second part of the prediction of the prophet fulfilled.

The relation of these occurrences in the book of Kings, 2 Kings XVI, is brief. The author of the books of Chronicles had access to more accurate sources of information, and gives a fuller account. He especially mentions the great overthrow, which Ahaz, as a punishment of his unbelief, suffered from Rezin and Pekah, although they were not able to capture Jerusalem; but were obliged to return without accomplishing their object, carrying with them, however, a great multitude of captives, whom, in consequence of the admonition of the prophet Oded, the Iraelites afterwards liberated. Many interpreters have incorrectly supposed, that the two relations refer to different expeditions. The greater fulness of the account in Chronicles does not justify this supposition, and the events follow each other in a perfectly natural order. See the clear representation of this subject by Lightfoot opp. t. I p 111, 2. ed. 1687. At least equally arbitrary is the assumption of Gesenius, that the addition in the book of Chronicles rests on no historical grounds, but is only rhetorical exaggeration *

Gesenius supposes, that the historical part of the passage, v 1—16, was not written by the prophet himself, but by some later collector, or reviser of his prophecies. He relies principally upon the circumstance, that v. 1 is repeated almost verbatim 2 Kings 16: 5. But there is nothing against the supposition, that the verse is here original. This is favored by the fact, that in the books of Kings, instead of the more difficult יָכֹל we find the easier יָכְלוּ. Gesenius objects that the concluding words, "but he could not take the city," do not stand in their proper place in Isaiah, since all that is related, v 2 etc. must have occurred before this final result. But it is easy to assign the reason, why Isaiah might here anticipate it. V. 1 is merely an introduction to the whole narration. It gives in general, the historical circumstances, which occasioned the prophet to appear in public. The following verses relate merely the part which the prophet acted on the occasion, and the narrative closes, as soon as he has fulfilled his commission. The composition of this portion by a later hand is the more improbable, since Gesenius himself asserts, that v. 17 etc. was composed by the prophet, for this paragraph presupposes the foregoing, and is altogether disconnected and unintelligible without it. This much, however, is true, that this portion cannot have been composed by the prophet at the same time with the rest. That it was written at a somewhat later period, appears from its giving the result, verse 1

V. 1. The verb עָלָה *to ascend,* is spoken of going to Jerusalem, even when the region from which the traveller comes does not lie lower than the city; probably on account of its moral elevation. לַמִּלְחָמָה עָלֶיהָ, *for war against it,* i e to make war upon it. The noun instead of the infinitive —" But he could not fight against it ," it is here easy and natural to supply : " with happy result," i e " he

---

* That something more must have occurred than is recorded in the book of Kings, appears from the circumstance, that according to v 15 and 16 the deliverance from the confederate kings and their overthrow, were to take place within an interval of from two to three years

could not take it." Gesenius unjustly objects, that the verb נִלְחַם with עַל never means *to capture*, but only *to besiege*. The word retains this meaning here also, only the connexion, as in numberless instances, gives it a secondary meaning, so e. g. the verb יָשַׁב always retains its meaning *to dwell*, but yet in many passages it receives, by means of the context, the associated idea of security and prosperity. So the noun קֶשֶׁר *conspiracy*, chap. 8. 12, receives from the context the associated idea of *dangerous*. That the allied kings really besieged Jerusalem, appears from 2 Kings 16. 5, which passage cannot naturally be translated otherwise than "they drew towards Jerusalem to lay siege to it and pressed hard upon Ahaz, but could not take the city." The reason why the otherwise victorious kings could not take the city, probably was, that the intelligence of a threatened invasion of their own dominions by the Assyrians left them no time for a protracted siege. The verb יָכֹל stands in the singular, instead of which we should naturally expect the plural. It accommodates itself to the foregoing עָלָה. It may be either taken indefinitely, *one could* for *they could*, or we may supply as its subject, Rezin, the principal of the confederates.

V. 2. נחה is the third person feminine of the verb נוח *quiescere*. It is true, that the noun אֲרָם should here properly have the verb in the masculine, because it stands as a designation of *the people*, but *the land* is frequently put instead of *the people*, and then it requires the feminine. So here *Syria* for *the Syrians*. So likewise וַתְּהִי אֲרָם לַעֲבָדִים 2 Sam. 8. 6. Several interpreters translate: "the Aramaeans rely upon Ephraim." To this it is replied, that Syria was the more powerful, and Israel the weaker kingdom; an objection, which is not entirely removed by the remark of Rosenmüller, that it was possible for the Syrians to capture Jerusalem, only by uniting with the Israelites, since the kingdom of Israel lay between Syria and Judea. The word נוּחַ and עַל properly, *to rest upon any one*, is better explained after the example of Vitringa: so to have one in our power, that he shall be entirely under our influence. See Psalm 125: 3. Numb. 11. 26. Isa. 11: 2. It will then properly designate the relation of the more powerful confederates to the weaker. Chald. אתחבר *societatem iniit*, the LXX συνεφώνησε. Gesenius, after the example of Grotius, inappropriately translates: "The Syrians encamp in Ephraim." It was precisely the confederacy of the two kings, which alarmed Ahaz; v. 4, and that the Syrians should previously have remained long in Ephraim, the country of their allies, is improbable.

Besides, the word נוה with עֹל never occurs in reference to an encamping army, and אפרים cannot well be understood of the land, since ארם must be understood of the people.

V. 3. "Then said the Lord unto Isaiah: Go forth now to meet Ahaz, thou and Shearjashub thy son, at the end of the conduit of the upper pool, in the highway of the fullers' field." We must here first explain the geography. Among the fountains of Jerusalem the principal was the Gihon or Siloah, without the city, on the south-west side of Zion. The water of this sweet and copious fountain, was conducted by water courses into several pools and reservoirs. Two of these pools were called the upper and the lower, probably because the one received its water from the other. From the upper pool there was an aqueduct, תְּעָלָה, probably to another pool, from which the king's garden was watered. Near this aqueduct was the public highway, מְסִלָּה, this was called the way of the washers', or fullers' field, because it led to a field in which the fullers were accustomed to cleanse and dry their fulled cloth. On the one side of this highway was the aqueduct, on the other the fullers' field. The fullers had chosen this place, because it lay near the aqueduct. Comp. Bachiere Beschreibung von Palastina II, 1 § 149 seq. The interpreters here inquire, what could have brought Ahaz to this spot. The most probable answer is, that he went there to see whether by obstructing the fountain, or changing its course he could not deprive his enemies of water. This must have done them essential injury, since water is exceedingly scarce in the neighborhood of Jerusalem. The correctness of this answer is evident from 2 Chron 32: 1—4, where Hezekiah employs the same measure against Sennacherib, and from 2 Kings 18. 17, where Rabshakeh takes possession of this place. But what induced the prophet to seek the king precisely in this spot? Probably the great multitude of people, who were accustomed to assemble there. Besides, the king himself might have gone forth attended by many of his counsellors. It was important that the prophet should execute his commission in the presence of many witnesses. For what purpose did he take with him his son Shearjashub? This could not have been accidental, for then he would not have mentioned a circumstance in itself so unimportant. The reason must lie in the etymology of the name, since the child performs no part on the occasion. The prophet was accustomed to give his sons symbolical names, which had relation to the destinies of the people. See chap VIII. According to Gesenius, the name Shearjashub imports nothing further than *the remnant will repent* But then no reason could be given for his being taken thither. There is rather a double sense intended by the name Shearjashub According to the different meanings of the verb שוב *to return*, and *to repent*, it imports the remnant will return, and the remnant will repent. This double sense also occurs in the passage, chap. 10. 21, 22. The name referred to the prediction often uttered by the prophet, that in consequence of a divine chastisement the people should be carried into exile, but that a part of them would repent and then return King Ahaz and his people now feared nothing less than the total ruin of the State. Isaiah took his son with him ; " as the living evidence of the preservation of the Jewish people amidst the most terrible desolation of the greatest part of them." After he had thus sought to free their minds from the extreme of fear, he endeavored to raise them to joyful hopes, by a direct prophetic annunciation, which showed that the future threatened carrying away of the people was not in the least to be apprehended from the present invasion.

V. 4. " And say unto him " The praeter must often be translated as Imp when an imperative has preceded הִשָּׁמֵר וְהַשְׁקֵט properly *guard thyself and be quiet*. As much as to say, yet only now, or yet only above all things, be quiet. *Vulg vide ut sileas. Guard thyself*, serves to render a command, or prohibition more emphatic. So Judg. 13 4, " beware and drink no wine." Ahaz is admonished to trust in God, who would maintain the cause of his people, and not to show his unbelief by seeking foreign alliances. Calvin · " Jubet quieta et tranquilla esse mente, ut et exterius contineat sese et intus pacato sit animo Illi enim sunt fidei effectus Impietas nunquam est quieta, ubi vero fides est, illic tranquillus est mentis status, nec trepidatur ultra modum " Fear not, and let not thy heart be faint," despond not " before, or on account of, the ends of these two smoking firebrands " The enemies of the king considered in themselves were powerful enough They are therefore here called firebrands. But the extinction of their power and glory was near. The prophet is even on the point of announcing their approaching destruction by the Assyrians He therefore calls them ends of firebrands, which no longer blaze, but only glimmer Chrysostom δαλοὺς ξύλον καλεῖ τοὺς βασιλέας ὁμοῦ μὲν αὐτῶν τὸ σφοδρὸν, ὁμοῦ δὲ τὸ εὐχείρωτον ἐνδεικνύμενος. καὶ γὰρ τὸ καπνιζομένων διὰ τοῦτο προστέθεικε, τουτέστιν ἐγγὺς ὄντων τοῦ σβεσθῆναι λοιπόν—It is by way of contempt, that the king of Israel is not called by his own name. The Hebrews and

Arabians, when they wish to speak reproachfully of any one, omit his proper name, and call him merely the son of this or that, especially when his father was but little known and respected. So Saul names David in contempt the son of Jesse, 1 Sam. 20. 27, 31.

V. 5, 6. The verb קוּץ properly signifies *to experience disgust*, in Hiph. to cause disgust, and then, since disgust and anxiety are related feelings, to make anxious and drive to extremity. Schultens (animadvers. philol. ad h. l.) has shown, that in the Arabic writers, *taedio afficere urbem*, is used precisely of besieging and distressing a city. The suffix in נְקִיצֶנָּה relates to Judah, and not as some interpreters suppose, to Jerusalem understood, as is evident from the following וְנַבְקִעֶנָּה, which can be referred only to Judah. Of the son of Tabeal, whom the confederate kings wished to make regent, we know nothing further, nor is it important that we should. But is there not an incongruity in the assertion, that the kings wished to divide the land between themselves, and yet still set a king over it? Either the former is to be limited. the kings wished to cut off such portions of the country as were most convenient to each of them, and then to place a king over the remainder, or to divide the whole between themselves, by setting up a king who should be subject and tributary to both.

V. 7. Thou hast no occasion to fear on account of these pernicious designs of thy foes. " For thus saith the Lord God, it shall not stand, neither shall it come to pass." Chrysostom. ὅταν γάρ τι μέγα ἀπαγγέλλειν μέλλῃ, τῆς δυνάμεως ἀναμιμνήσκει τοῦ θεοῦ.

V. 8, 9. The sense of these verses is as follows. The revolution which these two kings contemplate, shall not be effected. No changes shall take place. The kingdoms of Damascus and Israel shall not be enlarged by the acquisition of the kingdom of Judah; and Jerusalem shall not become the seat of a Syrian or Israelitish prince. We will, for the present, leave unnoticed the latter part of v. 8, which is controverted. " For the head of Syria shall still be Damascus, and the head of Damascus Rezin, and the head of Ephraim Samaria, and the head of Samaria, the son of Remaliah." The expression, each one shall remain what he is, must be limited to his receiving no enlargement. The kings shall not now succeed in their purpose of enlarging their dominions, and hereafter they shall lose what they at present possess. The prophet subjoins אִם לֹא הַאֲמִינוּ כִּי לֹא תֵאָמֵנוּ, according to Luther's appropriate version, if ye believe not, ye continue not." The verb אָמַן "to be firm," in Niph.

"to be fortified, to have security," in Hiph "to make firm, to declare or believe a thing to be firm. Symm. ἐὰν μὴ πιστεύσητε, οὐ διαμενεῖτε Theodot ἐὰν μὴ πιστεύσητε, οὐδ᾽ οὐ μὴ πιστευθείητε, on which Theodoret remarks· τῆς γὰρ πίστεως ἡ σωτηρία καρπός. A parallel passage is 2 Chron 20 20, when Jehoshaphat says to the distressed people, הַאֲמִינוּ בַּיהוָה אֱלֹהֵיכֶם וְתֵאָמֵנוּ, "believe in the Lord your God so shall ye be secure" You have no occasion, says the prophet, to fear God has resolved to aid you, and defeat the designs of your enemies; no portion of your land shall be taken from you. Nevertheless, in order that you may obtain deliverance from God, you must believe his promise made through me, and place your confidence, not in the help of man, the aid of the Assyrians, but in God alone. Unless you do this, you shall not prosper. The faith, which the prophet here requires, despair of their own strength, and confidence in the divine power, and laying hold of the promise of God, is essentially the same with Christian faith, which is only a modification of it The erroneous interpretation of Grotius is insipid "an ideo non creditis, quia non confirmamini se signo aliquo conspicuo." That of Pluschke is unnatural, who makes these words the commencement of the following verse If ye will not believe without a sensible proof, then ask, Jehovah proceeds to say to Ahaz, a sign from thy God.—We come now to the addition "Within three score and five years shall Ephraim be destroyed, that it be no more a people" יֵחַת fut Niph from the verb חתת. מֵעָם that is מִהְיוֹת עָם. Similar is 1 Sam. 15 23 "He has rejected thee מִמֶּלֶךְ from the king, that is, so that thou art not king" See Ewald's Gramm p. 599. Jerome *desinet Ephraim esse populus.* This passage presents difficulties Hence several interpreters have supposed it to be corrupted, others (as Pluschke, Gesenius) have denied its genuineness. The reasons of the latter are the following 1 "The number 65 does not suit, for the kingdom of Ephraim suffered the first overthrow from Tiglathpilesar, soon after the present invasion, 2 Kings 15 29, 30, the other in about 19—21 years afterwards from Shalmaneser in the 6th year of Hezekiah, when the ten tribes were carried away 2 Kings 17 3, 4" Jerome, and the Jewish commentators long ago perceived this difficulty, and made various efforts to remove it. The explanation, which has been most approved, is that of Archbishop Usher (Annales V et N T ad a. 3327 p. 61. ed. Paris) The kingdom of the ten tribes was indeed greatly reduced by Shalmaneser, but still not deprived of all its inhabitants. That Israelites still remained in the land is clearly manifest from several passages, 2 Chron. 34 6, 7, 33. 2 Kings 23 19, 20 The entire extinction of the state and people of Israel did not take place, till Esarhaddon put new colonists from Babylon, Cuth and other regions in possession of the country, who expelled the ancient inhabitants. Comp 2 Kings 17 24 with Ezra 4. 2, 10 This happened exactly 65 years after it had been predicted by Isaiah After that period, the ten tribes, which had in all probability heretofore lived under their own laws, and unmingled with any other people, never again constituted a state of themselves. The objections of Gesenius to this explanation, are unimportant. Thus, when he says, It cannot be imagined why the prophet should have mentioned that remote, instead of the nearer and far heavier calamity; how much might in this manner be objected against the prophet! He had already announced the nearer calamity by calling the two kings ends of smoking firebrands, and yet he returns to it again He here suddenly casts a look at the final catastrophe of the hostile land, and thus combines in one view the commencement, and the termination of its misfortunes Thou hast no occasion to fear before the king of Israel. In a short time, from two to three years, see v 16, the misfortunes of the kingdom of Ephraim shall commence with the desolation of the land, and its condition shall be continually growing worse and worse, until at last, after 65 years it shall be entirely destroyed. Chrysostom: ἵνα γὰρ μὴ ἀκούων ὁ βασιλεὺς ὅτι μετὰ ἑξήκοντα πέντε ἔτη ἀπολοῦνται λέγῃ πρὸς ἑαυτόν, τί οὖν, ἐὰν νῦν ἡμᾶς λαβόντες τότε ἀπολοῦνται, τί τὸ ὄφελος ἡμῖν; θάρρει φησὶ καὶ περὶ τῶν παρόντων. ἁλώσονται γὰρ τότε παντελῶς νῦν μέντοι πλέον οὐδὲν τῶν οἰκείων ἕξουσι, ἀλλ' ἔσται ἡ κεφαλὴ Ἐφραίμ, κ. τ. λ. It is easy to perceive the design of this distinct annunciation. It must serve to console Ahaz, if he possessed the slightest faith. For although there was not in this later ruin of the kingdom of Israel, any more than in the significant name of Shearjashub, a proper assurance of deliverance from the present danger, yet must its definite prediction serve to lessen his fear of his enemies, whom he regarded as invincible, and also strengthen his confidence in Jehovah, by whose providence all things must be controlled, since he could cause the events of futurity to be foretold with such precision. The prophecy had moreover the general aim of all definite predictions: it was intended to prove that God, the Head of the theocracy, was almighty and infinite in knowledge, and confirm the divine mission of the prophet —But those, who are not satisfied with this solution of the chronological difficulty, and reject the passage as spurious, involve themselves in another far greater. For granting the designation of time to be false, how could it be supposed that any one who was disposed to interpolate would introduce it ? His object could have been no other than to produce authority for the prophet by attributing to him a prediction which had been plainly fulfilled. That the expedient here adopted by Gesenius is unnatural, is so very obvious as to require no further pointing out.

2. "The passage contradicts v. 16 of the chapter, where the depopulation of both hostile lands is represented as soon to take place." But this proves nothing, since the entire extinction of the people as a people, foretold in this verse, is something very different from the mere laying waste of the country.

3. "The use of so definite numbers is contrary to the analogy of all other predictions." This objection is refuted even by v. 16, the genuineness of which is not contested. There also the time of the overthrow is accurately, though not numerically defined. It is, however, true, that as a general rule, the relations of time and space are kept in the back ground in the prophetic vision. But this rule is not without exceptions. The prophets were sometimes instructed also as to the distance of time, by a special divine revelation. Isaiah himself, chap. xx, foretels, by means of a symbolical action, that after three years, the Egyptians and Ethiopians should be conquered by the Assyrians. Chap. 23: 15 he declares that Tyre, 70 years after its fall, should revive and flourish anew. Chap. 38. 5 he announces to Hezekiah, when dangerously ill, that God would add yet 15 years to his life. The seventy years, which according to Jeremiah, should elapse before the termination of the captivity, Gesenius regards as a round number. But as, according to the passages, Jer. 25: 11, 12. 29. 10, etc. no one could doubt that the captivity would last 70 years, so a comparison of Dan. ix and of 2 Chron. 36. 21, shows that the number was then understood as a definite determination of time, and that the captivity actually continued so long. And lastly we appeal to the numbers in Daniel. Even those who deny the genuineness of this book, cannot assert that it is contrary to the analogy of all the prophetic oracles, to give definite numbers.

4. "The words stand in an unsuitable place, and interrupt the necessary succession of the four members." Were this objection entirely correct, it would nevertheless prove nothing more, than the necessity of supposing, with several interpreters, a slight transposi-

tion, and of inserting these words after · "the head of Samaria is the son of Remaliah," v. 10. At any rate, a difficulty which consists in a mere matter of taste, is insufficient to prove the spuriousness or genuineness of a passage. But this difficulty is only apparent. Kocher justly remarks: "Atqui ego certe non nunc sed olim in artificii poetici virtutibus illud extraordinarium et ἀπροσδόκητον esse putavi, quo non leviter afficiantur et capiantur auditorum animi." The discourse of the prophets is not always governed by logical rules, but it follows the change of objects, as they appear in vision. Before the prophet proceeds with the sentence he had begun, and says that the king has at present as little to fear from Israel as from Syria, his view is suddenly directed to the final result of the calamity impending over the kingdom of Israel, and he cannot refrain from immediately announcing it, in order to animate the courage of the king, and prepare him the better to receive the prediction of the nearer deliverance. Had these words been subsequently interpolated, they would certainly not have been placed where they now stand, but at the end of v. 10, where they seem to belong.

But while the objections against their genuineness are thus insufficient, it is sustained by the authority of all the manuscripts, and old translations as well as every thing in general, that is opposed to the supposition that glosses have been incorporated with the text of Isaiah.

V. 10 "Moreover the Lord spake again unto Ahaz," i. e. the prophet spake in Jehovah's name and as commissioned by him.

V. 11. On hearing this discourse Ahaz was entirely silent; but his whole deportment gave the prophet to understand, that it had produced no impression. He therefore says to him: "ask for thyself a sign from Jehovah thy God, ask it from the depth or from the height." Theodoret ἐπειδὴ οὖν ἀπιστεῖς τοῖς εἰρημένοις καὶ ψεῦδος νομίζεις τὴν ἐμὴν ὑπόσχεσιν, ἐγὼ βεβαιώσω θαυματουργίᾳ τοὺς λόγους. Αἴτησον τοίνυν ὑπὲρ βούλῃ σημεῖον, εἴτε οὐράνιον εἴτε ἐπίγειον. Had Ahaz been a true theocratic prince, possessing the spirit of David, if his confidence in the invisible head of the theocracy had not before been unshaken, yet he must at least have believed the word of God by the prophet, even though not assured of its truth by an outward sign. But as such a firm confidence was not to be expected from him, God condescended to his weakness of faith; the prophet proposed to demonstrate the truth of his prediction by a miraculous event, to be designated by Ahaz, from which he might at the same time perceive the omnipotence of God, and the divine mission of the prophet. The word אות *sign*, σημεῖον, signifies in general, *a thing*, or *an event*, or *an action*, which shall serve as an assurance, that something future shall come to pass. 1. In some cases this assurance consisted only in this, that with a nearer event God caused a more remote one to be foretold, which presupposed the former as having taken place. So e. g. as a sign that the deliverance from Egypt should certainly be effected, God gives to Moses, Ex. 3: 12, the assurance that after that event, the people would sacrifice to him on mount Sinai. In this case the sign contains in itself nothing miraculous, but still it is suited to strengthen faith, inasmuch as it shows the certainty of the divine purpose, proves that the promise does not depend on the conduct of those to whom it was imparted, but is unconditional, and finally demonstrates, in general, that the whole of futurity lies open before God. 2. In other cases the assurance given by the sign consists in this, that the bare word is connected with something external, and thereby fitted to make a stronger impression on the senses. Here also there is nothing miraculous. We have an instance of this e. g. when Isaiah, chap. 8. 18, calls his two sons, to whom he had given symbolical names significant of the future destinies of the Jewish people, *signs and wonders*, i. e. striking or remarkable signs. See also Isa. 20. 3, where as a sign of the misfortunes, which in three years would come upon Egypt and Ethiopia, the prophet goes naked and barefoot for that space of time. 3. In another class of signs, an event, in itself considered natural, but one not to be foreseen by human sagacity, is predicted, the occurrence of which at an earlier period then furnishes the proof, that the prediction of a still more distant event will also be fulfilled. In this case, it is not the sign itself, but the prediction of it, which constitutes the miracle, and the evidence. Thus Samuel, 1 Sam. chap x, gives to Saul several signs, that God has destined him to be the king of Israel, e. g. he would meet two men in a place accurately designated, who would inform him, that the lost asses were found; farther on he would meet with three men, the first of whom would be carrying three kids, the next three loaves of bread, and the third a sack of wine, etc. 1 Sam. 2. 34 the sudden death of his two sons is given to Eli as a sign, that all the calamities threatened against his family, should certainly be inflicted. See also Jer. 44. 30. 4. In other cases the assurance was given by the immediate performance of a miraculous action, which transcending the ordinary laws of nature, silenced every doubt, either of the divine mission of the prophet, or of the omnipotence of God, and every suspicion of fraud. Thus e. g. Isaiah chap. 38. 8, caused the shadow on the sun dial of Ahaz to go back ten degrees, as a sign of the fifteen years yet to be added to the life of Hezekiah. Of this kind also were the signs which were granted to Gideon, Judges chap. vi, and also in many respects, the plagues of Egypt. Now it is impossible, that in the present instance, the sign can belong to any other than the last mentioned class. For if the prophet had been unable, or unwilling to give a proper miraculous sign, where is the fitness of the answer of Ahaz? How can the prophet, v. 13, bring against him the charge of offending, not merely men, but also God? Surely the confidence with which the prophet here offers a miracle to the king, must embarrass the opposers of revelation. Pluschke knows of nothing better to oppose to the fact, than the *a priori* objection, that it is unworthy of God, to produce a miraculous natural phenomenon for a limited human purpose, an objection which can have no weight with any one who regards this occurrence, not as standing alone, but as connected with the whole system of the theocracy. הַעֲמֵק שְׁאָלָה properly *make low, ask for, obtain by asking for thyself a miracle to take place on earth.* The form שְׁאָלָה is the Imper. with ה paragog, which is also to be understood after הַגְבֵּהַּ *make high.* According to others, it is the Infin. with ה par. as שִׁמְעָה and סְלָחָה Dan. 9. 19. Aquil. Symm. and Theod. appear to have read שְׁאוֹלָה *to the world below,* instead of שְׁאָלָה and translate βάθυνον εἰς ᾅδην. Many interpreters have followed them. But we do not perceive how Isaiah could give to the king a sign from Hades, unless it were the return of one of the dead; since in other places signs in heaven, and signs on earth are contrasted with each other. See Joel 3. 3. Matt. 16. 1. Isaiah leaves to Ahaz not merely the determination of the place where the sign should be exhibited, as Pluschke erroneously supposes, but also that of the sign itself. Rightly Le Clerc: "quidvis pete in terra vel in coelo fieri remque impetrabis." Theodoret makes the appropriate remark, that both kinds of miracles, which God here proposed to the choice of Ahaz, he performed for his pious son Hezekiah, since in the heavens he produced a phenomenon, which caused the retrocession of the shadow on the sun-dial of Ahaz, and on earth, in a wonderful manner, destroyed the Assyrians, and restored the king to health. Jerome remarks, that among the plagues of Egypt, the

ISAIAH 7:12.

lice, frogs, etc. were signs on earth, while the hail, the fire, and the three days' darkness were signs in heaven.

V. 12 "But Ahaz said, I will ask no sign, and will not tempt Jehovah." Chrysostom. πολλὴ τοῦ θεοῦ συγκατάβασις καὶ τοῦ βασιλέως ἡ ἀγνωμοσύνη. ἔδει μὲν γὰρ αὐτὸν ἀκούσαντα τοῦ προφήτου μηδὲν ἀμφιβάλλειν περὶ τῶν εἰρημένων εἰ δὲ καὶ ἀμφέβαλλε, κἂν σημεῖον λαβόντα πιστεῦσαι, ὅπερ πολλοὶ τῶν παρὰ Ἰουδαίοις πεποιήκασι καὶ γὰρ ὁ θεὸς φιλάνθρωπος ὤν, οὐδὲ τοῦτο παρῃτήσατο παρασχεῖν πολλάκις τοῖς παχυτέροις καὶ χαμαὶ συρομένοις καὶ τῇ γῇ προσηλωμένοις, οἷον ἐποίησε ἐπὶ τοῦ Γεδεών. Ahaz declines the proposal, as it was the weakness of his faith, which had caused the offer, so it was his unbelief, which led him to reject it. Ahaz gives as a reason, that he would not tempt the Lord, appealing to the passage, Deut 6 16./b To tempt God is the same as to put him to the proof; since unbelief requires, that he should exhibit his omnipotence in a visible way, and does not rest satisfied with the former demonstrations of his mercy, and with his word. But Ahaz would not have tempted God by asking for a sign, since one had been offered him by the prophet in the name of God. The answer of Ahaz can be regarded, either as one of bitter scorn, as if he had said, I will not put thy God to the proof in which he will be found wanting, I will not embarrass thee, by taking thee at thy word, or as the language of a hypocrite, who assumes the mask of reverence for God and his command. Thus Chrysostom and Calvin: "fingit se fidem habere verbis prophetae, nec quicquam requirere praeter verbum." The latter is the more correct explanation. For 1. It does not appear from the accounts of Ahaz, that he had despised the God of Israel, as having no existence; but rather that like most of the idolatrous Israelites, he regarded him indeed as *a* God, but only as one among many and not perhaps the most powerful, and therefore believed he must seek the favor of the others likewise. 2 It is highly improbable that Ahaz, granting his total unbelief in the present condition of the State, should have been so imprudent as publicly to insult the religion of the people, and thus rouse one part of them against himself, and discourage another. Had he been a thorough unbeliever, and set aside all regard for the people, Isaiah would hardly have escaped punishment for the reply in v 13; nor would Ahaz have answered the previous annunciation of the prophet, merely by a cautious silence. But here the question arises, why did Ahaz decline the offer of the prophet, why did he not rather ask from him a miracle, which he could not perform, if he were a false prophet, and which, if it should really take place, must put an end to all his anxieties. He may have had various reasons for his conduct. Had the prophet failed in the performance of his promise, not merely the piously disposed portion of the people, but the great mass of those also, who still maintained a certain external conformity to the religion of their fathers, would have been entirely disheartened. Had the prophet on the other hand really performed the miracle, it would not have benefitted Ahaz. In his unbelief, he looked only upon what was human, as certain, and upon all that was of God, as uncertain. He believed that he needed no other aid than that of the Assyrians. Total unbelief darkens the understanding. Had the plainest miracle been wrought, though it might have impressed him at first, he would soon have doubted respecting it against the testimony of his senses, and against all reason. To this must be added another ground, which lies in the religious notions of those times, and which was first particularly pointed out by Michaelis. According to the heathen notions on the subject of religion, every nation had its own gods. Those of one people were more, and those of another less powerful. Isaiah 10· 10, 11. 36. 18—20. 37: 10—13 If now Isaiah had performed a miracle, Ahaz might have believed him to have been sent indeed by the God of his country, who might have had the best disposition, but not the power to defend him. He held it, therefore, in any event, to be the best course, not to comply with the offers of the prophet, and quietly to prosecute the measures once resolved on, thinking perhaps that Isaiah would be deceived by the piously sounding expression. The prophet, however, thoroughly understood the king. Soft and mild before, he now became at once, when the honor of God was concerned, zealous and vehement.

V. 13. "And the prophet said: Hear ye now, O house of David, is it too little for you to provoke men, that you must also provoke my God?" We are here naturally led to inquire, to what the antithesis between God and men can refer. According to some, this is the sense: since it is a sin to grieve men by undeserved suspicion, how much more highly does he offend, who refuses to trust in God, in whose name I speak. So Chrysostom ὁ λέγει τοῦτο ἔστι, μὴ γὰρ ἐμὰ τὰ ῥήματά ἐστι, μὴ γὰρ ἐμὴ ἡ ἀπόφασις εἰ δὲ ἀνθρώποις ἀπιστεῖν ἁπλῶς καὶ ἄνευ λόγου βαρὺ καὶ ἐγκλημάτων ἄξιον, πολλῷ μᾶλλον θεῷ — καὶ τοῦτο δὲ ἔλεγεν ἵνα μάθωσι πάντες, ὅτι ἀνεξαπάτητος ἔμεινεν ὁ προφήτης, οὐκ ἀπὸ τῶν ῥημάτων παραλογιζόμενος

ISAIAH 7:13

τῶν εἰρημένων, ἀλλ' ἀπὸ τῶν ἐν τῇ διανοίᾳ τοῦ Ἀχαζ φέρων τὴν ψῆφον. But the prophet would then have said nothing, which he could not have said before, since Ahaz put no faith in the bare prediction, and yet the address of the prophet must especially refer to the rejection of the proffered miraculous sign. According to others (Vitringa, Rosenmuller, Pluschke) the sense is this: thou despisest not me, not men, but God; but according to this explanation also, the antithesis is not quite clear. The true interpretation seems rather to be the following. When Ahaz before refused to believe the bare prediction of the prophet, his transgression was more excusable, as Isaiah had not given an outward proof of his divine mission, so Ahaz in a measure sinned only against men, against the prophet, by unjustly suspecting him of falsely pretending to a revelation from God. Therefore Isaiah remained mild and calm. But when Ahaz rejected the offered sign, the case was changed. God himself was insulted by this rejection of his offer, through unbelief. Similar is the expression of Calvin: "Putabant sibi negotium esse cum hominibus. Atque ita doctrinam dei extenuare volunt. Cum igitur ita loqui solerent, propheta per concessionem homines vocat, qui sacrosancto docendi verbi munere fungebantur. Esto vos me hominem mortalem esse dicitis. Tale apud vos est judicium de prophetis dei. Sed an parum est, nos molestia afficere, nisi etiam deo molesti sitis? Contemnitis deum, qui mirabilis potentiae suae signum aliquod vobis dare paratus est." בית דויד as a collective takes the plural. There must have been in attendance upon the king other princes of the house of David, who were partakers with him in the guilt of unbelief. The appellation seems to have been chosen by design. Calvin: "eos hoc nomine vocat non honoris, sed contumeliae causa. Oblique enim defectionis ipsos accusat, quod degenerassent a pietate Davidis. Quod igitur ipsis honori esse debuerat, in gravem ignominiam cedit." הַמְעַט מִכֶּם not *is it a small thing to you*, but *is it too small*, or *too little for you*. מן is comparative. See Ges. Lehrg p. 690. The verb הַלְאָה means properly *to weary*, then *to make impatient, to reduce to extremity*; here spoken of God after the manner of men. The prophet says emphatically *my God*, the God whose true servant I am, and in whom ye hypocrites have no longer any portion.

Of v. 14—16, we give in the first place, that explanation, which appears to us to be the true one, and afterwards those which differ from ours, with the reasons for and against them.

V 14. Ahaz had refused the proffered sign, and the prophet was compelled to relinquish the hope of raising him to confidence in Jehovah. But he must have been desirous, that the deliverance should not be regarded when it came, as the work of chance, but ascribed to the mercy of the Supreme Ruler of the theocracy, and that the confidence of the pious in HIM should be confirmed. He therefore gives a sign, even against the will of Ahaz, whereby the confidence of every true member of the theocracy, in the prediction already given concerning the deliverance from the confederated kings, must be strengthened. I behold, he declares, the wonderful event of futurity, the birth of a divine Redeemer of a virgin. How can ye who expect him, fear so inconsistently, that the State will go to ruin? Kocher: "Ideo dabit dominus ipse vobis signum h. e. etiam nolentibus dabit, sed non impiis, quibus convincendis aliud sensusque feriens et conveniebat, et oblatum, sed per malitiam contumaciamque contemtum rejectumque erat. Ergo piis dabit—stabit deus promissis, implebit fidem, itaque et Davidis domus perstabit, neque de ea triumphaturus hostis, nedum eam destructurus est." "Therefore behold Jehovah himself will give you a sign: behold the virgin has conceived and bears a son, and she calls his name Immanuel." The particle הִנֵּה is used demonstratively, and often indeed, when the prophets pointed to objects, which they beheld, not by an external, but internal perception. The article also in הָעַלְמָה probably serves to designate the particular virgin, who was present to the inward perception of the prophet, the virgin *there*, unless we should choose to explain it with others, the virgin whom ye know. Abarbanel, from ignorance of the nature of prophecy, has derived an objection against the Messianic interpretation from הִנֵּה which refers to the present. Chrysostom better understood the passage. He says: οὐκ εἶπεν ἰδοὺ παρθένος, ἀλλ᾽ ἰδοὺ ἡ παρθένος, καὶ μετὰ ἀξιώματος προφήτῃ πρέποντος τὸ ἰδού. Μόνον γὰρ οὐκ ὁρῶντος ἦν τὰ γινόμενα καὶ φανταζομένου καὶ πολλὴν ἔχοντος ὑπὲρ τῶν εἰρημένων πληροφορίαν. τῶν γὰρ ἡμετέρων ὀφθαλμῶν ἐκεῖνοι σαφέστερον τὰ μὴ ὁρώμενα ἔβλεπον. The word עַלְמָה is derived in different ways. The older interpreters for the most part derive it from the verb עלם *to conceal*. A virgin is called *one concealed*, in respect to the manners of the East, where virgins are compelled to lead a life of seclusion. Thus Jerome: "Almah non solum puella, vel virgo, sed cum ἐπιτάσει virgo abscondita dicitur et secreta, quae numquam virorum patuerit aspectibus, sed mag-

Isaiah 7 14.

na parentum diligentia custodita sit." But it is far more appropriate to make a comparison with the Arabic غَلَم *to grow up,* from which comes غَلَام *adolescens,* and غَلَامَة *adolescentula,* as well as the Syriac ܐܰܠܶܡ *to grow up,* from which is derived ܥܠܰܝܡܬܐ *virgin.* After the example of the Jews, recent interpreters choose to assert, that עַלְמָה does not here designate a virgin, but only a young woman. Their reasons, which may be easily refuted, are as follows: 1. "The etymology shows, that the idea intended to be conveyed is not that of pure virginity, nor of the married or unmarried state." Here, as well as throughout this whole inquiry, the notion of a pure virgin, and that of an unmarried woman, are blended together. The former is not indeed required by the etymology of the word, but the latter certainly is, for עלמה derived from עלם *to grow up, to become marriageable,* can mean nothing else, than puella nubilis, a marriageable young woman. Jerome strikingly remarks, and in accordance with the etymology, that עלמה does not mean a virgin in general, but a virgin in early youth. 2. "For a pure virgin the Hebrews had another name, בְּתוּלָה. But it is highly improbable, that they should have had two entirely synonymous expressions for the same thing. But even בתולה itself, Joel 1. 8, is used for *a young married woman.*" This objection also is removed, if we only separate the ideas, which have been confounded, of a pure virgin, designated by בתולה, and of a young unmarried woman, designated by עלמה. In the passage quoted from Joel it is extremely doubtful, whether a young widow laments the death of her husband, or a virgin that of her betrothed. Even in the former case the passage would prove nothing. For we are not here permitted, without consulting the usage of the language, to draw a conclusion from a single word of similar import. Thus in German poetry, perhaps in a single instance, *jungfrau* could be used for *junge frau,* but it would occur to no poet to use *dirne* or *fraulein,* when speaking of a married woman. 3. "The usage of the language also is against the meaning *pure virgin.* If this meaning is not necessarily excluded in Ps. 68 26 and Canticles 6 8, it cannot possibly be the true one in Prov 30. 19." This objection also entirely fails of its object. We concede that in the cited passage of Proverbs, according to the most probable interpretation, the idea of a pure virgin is not expressed. But what is gained by this, since we do not claim for the word the sense of unspotted purity, but only that of the unmarried state. But the usage of the language most decidedly favors the latter meaning. This is undeniably the meaning in all the six places where the word occurs, besides this in Isaiah, viz., Gen 24. 3. Ex. 2. 8. Ps. 68: 26. Cant. 1. 3. 6. 8. Prov. 30. 19. In Arabic and Syriac also, the corresponding words are never used in reference to married women, and Jerome remarks: "lingua quoque Punica proprie virgo עלמה appellatur." 4. "The Jewish translators and interpreters assert, that עלמה means a young married woman. Aquila, Symm., Theod. translate νεᾶνις." This however can prove nothing. They thus translated from polemic zeal against the Christians, in order to wrest from them a proof passage. The LXX, who had no such motive, rendered עלמה by παρθένος.—This then is the result of our investigation · the word עלמה signifies *a young unmarried woman*, without having, in itself considered, any direct reference to unspotted chastity, which however in this connexion is of course implied.—The form הָרָה is not as Rosenmuller supposes a participle of the verb הוּר, which does not occur, but the feminine of the verbal adjective הָרָה *pregnant*. We may translate, either the virgin is pregnant, or the virgin becomes pregnant and brings forth a son. The participle יוֹלֶדֶת, standing for the present, as well as הִנֵּה, shows that the event, which was to take place in future times was present to the prophet.—The form קָרָאת may be 3d fem. for קָרְאָה, as in Jer. 44: 23. See Gesen. Lehrg. p. 417. Ewald Gram. p. 452. But still there is no objection to regard it as 2d fem. thou namest, as an apostrophe to the virgin, and then it becomes entirely regular. It was not unusual among the Hebrews for the mothers to give the names to the children. Gen. 4. 1, 25. 19· 37. 29: 32. There is, therefore, no good reason to suppose, with many of the older interpreters, that by attributing to the mother the giving of the name, it is indicated, that the child should have no human father. *She will name*, is moreover, in reference to the manner of that age, the same as, *they shall name*, or *he shall be named*. Thus Matth. καλέσουσι, Jerome *vocabitur*. We are not then to suppose, that the child should actually receive the name Immanuel as a proper name, since according to the usage of the prophets, and especially of Isaiah, that is often ascribed to a person or thing as a name, which belongs to him in an eminent degree, as an attribute. See chap. 9. 5. 61. 6. 62. 4. The name Immanuel may be understood in different ways. Several interpreters, as Jerome, e. g. referring to

Ps. 46. 8, 12. 89 25, find in it nothing more than the divine aid and protection. According to others, on the contrary, the name must relate to the assumption of our nature by God in the person of the Messiah, i. e. God become man. Thus Theodoret: δηλοῖ δὲ τὸ ὄνομα τὸν μεθ' ἡμῶν θεόν, τὸν ἐνανθρωπήσαντα θεόν, τὸν τὴν ἀνθρωπείαν φύσιν ἀνειληφότα θεόν. So likewise Irenaeus, Tertullian, Chrysostom, Lactantius, Calvin, Rosenmuller, and many others. The two interpretations are consistent with each other; indeed the prophet himself seems to have intended a double sense in the name. The name *God with us*, is indeed in the lower sense only a designation of the divine aid, which should be granted through the Messiah, but in the higher sense, it refers to God's becoming man in his person, by which he was first truly "with us." Chrysostom well observes: τότε γὰρ μάλιστα μεθ' ἡμῶν ὁ θεὸς γέγονεν ἐπὶ τῆς γῆς ὀφθεὶς καὶ τοῖς ἀνθρώποις συναναστρεφόμενος, καὶ τὴν πολλὴν ἐπιδεικνύμενος περὶ ἡμᾶς κηδεμονίαν. This then is the import of the words: She will call his name *God with us*; consequently, he will be fully entitled to this name, since in him and through him, God will be with us. That this higher meaning really belongs to the passage, plainly appears from the parallel passage, chap 9 5, where the Messiah is called אֵל גִּבּוֹר *the mighty God*, and where this eternal existence, and divine glory are contrasted with his temporal birth.

According then to the explanation now given, it is foretold in this verse, that the Messiah should hereafter be born of a virgin among the covenant people, and reveal God by a visible manifestation. Traces of the belief in the birth of the great Redeemer of a virgin— not to mention the obscure intimations in the prediction concerning the seed of the woman, who should bruise the serpent's head, are found in Micah 5. 2: "he will give them up, till she who shall bare hath borne" Nay more, traces of this belief are found among nearly all nations, and in all the ancient religions, especially those of Asia. See the collections in Huet demonstratio Evangelica prop. 9 cap. 9 § 4, p 693 ed. Amstelod 1680 ej quaestiones Alnetanae II, 15 p. 188 seq. Rosenmuller in the article. uber die Geburt des Heilandes durch eine Jungfrau in Gabler's Journal f. theol. Litter. II, 2 p. 353—67, 1806, and in the second ed of his Comm I p 302 seq. Gesenius on the passage

The arguments, for the correctness of the interpretation we have given, besides those hereafter to be adduced in opposition to that of the Jews and the recent interpreters, are chiefly the following

1. Were there no other evidence, the passage in Matt. 1 22, would alone be sufficient proof. Matthew, after he had related the miraculous conception of Christ, says: τοῦτο δὲ ὅλον γέγονεν, ἵνα πληρωθῇ τὸ ῥηθὲν ὑπὸ τοῦ κυρίου διὰ τοῦ προφήτου κ. τ. λ. According to the Evangelist, therefore, the prophecy can be referred only to Mary, the mother of Jesus. That Matthew by no means intended to speak in the way of accommodation, but has thus explained it in the strictest sense, is conceded almost unanimously by the recent interpreters. Pluschke justly observes, that ἵνα cannot here, as in many other cases, well be taken as ἐκβατικὸν, but must according to the foregoing τοῦτο δὲ ὅλον γέγονεν, be taken τελικῶς. It was one design of the events of the evangelical history, to place in a clear light the faithfulness and omniscience of God, by means of the exact accomplishment of the predictions of the Old Testament. See Matt. 26: 54, where Christ in order to show the necessity of his death, says: πῶς οὖν πληρωθῶσιν αἱ γραφαί; ὅτι οὕτω δεῖ γενέσθαι. It is true, that in order to invalidate this argument, an appeal has been made to the fact, that Matthew on other occasions quotes passages of the Old Testament, where there is not a fulfilment of prophecy but only a resemblance. Thus, e. g. chap. 2. 15 where a passage of Hosea, which certainly relates only to the people of Israel, is referred to Christ. But the difference in the forms of quotation is to be well considered. Chap. 2 15, we have barely ἵνα πληρωθῇ, which, as we have already seen in the general introduction, does not of itself justify the assumption that the prophet designed to give the proper explanation of the quoted passages, but here Matthew shows by the preceding τοῦτο δὲ ὅλον γέγονε, that he intends to give an interpretation, not merely to make an allusion. Further, in the passage chap. 2· 15, the simile is obvious; as under the Old Testament, the church of God in its members was called out of Egypt, so was it under the New Testament in its head, here, on the contrary, if we reject the Messianic explanation, the simile also disappears. For what point of connexion is there between the two occurrences; the wife of the prophet, according to the course of nature, conceives, and brings forth a son, who serves as a sign and symbol of the deliverance; and Mary a pure virgin miraculously conceives the Messiah, who accomplishes this deliverance? The *tertium comparationis* must surely, in every event, lie in the conception by a virgin, who still remained such.*

---

* Appositely Rosenmüller in Gabler's Journal l. c. "Such a mere fanci-

Isaiah 7. 14

2. That the Messianic interpretation was the prevailing one among the prophet's contemporaries, and therefore the true one, is evinced by the parallel passage in Micah 5 2, already quoted. Micah there first predicts, v. 1, the birth at Bethlehem of him, who shall be ruler in Israel, whose goings forth have been from of old, from everlasting. He then proceeds to announce the impending calamities of the people, " in the mean time, shall he give them up until she who shall bear, hath borne." The expression " who shall bear," presupposes the miraculous birth of the Messiah and evidently refers to a definite prediction, which had gone before Rosenmuller l c. "She is not indeed expressly called a virgin, but that she is so, is self-evident, since she shall bear the hero of divine origin, (from everlasting) and consequently not begotten by a mortal Both predictions throw light upon each other, Micah discloses the divine origin of the person predicted, Isaiah the wonderful manner of his birth " There is also a striking similarity in other respects between the two prophecies. According to both, severe sufferings shall precede the birth of the child Isa 7. 17, which shall terminate with his appearing; in both, the divine dignity is placed in contrast with the temporal birth

3. The Messianic prediction, chap. 9 5, so strikingly resembles this, as to oblige us to assume, that the subject of both is the same. " Behold a virgin has conceived, and brings forth a son"—" unto us a child is born, a son is given " " They shall call his name Immanuel," *Deus in terra*—he shall " be called Wonderful, Counsellor, Mighty God, Father of Eternity, Prince of peace."

The Messianic interpretation has been the prevailing one in the Christian church in all ages. It was followed by all the fathers and other Christian expositors till the middle of the 18th century; only some of them held, that besides its higher reference to the Messiah, it related in a lower sense to an event in the time of the prophet. Among the modern interpreters, it has been defended by Lowth, Koppe, Kocher, Dereser, Rosenmuller (ed. II.), Kleuker (biblische Sympathieen. Schleswig 1820), and Meyer (Blatter fur hohere Wahrheit VI. p 92—114.) The principal objections, which, after

---

ful application is in itself improbable, since it would here be without an aim, where that which was wonderful and divine in the event related, was both demonstrated and heightened, by the very circumstance of its being predicted by a prophet."

the example of the Jews, Isenbiehl, Gesenius and others, have brought against this interpretation, are the following

1. "It was the main object to give to the unbelieving Ahaz a sign, which would be immediately accomplished, and which lay as it were before his eyes. How could this be effected by the promise of the miraculous birth of the Messiah, which occurred many centuries afterwards? How could Ahaz receive a promise to be fulfilled at a later period, as a pledge of an event previously to take place?" It is of the highest importance here to observe, that although the prophet directed his discourse in the first instance to Ahaz and his house, as the representatives of the people, yet the sign was intended, not so much for him, as for the people in general, and especially for the pious portion of them. Chrysostom. καὶ φησι τὸ σημεῖον οὐχὶ τῷ Ἄχαζ δίδοσθαι λοιπόν, ἀλλὰ τῷ κοινῷ τῶν Ἰουδαίων δήμῳ. Παρὰ μὲν γὰρ τὴν ἀρχὴν πρὸς αὐτὸν τὸν λόγον ἀπέτεινεν, ἐπειδὴ δὲ ἀνάξιον ἐκεῖνος ἑαυτὸν ἀπέφηνε, τῷ κοινῷ τοῦ λαοῦ διαλέγεται. They feared at that time the total ruin of the State, as appears from the prophet's taking along with him his son Shearjashub, as well as from the purpose of the enemy to effect it, sufficiently manifest in v. 6. The prophet now reminds the people of their firm faith in the coming of the Messiah, and shows the inconsistency between this faith, and their fear of the entire subversion of the State. Since the king, he declares, has despised the miracle offered to him by me, God reminds you, through me, of that great event of the future, which is well known, though now forgotten by you, the wonderful birth of the Messiah. Let this be to you a sign of deliverance. For as certainly, as that shall take place, so entirely shall the State still be preserved. Thus Theodoret ἐπειδὴ ἐδεδίεσαν τῶν πολεμίων προσβολὴν καταλύσειν ἀπειλούντων τὴν Δαβιτικὴν βασιλείαν, διαγκωνίως διδάσκει, ὡς ἀδυνάτοις ἐπιχειροῦσι Δεῖ γάρ φησι φυλαχθῆναι τὸ Δαβιτικὸν γένος, ἕως ἂν ἔλθῃ ὁ ἀπόκειται, Gen. XLIX. And lastly, as to the objection, that the promise of the Messiah could be no assurance of safety, since he was not to appear till many centuries later, were it just, it would apply with equal force to all the predictions of the Messiah. Yet Jeremiah likewise, and Ezekiel consoled the people, when they were carried away into exile, by predicting the future restoration of the theocracy to a far more glorious condition through the Messiah, whose appearance was nevertheless many centuries distant. Indeed the time of his coming was not accurately known to the prophets themselves. when

they spoke of him, they beheld him present; see chap 9. 5: "unto us a child is given, a son is born," and though they did not presume definitely to fix the time of his appearing, which God had withheld from them in order that the prediction might have the more effect, yet they could scarcely have supposed, that it would be so long deferred. Finally, had they known the long time which must elapse before his coming, still the promise of the Messiah would always have been to the Jews a sure pledge, that their State could not be utterly ruined. We now proceed briefly to reply to some objections of Isenbiehl against this method of removing the first mentioned doubt. "The prophet here proposes truths to be remembered by the people, which needed confirmation. The sign was the ground of their conviction, and therefore must have been clear and plain." This objection is set aside by the well established fact, that the future birth of the Messiah, and the redemption of the people through him, were at that time the general belief It appears from the manner in which the contemporaries of the prophet, Hosea 3: 5, Micah v, predict the Messiah, that they also supposed him to be known to the people. This being the case, the truth predicted must have been clear and intelligible to them. "If the Messiah is here the subject of discourse, then nothing new is said to the house of David; consequently we have here neither a prediction, nor a sign, but only a rhetorical motive" It is true, that what is here said is new, only so far as what was old was delivered anew by God to the prophet, and confirmed anew by divine authority Every prediction of the Messiah was at the same time both old and new. Every immediate disclosure respecting future things, is a prophecy, whether they may have been known before, or not. According to the remarks already made, a sign is any thing, that seems to confirm the belief, that a future event will actually take place. But the promise of the Messiah not merely recalled to mind, but confirmed anew by divine authority, was perfectly suited to the purpose, at least in regard to that part of the people, who held the prophet as an ambassador of God, and to them particularly was his discourse directed "The ground of consolation suits all other circumstances equally well, and is too general The Messiah could be born of the family of Ahaz, without the preservation of the Jewish State in its existing condition, and the continuance of Ahaz on the throne. The Babylonish exile occurred, and yet the Messiah was not born Isaiah then would have employed a sophistical argument." The ground of consolation contained in this verse is indeed general. As the prophet, by taking with him his son Shearjashub, *the remnant shall return*, had endeavored, before he announced deliverance from the present calamity, to remove the fear of the total ruin of the State, though its inhabitants might indeed suffer a temporary captivity, so here also he prepared the mind for the prediction in v. 15, 16, of a speedy deliverance from the present danger, by first showing, that the apprehension of the entire ruin of the kingdom was groundless; a people to whom, though at a remote period a divine Redeemer should be sent, must even at present be under the peculiar care of God's providence.

2 "The biblical idea of a אות every where else, is entirely disregarded by this interpretation. It makes אות refer to a future event, but according to the usage of the language elsewhere, אות is a second predicted event, whose earlier fulfilment then becomes a certain pledge of the fulfilment of the former, on which it properly depends." We will not here repeat what we have said before concerning the import of אות. This objection is already sufficiently refuted by the single passage in Ex. 3. 12, in which, as well as in that before us, a future occurrence is constituted a sign. It there reads: "God said, I will be with thee, and this shall be to thee the sign that I have sent thee, when thou hast led my people out of Egypt, ye shall sacrifice to God on this mountain," that is, you may infer the certainty of the deliverance of the people, to be effected through you, from the circumstance, that after the happy accomplishment of the exodus from Egypt, you shall present offerings to me upon this mountain. See further Isaiah 37. 30. "And this shall be a sign to thee, (of deliverance from the Assyrians) eat this year that which groweth of itself, the next year, what springs up again wild; the third year sow and reap, plant vineyards, and eat the fruit thereof," i. e ye shall as surely be delivered from the Assyrians, as ye shall, etc. Moreover the future event, on which, in this case, the certainty of a present result was grounded, was regarded as so certain by the people, (which was by no means the case in the two instances cited) that an appeal to it must have been no less convincing, than the present performance of a miracle.

3 "The representations of misfortune which follow, v. 17, etc. do not correspond with so magnificent a prediction." This objection is no doubt the weakest of all. Every one who has only a bare superficial acquaintance with the prophetic writings, knows that they every where predict that the coming of the Messiah shall be preced-

ed by severe divine judgments and afflictions of the people. It is only necessary to compare chap. iv, ix, xi, and Micah v, where the description of the divine judgments precedes, and chap. ii, where, as in the present instance, the prediction of deliverance by the Messiah is given before the denunciation of the judgments, which should precede it.

4 "The relation, chap. viii, so nearly resembles this, that if the Messianic interpretation is there plainly untenable, we are tempted to believe, that it must be here also. The name and the birth of a child there, as well as here, serve as a sign of deliverance from Syrian domination. If we must there understand by the mother of the afflicted child, the wife of the prophet, and by the child one of his sons, so also must this same interpretation here be correct." This passage, far from proving the point intended, serves rather to refute the notion, that Immanuel was one of the prophet's sons. For it is not probable, that the prophet would have given two of his sons symbolical names which related to one and the same event; on the contrary, it is entirely suitable to the Messianic interpretation, that a visible sign should have been added to the invisible one, which consisted solely of the promise. Meyer observes: "the oral, indefinite sign was not sufficient; it should also be connected with and receive its visible seal, from a matter of fact." The relation differs also in many respects widely from that before us, and certainly has not the same resemblance to it, as chap. 9. 5—here the mother of the child is called עלמה, whereby only a virgin can be signified, there נביאה, here we have the bare annunciation of the birth of a child, there a full account in which we are told, that the prophet received direction from Jehovah to give his child a name significant of the speedy ruin of Israel and Syria. He further made a record of the transaction, and took credible witnesses, who after the fulfilment should testify to the day on which it was composed, and thereby confirm it; he moreover went in unto the prophetess and she conceived and bore a son, and lastly, in the passage before us, the mother names the child, then the father.

5 "Chap. 8. 18, where the prophet says that his sons are for signs and wonders in Israel, is in favor of the explanation, that 'his child was a son of the prophet and not the Messiah.'" But if Immanuel were not reckoned among the sons of the prophet, there would yet remain Shearjashub and Mahar-shalal-hash-baz, whom the prophet seems to have before him in the above mentioned passage.

V. 15, 16. "Milk and honey shall he eat until he knows to reject the evil and choose the good.—Nevertheless before the child shall know to reject the evil and choose the good, the land shall be forsaken, before whose two kings thou fearest." The explanation of these two verses caused the older interpreters much difficulty. The majority supposed, that (v. 15) the true humanity of the Redeemer, who should be born, is announced. The name Immanuel indicates the *divine*, the eating of milk and honey the human nature of the Messiah. Milk and honey were the common food of young children. The sense of the verse would then be · He shall be brought up and gradually come to maturity, like other children. Thus Jerome · "Dicam et aliud mirabilius : ne eum putes in phantasmate nasciturum, cibis utetur infantiae, butyrum comedet et lac." Calvin "ne existimemus ipsum hic quoddam spectrum imaginari, signa humanitatis declarat, quibus demonstrat Christum revera carnem nostram induisse." In like manner, Irenaeus, Chrysostom, Basil, and lastly Kleuker and Rosenmuller, the latter of whom regards this verse as a parenthesis. But this forced explanation is liable particularly to the objection, besides several others, that it is here entirely out of place to announce the true humanity of the Messiah, since it was already implied in the prediction that he should be born of a virgin ; and that, in an unnatural manner it interrupts the connexion between the 14th and 16th verses. These interpreters, for the most part, assume a change of the subject in v. 16. By נער Immanuel is not to be understood, but in the opinion of some, (as Kleuker) Shearjashub, who accompanied the prophet, while according to others, no particular child is designated by the word, but it is said in general terms, the desolation of the hostile land shall take place in a shorter time than that, which elapses between the birth of a child and the developement of his moral powers. Thus Calvin. But the supposition of a change of the subject cannot be admitted ; since one and the same characteristic, the ability to distinguish between good and evil, is ascribed to the subject in both verses. The sudden transition is moreover altogether abrupt and unnatural. Others, as J. D. Michaelis, refer v 16 also to the Messiah and resort to a *jamdudum :* before the Messiah comes to years of discretion, the land shall have been *long* forsaken. But this interpretation is so manifestly unnatural, that it need not be refuted. How then is it possible to make these two verses harmonize with the preceding? How can the prophet make the developement of the powers of a child, who should be born 700 years later, synchronize with the deliverance of the land from its enemies, which took place in a little time after his prediction? Rosenmuller has remarked, that the prophet really supposed the Messiah would be born in his time. But this expedient, at least as he understood it, is inadmissible. It is true, that the time of the Messiah's appearance was concealed from the prophets, but it was for this very reason, that they refrained from any positive determination of it. We can however show from sure grounds that the prophet did not expect the Messiah to appear so soon. For the sufferings to be inflcted by the Assyrians, foretold v. 17 etc., must plainly follow the deliverance from the Israelites and Syrians, and precede the appearing of the Messiah. And thus is it also in the remaining passages. It is true that in the vision of the prophet, the Messiah always appears as present, but at the same time, he every where announces that before his coming, heavy divine judgments and severe afflictions should overwhelm the people. According to chap. xi, the royal family of David shall then be fallen into entire obscurity, and a great part of the people be scattered throughout all lands. The view of Vitringa, Lowth, and Koppe, comes nearest the truth. According to them, the prophet employs the period between the birth of the Messiah, and the developement of his faculties, as a measure of time for the complete deliverance of the land from its enemies. It is of the utmost importance to observe, that v. 15 and 16 were spoken by the prophet in the same ἔκστασις as that, in which he beheld the Messiah v. 14, as present. His vision here, as in all other cases, has no concern with time. As the child appears before his prophetic eye already born, as in chap. 9. 5, he borrows from him his measure of time. He designs to say, that within the space of about three years, the two hostile kingdoms would be overthrown. This he expresses, by saying, that the same space of time would elapse before that event, as between the birth of the child, which he then beheld as present, and his coming to the age of discretion. Having made these general remarks, we now proceed to an explanation of particulars. It is asked in the first place, what we are to understand by eating milk (חמאה not butter, but thick and curdled milk, and honey.) Several interpreters take this as a designation of wealth, and abundance. Pluschke: "when the child shall have come to years of discretion the treasures of peace, abundance, and luxury, shall again be found in Jerusalem." But these interpreters have confounded the two very different modes of expression, viz. to eat milk and honey, and to flow with milk and honey; and v. 22 plainly shows, that the eating of milk and honey must be regarded as a consequence of a general devastation of the country. The fields being laid waste, those who remained must lead a nomadic life, and be sustained by wild honey, and the produce of their herds, which would now be more numerous than before in consequence of the great abundance of pasturage. The word לְדַעְתּוֹ several translators render. 'when he shall know.' Others more correctly, 'until he shall know.' The phrase, 'to know to choose the good and refuse the evil,' signifies the very commencement of moral consciousness in the child, at the age of from two to three years Deut 1: 39 Jonah 4 11. The verbs מָאַס and בָּחַר are construed with the accusative or more frequently with בְ of the person. The sense of the verse therefore is the existing generation, whom this child, whose birth was viewed by the prophet as present, represented, would not for some years to come obtain the quiet possession of the country, but would be obliged to live on the produce of their herds, which would find abundant pasturage in the devastated land. Next v. 16, follows the prediction, that nevertheless before the close of this period, the ruin of the two hostile kings, and the desolation of their lands (by the Assyrians) would ensue. So that afterwards, the products of the country which would in the mean time be cultivated, could again be quietly enjoyed. כִּי in the sense of *yet*, as chap 8: 23   קוּץ with מִפְּנֵי, *to be distressed, to fear before any one.* The land will be forsaken, that is, it will be laid waste, and deprived of its inhabitants   אֶרֶץ embraces here, at the same time, the land of Israel, and Syria, as is evident from the following words : *before whose two kings thou fearest.*

The prophet had thus far predicted only joyful events. He had foretold the deliverance of the land from both the hostile kings, and as a pledge for the fulfilment of his prophecy, he had appealed to a still more joyful event to be expected in future times. He now pauses for a while, as appears from the absence of a connecting word between v 16 and 17. His vision is filled with mournful images. New foes, the Assyrians and Egyptians, inundate the land, and convert it into a desert.

Gesenius chooses to think, that this prophecy of the desolation of Judea by the Assyrians and Egyptians was never fulfilled, and is to be regarded as merely a prophetic threatening. His argument is, that the distress brought upon the Jews by Tiglath-pileser in the reign of Ahaz, in respect to which comp. 2 Chron. 28: 20 etc, was too inconsiderable to be regarded as the fulfilment of this prediction He asserts, that we are not to seek for its fulfilment after the time of

Ahaz, since it is expressly said: "Jehovah will bring upon *thee.*" But to this objection it may be justly replied, that Ahaz is not here mentioned as an individual, but as sustaining the royal dignity, in contradistinction to the people. 'Upon thee, and upon thy people,' is equivalent to. 'upon the people, and their king.' Thus, even when divine judgments, which are not to be inflicted for centuries, are threatened, it is always said 'Jehovah will bring upon you, etc.' although none of the sinners present would live till the prediction should be fulfilled. And this is entirely consistent with the peculiarity of the prophetic vision, already often referred to, that every thing appeared to the prophets as present. Transgression, and its punishment, were exhibited to their spiritual vision, without their perceiving in general the distance of time between them. And when the punishment had several gradations, they were left unnoticed, because its commencement and completion were blended in one picture. For an example, we refer to Jer. 50. 51, where the capture of Babylon by Cyrus, and its final and total ruin, are combined in one description. So here the prediction of the approaching calamity to be caused by the Assyrians, embraces the whole chain of misfortunes, which began with Tiglath-pileser, and ended with Nebuchadnezzar. (The king of Babylon is expressly called, 2 Kings 23. 29, the king of Assyria, and the best Greek writers also take Assyria in a wider sense.) It was the Assyrians, from whom the Jews thenceforth suffered most. The wretchedness also is included, which Sennacherib under Hezekiah, and Esarhaddon under Manasseh, brought upon the land.

The prophet intimates, that the calamity to be inflicted by the Egyptians would not be so great, since he does not mention it in v. 17, but speaks solely of the Assyrians, upon which Gesenius unjustly grounds his assertion that the words את מלך אשור are to be taken as a gloss.)* Having briefly noticed the Egyptians in v. 18, 19, he entirely loses sight of them afterwards. Eichhorn (Bibl. f. Bibl. Litt. IV. p. 465) justly remarks "The prophet loses sight of them so quickly, because, being already deprived of half their power, they only seldom, and as it were in passing, came into view." As Palestine lay between Egypt and Assyria, it must suffer in every war in which both powers were engaged. In this respect also the fulfilment of the

---

* The difficulty, that the words את מלך אשור cannot be taken as epexegetical of ימים is removed by the remark, that before the last member is again to be supplied · 'Jehovah will bring, or cause to come upon thee—the king of Assyria.'

prophecy was gradual. It was most completely accomplished, when Pharaoh-Necho, king of Egypt, on the occasion of a war with the Babylonians, conquered the land of Judea, and made it tributary after king Josiah had fallen in battle, 2 Chron 35. 20. 2 Kings 23. 29.

The figure, which the prophet employs to represent the invading foes, is taken, as Eichhorn rightly observes, from the nature of their respective countries Egypt, especially at the mouths of the Nile, abounds in vermin and insects. Hence the host of the Egyptians appeared to the prophet, as an enormous swarm of flies "From the marshes of the Euphrates, he sees the Assyrians advance in swarms of wasps and hornets"

Having finished our explanation of the chapter, we must now devote a few moments' attention to those explanations of v. 14—16, which differ in essential points from that which has been given They may be divided into two classes.

I Several interpreters do not indeed deny the reference to the Messiah, but they suppose the prophet had in view, *in the first instance*, an occurrence of his own time. They believe there is here a double sense. The prophet in speaking of a child of his time, was led by divine Providence to use expressions, which are far better suited to Christ, and are applicable to this child only in a very inferior sense. Thus it was interpreted in the time of Jerome, by an anonymous writer, whom he censures, on account of it "Quidam de nostris judaizans Esaiam prophetam duos filios habuisse contendit, Jaschub et Emmanuel. Et Emmanuel de prophetissa uxore ejus esse generatum, in typum domini salvatoris, ut prior filius Jaschub, quod interpretatur relictus sive convertens, Judaicum populum significet, qui relictus est et postea reversus, secundus autem i e Emmanuel et nobiscum deus, gentium vocationem postquam verbum caro factum est et habitavit in nobis" This interpretation was defended, among others, by Grotius, Richard Simon (histoire crit. du texte du N. T. Cap 21 Bd. 1. p 440 seq, the German editor of the critical writings of Simon on the N T, and the lettres choisies III. 1 26, 27), and Le Clerc. But this view was plainly owing to the seeming difficulties of the strict Messianic explanation It arose, partly from inability to remove them, and partly from a desire to sustain, at least in some degree, the authority of the evangelist Matthew. It has already been shown, that if the prophecy was properly fulfilled in the time of Ahaz, no reason whatever can be found, in the text of the prophet, for a higher reference to the Messiah, since even all resemblance thus disappears. The Messianic and non-Messianic interpretation, totally differ as to the meaning of the words. According to the former, עלמה is a virgin, who remains one even after her conception; according to the latter, one who is no longer a virgin, the former regards Immanuel as *Deus in terra*, the latter merely as a symbol of the divine assistance. If therefore we adopt the former, there can be no reference to the time of the prophet; if the latter, it exhausts the sense, and nothing remains to show, that we have here a type of the Messiah. See the subject further pursued by Isenbiehl, (neuer versuch uber die weissagung vom Immanuel, 1778 p. 150 seq) Dathe, who perceived these difficulties, but still could not resolve to follow the strict Messianic interpretation, has resorted to a very peculiar expedient. He supposes (prophetae majores ad h. l) that Isaiah speaks literally of a virgin of his time, who as a true virgin (modo miraculoso) should bare a son in confirmation of his prediction. Then indeed there would be a resemblance to the birth of Christ; but surely no one would join with him in its purchase at such a price. See in opposition Michaelis Or Bibl XV, 66. To a certain extent Lowth, Koppe, and Meyer, belong to this class of interpreters. According to them, the prophet does not indeed speak of a particular child, who should be born in his time, but still he connects the destinies of his country with the name, and destinies of a child, whose conception he represents to himself at this moment as possible. "The meaning which would most readily occur to Ahaz, says Meyer, was this · When now a maiden marries, becomes pregnant, and bears a son, she may call his name *God with us*, since God will then be with us." Nevertheless the prediction shall in the end refer to Christ "The prophecy," says Lowth, "is introduced in so solemn a manner; the sign is so marked, as a sign selected and given by God himself, after Ahaz had rejected the offer of any sign of his own choosing, out of the whole compass of nature, the terms of the prophecy are so peculiar, and the name of the child so expressive, containing in them much more than the circumstances of the birth of a common child required, or even admitted; that we may easily suppose, that, in minds prepared by the general expectation of a great Deliverer to spring from the house of David, they raised hopes far beyond what the present occasion suggested; especially when it was found, that in the subsequent prophecy, delivered immediately afterwards, this child, called Immanuel, is treated as the Lord and Prince of the land of Judah Who could this be, other than the Heir of the throne of David? Under which character, a great and even a Divine person had been promised." We have quoted this passage at length because it states in a very admirable way, the various grounds of the Messianic interpretation. As for the rest, neither of the defenders of this hypothesis has shown the necessity of the inconvenient supposition of a double sense, while the difficulties of the exclusively Messianic interpretation, which seem to have induced them to resort to this expedient, have already been removed. This hypothesis also is, in fact, subject to the difficulties, which as we have seen, attend that of Grotius and others, and an explanation which takes אות in a literal sense cannot, as we shall hereafter see, be justified.

II. The non-Messianic interpretation remained for a long time, the peculiar property of the Jews,* until an attempt was made by John Ernst Faber zu Harmar's Beobachtungen uber den Orient I. s 281 seq., to introduce it into the Christian church. The catholic commentator Isenbiehl followed him in the treatise already quoted, in consequence of which he was thrown into prison. He had borrowed its principal points from the prelections of Michaelis, who also rejected the Messianic interpretation, on account of the difficulties attending it, which he could not remove, on account of ignorance of the prophetic vision, in which from deficiency of imagination, he was unable to place himself. Since that time the non-Messianic interpretation has been quite predominant, so that v. d. Palm himself hesitates, and exhibits the different explanations for the choice of his readers. These interpreters again disagree among themselves respecting the עלמה, who was to bear Immanuel.

1. The more ancient Jews make the *Almah*, the wife of Ahaz, and Immanuel, king Hezekiah. This interpretation prevailed among them even in the time of Justin. Comp. dial c Tryphone Vol II p. 180 ed Wirceb. But Jerome easily refuted it, by showing that Hezekiah must have been, at the time, at least nine years old. Kimchi, and Abarbanel now resorted to the supposition of a second wife of Ahaz, and Kelle among the moderns coincides with them. (Proben

---

* Gesenius mentions Pellicanus as the first defender of the non-Messianic interpretation. But this assertion seems to have been occasioned by a cursory view of a remark by Cramer on Richard Simon's krit Schriften I p 441, where the words "This historic explanation was also advanced by Pellicanus," do not refer to Isaiah, but Daniel. Nor is there any better historical authority for the intimation, that Theodore of Mopsuesta, rejected the Messianic interpretation. The passage from him cited by Paulus Comm I p 129, is entirely of a general character.

einer Deutschen Darstellung der heiligen Schriften in ihrer Urgestalt p. 12.)

2. According to others the עלמה was a virgin not to be accurately determined by us, who was present in the place where Isaiah and the king held their conference, and to whom Isaiah pointed with his finger. As surely, declares the prophet, as that shall soon happen, which I now predict of this virgin, so surely shall that also be fulfilled which I have before predicted respecting the issue of the war. Thus Isenbiehl, Bauer, Cube, and Steudel, in the Programm known to us only by the title loci Jes 7 1—9 6 *interpretandi tentamen* But not to mention other objections, it seems not exactly suitable and proper for the prophet, in presence of the king and the people to predict to a virgin her pregnancy.

3. Others regard עלמה not as an actual, but only as an ideal virgin We will give this view in the language of Michaelis "By the time when one who is yet a virgin can bring forth, (in nine months) all will be happily changed, and the present impending danger so completely passed away, that if you yourself were to name the child, you would call him Immanuel." Thus Eichhorn (Bibl. f bibl. Litt 4 s 450—67) Paulus, Hensler, and Ammon (Christologie p 84). But according to this interpretation we see not wherein the אות would consist, since a mere poetic image, cannot serve as a confirmatory sign.

4. Others still conjecture the *Almah* to be the prophet's wife. Thus Abenezra, Jarchi, Faber, Pluschke (Immanuel, Paralele zwischen Isa. vii and Matt i Analekten v Kiel u. Tschirner I 2 p 43 ff) According to him the sense is as follows. "the prophet's wife, or betrothed virgin, shall conceive and bear a son, who shall be called God with us, (in about nine months the people shall be already delivered); until the child shall know good from evil, (a period of some years) men shall eat milk and honey (the land being uncultivated, they shall live upon the produce of their flocks, and the spontaneous productions of nature); but then the land of the two kings shall be laid waste." The sign was to be gradually developed, and contained two distinct purposes, the deliverance of Judea within nine months, and the ruin of the hostile kingdoms within about three years. The chief objections to this view, besides the arguments already advanced for the Messianic interpretation, are the following, which are likewise applicable, in part, to the three other hypotheses to which we have referred.

a) Since the word עלמה designates only a virgin, and never a young married woman, it is impossible that the wife of the prophet, the mother of Shear-jashub, who was already sufficiently old to accompany his father, could be thereby intended. Gesenius himself is obliged to confess the weight of this objection. He declares himself inclined to the supposition, that the former wife of the prophet was dead, and that he had afterwards betrothed another virgin. But this is a mere fiction. Chap. 8, 3, the wife of the prophet is called simply הנביאה. Besides, we cannot perceive how the prophet could be desired to be understood, if he chose to designate his supposed betrothed by the general expression, "the virgin." We must then, at least suppose with Pluschke, that he took her with him, and pointed to her with his finger, but of this there is no trace in the narrative, nor would it have been proper, and in accordance with oriental manners.

b) That a son of the prophet, or in general any other person except the Messiah, is here referred to, is excluded by the circumstance, that, chap. 8, 8, Palestine is called the land of Immanuel, which is of itself a sufficient refutation of the third hypothesis. Grotius, Pluschke, and Gesenius, resort to the supposition, that ארץ may here signify *native land*. The word it is true can sometimes have this meaning by virtue of the connexion, but these interpreters are not able to inform us, for what purpose the prophet should have here directed his discourse particularly to his son Immanuel.

c) We have already shown, that the word אות does not always signify a miraculous event. But the word, as is shown by לכן, must still so far be used in this sense here, as to designate something whereby the people and king would really be assured of the coming deliverance. Such a sign, as we have already seen, the predicted birth of the Messiah in future times really was. But the prophet would have exposed himself to ridicule, if he had introduced, with such solemnity and such lofty expressions, an event so natural as the birth of his own son. It might indeed be said, the birth of his son predicted by the prophet could have given the Israelites a pledge for the remainder of the prophecy; inasmuch as the prophet could not foresee by human sagacity, whether the Lord would give him a son or a daughter. But then the solemnity of his whole manner, which requires something of greater moment, remains inexplicable, and the opponents cannot avail themselves even of this expedient, since they must then allow the prophet to have been something more than a mere politician. Pluschke l c p 67 supposes the prophet to have ventured on a bold conjecture. But then it might easily have happened to him, as in the well known case at Worms, (comp. Eisenmenger entd. Judenth II p. 664 seq.), and if his conjecture had failed, he would have lost all his reputation

d) Gesenius, who makes the sign refer to two events, instead of one according to the Messianic interpretation, supposes that a period of about three years was to elapse, between the deliverance from the enemies, which was to take place in nine months, and the renewed cultivation of the land. But no reason can be perceived, why the people may not have returned to the cultivation of their fields, as soon as their enemies had withdrawn. Chap. 37 30, Gesenius himself explains the words· "eat this year, what grows of itself; the next year, what springs up again wild: the third year sow and reap, plant vineyards and eat the fruit thereof," as follows: "two years the land has now been laid waste by enemies, so that it has been neither sown, nor reaped, but in this third year, being freed from your enemies, ye shall again sow and reap," and gives as a reason why the imperatives, sow, reap, plant, must not be referred to the future, that Sennacherib according to v 36, 37, immediately after withdrew, and then there was nothing to hinder the cultivation of the land.

e) According to the interpretation of Gesenius, the space of about three years intervenes, between the deliverance of Judea, and the desolation of the two hostile kingdoms But this cannot be, since it was precisely the irruption of the Assyrians into Syria which brought deliverance to Judea, 2 Kings 16: 9.

Isaiah 8: 23 — 9.6

The prophecy, chap. 8 1—9.6, forms one connected whole, it corresponds in many respects, with that contained in chap vii, the occasion of both is the same, the invasion of Judea by the confederated kings of Israel and Syria; the contents and object are quite similar; in both we have the prediction of the speedy deliverance from the Syrians and Ethiopians, and their overthrow by the Assyrians, and of the calamities which the Assyrians should afterwards bring upon the land, the reference to a wonderful divine child, who should establish a kingdom of peace, and whose future appearance furnishes a certain pledge, for the preservation of the State in every danger. There is even an allusion here in v 9, 10, to the name given to this child in chap. 7. 14. But notwithstanding all these points of resemblance, the prediction now before us is not entirely contemporary with the foregoing, as several interpreters have erroneously supposed. It rather appears from the difference between chap. 7. 15, 16 and chap 8 4, in the determination of the time, which should elapse before the ruin of the two confederate kings, that this prophecy must have been spoken from a year to a year and a half later

The course of the prophecy is as follows. The prophet, v. 1—4 represents the speedy destruction of the two hostile kings by a symbolical transaction, with a view to make the bare word spoken in chap vii an object of sense, and thus deepen its impression. The prophet was commanded by Jehovah to write on a tablet or parchment-roll in large characters, that every one could read, the words, Mahar-shalal-hash-baz, 'the spoil hastens, the plunder quickly comes,' i. e the time when the Assyrians shall lay waste the dominions of the two hostile kings is already near. He was then to cause the prophecy, like a judicial document, to be confirmed by the authority of credible and respectable witnesses, in order that after the fulfilment, he might exhibit it to the unbelieving multitude, and remove from himself every suspicion of a *vaticinii post eventum* The prophet complies with the divine command, and takes for witness, the high priest Uriah, 2 Kings 16 10, and Zechariah He then receives from Jehovah the further command to name a son, who was born to him at that time, Mahar-shalal-hash-baz; since before this child could speak the name of father and mother, the two hostile lands should be laid waste by the Assyrians* With respect to the fulfilment, sufficient has been said in our remarks on chap vii By the spoil of Samaria, v. 4, is not to be understood, the spoil which should be carried away from the city, but from the province of Samaria So also in other passages, 2 Kings 17. 26 23. 19. Jer. 31. 5, the land is call-

---

* Some interpreters, as e g Calvin suppose, that the symbolical action here mentioned was not performed outwardly, but only in the internal contemplation of the prophet At all events, it can be shown that this was the case with most of the symbolical actions of the prophets They were then committed to writing by the prophets, and were of the same utility to the people, as if they had been actually performed Thus the symbolical action in Hosea chap i—iii, which is quite similar to this, certainly took place only in the mind of the prophet But, that the one, which is here related, nevertheless really took place, seems evident from v 18

ed by the name of the capital. This remark refutes the assertion of Gesenius, that the prediction, as far as it related to the kingdom of the ten tribes, was not fulfilled until about 18 years after the time fixed by the prophet.

In v 5—8 there follows a prediction of the calamity, which as a punishment from God, should be brought upon Judah, as well as Israel, by the Assyrians, from whom Ahaz and the ungodly portion of the people expected nothing but deliverance. The enemies shall overspread the whole land. The prophet here, however, by addressing Immanuel, the future great restorer of the theocracy, and calling the land *his* land, shows, that the visible theocracy, whose concerns he already directed, could not be brought to ruin, nor the land in which he should, at a future time, be born, remain desolate.*

---

* The question naturally occurs, what is to be understood by העם הזה v 6. Some interpreters understand by these words merely the kingdom of the ten tribes, others the kingdom of Judah, and lastly others suppose the discourse to be addressed at the same time to both, and the divine punishment to be threatened against both in the following verses. The latter opinion, in all probability, is the true one. The section cannot relate to the Jews alone, for it could not be brought as an accusation against them, that they took pleasure in Rezin. Several interpreters (Michaelis, Paulus, v d Palm, Gesenius), have indeed supposed, that a party had been formed among the Jews, who despised the royal family of David, and favored the enemies of their country. But of this there is no evidence whatever, and even were it so, how could the prophet charge the offence of some few individuals upon the people and represent it as the ground of their punishment? But the supposition, that a great part of the people, weary of the existing government, would have readily submitted to the hostile kings, is inconsistent with chap 7 2, where it is expressly asserted, that Ahaz with his whole people was greatly terrified. In chap vii, moreover, the invasion of the Assyrians is not by any means, as would then have been the case, represented as a punishment for rebellion against the royal house of David, but for the want of a theocratic disposition, manifested by the king and his people in seeking aid from the Assyrians. Further, that there is a joint reference to Israel appears also from v 14, where the two houses of Israel are spoken of, and lastly the prediction of prosperity, v 23, which relates directly and chiefly to one part of the kingdom of the ten tribes, shows that the corresponding threatening must in like manner relate to the same kingdom. It is otherwise impossible to see what could have induced the prophet to announce prosperity to these regions. But it would be equally erroneous to refer the discourse, with the author of the Exeg Handb and others, to the Israelites alone. It is evident, that the address must have been chiefly directed to the Jews, even from the fact, that v 11 and 12, the apostate portion of the Jews, the untheocratic multitude, are twice called *this people*, and still more so from the circumstance, that according to v 8 the punishment was to fall

He says this still more plainly v. 9, 10. He here addresses the people hostile to the theocracy, in the first instance the Assyrians,* and announces that their efforts to destroy the covenant people were in vain, since the future great deliverance which Jehovah would accomplish through Immanuel, whose name is alluded to, was a pledge even of his present help. God must even now, in an inferior sense, be with a people, with whom he would be hereafter in the truest

---

upon the Jews also, who must consequently have borne a part in the crime mentioned in this verse. We must therefore conclude with Vitringa and Lowth, that the verse refers to both Jews and Israelites. The offence in the first member, the despising of the waters of Siloah, can be referred at the same time to both. The interpreters, for the most part, understand by the soft flowing waters of Siloah, the royal house of David reigning within narrow limits and already on the decline, but without good reason. Contempt of the royal house of David, in itself considered, was no crime; and the prophet here as in chap. vii, reproaches the people for having put their trust in human aid, instead of the power of God. Were the prophet speaking merely of despising the royal house of David, his reproach would not affect Ahaz, upon whom it ought however chiefly to fall. Rather by the soft flowing waters of Siloah, which though neither abundant, nor splendid, were a great blessing to the inhabitants of Jerusalem, in contradistinction from the roaring waters of the Euphrates, which laid waste the adjacent country by overflowing its banks, we are to understand the kingdom of God among the Jewish people in so far as it was manifested in the kingdom of the house of David, which, though outwardly humble and without splendor, would yet afford the people more support, security and blessings, than the most powerful foreign kingdoms, if they did not through unbelief sin against its king and make themselves unworthy of his protection. The fountain of Siloah is here appropriately used as an image of the theocracy; for it issued forth at the foot of the holy hill of Zion which was the seat of the theocracy, just as the Euphrates is employed as an image of the kingdom of Assyria, since it is the chief river of that country. Now Ahaz and the untheocratic portion of the people had become guilty of contemning the theocracy, inasmuch as looking only at the appearance of things, instead of raising themselves above this by faith, they had sought help from the Assyrians. The Israelites had committed the same offence, by combining with its enemies against the theocracy, which they hoped easily to overthrow. The crime mentioned in the second member, of taking pleasure in Rezin and the son of Remaliah, was peculiar to the Israelites. Instead of trusting in Jehovah alone, the Israelitish people were proud of their own might and that of Rezin their ally. The inundation by the Assyrians, which the prophet foretold, came upon the kingdom of the ten tribes under Tiglathpileser and Salmaneser, and upon Judah under Sennacherib

* Not the Syrians, as several interpreters suppose. For the connexion of this verse with v. 23 shows, that the prophet here had in view the common enemies of both houses of Israel, v. 14.

sense. Thus Calvin justly remarks: "constituendus est propheta velut in specula, unde cladem populi et Assyrios victores atque insolenter exultantes conspiciat, Christi vero nomine et conspectu recreatus, omnium malorum obliviscatur, quasi nihil passus sit, omnique miseria liberatus insurgat in hostes, quos dominus erat statim periturus."

The prophet could now have announced, as he usually does elsewhere, immediately after the inferior deliverance the higher one by the Messiah; just as in the second part, he commonly connects the prediction of the deliverance from the captivity with that of the times of the Messiah. In order however to awaken the ungodly from their false security, and inflame the zeal of the pious, he here suspends the prediction of salvation, and gives v. 11—22, the *subjective* conditions, on which it is to be imparted, and at the same time predicts the fearful calamity which will fall upon that portion of the people, who fail to fulfil them. The deliverance, says the prophet, which I announce to you, depends not on human conjecture, but on a divine revelation; still God has, at the same time, taught me the conditions, which you must perform before it can be obtained.

The prophet here employs, v. 11—15, peculiar imagery, or rather the revelation respecting what must be done by the people is conveyed to him in a peculiar form. The prophet has a conference with God in a vision, (בְּחֶזְקַת יַד יְהוָה.) In this interview, he himself represents the better part of the people, who were ready to receive the word of Jehovah, in contradistinction to those (הָעָם הַזֶּה), whether honorable, or ignoble, who rejected his authority. For this reason, Jehovah speaks to him in the plural. He admonishes him to repose his confidence in himself alone, and not like the unbelieving part of the nation to sin against him by distrustful fears of human power and earthly foes. As he would be to the unbelieving, apostate portion of the people in both kingdoms, a severe judge, and bring upon them a heavy destruction, so would he be the faithful helper and Redeemer of the believing and obedient.* After Jehovah has thus addressed the better portion of the people in the person of the prophet, he directs his discourse v. 16, particularly to him. He commands him to exhort

---

* This passage is several times cited in the N. T. Luke 2:34, 1 Pet. 2:7, Rom. 9:32, 33. It is also referred to the Messiah by the Jews, comp. Jalkut on h. l. fol. 43 c. Raym. Martini, pug. fid. p. 343 ed. Carpzov. It may justly be called *Messianic*, inasmuch as the truth of this declaration will be especially manifest at the time of Christ's appearance.

his disciples i. e. those who rely solely on his word and his revelation, his true worshippers (see chap 54 13) to perseverance in the revealed religion and the observance of his law *

With v. 16 the admonition, thus clothed in the form of an address of Jehovah to the prophet, is concluded; v. 17 etc., the latter then addresses himself to the people, and especially to those, who feared God He declares to them his firm confidence, founded on the divine promise, that though Jehovah would now cause the people to feel his heavy displeasure, yet he would not suffer them to be destroyed. He appeals to the names of himself and his sons, which were prophetic of salvation, Isaiah, the salvation of God, Shear-jashub, a remnant shall return, and Maher-shalal-hash-baz, which could serve the people, for אתות and מופתים, for types of future events, Isaiah 20 3 Zech 3 8, and impress upon them, in a sensible manner, the truth that Jehovah could not forget his people, and suffer them to perish. He exhorts them to rely on God alone, and not in an unlawful manner, to seek from other sources a knowledge of the future. He requires in general a firm adherence to the revealed will of God, and concludes with a lively description of the affliction which would come upon the people, if they did not perform the conditions of the covenant, and submit themselves entirely to the authority of the supreme Lawgiver. This threatening has been fulfilled, at all times, when the people have been visited by the purifying chastisement of God, but was especially carried into execution when Jerusalem was destroyed by the Romans

---

* The expression in this verse is metaphorical. Writings of importance were bound up together, sealed, and preserved in a case. The divine revelation is accordingly represented as such a writing to be bound together and sealed, the hearts of believers, upon which it should be impressed, under the image of a case, in which the writing thus bound and sealed is deposited Gesenius prefers to understand by תעודה and תורה the consoling prediction v 1, he takes "bind and seal," literally The prophet, he supposes, receives command, to bind up and seal the prophecy until its fulfilment But were this interpretation adopted, the verse would greatly interrupt the connexion, besides it cannot in general be proved on philological grounds, that by תעודה and תורה a consoling prophecy only would be designated and that such is not the import of the words in this place appears from v 20, where according to the explanation of Gesenius they are used to signify the law How it could be asserted, that their sense is different in the two places, is hard to be conceived The interpretation of בלמדי by, *with consultation of my disciples*, is also unnatural Aquila expresses the true sense of the passage ἔνδησον μαρτύριον, σφράγισον νόμον ἐν τοῖς διδακτοῖς μου.

Isaiah 8:23.

When the prophet had thus excluded the ungodly part of the people from the salvation, and admonished those who feared God, to render themselves fit to receive it, he continues, v. 23, the prediction of salvation, interrupted at v 10. The inferior is followed by the higher deliverance, which he represents, as usual, by images taken from the earthly theocracy After severe sufferings, the people shall experience a time of prosperity. The blessings of this period shall be chiefly enjoyed by the province of Galilee—the region of Israel, hitherto the most deeply sunk in misery and ignorance. The covenant people, from among whom according to the preceding threatening the ungodly have been excluded, will experience a wonderful deliverance, and be blessed with joy and peace All the blessings will be conferred through a miraculous child, whom the prophet, chap. 7 14, had named Immanuel, and to whom, v. 8 and 10, he had again referred. At the same time man and God, born and eternal, a descendant of David and the Son of God, mighty in counsel and in action, the Restorer of peace to mankind at war among themselves, he will extend, without limit, his eternal dominion, not by force like earthly conquerors, but by righteousness.

V. 23. " For darkness shall not be upon the land, upon which there is distress; as the former time has dishonored the land of Zebulun, and the land of Naphtali, so shall the time to come honor it, the region on the border of the sea, by the side of the Jordan, Galilee of the Gentiles." כי is by most interpreters regarded as an adversative particle referring to the preceding verse. But it may also well be taken in its usual sense *for*, with reference to v. 9, 10, 17, 18. The prediction of salvation had only been interrupted by the insertion of other matter. The words מועף and מוצק are properly participles in Hoph. but they here stand in the place of nouns Most interpreters give to מועף the meaning, *darkness* That the verb means, *to be dark*, seems certain from Job 11: 17, and the derivative עיפה. Some on the contrary, as Augusti and Jahn, understand by it *weakness*, appealing to 1 Sam 14 28 and Judges 4· 24, where the verb occurs in the sense *to become weak*, to the Syriac עוף which has this meaning, the kindred Hebrew יעף and the derivative עיה. Certainly darkness and trouble seem to make no very fit antithesis The adverbs *hereafter* and *now*, as appears from what follows, are to be supplied The suff. in לה as well as the suff. in בה v 21, refers to ארץ understood. The כ in כעת is the same as כאשר. The Hebrews and Arabians often attribute to time, as an action, that which happens in it. See the numerous examples by Schultens on Job 3 3, 10 30 17. The verbs הָקֵל, properly, *to make light*, then, *contemptible, to cover with disgrace*, and הכביד *to make heavy*, then metaphorically, *to honor*, a sense properly peculiar to Piel, in which however Hiph. also occurs Jer 30 19, stand in contrast with each other. Other interpreters, appealing to the circumstance, that there is no analogous case, where כ is used precisely for כַּאֲשֶׁר, translate: 'as Jehovah in former times has made contemptible the land of Zebulun, and the land of Naphtali, so will he make it honorable in the time to come.' The particle כ is then not used by way of comparison, but to determine the time, as is often the case. As subject, Jehovah is to be supplied, or we may with Augusti take both verbs impersonally. 'he has made contemptible,' for 'one has made contemptible,' i.e. 'it has been made contemptible.' Before הָאַחֲרוֹן then כְּעֵת is to be supplied. It can however be taken also in the accusative, as an answer to the question *when*. That the passage possesses more poetical beauty, according to the former explanation, cannot be questioned. Also כ in several places has the sense of כַּאֲשֶׁר, if we only supply the ellipsis. Thus directly below in chap 9 3 "thou hast broken his yoke כְּיוֹם מִדְיָן, as thou hast broken it in the day of Midian;" 1 Sam. 8:5 "Give us a king כְּכָל־הַגּוֹיִם: as all nations have a king." See Ewald Hebr Gramm. p 614. The form אַרְצָה, has a paragogic ה, not to be confounded with ה local, which is elsewhere subjoined to אֶרֶץ. See Gesen. Lehrg. p 545. The appellations in the last number stand in apposition to אַרְצָה זְבֻלוּן וְאַרְצָה נַפְתָּלִי.—'the land of Zebulun and Naphtali,' and designate the same region. The tribes of Zebulun and Naphtali dwelt at the sea of Gennesareth, the יָם כִּנֶּרֶת, which is here to be understood by יָם. The tribe of Zebulun had the sea for its eastern border, that of Naphtali for its southern. Hence the region of the two tribes was called the way of the sea, דֶּרֶךְ הַיָּם, or the country along the sea. In like manner דֶּרֶךְ in the accusative, *adverbiascens*, Josh. 2 7. 4 15. Both tribes had, at the same time, the Jordan for a boundary. Hence their district is called עֵבֶר הַיַּרְדֵּן, 'the land by the side of the Jordan.' It is true, this appellation commonly signifies 'the land beyond Jordan,' or 'the region of Perea;' but here this cannot be the meaning, since these words are explanatory of the land of Zebulun and Naphtali, and must be synonymous with גְּלִיל הַגּוֹיִם. But all Galilee was on this side the Jordan. We must therefore take עֵבֶר in the sense: *side*, which it often has See Gesen. s. v. It here stands in the Accus *adverbiascens*. The name גְּלִיל הַגּוֹיִם, properly an appellative, the circle of the Gentiles, according to several interpreters, designates only one particular part of the province of Galilee in later times. But in this passage, which is the only one where the appellation occurs, there is nothing which favors this limitation. See Bachiene, Palastina II, 4 p 12 seq. The province was called Galilee of the Gentiles, because its inhabitants were then already intermingled with them. But in how far was this region, which was chiefly held by the tribes of Zebulun and Naphtali, made contemptible? The language seems to relate partly to its outward calamities, partly to the moral degradation of its inhabitants. 1 The district of these two tribes constituted the border-land, towards the heathen nations, the Galileans were therefore always first exposed to the assaults of enemies. Thus under king Asa, they experienced a severe overthrow from Benhadad, king of Syria, 1 Kings 15. 20. In the time of Isaiah it was they especially, who suffered in the Assyrian invasion under Tiglath-pileser, 2 K 15 29. Although this event could not yet have taken place, since Isaiah, v. 4 and 5—7, represents the invasion of the land of Israel by the Assyrians, as still future, and the Jews were still harassed by the Israelites and Syrians. he may nevertheless have referred to it, since he foresaw that the predicted invasion of the Assyrians, would first fall upon the region of Galilee. 2 The Galileans not only dwelt in the vicinity of the heathen, but a multitude of the latter had always remained in the country, Judges 1 30—35, from the time of their taking possession of it. Solomon gave to Hiram, king of Tyre, twenty cities in Galilee, 1 Kings 9 11. But the Phenicians with whom they held commercial intercourse, and with whom they dwelt intermingled, were among the most corrupt of all the heathen nations. That the reproach of Galilee consisted especially in this mingling of its inhabitants with heathen, who exerted the most baneful influence upon them, Isaiah himself seems to indicate by the appellation, 'Galilee of the Gentiles,' which has erroneously been regarded as a geographical name. Thus Theodoret Γαλιλαίαν δὲ τῶν ἐθνῶν καλεῖ ὡς καὶ ἀλλοφύλων συνοικούντων τοῖς Ἰουδαίοις. διὰ τοῦτο καὶ ἐν σκότει πορευομένους καὶ ἐν σκιᾷ θανάτου καὶ χώρᾳ οἰκοῦντας ὀνομάζει τοὺς τῆς χώρας ἐκείνης οἰκήτορας καὶ τοῦ θείου φωτὸς ὑπισχνεῖται τὴν αἴγλην. To this must be added its great distance from Jerusalem, where the power of religion was chiefly concentrated, notwithstanding the corruption of a portion of its inhabitants. Consequently the pure knowledge of religion, was in a great measure lost among the Galileans, and ignorance and superstition occupied its place. Hence arose the general contempt, in which they were held in the time of Christ, John 1 47. 7 52 Matt. 26 69 But wherein consisted the honor, or the glory which in future times should be conferred upon this despised people? The evangelist Matthew gives us the answer. He says, chap 4 13, the prophecy was fulfilled, when Christ fixed his residence at Capernaum in Galilee, within the borders of Zebulun and Naphtali. Christ passed the greatest part of the time of his public ministry in Galilee; there lay Capernaum, his ordinary place of abode; in Galilee were most of his disciples; there he performed many miracles, there the preaching of the gospel met with much success; and even the name of Galileans was transferred to the Christians in the first centuries. Theodoret strikingly observes. ἡ Γαλιλαία γὰρ τῶν ἱερῶν ἀποστόλων ἦν πατρίς· ἐν ἐκείνῃ τὰ πλεῖστα τῶν θαυμάτων ὁ δεσπότης εἰργάσατο· ἐκεῖ τὸν λεπρὸν ἐκάθηρεν· ἐκεῖ τῷ ἑκατοντάρχῳ τὸν οἰκέτην ἀπέδωκεν ὑγιᾶ· ἐκεῖ τὸν τῆς Πέτρου πενθερᾶς κατέσβεσε πυρετόν· ἐκεῖ τὴν Ἰαείρου θυγατέρα τὸν βίον ὑπεξελθοῦσαν ἐπανήγαγε πρὸς ζωήν· ἐκεῖ τὰ τῆς θαλάσσης ἐστόρεσε κύματα· ἐκεῖ τοὺς ἄρτους ἐπήγασε· ἐκεῖ τὸ ὕδωρ εἰς οἶνον μετέβαλε. It is evident, that this honor was not to be conferred upon Galilee at an earlier period, partly because the Galileans, as Michaelis (A T. VIII, p. 48 seq) has shown, then enjoyed no special prosperity, and partly because, according to chap 9· 5, the Galileans, as well as the rest of the covenant people, were not to obtain this salvation until the appearing of the great King, who had been promised. Altogether similar is the passage, Micah 5 1, properly compared with this by Gesenius. As there, the birth of the Messiah shall confer honor upon the hitherto obscure Bethlehem, so here, shall Galilee, hitherto held in contempt, upon which the Jews cast the reproach, that no prophet arose there, be raised to honor and rendered illustrious by the manifestation of the Messiah. This passage gave rise to the opinion of the Jews that the Messiah would appear in Galilee. See Sohar p. I, fol. 119 ed. Amstel fol. 74 ed Solisb. יהגלי מלכא משיחא בארעה דגליל *revelabitur Messias in terra Galilaea.*

Chap. 9 1. "The people that sit in darkness, see a great light, upon them who sit in the land of the shadow of death, a light arises." הָעָם, the people, are the Galileans, the inhabitants of the region mentioned in the foregoing verse; for there is no reason to suppose a change of the subject: still however it appears, that here as well as afterwards, there is at the same time a reference to the rest of the Jewish people. The land appears to the inward vision of the prophet enveloped in thick darkness, which is suddenly penetrated by a clear light, as the darkness of night by a flash of lightning. Light and darkness supply the orientals with a twofold metaphor, being employed to express physical good and evil, prosperity and adversity: and also moral good and evil, righteousness and truth, sin and error. In the former sense, they occur e. g. Job 18. 18, where it is said of the ungodly: "he shall be driven from light into darkness," and chap 21. 17. In the latter sense, the Messiah, chap 42. 6. 49. 6, is called the light of the heathen, he who removes the spiritual darkness of sin and error, as the sun disperses natural darkness, John 1. 9. 8. 12. In the latter sense also it is said, chap 60. 2: "Behold darkness covers the earth, and gross darkness the people," and the extension of true religion among the heathen through the Messiah, is represented as a coming to the great Light which has risen upon the covenant people. According to Malachi 4. 2, in the time of the Messiah the sun of righteousness shall arise upon the pious. The question now occurs, in which sense the figure is here to be understood. The recent interpreters, for the most part, stop at the former, prosperity and adversity, but erroneously. As the disgrace, in the foregoing verse, signifies not merely physical evil, but at the same time, and indeed chiefly, sin and error, so also must the corresponding darkness be taken in an equally comprehensive sense. Both meanings of the metaphor, therefore, are here to be combined. The people physically and spiritually miserable shall be enlightened, sanctified, and blessed by the coming of the Messiah. The same double sense occurs also in the splendid passage, chap 60. 1: "Arise, shine, for thy light is come, and the glory of the Lord is risen upon thee." The words חשך and צלמות are commonly used in connexion, to signify the thickest possible darkness. עם as a collective is connected with the plural, ההלכים. The preterites ראו and נגה are explained by the circumstance, that events really future appeared to the inward vision of the prophet as already passed. The light has already expelled the darkness. ישבי as in the Nomin. Absol., *as to the dwellers;* the Stat. Const. is often used, as here, where the connexion is intimate, though not made by a genitive, especially before prepositions.

V. 2. The glory of the time of the Messiah is present to the pro-

354 ISAIAH 9:2.

phet: he beholds the covenant people increased in numbers, freed from all suffering, and filled with joy, in a transport he turns to Jehovah and celebrates what he has done for his people. "Thou increasest the people, to whom before thou gavest little joy; they joy before thee, according to the joy in harvest, and as men rejoice when they divide the spoil." Several interpreters, as Calvin, Vitringa, Le Clerc, suppose that the prophet here, and in the two following verses, speaks in the first instance of prosperity near at hand, of the rapid increase of the Israelites after their return from the Babylonish exile, in which the inhabitants of Galilee also must have participated, as may be inferred from the accounts of Josephus respecting the great population of that province in his time. He says de b Jud 1, 20, 3: πόλεις πυκναὶ καὶ τὸ τῶν κωμῶν πλῆθος πανταχοῦ πολυάνθρωπον διὰ τὴν εὐθηνίαν, ὡς τὴν ἐλαχίστην ὑπὲρ πεντακισχιλίους πρὸς τοῖς μυρίοις ἔχειν οἰκήτορας. Vitringa directs our attention to the fact, that the Jewish people, after the exile, not only filled Judea, but also spread themselves in Egypt, Syria, Mesopotamia, Asia Minor, Greece, and Italy. But although the prophets frequently blend in this manner an inferior and a higher deliverance, as e g in the second part of Isaiah, where the blessings immediately after the exile, and the blessings of the Messiah's time, are often not carefully separated, yet there appears to be here no sufficient ground for the supposition of a double reference; all perfectly agrees with the time of the Messiah, if we do not mistake the figurative character of the prediction, and at the same time bear in mind, that here, as in most of the prophecies of the Messiah, the feeble beginning of his kingdom is closely connected with its glorious completion. The extension of the theocracy, by the reception of the heathen, often appeared to the prophets under the image of a great increase of the people. See chap. 2. 2—4 54· 1, etc. 66 8, etc. Ez. 37 26, and other places. The words לֹא הִגְדַּלְתָּ הַשִּׂמְחָה are to be translated, *whose joy thou didst not before enlarge.* This is a Litotes for, *upon whom thou hast heretofore inflicted heavy sufferings.* Before לֹא is to be supplied אֲשֶׁר and הַשִּׂמְחָה with the article stands for שִׂמְחָתוֹ. So Symmachus: ἐπλήθυνας τὸ ἔθνος, ᾧ οὐκ ἐμεγάλυνας. Instead of the reading of the text לֹא the marginal reading is לוֹ, and this was followed by most of the old translators (LXX Chald Syr). It is then to be translated: *thou hast made their joy great.* Several suppose the reading in the text to be the true one, but that לֹא here, as also in some other places, by a careless mode of writing is put for לוֹ. There is however no reason to reject the first explanation, which gives a meaning so appropriate. The prophet in what follows expresses first the nature of this joy and then its greatness under two images. The joy on account of the blessings received is a joy before God, a holy joy, שִׂמְחוּ לְפָנֶיךָ. The expression is taken from the sacrificial feasts in the courts before the temple, at which the partakers rejoiced before the Lord, לִפְנֵי יְהוָה, Deut 12 7 14. 26 Joy in harvest, and in dividing the spoil, is elsewhere also employed, as a metaphorical designation of the highest joy. The time of harvest in Palestine, especially when the harvest was abundant, was one of great rejoicing The reapers sang songs and those who passed by gave them a benediction, in which they wished them prosperity. The joy of an abundant harvest must have been the greater, because according to the theocratic law of a visible retribution, it served as a proof of the divine mercy, while on the contrary a failure of the crops, was a manifestation of the divine displeasure Jahn Arch. I, 1 § 71 On the division of the spoil, see Jahn II, 2 § 246

V. 3 "For his heavy yoke, the staff, which smote his neck, the rod of his driver, thou hast broken as in the day of Midian." In this verse the reason of the joy of the people is given. Jehovah has accomplished for them merely by his own power, without human means, a glorious deliverance, and redemption This deliverance of the theocracy from all its enemies, which has only commenced, and the completion of which is still to be expected, is here represented under the image of a deliverance from powerful oppressors; such as were the Assyrians at an earlier, and the Babylonians at an later period. But that it must not be regarded as a mere temporal deliverance, is evident from v 4—6, according to which its author shall be the Messiah, the Prince of peace; his kingdom, a kingdom of peace, extended over the whole earth, and not as the kingdoms of the world by force, but by justice and righteousness עֹל סֻבֳּלוֹ, properly, *the yoke of his burden, the yoke which he bears*. The ground form is סבל. The Dagesh forte is merely euphonic On this account, in the place of the Sheva simple, there is a composite Sheva, because the reduplication requires the moveable Sheva to be plainly uttered. See Ges. Lehrg 77 87 מַטֵּה שִׁכְמוֹ *the staff which strikes the neck, or back*. Vitringa and Rosenmuller, taking for granted that שכם can mean only *shoulder*, erroneously suppose that מַטֶּה is here synonymous with מוֹטָה *yoke*. מטה in all places means *staff*, and this signification here accords well with the following שֵׁבֶט. The great deliverance to be hereafter accomplished by Jehovah, is finally compared with a deliverance, which he formerly vouchsafed to the covenant people, the deliverance of the Israelites under Gideon from the dominion of the Midianites, Judges 7: 19, etc. יוֹם stands in the accusative, in answer to the question, *when;* כְּיוֹם מִדְיָן therefore, *as in the day of Midian.* The day of Midian is the day which has been rendered memorable by the overthrow of the Midianites. In Arabic, *day* often stands precisely for *day of battle.* The question now arises in what consists the *tertium comparationis* of the earlier and the later redemption. Herder thinks that it consists in the sameness of the place. He says (Heb. Poesie II, 436) "The images are taken from the times of Midian, and of the victories of the judges. As it was in the northern part of the land, that the great deliverance was effected, as it was in the dark forests of Naphtali and Zebulun, that the light of freedom arose upon the whole land; so also now shall the light of freedom here arise." This is indeed a beautiful point of comparison, but still it must not be regarded as the only one. It was characteristic of the deliverance from the Midianites, that it was not effected by human power, but by the most evident interposition of God. So also shall Jehovah accomplish the far greater redemption to be effected by the Messiah, of whom Gideon was a type, not by human means, not by the force of arms, but in a miraculous manner, and thus establish the kingdom of peace on earth. Thus Calvin: "notandum est, dominum sic interdum nobis adesse, ut mediis ordinariis utatur, quae impediunt, ne apertam ejus manum conspiciamus. In hac autem Gedeonis victoria potentia domini aperte cernebatur, quod sine ulla hominum ope hostes delevisset. Quid enim habebat Gedeon praeter strepitum lagenarum, quo vix pecora abigi potuissent? Illustre igitur specimen potentiae suae tunc edidit dominus. Itaque illi victoriae hanc redemtionem comparat, quoniam in ea dei manus aperta et nuda conspicietur, sicut in die Madian." So also the author of the ex. Handb.

V. 4. In this verse, the idea is further unfolded, that the great redemption shall be accomplished, not by earthly weapons, but in a miraculous manner by the power of God. "For all war-shoes put on at the noise of battle, all garments dipt in blood shall be burnt, shall be the food of fire," literally: for with respect to all the war-shoes of those shod at the noise of battle, and all the garments of war stained with blood, they shall be for burning, for the consumption of fire. כִּי relates to the words: *as in the day of Midian.* The great future redemption will be like the deliverance under Gideon; because far from being accomplished by force of arms, with it all contention,

Isaiah 9: 4, 5

and war will cease. Calvin "dominus enim multorum opera non utetur, sed e coelo sibi victoriam pariet." Most interpreters suppose, that the image here employed, is taken from the custom among several nations, of burning the weapons, and bloody garments after a battle See Virg En. VIII, 561, 62. Lowth on the passage But it by no means appears, that this practice prevailed among the Hebrews, from the passages cited in its favor, Ps 46 10 Ez 39. 9, besides the allusion here would be entirely unsuitable; since the subject of discourse, as is shown by the particle כִּי, is not a peace which follows a conflict, but a peace which shall be introduced by Jehovah without a conflict Gesenius therefore justly regards the figurative expression, as a general designation of the commencement of that peace, which shall never end. The sense. all the preparations for war shall then be burnt, as being of no further use. This explanation is in harmony with the numerous parallel passages, in which peace is represented as a characteristic mark of the time of the Messiah, when even in nature itself, contention, war, and destruction, shall cease See e. g. chap 11. 6, 7. Ps 72 Micah 5 9—13. Zech. 9 9, 10. From the commencement of the Messiah's kingdom this peace has existed in the disposition of its members; at the end of this kingdom, it will also outwardly prevail, and the fulfilment of this, and similar prophecies has therefore but just commenced The ἅπ. λεγ. סְאוֹן often misinterpreted, is explained by a comparison of the Syr Chald. Eth and signifies a soldier's shoe, or half boot, which formed a part of his armor, Jahn Archaol. II, 2 p 412. The verb סָאַן is a denominative, and signifies *to draw on such a war-shoe*. רַעַשׁ *disquiet, noise*, stands here for the tumult of battle. Rosenmuller translates בְּרַעַשׁ *cum strepitu*, and refers it to the rattling of the war-shoes, which however does not appear altogether appropriate. שִׂמְלָה *garment* receives here from the connexion, the special meaning, *war-garment*. Shoe and garment stand as *species pro genere*, for all warlike preparation. מְגוֹלָלָה part. Po. from גָּלַל properly *rolled about*. The ו in וְהָיְתָה is the Vav apodotic. The foregoing nouns stand in the nominative absolute

V. 5. "For unto us a child is born, unto us a son is given, and the government shall be upon his shoulders, and his name shall be called Wonderful, Counsellor, Mighty God, Father of eternity, Prince of Peace" The prophet has hitherto spoken only of the salvation, which should be extended from Galilee over the rest of the land, the author of this salvation here first appears before him in all his exaltation, and glory. We first give the explanation of this, and the following verse, and shall afterwards examine the hypothesis, which makes Hezekiah, instead of the Messiah, their subject. For the present, we take it for granted, that the Messianic interpretation is the true one. The prophet, as in chap. 7. 14, beholds the great Redeemer, as already born. Hence the preterites יֻלַּד and נִתַּן. If any one chooses to infer from them, that the subject of the prophecy must, at that time, have been actually born, he must also, on account of the preterites, v. 1, etc. assume, what no interpreter has done, that the predicted prosperity had already been conferred upon the Israelites. בְּ here seems to possess peculiar emphasis. We may either explain it with Vitringa unto us a son is given, namely a son of him who has given him, or we may suppose with Herder, that בְּ here emphatic, as בַר in Ps. 2. 12, signifies a son of God.—" On his shoulder the government shall be." In this prophecy the Messiah in glory presents himself to the prophet, and not as in other prophecies, in the form of a servant. The figurative expression here, as well as chap. 22. 22, is not taken from the idea, that the government was regarded as a burden, but rather from the circumstance, that the insignia of dominion, the mantle with which kings, and other great men were clothed when they appeared in public, was worn upon the shoulders. The regal dignity was not considered as a burden, but as an ornament of which the king was the bearer. Pliny. " cum abunde expertus pater, quam bene humeris tuis sederet imperium." The passage Cic pro Flacco c. 38. " de salute omnium nostrûm, de fortunis civitatis, de summa republicae taceo? quam vos universam in hoc judicio vestris humeris, vestris inquam, humeris, judices, sustinetis," which is commonly quoted in favor of the first mentioned opinion, is not to the purpose, since dominion is not here the subject of discourse. As the subject of וַיִּקְרָא, either Jehovah may be supplied, or which is better, it may be taken impersonally. Le Clerc justly remarks: " quisquis de eo loquetur vocabit eum." *One calls him* is then, according to the usage of Isaiah, as much as to say he will justly bear this name, or simply: he will be. The Jewish interpreters, in despair of being able to refer the following predicates with any show of probability to Hezekiah, would make them designate him, who gives, and not him who receives the name; to the latter only שַׂר הַשָּׁלוֹם belongs· the Wonderful, the Counsellor, etc names him, the Prince of Peace. But this unnatural interpretation is contradicted by the accents, there must then be an Athnach under

אֲבִי עַד. Besides, the mention of so many names of Jehovah is here entirely out of place, and in all other instances the noun placed after קָרָא שְׁמוֹ designates the person who receives, not the one who gives the name. With respect to the following names it is in general to be observed that the recent interpreters, viewing them with too little regard to their mutual connexion, have not reflected that though the reference of some of them to a human subject were possible, yet this is excluded by the connexion in which they stand with the rest. The first name is פֶּלֶא. This word properly signifies as an abstract, *miracles*, and is especially employed to denote the wonderful works, by which God glorified himself in the history of the Israelites. Here it stands, as the abstract for the concrete, as a stronger expression, for *miraculous* It imports, that the great king, in his being, and in his works, will be exalted above the ordinary course of nature, that his whole manifestation will be a miracle. This meaning of the word is confirmed by the parallel passage, Judges 13 18, where the angel, who announces the birth of Sampson, says wherefore askest thou after my name; it is Wonderful פִּלְאִי, i. e. my whole nature is miraculous, full of mystery, and therefore cannot be designated by any human name. Pluschke, except that he refers the name too exclusively to miraculous works, and not to the supernatural character of his being, justly remarks "he shall be called Wonderful on account of the great events, which will take place in the beginning of his reign, and during its continuance, resembling those mighty works of God, which Israel had seen and experienced in former times, when, e g they were led out of Egypt, through the sea, through the wilderness, and through the Jordan." According to Jahn and Gesenius, the word here means nothing more, than remarkable, distinguished, extraordinary. But as פֶּלֶא is the standing expression for miracle, see e g. Ex. 15· 11. Ps 77: 12, 15 78: 12. Dan. 12. 6, so here especially, where it stands in connexion with other names of so high import, are we, least of all, justified in taking the word in an unusual sense. The second name יוֹעֵץ, is a designation of wisdom, and intelligence. According to Gesenius, together with the meaning, counsellor, it has also that of curator. But this is contradicted by the parallel passage chap 11 2 What is there expressed by רוּחַ עֵצָה וּגְבוּרָה, *the spirit of counsel and might*, is here signified by יוֹעֵץ and אֵל גִּבּוֹר. Supernatural wisdom and divine power, as the two chief virtues of a Ruler, shall adorn the great king The third name is אֵל וּבּוֹר, *the mighty God*. Gesenius *the mighty hero*.

אֵל has indeed this meaning also; but that this is not its sense in the passage before us, is evident both from chap. 10. 21, where the two words likewise occur in the sense: *mighty God*, and from the following name which also ascribes a divine attribute to the king. We have already seen in the general introduction, that the doctrine of the true deity of the Messiah, was already known under the old covenant, and also that the name Immanuel signifies, God become man. When Gesenius reminds us, in case the meaning *God* is here adopted, of the custom of the orientals, to ascribe divine attributes to kings, he entirely overlooks the difference between the Hebrews and all idolatrous nations. The name Son of God, in the Old Testament sense of representation and subordination, justly belonged to the theocratic kings as well as to other magistrates. But had Isaiah called an earthly king God, or given him divine predicates, he would have acted in direct opposition to his duty to defend the rights of God from every encroachment, and have rendered himself unworthy of the dignity of a prophet. Pluschke endeavors in another way to set aside the deity of the king: "In my opinion," he says, "this name is altogether symbolical. The Messiah shall be called strength of God, or strong God, divine hero, in order by this name to remind the people of the strength of God." But this explanation is refuted by the very connexion in which גבור אל stands with יועץ. As the latter must signify the wisdom of the king, so must the former, according to the parallel passage, chap. 2. 2. signify his strength. In opposition to the accents, several interpreters would separate the two words אל and גבור from each other. Thus of old, Aquila ἰσχυρός, δυνατός, and Jahn *deus, fortis*. —The fourth name is אֲבִי עַד literally: *Father of eternity.* This allows of a two-fold explanation. Either, we may suppose, according to a frequent usage of the Stat. Con. that Father of eternity, is the same as Eternal Father; and the meaning would be, that the Messiah will not, as must be the case with an earthly king, however excellent, leave his people destitute after a short reign, but rule over them, and bless them forever. Or we may explain it by the usage of the Arabic in which he who possesses a thing, is called the Father of it, e. g. the father of mercy, the merciful. We have the more reason to suppose this usage adopted here, since in respect to proper names especially it very often occurs in Hebrew. Thus e. g. אֲבִי אֵל *Father of strength*, strong; אֲבִי דֵּע *Father of knowledge*, intelligent; אֲבִי הוֹד *Father of glory*, glorious; אֲבִי טוֹב *Father of goodness*, good; אֲבִי נֵעַם *Father of compassion*, compassionate ; אֲבִי שָׁלוֹם *Father of peace*, peaceful. According to all these analogies, Father of eternity, is the same as, eternal. According to both explanations, the latter of which is much to be preferred, a divine attribute is here ascribed to the Messiah. For although merely the longest duration, of which a thing is in its nature capable, is sometimes expressed in Hebrew by the idea of eternity, yet this limitation must always be shown by the context; thus e. g. in the passage Deut 15. 17, "he shall be thy servant forever," for during life. Here on the contrary, not only is there no intimation in the context of such a restriction, but its connexion with the remaining appellations, compels us to take this name also in its most comprehensive sense. The eternal reign of the Messiah, in contrast with the temporal reign of the human rulers of the theocracy, is made especially prominent also in Ps LXXII, which bears throughout a strong resemblance to this prophecy. That there the word *eternal*, in v 17, is to be taken in the stricter sense is evident from the additional phrase: "as long as the sun endureth." Paulus and Jahn interpret: Father of his age; but this is entirely arbitrary, since עַד never occurs in this sense. The explanation of Herder besides being ungrammatical is extremely forced: "my Father to eternity;" that is, he will thus address Jehovah. It would then, at least, have read אָבִי. Contrary to the analogy of the other names, Pluschke: everlasting Father, to remind them that God is the everlasting Father of his people.—The fifth name is שַׂר שָׁלוֹם, '*Prince of Peace*' In this name there is plainly an allusion to the name Solomon, *the peaceful*, which is perhaps directly given to the Messiah in Ps. LXXII. As under the reign of Solomon, the theocracy enjoyed an outward and temporary peace, so under that of his great successor and antitype, it shall enjoy a real and everlasting peace. In like manner also in the blessing of Jacob, the Messiah is called שִׁילֹה *peace-maker*.

V 6 "Without end will the dominion, without end will the peace increase on the throne of David and in his kingdom, that he may establish and sustain it by justice and righteousness, from henceforth to eternity. The zeal of Jehovah, the Almighty will do this." The word מַרְבֵּה, *increase*, is a noun after the form of מַשְׁקֶה and מַרְאֶה properly a participial form. In the middle of it is a ם final, which was at first in all probability accidental, but was afterwards supposed to contain great mysteries. On the "throne of David and over his kingdom, that he may establish it, etc." is a concise mode of saying: this increase of power shall proceed from the Messiah, who sitting upon the throne of David shall extend it over his kingdom, the theocracy, which he shall be constantly intent upon sustaining by justice and righteousness. The sense through the great descendant of David, the Messiah, the theocracy shall forever be increasing in extent, and after all opposition shall be subdued, its members shall be blessed with perfect inward and outward peace. But this dominion, unlike the kingdoms of the earth, shall be founded, established, and administered, not by force, but by righteousness, which shall move the hitherto hostile nations to yield to it a willing and joyful submission. (See the parallel passage, Ps 72·12, where the voluntary submission of the heathen nations, is also represented as the effect of the righteousness, mildness, and compassion of the great king.) While the kingdoms of this world pass away, the kingdom of the Messiah will be eternal, as its King. Comp. Ps 72·17.—In the last words· "the zeal of Jehovah will effect this," the word קִנְאַת may be taken in a twofold sense; we may either, with Heider, understand by it the zeal of God for his honor, which moved him to fulfil his promise to the covenant people of a future great descendant of David, and at the same time also to vindicate his honor in opposition to the idols, or the zeal of love, a sense in which it often occurs, e. g. Cant. 8·6. The raising up of so illustrious a king, the establishment of his everlasting kingdom, the subduing all opposition to it, is a work of the love of God, which moves him to have compassion on his people, who for their own works had deserved an entirely different fate.

We have here, in conclusion, still to add some general remarks, as to the subject of v. 5, 6. The older interpreters unanimously acknowledge the Messiah as such; this also was the view entertained by the Jews in ancient times. The passage is referred to the Messiah by the Chaldee Paraphrast, the commentary on Genesis at chap. 41·44, known under the name of Bereschit Rabbah, in Raym Martini pugio fidei Th III, Abschn. 3 cap 14 § 6, and by Rabbi Jose Galilaus, in the book Echa Rabati, a commentary on the lamentations of Jeremiah in Raym Mart I. c III, 3. cap. 4, § 13 * Ben Sira fol 40 of the Amsterdam edition 1679, numbers among the eight names of the Messiah those also taken from this passage, Wonderful, Counsellor, Mighty God, Prince of peace. Among the more modern Christian interpreters, this interpretation has been held

---

* א״ר יוסי הגלילי אף שמו של משיח נקרא על שמו על שם עד אבי עד שר שלום. Rabbi Jose of Galilee says the name of the Messiah is also שלום, as it is said Isa 9·6, Father of Eternity, Prince of Peace.

by Cube, Dathe, Michaelis, Döderlein, Lowth, Koppe, Pluschke, Kuinol, Herder, v. d. Palm, Rosenmuller, Umbreit, (in den theol Studien und Kritiken 1, 2 p 307) and others. The later Jewish critics on the contrary, were offended, that the Messiah is here described as God, contrary to their system of doctrine. On doctrinal grounds, therefore, they relinquished the received interpretation, and sought to make the passage agree with Hezekiah, but in the end were obliged to resort to the grossest perversions. Among them R. Lipmann, however, allows the Messianic interpretation to be in a manner valid Perceiving that the prophecy cannot relate exclusively to Hezekiah, he extends it to all his successors of the line of David, including the Messiah, by whom it shall be most completely fulfilled Grotius was the first among Christian commentators to relinquish the Messianic interpretation Le Clerc himself acknowledges, that these predicates agree with Hezekiah only *sensu admodum diluto*. The explanation which refers the prophecy to Hezekiah has found in recent times, on the contrary, several defenders; among others Hezel, Hensler, Paulus, the author of the Exeg Hanb. Jahn (append. herm II, p 133 seq see the refutation of his unnatural explanation by Gesenius) and Gesenius, who has modified this hypothesis by the supposition, that the prophet connected his Messianic expectations and wishes with Hezekiah, and expected them to be realized in him

Leaving out of view for the present this modification, it is inconceivable how any one, except from doctrinal prejudice, should regard king Hezekiah as the subject of this prediction. Against him, and in favor of the Messiah, the following are the most important arguments.

1 The testimony of the New Testament. Gesenius indeed asserts that there is the less occasion to adopt the Messianic interpretation, since the New Testament gives no evidence in its favor; but he is here in an error. For if, as we have seen, chap 8. 23 and 9 1, according to the testimony of the New Testament and internal evidence, must be explained of the honor and the blessings which should be conferred on despised Galilee by the Messiah, it cannot well be perceived how the author of this honor and these blessings, described in v 5, 6, can be any other than he.

2 It is decisive against Hezekiah, that the discourse is not here concerning prosperity destined merely for the kingdom of Judah, but concerning a glorification, chiefly of the province of Galilee,

which belonged to the kingdom of the ten tribes, and over which Hezekiah neither had, nor could have any influence.

3. The attributes here ascribed to the great king afford a strong argument against Hezekiah, and every earthly ruler. Herder well observes (Heb. Poesie II, p 437): " could the prophet more plainly show to whom he refers? Surely it is not to Hezekiah or Hezekiah's son, as if he were writing a birth day ode ; he speaks of a king, who himself bears all the names and blessings of the house of David, and introduces the promised golden age " If we consider the prophecy only as a human conjecture, how could the prophet to whom so great political sagacity is ascribed on other occasions, and by which it is thought his fulfilled predictions may be explained, expect Hezekiah, who was then about ten years of age, and who came forward under such unfavorable circumstances, to realize the hopes, which he had expressed concerning the future ruler, extend his kingdom without limit and found an everlasting dominion? How could he ascribe divine attributes to Hezekiah, a feeble mortal, and thus insult the majesty of God, whose servant he was? It would have been only senseless flattery, which must have appeared to Hezekiah himself as satire, for Isaiah to utter such language, but his character as it is established by history, secures him against every suspicion of this sort When it is said that the Israelitish kings also, in Ps II, XLV, LXXII, CX, are the subject of similar ideal hopes, or flattery equally gross, it is erroneously and without regard to the natural meaning of these Psalms, and the authority of Christ and his Apostles, assumed that they are not to be explained of the Messiah, but of an earthly king. Even among the idolatrous heathen, the practice of ascribing divine names and predicates to kings, first originated in a later and corrupt age, and in what light this practice was viewed by the Jews, let the example of Josephus show, who, Arch. XIX, 8th, 2d, regards the death of Agrippa, as a punishment for not disapproving the conduct of the people, who cried out to him as a god.

4. In favor of the Messiah, is the similarity of this prophecy with other Messianic passages, viz, with the Psalms before quoted, especially Ps LXXII, and with the remaining Messianic predictions in the first part of Isaiah The same characteristics are here ascribed to the Messiah, which constantly occur in the prophecies respecting him, perpetual peace under his reign, its vast extension, his everlasting dominion, etc

5 Against Hezekiah is the parallel passage, chap 7 14 We

have before spoken of the similarity of these two places, and shown that both must belong to one and the same subject. If then, as is generally confessed, Hezekiah cannot be the subject of the former, neither can he be of the latter.

But against the supposition, whereby Gesenius has endeavored to combine the Messianic interpretation, with that which makes Hezekiah the subject, we may urge, that no analogous example can be produced, where a prophet had connected his hopes of the Messiah with a definite subject, by which they were not realized. Allowing the exact distance of time which separated them from the Messiah to have been unknown to the prophets, so that they might have believed, as the Apostles did, concerning the second coming of Christ, that his manifestation *could* take place even in their time, still no proof can be found in any passage, that, going beyond what was communicated to them from above, they predicted that it actually *would*. But it is the more improbable that the prophet should have placed his Messianic hopes on Hezekiah, since according to chap 7·14, and according to the passage before us, the Messiah was to be a higher, and more than human being, which it would have been difficult indeed for the prophet to suppose of Hezekiah. Moreover the view of Gesenius being assumed as correct, we must in like manner refer all the Messianic predictions of the prophet to Hezekiah and thereby involve ourselves in many absurdities.

The objections which have been brought against the Messianic interpretation, disappear of themselves before a correct insight into the nature of the prophetic vision. The most common of these objections is, that the whole connexion requires a present and not a future subject, and that we must therefore refer the whole to a prince of the royal family, already born; but Lowth has long since justly remarked in reply, that it is the constant practice of the prophets to place temporal, in connexion with spiritual deliverances. As Isaiah, in the second part of his prophecies, always connects the deliverance from the captivity, with the deliverance by the Messiah, and passes over from the former to the latter, and as towards the close of chap. x, he describes the overthrow of the Assyrians, and then chap xi, abruptly speaks of the Messiah's kingdom, so here, he suddenly directs his view to the higher benefit, after chap viii, ix and x, he has described the inferior one. Every deliverance in the nearer future, suggested at the same time to the prophets that great deliverance in the more distant future, which was the occasion of the former, and the pledge of its accomplishment. The distance of time does not thereby come into consideration, because it is neither known, nor regarded by the prophets, who behold all events of futurity combined in one picture. Another objection against the Messianic interpretation, that here political expectations lie at the foundation, and the discourse is not concerning a moral kingdom, arises, partly from a literal and false understanding of the prophecy, and the disregard of its metaphorical character, and partly from ignorance of the nature of the kingdom of Christ, of which Christ is king and sovereign in the most proper sense, since by his humiliation, and the redemption thereby accomplished, he has obtained the right to exercise dominion.

Isaiah XI and XII.

This section constitutes a part of a larger whole, which begins with chap. 10: 5. The contents of this whole portion are as follows; the prophet had before repeatedly described the calamity, which the Assyrians, an instrument in the hand of the Lord, should bring, first upon Israel, and then upon Judah. The foregoing portion, chap. 9: 7—10: 4, though not contemporaneous with this, yet certainly not without design placed in connexion with it, was probably composed after the Syrians confederated with the Israelites, had already been overthrown by the Assyrians. In it the prophet had threatened the Israelites with the devastation of their country, and the final and total annihilation of their State, which were impending on account of their transgressions. This threatening had already been fulfilled in the period, which had elapsed between this prophecy and the foregoing. The king Tiglath-pileser, after the conquest of Syria, had invaded the kingdom of the ten tribes, and carried away a part of its inhabitants, into captivity; Salmanezer at a later period had taken Samaria, and almost put an end to the kingdom of the ten tribes, since only a few of its citizens were left in the land. Judah also under Ahaz, had already suffered much from the Assyrians, from whom that help had been foolishly sought, which Isaiah had in vain exhorted them to seek from God alone. But they had reason to apprehend still greater calamities from the same quarter. Under these circumstances, the prophet came forward, and delivered the present discourse, whose object is to animate the drooping courage of the people, to inspire them with firm confidence in God, who can, indeed, inflict heavy judgments upon them, since according to the law of visible retribution, which prevailed in the theocracy, sin and apostasy must not remain unpunished, but, who would never suffer them to be utterly destroyed, because their destination to receive the Messiah among themselves, had not yet been fulfilled.

The whole discourse is of a joyful character; the prophet had no more occasion to threaten, since his former threatening had now become a reality, and all was dismay before the approaching invasion of the king of Assyria. A twofold deliverance of the covenant people was presented in vision to the prophet, the latter and greater, as it presupposed the former, served to confirm it.

The first part, chap 10 5—35, is chiefly directed against the king of Assyria. This king, unconscious of his destination to be an instrument in the hand of God for the punishment of his rebellious people, had attributed all his victories to himself, he believed he might, with ease, entirely subdue the covenant people, and audaciously derided the Almighty God of Israel, as a powerless being, who could not help his people He shall therefore suffer a terrible overthrow, v 5 27 It is true, that he shall succeed in penetrating to Jerusalem, but while he prepares to capture the city, he shall be overtaken by the vengeance of Jehovah, v 28 34. How strikingly this prediction was fulfilled is well known See chap. xxxvii

The second portion, chap xi and xii is closely connected with the foregoing This is evident from its commencing with Vav copulative, and from the manifest reference of the figure in the first verse of chap xi, to that in the last verse of the preceding chapter, the Assyrians had there been compared to a magnificent forest, which should be cut down by the hand of Jehovah; here on the contrary, the house of David appears, as a tree which had been felled, from whose roots a small shoot would spring forth, and insignificant at first, grow up to a stately tree This portion is chiefly occupied with the description of the illustrious attributes of the great Restorer and king, and the nature of his kingdom Reinhard and others are disposed to derive from this, a proof against its connexion with the foregoing, but unjustly, since it is the custom of the prophets to connect with the representation of the inferior and nearer deliverance, that of the greater and more distant

The contents are as follows. From the house of David, fallen into total obscurity, a Ruler shall hereafter arise, who though lowly and obscure at first, will attain to great glory. The Spirit of God, who shall dwell constantly with him, will furnish him with all those endowments, which the discharge of his official duties required. By the aid of this Spirit, he will easily discriminate between the pious, and the ungodly, he will search the heart, and therefore will not, like worldly kings, be deceived by the outward appearance. While he becomes the patron of oppressed innocence, and maintains the rights of those, who cannot procure justice for themselves, he will destroy the ungodly, not like earthly kings by outward punishment, but by the bare word of his mouth; instead of worldly splendor, righteousness and faithfulness shall be his highest ornament. V 1—5 When the prophet has thus described the person of the great Restorer, he proceeds to speak of the character of his kingdom. Under his reign, even in the irrational part of the creation, all discord and destruction, introduced by sin, shall cease, sin, and crime, shall be known no more; his dominion will not be confined to the ancient covenant people; the heathen before devoted to their idols, shall reverently turn to Him. V. 6—10. While the prophet in the first part of the chapter has spoken rather of the Messiah in general and his kingdom, in v. 11—16 he announces by a figure taken from the theocracy, what he will accomplish especially for the covenant people, for whom indeed the prediction was in the first instance designed. The restoration of the Jews, dispersed, as the prophet foresees, in the time of the Messiah's appearing, into widely different lands, as it has in part already taken place and shall be completed before the end of the world, is represented under the image of their being led back to the holy land, at that time the seat of the kingdom of God, successively connected with it in the vision of the prophet. The harmony and love, which will unite the covenant people with each other in the time of the Messiah, are represented under the image of the extinction of the most fatal dissension of former times—the enmity between Ephraim and Judah, the prosperity which the people shall enjoy, under the figure of the conquest of hostile neighbors, taken from the prosperous reign of David, and the removal of all hindrances of their prosperity under the figure, furnished by the history of the redemption from Egypt, of the drying up of the Red Sea and the river Euphrates. In chap. xii follows a song of thanksgiving, which the prophet puts into the mouth of the redeemed.

Several recent critics (Vater, Comment. in Jes. xi, Rosenmuller and De Wette Einl p 234) have doubted the genuineness of a part or the whole of chap xi and xii. On the contrary it has been defended by Beckhaus (Integritat der prophetischen Schriften p. 77 seq), Jahn, (Einl. II, 474), Bertholdt (Einl. 1392), Gesenius, on the passage. The only tolerably plausible objection to the genuineness of these chapters, is, that the prophet, v 1. speaks of the royal family of David, as sunk into entire obscurity, and of the Jews, as well as of the Israelites, v. 11, etc as though they had already been carried away captive into the most distant lands. This objection could not be sufficiently refuted by Gesenius, with his views. But it loses all force as soon as we apply to it the remark, which will be proved to be just in the introduction to the second part, that the prophets frequently transfer themselves into the future, which then became to them in vision, the present. And thus the prophet here describes the condition of things, not in his own time, but in the time when the great promised Redeemer should appear.

The reference of the prophecy to the Messiah is so plain, that after the example of the Chaldee Paraphrast, most Jewish interpreters as Jarchi, Abarbanel, and Kimchi, defend it. Their testimony is collected in a treatise by Seb Edzardi, undecimum cap Esaiae Christo vindicatum adversus Grotium et sectatores ejus, imprimis Herm. v. d. Hardt. Hamb 1696. Among modern interpreters it has been defended by Michaelis, Doderlein, Koppe, Lowth, Kube, Beckhaus (Integritat der proph. Schr p 77 seq) Reinhard (explanatio loci Jes. XI, v 1—5 Wittemb 1783, wieder abgedr. in Velthusen, Kuinol, Ruperti Comment. theol V. 1 und in Reinhard's opusculis theol ed Poelitz v. II) v d Palm, Dereser, Jahn (append. Hermeneut II. p 123 seq) and others. Eichhorn, Bauer, De Wette, and Gesenius, also belong in some degree to the defenders of this interpretation, although they do not find the historical, but only an ideal Messiah in the prophecy.

Nevertheless several interpreters have felt themselves obliged to relinquish the natural explanation, and seek for another subject of the prophecy. But few have been in favor of the interpretation, which makes Zerubbabel the subject, and it is so absurd as to deserve no further notice.* By a larger and more respectable number, how-

---

* It is already mentioned by Theodoret· ἄξιον δὲ θρηνῆσαι τὴν Ἰουδαίων ἐμβροντησίαν, οἱ τῷ ζοροβάβελ ταύτην προσαρμόζουσι τὴν προφητείαν.

ever, it has been referred to Hezekiah. This interpretation is mentioned even by Ephraem the Syrian; among the Jews it was followed by Moses Hakkohen, and Abenezra; among the Christian interpreters, Grotius was the first to adopt it, though at the same time, he supposed the prophecy to have a higher reference to the Messiah, (Redit ad laudes Ezechiae, sub quibus sublimiores latent Messiae laudes). He was followed by Dathe, its exclusive reference to Hezekiah was asserted by Hermann v. d. Hart in a treatise published in 1695, which was condemned, and by Bahrdt, Hezel, Paulus, Hensler, Augusti, Holzapfel, and others among the recent commentators.

The objections to the strict Messianic interpretation, urged by these interpreters, and also by those who maintain its reference to a mere ideal Messiah, are inconclusive. They have originated in a great measure from overlooking the metaphorical character of the prophetic style. "Traits," says Gesenius, "like those in v. 4 and 5 exclude every other subject but a political Messiah, and king of the Israelitish State." But we have already shown, in the general introduction, that persons of the Old Testament must necessarily have formed the ground work of that idea of the Messiah, which was presented to the prophet in vision, that this idea must, as it were, have been embodied in those persons. As now in other places, the Messiah appears as prophet and high priest, because that part of his office which is related to the office of prophet and high priest under the Old Testament presented itself to the prophet, so here, and in many other places, he appears for similar reason under the image of a king. It must not be overlooked, that with the exception of the allusion to the obscurity of his origin in v. 1, the whole prediction exhibits the Messiah in glory, and that, consequently, we must not compare what is here said of him with his appearance in a state of humiliation in the New Testament, but we must compare it with the description of him, as exalted to the right hand of the Father, and invested with universal dominion; and thus when the theocratic drapery is removed, perfect agreement will be found to exist between the prophecy and its fulfilment in Christ.

The reasons for the Messianic interpretation, and against making Hezekiah the subject of the prophecy, are the following:

1. This interpretation has the testimony of tradition in its favor, preserved to us by the Chaldee Paraphrast. He translates the first verse וְיִפֹּק מַלְכָּא מִבְּנוֹהִי דִישַׁי וּמְשִׁיחָא מִבְּנֵי בְנוֹהִי יִתְרַבֵּי. The New Testament also shows that this was the usual interpreta-

tion; even without an express citation, appellations taken from this prophecy are ascribed to the Messiah, see Apocalypse 5. 5. 22. 16 ἡ ῥίζα Δαβίδ.—To this must be added the distinct testimonies of the New Testament, which show that its authors approved the traditional interpretations. Rom 15. 12, Paul quotes this prophecy, and proves from it the calling of the heathen. 2 Thess 2 8, he employs the words of v. 4 and ascribes what is said in it to the Messiah.

2. The comparison of parallel passages leads every unprejudiced mind to make the Messiah the subject of the prophecy. From the great mass of these we will select only a few. The Messiah is here represented under the figure of a shoot or branch. But this was so common an image for him, that the epithet sprout or branch became almost a common name. See chap 4 2. A very striking resemblance to the 1st verse of chap. XI is found in chap 53 1, where, in order to designate the lowliness of his first appearance, the Messiah is in like manner compared to a feeble and tender shoot. The predictions in chap. II, IV and IX, have the greatest resemblance to this, and cannot be referred to any other subject without violence. So also the prophecy in Micah 5 1. In general the reception of the heathen into the kingdom of God, the holiness of its subjects, the cessation of all hostility, are traits which are constantly recurring in the Messianic predictions.

3. There are some features in this prophecy, which indicate a more than human dignity in its subject. According to v. 4, he slays the wicked, not like earthly rulers by outward means, but by his bare word, an expression which is elsewhere used in reference to Jehovah. The heathen in v. 10, are represented as coming to him to render him religious reverence.

4 It appears from chap 10. 11, that this whole portion could not have been composed earlier than the sixth year of Hezekiah. For in this year Samaria was captured, which here is presupposed to have already taken place. It may even be made probable by many reasons that it cannot have been composed *long* before the invasion of Judah by Sennacherib, in the fourteenth year of Hezekiah; while it must have been composed previously to that event, since it is predicted as still future. Hezekiah had therefore certainly reigned a considerable time, when the prophecy was made known. Hence it is impossible, that he can have been its subject, since it promises a *future* sprout of David. It is true that the defenders of the explanation, which makes Hezekiah the subject, seek to avoid the difficulty by

taking the verbs in v. 1 as preterites, and then understanding the remainder as present and future. But Gesenius well remarks in reply to this· "the understanding of the passage partly as present, partly as future, appears to be inadmissible and arbitrary, especially when the passage is viewed in connexion with chap. x, as indeed the Vav v. 1 וְיָצָא requires. As the interchangeable praeters, futures and participles must there be constantly understood in the future, (see especially v 34) so must they also here; and according to the prevailing *consecutio temporum*, וְיָצָא with a future in the parallel member cannot be taken otherwise." As the prophecy was composed long after Hezekiah began his reign, the assertion of Hensler is groundless, who supposes, that though the passage should be translated in the future, it may yet be understood of Hezekiah; it may foretell, that he will one day take the throne of his father and reign in wisdom.

5. If the reference of chap ix to Hezekiah appears untenable, because the prophet could not without the basest flattery, ascribe to Hezekiah the language he there employs, this objection is still stronger here. When that prediction was composed, Hezekiah was not yet grown up, and we can more easily conceive, if we leave out of view the true notion of a prophet, how ideal hopes could be connected with his person. But at a time when Hezekiah, who was indeed a pious king, but not otherwise very distinguished, and who so greatly needed the counsel of the prophet, had already long sat on the throne, how could Isaiah have attributed to him gifts of the Divine Spirit, which only flattery could have ascribed even to a David? How could he expect that under his reign the golden age would arrive and all transgression cease, that all the heathen nations should come and devote themselves to his service?

6 That the prophet does not speak of a present, but of a future sprout of David, appears from v. 1; the subject of the prediction is there represented under the image of a sprout, feeble at first, which springs up from the roots of a tree, which had been felled. It is thereby plainly indicated, that the royal house of David at the time of the appearing of the great object of expectation, would have entirely declined and be sunk in obscurity. This agrees well with Christ, but not with Hezekiah. Gesenius replies, that shoots spring up from the roots of trees that are yet alive, and hence we are not obliged to think only of a tree which has been cut down. But as we shall see in our explanations of the verse, the prophet is speaking

precisely of a tree which had been cut down; the figure would certainly otherwise have been most unfitly chosen. In addition to this, even the very circumstance, that the sprout shall not arise from the stem of David, but of Jesse, indicates that at that time the royal family of David will have again fallen into the obscurity of private life. Gesenius further supposes, but we see not with what propriety, that the dynasty of David, even in the time of Isaiah, might be compared to a tree which had been cut down. The family of David still maintained its dignity unimpaired, the misfortunes under Ahaz had not so much affected them as the whole people. The comparison with a tree cut down to the roots would naturally signify, not the mere decline of the house of David, but rather the entire cessation of its dominion. The existence of the kingdom of Judah, as Gesenius asserts, is, indeed, presupposed in the oracle, although the prophet sees a large portion of the people scattered through all lands; but that, the continuation of the royal house of David need not necessarily be connected therewith, is shown by the state of things, at the time when Christ appeared; when precisely according to this representation, the kingdom of Judah still existed, but the family of David had long before lost the dominion. When Gesenius appeals to the circumstance, that Amos also, a contemporary of Isaiah, chap. 8 11, speaks of the house of David as already fallen, it is easy to perceive, that the prophet does not represent the condition of things in his own time, but in that of the great Redeemer, whom he foretells in the cited passage.

7. V. 12 etc. the return, not merely of the subjects of the kingdom of Israel, but also of the Jews from all the regions of the earth, where they have been dispersed, is foretold. This must relate to a far later period, than that of Hezekiah; for in his time no carrying away of the Jews had as yet taken place. The remarks of Gesenius in reply will be refuted in the explanation of the passage.

As in most prophecies of the Messiah, so also in the one before us, no regard is paid to the gradual development of his kingdom The fulfilment, therefore, has only commenced, and will be completed in the future, when, after the fulness of the Gentiles shall have been brought into the kingdom of God, and apostate Israel converted, the consequences of the fall, even in external nature, shall be done away.

V. 1. The prophet announces in the commencement, that the fate of the royal house of David, should be totally different from that of the Assyrians, which he had just foretold. The Assyrians were abased, when they were most highly exalted, the royal house of David shall be exalted, when sunk the lowest. "And a rod goes forth from the stem of Jesse, a branch from his root bears fruit." The word חֹטֶר occurs besides only in Prov 14 3, and signifies there, *a rod* Aram. חוּטְרָא *baculus.* Arab. خُطْر *branch.* The image of a sprout for a descendant is very common. See chap. 4. 2, and the examples from profane writers by Reinhard on this passage. Hensler endeavors to prove that גֶּזַע does not mean a trunk of a tree that has been cut down, *truncus,* but only the trunk of a tree in general, *stipes.* But this is in opposition, 1 to the etymology; the word is derived from גָּזַע equal to גָּדַע *to cut off,* or *cut down.* 2 To the Hebrew usage,—the word occurs besides only in Job 14 8 and Isa 40 24. In the latter place some interpreters indeed wish to give it the meaning *trunk*, in general; but entirely without reason. See Rosenmüller on the passage. 3 To the connexion. It is said in the second member, a sprout from his roots shall bear fruit. Unless we choose to explain this altogether unsuitably of a wild shoot, which springs up from the roots of a tree that is still standing, we must understand by the word a trunk, which had been cut down to the roots. 4 To the dialects. In the Talmud, and in Syriac, the word signifies: *truncus.* In Arabic the root جَزَع has the meaning: *secuit.* After all these proofs, it is of little consequence, that the Arabic جَذَع sometimes stands for *trunk* in a wider sense. Also Aquila, Symmachus, and Theodotion translate: κορμός, *truncus.* The question now arises, why the Messiah is here represented as the sprout of Jesse, when in other places he is called the sprout of David. Vitringa gives as the reason, that the Messiah should be born at Bethlehem, which was the dwelling place of Jesse, but not of David. See Micah 5: 1. But far more in accordance with the figure, others remark, that the prophet hereby wished to indicate, that the family of David would then have so much declined, that it would be more appropriately designated after its humbler, than its royal ancestor. Calvin. "Davidem ipsum non nominat, sed potius Isai. Adeo enim imminuta erat illius familiae dignitas, ut rusticana potius et ignobilis, quam regia videretur." נֵצֶר *branch, sprout.* The suff in מִשָּׁרָשָׁיו refers to the stem of Jesse. The expression: "a branch from his

Isaiah 11 : 1, 2

roots will bear fruit," is as much as to say, a branch sprung from his roots will grow up to a stately, and fruitful tree." By this image it is foretold, that the Messiah before he should attain to glory, would be obscure and lowly. A parallel passage is found in Ez. 17. 22, 23. There the Messiah is compared to a tender twig, which planted by Jehovah on a high mountain, puts forth boughs, and bears fruit, so that all the fowls dwell beneath it. It is scarcely necessary to mention, that figure and reality are blended together in the verse. It would be paraphrased thus: " as a tree, which had been cut down, sends forth a young shoot from its roots, which, insignificant at first, soon increases to a stately, and fruitful tree, so also a king will arise from the family of David, buried in neglect and obscurity, who, inferior and unnoticed at first, will afterwards attain to great glory."- Interpreters, from not observing this mingling of figure and reality, have been led to many erroneous explanations; thus e. g. Vitringa asks: Who the roots of the house of David can be? and understands by them the most distinguished of his descendants; and J H. Michaelis explains יִפְרֶה by *spirituali sobole augebitur*, etc

V. 2. "Upon him rests the spirit of Jehovah, the spirit of wisdom and insight, the spirit of counsel and strength, the spirit of knowledge, and of the fear of Jehovah." The sense he will possess in abundant measure the Spirit of God, and as particular manifestations of it, the qualifications mentioned. The Spirit of Jehovah, the spirit of wisdom, is the same as the spirit of Jehovah who imparts wisdom, etc. The genitive here does not denote possession, but effect. So Ps. 4· 2 אֱלֹהֵי צִדְקִי, *the God of my righteousness*; 2 Cor. 1 3 ὁ θεὸς πάσης παρακλήσεως. Reinhard, who in his whole explanation of this verse is influenced by the mistaken hypothesis, that it exhibits the Messiah as a prophet, erroneously supposes, after the example of the Chaldee, that רוּחַ יְהוָה means specifically the prophetic spirit; and appeals to passages like chap 40· 1. 61 1. But we have seen already, that the Messiah is not here exhibited as a prophet, but as a king. רוּחַ יְהוָה different from רוח אלהים, inasmuch as Elohim is the general, and Jehovah the theocratic name of God, is the power, with which God qualifies his instruments for the advancement of his kingdom, and exalts and consecrates their natural endowments; which gives skill to the theocratic artificer, the view of futurity to the prophet, and wisdom and all the virtues of a ruler to the theocratic king. See 1 Sam 16 13 Calvin " Tametsi Christus his donis minime indigebat, quia tamen induit carnem nostram, oportuit ipsum his locupletari, ut deinde participes efficeremur omnium bonorum." Perhaps the circumstance, that the Messiah is first said to be endowed with the Spirit of God in general terms, and that then particular gifts are mentioned by way of example, indicates that he would not, like all other servants of God, be endowed with any particular gifts. Theodoret: τῶν μὲν γὰρ προφητῶν ἕκαστος μερικήν τινα ἐδέξατο χάριν, ἐν αὐτῷ δὲ κατῴκησε πᾶν τὸ πλήρωμα τῆς θεότητος σωματικῶς, καὶ κατὰ τὸ ἀνθρώπινον δὲ πάντα εἶχε τοῦ πνεύματος τὰ χαρίσματα. Although the word רוּחַ is elsewhere spoken of the Spirit of God, when it takes possession of the mind, see Num. 11 25, yet here it seems to be peculiarly emphatic. The prophets were powerfully seized by the Spirit, and then again deserted; but his influence with the Messiah shall be uniform and permanent. What Isaiah expresses by the word נָחָה, John expressed by the Greek μένειν, John 1 32, 33. 14: 16, 17, probably with distinct reference to this place. Jerome: "in quo requievit spiritus domini id est aeterna habitatione permansit, non ut avolaret et rursum ad eum descenderet, sed juxta Joannis baptistae testimonium, jugiter permaneret." In respect to the particular gifts mentioned, it is to be remarked, that the prophet does not design to specify *all* the perfections of the Messiah; he rather mentions only some few, after he has included all the rest in the general one, the spirit of Jehovah. Thus e. g. righteousness is wanting here. Further, we are not to proceed upon the principle that all here mentioned, were distinguished from each other with philosophical accuracy, by the prophet. Such accurate discrimination is not to be found in general among the Hebrews, with whom, that blending together of the qualifications conferred by the Spirit and of the theoretical and practical, which took place in real life, is also plainly expressed in the language. There is indeed a certain difference between the expressions selected, yet it is not such, that one would exclude the others. On the contrary, the first attribute, חָכְמָה *wisdom*, includes nearly all the rest. The meaning of wisdom, especially among the Hebrews, is very comprehensive. It is always at the same time practical and theoretical. It comprehends the knowledge of what is good and desirable, and corresponding sentiments and conduct. It also includes prudence, or the ability to select the best means for the attainment of the best ends. חָכְמָה is here coupled with בִּינָה *insight*, the gift of a judging and discriminating sagacity. There is a difference between them in regard to

ISAIAH 11:2, 3   377

the objects to which they refer; inasmuch as the former designates the moral, the latter the pure theocratic virtue of knowledge. While the first and last couple of attributes are such as the king must possess as a man, the second couple are especially requisite for kings as such, in order to the successful administration of their government. עֵצָה *counsel*, signifies the power of forming a quick and wise resolution even in the most difficult cases גְּבוּרָה *strength*, the power to carry this resolution into effect; the great king shall be mighty in counsel, and in action. We are not to understand by גְּבוּרָה bravery in war, since the kingdom of the Messiah is the kingdom of peace; he needs no worldly courage, or weapons against the ungodly, but he slays them, as it is said, v 4, by the breath of his mouth. As here, עֵצָה and גְּבוּרָה are placed in connexion, so in chap. 9:5 the Messiah is called in reference to the first attribute, יוֹעֵץ *counsellor*, and in reference to the second אֵל גִּבּוֹר, *mighty God*. Reinhard and also Jahn, proceeding upon the false assumption that all these attributes designate a prophet, understood by עֵצָה *the gift of prophecy* He takes גְּבוּרָה in a special sense, for the power to work miracles, contrary both to the connexion, and the usage of the language, although the power to work miracles is indeed included in the general attribute of strength Of the last two attributes, the knowledge and the fear of Jehovah, (after דַּעַת, יהוה is to be supplied from what follows), both together convey the idea of religion so far as it comprehends 1 a knowledge of God, and 2. a corresponding disposition. Both are always viewed in Scripture as connected; without the fear of God, which does not exclude love to him, but implies it, there can be no true knowledge of Jehovah Hence the expressions here used for a part, are employed in other places to designate the whole Ps. 19. 9 Hos. 4 1 6 6.

V. 3. "He will easily understand the fear of God; he will not judge after the sight of his eyes, nor punish after the hearing of his ears" The verb רִיחַ is sometimes construed with the accusative of the thing, sometimes as here with the prep. בְּ. To smell is here used metaphorically, for a quick and penetrating judgment and knowledge. The word also occurs elsewhere in a figurative sense, thus Job 39. 25, where it is said of the horse, "he smells the battle from afar." In other languages also the word "smell" is used metaphorically, when any one from certain marks, conjectures what appears to be concealed. Thus Cicero frequently uses the word *odorari*. The sense then is . the king whose insight and wisdom are praised in the foregoing verse, will possess the gift of the discerning of spirits in so high a degree, that he will distinguish at first sight the pious and the ungodly See John 1: 48, 49. Luke 7: 39 In favor of this interpretation we observe, 1. That the verb הריח plainly corresponds to מראה עיניו in the second, and משמע אזניו in the third member, and therefore must have the meaning, *to smell* 2 That the second and third members will then agree well with the first, since they will be only a further development of it. The subordinate idea of agreeableness may also be ascribed to the verb, which the verbs of sense often have, when combined with ב; thus הריח with ב *to smell with pleasure*, Ex. 30. 38. Lev. 26. 31. This explanation is given by Vitringa, Lowth and Kocher: "Imbutos dei timore, quo solo delectabitur, nunquam fallente judicio nec illusuris sensibus ab impiis discernet" Others, as (Vogel, Rosenmuller, Jahn, Gesenius,) following in a measure the example of Abarbanel "ubi reges alii delectantur odore florum et aromatum, rex Messias delectatur בריח יראת יהוה take the verb in the sense of being well pleased with any thing, thus making that the *only* meaning, which we regard as a secondary one. he will have his pleasure in the fear of God. But the passage Amos 5 21, to which they appeal, is not conclusive, since the words: "I will not smell your solemn assemblies," may there mean: I will not *even* smell them, I will have nothing whatever to do with them, as an expression of the strongest disgust. Besides, according to this explanation, this member does not well agree with the second and third, which likewise speak rather of the knowledge of the fear of the Lord, than of being well pleased with it. Other interpretations are still less to be approved. Thus after the example of Le Clerc, Paulus, Herder, v d. Palm and others translate: his breath is in the fear of God, or he draws each breath in the fear of God, since from a comparison of the Arabic اروح, they assume a meaning of the verb הריח which it never has in Hebrew. Others, as Michaelis, Cube, Doderlein, Hensler, Koppe, Kuinoel give to the verb the meaning, which likewise does not belong to it, *to excite, to animate*, and translate, referring to the LXX (ἐμπλήσει αὐτὸν πνεῦμα φόβου θεοῦ) and the Vulgate (replebit illum spiritus timoris domini;) and he, i. e either the spirit of Jehovah or Jehovah, fills him with the fear of God, since most of them read וְהֵרִיחוֹ the praeter, instead of the infin But it is decisive against their interpretation, that this had been already ascribed to the spirit of God in the end of the foregoing verse, and the prophet would then say the same thing twice. Reinhard is still further from the truth, who, while he confesses, that the verb הריח does not occur in this sense, understands by it, *to be angry,* and translates: "ipsa ejus indignatio non erit a religione abhorrens." The two following members contain a consequence of the first. Vitringa thus renders: therefore he will not judge after the outward appearance, etc. The sense: Since the Messiah searches the heart, he will not judge with the danger of erring, merely according to the superficial appearance, or hearsay evidence, as the best earthly kings often must, but this decision will always be correct. Jahn takes the phrase שָׁפַט לְמַרְאֵה עֵינָיִם as synonymous with נָשָׂא פָנִים, which is of frequent occurrence, πρόσωπον λαμβάνειν, non respiciet divites et potentes, nec pauperes et miseros, verbo sine omni partium studio judicabit, Levit. 19. 15; but a comparison of the last member shows, that the prophet is not speaking of favoritism, but of being deceived by the outward appearance and false reports. In like manner 1 Sam. 16: 8, it is said of God, as it is here of the Messiah, "The Lord seeth not as man seeth, for man looketh on the outward appearance, but the Lord looketh on the heart." The verb הוֹכִיחַ need not be taken as precisely synonymous with שָׁפַט, but as retaining its usual meaning, *to punish,* the case is somewhat different in the following verse, where the subjoined ל modifies the sense.

V. 4. A just worldly king suffers himself to be bribed by nothing external; he protects suffering innocence, and restrains by punishment the oppressions of the wicked. Thus also, will the Messiah protect the poor and innocent sufferers, and destroy the ungodly. "He judges with righteousness the lowly, procures impartial justice for the meek in the land, he smites the earth with the rod of his mouth, slays the ungodly with the breath of his lips." The word דַל *low, poor,* as appears from the parallelism with עֲנָוִים, occurs here with the accessory idea of innocence, humility and virtue, as is commonly the case with words that signify poverty and lowliness; while those which signify wealth and power, have often the accessory idea of wickedness and oppression. בְּצֶדֶק not as Reinhard supposes, *benignly,* but with righteousness, without respect of persons. The verb הוֹכִיחַ Reinhard after Vitringa takes in the sense: *to convince of error, to instruct,* and refers it to conviction respecting the doctrine of salvation, to moral reformation. But this is entirely opposed to the context: the Messiah is here spoken of not as a teacher, but as a judge and king. It can here have only the common meaning with לְ of the person, *to punish*. Thus Le Clerc: "castigabit recte pauperes i. e. non castigabit ex contemtu, vel calumniis, sed quum jure castigari poterunt, contra quam solet fieri. בְּמִישׁוֹר cum rectum et aequum erit eos castigari." Or, which seems to be better, לַעֲנָוֵי may be taken as the dativ. commodi: he will punish for the benefit of the humble, i. e. he will maintain their rights. The meaning: to pronounce sentence, which Rosenmuller here assumes, is not sufficiently established. The עֲנָוֵי הָאָרֶץ *mansueti terrae* are the πραεῖς Matt. 5. 5. The primary sense of the word is: humility and meekness; the secondary: suffering, while the reverse is the case with respect to דַּל. That the Messiah would especially interpose for the poor and wretched is asserted also Ps. 72: 4, 12. Zech. 11: 7, etc., and this feature, taken from a pious head of the theocracy, and interwoven with the portrait of the future Messiah, is found ennobled and spiritualized in the character of Christ. — In the second part of the verse אֶרֶץ is limited to the ungodly by the contrast with דַּלִּים and עֲנָוִים, and by the parallelism with רָשָׁע. The ground of this designation constantly used in the N. T. κοσμος, seems to be, that the ungodly on earth are so much superior in number and power, that the little band of the pious entirely disappear before them. The phrase *with the rod of his mouth*, which has perplexed interpreters, and even led some of them to change the text, is easily explained by the supposition of a silent antithesis. שֵׁבֶט *staff*, often stands, as an instrument of punishment, for *rod of correction*. Earthly kings employ against transgressors outward instruments of punishment,—the Messiah punishes by his bare word, which alone is sufficient to "slay the wicked." That we are not here with Reinhard and others to understand merely severity in punishing, (rod of his mouth, equivalent to, *sententiarum severitas*,) is shown by the following member, where likewise especial importance is given to the circumstance, that the Messiah should inflict punishment by his bare word. רוּחַ שְׂפָתָיו *the breath of his lips*, the same as bare word, bare command, similar to רוּחַ פִּיו which elsewhere occurs, Ps. 33. 6. That which is here spoken of the Messiah is in other passages attributed to God; thus Job 15. 30, it is said of the ungodly וְיָסוּר בְּרוּחַ פִּיו "he shall perish by the breath of his mouth." The Chaldee paraphrast translates: et verbo labiorum ejus morietur Armillus improbus. (וּבְמַמְלַל סִפְוָתֵיהּ יְהִי מָמִית אַרְמִילוֹס רַשִׁיעָא) He understands therefore the collective רָשָׁע as singular, and makes it refer to the Armillus (ἐρημόλαος s. v. a עַם מַחֲרִיב *vastator populi*,) the monstrous and last enemy of the Jews, who wages cruel wars with them, and slays the Messiah Ben Joseph, but shall at last be slain by the bare word of the Messiah Ben David, Buxtorf Lex. Chald. c 221—24 Eisenmenger entdecktes Judenth II, 705 seq Paul employs those words 2 Thess. 2: 8, in describing the destruction of Antichrist by the Messiah, who nevertheless, like the רָשָׁע in this verse is probably not an individual, but the enemies of Christ collectively See Koppe on this passage. The apostle justly refers the expression of the prophet to the highest manifestation of penal justice on the part of the Messiah against the highest manifestation of ungodliness, without thereby excluding its reference to all other enemies of the kingdom of God, and to all other times. As the fulfilment of the promise of the blessing, which the Messiah would confer on the poor and the meek extends through all history, so also does the fulfilment of the threatening against the ungodly

V. 5 "Righteousness will be the girdle of his loins, and faithfulness the girdle of his waist" A silent contrast here also lies at the foundation. While temporal kings are clothed with worldly magnificence, and invested with worldly ornaments, the glory of the Messiah will be spiritual, his most beautiful ornament, righteousness and truth. Calvin: "Non apparebit instar regum purpura indutus et diademate, aut praecinctus baltheo, sed justitia et veritas in eo apparebunt." The representation of attributes under the image of garments is very frequent in the Old and New Testament, e. g chap 59. 17. Job. 29 14. Ps. 131. 9, and many passages in the epistles of Paul צֶדֶק *righteousness*, the most illustrious attribute of earthly kings, is every where made particularly prominent among those of the Messiah. For example, chap 53 11. Jer 23· 5. 33. 15 Ps. 45 5 72 2, אמונה *truth, faithfulness*

6 After describing the person of the illustrious king. the prophet proceeds to describe his kingdom On v 6—8, the question arises, whether the representation is to be considered throughout as metaphorical, or as in some measure literal, in other words, whether the prophet would represent only metaphorically the cessation of all hostility among men, or whether he expected in the time of the Messiah, the actual cessation of all enmity, all destruction, all that is hurtful, even in the irrational part of the creation. The former view was adopted by most of the older interpreters Thus Theodoret remarks: διὰ τῶν ἡμέρων καὶ ἀγρίων ζώων τροπικῶς τῶν ἀνθρωπείων ἠθῶν ἐδίδαξε τὴν διαφοράν. He refers all to the union of those in the

Christian church, who were by nature far from each other, and on terms of mutual enmity. Jerome even regarded the opposite interpretation as a sort of heresy: "Haec quoque Judaei et nostri Judaizantes juxta litteram futura contendunt, ut in claritate Christi, quem putant in fine mundi esse venturum, omnes bestiae redigantur in mansuetudinem et pristina feritate deposita lupus et agnus pascantur simul," etc. He gives the sense, on the whole, the same as Theodoret, and differs from him only at times in allegorizing the particulars. Similar is the explanation of Calvin. "Similitudinibus istis declarat, nullum in populo Christi affectum nocendi, nullam ferociam aut inhumanitatem fore." So also Vitringa, Michaelis, Jahn and others. But nevertheless, the literal interpretation defended by several Jewish interpreters, and which first presents itself to every unprejudiced critic, claims an undeniable superiority, provided it does not adhere too closely to the particular images, but merely embraces the fundamental thought, the removal of all destruction even from the irrational creation, and its return to its original condition. The principal reasons in its favor are the following. 1. The parallelism with the condition of the creation before the fall, as it is presented to us in holy Scripture. Surely it cannot be without cause, that in the history of the creation, such peculiar stress is laid upon the fact, that every thing created was very good. This supposes, that the irrational creation was in a condition different from the present, in which it gives us, in some measure, a true representation of the first apostasy, and in which every hateful vice has its likeness and representative in the animal kingdom. According to this history beasts of prey did not at that time possess their present ferocious nature: they acknowledge in Adam their lord and king, peacefully collect around him and receive from him their names. Gen. 2: 19, 20. The whole animal creation bore the image of the innocence and peace of the first man, and the law of mutual destruction was yet unknown. According to chap. 1: 30, grass only was appointed as the food for beasts, and herbs, besides the fruits of the trees, etc. for men. The serpent had not as yet its frightful form, and man was not afraid of intercourse with it. See chap 3: 1, 14. Now as sin, whose influence extended through all nature, and subjected it to a curse, chap. 3: 17, so that it no longer testifies merely of the existence of God, but also of the existence of transgression, produced the outward dissension, war, and destruction, which exist in irrational nature; so also we may venture to hope, that when in the time of the Mes-

Isaiah 11:6—8.

siah, according to the expectation of the prophet, v. 9, the cause, inward discord, will be removed, the effect also, outward dissension, will cease. The prophet even appears in particular characteristics to refer distinctly to the history of the creation, comp. v 7, (lions shall eat straw like the oxen,) with Gen 1· 30 v. 8, (the sucking child shall play upon the hole of the asp,) with Gen. 3. 15 2 The comparison of other passages of Scripture, according to which likewise, after the removal of moral evil from the rational creation, the removal of the reflection of it in the irrational shall follow. See chap 65 25. 66. 22 But especially, Rom. 8 19, etc. 3. A comparison of the notions derived from an original tradition respecting this subject, among heathen nations. Not only, as we have seen in the general introduction, is the idea in general of a future renovation of nature found among them, but even precisely the same characteristics as are here presented. We here introduce only a few, of the numerous passages collected from Greek and Roman writers, by Le Clerc, Lowth, Gesenius, and others. Virgil says in his representation of the golden age, Eccl 4. 21 etc 5. 60, "Occidet et serpens et fallax herba veneni occidet."—" Nec magnos metuent armenta leones," —"Nec lupus insidias pecori"—Horat Epod 16 53 "Nec vespertinus circumgemit ursus ovile, nec intumescit alta viperis humus." Theocrit Idyll. 24. 84· ἔσται δὴ τοῦτ' ἆμαρ, ὁπηνίκα νεβρὸν ἐν εὐνᾷ—καρχαρόδων σίνεσθαι ἰδὼν λύκος οὐκ ἐθελήσει

V 6. "Then the wolf dwells with the lamb; the panther lies down with the kid; the calf and the lion and the fattened beast are together, a little child leads them."

V 7 "The cow and bear go to the same pasture, their young ones lie down together, the lion shall eat straw like the ox." יַחְדָו is to be supplied in the first member This verse is repeated almost verbatim in chap 65· 25

V. 8 "The sucking child plays on the den of the asp, and the weaned child thrusts his hand into the hole of the basilisk." שִׁעֲשַׁע to delight himself, to play   פֶתֶן is the asp of the ancients, a small, but very poisonous serpent, whose bite kills without pain by an overpowering sleep. See Oedmanns verm. Samml. 5 p. 81 seq The ἅπ. λεγ. מְאוּרָה receives through the connexion and the parallelism with חֻר its definite meaning According to Gesenius it is kindred with מְעוּרָה = מְעָרָה hole. But it is more naturally derived from אוּר to give light, whence comes מָאוֹר. According to which it would not properly be the hole itself, but its entrances, pars luci ex-

posita; in like manner as צֹהַר *light*, Gen. 6: 16, means: openings for light, windows. The translation *eyes* by Jahn, and *feelers* by Michaelis, is as unfounded as incongruous. The word צִפְעוֹנִי signifies the cerastes, one of the most poisonous of serpents. Bochart. Hieroz II 1 3, c. 10. The ἅπ λεγ הָדָה is explained by the Arabic هَدَىٰ *direxit*.

V. 9 This peace in outward nature is a consequence of the inward peace, which will prevail in the kingdom of God, after the annihilation of all that opposes his will.—" They shall not do evil, and shall not sin on all my holy mountain, for the land is full of the knowledge of the Lord, as the waters cover the bottom of the sea." The words רוּעַ and שָׁחַת have in Hiph an intransitive meaning, properly: to make bad, and corrupt, namely, the conduct, or the way. הַר קֹדֶשׁ *the holy mountain*, is the usual appellation of mount Zion But that it must here designate the theocracy, of which it was the seat and central point, is evident from the following כִּי, which gives the reason and would otherwise be inappropriate, even if only the land of Judea were to be understood by the word הָאָרֶץ. Eichhorn well observes: as far as my kingdom extends. So likewise Kuinol. On the contrary Jahn asserts, without reason, that הַר קָדְשִׁי here means precisely the mountainous region of Palestine The word retains its customary meaning, (see Gesenius) but in the vision of the prophet the kingdom of God was presented under the image of its centre and seat In the second member, the cause is given, which has produced this great change; it is not external force, which can restrain merely the outbreakings of sin; but it is a consequence of the knowledge of God, diffused by the Messiah, and the fulness of the divine life supplied through Him. The general outpouring of the Spirit, and the holiness resulting from it, which was imparted only to a Jew under the Old Testament, are uniformly given as a characteristic mark of the Messiah's time See e g chap. 32 17, 18 54 13 Jer. 31. 34. Joel 3 1. It is uncertain here, as in other similar passages, whether הָאָרֶץ designates the land of Judea alone, or the whole earth If the former, the prophet does not describe the extension of the divine life throughout the world, until the following verse. See chap 4 2 We may best translate it by the equally indefinite expression, *the land*, the prophet himself would have found it difficult to decide, which interpretation is the true one, he was not concerned with its local limitation, but with the fact itself, the abundant and general effusion of the Holy Spirit. The verb מָלֵא with the Acc. of that of which any thing is full. The verbal noun דֵּעָה is here construed with the case of the verb, from which it is derived. In like manner, e. g. Hos. 3. 1 : כְּאַהֲבַת יהוה אֶת־בְּנֵי יִשְׂרָאֵל, "as Jehovah loves the sons of Israel." Gesen. Lehrg. p. 688. The knowledge of God includes love for him, and devotion to his service. יָם stands here inaccurately, for *bottom of the sea,* and there is no occasion to multiply the proper senses of the word.

V. 10. The central point of this divine life is the great King, from whom it proceeds.—" And it will come to pass at that time, that the heathen shall betake themselves to the root of Jesse, which stands as the banner of the people, and his rest will be glorious." The verb דָּרַשׁ with לְ, אֶל and with אֵת is used in two senses, generally to turn to Jehovah, or to the idols in order to seek protection, help and counsel, to manifest reverence, (thus דרש את יהוה Ps. 9. 11. 14: 2. 22. 27. 34. 5. Jer. 8· 2, with לְ 2 Chron. 15· 13, with אל Job 5. 6), and specially to ask counsel of any one, either Jehovah or the idols, as an oracle. (Thus Gen. 25. 22. Deut. 18· 11, and especially above, chap. 8. 19, הֲלֹא־עַם אֶל אֱלֹהָיו יִדְרֹשׁ " shall not a people seek an explanation from their God ? ") Jahn unjustly objects to the latter meaning in this place, that it is unsuitable to speak of consulting a root as an oracle. That the prophet however had already laid aside the figure is manifest from the words which follow. " and his rest shall be glory," which also relates not to the image of the root, but directly to the person, who had been represented by it. If we adopt this meaning, the sense will be· the nations, who have heretofore sought for responses from their idols in vain, will now look to the Messiah alone for instruction, in the things of God. Some interpreters then suppose, that here is an allusion to Solomon, whose wisdom attracted a multitude of strangers; others think, that as in former times, the answer of God was given out of the holy of holies from the place above the ark of the covenant, Num. 7. 8, 9, so now it shall be sought from the Messiah. But however the expression may be understood, at all events, it implies a religious seeking of the Messiah, and ascribes to him more than human dignity. Hos. 3. 5. The שֹׁרֶשׁ stands in the nomin. absol ; with respect to the root of Jesse, they shall seek to it, etc. The root here signifies by synecdoche. the tree which springs up from the root. Comp. chap. 11: 1. 53. 2. Rev. 5. 5. 22: 16. נֵס, *a standard,* is a high pole with waving banners, which in times of distress was erected on lofty hills, as a sign for the people, or for the warriors to assemble ' See Jahn Archaeol p. 465. The Messiah is here compared with such a standard, around which the nations should assemble, which had heretofore been far from salvation. And thus shall be fulfilled the prediction of the dying Jacob, Gen 49 10, that the nations should be obedient to the Messiah מְנוּחָה *resting-place*, then *dwelling*, *residence*, spoken of the temple, as the palace of God, Ps 132 14 כָּבוֹד *glory*, as in chap 4 5, the abs instead of the con. for *honored*, *glorious*. As of old the tabernacle and the temple were honored and glorified as the seat of the gracious symbol of the divine presence; so shall it be now with the dwelling-place of the Messiah, of the *deus in terra* The image is taken from an illustrious earthly king, whose residence is honored by worldly splendor, the embassies of foreign nations, etc. We need not ask what is here meant by the dwelling-place of the Messiah. The sense without a figure: the Messiah will be honored by all people, as their king and Lord. Regardless of the metaphor, Jerome translates: *et erit sepulchrum ejus gloriosum*, and Theodoret also here finds the glorification of Christ after his burial.

The prophet having hitherto represented the blessings of the Messiah's kingdom more in general, and with especial reference to the heathen nations, confines himself, in the following portion, exclusively to the benefit which, through him, should be conferred upon the Jews An entirely similar appearance is presented by the two closely connected predictions of the Messiah, chap II and IV, the former of which has respect especially to the heathen, the latter exclusively to the Jews With respect to the interpretation of the whole portion, two principal views especially may be distinguished. It is understood for the most part literally by some, and figuratively by others. 1 The first view is entertained by very different classes of interpreters; in the first place by the Jews, who hope the Messiah will bring back their dispersed people to Palestine, and there establish a splendid worldly kingdom, then by Christian interpreters, as Michaelis and others, who infer from this and similar passages, that the Jews at some future time, after their conversion to Christ, will be restored to their native land and there form a Christocracy, as they had a Theocracy before; and lastly by most recent interpreters, as Rosenmuller, Gesenius and others, who find here an expectation of the prophet, which has not been confirmed by history, of a splendid, visible restoration of the outward theocracy by the Messiah 2. Those who maintain the figurative character of the whole representation suppose, that under theocratic images, the spiritual deliverance of the Israelites by the Messiah, and their reception into His kingdom, are here described. Among these again there is a difference Some regard the complete fulfilment as having already taken place by the introduction of Christianity. Thus Jerome "ut nequaquam juxta nostros Judaizantes in fine mundi, quum intraverit plenitudo gentium, tunc omnis Israel salvus fiat sed haec omnia in primo intelligamus adventu ;" others, as Lowth, suppose the whole prophecy relates to that future general conversion of the Jews, which the New Testament also leads us to expect.

We are induced to join the advocates of the second view, in opposition to those of the first, by the following reasons 1. The literal interpretation cannot be consistently *carried through* When it is said, v. 15, 16, that in the time of the Messiah, Jehovah will dry up the Red Sea, and divide the Euphrates into seven streams, and make it so shallow that men may pass over it with shoes, no interpreter thinks of understanding this otherwise than figuratively But since the foregoing representation has an entirely uniform character, the charge of capriciousness, certainly falls rather upon the advocates of the literal, than of the figurative interpretation. 2. The defenders of the former must suppose, that the prophet pointedly contradicts, not only the other prophets, but even himself also. According to that, for instance, the prophet v. 14 would say, that the Israelites in the time of the Messiah, will carry on prosperous wars against the Philistines, Arabians, Edomites, and Moabites, and reduce these people to subjection On the contrary, according to v 6—8 of this same prophecy, the kingdom of the Messiah is so entirely a kingdom of peace, that contention shall cease, even in the irrational creation; according to v. 10, the heathen also shall share in its blessings; according to chap 2 2, all nations shall flow together to mount Zion, chap 9 4, it is given as a characteristic of the Messiah's time, that with its introduction all war and contention shall cease ; the Messiah v. 5, bears the name of the Prince of Peace , and according to v. 6, through him peace shall be extended over the whole earth, and his kingdom established by righteousness, and not by the force of arms. 3 Even granting what cannot here be conceded, that the prophet did not himself entirely see through the figurative covering in which the subjects were presented to him in vision, we should still, since he was only an instrument, be perfectly justified in availing ourselves of the light which the fulfilment gives in discriminating between the figure and the reality. But the fulfilment shows, that under images taken from the outward theocracy, the prosperity of the covenant people, after their conversion to Christ, is here described.—With respect to the difference between the defenders of the figurative interpretation, we must join with Vitringa, who unites both opinions by the supposition, that the fulfilment of the prophecy has indeed already commenced by the reception of many of the Jews dispersed among all nations of the earth, at the first establishment of Christianity; but will be carried forward through all ages, and only completed at the end of the world, by their general conversion. The prophet announces in general terms the reception of the Jews into the Messiah's kingdom, and their participation in its blessings; the limitation to a particular time was certainly as far from his purpose here, as in what he says, v. 10, of the heathen.

Jahn understands only v. 1—10 as a prediction of the Messiah; in the portion commencing with v. 11, the prophet makes an abrupt transition to the deliverance from captivity, and the victories of the Maccabees. But this assumption is occasioned entirely by the erroneous supposition that the prophecy must be literally understood throughout. To separate the paragraph in this way from the foregoing does not agree with ביום ההוא v. 11, and is altogether unnatural, still we may suppose, that these occurrences were at the same time within the hope of the prophet's vision, and that he borrowed his images from them.

V. 11. Not only the heathen, but also the Jews dispersed in all lands, shall be brought back, and received into the kingdom of God. —"Then will the Lord stretch out his hand the second time, to deliver the remnant of his people, which shall be left, from Assyria, from Egypt, from Pathros, from Cush, from Elam, from Shinar, from Hamath, and from the islands of the sea." ביום ההוא, entirely indefinite, then, namely in the time of the Messiah's kingdom. After the verb יוסיף he will proceed, the action, which is to be repeated, is omitted, as is often the case elsewhere, see Gesenius s v., לשלח is to be supplied שנית, the second time refers to the deliverance from Egypt, as appears from v. 16. The prophet compares together the greatest temporal, and the spiritual redemption of the covenant people. See Micah 7. 15. Hos. 2. 15. 1 Cor. 5. 7. קָנָה to ransom, especially used concerning Jehovah, when he delivers the covenant people from the power of their enemies, as well as מָכַר to sell, when he gives them up to their power. The phrase אֲשֶׁר יִשָּׁאֵר מֵאַשּׁוּר, as Vitringa justly remarks, is a concise expression for . who shall have remained in Asher etc., that they might be collected from these lands. פתרוס as Bochart (Phaleg. IV, c. 27,) and Jablonski (Pantheon Aegypt. III. p 123), have shown, is the Thebais, or Upper Egypt, which elsewhere also is distinguished from Egypt Proper, comp. e. g. Plin h n. 18. 18.—"Excellentius Thebaidis regionis frumentum (quam Aegypti), quoniam palustris Aegyptus." כוּשׁ is the Arabic, and the African Ethiopia or Abyssinia, which were inhabited by the same race of people; the Arabic is the mother country from which a colony emigrated to the African. See Michaelis, Spiceleg. Geogr. Hebr. ext I, p. 143 seq. עֵילָם, properly the province Elamais in southern Media, stands also in several other places in a wider sense, and here, where the names of countries are in general used indefinitely, and where accurate geographical discrimination is not to be thought of, it signifies all Media and Persia שִׁנְעָר, properly the name of the region around Babylon; here in a wider sense, of all Mesopotamia. By חֲמָת, one of the most important cities of Syria, all Syria is designated. The expression אִיֵּי הַיָּם is very indefinite; it signifies in the first instance all the islands and coasts of the Mediterranean sea; but then also, all that lies beyond them, in general all Europe That the prophet mentions these particular countries, only as a part for the whole, and by way of example, in order to show, that the Jews shall be scattered through all lands, even those the most remote, appears from the following verse, according to which they shall be collected from all the four ends of the earth. The question now arises, whether the dispersion of the Hebrews here described, really existed in the time of the prophet, or whether transporting himself in spirit, as in v. 1, into distant times, he represents the later dispersion of the Jews as it took place, when the Israelites had already been carried captive into Assyria after the Babylonish exile, and especially after the destruction of Jerusalem. The latter is the opinion of by far the larger number of interpreters; Gesenius has endeavored to defend the former. But his arguments can satisfy only a few. It is important to remark, that but little is accomplished when it is shown, that in the time of the prophet individual Jews were to be found in all the countries enumerated. For the whole description of the prophet shows, that he presupposes a dispersion of the whole nation, even though we were not to connect with it the total depopulation of Palestine. It is true that the ten tribes were already carried into captivity, but the kingdom of Judah, the members of which likewise, v. 12, appear among the dispersed, had not as yet suffered this calamity to any considerable extent But the few Jews, who, according to Joel 3 11 and Amos 1· 6, 9, had been sold as slaves by the Philistines, and the Phenicians, and others, who possibly in times of distress may voluntarily have fled from their own country, of whom however there is no historical account, do not here come under consideration. Then Gesenius has entirely failed to prove, that, in the time of the prophet, individual Jews were to be found in all the countries enumerated. He supposes, e. g. in total contradiction to the relation, 2 Chr. 14 9, etc., that in the war with the Ethiopians under king Asa, the Jews were carried away prisoners to Ethiopia It is there expressly said, that the whole hostile army was destroyed —But why does the prophet here, like Micah, 4 6, 7, represent the reception of the dispersed Israelites into the kingdom of the Messiah, under the image of their restoration to their native land? The answer is, that as the kingdom of God must of necessity have a *substratum* in the vision of the prophet, because images only, and not abstract ideas, can be exhibited in vision, so the seat of the ancient theocracy appears to him as the central point and capital of the Messiah's kingdom, whence also this kingdom takes its rise. As now, chap. II, he represents the reception of the heathen nations into the kingdom of the Messiah, as their journeying to Mount Zion, so here the reception of the dispersed Jews is described as a return to their native land We are not here to have respect to the locality, since this belongs merely to the *form* of the vision, but to the fundamental idea, the sin and apostasy of the Jews, for which they were expelled from the old theocracy and its blessings, to which the possession of the land of Canaan especially belonged, and repentance and conversion, whereby they gain admission into the Messiah's kingdom, and participate in its blessings.

V. 12 " And the Lord lifts up a standard to the heathen nations; and collects the exiles of Judah, and gathers together the dispersed of Israel from the four ends of the earth." The erection of a standard for the heathen nations, is not here, according to the opinion of several of the older interpreters, as in v 10, a sign for them, that they should themselves assemble in the kingdom of the Messiah; a comparison of the parallel passages, chap 49 22. 62: 10, shows rather, that the object, for which the heathen are to be collected is, that of conducting the dispersed Jews to their native land The sense without a figure: the heathen people, the same, who according to v. 10, have already become members of the Messiah's kingdom, shall then be actively employed in obedience to the command of the Lord, in promoting the reception of the despised Jews into his kingdom. After נפצות J. H. Michaelis supplies *sheep*, Le Clerc משפחות *families*, Rosenmuller נכשות *souls*. But Gesenius here properly applies a usage, according to which totality is expressed by the combination of the masculine and feminine. Thus chap. 3: 1, בָּשִׁיעֶךָ, וּמַצֵנָה properly, the male and the female support, stands for every kind of support. See examples from Arabic writers, in Gesenius on the passage. Thus also here, the men of Judah, who had been driven away, and the dispersed women of Israel, for all the dispersed of Israel and Judah. The two parts, which make out the whole, are divided between Israel and Judah, although each properly belongs in the same manner to both. Similar is the passage in Zech. 9:17, "corn shall make the young men cheerful, and new wine the maidens," for corn and new wine shall make the young men and the maidens cheerful.

V. 13. "The jealousy of Ephraim ceases; and the inimically disposed of Judah are cut off, Ephraim will not envy Judah, and Judah will not be hostile to Ephraim." The words צררי יהודה יכרתו are translated by Augusti, after most of the older interpreters, the adversaries of Judah shall be exterminated. But the parallelism requires, that like as וסרה קנאת אפרים corresponds to אפרים לא יקנא את יהודה, so also וצררי יהודה יכרתו should correspond to ויהודה לא יצר את אפרים, against which, the remark of Kocher is not conclusive: that the prophet here speaks rather of the cessation of the hostile disposition of Ephraim against Judah, than of Judah against Ephraim, because Judah had the greater right, Ephraim the greater guilt. Schultens (Animadvers. phil. ad. h. l.) who is followed by Rosenmuller, compares the Arabic ضَمَّ III *zelotypus fuit* and translates: those who are jealous of Judah. But there is no occasion to depart from the common acceptation of the verb צרר *to be hostile*, in which it immediately after occurs. The genitive often stands in Hebrew, where we use the preposition *among*. Thus אביוני אדם *the poor among men*, זבחי אדם *those who sacrifice among men*, Hos. 13:2. Comp. Gesen. Lehrg p. 678. So here also the adversaries of Judah, are the inimically disposed (against Ephraim) in Judah. Between the two tribes of Judah and Ephraim, the latter of which considered all advantages as its own,- which, by any means the whole tribe of Joseph could have appropriated to itself, there existed constant jealousy and collision. Comp Michaelis Mos. R § 47. This hostile disposition at last fully broke forth, after the death of Solomon, when Jeroboam, an Ephraimite, separated from Judah the remaining tribes, with the exception of Benjamin and Levi The new kingdom took the name of Ephraim after the most powerful tribe From this time, peace and harmony seldom existed between the two kingdoms, until at last the Ephraimites were carried away into captivity —Now this schism between Ephraim and Judah was the most destructive, and deplorable in the whole history of the Hebrews. The prophet therefore could choose no more suitable image to express the idea, that when the covenant people should be received into the kingdom of the Messiah, all internal jealousy and enmity among them would cease, that common love for the great Redeemer would unite all in the bond of harmony. Parallel passages, in which the same figurative representation prevails are, Hos. 1 11. 2 1 Ez 37 22. Jerome: "Eo tempore nequaquam Ephraim et Judas, qui nunc me prophetante hostili odio inter se dissident, inimici erunt, sed juxta Ezechielis prophetiam duae virgae in unam virgam copulabuntur et jungentur in Christi ecclesiam, qui prius fuerant separati."

V. 14 "They fly then upon the shoulders of the Philistines westward, plunder together the sons of the east; they will assault Edom and Moab; the sons of Ammon will obey them." The image in the first member is taken from birds of prey, and is illustrated by the parallel passage, Hab. 1: 8, where it is said of the Chaldeans: "they fly along as the eagle, who darts on his prey." The Qamets in כָּתֵף, is here treated as though it were impure, although the Stat constr. elsewhere is commonly כְּתֵף Examples of similar irregularities, may be seen in Gesenius Lehrg p 562 Anm 2. It is unnecessary to suppose, that the Stat. constr here stands for the Stat. absol ים *scá*, the west side, since the Mediterranean sea lies on the west of Palestine; sons of the east, are by way of eminence, the Arabians dwelling to the east of the Israelites, and from whose predatory invasions they had much to suffer. שָׁלַח יָדָיִם *to lay the hand on, to make a hostile attack.* מִשְׁלוֹחַ יָדָם *the object of their attack* Obedience, the abstract instead of the concrete, for subject — We have already seen that this verse cannot be literally understood, but must be taken in a figurative sense The question now occurs what

Isaiah 11 : 14—16.

is signified by the figure. Most interpreters refer it to spiritual victories, in the conversion of these people, effected by the Hebrews. Thus Jerome: "Hae enim gentes tempore, quo Jesaias prophetabat, adversariae erant populo Judaeorum et idcirco nunc dicit, quod postquam surrexerit radix Jesse, ut regnet in gentibus, tunc—dent Apostolis manus et in locis idololatriae Christi ecclesiae suscitentur." But although spiritual conquests are elsewhere designated by the image of war, see chap 53 12, yet this explanation seems here to be inadmissible, because according to the whole context, the prophet speaks of the prosperity, which the Israelites themselves should enjoy after their reception into the kingdom of the Messiah. The true interpretation is rather the following. The nations mentioned were the most dangerous enemies of the theocracy, whom God employed for the chastisement of the apostate Israelites. When the people manifested genuine dependance on Jehovah, these enemies were not the object of dread; such a splendid period was that e. g. in the time of David. From these the prophet borrows an image to embody the thought, that the people when they should have submitted to their great king, would enjoy the divine protection, a rich measure of the divine mercy and complete security. The consequences of a return to God in the time of the Messiah, are represented under the image of the consequences of a return to God, during the former theocracy.

V 15, 16. The removal of the hindrances, which will stand in the way of the future redemption of the Israelites, is represented under the image of the removal of those, which obstructed their former deliverance from Egypt. "Jehovah covers with a curse the tongue of the sea of Egypt, and waves his hand against the river, with his vehement wind, and smites it into seven brooks, that a man may go through with shoes." Many interpreters—Lowth, Rosenmuller, etc suppose that the verb הֶחֱרִים is here synonymous with הֶחֱרִיב *to dry up;* and appeal to the frequent interchange of the vowels of the same organ. But the verb הֶחֱרִים is of too frequent occurrence to require us here to give it another meaning, and moreover its usual sense is far more suitable, than the one assumed. To cover with a curse, imports as much as, entirely to destroy, since total destruction was a consequence of the anathema.— The tongue of the Egyptian sea is the head of the Arabian gulf. This makes towards the north two smaller and narrower gulfs, of which the one situated to the westward, through which the Hebrews formerly passed, ends at Suez.

This bears also in Arabian geographies, the name *tongue*, which occurs in Hebrew as the name of a gulf of the Red Sea, Josh 15 2, 5. 18: 19. By הַנָּהָר *the river*, by way of eminence, the Euphrates is designated; the Nile, which Vitringa, Augusti and others find here, never bears simply this name; even in chap. 19. 5, the word is defined, by being employed in a prophecy against Egypt The meaning of the word עָיָם, cannot indeed be ascertained with certainty, as the kindred dialects afford no aid, still the meaning: *vehemence*, is favored by the connexion, the authority of the ancient translators, and perhaps also a comparison with the adjective אָיֹם *fearful, terrific*. With the vehemence of his wind, i e with his vehement wind The ground of the figure is a personification of the river; Jehovah appears as a mighty hero, who waves his hand, armed with a frightful wind, like a sword, against the opposing stream. Hence also the following הִכָּה. There is here an allusion to Ex. 14 21, according to which the Lord dried up the Arabian gulf by a strong wind. He smites it to seven streams, for: so that it is divided into seven streams The image is here taken from great rivers, whose waters are conducted into a multitude of channels. Lowth appropriately compares the account of Herod 1 189 Cyrus on his march to Babylon lost, in a rapid stream, one of his sacred white horses He became enraged by the accident, and regarding the stream, as in the present instance, as an enemy, threatened to reduce it so much that even women could easily ford it He set his whole army at work, and conducted the water of the river into 360 ditches, on both sides of it The prophet therefore here promises that Jehovah in future times will open a passage for the Israelites through the Red Sea and the Euphrates, in the same miraculous manner, as he had done before through the Red Sea and the Jordan. The sense is simply: no obstacle to this redemption shall be so great, that Jehovah will not remove it by his omnipotence, as in his former deliverance of his people from Egypt

V. 16 " And there shall be a way for the remnant of his people, who shall be left from Assyria, as there before was for Israel, when he came out of Egypt." After מֵאַשּׁוּר, we must supply the remaining countries, mentioned in v 11, in which the Israelites are dispersed, the prophet here omits to repeat them for the sake of brevity. The entire similarity of the expression points to the former description

As the hymn of thanksgiving of the redeemed people chap. XII, is of a more general character, and like many of the Psalms applicable to any great deliverance and contains but few individual traits, we have no occasion to explain it.

General Preliminary Remarks on Isaiah XL—LXVI.

The second part of Isaiah must be ranked with the most splendid, and for us the most important portions of the Scriptures of the Old Testament. No part of these writings contains so little that is local and temporary; none shows so clearly the connexion between the preparatory and the ultimate dispensation;—none lingers with such delight on the description of the time, when after the great separation between the ungodly and the pious part of the ancient covenant people, the latter shall be united with the heathen in one sanctified, and blessed church of the Lord; none presents the exalted founder of the New Covenant, which is not like the old to be limited to a single people, so clearly to our view both in his humiliation and in his glory.*

We have seen in the introductory remarks on Isaiah, that the prophet probably lived for some time under the reign of Manasseh. If now we assume that he composed the second part of his prophecies in this latter period of his life, its character will be the more intelligible, and all its peculiarities will be explained.

1. This supposition accounts for the difference of the representation in the first, from that in the second part. Between the last prediction of the first part and the second part, there is then an interval of from fourteen to twenty years. But as the tone of the mind changes with years, so also does the style. Although the second part is in no respect inferior to the first in beauty of description, still the representation is more flowing, the tone milder and softer. In place of the compression and conciseness of the first part, in which the author, as it were, struggles with the language, and only briefly suggesting his images, passes on from one to another, an agreeable copi-

---

* With particular reference to the second part, Jerome praef. ad Iesaiam, says of Isaiah "Non tam propheta dicendus est, quam Evangelista. Ita enim universa Christi ecclesiaeque mysteria ad liquidum persecutus est, ut non putes eum de futuro vaticinari, sed de praeteritis historiam texere.

ousness succeeds; the images are finished and painted with the loveliest colors even to the minutest features. While the two parts are essentially one, and closely resemble each other in many points, there is a difference between them, like that between Deuteronomy and the other books of the Pentateuch, or the Epistles of John, which he probably composed at an advanced age, and his Gospel.

2. We may in this way explain the point of view assumed by the prophet. Isaiah, when arrived at an advanced age, probably committed the active employments of the theocracy to his younger associates in the prophetical office. He transferred himself from the present, which afforded little that was consoling, to the future, in which and for which alone he lived, assured that the legacy which he should leave to posterity, would bring forth the fruits, which in his labors for the benefit of the present generation, he had so often failed to realize. He places himself in the time clearly predicted in his former prophecies, when Jerusalem was already captured by the Chaldeans, the land laid waste, and the people in the distant region of Babylonia, longing for their native home. In this period of time he thinks, feels and acts; it has become to him the present, from which, although he not unfrequently casts a look upon the real present, he beholds the distant, and most distant future, nearer. He directs his discourse to his unhappy countrymen in exile, he exhorts, rebukes, and consoles them, by unfolding the prospect of a happier future.

3. This supposition explains the *arrangement* of the second part. While the first part, embracing the predictions which the prophet uttered during his exertions for the benefit of the present times, consists of individual prophecies, delivered at different times, and on various occasions, and at first separately made public, but afterwards being distinguished from each other by superscriptions, or some other intelligible method, combined in a single collection; in the second part, on the contrary, which was not called forth by external occasions, the individual portions cannot be so easily distinguished; it is more as if the whole had been uttered at the same time. The proof of the unity of the second part is furnished, even by the following representation of its contents. The objects of prophecy are throughout the same. Even the language and mode of representation are far more uniform, than in the different portions of the first part. If the prophet did not, at one and the same time, receive and commit to writing the revelations recorded in this part, yet it is certain that no long period elapsed between them, and that he did not make

known the separate discourses to the people, but chose to leave the whole as a legacy to posterity.

All was communicated to the prophets in vision, and therefore in the present, distance of time was in general not known to them; hence it happens, that events connected by an internal resemblance, in reality far distant from each other, seem to be closely connected, or even blended together, and must be first separated by the interpreter, who can compare the prediction with the fulfilment and refer those events to the different times to which they belong, which had no relation to time, as they appeared to the prophets. Whoever, without adopting this principle which lies deep in the nature of the entire prophetic vision, and has been further developed in the General Introduction, attempts the interpretation of the second part of the prophecies of Isaiah will behold throughout nothing but darkness, where under its guidance, the clearest light would appear.

These predictions relate chiefly to two objects. The prophet first consoles his people by predicting their deliverance from the Babylonish exile; he represents this under the most agreeable images, which are often suggested by the deliverance from Egypt; he names the monarch, who sent by Jehovah, should punish the oppressors of his people for their insolence, and restore the latter to their native land. But he does not stop at this inferior redemption. With the prospect of deliverance from the captivity of Babylon is connected, that of redemption from sin and error by the Messiah. Sometimes both objects appear intermingled with each other, sometimes one alone is exhibited with peculiar clearness. To the latter object especially, does the prophet sometimes so exclusively direct his view, that for a time, enraptured with the glory of the spiritual kingdom of God and its exalted founder, he loses sight of the less distant future. In the representation of this spiritual redemption also, the relation of events to time is disregarded. Now the prophet beholds its author in his humiliation and suffering, now the most distant period of the Messiah's kingdom is presented to the ravished view, in which the human race estranged from God shall be brought back to Him, and after the annihilation of all opposition to God, outward and inward peace shall prevail, and all evil introduced by sin shall be abolished. Elevated above time and space, from the eminence upon which the Holy Spirit has placed him, he extends his view over the whole progressive development of the Messiah's kingdom, from its obscure commencement, to its glorious completion.

Genuineness of Isaiah XL—LXVI

Through all past centuries, the second part of Isaiah had been regarded as incontestably his, by the Jewish synagogue, as well as the Christian church. The attempt was first made in the last quarter of the 18th century to contest his right to its authorship. The first intimation, which however was little regarded, was given by Koppe, who made the remark on chap. L, that Ezekiel, or some other prophet living in the time of the captivity, might perhaps have been its author. A distrust of the genuineness of the whole of the second part was first distinctly expressed by Doederlein in the Auserlesenen theol. Bibliothek Bd. I. H. 11, p 832. The most complete effort to establish this view was made by Justi, first in Paulus Memorabilien IV. s. 139 seq., then in his vermischten Abhandlungen uber wichtige Gegenstande der theol. Gelehrs. Bd. I. p 254 seq., Bd. 2 p 1—80. Henceforth it became quite predominant. It was eagerly embraced by the recent critics, because it stood in a necessary connexion with their idea, that the prophets enjoyed no immediate divine influence, and therefore could know nothing of the future except what might be deduced beforehand from the events of their own time by calculation and political sagacity. Among the defenders of this hypothesis are especially to be mentioned, Eichhorn, Rosenmuller, Paulus, Bauer, Bertholdt, De Wette, and Gesenius. Comp. the history of this interpretation in Bertholdt, Einl IV. s. 1371. But these critics again differ from each other in this respect, that some of them assume a plurality of writers, while others ascribe the whole to a single author. The latter opinion however seems now to have become pretty generally prevalent.

With respect also to the time of its composition, there is not an entire uniformity of views. Yet all agree that the prophecies of the second part cannot have been committed to writing till near the termination of the captivity. Gesenius, to whom, leaving the earlier opposers unnoticed, we may almost exclusively direct our attention, calls the second part the work of an anonymous prophet, living towards the close of the exile, who directed these words of comfort, of exhortation and reproof, to his contemporaries in the Babylonish captivity, and probably, after the manner of all the later prophets, in writing, or in other words, as a prophetic epistle to the exiles.*

Among the defenders of its genuineness, are to be mentioned Piper (in the work: Integritas Jesaiae a recentiorum conatibus vindicata Greifswalde 1793), Beckhaus (die Integritat der prophetischen Schriften des A. T. s. 152 seq), Hensler (in den Anmerkungen zu seiner Uebersetzung des Jesaias), Jahn (in der Einleitung),† Dereser (in der Einleitung zu seiner Bearbeitung des Jesaias als Fortsetzung des v. Brentanoschen Bibelwerkes), Greve (in den Prolegom z. d. Sch : Ultima capita Jesaiae Amsterd. 1810 4to), and lastly, Jo. Ulr. Moeller (in a distinct work De authentia oraculorum Jesaiae c 40—66 Coppenh. 1825, 240 s. 8) By means of the learned and acute treatise of Moeller the investigation was much further advanced It is however to be lamented, that the author has much weakened the impression of his argument, by too frequently yielding to conjectures which are uncertain, and contradicted by the feelings of every sound interpreter. We must not entirely pass over this investigation here, since the decision respecting the Christology of Isaiah must always be varied according to its different results

We will therefore as briefly as possible, first exhibit and refute the arguments of the opponents of the genuineness, and then present the positive proofs by which it is established. We shall thankfully avail ourselves of what is tenable in the treatise of Moeller; the grounds of the opponents we bring forward mostly in the words of Gesenius, who has subjected them to a revision, and saved us the trouble of noticing many very weak arguments, which were formerly urged.

1. "All historical intimations respecting the condition of the people point to the time of the exile, not to that of the prophet. Jerusalem is in ruins, the land desolate, the people rejected of God, the kingdom of the Chaldeans, so little powerful in the time of Isaiah, has attained the highest summit of its greatness, but notwithstanding, is near its overthrow by Cyrus All this however is not represented as something future, but as existing in the time of the prophet, as the present condition of the Jews, and the surrounding nations, with

---

* Entirely similar Rosenmüller in Gabler's neuestem theol Journal II 4, p 334

† In part also the Author des ex Hdb p XXIII seq comp. Augusti, Einl. ins A T § 204

which condition the predictions concerning the future are afterwards connected. Yet Isaiah, according to the analogy of the other predictions, must have commenced with the present, and connected with it his prophecies of the future. But even the most distant possibility that Isaiah could have been the author is removed by the circumstance, that the captivity is not *foretold*, but the point of view is taken in it, in the same manner as that of Isaiah in his time." This whole objection owes its origin to a want of just conceptions of the nature of prophecy. The knowledge of the prophets is supposed to have been received in the usual way by the understanding, when it was rather intuitive or communicated in vision, as is sufficiently indicated by the name *Seers?* The prophets, to whom, as we have seen in the General Introduction, all communications were made in vision, were in an ecstasy,—they lived in the events which they announced, and the events lived in them. They either took their station in the present, and thence beheld the less distant future, or they took their station in the nearer future, and thence extended their view to the more remote. In the latter case, the nearer future is represented by them as present, and from which they view that as past, which in reality is still future; it lies before them with such intuitive clearness, that they live and act in it. We here adduce only some few from the great mass of examples, which serve to confirm this remark.* The prophet Hosea, chap. XIII, had predicted to the Israelites heavy judgments of God, the devastation of the land, and the carrying away of its inhabitants by powerful enemies. Chap. 14 2 etc., he transfers himself in the spirit to the time when these judgments have already been inflicted. He anticipates the future as already happened, and exhorts, not indeed his contemporaries, but those upon whom the calamity was already fallen, to sincere repentance. "Return, O Israel, to Jehovah, since thou hast become wretched (כָּשַׁלְתָּ Practer) by thy iniquity." The blessings of Jehovah, on the contrary, v 5 etc. he represents as future. The prophet Micah, 4 8, says: "and as for thee, thou tower of the flock, hill of the daughter of Zion, unto thee shall the former dominion come, the dominion over the daughter of Jerusalem." When the

---

* A striking proof is furnished in the farewell ode of Moses, Deut. XXXII, comp e g v 7 and v 30. On the latter verse Le Clerc remarks "Haec quasi praeterita cantico deplorat Moses, quod ea ita futura praevideat, et quasi in illas aetates futuras se animo transferat eaque dicat, quae tum demum debebant dici."

prophet, a contemporary of Isaiah, here speaks of a former dominion, and prophesies that it shall be restored to the house of David, he transfers himself from his own time, in which the royal family of David still existed and flourished, to the time of the captivity, of which he had just spoken, and during which the dominion of the house of David should cease. V. 9 it is said "Now, wherefore dost thou set up a cry of lamentation? Hast thou no more a king? or have thy counsellors perished? Yea, pain has taken hold on thee, as one that travails." The prophet here addresses the Jewish people in the Babylonish exile. The time of their being carried away is to him the present, that of their deliverance, the future, see v. 10 "There wilt thou be delivered, there will Jehovah, thy God, redeem thee." Chap. 7. 7, Micah introduces the people already carried into exile, as speaking, and makes them declare at the same time the justice of the divine chastisement, and their confidence in the divine mercy. In the answer of Jehovah also, v. 11, it is presupposed, that the city is already destroyed, since he promises that its walls shall be rebuilt. Isaiah himself in the prediction against Tyre, chap. xxiii, beholds the approaching siege of the city by Nebuchadnezzar as present; the flight of its inhabitants, the impression which the news of their calamity makes upon the nations in alliance with them, etc., he describes as an eye-witness. From the nearer future, become to him as the present, he then extends his view to the more distant. He predicts, that after seventy years, reckoned not from the actual, but from the imaginary present, the city should again rise to its former greatness, he extends his view still further, and he sees how finally the Tyrians, in the days of the Messiah, embrace the true religion. Chap. LIII, he takes his position between the sufferings and the glorification of the Messiah; the sufferings appear to him as past, he represents the glorification as future.—These examples, which might easily be increased by innumerable others, may suffice to refute the assertion, that it is contrary to the nature of prophecy, for a prophet, taking his position in the nearer future, to view that as present, and thence look forward to the more distant future.

Bertholdt Einl. p. 1384 confesses, "that other prophets also, frequently transfer themselves in the spirit into later times, especially into the ideal times of the Messiah," and therefore in the main relinquishes the objection; he argues only from the circumstance, that they return again to their own times, while Isaiah continues to dwell in the later period, but we shall hereafter see, that he also, in many instances, returns from the fictitious present, to the real.

2 "Before Isaiah could predict a return from the captivity, he must of course have foretold the carrying away." It is a sufficient reply to this, that it is presumptuous to wish to prescribe to God, what revelations he shall impart to his prophets, that Isaiah could assume the carrying away to Babylon, as already sufficiently known from the predictions of other prophets, particularly from those of his contemporary, Micah, that indeed this event is also contained in the second part of Isaiah, as well as the return, only the former appears as past, because the prophet takes his position in the time of the exile; and lastly, that in our collection we certainly do not possess all the predictions of Isaiah, who may well have prophesied much concerning the exile, which has not come down to us. Suppose therefore, that in the first part, there were no clear predictions of the carrying away of the people, this objection would nevertheless be inconclusive. There are however such predictions. We first appeal to chap xxxix, where the carrying away to Babylon is foretold to king Hezekiah by the prophet in clear and positive terms, which cannot possibly admit of another interpretation. The suspicion expressed, though with hesitation by Gesenius, comp. p. 1006, that this prediction may have been first committed to writing at a later period, and more accurately expressed after the event, rests on mere caprice, and does not affect the object for which it was intended: it does not remove the troublesome fact, that an event had at that time already been foretold, which lay entirely beyond the political horizon of the age, and could have been foreseen by no human sagacity; for Micah 4: 9, 10, predicts with equal definiteness the carrying away to Babylon, and the deliverance from the Babylonish exile, 150 years before the event, and when Babylon stood in no hostile relation to Judah. There are besides, several predictions which cannot without the greatest violence be otherwise understood than, as referring to the devastation of the land by the Babylonians, and the carrying away of its inhabitants, and in which at the same time the return is predicted as approaching. Thus chap. v and 6. 11—13, whose genuineness is universally confessed.

3 "The prediction of events so distant was unintelligible to contemporaries, and therefore without object." As this is an *a priori* objection, it is, therefore, of but little importance. It arises from an entirely false understanding of the design, for which the prophets

were appointed. It may indeed be conceded, that these predictions were not perfectly clear and intelligible to the contemporaries of the prophet.—This, in general, was not to be required in prophecies, which first receive their full light from history. Even the prophet himself, in his ordinary state, might not be able to form an entirely clear conception of the contents of his predictions. But still such a prediction was not on that account by any means without an object. Although the contemporaries had no entirely clear understanding of its import, yet they had such an one as sufficed to accomplish its moral purpose. No contemporary of Isaiah, e. g., could read the second part of his prophecies, without perceiving therein, the penal justice of Jehovah in giving up his people a prey to their enemies, and his love in redeeming them. The point of view, which the prophet assumed, would be to his reader throughout the less uncertain, since he had immediately before predicted the Babylonish captivity as future ; in the reference to the manner of the carrying away, and of the deliverance, the person of Cyrus, etc., much might remain to him obscure. In like manner every one who did not voluntarily shut his eyes upon the light, could perceive the atoning death of the Messiah in the 53d chapter, though the particular circumstances connected with it, remained in part concealed. Besides, the prophecies were by no means designed especially for the present generation. They were not even all published by the prophets. The whole second part of Isaiah, e. g., was probably never recited in public. Committed to writing at the command of God, they were suited to posterity, who would understand them the more clearly, since to them the nearer future, in which the prophets had taken their position, would be the present. The Jews in the Babylonish exile must have been preserved from total despondency, and strengthened in their reliance on God, by the distinct prediction of their return, and thereby moved to prepare themselves for the promised redemption, by repentance and fidelity towards Jehovah. But as these and other predictions, strengthened the faith of the people of the old covenant, so do they afford the same benefits in a still higher degree to us, who have it in our power every where to compare the prophecy with the fulfilment, and perceive their exact agreement. And thus, although our faith in God and Christ is not grounded on this, it yet receives from it a firmer support and consistency ; whoever thinks he stands in no need of such aids, needs them the most.

4 "The prophet appeals to former predictions of the return of

the people from captivity, which were now fulfilled, and to which he subjoins new ones Chap 42· 9 45 19. 46 10 48 : 5, 6. " This presupposes a later prophet, contemporary with the events." This objection is very obscurely expressed How then could the predictions of the return from the captivity be already fulfilled, while it still continued ? Besides, according to the opinion of Gesenius, the author made known his prophecies before the termination of the captivity. The commentator moreover contradicts himself, when he finds reference here to the predictions of far earlier prophets, who foretold the captivity and the deliverance from it. He must then concede, what he elsewhere denies, that they were in general prophecies, in which future events were foretold so definitely, and so long beforehand, as to afford a sure proof of the omniscience of God —How little the cited passages prove, what they ought to prove, is evinced by an unprejudiced examination. Chap 45 . 19 46 . 10, Jehovah, in order to show his superiority to the vain idols, appeals to his omniscience, manifested in the fulfilment of the predictions of his servants, the prophets These declarations of Jehovah are altogether general; referring as well to earlier prophecies already fulfilled, those of Isaiah himself, e g , concerning the ruin of the Assyrians, as to those of the present time, whose future accomplishment would demonstrate the omniscience and the omnipotence of God —Chap 42 . 9 48. 5, 6, Isaiah appeals to former predictions, already accomplished, and whose fulfilment could give the people a pledge for the fulfilment of the prophecy respecting the return from the captivity, which he now delivers to them It may here, we admit, be supposed that the prophet in appealing to the prophecies already fulfilled includes also those respecting the carrying away into captivity ; but then this he might very well do since he takes his position not in the actual present, but in the future, which appeared to him as the present The prophet, chap xxxix, had foretold the Babylonish exile While he now transfers himself in the spirit into this time and directs his discourse to the people in exile, he beholds and can appeal to as already fulfilled, what in reality was yet future, but would give to the captive people, when accomplished, an assurance of the fulfilment of his predictions relating to the more distant event.

5 " What the prophet says of the present is correct, and very circumstantial His description of the future is ideal and consists of joyful and animated hopes far beyond reality Were the work composed by Isaiah, it must have been written by divine assistance. But

then its author must have known the future also. What a contrast between the condition of the miserable colony under Ezra and Nehemiah, and the splendid description of the coming prosperity." It is in the first place incorrect, that in the part of the prophecy, which relates to the condition of the people in the Babylonish exile, any thing so special (the name of Cyrus excepted, of which hereafter), occurs, as to evince, that the prophet had a more accurate knowledge of that period than of later times. The mention of the name of Cyrus is at all events counterbalanced by the passage, chap 44. 27 Gesenius himself l c p 88, finds in this passage a distinct allusion to the turning aside, and drying up of the Euphrates in the neighborhood of Babylon by the well known stratagem of Cyrus. Herod. 1, 185 190 Xenoph. Cyrop 1 VII He must therefore here acknowledge a prophecy, inexplicable by natural causes, since he himself maintains, that the second part was composed before the capture of the city of Babylon — It is not to be mistaken, that the author of the greater and higher redemption, the eminent servant of God, the Messiah, is yet more definitely and plainly designated, than Cyrus the author of the inferior deliverance; at the same time, every unprejudiced critic must confess, that the personal Messianic predictions of the second part, far from being ideal representations, have been fulfilled with circumstantial accuracy —The objection, however, that the greater portion of what extends beyond the time of the exile, remains unfulfilled, is applicable indeed to those, who, as Jahn and others, seek for the complete accomplishment of the prophecies, which promised prosperity, in the times immediately after the exile Gesenius is right, when he maintains, that it would be in the highest degree capricious to represent all, that is contained in these prophecies, to have been at that time fulfilled. But this objection loses all its significancy, as soon as we assume two objects of the promise, the return from the Babylonish exile, and the happiness of the Messianic times, which are not always accurately distinguished in the vision of the prophet, but frequently presented under the same images. - There is then nothing more to be said respecting ideal representations and enthusiastic hopes, but we justly expect the accomplishment of the yet unfulfilled part of the prophecies, though without overlooking their figurative character, from that God, who has shown their divine origin by the fulfilment of a great portion of them, and confirmed it by the entirely corresponding predictions of the New

Testament, respecting the last times. At least the opposers must refrain from urging this objection, until time has shown the non-fulfilment of the prophecies. *Adhuc sub judice lis est.* But that the larger portion of these predictions properly refer to the time of the Messiah, is proved by a comparison of them with other passages, to which the Messianic interpretation is given by the opponents themselves, e. g. with chap. IX and XI. As there, the prospect of the Messiah's kingdom is subjoined to the promise of deliverance from the Assyrians; so is it here the prediction of deliverance from the Babylonians. The prophet describes the picture lying before him, without regard to the determination of time. It is no more asserted here, that the time of the Messiah would immediately succeed the Babylonish exile, than it is there said, that the temporal deliverance from the Assyrians, would be immediately connected with the spiritual redemption.

6 "It may be assumed with certainty, that these oracles ascribed to Isaiah were not yet in existence in the time of Jeremiah. Otherwise this prophet, who suffered much ill treatment for having predicted the captivity, would no doubt, have appealed to such a predecessor." This *argumentum a silentio*, which of itself proves nothing, allowing it to be generally conclusive, would here prove too much, namely, that the first part of Isaiah also, did not exist in the time of Jeremiah, nay, that even all those prophetic writings were at that time unknown, in which a carrying away into captivity in general is mentioned, since it is only of such an event, and not of the carrying away into the Babylonish exile, that Jeremiah has spoken. He could have appealed, with far more effect, to the predictions of the carrying away into the exile, contained in the first part, particularly to chap. v, and to the most definite of all chap XXXIX, than to the latter part, in which this event is no longer predicted, but presupposed, and which is far more occupied with joyful hopes, than with threatenings. And it was on account of these latter, according to chap XXVI, that Jeremiah was assailed, and he was defended by his friends with an appeal to the similar prediction, Mic. 3: 12. It may with just the same reason be asserted, that the more definite prediction, Mic. 4: 10, was not then in existence, for otherwise the friends of Jeremiah would not have omitted to appeal to it. But if it cannot be asserted, who would be willing to deny that Jeremiah, or his defenders, on some other occasion, did appeal to the predictions

of Isaiah? But we shall hereafter see, that the acquaintance of Jeremiah with the second part, is beyond a doubt, since he has both used, and imitated it.

7 "Although the style of the author is in general pure, yet it, nevertheless, exhibits some Chaldaisms, and expressions belonging to a later period." For reply to this, we offer the following general remarks. The proof from alleged instances of later words and phrases is very doubtful. We have too few written monuments of Hebrew literature, to permit us accurately to determine the treasures of the language, belonging to each particular age. If a word be met with for the first time in later writings, this is by no means a proof, that it had not been in use before. It is of more weight, when forms of words occur, which seem to belong only to the later Chaldaizing dialect. But in this case also, there must be other and stronger reasons to render the evidence of a later composition conclusive. We know too little, when the influence of the Chaldee language on the Hebrew commenced, to be able to decide, that any particular form could not, before a given time, have found its way into the Hebrew. It is true that this influence was first chiefly exerted in the period immediately before the exile. As both nations however, were long before connected with each other, particular Chaldee forms may equally early have been transferred to the Hebrew. But how little this proof is entitled to even the appearance of weight, is manifest from the circumstance, that it is entirely given up by most opposers of the genuineness. Paulus asserts that the language in these chapters, is certainly as pure, as in those of Isaiah himself. Bertholdt Einl. p 1363 seq., candidly confesses, that they contain no single trace of a later usage. Nor has Eichhorn produced any example. Gesenius, perceiving how strongly it would argue in favor of the genuineness of the second part, if in respect to the language, it belonged entirely to its first period, although he confesses that he could not find many instances of a later usage, has yet brought forward some few. But among the examples cited, there is scarcely one which can be proved to belong to a later period.

In the first place, that must be set aside, which this second part has in common with writings, whose antiquity is indeed contested by recent critics, but with arguments so doubtful, that they must themselves justify us in requiring, that the alleged later usage of these books should not be brought as a proof of a later usage in other books. If we reject what the second part of Isaiah has in common with these, especially with the book of Job, we dispose at once of a considerable part of the examples cited. Those that remain, we will separately examine. The verb עָמַד, chap. 47. 13, has the sense *to arise*, the same as קוּם, which is the prevailing one in Chaldee. But this sense is only an arbitrary assumption; the verb עֲבֹד v. 13, can have no other meaning than that in which it occurs in a similar connexion v. 12, where Gesenius himself translates it, not *to stand up*, but *to stand firm*, just as he has rendered it *to stand*, in the parallel passage 44· 11. In all these passages, the meaning *to stand firm*, is the appropriate one, in which the verb, e. g. occurs in Amos 2. 15.—A second Chaldaism is found in the meaning of the verb בָּחַר, chap. 48. 10. But 1. It is probable, that the meaning *to prove*, there given to the verb, belongs, not merely to the Aramaean, but also to the Hebrew usage, since it occurs in the same sense in Job; and 2. It is in the highest degree uncertain, whether, in the passage cited, the word really has this meaning. The best interpreters, with the exception of Gesenius, retain the usual sense. The verb בָּחַר in these chapters, so frequently occurs in the sense *to choose*, that it is very improbable that the prophet in this single passage has used it in a different sense. The explanation *I chose thee in the furnace of affliction*, i. e. I loved thee, even when I punished, in order to purify thee, is entirely in accordance with the parallelism.—It belongs also, it is said, to the later usage when, chap. 54: 15, the particle הֵן occurs in the sense *if*, instead of the older meaning *see*. But the particle occurs in this sense in four places even in the Pentateuch, e. g. Lev. 13. 56, see Gesenius s. v. Only the more frequent use can be peculiar to the later period; but in Isaiah, it does not occur in this sense except in the single passage cited, and not even there with certainty.—The expression, *people and tongues*, chap. 66. 18, is altogether Chaldaic. But *tongue* stands for *language*, even in Gen. 10. 5, and in other passages, and it is difficult to perceive, how there can be any thing Chaldaic, in so naturally connecting together these two words, of which there is only this single instance in Isaiah. In the passages of Daniel, on which Gesenius relies for proof, the two words גּוֹיִם and לְשׁוֹנוֹת which Isaiah here uses, do not once occur in connexion, but the three words עַמְמַיָּא, אֻמַּיָּא and לִשָּׁנַיָּא.— The word יֶתֶר, chap. 56. 12, in the sense *very, exceedingly*, corresponding to the Chald. יַתִּיר, is a Chaldaism. But Gesenius himself confesses on this passage, that this meaning is not necessary, and it may also be regarded as a noun, in the sense of *abundance*. Thus

Rosenmuller "יֶתֶר est περισσόν, *quod abundat.*" But if we were to take יֶתֶר in the Accus adverb. in the sense *abundantly*, there would then be no Chaldaism here, since עַל יֶתֶר occurs in the same sense Ps 31. 24, and the preposition makes no difference.—In chap. 61. 10, the verb כָּהַן elsewhere, *to serve as a priest, to be a priest*, means, as in Syriac, *to make rich, splendid*, but there is no occasion to give to the verb כִּהֵן, which is every where a denominative of כֹּהֵן, another meaning in this single instance. Kimchi and Jarchi, in Rosenmuller on this passage, explain the words כְּחָתָן יְכַהֵן פְּאֵר, after the example of the Chaldee and Aquila thus: as the bridegroom makes priestly the ornament of his head, i. e. puts on a head-ornament of priestly splendor; and Gesenius opposes nothing to this explanation. But if we adopt the meaning alleged by Gesenius, there is even then no occasion, according to the general remarks that have been made, to suppose a Chaldaism.—The confounding of אוֹת with אָה, which occurs in two places, is never found in the older prophets. But it is sufficient if it occurs only in the older writings generally. It is found however, even in Genesis 34. 2 Josh 14. 12, and other passages cited by Gesenius s. v. Here also, it is at most only its more frequent occurrence, that can be regarded as peculiar to the later usage, and there is no occasion to suppose, with Jahn, a mistake in transcribing, though it is generally in such pure orthographical varieties that this most easily occurs.—Examples of the position of the verb after the object, as in chap. 42: 24. 49. 6, which are said to be Chaldaisms, are found in equal number, even in earlier books. Comp Ewald Grammatik, p 635.—The verb קָרָא in the sense *to preach, to announce*, chap 42. 2, by no means belongs to the later usage. It is found in this sense in Joel 4. 9, קִרְאוּ זֹאת בַּגּוֹיִם, *proclaim this among the nations*, and also Lev 25: 10.—The noun צָבָא in the sense *military service*, occurs not only in the book of Job, but several times also in the book of Numbers, e. g. chap. 1. 3.—The use of הַ as a relative, in the single passage, chap. 56. 3, is not exclusively peculiar to the later usage, but occurs also Josh. 10. 24. Judges 13. 8. 1 Sam 9: 24.—Only a single form of a word occurs אֶגְאַלְתִּי for הִגְאַלְתִּי, chap. 63. 3, which has probably been justly explained as Aramaean, and in which Jahn supposes there is a mistake of the transcriber for אֶגְאָלָה, as אֲרַמְסֵם precedes. But suppose, that some few traces besides of Syriac and Chaldaic usage might be found by an acute observer, what would they prove? The Aramaean was at that time so well known, that the ambassadors of king Hezekiah, Isa.

36. 11, could propose, that the conference should be carried on in the Syrian language. Bertholdt therefore has the candor to confess, that Isaiah could have intermingled in his discourses, here and there an Aramaean word, or an Aramaean form. He says, l c p 1374, "that it must be conceded, that in the times of Ahaz, Hezekiah, and Manasseh, circumstances were such, that any writer, unless he carefully sought to avoid it, might lose the purity of his Hebrew style, through the influence of the Aramaean."—This argument then, has no validity, 1. Since the examples adduced, partly rest upon false interpretation, and partly, one only excepted, do not belong exclusively to the later usage, and, 2. Because individual Chaldaisms may have been already in use in the time of Isaiah.

8. "The style, the circle of words, and the phraseology in these portions, have much that is peculiar, which is not found in the genuine Isaiah." Here again, much has been believed to be proved, when a few words and expressions have been produced, which are regarded as peculiar to the second part. But in this way can the spuriousness of any portion of any composition be evinced. Who shall require a writer always to use the same words and modes of expression? What writer, whose mind was not entirely barren, would always repeat his old expressions, and never intermingle new ones? Especially, when his earlier and later productions are separated by so long an interval, as in the case of Isaiah; and, when the change of subject rendered the use of new words and expressions almost indispensable. With equal justice, this argument may be turned against our opponents. When, in a doubtful portion of a writer, precisely the same stock of words and expressions only, is to be found, as in other portions proved to be genuine, it may be said, that this very uniformity, betrays the anxious and slavish imitator, who has studied to produce an accurate outward resemblance, in order to pass off his own for that of the author, and to conceal its want of inward agreement. Of that which has been cited, we will here touch only upon what has some plausibility in its favor. Reliance is placed first on the appellation עֶבֶד יְהוָה, *servant of Jehovah*. No one would seek to prove any thing from the bare occurrence of this appellation. It not only often occurs in the remaining books of the Old Testament, but also in the first part itself, and indeed chap. 20 3, as an appellation of the prophet, chap 22· 20, of another pious Israelite, called to an office under the theocracy. But the occurrence of this appellation, might well have weight, if it were really

employed to designate the prophets collectively. But this, as we shall see on chap. LIII, is a supposition which is not sufficiently established.—אִיִּים in the sense *distant lands*, is found also in the first part chap. 24: 15. But that in the passages of the second part the prophet always had in view the dark, and to the Hebrews, immeasurable West, and that consequently, אִיִּים does not here occur in a *simply* indefinite sense, Gesenius himself remarks s. v.—Peculiar to the second part also, is the use of the nouns צֶדֶק and צְדָקָה in the sense: *salvation, help, deliverance, victory*, synonymous with יֵשַׁע and יְשׁוּעָה. But Gesenius himself, II p. 136, in a measure retracts this assertion, when he doubts whether צֶדֶק could any where stand without regard to the original meaning of the word, to express also the prosperity and triumph of the unrighteous. A more accurate comparison of the passages cited by Gesenius, shows also, that in them we may be perfectly satisfied with the usual meaning *righteousness*; sometimes with the secondary idea, founded in the Hebrew mode of thought, of the consequences of righteousness; a meaning which has been retained also by the earlier critics. Chap. 41: 2, the words צֶדֶק יִקְרָאֵהוּ לְרַגְלוֹ are to be translated: *righteousness comes to meet him at his foot*, i. e. wherever he goes. The sense: righteousness will be his inseparable companion; the image being taken from an attentive servant, who does not wait to be called, but willingly presents himself for service. V. 10, בִּימִין צִדְקִי is not to be translated by: *my victorious*, or *sustaining*, but by: *my righteous right hand*. Jehovah's righteous right hand, is that with which he accomplishes his righteous purposes, and in this instance delivers the Jews from their unjust oppressors.—In chap. 45: 8 also, there is no necessity to depart from the usual meaning; the sense: by the mercy of Jehovah shall righteousness and prosperity be diffused through the earth. This is represented, as though the heavens were to send down righteousness, as a refreshing rain or dew after a long drought, and the earth thus made fruitful, were to bring forth an abundant harvest of righteousness, and prosperity. See Ps. 85: 11, 12, and 72: 3, where righteousness and prosperity are connected in the same manner, and Rosenmuller *in loco*. With respect to chap. 45: 13, see on chap. 42: 6.—Chap. 46: 13, the righteousness of Jehovah is his faithfulness in the fulfilment of his promises and assumed obligations. Chap. 48. 18, it is only necessary to add to the main idea of righteousness the secondary one of its consequences, which are in a measure identical, since righteousness itself is prosperity. Chap. 51: 5, righteousness stands in the parallelism with salvation, the righteousness, which shall be imparted to the heathen from above, and in which, and its consequences, their salvation consists. On chap 54· 17, Rosenmuller justly remarks צִדְקָתָם hic est, quod iis ex sententia justi judicis debetur. Chap 56· 1, again the righteousness of God, is his faithfulness in the performance of his promises. Chap 58: 2, the מִשְׁפְּטֵי צֶדֶק are not the judgments of salvation, but the judgments of God's righteousness. Chap 62 1, 2, also, there will be no occasion to give up the sense, *righteousness*, if we bear in mind, that it was altogether common in those times, to infer guilt from suffering, and innocence from prosperity, and consequently that the deliverance and happy condition of the people, at the same time, justified them in the sight of their enemies.—The remaining instances, which are far less important are accurately, and thoroughly refuted by Moller, l. c p 188 seq Several phrases, which often return, the frequent reduplication of words, the custom of subjoining a greater or smaller number of epithets to the names of Jehovah or Israel, are merely a result of what admits of an easy explanation, the diffuseness, and the repetition which characterize the representation in the second part, and need not therefore be particularly vindicated

9. "The style is here, nearly throughout, easy, flowing, clear, but has something of diffuseness and repetition, while on the other hand, that of the genuine Isaiah, appears far more concise and vigorous, full of unfinished thoughts and images, but harsher and less correct." We have already conceded above, that this difference really exists, though it has been magnified by the opponents of the genuineness, and at the same time have assigned the cause, to which it is chiefly owing. Secondary causes were, the difference of the subject, and of the tone of the writer's mind; when he reproves and admonishes the present age, and when he utters promises, and offers consolation for the future, there must of necessity be a difference in the modes of representation Where the subject is the same, there is also a striking agreement with respect to the representation, between the first and second part Thus it is especially in respect to the times of the Messiah, where even the minutest features correspond. So e g chap. 65· 25 in the same manner as 11. 6, the circumstance is made prominent, that the wolf and the lamb shall feed together. The reproving and threatening tone, which is peculiar to the portions which are certainly genuine, is found also in chap 56: 9—57: 12. 58. 1—7. 59. 1—8. 65 11—14.

10. "If all other arguments were of no validity, yet the bare mention of the name of Cyrus. chap 44. 28 45. 1, is sufficient to disprove the genuineness. The prophets are accustomed to designate the persons, whose future appearance they announce, according to their characteristics, but they never mention their names." To this we make the following reply. The name Cyrus is in all probability an appellative, which was an honorable distinction of the Persian kings; in the same manner, as Pharaoh among the Egyptians, or Abimelech among the Philistines. This name was universally explained by *Sun* among the Greeks, (Ctesias. Plutarchus in Artaxerxe c. l.) and indeed justly, since خور still signifies *Sun*, in modern Persian. Comp. Gesen s v v. Bohlen Symbol ad interpret S cod ex ling Pers. p. 20. Reland de vet ling. Persar p 166 seq According to the account of Strabo, Cyrus before he ascended the throne, was called Agradatus, and according to *Schickardi Tarch* p 123 in Gesen l. c., a still later Persian king Bahram, likewise bore the surname كرش. When therefore Isaiah here predicts the deliverance through *Koresh*, his prophecy is no more definite, than the predictions of the first part, chap XIII, XIV, XXI, in which he foretells the overthrow of the Babylonish monarchy by the Medes and Persians. That afterwards Cyrus chiefly received this name to the exclusion of his proper name, arose from his splendid exploits, he was called κατ' ἐξοχὴν *the great king*. It was owing to the special guidance of Divine providence, that Isaiah used this name, which he might have learned from Persian travellers, or as Hensler supposes, from the Medes, who served in Sennacherib's army Comp Hensler's Jesaias p 247, 363. Jahn's Archaologie II, 2 p 286. To this our opponents can make no satisfactory reply. But suppose the name Koresh, were really a proper name, and no other prophecy could be produced, in which a person, who was to appear at a future period, was mentioned by name, still this would be no proof of spuriousness. For who shall prescribe to God the rule, which he shall follow in making his revelations? Who shall say that he may never depart from his usual method of proceeding? If while as a general rule, he unfolded the future to the prophet, without fixing the time, when events were to take place, he still in particular instances, accurately determined the number of years between the prophecy and its fulfilment; he surely might with the same propriety in a particular instance reveal the name of a future person, who should

exert a special influence on the affairs of his kingdom. Indeed the mention of a name no more transcends the powers of nature, than the prediction of any one particular historical circumstance, as chap. 44: 27.—But the assertion of the opponents, that no analogous case can be shown, is altogether erroneous. We have an instance, 1 Kings 13 2 A prophet there foretells to Jeroboam, who had erected an idolatrous altar, that a son should be born to the house of David, named Josiah. He will offer upon the altar the priests of the high places, who burn incense thereon. Since king Josiah is there called by name, 300 years before his appearance, how can it seem strange to find here the name of Cyrus about 150 years before his appearance But if our opponents wish to assert, that the name of the king Josiah in the book of Kings is an interpolation of a later period, the assertion would be entirely arbitrary. In this way no proof could ever be adduced against them But then they must also give up their appeal to the name of Cyrus, for what could they say in reply, if we should declare the name of Cyrus in these two places to be the gloss of a later reviser? Although we are far from doing this, yet it would not be greater capriciousness, than that, which they practise on the passage in the book of Kings, and that whereby, as we shall immediately see, they declare the characteristic peculiarities, which the second part has in common with the first, to have been added for the purpose of producing conformity.

These objections, which we have here conscientiously cited in their own words, are all that have been brought forward by the latest and ablest opposers of the genuineness; their untenableness cannot be compensated by the confidence with which the spuriousness is asserted.

We now proceed to lay down the positive proofs in favor of the genuineness

1. It is a fundamental principle of the higher criticism, that the whole of writings, as well as their particular parts, must be held as the work of the author, to whom they are ascribed, until his authorship has been disproved, either by internal or external evidence. That this has not been done in the present instance, we have already shown, while the second part is attributed to Isaiah, by the very circumstance of its being found in the collection, which bears his name We can prove by certain testimony, that Isaiah was unanimously acknowledged as the author in the Jewish synagogue. The oldest is that of the son of Sirach, chap. 48. 22, etc. Isaiah, the

great prophet, it is there said, filled with the spirit, looked into the most distant future, and consoled the mourners in Zion. This can refer, as even Gesenius (Th. I S. 37) concedes, only to the second part. In the New Testament Isaiah is mentioned as the author, as often as a passage is cited from the second part. It may be said, that the writers of the New Testament only followed the prevailing mode of citation, without thereby expressing any opinion respecting the genuineness. But passages, such as Rom. 10: 20, show that they actually regarded Isaiah as the author of the second part. Josephus and Philo also acknowledge him, as the author of the whole collection.

2. The fact which is assumed in reference to Isaiah, when it is asserted, that a multitude of heterogeneous pieces are mingled with the genuine portions, is without any demonstrable analogy in the Hebrew literature. An appeal is made to the Songs of Solomon—but the view of those, who regard this as a collection of odes by different authors, is almost universally relinquished in recent times, and it is acknowledged as the work of one only. The book of Proverbs is appealed to, but here also the supposition, that Solomon is merely a collective is without foundation. But in the prophetic literature not even an attempt has been made to show any thing analogous. It is confessed, that all the portions contained in the collections, which bear the names of Jeremiah, and Ezekiel, are the productions of these authors; in the minor prophets also, no similar appearance is to be found, though some have assailed with weak objections the second part of Zechariah. True the absence of analogy can decide nothing,—an instance of the kind, though the only one, may be still that in Isaiah. But yet it enables us to see how strong must be the arguments, which could compel us to yield to the assertion of our opponents.—In addition to this, however, they have yet to contend with the difficulty of assigning an object, which the collector of these prophecies could have had in view. They all agree, that he must have been conscious, that they were not the work of Isaiah. This they are obliged to confess; since their supposed collector, and the author of the second part, must have been contemporaries. According to Eichhorn, the genuine portions of Isaiah were not sufficient to fill a roll. But then who tells us that only great rolls were used? And if one wished to add any thing to Isaiah, why should he not as well have distinguished it, from what belonged to this prophet, by an intervening space and superscription, as the minor prophets

are distinguished from each other, although they equally form but one collection. It cannot be said in reply, that the name of the author could not be mentioned, because he was not known. For the name of so distinguished a prophet could not have been unknown to the collector, especially, as at that time, the prophetic order was almost extinct. Others, as Doderlein. suppose that the author of the second part may have likewise borne the name of Isaiah, and that this was the cause of the reception of his prophecies among those of the older Isaiah. But that a second Isaiah, son of Amos, lived at the time of the exile is a mere fiction, sustained by no historical testimony, and would surely be a remarkable coincidence; had such been the case, however, the identity of the name could have been no reason for the collector to combine the productions of both, without the slightest remark. Others talk of a *pia fraus*, of the collector; he aimed to give to the prophecies of one of his contemporaries, a higher authority by attributing them to Isaiah. But such a *pia fraus*, could not have escaped detection; had the author lived at the time of the Babylonish exile he must, on account of his distinction, have been as well known to those, whom the collector designed to deceive, as to him. — Others still suppose, that the threatening nature of the prophecy, chap. xxxix, may have been the reason, why the second part, which is of a consoling character, was attached to it. But this singular proceeding of the collector, can be sustained by no analogous example, and besides no reason can then be given, why the second part of Isaiah might not just as well have been inserted in any other collection of prophetic writings since several of the prophets predict the Babylonish exile; why it might not have been appended, for instance, to Micah or Jeremiah, who speak with the greatest definiteness of that event. Gesenius perceiving the difficulties of all these suppositions, ascribes it to accident. But this is merely an acknowledgement, that the fact admits of no explanation. Gesenius suggests the possibility, that the union of these anonymous oracles with those of Isaiah on the same roll, might be sufficient reason with a later possessor, to ascribe to this prophet all the roll contained; but then the question immediately arises, how came the collector, to combine them both on one roll?

3. In this portion of Isaiah there are many peculiarities of language, which it has in common with the first part, but which are either not found at all, or only seldom in the other books of the Old Testament. Of these Jahn l. c. p. 460 seq., and Moller p. 59 seq.

give a collection made with diligence. We here produce but two examples The first is the standing name of Jehovah קְדוֹשׁ יִשְׂרָאֵל *the Holy One of Israel*, throughout the whole book, occurring in the second part, as often as in the first. This name occurs elsewhere, in all the Old Testament, but five times, viz Ps 71· 22., 78· 41 89· 19. Jer 50 29 51· 5 In the two latter passages, it does not properly belong to Jeremiah, but to Isaiah, whom Jeremiah has imitated in these chapters. How very peculiar to Isaiah this appellation was, appears from the circumstance, that it is found in his address in 2 Kings 19· 22, although it occurs no where else in the books of Kings. The second idiom, to which attention was first drawn by Gesenius himself, is that in the second part, as well as in the first, "to be named," stands extremely often for " to be." These peculiarities have occasioned the opposers much difficulty They confess that they cannot possibly be accidental   Comp. De Wette Einl S. 231. Gesenius Einl. zu dem zweiten Th. p. 29. The evasion, to which they have recourse, is very unnatural. They assert that these peculiarities proceed from a conforming hand, which has been active in shaping the whole. But this is the extreme of caprice Then, in general, no question of the higher criticism can be decided by the character of the style; since the liberty, which the opposers of the genuineness of a portion assume to themselves, they must also concede to its defenders.—It is altogether unnatural, and inconsistent with the spirit of that age, as represented by the opponents themselves, to suppose that the collector, or whoever else it was, should have set himself down, and collected particular words and phrases, from the first part, and inserted them, instead of others in the second And what could have been his motive for this procedure? It happened by mere accident, as the opposers themselves assert, that the second part was joined to the first, consequently, he could not have designed thereby to make the second part pass with more plausibility for a work of Isaiah And even allowing this to have been his object, he could not expect to accomplish it, on account of the character of the readers of his time For who had then a taste for a critical comparison of the diversities of style, as it is now practised?

4. Against the opinion, that the second part of Isaiah was composed in the time of the exile, its style furnishes an argument, which is not to be contemned. The influence which the Aramaean language had previously exerted on the Hebrew became from the nature of the case very considerable with the Babylonish exile. During

this period, the Hebrew already began to be the language of the learned. A considerable Chaldee element is contained even in the writings of Jeremiah, who lived before the exile and at the commencement of it not in Babylonia but Jerusalem; and there is still more in those of Ezekiel, who spent his life in the exile. But in the so called Pseudo Isaiah, we must expect a far greater degree of this Chaldaic influence. According to our opponents, he prophesied at Babylon about the last year of the seventy years' captivity. He was therefore never in Judea, he lived from his youth among a foreign people. But now we find a style, which according to the confession of the opponents themselves, equals in purity, and elegance the productions of the most flourishing period of the Hebrew literature. That the Pseudo-Isaiah may have *retained* his language pure, we cannot say with our opponents, since he could not *retain* what he never possessed, and that he may have formed his style after the model of older writings, is not sufficient to explain the fact. It seems impossible in times so very unfavorable to learned studies, so entirely to resist the influence of the circumstances, in which he was placed, that they should not be visible, in a composition of such an extent. When an appeal is made to the book of Job, as a similar instance, the later age of this most ancient of all the productions of Hebrew literature, is erroneously presupposed. When also it is asserted, that many psalms belong to the time of the captivity, whose diction is entirely, or almost pure, the most of them are in like manner capriciously assigned to this period. Those which actually belong to it, can prove nothing. For in a poem consisting of only a few verses, it is not conceivable, that many Chaldaisms could occur. Nor can any evidence be drawn from the books of Kings; partly, because not a few Chaldaisms are found in them, and partly, because in their composition older contemporaneous sources were made use of whose words were adopted.

5. The first and second part have also many other peculiarities in common. Both delight to subjoin to the prophecies hymns of thanksgiving. It is true, that examples of this sort are found in other prophets, but yet proportionably not so frequent. In both parts visions and symbolical actions occur but seldom. The first part contains only a single vision, chap. VI, the second, in like manner contains but one, chap. LXIII. Both exhibit the same simplicity and artlessness, not the redundancy, which prevails in the later prophets. In the first part there are but two symbolical actions, chap.

VIII and XX; in the second part but one, chap. 62· 6, where the prophet says, that he would place watchmen, who should pray on the walls of Jerusalem, which yet is properly rather a figure, than a symbolical action. This peculiarity must appear striking, as one common to both; it affords so much the stronger proof of the genuineness of the second part, since we should expect to find in that, visions and symbolical actions, had it been composed during the time of the Babylonish exile. These abound in the later prophets, viz. in Jeremiah, Ezekiel, Zechariah, and Daniel. To this, it is indeed replied, that in the prophets Haggai and Malachi also, who lived at a later period, these peculiarities do not occur. But this is not conclusive, since the predictions of the former, which have come down to us, consist of but two, those of the latter, of but four chapters. Finally, throughout the second part, we meet with the same figures, the same thoughts, the same historical examples, which are peculiar to the first. A single instance, considered by itself, cannot of course be conclusive; but the collection of examples by Jahn, Beckhaus, and especially by Moller, l. c p. 71, may well serve greatly to confirm the unprejudiced, in the conviction of the genuineness, derived from other arguments.

6. If the author of the second part lived about the end of the exile, it is very strange, that he has made so few special references to this period, and is silent respecting so many things, which, one would think, he must of necessity have noticed. Even in reference to Cyrus, how enigmatically is every thing represented! It is only by the aid of the fulfilment, that we can obtain any clear idea who this Cyrus was, and in what way, he was to deliver the people of Israel. What could induce the prophet, who is said to have prophesied at a time, when the Medes and Persians were already advancing against Babylon, to suppress the names of these people, whom the *alleged* older Jeremiah had already mentioned, chap 51 11, 28?

7. On the contrary, there is a multitude of references, which by no means agree with the condition of things about the termination of the exile, but necessarily require the age of Isaiah, or at least the time preceding the exile. If Isaiah is the author, these passages may be easily explained. It is true, that he had transferred himself in the spirit into the time of the exile, and this had become to him the present. But still it must awaken suspicion, if the real present had not sometimes prevailed, and attracted to itself the view of the prophet. This was indeed the case. The prophet often returns

from his assumed position, to the circumstances of his own time. He now beholds the condition of the unhappy people in their captivity; now the State still existing in his time, but inwardly disordered by idolatry and apostasy. These apparent contradictions can be explained only by the supposition that Isaiah is the author. We must here go into particulars. For the most part, Jerusalem appears to the prophet as already destroyed, as also the other cities of Judea, and the country as laid waste. But on the contrary, it is said, chap. 40 9: "O Zion, get thee up on a high mountain. Say to the cities of Judah: behold your God," and chap. 41. 27: "I am the first who saith to Zion. behold it is there, and give to Jerusalem messengers of joy." Here Jerusalem and the cities of Judah are spoken of, as not being yet destroyed. Gesenius, in order to evade this argument, would understand these passages of the former inhabitants of Jerusalem and the cities of Judah. Comp. Th. 2. s. 31. But, allowing that Zion might stand for the inhabitants of Zion, who had been carried away, it is still difficult to conceive, how Zion could address the cities of Judah, when they had long ago been destroyed, while on the supposition, that Isaiah was the author, it is easy to understand, how he could return to the present from the situation to which he had transferred himself. But even the supposition, that Zion might be put for its inhabitants in exile, is incapable of proof, and is not sustained by the passages cited by Gesenius, Jer 51 10 and Zech. 2: 10; since the 51st chapter of Jeremiah was composed in the fourth year of Zedekiah, when Jerusalem had not yet been entirely destroyed (comp. Bertholdt Einl IV, p. 1432); while the prophecies of Zechariah were not written till after the city had been rebuilt —Chap. 43 22, Jehovah declares, that he will have mercy on the people, although on account of their conduct, they had not deserved his help. He brings against them, viz, the charge, that far from rendering to Him that inward service, which the law required, and worshipping Him in true holiness, they had even neglected his outward worship through sacrifices "Thou hast not brought to me the lambs of thy burnt offering, thou hast not honored me with sacrifices;" etc But how can Jehovah charge the people in exile with the omission of a service, which, according to his own law, they could render only in their native land, in the temple consecrated to Him, which was then destroyed?

Chap 48 6—8 the prophet declares, that the destruction of Babylon, and the deliverance of the Israelites, had been predicted by no prophet before him. Chap. 41 : 26, also, he appeals to the fact, that he was the first to foretell these events, which no one had before conjectured. How could a prophet, who lived in the last year of the Babylonish exile, say this when Micah long before, chap 4 10, had predicted in plain terms, not only the carrying away into captivity, but also the restoration from it, when Jeremiah had already made known, chap 50. 51, his far clearer predictions, in which not merely the overthrow of Babylon, and the deliverance of Israel in general were foretold, but also the people who should accomplish these results, were named, and the attending circumstances particularly related? Gesenius (Th 2. p 32), seems to desire to refer the words merely to the mention of the name of Cyrus. But this name had not immediately preceded, and besides, we cannot see how a prophet who delivered his predictions immediately before the capture of Babylon,—after the older prophets had already distinctly announced, that the ruin of the city should be effected by a Medo-Persian army, and after Cyrus at the head of this army, had gained many victories and conquered several nations,—could without exposing himself to general ridicule, boast in many words that God had revealed to him, that Cyrus should deliver the covenant people from the power of the Babylonians. Every one surely could know this, since Jeremiah had accurately given the very time Gesenius himself asserts l. c. p. 33; "The position of the prophet is no other than that when in consequence of the splendid victory of Cyrus, and his advance upon Babylon, the sure hope, yea the conviction gradually arose in the minds of the Hebrews, that this storm would soon fall upon Babylon, and at the same time prepare the way for the deliverance of the people." Chap 52 4, it is said, "Thus saith the Lord, My people went down at first into Egypt to sojourn there, and the Assyrian oppressed them at the end." Isaiah only, and not the Pseudo-Isaiah, to whom the oppression of the Assyrians was not the last, could write this. The prophet contrasts the first deliverance of the people, that from the Egyptians, and the last, that from the Assyrians, which was effected in his time. Gesenius, in order to remove this stone out of the way, translates בְּאֶפֶס *for nought, absque ulla causa*, as the Vulgate has it. But this expedient is inadmissible here and בְּאֶפֶס stands in manifest antithesis with בְּרֵאשֹׁנָה.— Chap LVII, the Israelites are reproved for their idolatry, and it is said v. 5 "Inflaming yourselves with idols, and slaying the children in the vallies." In these words there is a plain reference to the age of Isaiah, in which children were slain in the vallies in honor of the idols. That this was done under Ahaz, appears from 2 Chron 28: 3, and under Manasseh, from 2 Chron. 33. 6 All the remaining passages, in which such sacrifices are mentioned, as e. g. Jer. 7. 32. 19 5, refer also to the time, when the Jews were yet in Palestine But this abominable custom ceased with the carrying away into exile The exile had the effect of giving the Hebrews the deepest abhorrence of idolatry, since they saw in that event, a punishment of this crime, and hoped on the contrary, by true reliance on Jehovah, to regain their former prosperity. All the written memorials of the later Jews, e. g. the books of Ezra and Nehemiah, and the books of the Maccabees, bear testimony to this abhorrence of idolatry, which was produced by the Babylonish exile. It appears even from the circumstance, that hell was called by the name of the valley, in which the rites of Moloch had been formerly practised. Gesenius here proceeds in a complete circle . "Wherefore," he asks, "the constant warfare against the worship of idols, if a great part of the people were not given to it?" This is exactly the point in question, whether a warfare against idolatry is conceivable, and whoever asserts this must otherwise show, that in the time of the exile idolatry, and particularly (what is still more incredible) the burning of children in honor of idols was practised at that time. When the same critic further says, that from a people, who had always been inclined to idolatry, nothing else could be expected, while living among gross idolaters, he opposes mere groundless probabilities, to the testimony of history. For to say nothing of the religious excitement, which was awakened in the minds of the Hebrews by the exile, hatred of their oppressors, and national pride, would of themselves have kept them from every approach towards imitation Although the Jews, so long as they lived as an isolated people, eagerly embraced every foreign mode of worship, yet the whole history of their earlier and later dispersions among other nations, exhibits only one continued example of the most steadfast perseverance in the religion of their fathers —Even among the opposers of the genuineness, several have been obliged to acknowledge the weight of the argument from this passage De Wette (Einl. p. 232) confesses, that it seems to refer back to the age of Isaiah Eichhorn (Hebraische Propheten Bd 1 p. 415) concedes, that the portions, chap. 56 10—57: 21 and chap 66 1—17, on account of the reproof of idolatry which they contain, could not have been written at the time of the captivity, but belong to that of Manasseh. But now, since the whole second part of Isaiah, as Gesenius (Th 2, p. 5 seq) himself has proved, is connected by an inseparable unity, so must the whole necessarily belong to an earlier period, if this is demonstrable of any single portion.—In chap 57 9, it is brought as a charge against the Israelites, that they have not only sinned against Jehovah by idolatry, but also by soliciting the aid of distant kings, by embassies and costly presents, instead of placing their hope on Him alone This is a charge which Isaiah, in the first part, often brings against the people, but which could have had no meaning at the time of the captivity, when the oppressed people, who had then lost their national independence, could have done nothing like this, even had they been disposed —Chap 57 11, Jehovah says, that, with great patience, he has long borne with the sins of the people, but that, instead of repenting in consequence, they had only become more confirmed in their transgressions. Comp Rosenmuller T. III, p. 441. How does this accord with the time of the Babylonish exile, when the people groaned under the heavy judgments of God, and during seventy years had experienced not his long-suffering, but his righteous chastisement? The whole contents of the 66th chapter, lastly, prove it to have been composed at a time, when the temple was yet standing, and the Mosaic worship, and at the same time the worship of idols, were still practised. The prophet, in this chapter, contends with those, who believed they might merit the favor of God, by outward observances, by sacrifices, and similar means But at the time of the exile, this error reproved by the prophet, could have had no existence, since the service of the temple, and the offering of sacrifices had ceased, and the prophet therefore, would only have been beating the air —We have here produced only that which cannot be even plausibly controverted by opponents. There is much besides, that cannot, without great violence be referred to the time of the Babylonish exile.

8. The assertion, that the author of the second part, prophesied in the last year of the captivity, is refuted by the fact, that Jer L, LI, has undeniably used and imitated his writings. This Jahn has shown by a careful comparison, Jahn Einl. T II, p 463, and the remarks of Bertholdt and Gesenius in reply, are not adapted to invalidate the result, at which he has arrived In the predictions of other prophets also, plain traces of the imitation of this part of Isaiah may be shown, but we can here no longer pursue the investigation

Contents of Isaiah XL—LXVI.

In order that the mutual connexion of the Messianic predictions may be seen, it will be of service here to premise a condensed representation of the contents of the whole second part.

Chap. 40 1—11, forms a kind of introduction. The prophet begins with a command of God to his messengers, to announce to the unhappy people, that the divine punishment for their sins, is now about to terminate, and the time of reconciliation and mercy, to commence, v. 1, 2. He next represents the deliverance of the people, which God would accomplish, under an image taken from the relations of earthly kings. He represents a herald, as going forth, who demands a way to be prepared in the pathless desert for Jehovah, who would march at the head of his returning people, as of old he led the Israelites on their journey out of Egypt, v. 2—5. This will as surely happen, as Jehovah has promised it, the Almighty and Omniscient, whose word stands forever, while all created beings are frail and transitory, and therefore deserve no confidence, v 6—8 The prophet requires Jerusalem to announce to the remaining cities of Judea, the news of Jehovah's glorious assistance, v. 9—11

"The deliverance from Babylon is clearly predicted, but at the same time, it is employed as an image, to designate a deliverance of an infinitely higher and more important character." As Isaiah scarcely ever speaks of the inferior deliverance without alluding to the higher, so is it here. The prediction of the forgiveness of sins, of the restoration of the people, of the manifestation of the glory of God, will be fulfilled in its highest and most complete sense only through the Messiah. This concurrent reference to the higher deliverance, is proved, partly by the nature of prophecy itself, and partly by the most distinct testimonies of the New Testament, Matt 3 3. Mark 1. 3. Luke 3. 4. John 1· 23. In these passages, v 3 is referred to John the Baptist. He was called to remove the obstacles, which retarded the revelation of the glory of God in the Messiah; he occupied the first place among the heralds, who prepared the way of the great king. The wilderness, in which he should prepare this way, was the Jewish people, sunk in sin and error

V 12—31. The prophet is led by the prediction of the illustrious proof of Omnipotence, which God will give in the deliverance of

describe the divine omnipotence, majesty, and glory. He makes of this a twofold application. He first shows from it, v. 18—26, the vanity and folly of the worship of idols, to which he was induced, partly by the circumstances of his time, and partly by the foresight of the temptations to idolatry, to which the people of Israel would be exposed in the exile, in the midst of an idolatrous people. Next he derives from it, v. 27—31, an exhortation to his people to persevering confidence in this, their almighty and all wise God, who comes though often late to help by his power the weakness of those who trust in him.

Chap. XLI, relates as well as the foregoing, chiefly to the first great object of the predictions of the second part, the deliverance of the Jews from the Babylonish exile by Cyrus. The discourse is addressed first, to the idolatrous nations, who should learn the vanity of their idol worship from this manifestation of the omniscience and omnipotence of God. If they could not attribute to natural causes, the prediction of the appearance of Cyrus, which Jehovah by his prophets had so long foretold, as it now came to pass, and if they could produce no similar prophecy given by their idols, then they must confess, that Jehovah really sent him, whom he promised to send. They would be the more obliged to this, since their gods afforded them no help against the mighty conqueror, while the people of Israel, who were regarded by all as lost, received through him their long promised deliverance.—Secondly it is addressed to the Jews in exile, who are consoled by the annunciation of the approaching deliverance, and the prosperity which is to follow. Jehovah appears, in the first verse, as the speaker, and summons the idolatrous nations to enter into judgment with him. He demonstrates the righteousness of his cause, from the sending of the powerful king Cyrus, whom nothing can resist. Instead, however, of being thereby brought to an humble acknowledgment of their error, and of the omnipotence of Jehovah, in deep distress they seek assistance from their idols, but in vain, v. 5—7. Jehovah then turns to the people of Israel, and consoles them by the promise of deliverance, and of the destruction of their foes, v. 8—16, in connexion with the assurance, that their affliction should be followed by great prosperity, v. 17—20. (V. 14—16, the prophet announces to the people, after he has before predicted a deliverance, which should be procured for them, by other instruments, which God would prepare, that at some future time, they should subdue even their powerful enemies. The fulfilment is to be sought in the first instance in the time of the Maccabees. They not only contended successfully against the Syrians, but also subdued the neighboring nations, who had been most hostile to the people of Israel. The arrangement of the prophecy is agreeable to the course of time, the deliverance from the exile by Cyrus is first announced, then the victories of the covenant people themselves.—In the representation of the prosperity, which shall follow the deliverance from adversity, the times immediately after the exile are merely the foreground, and furnish but an imperfect fulfilment. The blessings here promised will be imparted, in the complete and spiritual sense, by the Messiah.—Jehovah then again addresses the worshippers of idols, and requires them to demonstrate the omnipotence and omniscience of their idols in opposition to him, as he shows his omnipotence and omniscience by the sending of Cyrus, and the prediction of him by his prophets.

Chap. 42. 1—9, forms a section by itself. The representation of the great human author of the temporal deliverance, gives the prophet occasion here to sketch in contrast with him, the image of the great divine author of the spiritual redemption. He then returns to the interior deliverance, and dwells chiefly upon it, until chap. 48. 22. He occupies himself throughout this whole portion almost entirely, with the same objects, the conquests of Cyrus, the overthrow of the Babylonish dominion, the undeserved deliverance of the Israelites, the controversy with idolatry founded on these events. This whole portion can be divided into several parts, in which however much must be arbitrary.

Chap. 42. 10—43. 7, form the first portion. After an exordium, v. 10—12, in which all the inhabitants of the earth are required to praise the glory of Jehovah, that manifestation of this glory is represented, which gives to the prophet an occasion to make this demand. Jehovah, after having long restrained himself, will suddenly come forth to annihilate his foes, and at the same time redeem his unhappy people, while all the worshippers of idols are left without defence and aid, v. 13—17. The people of Israel are next addressed. They are admonished, now at least, to rouse themselves from their stupidity, and attain to true knowledge and conversion. Notwithstanding all that God had done for the people of Israel, notwithstanding the revelations and the proofs of mercy, which he had given to them, they had still hardened themselves, and shut up their heart against every good impression. Finally, must Jehovah therefore give them up to punishment and all misery, without their being thereby reformed, v. 18—25. But nevertheless, Jehovah cannot leave the people, still always dear to him, in their well deserved wretchedness. He will deliver them from the servitude, in which other great and powerful nations, given as it were as a ransom for Israel, shall take their place, and conduct them back to their native land, from all the regions in which they had been scattered, chap. 43. 1—7.

V. 8—13, from this great work, of the deliverance of the Israelites, and the overthrow of their enemies, which had been long and accurately predicted by Jehovah, through his prophets, Isaiah proves, in opposition to the apostate, unbelieving portion of the people, and the idolatrous nations, the omnipotence and omniscience of Jehovah, and the vanity of idolatry. Then follows a new description of the redemption. Jehovah as the protector and covenant God of the Israelites, will demand back his rightful property, and overthrow Babylon for their sake. The blessing to be conferred upon them will be so great, that the former one, the deliverance from Egypt, shall be thereby entirely forgotten. Jehovah will remove all difficulties, v. 14—20. The Israelites could easily imagine, that Jehovah delivers them on account of their merit. This carnal prejudice, the prophet sets himself to oppose, v. 21—28. Jehovah glorifies himself in the Israelites, for his own honor, in order that their history may be a speaking proof among the heathen, of his omnipotence and majesty. Far from having obtained this deliverance by their merit, they have rather so sinned against their God, as to add even outward to inward apostasy; and withhold from him, not merely the worship of the heart, but even external homage. As they have procured their misery by their sins, so will they be indebted for their deliverance from it, to the mercy of Jehovah alone. Chap 44 1—5 contains a new description of the divine mercies. After their calamities are over, Jehovah's rich blessing will be conferred upon the people. He will pour out his Spirit upon them, and many heathen shall acknowledge and worship the God of Israel, as the only true God. The divine blessings, to be imparted at the deliverance from the captivity, are here blended with those to be imparted at the appearing of the Messiah. The effusion of the Spirit, and the conversion of the heathen, are always given as a mark of the Messiah's time.

V 6—11, again, as usual, the omnipotence and omniscience of the only true God, and the vanity and folly of idol-worship, are proved from the redemption of his people, which had long been predicted by Jehovah, and the overthrow of the idolatrous nations. The absurdity of idolatry is then strikingly displayed in a splendid description, v. 12—20. This is followed by an exhortation to Israel, founded on the nothingness of idols, and the true and exclusive Deity of Jehovah, to worship him in truth, strengthened by the annunciation of the speedy deliverance, whose author, Cyrus, is expressly named, v. 21—28.

Chap. XLV. Jehovah, who long before his appearance, clearly designated Cyrus his anointed, and even called him by name, so that there might be no doubt of his having been sent by Him, will arm him with power, and grant him the victory, for the double purpose of delivering his people through him, and then of causing himself, the Almighty, to be acknowledged and worshipped as the only true God, v. 1—7. Righteousness and rich blessings shall abound upon earth, v. 8. This relates in the first instance to the reign of Cyrus, which was distinguished by righteousness in comparison with those that had preceded, for example, those of the severe and cruel kings of Chaldea, but connected with this in the view of the prophet is the prospect of the times of the Messiah. The heathen nations would act a foolish part should they wish to enter into judgment with God, respecting this manifestation of his favor to the Israelites. He who is Almighty, who has made heaven and earth, who has shown his omniscience by his predictions, needs give to none of his feeble creatures, an account of his conduct. According to his unsearchable counsel, he has chosen Cyrus for the deliverance of the Israelites, nay, he will in future times, make the covenant people, who now appear so weak and helpless, victorious over the most powerful and richest of the heathen nations. No man may venture to fathom the counsels of that God, *who hideth himself*, v. 9—15.* The deliverance of the Israelites, con-

---

* The reprimand of those who presume to find fault with the divine government of the world, is, for the most part, referred by the interpreters to the murmuring and unbelieving Jews, who were dissatisfied with the purpose of God concerning them, and especially that instead of preventing their exile, he only promised them deliverance from it, or that the deliverer he had destined for them was not an Israelitish, but a heathen king. But this supposition is contradicted by the whole context. Such a murmuring of the Jews is by no means probable. The joyful news of deliverance makes it certain, that they forgot every thing else. The whole of this reproof appears, on the other hand, far more suitable when referred to the heathen nations. The prophet in the foregoing verses, had said, that the sending of Cyrus had for its object the deliverance of the Jews, while the heathen nations should be

nected with its prediction by Jehovah, will put to shame all the worshippers of idols. Hence Jehovah takes occasion to invite the idolaters to forsake their folly and worship him, the only true God, and solemnly declares, that the time will yet come, when the knowledge and worship of the true God shall prevail among all the heathen nations, and the now apostate portion of the Jewish people, v 16—25 The whole chapter may therefore be divided into three parts, the prediction of the conquests of Cyrus, the reprimand of those, who would call God to an account, the proof of the vanity of idolatry.

Chap XLVI begins with the overthrow of the Chaldaic dominion The idols of Babylon are thrown down and removed Israel, whom Jehovah had protected from his youth, and will still protect, in a manner very different from that, in which the idols protect their worshippers, may hereby learn the folly of the worship of idols and images, the worthlessness of which appears, even from the way, in which the idols are formed, v 3—7. Those of the people, who have forsaken Jehovah, and polluted themselves with the worship of idols, may therefore return to him, who, in the former history of Israel, has shown Himself to be the only true God, who alone foretells future events long before, and accomplishes them himself, who will also prove himself the only true God by the sending of Cyrus, and will soon deliver his people, v. 8—13.

Chap LVII is wholly occupied with the capture of Babylon, and the subversion of the monarchy of the Chaldees. Babylon, the proud and luxurious city, shall be robbed of all her glory and sink in wretchedness and degradation, v 1—5, 8, 9, 11 She relies indeed with proud confidence on her magic arts, and incantations, and believes herself thus secure from every danger But in vain Destruction shall overtake all her magicians and conjurers, v 9, 12—14. Her allies also, instead of coming to her aid, will leave her to her miserable fate, v 15 The reason, for which this divine punish-

---

brought into subjection to him Such favor towards the covenant people, might appear to the heathen, as unrighteous and arbitrary The objection, that the idolatrous nations, who did not acknowledge Jehovah as a true God, could not complain of injustice suffered from him, is inapplicable The prophet does not controvert, what they actually said, but what they might have said with some appearance of right, had they acknowledged Jehovah —V 14, by a customary figure taken from the earthly theocracy, the reception of the heathen nations among the people of God is described, as if the richest and most powerful of them were to be conquered by the Israelites Here also the time of the Messiah is again brought into view

ment is sent upon her, is the inhuman severity, with which she had treated the covenant people, who had been delivered over to her power by Jehovah, to be chastised indeed, but not so severely, and v. 6, that proud self confidence and forgetfulness of God, in which she acknowledged no higher power, and believed that her own strength could secure to her a firm and eternal existence, v. 7, 10. The whole chapter is throughout a continued allegory. According to the usual custom of the Hebrews, of personifying cities and countries as matrons, Babylon is represented as a lady, who, having grown up in wealth, pleasure, and luxurious living, is suddenly bereaved of her husband and her children, and involved in the deepest poverty and humiliation

Chap xlviii, the discourse is directed to the people of Israel, particularly to the hypocritical portion of them, who worshipped God, outwardly, but idols in their hearts Jehovah shows in opposition to them, his infinite power and wisdom, from the accurate fulfilment of his former predictions, declaring it to have been the object of them, to render it impossible for the events, when they should take place, to be ascribed to idols, v 1—6 He gives to his people a fresh and splendid proof, that he alone is the true God, and as such has a righteous claim upon their perfect devotion to himself, by a new prophecy never made known before, that his people, who on account of their sins, had been sent into exile to be purified, should be redeemed by his mercy, and for the glory of his name The Chaldeans, the enemies of his people, shall be overthrown by a mighty king, to be sent by himself Ever since the establishment of the theocracy, God has given to his people the most distinct predictions, publicly made known, and has accomplished them by his omnipotence, and now he has sent his servant Isaiah, endowed with his spirit, that by a new and remarkable prediction, he may bear testimony to his omniscience and omnipotence, v 7—16. Had the people of Israel been obedient to Jehovah, their faithful Lord and God, they would have enjoyed a rich blessing, v 17—19 Now he has been compelled on account indeed of their sins, to give them up for a time to wretchedness. But he will nevertheless again have compassion on them, redeem them, and bring them back in prosperity to their native land The ungodly however shall have no share in this mercy, v. 20—22

From chap. xlix onward, the temporal deliverance, which had hitherto been the principal object of attention, is kept more in the back ground, and the spiritual redemption is chiefly, though not exclusively, presented to the vision of the prophet. V 1—9, he describes its author in contrast with the author of the inferior deliverance, and introduces him as speaking. Henceforth until the end of the portion, chap 50 3, the glorious deliverance is described, which Jehovah will vouchsafe to his people. But here, what appears in history, as occurring at different times, was represented to the prophet in a single vision. The reestablishment of the State after the exile, and the enlargement of the theocracy by the Messiah, its increase and its final glorification appear to him combined in one picture. Signal prosperity, and a rich blessing shall be conferred upon the theocracy; although it seems near its extinction Yet Jehovah will have mercy upon it, restore it to far greater splendor, than it ever possessed before, and bring back its scattered members from all regions of the earth; for he can no more forget his people, than a mother her child, v 10—16 By a miracle of the divine omnipotence, the theocracy shall flourish most gloriously, at the very time, when it seemed on the point of total extinction The enlargement of the church will be so great, that it can be explained by no natural causes, v. 17—21 The heathen and their kings shall become its friends, and promote its prosperity, v 22, 23. No power of the enemies of the divine kingdom shall hinder the fulfilment of those promises, v 24—26. Jehovah has indeed, for the present, rejected his people, on account of their sins, but he, who is Almighty, can and will redeem them, chap 50 1—3

Chap 50. 4—11. The author of the spiritual redemption, the Messiah, again appears before the spiritual eye of the prophet, and is introduced as speaking.

Chap 51—52. 12, constitute one connected portion. The prophet consoles the small and oppressed community of believers, by the prediction of a rich blessing, and great glory, first at the deliverance from the captivity of Babylon, and, in a complete sense, at the appearing of the Messiah The pious portion of the people, the true Israel, are addressed The prophet exhorts them to persevering confidence in God, and appeals to the example of Abraham, who, as an individual, was called of God, and became by his mercy the ancestor of a great people By the same divine mercy should the covenant people also be comforted, v 1—3 God in future times will yet glorify the now fallen theocracy, by imparting to the heathen the knowledge of the true religion, and reducing them again to subjection to his authority, which they have hitherto rejected. Though every thing else should fail, Jehovah's merciful promises are sure forever, v. 4—6. Therefore the people of God must not despond, although assailed by persecution and reproach; destruction overtakes their persecutors; for them eternal salvation is appointed, v. 7, 8. The church is then introduced as speaking, and beseeches Jehovah to glorify himself in her anew, as he had just promised, and rescue her from her distresses, by that same omnipotence, by which he had before delivered his covenant people from Egypt, v. 9—11. Jehovah in reply, exhorts the church to be steadfast, by reminding her, that her enemies are feeble mortals, but her protector is the Almighty God, and announces, that he will soon effect the deliverance of his church from her foes, by that same omnipotence, which he displays in the operations of nature, v. 12—15. V. 16 Jehovah, in accordance with the dramatic character of the whole discourse, addresses the Messiah, and assures him, that he will endue him with power, and sustain him by his omnipotence, in order that he may effect a great change in the condition of things, and glorify the theocracy. (In this verse a change of the person addressed must in any case be supposed. In opposition to Rosenmuller, who understands the passage of the community of Israel, see Gesenius on the same. Gesenius proceeding here upon his groundless hypothesis, that the prophets, were to be the founders of the new ideal state, supposes the object of address, to be the prophetic order. In reply see on chap LIII. The person addressed can be no other than the Messiah. Comp. the parallel passages chap. XLIX, especially v. 2, and chap L, especially v. 4 and 5. In the foregoing chapter, the Messiah appeared as the speaker, in this chapter, Jehovah takes up the discourse; he addresses the church, she answers, he replies, he then turns to the Messiah, and gives him the command to accomplish what had been promised to the church.) V. 17—23 the address is again directed to the unhappy people in the Babylonish exile; Jerusalem has drunk of the cup of God's wrath; but it shall now pass from her to her proud oppressors. Chap 53 1—6. As Jehovah had before delivered his people from the power of the Egyptians and Assyrians, so will he now deliver them. V 7—12, the prophet places himself in spirit in the time when this redemption shall be accomplished, he hears the messenger proclaim; he summons to depart. Still it is to be remarked, that as in the first part of the portion, chap 51 1—16, the prospect of redemption through the Messiah, is most prominent, so in the latter part, is that of deliverance from the captivity

Chap 52 13—53 12, the exalted author of the spiritual redemption is described with the clearness of the fulfilment, in his humiliation and in his glory

It had been promised, chap 52. 15 and chap 53 10—12, that the kingdom of the Messiah should be widely extended over the heathen nations This is enlarged upon chap LIV. The church of God is addressed, which under the old covenant was confined to a small number of true believers, often oppressed and apparently forsaken by Jehovah, because involved in the theocratical judgments sent upon the ungodly. See v. 17. chap. 51: 1 etc. She is represented under the image of an unfruitful wife, who now receives many children; Jehovah her husband, who had rejected her, will become reconciled to her; her family shall be increased by the accession of the heathen, v 1—10. The church thus enlarged, shall be glorified by Jehovah, and be internally and externally blessed; all her members shall be taught and justified by Jehovah, who will defend her against all her enemies, v. 11—17. Although the deliverance from the Babylonish exile, may have been continually before the eye of the prophet, yet there are only some indistinct references to it. It is important to observe, that as the prophecy embraces the feeble beginning of the kingdom of God and its glorious completion, its fulfilment is, in part, yet to be expected See Apoc 21. 18—21.

Chap LV. Those who seek salvation are admonished to accept the blessings of Jehovah, which are freely offered, and are more precious than all the good things of earth, instead of longer wearying themselves in vain in their own ways, v. 1, 2. Jehovah will, in particular, enter into a covenant with them, through the second David, the Messiah, which shall not like the former, last only for a short time, but endure forever, and secure to its members life and salvation, v 3 This second David shall not, like the first, rule only a single small nation, Jehovah has subjected all the heathen to his dominion, and they shall join themselves to the community of Israel, v 4, 5 (By David, v. 3, must be understood, the great descendant of David, the Messiah, who is so named in Ezek 34· 37 37: 24, 25. Jer. 39 9 Hos. 3· 5. For the suffix in נְתַתִּיו can only be referred to him. But that the Messiah is to be understood, by the teacher, commander and lawgiver of the heathen in this verse, is unquestionable, and acknowledged by the best interpreters, and even by Kimchi, Jarchi, and Rosenmuller. Gesenius makes but one, and that a groundless, objection : "that the idea of a personal Messiah, is nowhere expressed in the second part of Isaiah, and that he entertains only the general Messianic expectations " He translates · "that I may make with you an everlasting covenant—may show to you, as to David, lasting mercy. Behold I have made him a Ruler of the nations, a Prince and Leader of the people;" and refers v. 3, as well as 4, to David himself To this we reply, 1. That the חַסְדֵי דָוִד הַנֶּאֱמָנִים, the enduring, not transient mercies of David, plainly correspond with בְּרִית עוֹלָם and stand in contrast with the transient mercies which had been shown to the typical David, and through him to the people. 2 The designation of David as a teacher,* a leader, and lawgiver of the heathen people is unsuitable, and can be justified by no parallel passage ; while the Messiah is thus represented in numerous places 3. That v. 5, according to this explanation, is separated from v. 4, which is inadmissible, since the לְאֻמִּים v. 4, over whom David is placed as ruler, are obviously the same, who v 5 hasten to join themselves to Israel)—But he only can have a part in this kingdom, who glorifies Jehovah by true righteousness. Therefore let all the ungodly truly repent, and seek the forgiveness of their sins from him who is so rich in mercy and compassion, v. 6, 7. It might appear incredible to the small and oppressed church, that she should be so glorified and extended over the heathen nations Jehovah therefore meets this doubt by showing that his counsels transcend all the thoughts of mortals, that what seems difficult and impossible to them is easy to him, and that therefore Himself and his work must not be judged by the views of men, v. 8, 9. The divine promises of mercy cannot fail of their accomplishment ; they must prove powerful and efficacious, in like manner as the rain and snow according to their own nature must moisten the earth, and make it green and fruitful. A luxuriant harvest must spring forth from the seed of the divine word, v 10, 11. The church of God shall be delivered from the oppression under which she now sighs, and be glorified (In an incomplete sense, by the deliverance from captivity, in a complete one, through Christ)

---

* So is עֵד in all probability to be translated , comp Rosenmüller and Kimchi, who render it by *is qui monet et redarguit* , the translation *prince*, preferred by Gesenius, does not accord with the usual meaning of the word *witness*

The portion chap 56. 1—8, is connected with the foregoing. Jehovah again exhorts to a worthy preparation for the coming prosperity, by genuine righteousness, and obedience to the divine commands. (According to the custom of the prophets of putting a part for the whole, the observation of the sabbath is mentioned as an individual example,) v 1, 2. The kingdom of God, when the salvation has appeared, shall be no longer bounded by outward limits, and admission into it shall no longer depend on outward conditions (These thoughts the prophet individualizes by announcing the abolition of the law, Deut. 23· 2—8, which excluded certain foreigners, and of that Deut. 23 1, which excluded eunuchs from admission into the theocracy.) Reception into the theocracy shall rather depend on a purely spiritual condition, on an entire subjection to the divine will, and cheerful obedience to the divine commands, v 3—5. (The observation of the sabbath here again serves merely as an example, the part being put for the whole, or rather a single divine institution, in force under the old covenant, serves as a designation of the divine law in general, as appears from the parallelism "who choose the things that please me, and take hold of my covenant." The heathen shall have free access to the theocracy, and participate in all the privileges of the members of the kingdom of God, on condition of fulfilling its obligations, v 6, 7. (This thought is exhibited under images taken from the ancient theocracy, by saying, that the heathen will then have free access to the temple, and their offerings be well pleasing to God) The Lord will not merely collect the Israelites from their dispersion, but also enlarge the theocracy by the reception of the heathen nations, v. 8.*

---

* Gesenius supposes, that there is here a contradiction between the prophet and Ezekiel The latter, a son of a priest, he thinks was more contracted in his principles, and desired to know nothing of foreigners in the new colony But this opinion rests on a false and literal understanding of the metaphorical expression of Ezekiel chap 44 9, where the phrase "of an uncircumcised flesh," is sufficiently explained by that "of an uncircumcised heart," and where circumcision by a figure common with the prophets, serves as a symbol of purity of heart That Ezekiel, no less than all the other prophets, expected the reception of the heathen into the theocracy in the time of the Messiah, is evident from chap 17 22—24, where the Messiah is represented as a lofty cedar tree, under which all the fowls dwell, also from chap 47 1—12, and other passages When Gesenius further represents the conduct of Ezra and Nehemiah as in opposition to the principles here expressed by Isaiah, it may be said in reply, that they would not presume to undertake that, which accord-

A new section begins with chap 56: 9, and extends to chap. 57: 21. The prophet had predicted in the preceding section the great honor to be conferred on the theocracy, and the reception of the heathen nations into it, at the same time expressly declaring, that only those who feared God should partake of the blessings to be imparted by Jehovah. He now sketches a picture of the prevailing depravity, in order to show, that the greater part of the nation, should it continue in its present corruption, need entertain no hope of a participation in these blessings. The condition of the people in his own time, and not in that of the exile, is here described by the prophet. Foreign enemies shall lay waste the land of Israel, v. 9. (These enemies appear under the figure of wild beasts, the Israelites under that of a badly guarded flock. Jer. 12: 7. Ez 34: 5.) For the prevailing corruption calls forth the divine chastisement. The teachers and rulers of the people neglect the duties of their station, their covetousness is insatiable; they lead a luxurious and dissipated life, v. 10—12. The righteous are removed out of the way with impunity, and have already almost entirely disappeared, chap 57: 1, 2. Idolatry, here, by a customary figure, represented as adultery, as infidelity towards Jehovah the rightful husband of the church, is practised by the apostate people, openly and in secret, v 3—8. Instead of seeking help from Jehovah, their faithful covenant God and protector, the people solicit the aid of foreign kings by embassies and presents, and summon their last energies in vain to help themselves, v 9, 10. A foolish fear of objects from which nothing was to be apprehended has brought the people to these futile purposes, and this forgetfulness of God, in which they have only been confirmed by his long suffering, v. 11. But now will Jehovah cease to exercise this long-suffering, and visit them with heavy punishment, from which all their idols and all their human allies shall not deliver them.* Afterwards Jehovah will again have mercy upon them But

---

ing to the uniform doctrine of the Old Testament the Messiah was to accomplish, that rather in respect to their own agency, they were strictly bound to the law which was designed for the whole duration of the old covenant.

* A comparison of v 9, of the preceding chapter shows, that nothing else than the carrying away into the Babylonish exile can be intended by the judgment here threatened. Gesenius has not informed us, who other than the Babylonians are the enemies, who according to v 9, should destroy Israel But if the desolation by the Babylonians is here described as future, how can a prophet who lived at the end of the exile have been the author?

his salvation, which he tenders at the same time to Jews and heathen, (comp v. 19 with Eph. 2· 17,) will not be imparted to the whole people, but only to that portion of them who fear God. The ungodly remain excluded from it, and are to suffer still heavier punishment, v. 13—21.

Chap LVIII. Continuation of the complaint. Another part of the nation it is true persevere in outward conformity to the religion of their fathers; but they entertain the hypocritical opinion, that by outward religious observances, without true repentance, and reformation of heart, that by serving God with outward fasts, and rigid outward observance of the sabbath, they can acquire a righteousness before him, and thereby give themselves up without restraint to every vice. It is only by sincere reformation, that the divine mercy will be imparted to them, and they will obtain a rich blessing, and deliverance from the evils which the apostasy of the people brings upon themselves. (V. 12, the desolation of the land, which the prophet, chap 56: 9 and 57. 12, 13, transferring himself from the imaginary to the actual presence, had predicted as future, appears to him in vision as already accomplished. Gesenius erroneously infers from the expression, *old waste places*, that this portion was not composed until the end of the captivity, see Deut 32 7, v. d Palm finds in the verse only a general figurative description of a renovation of the State, and its exaltation to greater prosperity. Nothing can be a surer proof of the flourishing condition of a State, than when the dwelling places, which have long ago been laid waste are rebuilt, and even the highways changed into inhabited places, etc.)

Chap LIX, also the threatening is still continued. The people were always inclined to seek the causes of their misfortunes, not in themselves, but in God. The prophet therefore meets their doubts, by showing that the infinite power and wisdom of God are always the same, but he cannot send deliverance to the people, and must give them up to suffering, on account of their unrighteousness, violence, wickedness, and sanguinary disposition, v. 1—15. For this depravity severe divine punishment shall overtake the people, but God's chastisement shall also be extended over the heathen nations, v. 16—19. But finally, for the penitent portion of the people, a Redeemer shall appear; a new everlasting covenant shall be ratified, the Spirit of Jehovah shall be imparted, v 20, 21. (That by גואל v. 20, only the Messiah can be understood, is so obvious as to be acknowledged even by Abenezra, Kimchi, and Rosenmuller. Comp.

Rom 11. 26 Gesenius has not explained his view of the passage. On the one hand, it must have been difficult for him to substitute, with the least plausibility, any other subject for the Messiah,—the following verse will not allow Cyrus to be thought of—on the other hand it must have cost him a struggle, to retract his hypothesis, according to which, in the second part of Isaiah, a personal Messiah was never thought of.

Chap. LX. The subject of the last verse of the foregoing chapter is enlarged upon. Under an abundance of images taken from the earthly theocracy, the glory of the new kingdom of God is represented, in which all the heathen nations shall participate. There are only indistinct references to the deliverance from the Babylonish exile. The prophet addresses the believing penitent portion of the people of Israel, who constitute the essence of the old and the foundation of the new theocracy. (See chap. 51 1 According to chap. 57: 20, 21 and chap 59 20, the ungodly shall have no part in the salvation) While darkness covers the whole earth, a splendid light arises upon the congregation of Israel, and it is made glorious by the gracious presence of the Lord, v 1, 2. (The darkness is the image of sin, error, and evil, the light is the image of mercy and righteousness, the knowledge of God, and salvation.) The heathen nations and their kings hasten hither to receive the beams of this light, v. 3 The journeying of the nations to Zion is next represented, v. 4—11 and v 13, to do homage to Jehovah, and Israel as his people. They draw near in numerous companies—bring back the dispersed Israelites with the carefulness of a nurse towards the child entrusted to her care (A feature in the first instance taken from the deliverance from the captivity, and referred to the chief object of the prophecy, the time of the Messiah, and is nothing more than a figurative designation of the reverence which the heathen, when received among the covenant people, will cherish towards them) They come from the east and the west, with camels and in ships, and bring rich presents; each people the most costly productions of their country, the Sabeans gold and incense, and the Nomadic nations of Arabia, herds. (It can scarcely be necessary to remark, that the whole representation is figurative throughout. The reception of the heathen into the theocracy is metaphorically described, as their going up to Jerusalem, which was its seat in the time of the prophet. Gifts in the East are signs of reverence; the fundamental thought is: the heathen will show the deepest reverence for Jehovah, and his people among whom they desire to be received. The mention of particular nations, serves merely as a part for the whole.) So great shall be the splendor and renown of the theocracy, that even its former most bitter enemies shall submit to its dominion, v. 12, 14. Former contempt and enmity shall be succeeded by general reverence and love, v. 15, 16. Great prosperity, peace and righteousness shall abound among the covenant people, whose numbers shall continually increase, v 17, 18, 21, 22. Jehovah himself will dwell among his people, the splendor of his mercy will dispel all darkness, v. 19, 20. The prediction, whose fulfilment commenced at the first appearing of Christ remains in a great degree still to be accomplished, Rev 21. It will be completed when the fulness of the Gentiles shall have been brought into the kingdom of God, when all which opposes that kingdom shall have been destroyed, and its glorification begun.

Chap LXI. The Messiah is introduced as speaking He announces to the true church of Jehovah among the Israelites, that Jehovah had commissioned him, not merely to announce, but also to impart to her deliverance from her present misery, together with righteousness and joy, v 1—3. (That the Messiah speaks and not the prophet, as the recent interpreters suppose, appears from a comparison of the parallel passages, chap. 42 49, 50, as well as from Luke 4· 21, where Christ himself, in the synagogue at Nazareth, declares that the prophecy relates to him) The fallen theocracy will then be reinstated and exalted to a high degree of glory The heathen will reverently devote themselves to its service; for the righteousness of Jehovah requires him to make it honorable and glorious, v. 4—9. The church answers, v. 10, 11, and expresses her joy at the promise which is given, as well as her firm confidence in the fulfilment. In this chapter also, the images are taken from the earthly theocracy, and the renovation of the State after the Babylonish captivity (v 4), or this event may have been at the same time before the vision of the prophet

Chap LXII. The prophet, with whom all believers should join, ceases not to pray to Jehovah to accomplish the redemption of his church, first by delivering them from exile, chiefly by sending the Messiah, v. 1, 6, 7. The church shall be highly favored and glorified, v. 2—5. No enemy shall again disquiet and injure her, v. 8, 9. Restored to her native land, and rewarded by Jehovah for all the sufferings she had endured, she shall be a holy nation devoted to his service, v. 11, 12.

Chap 63· 1—6 With the description of the glorification of the church of God predicted in the foregoing chapter, there is here connected the prediction of the subjection of her enemies. They here bear the name of Edom, according to the custom of the prophets, of which we have already treated in the general Introduction, of designating the enemies of the Messiah's kingdom by the name of a people peculiarly hostile to the former theocracy. That such were the Edomites is manifest from Lam. 4: 21, 22. Ez. 35 Ps 137 7. Obad. v 11. (Gesenius, after some other interpreters, understands the whole in a literal sense, and supposes the prophet speaks of an actual slaughter which Jehovah would cause among the literal Idumeans. But against this interpretation, there is, 1 The comparison of numerous similar passages in the prophets, in which, as in the present instance, the description of the blessings of the Messiah's time, is followed by the threatening of a *general* punishment of the enemies of the theocracy. See Joel chap 3 Ez 38 39. Mic 5: 14 etc 2 V 6 of this chapter, where Jehovah says he has trodden down *nations*, גוים, which, as well as the lofty character of the whole passage, argues in favor of a general infliction of punishment. 3 Lastly, the comparison of chap xxxiv, where, v 1—4 a general judgment of the nations is announced, and v. 5 Edom is plainly mentioned, only as an individual example, a part for the whole See Rosenmuller on the passage The style of this portion is dramatic, and the imagery highly poetical. The prophet in vision beholds a powerful hero approach, in garments stained with blood, and asks who he may be. The hero gives an answer, which manifests his divinity, v 1. The prophet again inquires, wherefore then his apparel is so red, as if he had trodden the wine-press, v 2 The divine hero replies, that his garments are red with the blood of his enemies, which he had destroyed, not as in former times by human instrumentality, but by an immediate effect of his omnipotence, v. 3—6. That the fulfilment of this prophecy, whose figurative character throughout cannot be mistaken, is in a great measure still future, appears from a comparison of the Apoc 14 18 etc. and 19 12 etc. where it is repeated almost *verbatim*.

Chap. 63 7 and LXIV, to the end The prophet transfers himself in the spirit to the time, when the unhappy people have been rejected for their sins, and carried into the Babylonish exile, and he directs in their name a penitential confession to Jehovah, and a prayer for mercy and redemption The course of thought is as follows The people call to remembrance with grief, the great blessings which Jehovah had formerly conferred upon them by his visible Revealer (מַלְאַךְ פָּנָיו v 9), v 7—9 They confess, that they have lost these blessings by their own fault, by their apostasy, which justly deserves punishment. v 10 They cast back a longing look to the period, when Jehovah glorified himself in them through Moses, and granted them his miraculous aid, v. 11—14. They fervently pray for mercy, reminding God of his former relation, and former love, which he could not now entirely deny, when his people are forsaken of all human help, v. 15, 16. They pray Jehovah, that he would no longer deprive them of his gracious assistance in their conversion, that he would consider the mournful condition into which they, his people, whose weakness would be, at the same time, regarded as a proof of his own, have fallen, as well as the desolation and profanation of his sanctuary, v 18, 19, and that he would aid them, as he had so often done in a wonderful manner before, by his omnipotence. Chap 64 1—3. The guilt of their misfortunes rests with the people alone, and not with Jehovah. The holy and righteous Jehovah can favor only those who obey his commands, but the people are sunk in sin and vice, which cannot fail to subject them to the divine chastisement, v. 4—6 But while the people humbly acknowledge this, they pray Jehovah, that he would nevertheless remember his ancient love for his unfaithful children, and forgive their transgressions, v 7, 8. They seek to move him by a new representation of the affliction which has overtaken them, v. 9, 10, and finally ask him, whether he can longer remain a silent spectator of their sufferings, v 11.

Chap. LXV contains the answer of Jehovah to the prayer of the people in the foregoing chapter, and a justification of his conduct towards them He first shows his mercy and compassion from the calling of the heathen, whom he had destined, though they have neither deserved, nor sought the blessing, to be received as members of his kingdom, v. 1. (That v. 1 must be referred to the calling of the heathen, as Vitringa, Lowth, Dathe, Koppe, and others suppose, and not to the calling of the Jews, as Grotius, Rosenmuller, and Gesenius assert, is manifest from the distinct testimony of the Apostle Paul, Rom. 10. 21, 22, where v 1 is referred to the heathen, and v 2 to the Jews, and also from the words themselves, which require this reference For the גוי לא קרא בשמי, *the people which are not called after my name,* cannot be the people of Israel. For should we (though for this there is no sufficient reason) translate with Gesenius "a people that does not name itself after my name," yet the remark of Gesenius, that the apostate portion of the people no longer wish to be called Jehovah's people, is contradicted by the passage, chap. 48: 1, 2, from which it appears, that in their carnal national pride they still always attributed a peculiar value to the dignity, and the name of a people of God. See Gesenius on the passage. The inward apostasy, and the claim to the outward privileges, harmonize well with each other. Comp chap. 66: 1—6.) He next shows his mercy and compassion from his numerous efforts to bring the people of Israel to happiness. But since they have rejected all that he has done for them, since they have defiled themselves with every species of idolatry, and with the conceit, moreover, of peculiar holiness obtained thereby, his justice requires that he should punish them, and visit upon them their own sins, and the sins of their ungodly forefathers, the measure of whose iniquities they have filled up, v. 2—7. But still he has not rejected the whole people, but will redeem and bless the pious portion of them, v 8—10. (This promise refers indeed immediately to the deliverance from the captivity; but it extends at the same time, and, as is shown by what follows, chiefly to the time of the Messiah, the obscure beginning, and splendid completion of whose kingdom are combined in the view of the prophet. Then the different fate of the pious, and of the ungodly portion of the people, as here announced, became most signally manifest. The sincerely pious received a part in the blessings of the Messiah's kingdom; the chastisement was inflicted on the ungodly portion of the people, under which they even now sigh.) Severer punishment, on the other hand, than they have hitherto suffered, shall overtake the ungodly, and the apostate portion of the people. Given up to all misery, their fate will be the more insupportable, because they must witness the prosperity of their favored brethren, v 11—15. The latter will then participate in the great blessings, exhibited under the most splendid images, which God after he has glorified his kingdom, will confer upon its members. An entirely different state of things shall ensue for their benefit; sin with its consequences, sickness, early death, destruction in the irrational part of the creation, and in general all evil shall cease; the condition of human nature before the first apostasy shall return; God shall be joined with his people in the most intimate fellowship, v. 16—25.

The contents of chap. LXVI are similar to the preceding. It describes the rejection and punishment of the ungodly part of the nation, as well as of all enemies of the kingdom of God, the blessedness of the pious portion and their union with the heathen to form a spiritual kingdom of God, a nation of priests of Jehovah. The Jews in the time of the prophet placed their trust especially in outward works of piety, and were proud of their temple, and their worship. The prophet declares, that Jehovah, the Lord of heaven and earth, can easily dispense with the temple and its service, which were instituted merely in condescension to the weakness of men, that he is pleased only with a contrite heart, which he requires, as the only sacrifice worthy of himself; that sacrifice presented without a believing disposition, would provoke his severe displeasure, and be regarded by him with the same abhorrence as gross idolatry, v. 1—3.* He then denounces against these hypocrites, who will not cease from their ungodly course, and who despise and persecute their pious brethren, the severest punishments from God, v. 4—6. The church of God, on the other hand, here personified as a wife, who easily brings forth by Jehovah's help, shall wonderfully increase, and shall be consoled and glorified by Jehovah, v. 7—11. While God confers upon his church the richest blessings, he will destroy his enemies, and the enemies of his kingdom by his heavy judgments, v. 12—17. (The destruction of Jerusalem, together with the prospect of the last great theocratic punishment.) Messengers, furnished with the proofs of their divine mission, shall then be sent forth from the pious portion of the people, who have obtained salvation for the conversion of the most distant heathen; these shall be brought as an acceptable offering to Jehovah, received into the theocracy, and enjoy all the privileges of the older members of the kingdom of God; all carnal prerogatives shall cease, v. 18—21. As long as the new heaven and the new earth, to be erected by Jehovah shall endure, so long also shall the church exist, devoted to Jehovah, and worshipping him in sincerity. On the contrary, everlasting torment overtakes those, who, as enemies, are excluded from the kingdom of God and its blessings, v. 22—24.

---

* That such a warfare against outward religious services connected with inward depravity, agrees only with the times when the Levitical service still existed, is self-evident, and is acknowledged even by Eichhorn (hebr Propheten Th I s 423 seq) who was compelled to assign this portion to the times when the kingdom was still in existence.

Isaiah 42 : 1—9.

The prophet, in the two foregoing chapters, had chiefly pointed to the deliverance from the Babylonish exile; but still his spiritual eye had already, from time to time, rested on the greater event, of which that must serve as a type. He had plainly designated the instrument who should effect the first deliverance, he should be a righteous king from the distant east. The author of the spiritual deliverance in all his sublime humility, now appears at once before his enraptured vision, he directs the sorrowing people to him, and describes him, v. 1 —9. He then returns to the nearer future, and describes anew the deliverance from the captivity, the contemplation of which generally prevails until chap. XLIX.

It will be perceived from what has been said, that we can separate this section from the foregoing and following, as a distinct portion, although there is a connexion between them, which is not to be mistaken, founded on the association of the images in the vision of the prophet.

The arrangement is as follows. Jehovah is introduced as speaking throughout the whole. V 1—4, he speaks of the Messiah in the third person; he points as it were to him, and recommends him to the world. As the beloved, and chosen servant of God, endowed with the fulness of the divine Spirit, and sustained by God, he will be a helper of all those who feel themselves poor and wretched, going about, and laboring in meekness and lowliness, and as wise as he is stedfast, in accomplishing the commission entrusted to him by God, he will establish the true religion among all nations of the earth, who have heretofore been estranged from God. Jehovah then, v. 6, 7, turns to the Messiah, and addresses him, after the prophet, in v 5, has called the attention of his hearers to his omnipotence, as the pledge for the fulfilment of so great, and apparently almost incredible a prediction. He declares to him that it is his high destination, to be realized through his almighty aid, partly to establish a new and better covenant with his ancient people, partly to enlighten the heathen nations, and in general to redeem and bring back to God, the whole human race, lying in the bondage of sin and error. V 8, 9, Jehovah turns to those to whom the prophecy had been given, and awakens their attention to its object. It should serve after its fulfilment, like the former predictions already fulfilled, to place in a clear light before the covenant people exposed to many temptations to idolatry, and thus to preserve them in their fidelity to him, the superiority of Jehovah, the Allwise and Almighty, over vain idols, who can give to their worshippers no disclosures respecting the future. This portion has, as the view of its contents which has been given shows, a very dramatic character, which is founded in the nature of the prophetic vision. (See the general Introduction.)

We have presupposed in the exhibition of its contents the Messianic interpretation of the portion to be the true one. We must now return to the position of inquirers, and bring forward and examine the different opinions that have been advanced respecting the subject of the prophecy.

In the interpretation of the whole prophecy every thing depends on the question: who is to be understood by the eminent servant of Jehovah, who is described in v. 1—7. The opinions of interpreters on this point are divided, which is nevertheless, owing rather to preconceived doctrinal views, than the nature of the case itself. From the mere appellation nothing can be determined. A servant of Jehovah (עֶבֶד יְהוָה) is every one, who acknowledges Jehovah as his Lord, every pious worshipper of God; but then those are especially so named, who are called by him, whether with or without their own knowledge, to execute a particular commission in his arrangements for the salvation of men. See on chap. LIII. A more accurate determination of the person, if his name is not mentioned, must therefore, in each instance be derived from the attributes ascribed to him. In reference to the prophecy before us, there is here still one remark to be made. The עבד יהוה described in this passage, is manifestly the same, who is brought before us chap. XLIX, L, LIII, LXI. This is acknowledged by the best interpreters. We must not therefore be satisfied with showing that the characteristics here given can scarcely be found in any other person, but we must add to these all that is said in the designated passages respecting the עֶבֶד יהוה. Had this been observed many erroneous interpretations of this passage would have been prevented.

As it is, five different views respecting the subject of this prophecy may be noticed. It has been supposed to be, 1. The Jewish people. This hypothesis is as old as the Septuagint version. They translate Ἰακὼβ ὁ παῖς μου, ἀντιλήψομαι αὐτοῦ, Ἰσραὴλ ὁ ἐκλεκτός μου, προσεδέξατο αὐτὸν ἡ ψυχή μου. They have introduced their interpretation into the text by interpolating the words 'Ἰακώβ and 'Ἰσραήλ. Among the Jewish interpreters Rabbi Sal Jarchi follows this explanation, but so modifies it, that he understands by עֶבֶד יְהוָה collectively. *the righteous in Israel*, among the recent interpreters, Eckermann, Rosenmüller in the second edition of his commentary, Paulus and Ammon; the last two with the same modification as Jarchi. They rely chiefly upon the circumstance, that the appellation *servant of God* in other passages, also, and particularly in v 19 of this chapter, is manifestly ascribed to the Jewish people, which however, considering the general import of the expression, and the manifold ways in which it is employed, is saying but little. Against this interpretation, to say nothing of the objections to be derived from the parallel passages, we urge, a) that v 6, the servant of Jehovah is plainly distinguished from the people. (See chap 49: 56.) How can Jehovah say of the people, that he will make them a mediator of the covenant *with* the people? b) That the description of the servant of God as one, who is meek, mild, quiet, and humble, v 2, 3, is in striking contrast with what the prophet elsewhere says respecting the character, and manners of the people of Israel. c) That neither here nor in any of the parallel passages is עֶבֶד יְהוָה joined with a plural, but always with the singular, while in the case of the collectives elsewhere, and especially in the passages where the Jewish people are personified as an individual, the singular and the plural are interchanged. Finally, how little this interpretation is capable of being carried through, unless manifest violence be done to the words, let the example of its latest defender, Rosenmuller show, l. c III p. 71 He says in opposition to Telge, who makes the unnatural supposition, that the prophet speaks, now of the people, now of their king the Messiah: "in eo minus illi assentiri possum, propterea, quod talis oratio anceps et lubrica futura esset, qua bonum scriptorem uti posse, aut unquam usum fuisse vix est credibile." On the contrary, in opposition to himself, he agrees with Jarchi in the explanation of the words, לֶאֱמֶת יוֹצִיא מִשְׁפָּט, v 3 "rex eorum non diripiet pauperes, nec egenos debilesque concutiet." He compares Isa. 11 4, where it is said of the Messiah וְשָׁפַט בְּצֶדֶק דַּלִּים, and approaches therefore, almost involuntarily, the true interpretation, the defenders of which are driven to no such inconsistencies.

2. Others understand by the עֶבֶד יְהוָה Cyrus, e. g. among the Jewish interpreters Saadias Gaon, among the moderns Vogel, Koppe, Hezel, Hensler, Augusti (in dem exeg. Handb.,) Bauer.

They rely chiefly upon the fact, that in what precedes, and also in what immediately follows, the subject of discourse is likewise the deliverance to be effected by Cyrus, which, however, after the general remarks which have been made respecting the nature of the second part of the predictions of Isaiah, proves nothing. They also appeal to the fact, that Cyrus, chap. 45. 1, is called the anointed. chap 44 28 the shepherd of God, and although he elsewhere never bears the name עֶבֶד יְהוָה, is yet designated by all the characteristics which constitute the idea of a עֶבֶד יהוה. But besides the consideration that these critics themselves prove the erroneousness of their explanation, inasmuch as they are obliged to assume another subject in the parallel passages, (no one has yet ventured to explain chap LIII of Cyrus) it is liable to insuperable difficulties arising from the passage itself Cyrus is indeed always represented as a king sent by God for the deliverance of his people, but never as a mediator of a new covenant between God and the Israelites, never as the founder of the true religion How do the words, " I have put my spirit upon him," agree with Cyrus? It is true that Koppe supposes that in ancient poetry, this is the same as. I help him; I give him courage and power to conquer for my people. But as this use of רוּחַ יהוָה in general is incapable of proof, so here, the connection throughout allows it to mean only the prophetic spirit, who qualifies for establishing the true religion How do passages like v. 2, 3, where the servant of Jehovah is described as quiet, mild and gentle, agree with Cyrus, the conqueror, who shed rivers of blood? The erroneousness of the whole hypothesis plainly appears, when the explanation, which Koppe gives of these verses, is compared with the text. According to him, they express nothing more than: he was the gracious ruler of the Jews, and of all the nations formerly subject to the Babylonians, who voluntarily submitted to his sceptre

3. According to others the prophet Isaiah, who, chap 20: 3, is called עֶבֶד יְהוָה, is the servant of Jehovah. So among the Jewish interpreters Abenezra, among the moderns Grotius, and after him Dathe, Doderlein, and Rosenmuller in the first edition of his commentary But it is only necessary to look for a moment at the explanation of Grotius, to be convinced of the violence which is practised to bring the reluctant text into subjection to this hypothesis Should we overlook the parallel passages, chap. XLIX, etc, where Isaiah could not say of himself, without ridiculous extravagance, what is attributed to the servant of Jehovah (see e g 49: 5, 6), still even what is here

affirmed, is too great to be referred to himself, without a degree of exaggeration, and a misapprehension of his calling, not to be charged upon the humble prophet. How, for instance, could the establishment of a new covenant with the people of God, and the conversion of all the heathen nations be ascribed to Isaiah; especially, as in other places, he expects both from the Messiah, and as his whole agency was confined to the Jewish people, and never extended to the heathen nations? In order to remove this difficulty, an appeal has been made to passages, as Jer. 1. 10, where it is commanded the prophet to do that which they were to predict. But to this Michaelis has well replied "This is true, but in that case it is a single expression, not continued so long as in this instance; it is not customary so to lengthen out a figure, and let any one only read this, and the 49th chapter, and he will easily feel the difference, and cannot well deny that the discourse is concerning one who shall actually convert the heathen." Some of the defenders of this explanation, perceiving the difficulty, choose that what is said should refer only in a lower and imperfect sense to Isaiah, and in a higher and perfect one to the Messiah, but we cannot perceive any inducement to adopt such an hypothesis, which only involves us in unnecessary embarrassment, without in the least degree obviating the difficulty.

4. After the example of Rosenmuller (in Gabler's neuem theol. Journal II, p. 340), who, nevertheless, has since changed his opinion, and De Wette (de morte expiatoria p. 26) Gesenius supposes, that here, as well as in the parallel passages, the subject of the prediction is the prophets taken collectively. But it will be shown on chap. LIII, that such a *collectivum* of the prophets exists only in the imaginations of certain critics. We here only call to mind the remark already made above, that a collective body as the subject is excluded by the very circumstance, that here, as well as in the parallel passages, the עֶבֶד יְהוָה is never connected with the plural, but always with the singular, and also that this hypothesis is in opposition to the whole analogy of the prophetic writings, in which the establishment of a new covenant with the people of Israel, and the conversion of the heathen is never attributed to the prophetic order, but always to the Messiah alone.

5. A great multitude of interpreters, far more numerous than the defenders of all the hypotheses which we have mentioned, refer the prophecy to the Messiah. Thus of old the Chaldee paraphrast, the faithful preserver of the exegetical tradition, so among the later Jew-

ish interpreters, D Kimchi, and Abarbanel, the latter of whom says of the non-Messianic interpreters, שכל אלה החכמים הוכו בסנורים, "all these interpreters are smitten with blindness" That this explanation was the prevailing one among the Jews in the time of Christ, (the Alexandrian Jews are here not taken into consideration, because they had less regard for tradition) appears from Luke 2. 32, where Simeon, with reference to v. 6, calls the Messiah $φῶς εἰς ἀποκάλυψιν ἐθνῶν$. Still more explicit are the passages Matt 3 17, in which, the words proclaimed from heaven at the baptism of Christ, $οὗτός ἐστιν ὁ υἱός μου ὁ ἀγαπητός, ἐν ᾧ εὐδόκησα$, were taken from v. 1 of this section, in order to point out that he who had now appeared could be no other than the one foretold by the prophets many centuries before, Matt. 17· 5, where at the glorification of Christ towards the end of his ministry, with a view to confirm the faith of the apostles, the same words resounded from heaven by which, in the beginning of his ministry, he had been commended to the covenant people; and lastly, Matt. 12· 18, where v. 1—3 are cited almost verbatim, and referred to the Messiah. Relying partly upon these authorities, and partly on the natural sense of the passage, the Christian church from the beginning, has referred this prophecy to Christ, and even interpreters, as Le Clerc, who elsewhere endeavor, when practicable, to set aside the Messianic interpretation, are here found among its most decided defenders. Among the modern interpreters, it was held by Lowth, Michaelis (who in his ubers. d. A. T mit Anm. fur Ungelehrte Bd. 8, p 217, gives very valuable remarks respecting the fulfilment of the prophecy), V d Palm, Dereser, Steudel (in dem Osterprogramm von 1826 zu Jes 53, p. 6 seq.), Umbreit (uber den Knecht Gottes im letzten Abschnitt der Jesaianischen Sammlung, in den theol. Studien und Kritiken herausg. von Ullmann und Umbveit I, 2 p 302 ff), and others. The objections, which have been brought against the Messianic interpretation, are of little weight. We borrow them from Gesenius He says: 1. "The Messiah is excluded, since the subject is not merely a teacher of the heathen, endowed with the Spirit of God, but also the Deliverer of Israel" But this objection rests entirely on an erroneous and literal understanding of the 7th verse Gesenius himself explains the first part of it, *to open the blind eyes*, figuratively. He remarks, "in the intellectual sense, therefore to teach the ignorant." No reason can be given, why he should refer the second part to the deliverance of the people from exile, and not to the redemption of mankind from sin and error. Rosenmuller is at least more consistent, who understands עֵינַיִם עִוְרוֹת also in some measure literally, though in a sense that cannot be justified. The correctness of the spiritual interpretation is evident from the fact, that "*those who sit in darkness, or in a dark prison,*" manifestly corresponds to "*the light of the heathen,*" in the foregoing verse. If in the latter case, we are to understand, as all confess, a spiritual light, then must the darkness, and the prison, which this light is to illuminate, be spiritual also. 2. " It is further to be observed, that this עֶבֶד יְהֹוָה is not predicted as a future person, but is spoken of as one already present." This objection arises from ignorance of the nature of the prophetic vision, of which we have treated in the general Introduction, in which every thing appeared as present. It is to the inward, and not to the outward vision that the particle הֵן *behold*, v. 1, relates. That the perception of the prophet had no regard to time, appears even from the interchange of the praeter and future tenses. Had the prophet been speaking of a person externally present, he would surely not have chiefly employed the future.

The Messiah should combine in his own person, in a higher and more complete sense, the three theocratic offices of prophet, priest, and king. Should we divide the predictions, accordingly as one or the other of these offices prevailed in the view of the prophet, that before us would plainly belong to those, in which the Messiah appears chiefly as a divine prophet. J. H. Hottinger has treated this passage at large in a distinct dissertation. dissertatio de servo dei electo ad Es 42. 1 seq Marburg 1709, reprinted in the Thesauro novo dissertat. exeg. t I, p. 890 seq.

V. 1. Jehovah speaks; he points to his Son, and represents him as the Redeemer appointed for the salvation of the world.—" Behold my servant, whom I uphold, mine elect, in whom my soul delighteth, I have put my spirit upon him : he shall bring forth judgment to the Gentiles." *Servant of Jehovah* is the name here given to the Messiah in the state of humiliation. Matthew has instead ὁ παῖς μου, which is of equal import, if the appellation *Son of God* be taken in the Old Testament sense, of subordination and representation. Thus e. g. the judges and kings under the theocracy could be called *sons*, as well as *servants* of God.* The verb תָּמַךְ construed with the ac-

---

* That Matthew employed the word παῖς in the sense *son*, and not with the LXX in that of servant, appears from a comparison of chap 3. 17 and 17. 5, where παῖς is exchanged with υἱός.

cusative and with בְּ ; *to seize*, and then, since we seize by the hand one whom we wish to hold fast *to hold, hold fast*, finally, *to protect, sustain*. The verb here signifies: peculiar care and love, and the sense is correctly given in the translation of Matthew ὅν ᾑρέτισα. The LXX, however, render it more appropriately ἀντιλήψομαι αὐτοῦ. Theod. ἀντιλήψεται αὐτόν. Grotius takes the verb passively, *quo innitor*. But it does not so much signify: to rely upon, as to sustain any one. The phrase רָצְתָה נַפְשִׁי, *my soul delighteth*, is elliptical for the full form אֲשֶׁר רָצְתָה נַפְשִׁי בוֹ. The בוֹ is omitted, because it immediately precedes. The verb רָצָה like many other verbs, by virtue of a certain modification of the meaning, can be construed with the Accus. as well as the preposition בְּ, with the former to find any thing agreeable, with the latter : to have pleasure in any thing.—The words "I have put my Spirit upon him," contain the condition of what follows, "He will bring judgment among the heathen." Hence the praeter is used in the first, and the future in the second instance. The Messiah shall be endowed for the execution of his commission, not with one particular power, but with all the fulness of the Spirit of God. A parallel passage is chap 11.2, where it is said of the Messiah, וְנָחָה עָלָיו רוּחַ יְהוָה, "and the Spirit of Jehovah rests upon him," and chap. 61 1, where the Messiah says of himself (see Luke 4 18), רוּחַ אֲדֹנָי יְהוִה עָלָי, " the Spirit of the Lord God is upon me." Before Christ entered upon the duties of the office committed to him by God, he received the Spirit at baptism, Matt. 3: 16, and that not in a limited degree, but in all its fulness, John 3 34. The words מִשְׁפָּט לַגּוֹיִם יוֹצִיא Gesenius translates : He shall announce justice to the nations. But Steudel (l c p 7) well remarks, on the contrary, that יָצָא in Hiph cannot properly mean: *annunciare, promulgare*. There is no reason for departing from the usual sense. Rather the extension of the מִשְׁפַּט יְהוָה among the heathen by the Messiah, forms an appropriate contrast with its restriction to a single people under the Old Testament. The question however now arises, in what sense the word מִשְׁפָּט is here to be taken. Steudel paraphrases thus " faciet ut prodeant (rata sint) inter gentes, quae (in usu) esse fas est." He therefore understands by the introduction of מִשְׁפָּט merely the introduction of a state of things in accordance with justice and law. But this is liable to the objection of v d Palm: " all the attributes of this exalted person are those of a prophet, a teacher of the people, the word מִשְׁפָּט must therefore be so explained, as to be applicable to such a character." A further objection is suggested by v. 4, where מִשְׁפָּט stands in the parallelism with תּוֹרָה, which there plainly signifies the whole compass of doctrine, and cannot without violence be explained by *decretum*, as Steudel proposes. See Mic. 4. 2, where מִצִּיּוֹן תֵּצֵא תוֹרָה stands in the parallelism with דְּבַר־יְהוָֹה מִירוּשָׁלָיִם. Other interpreters, therefore, have with good reason supposed, that the word מִשְׁפָּט has the meaning, *religion* This sense can be easily derived from its usual acceptation. The word generally signifies, *right, precept, law*, but it is customary for words, which signify law to be employed to designate likewise the whole of religion, partly because religion gives the rule by which the life must be governed, partly because under the old covenant it subsisted in the law See on chap 2· 3. Thus תּוֹרָה, and thus νόμος in some passages of the New Testament. The word מִשְׁפָּט undeniably occurs in this sense in the parallel passage 51·4 "for a law goes forth from me, and my judgment," i e "my religion I will establish for a light of the Gentiles." See Ps 25: 9 2 Kings 17. 26.

V. 2. "He shall not cry, nor be loud, not cause his voice to be heard in the street" After יִשָּׂא, is to be supplied from the following member, קוֹלוֹ, *his voice* In this way the verb נָשָׂא thus occurs in several passages elliptically, without being followed by קוֹלוֹ. In this verse the quiet, mild, and humble character of the Messiah is represented, in opposition to the hypocritical and ostentatious teachers, who seek to make for themselves a party among the people by clamor. In this sense Matthew also introduces the passage, after he relates how Christ avoided outward display and contention This disposition was symbolically represented by the sending of the dove at his baptism. Calvin: "Quietum fore significat, ut vulgo dicere solemus de placido homine et quieto. il ne fait pas grand bruit Nec enim venditabat sese populo, quin saepe miracula sua vulgari prohibebat, ut ejus imperium atque auctoritatem omnes longe diversam esse intelligerent ab ea, quam reges aut principes sibi conciliant, rumore de se conciliato ad captandum favorem multitudinis" After the example of Grotius, Rosenmüller erroneously says "Sicut qui ira exardescunt, qui solent ita altum loqui, ut vox eorum extra domum a praetereuntibus audiatur" On the contrary, Le Clerc has remarked that the subject of discourse is neither anger nor loud speaking in an apartment

V. 3 "The bruised reed he will not break, the glimmering wick he will not extinguish, he will firmly establish religion" The sense

ISAIAH 42.3   453

of the verse: he will not seek to spread the true religion by violent measures, better suited to stifle the feeble germs of goodness, than to nourish and bring them to a happy increase; but with meekness, tenderness, and forbearing indulgence, he will endeavor to bring all those to salvation who do not harden themselves against it. Two things may be signified by the glimmering wick, and bruised reed. According to many interpreters, they designate men in whom only feeble remains of goodness still exist, and who may be entirely alienated from it by harsh treatment, while they may yet be won by mildness adapting itself to their present condition. Accordingly to break a bruised reed, is the same as, utterly to harden those who are already corrupted. Thus, among others, Calvin. "Christus imbecillitati nostrae succurrit. Ubicunque enim emicat aliqua scintilla pietatis, eam fovet atque excitat. Nam si nobiscum summo jure ageret, in nihilum redigeremur. Quamvis igitur vacillent homines ac claudicent, quamvis etiam quassati aut luxati sint, tamen eos non statim abjicit, quasi prorsus inutiles, sed diu perfert, quoad firmiores et constantiores reddiderit.—Hoc igitur exemplo debent ministri Evangelii, cum ejus vices sustineant, mansuetos se praebere et sustinere infirmos et placide ducere in viam, ne extinguant in eis igniculos pietatis, qui vel paulummodo emicant, sed potius inflamment totis viribus." According to another interpretation, related indeed to this, the bruised reed and glimmering wick, signify those who, humbled by outward affliction, and brought to a consciousness of their sins, feel themselves poor and wretched. To break a bruised reed is then the same as to make the unhappy still more wretched. The Messiah, according to this interpretation, will not by his severity drive to despair, those who under the burden of their sins, draw near to him with a broken heart; but will encourage them by his love, mildness, and forbearance. Thus Luther. "that is, he does not cast away, nor crush, nor condemn, the wounded in conscience, those who are terrified in view of their sins; the weak in faith and practice, but watches over, and cherishes them, makes them whole, and affectionately embraces them." The latter interpretation is favored by the parallel passages, "he binds up the broken hearted," chap. 61. 1, and "he knows how to strengthen the weary," chap. 50. 4. In order to illustrate the image here employed, v. d. Palm compares 1 K. xix. The old prophets, he says, were sometimes like a storm of wind, sometimes like a gentle breeze, that breaks no bruised reed, and extinguishes no glimmering wick. Of the latter class should be the eminent servant of God. פִּשְׁתָּה, *flax*, then *a wick made of it.* כֵּהָה, *going out,* from the verb כָּהָה, *to go out, to be weak, small, dim.* The LXX λίνον καπνιζόμενον. Vulg. linum fumigans. Aq. Symm. Theod λίνον ἀμαυρόν. Matthew λίνον τυφόμενον, all designations of a light, which, when it is near being extinguished, burns obscurely, and throws out smoke. The words פִּשְׁתָּה כֵהָה, stand in the Nom. absol. hence the suffix in יְכַבֶּנָּה. The last words of the verse are interpreted in very different ways. At all events מִשְׁפָּט, must be taken in the sense in which it occurs, v. 1, and is repeated v. 4. Many interpreters translate לֶאֱמֶת by *secundum veritatem:* He will inculcate religion in truth, that is, faithfully or truly. Some, as Le Clerc, then find here a contrast with the former constitution of religion, which, considered in itself, was not perfect, but adapted to the necessities of the human race still under the dominion of sense, and moreover in many ways disfigured by human additions. Others, as Calvin, perceive an antithesis with the foregoing members of the verse. He will indeed be mild and forbearing, but yet will surrender nothing of the truth: "Quamvis ergo Christus infirmos sublevet ac sustineat, tamen longe abest a blanditiis, quibus vitia aluntur. Corrigenda igitur sunt peccata sine adulatione, qua nihil magis alienum ab ista mansuetudine esse potest." This interpretation has, indeed, something to recommend it, ל also sometimes denotes a state, or condition, thus, for example, לְבַד *alone,* לָבֶטַח *securely,* לָנֶצַח *always;* but on the other hand ל here plainly indicates the *terminus ad quem,* to which the religion should be brought. There are still stronger objections against the translation of Gesenius: "with mildness he declares justice." The word אֱמֶת as will be evident from a careful examination of the parallel passages adduced by Gesenius, never has the meaning, *goodness;* even in the connexion חֶסֶד וֶאֱמֶת, it signifies only faithfulness, purity, and veracity. And as we have already seen יוֹצִיא cannot well signify, precisely: he will announce. Hensler and Augusti interpret: he will cause justice to be done to the innocent, literally he commands righteousness to appear in favor of honesty. To this we reply, that the word מִשְׁפָּט, must then be taken in an unusual meaning, and that עֶבֶד יְהוָה is here represented rather as a teacher, than as a king. This feature, therefore, would not suit the image. The same objection lies also against the interpretation of Rosenmüller, who makes יוֹצִיא מִשְׁפָּט, the same as יְשַׁפֵּט, and the sense: justus existet judex, neminem injuria afficiet. It may be most naturally translated: he will conduct religion to truth, that is: he will cause religion to be truly and firmly established on earth. Thus with a slight difference in the understanding of לָאֱמֶת, Michaelis, in den bibl. Hal "ad veritatem non notat modum, aut qualitatem judicii, sed convictionem conscientiarum, ut veritas esse agnoscatur." Similar is the explanation of V. d. Palm he shall place religion in the light of truth. Thus Matthew, also explains it, who has given an independent translation of this verse· ἕως ἂν ἐκβάλῃ εἰς νῖκος τὴν κρίσιν, until he has conducted the true religion to victory; κρίσις as a verbal translation of מִשְׁפָּט, in the sense of decree, law of God, positive religion; Wisdom 17: 1. LXX, Deut 11· 1. Ex 15 25 2 Chron 35 13. The phrase εἰς νῖκος, according to our interpretation, corresponds entirely, with לָאֱמֶת, and it is therefore altogether unnecessary to resort to the conjecture of Gesenius, and others, that Matthew has followed a gloss for לָאֱמֶת לָנֶצַח, and translated this according to the Aramaean usage: unto victory. By the addition of ἕως, Matthew indicates the connexion between the last and first two members of the verse. Precisely by his gentle, and mild nature, shall the Messiah gain the victory for truth.

V. 4 "He will not be discouraged, nor hasty, until he hath established righteousness on the earth, and the distant lands shall place their hope in his doctrine." The sense: with fervent zeal, and wise discretion he will labor for the extension of his kingdom, and not rest until he has accomplished his object, the establishment of true religion on earth. Gesenius, after the example of many other interpreters, takes יָרוּץ as derived from the verb רָצַץ *to break in pieces*, for יָרַץ. It is true, that in some cases the verbs עע borrow their forms from the verbs עו.—Thus יָרוּן for יָרָן Prov 29· 6. יָשׁוּד for יָשֹׁד Ps 91 6. (Comp. Gesen. Lehrg p 369.) We must then give to the verb here a passive sense he will be broken. In this sense it seems to occur in Kal. Eccles 12 6 יָרוּץ would then be about synonymous with יִכְהֶה. The sense: he will suffer himself to be checked in zeal by nothing. It is probable, that the word was thus explained by the Chaldee paraphrast, who has לָא יִלְאֵי, *non laboravit*. LXX οὐ θραυσθήσεται. It is in favor of this interpretation, that it makes this verse correspond with the foregoing. As יִכְהֶה with כָּהָה, so יָרוּץ corresponds with רָצוּץ. This agreement is still greater, when we give to the verb כָּהָה with v. d. Palm the original meaning: *to be extinguished*. He will not extinguish and will not break in pieces, i. e. he will neither be broken, nor extinguished, according to v. d. Palm's explanation: the efforts of his enemies shall not prosper, until his doctrine has been planted and taken root, so that it can no more be extirpated. But nevertheless, the preference seems to belong to another interpretation, which we have followed in the translation, and which is recommended especially by Vitringa, with whom Rosenmuller agrees. It supposes the verb יָרוּץ to be the future in Kal, from רוּץ *to run*, as a regular form, and used in its customary signification He will not run, that is his zeal for the extension of his kingdom will be combined with wise consideration and discretion; he will do nothing rashly. Thus of old, Aquila and Theodotion, according to the account of Jerome· *non curret*. The verb is not then synonymous with יִכְהֶה, but it forms a suitable antithesis to it· he will not become disheartened, or his zeal will not abate, but neither will he act rashly. Matthew has omitted this, and the following member, because they contain nothing that directly served his purpose. The words עַד יָשִׂים בָּאָרֶץ מִשְׁפָּט, Rosenmuller translates· "donec omnia ab eo juste instituta et ordinata fuerint." But to this we object, that מִשְׁפָּט must here have the same meaning as in the former verses, in favor of which also is the parallel שׂוּם תּוֹרָה מִשְׁפָּט *to establish judgment*, the same as to introduce the true religion.—The words וּלְתוֹרָתוֹ אִיִּים יְיַחֵלוּ are translated by many interpreters· *the distant lands will hope in his doctrine*, as something to be imparted to them in future But then the sense is not altogether appropriate. How could the heathen place their hope on the doctrine of the Messiah before it had been announced to them The thought of an unconscious longing and desire, which Le Clerc here finds, was certainly foreign from the prophet He remarks: "cum neque Judaismus, neque ethnicismus sapientibus et probis satisfaceret, exspectabant melius quidpiam a deo" We must therefore here give to the verb יִחֵל the meaning: *to trust in any thing*, which it frequently has. See Ps. 31 25 119. 74 Gesenius s. v. The sense: they will eagerly receive his doctrine, believe in it, and ground upon it all their hopes It will then be declared in both members, that the doctrine to be propagated by the Messiah will not be confined to the narrow bounds of Palestine, but imparted to the whole heathen world, and eagerly embraced. Matth. has translated the words· καὶ τῷ ὀνόματι αὐτοῦ ἔθνη ἐλπιοῦσι; so likewise the LXX, whom he probably followed. But it is not necessary to suppose that he and they had before them a different reading. *On his name*, is the same as, *on him* But whoever, in the true sense, places his hope on the doctrine of the Messiah, places it on him. אִיִּים *islands, coasts,* here as frequently, an indefinite designation of the most distant lands.

V. 5. Here commences a new discourse of Jehovah. He had before pointed to the Messiah, and spoken of him in the third person; v. 5—8, he addresses the Messiah himself, and announces to him his destination. The introduction of so many appellations of God in this verse is not without a cause. Calvin: "Confirmat id, quod dixit initio capitis de regno Christi, omnia videlicet per ipsum restituenda atque instauranda esse. Quod cum incredibile videri posset, magnificam hic descriptionem subjunxit de potentia dei, qua fides nostra confirmari debet, cum praesertim externus rerum status omnino adversatur."—"Thus saith the Lord Jehovah, who creates the heavens and stretches them out, who spreadeth abroad the earth with its productions, who giveth breath to the people that inhabit it, the breath of life to those who walk thereon." It is not necessary to translate the participles ברא and נוטה by the imperfect. Preservation with the Hebrews is a continual creation. Jehovah daily stretches out the heavens anew.—The plural נוֹטֵיהֶם is explained by the circumstance, that participles and adjectives, when they relate to a subject, which designates God, are sometimes put in the plural. Thus Job 35, 10 אַיֵּה אֱלוֹהַּ עֹשָׂי, Ps 121, 5, יְהוָֹה שֹׁמְרֶךָ, *Jehovah is thy keeper*. Comp. Gesenius Lehrg. p. 664. Rosenmuller takes נוֹטֵיהֶם as part sing. The last radical ה has passed over into י before the suffix. But רֹעֵיהֶם Zech. 11, 5, to which he appeals, is not satisfactory, since there also the plural occurs. In the words · who spreadeth out the earth and its productions, we have an example of the figure called Zeugma. The verb cannot also refer to the productions, צֶאֱצָאִים, but a verb must be understood, as · to bring forth. After the example of Vitringa, Rosenmuller takes the verb רָקַע in the sense: to make firm. The meaning however · to spread out, is more suitable. See what Busching has said on this passage in opposition to Vitringa.—According to Kimchi, whom Rosenmuller follows, נְשָׁמָה relates only to men, רוּחַ only to the beasts. But it is not to be doubted, that the prophet understood by those who walk upon the earth, men also.

V. 6. "I Jehovah have called thee in righteousness; I will take thee by the hand, and guard thee, and make thee the mediator of the covenant with the people, for the light of the nations." בְּצֶדֶק is very differently understood. It is spoken in a similar connexion of Cyrus, chap. 45, 13, where Jehovah says, "I raise him up בְּצֶדֶק."

We may explain it most naturally with Vitringa in righteousness, i. e. since my righteousness, integrity and truth require it. It is true, that the sending of the Messiah, as well as that of Cyrus, was indeed a pure work of the divine mercy, but when God has once given his merciful promises, his righteousness demands that he should fulfil them. Thus by the righteousness of God, his faithfulness in the fulfilment of his promises is frequently designated. Others translate: to practise what is right, to administer justice. Gesenius even: for prosperity; defining the meaning of the preposition בְ in the same arbitrary manner, as that of the noun צֶדֶק, which never means simply: prosperity. Rosenmuller: I have called thee in righteousness, i. e. thou mayest surely trust, that I will fulfil my promise to protect thee. He therefore understands צדק in the same way as we do, only he refers it, not to the promises made to the people of Israel, but to those made to the Messiah. The opinion of Steudel appears to be erroneous, who, l. c. explains בְּצֶדֶק by *profecto*, appealing to chap. 45: 19, where צדק signifies *truth*. For should it be granted, that בְּצֶדֶק may mean *profecto*, yet this sense would here be unsuitable, and render the discourse insipid —הֶחֱזִיק בְּיַד, *to take by the hand*, is the same as to guard, and keep. In the words וְאֶתֶּנְךָ לִבְרִית עָם לְאוֹר גּוֹיִם a twofold destination of the servant of God is declared. 1. He shall ratify a new covenant with the ancient covenant people; and 2. He shall enlighten the heathen, who have heretofore been excluded from communion with the true God. The words עָם and גּוֹיִם stand as usual in contrast. The expression: "I will make thee for a covenant of the people" is very concise. According to Vitringa, whom Hensler follows, "for a covenant of the people" stands for לְהָקִים בְּרִית עָם, to procure for the Jewish people that which was promised to them in the covenant made with Abraham. But this reference is very far-fetched, and is contradicted by the parallel passage, chap. 49: 8, where the Messiah is called the covenant of the people, plainly with reference to the new covenant to be established. So also is the Messiah here called the covenant of the people, because the covenant should be ratified through him, and depended on him alone. The nature of this new covenant, to be ratified with the covenant people, may be learned from Jer 31: 31. The new covenant to be established by the Messiah, as was the old by Moses, shall be the covenant of mercy and of the Spirit, under which, as Ezekiel foretold, God shall write his law in the hearts of believers, and give them hearts of flesh instead of stone. As the servant of God is here called the Covenant of the people, because the covenant depended on him, and was to be established by him, so is he immediately after called the Light of the heathen, because through him the heathen were to be enlightened. Similar is what is said of him by Micah, 5 4, וְהָיָה זֶה שָׁלוֹם "and he shall be peace," for . giver of peace, and Eph. 2 14 αὐτός γάρ ἐστιν ἡ εἰρήνη ἡμῶν. Rosenmuller explains it differently, after the example of Doderlein. According to him עָם is a collective, and designates either the heathen nations, or, as v. 5, all mankind He explains· "tu foedere et tecum et inter se consociabis populos, qui omnes tua instituta recipient." Against the reference to the Jewish people he objects, that the prophet must then have said, either עַמִּי with the suffix, or הָעָם with the article But this reason is not sufficient, since 1. the article or the suffix in the poetic portions, is very frequently omitted, comp Ges. Lehrg p 652, and 2. the insertion of the article or of the suffix was here unnecessary, because עָם was rendered sufficiently definite without, by the contrast with גוֹיִם. This continual contrast requires us to understand by עָם the covenant people. But this interpretation is rendered completely certain by a comparison of the parallel passage, chap 49 6—8, where the servant of God is likewise called בְּרִית עָם without the article and אוֹר גּוֹיִם, and where עָם stands as synonymous with יִשְׂרָאֵל and יַעֲקֹב, and with שִׁבְטֵי יַעֲקֹב and יִשְׂרָאֵל נְצִירֵי. There also, as well as here, a twofold destination is assigned to the Messiah, to act upon the covenant people, and the heathen nations The same difficulties, and others besides, oppose the interpretation of Steudel, who with Rosenmuller, refers עָם to the heathen nations, but understands בְּרִית differently. According to Rosenmuller . I give thee for a covenant of the heathen people, is the same as· I establish through thee, a union of the heathen nations with thee, and with one another. According to Steudel, on the contrary, who translates· "te eum, per quem satisfiat foederi cum populis sancito," this sense arises· I fulfil through thee, the conditions of the covenant formerly established with the heathen. This will then refer to the promise made to Abraham, that through him all nations of the earth should be blessed. But the covenant made with Abraham cannot possibly be represented as made with the heathen. This is altogether contrary to the doctrine, as well as the *usus loquendi* of the sacred writers.—The servant of God is called a Light to the heathen, not merely in reference to his doctrine. As sin, error, and superstition, in which the heathen world was sunk, are figuratively represented as a thick darkness; so the Messiah, who by his doctrine and his Spirit, supplies the efficacious means of illumination and of sanctification, is described as a great Light, as the Sun of Righteousness, which was destined to dispel this darkness. See chap 9: 1.

V. 7. "That thou mayest open the blind eyes, bring forth from confinement those who are chained, and out of prison, those who sit in darkness." What is here given as the destination of the servant of God, relates as well to the Jews as to the heathen. To open the eyes means . to see; to open the eyes of any one : to make him see. But the removal of spiritual blindness by the Messiah signifies not merely the giving of a pure system of religion through him, but especially the imparting of that inward illumination, which always appears in Scripture as necessarily connected with sanctification, and constituting, as it were, an essential part of it. This inward connexion of knowledge with the will, in reference to its depravity and its cure, runs through the whole Scripture. Rosenm supposes, that by the blind eyes, those are designated who are confined in dark prisons; but he has justified this unnatural interpretation by no favorable passage. The same sense is expressed in the second part by another figure. The remarks of Theodoret on this verse are very appropriate: τυφλοὺς ἐνταῦθα τοὺς τὸ ὀπτικὸν τῆς διανοίας κακῶς διακειμένους καλεῖ· τοὺς δὲ αὐτοὺς καὶ τοὺς ταῖς ἁμαρτίας πεπηδημένους σειραῖς καὶ τῷ σκότει τῆς πλάνης κατεχομένους· τούτους τοῦ ζόφου τῆς ἀγνοίας ἐλευθερώσας καὶ τῆς ἁμαρτίας τὰ δεσμὰ ῥήξας, προσήγαγε τῷ τῆς ἀληθείας φωτί.

V. 8 Jehovah now turns from the Messiah to the people to whom the prophecy was imparted, and gives the object of it : "I am the Lord, that is my name, and my glory will I not give to another, neither my praise to graven images" The sense I am the only true God, who cannot allow that the glory due to Him, should be given to others; therefore have I delivered this prophecy. The name Jehovah designates God as the self-existent and unchangeable, especially in reference to his promises. And as the idea of the true God is included in this name, it is often used to designate him in opposition to the idols See for example Ps. 96 5

V. 9 "Behold the former things are come to pass and new things do I declare, before they spring forth I tell you of them" ראשנות, *the former*, are the former prophecies already fulfilled, partly of other prophets, partly of Isaiah himself. To them God appeals in order to awaken faith in the truth of those, which will not be fulfilled for many years. By חֲדָשׁוֹת, *that which is new*, is then to be understood particularly the great deliverance here announced, to be effected by the servant of Jehovah, which was prefigured by the deliverance from the Babylonish exile. בְּטֶרֶם תִּצְמַחְנָה, *before they spring up*, shows that the seeds of the events announced did not exist in the present, and therefore they could not have been predicted by human sagacity and calculation.

Isaiah 49: 1—9

As the prophet had before plainly described Cyrus, the author of the first deliverance, and even called him by name, so here he introduces the author of the second deliverance, the Messiah, as himself speaking and announcing his office and the design of his mission. In this prediction, as well as in the parallel passages, chaps XLII and L, it is the prophetic office of the Messiah, which especially engages the attention of the prophet. After all nations of the earth have been summoned to attend to a prediction which concerns them all, and not the covenant people alone, the speaker v. 1—3 declares, that he has not presumptuously assumed his office, but has been solemnly chosen and called to it by Jehovah, endowed by him with the requisite qualifications, and finally after having been long concealed with him, has been sent to execute his commission, with the promise that Jehovah would glorify himself in him, as his servant and ambassador, and not forsake him. The result appeared at first, not to correspond with this promise. It seemed as if all that the servant of God had done were in vain, but his confidence in Jehovah is not thereby weakened, v. 4. How well grounded this confidence is, Jehovah shows by assigning him as a sort of indemnity for the unbelief of the covenant people, a far greater and higher destination, that of enlightening and blessing all the heathen nations, and by exalting him from the deepest disgrace to the highest glory, and making him the mediator of a new covenant, v. 5—9.

Hitherto we have presupposed the Messianic interpretation of the portion to be the true one; we must now examine the various explanations of it. We remark in the outset, that this portion must not be considered by itself, but in connexion with the parallel passages, chaps. XLII, L, LIII, LXI, and therefore, that he only can be properly regarded as its subject, to whom the predicates belong, which occur in all the specified places. 1 According to some (Paulus, Doederlein, Augusti in dem exeg Handb) with whom Rosenmuller in the second edition of his Scholia concurs, the people of Israel are here introduced as speaking. According to these interpreters, the whole people are here represented as a prophet, and the fundamental idea is, that the Israelites will in future times become the instructors of the heathen, and spread the true religion through the earth. It is a strong presumption against this interpretation, that even those Jewish commentators who explain chap. LIII. of the Jewish people, have not ventured to apply it here It is in opposition to v 5, where the servant of Jehovah is distinguished from Jacob and Israel, v. 6, where he shall restore and bring back the tribes of Jacob, v. 8 and 9, where he is to be the mediator of a new covenant between Jehovah, and the people of Israel, and liberate the captives from prison The unnatural explanations, by which Rosenmuller endeavors to evade these difficulties, will be noticed in our explanation of the passage. See on the contrary Gesenius l c p. 123 seq If we suppose, that the Jewish people, appointed as the instructors of the heathen, are here brought forward as speaking, it is impossible to see how they can say v 4, that they have hitherto labored in their calling in vain, and have seen no fruit, since they have as yet made no attempt to convert the heathen The defenders of this interpretation appeal indeed to v. 3, where the speaker is expressly called Israel, but we shall hereafter see that by this appellation neither the prophet nor the prophetic order, but only the Messiah can be intended. 2 According to others, the person who speaks is the prophet himself Thus, after the example of Jarchi, Abenezra, Kimchi, and Grotius, and among the recent interpreters, Koppe, Hensler, Beckhaus (Integritat der proph. Schr p. 168), Staudlin (neue Beitrage p 258—60), and Steudel. But it is difficult to conceive how the prophet could have formed such extravagant expectations, as the passage, if referred to him, would express. Isaiah, as well as all the other prophets, was sent to the Jews, and not to the heathen. Here, even in the outset, the most distant lands, and all the heathen nations are summoned to give their attention. It is said that the conversion of the Israelites is too little for him; he shall be a light for all the heathen, from one end of the earth to the other. Kings and princes shall prostrate themselves before him with the deepest reverence. Nor v. 3, could the

prophet be called Israel. 3. Gesenius, clearly perceiving the unsoundness of both interpretations, chooses that the subject of the prophecy should not be the prophet alone, but the collective body of the prophets, which are here represented by him. He nevertheless here, far more than in the parallel passages, carefully covers over his view, with that which makes the prophet alone the subject, in order to avoid the difficulties, which stand in the way of the supposition, that a personification would be introduced as speaking. But the groundlessness of the assumption of such a personification of the prophetic order, will be shown on chap LIII. Every thing here proves, that the subject is an individual, and not a mere personification. There is no interchange of singular or plural suffixes. V. 1, "Jehovah has called me from my mother's womb, from the bowels of my mother has he made mention of my name." V. 2 agrees with this hypothesis, only when the concealing of the sword in the shadow of his hand, and the arrow in the quiver, is made to signify the divine protection, which is inadmissible.—The prophets taken collectively can by no means bear the name of Israel, which in the third verse is attributed to the person who speaks. This Gesenius himself confesses, and resorts to the extremely unnatural evasion of denying the genuineness of the word, in opposition to all critical authority. V. 6 furnishes the same argument against the prophetic order, as against the individual prophet. The prophets never considered themselves as called to exert an influence upon the heathen, but always expected the heathen to be converted by the Messiah. The splendid hopes, v. 7, can no where be proved to have been entertained by the prophets; finally it is an assertion totally foreign to the doctrine of the Old Testament, that the prophets should be represented, v. 8, as mediators of a new covenant between God and the people of Israel. 4. The Messianic interpretation here, as well as in the parallel passages, was universally adopted in ancient times. That the Jewish interpreters abandoned it, need not surprise us. The Christian church has maintained it for nearly eighteen centuries, relying both on internal evidence and the authority of the New Testament. Even interpreters like Theodoret and Le Clerc, who are in general more inclined to deny actual references to the Messiah, than find them where they do not exist, regard the Messianic interpretation of this passage as placed beyond a doubt. The former says:
ταῦτα ἐκ προσώπου εἴρηται τοῦ δεσπότου Χριστοῦ, ὅς ἐστι σπέρμα τοῦ Ἀβραὰμ κατὰ σάρκα, δι' οὗ τὰ ἔθνη τὴν ἐπαγγελίαν ἀπέλαβε.—

This interpretation is maintained by Michaelis, Lowth, Kocher, and v. d. Palm among the moderns.

It is remarkable how little those, who have given it up, have thought of proving it erroneous by arguments. Rosenmuller remarks nothing further in opposition to it than *aliene ab orationis contextu*, an objection which has been refuted in the general introductory remarks to chap. XL—LXVI. Gesenius argues, that the Messiah could not be introduced as speaking, as would here be the case. But it cannot well be conceived, how this can be urged as an objection by those who themselves maintain, that a personification, either the people of Israel or the prophetic order, is introduced as speaking. If a difficulty is created because a real person is thus introduced, without any particular notice being given, how can the abrupt introduction of a fictitious person be justified? But it is very customary with the Hebrew poets to introduce a person in this manner without notice. See e. g. Ps. II, where at one time the poet, then Jehovah, and then again his great Anointed speaks. As in chap. XLII, Jehovah directs his discourse to the Messiah as present, so here the Messiah himself appears, and addresses the heathen nations.—It has already been shown in the general Introduction, that the prophetic style has a dramatic character, owing to the circumstance that every thing was communicated to the prophets in vision and in the present time. Finally, Gesenius still remarks, that the Messianic interpretation is inconsistent with the contents of v. 8 and 9. But to insist on understanding literally what is there said, is to manifest ignorance of the metaphorical character of prophecy. Compare the remarks on chap. 42. 7.

In favor of the Messianic interpretation we mention 1. The accurate agreement which exists between the prophecy when thus explained and its fulfilment. This requires no further evidence here, since it is already manifest from the representation which has been given of the contents. 2. The comparison of the parallel passages mentioned, which can be referred to no other subject than the Messiah, and 3. The authority of the New Testament, Acts 13. 47. Paul and Barnabas show from this passage the destination of Christ to be the Saviour of the heathen, and the propriety of their conduct in offering to them the salvation, which was despised by the Jews. In 2 Cor. 6: 2, v. 8 is quoted, and referred to the time of the Messiah. There is an allusion to this passage Luke 2. 30—32.

There is here still to be noticed a difference, which exists among the Messianic interpreters. The majority regard the Messiah as the only and constant subject of the whole portion. Others on the contrary, suppose a concurrent reference to the church, either throughout the whole portion, or from v. 7 onward; or they entirely separate v 1—7 from the remainder, and refer v. 8, etc. to the people of Israel. The first opinion is adopted particularly by Calvin. He remarks on v. 8. " Propheta sic totum ecclesiae corpus alloquitur, ut a Christo incipiat, qui caput est Hoc ab interpretibus animadversum non est, nec tamen aliter potest hoc caput eodem tenore explicari. Hoc facile ostendit Paulus, qui 2 Cor vi hanc sententiam ad totam ecclesiam accommodat." Vitringa advocates the second, in support of which he appeals in like manner to 2 Cor vi. But although what is here said of the Messiah is in a great measure applicable also to the church and its members, inasmuch as the history of the Head is repeated in that of the member, and they also are conducted to glory through reproach, contempt, and humiliation,* yet there is no sufficient reason to suppose, that the prophet here intended such a concurrent reference. Had he done so, this reference must have been continued through the whole, and expressions could not have occurred, which (as that in v. 8, " I make thee the mediator of the covenant of the people,") even according to the opinion of these interpreters, must relate exclusively to the Messiah. The passage 2 Cor. 6 2, is not conclusive in favor of this hypothesis, because it is not necessary to refer the pronouns σου and σοι to the church. Paul exhorts the Corinthians to embrace with true zeal the grace that was offered to them. He reminds them, that now the time has arrived, which God had foretold by the prophet Isaiah, the time when God has heard and succored the Messiah, i e. has exalted him to glory after his sufferings, and has commenced the establishment of his kingdom through him. He exhorts them therefore, not to suffer this time to pass by without improvement. The pronouns here, σου and σοι, as well as the suffixes in Isaiah, refer to the Messiah. The latter opinion, that the proper Messianic prediction includes only v. 1—7, has been defended by v d Palm. But not to mention other errors, it is inconsistent with בְּרִית עָם v 8, which v. d. Palm himself, chap. 42: 6, explains of the Messiah, and which he cannot disprove of him ex-

---

* It is hereby sufficiently explained how the prophet in other passages speaks of the people partly in the same expressions, he here employs in reference to the Messiah, a circumstance which Rosenmüller erroneously regards as proof, that the people are the subject of the prophecy.

cept by an arbitrary change of the text (He proposes to read בְּרִית עוֹלָם.)

V. 1. "Listen, ye distant lands, unto me, and hearken, ye people, from far; the Lord hath called me from the womb; from the bowels of my mother hath he made mention of my name." The prophet here contemplates the Messiah, at the time when he had already appeared in the flesh, and experienced many proofs of the unbelief and obduracy of the Jews. See v. 5. These, as well as the great contempt which he experienced from the covenant people, are represented as having already taken place, on the contrary, the enlightening of the heathen, which he is to effect, the reverence of kings towards him, etc. are described as still future. In like manner in chap. LIII, the humiliation appears to the prophet as past, the exaltation as future. See remarks on the place. אִיִּים here occurs again in the indefinite sense of, *distant lands,* yet so as to imply that the dark and immeasurable regions of the west were before the vision of the prophet. מֵרָחוֹק properly, *from far,* dwelling afar off, just as מִקֶּדֶם properly, *from the east,* far eastward, on the east side. Gen. 11. 2. 13. 11. Ewald Gramm p. 601. The reason why the Messiah addresses the heathen nations is found in v. 6. Through him they shall obtain salvation. In the words. "Jehovah hath called me from my mother's womb," the stress is laid, rather on the calling itself than on the particular time at which it took place. The speaker gives great importance to the fact, that he had not presumptuously assumed his office, but had been called to it by God. Calvin: "Non definit propheta initium temporis, quasi deus ab utero demum coeperit ipsum vocare, sed perinde est ac si diceret, priusquam ex utero prodirem, statuerat deus me subiturum hoc munus. Quemadmodum etiam Paulus se ab utero segregatum dicit, cum tamen ante creationem mundi electus esset." The Messiah here mentions his divine appointment, the gifts which God had bestowed upon him, and the protection which he had promised, in order the more to awaken the attention of the Gentiles to what he was about to announce to them. מִבֶּטֶן *from my mother's womb,* when I was not yet formed in my mother's womb, even before my birth. Vitringa mistranslates. before the womb of his mother, and before he was in the bowels of his mother. See on the contrary, v 5, and chap 44. 2, 24. Parallel are Jer. 1. 5, where Jehovah says that he had destined Jeremiah for a prophet, before he had formed him in the womb of his mother and before he was born, and Gal. 1. 15, (ὁ θεὸς, ὁ ἀφορίσας με ἐκ κοιλίας μητρός μου καὶ καλέσας διὰ τῆς χάριτος αὐτοῦ), where, also, the being called from the mother's womb is put in opposition to the presumptuous intrusion into an office not conferred by God. The last words: "He hath made mention of my name from my mother's bowels," have been literally understood by several interpreters. They are supposed to predict the circumstance, that Mary was commanded by an angel before the birth of the Messiah, to call him Jesus, Saviour, Luke 1·31, and that the same command was given to Joseph in a dream, Matt. 1:21. So Jerome. "Dominus inquit ab utero vocavit me et de ventre matris meae, recordatus est nominis mei. Quod nunc interim audientibus videtur obscurum, postea autem cunctis gentibus notum fiet, quando Gabriel Joseph de partu dixerit virginali; et vocabis nomen ejus Jesum, ipse enim salvum faciet populum suum." Likewise Le Clerc, Vitringa, Michaelis, and others. Others, on the contrary, suppose הזכיר שם to be synonymous with קָרָא *to call*. They appeal to Exod. 31·2, where Jehovah says, he has called Bezaleel by name, i. e. chosen him. Both explanations, the special and the general, may be easily combined by the supposition, that here as well as in many other instances, expressions which admit of a general meaning, and were probably so understood by the contemporaries of the prophet, are literally and specially fulfilled under a particular guidance of divine providence. See on Zech 9: 9.

V. 2. "And he hath made my mouth like a sharp sword, in the shadow of his hand hath he hid me, and made me a polished shaft, in his quiver hath he hid me." The mouth stands for discourse; a powerful and penetrating discourse is compared to a sword, because it pierces the soul as a sharp sword does the body. See the striking examples of the use of the metaphor of a sword and bow to designate an impressive discourse, taken from the Greek writers by Lowth on this passage, and from him by Gesenius, etc. From the sacred Scriptures we extract especially the following. Ecc. 12 11· "The words of the wise are as goads, and as nails fastened by the masters of assemblies." Heb 4 12: "The word of God is quick and powerful, and sharper than any two-edged sword, and piercing even to the dividing asunder of the soul and spirit and of the joints and marrow." In Rev 1 16, probably with reference to this passage, the characteristic of Christ here spoken of is exhibited under the figure of a sharp two-edged sword proceeding from his mouth. So likewise chap 19 15.—The sense is the same when the Messiah calls himself an arrow. As the arrow pierces the heart of the outward man, so does he pierce the heart of the inner man; no enemies can stand before him; they must be slain, either that they may live in a higher sense, or that they may die forever. Theodoret: ὁμοίως καὶ ταῦτα τροπικῶς κέκληκε, βέλος μὲν αὐτὸν τὸν τιτρώσκοντα τὰς ἐρώσας αὐτοῦ ψυχὰς, ὧν ἑκάστη βοᾷ· τετρωμένη ἀγάπης ἐγώ חֵץ בָּרוּר, either *a chosen*, or *a polished sharp arrow*. See Jer. 51: 11 The first interpretation is followed by Jerome, Vitringa, and others, the latter is recommended by the circumstance, that a sharp arrow corresponds better with a sharp sword.—As the two figures of the sword, and of the arrow correspond, so also must the other two have a corresponding sense We cannot, therefore, with many interpreters, as Grotius, Gesenius, etc refer the words, "He hath hid me in the shadow of his hand," to the protection which Jehovah extends to the Messiah; since in the second figure the phrase, "He hath hid me in his quiver," cannot have this sense, as Le Clerc and Vitringa have shown. The image would then, at any rate, have been very unfitly chosen, since the arrow is not placed in the quiver to be protected, but to be ready for use in the time of action. Besides, in the first figure, the simile of a sword must be carried through as well as that of an arrow in the second The image, therefore, according to this explanation, would be unsuitable, even so far as this member alone is concerned. For the sword, as Vitringa justly remarks, is here represented, not as sheathed, but as drawn; but a drawn sword needs no protection, it is not a thing to be defended, but one with which a man defends himself. Far more congruous therefore is the opinion of those, who after Abenezra and Vitringa, suppose that the shadow of the hand of God, is what here covers and hides the sword, and serves, as it were, for its sheath. The image is perhaps taken from a dirk, which a man carries concealed in his hand, and in the moment of attack suddenly draws forth. The two figures thus explained, can be fitly referred neither to the prophet (Cum Jesaias hoc tempore vitia oppugnaret, sagitta illa dei jam erat emissa Cleric), nor to the people of Israel. But on the other hand, according to the Messianic interpretation, all is suitable and clear. Before his appearing the Messiah was concealed with God like a sword kept in its sheath, or like an arrow lying in the quiver. When at last he came forth from his concealment, he pierced the hearts of men like a brandished sword, or an arrow shot from a bow.

V. 3. "And said unto me: Thou art my servant, O Israel, in

whom I will be glorified." These words occasion the non-Messianic interpreters great difficulty. It is best obviated by those who suppose the person speaking to be the people of Israel; but this interpretation, as we have seen, is elsewhere liable to so many objections, that it is rejected by nearly all commentators. The bare mention of the explanations of those, who regard the prophet as the subject, is sufficient to show that they are altogether unnatural. After the example of Grotius, Dathe supplied the preposition לְ before יִשְׂרָאֵל. "it is for Israel's benefit, that I will glorify myself in thee." An explanation, which besides being altogether forced, is totally inadmissible on philological grounds. As little justifiable is the interpretation of Saadias, which supposes a similar ellipsis. "thou art my ambassador to Israel," and in which, moreover, the meaning of עבד is arbitrarily modified. According to others (Doderlein in der 2ten Ausg.) Isaiah is here called an Israelite in the full sense of the word, a true descendant of Israel. See John 1 18. But then the word must be יִשְׂרָאֵלִי, since יִשְׂרָאֵל is always, either the name of the ancestor, or of the people. Others (Hensler, Staudlin) after the example of Kimchi, regard the words as an abrupt address to Israel "thou art my servant, and I will glorify myself in thee, O Israel." But it is easy to perceive, that this interpretation, which entirely destroys the parallelism, is erroneous. This sentence would then stand entirely in the wrong place. For since the speaker addresses himself to the Gentiles, nothing belongs here, but what has respect to the relation of Jehovah to his servant, and tends to fix their attention upon him. What Jehovah purposes concerning the people of Israel is here out of place. Explanations like that of Koppe, which separate the sentence from the third verse, and connect it with the following, as an address of the prophet to his people: "O Israel, how could I be glorified by thee, but I must lament, in vain do I labor, etc.," refute themselves.—Gesenius himself, perceiving the erroneousness of all these explanations, confesses that the translation that has been given is the most simple, l. c p. 122 and 126. He therefore prefers to cut the knot, which he cannot untie. After the example of Michaelis, he denies the genuineness of the word, against the authority of all the old translations and manuscripts, one only excepted, to which he himself gives no weight. He is contradicted by the circumstance, that the second member necessarily requires a word corresponding to עַבְדִּי.—The Messianic interpretation entirely removes this difficulty, and with it the necessity of resorting to such violent measures. It has already been shown in the general Introduction, that in the Messianic predictions, not merely are the figures borrowed from the things and persons of the old covenant to represent those of the new; but also the persons of the new are expressly called by the names of those of the old, when the latter were types of the former, or resembled them in their nature or names. The enemies of the new theocracy bear the names of Edom, Moab, Ashur; John the Baptist, the name of Elias; the Messiah himself is frequently called David; and Isaiah gives him the name of Prince of Peace, which is of the same import with Solomon. And in like manner, in the passage before us, he is called also Israel. But it may be asked, wherein consists that resemblance of the Messiah to Israel, on account of which he here receives his name. Most Messianic interpreters here find a reference to Gen. 32: 28, according to which, the name Israel, one who contends with God, was given by Jehovah to Jacob, after his wrestling with him. Christ deserves this name in its highest sense, since by his vicarious life and sufferings, he mightily contended with God and prevailed. Thus Vitringa and Lowth. The explanation of Le Clerc is similar: " attendenda est significatio vocis Israel; contendens cum deo, quae videtur omnino spectari. Sic Gen. 49. 8, tu es Juda, et Matt. 16. 17, tu es Petrus, manifesto respicitur ad significatum eorum nominum. Pariter hic; tu es Israel, est, id facies, quod fecit יִשְׂרָאֵל, quando contendit cum deo כַּאֲשֶׁר שָׂרָה עִם אֱלֹהִים. Fecit autem hoc Christus, cum mediator dei et hominum constitutus, precibus suis cum deo contendit, ut pater humano generi ignosceret." It cannot be objected to this interpretation, that it attributes to the prophet a knowledge of the work of redemption, which does not belong to the Old Testament. For the prophet in chap. LIII describes this work with the clearness of history. But nevertheless, those may be more correct, who do not seek the resemblance merely in this particular point. As the Messiah is called David principally because he should be the head of the spiritual theocracy, as David was of the earthly; so here he seems to bear the name of Israel, principally because he is to be the father of the spiritual people of God, as Israel was the father of the Jewish people. See chap. 53. 10. Other resemblances besides, as piety and devotedness to God, the passing through suffering to joy, etc. may have been considered. Those depart further from the truth, who suppose the Messiah to be called Israel, either because he represented the whole people, or because he is their king; or else as the seed promised to Israel, in whom all nations of the earth should be blessed, Gen 28 14. The view of Abenezra is similar to the first of those just mentioned, though he refers the appellation to the prophet, which is still more objectionable. "tu Israel i. e tu minister meus, qui in oculis meis reputatus es instar totius Israelis."* The words אֲשֶׁר בְּךָ אֶתְפָּאָר can be translated either *by whom*, or *in whom I will glorify myself*. Christ, as John frequently says, glorifies the Father, and is glorified by him. But in favor of the latter interpretation is the parallel passage, chap 44 23, כִּי גָאַל יהוה יַעֲקֹב וּבְיִשְׂרָאֵל יִתְפָּאָר, "Jehovah redeems Jacob and glorifies himself in Israel," where the verb is closely connected with the object of the glorification with בְּ. It is also more agreeable to the connexion, (see on v 1) that the glorification of the Messiah by God, rather than the glorification of God by the Messiah, should be here introduced. For the same reason, the idea of obedience to God is not the prominent one in the appellation *my servant*, but the idea of God's love towards him, and of his protection

4. "And I said I have labored in vain, for nothing and without use have I expended my strength, but my judgment is with Jehovah, and my reward is with my Lord." The Messiah having in the foregoing verses, spoken of his dignity and divine nature, now prepares the way to make known his destination to be the light, and the salvation of the heathen, to whom the whole discourse is directed. He laments over the little fruit which he saw in the commencement of his efforts among the Jews, but consoles himself by trusting in the righteousness of God, that the faithful performance of the work entrusted to Him, cannot go unrewarded. In the same manner as here, the unbelief of a great part of the Jewish people is clearly foretold in the prophecy, chap LII, LIII. Jerome remarks Haec universa dicuntur, ut liberum hominis arbitrium monstraretur. Dei enim vocare est et nostrum credere, nec statim si nos non credimus, impossibilis deus est, sed potentiam suam nostro arbitrio derelinquit, ut juste voluntas praemium consequatur." He therefore supposes this verse to be connected with the foregoing "Dicente autem mihi patre ista, quae retuli, ego respondi ei: quomodo in me glorificatus eris, quia in vacuum laboravi, etc." אָכֵן, an adversative particle, *but, nevertheless* מִשְׁפָּט *right*, here, that which can be justly demanded, because the condition on which it was promised has been fulfilled,

---

* In like manner Umbreit theol Stud und Krit I, 2 p 319.

righteous reward. It is with Jehovah, it is there safely preserved, to be imparted to me in his own time פְּעֻלָּה *work, performance,* then *reward.* See Lev. 19. 13 Ps 109. 20

V 5 "And now Jehovah speaks to me, who formed me from the womb to be his servant, that I should bring back to him Jacob, but Israel would not be gathered, and I was esteemed in the eyes of Jehovah, and my God was my strength." What Jehovah has spoken does not follow till the 6th verse, which, on account of the long interruption, again commences with וַיֹּאמֶר *he, I say, has spoken.* The declaration of Jehovah relates to the appointment of the Messiah to be the Saviour of the Gentiles. In this verse two reasons are given why this was to be the destination of the Messiah; 1. The Jews, to whom he was sent first, refuse to be converted, and 2. The servant of God stands so high in his favor, and so entirely enjoys his protection, that God cannot withhold from him the full reward which his work deserves. The words, "and now Jehovah speaks, etc." are of the same import as and this hope, which I cherish, that Jehovah will not suffer my work to go unrewarded, is not vain; it is ratified by a distinct divine promise, which assures me, that I have received the heathen for a possession, as an equivalent for the unbelieving Jews. It is represented, as though the Messiah had first received the promise, that he should convert the heathen, after his efforts had proved fruitless among the Jews, because this promise was then first carried into effect. The words " who formed me from my mother's womb, etc" are the same as: who appointed me before I was born, to be his servant and instrument in the conversion of the Jews. The verb יָצַר is spoken of the divine purpose and foreordination, chap. 46 11 —Rosenmuller, from regard to his hypothesis, that the Jewish people is the subject, will not allow that the words לְשׁוֹבֵב יַעֲקֹב אֵלָיו are connected with עבד, and should be translated that I should bring back Jacob to him He refers them to Jehovah, and takes לְשׁוֹבֵב as a Gerund: "reducendo s. °qui reducit ad se Jacobum " He understands in the same manner the Infin. with לְ in the following verse But although the Infin. with לְ sometimes stands for the Gerund, yet as Gesenius remarks (Lehrg p. 785), this usage is rare, and is never so frequently repeated Besides, according to this interpretation, this verse, as well as the following, will be entirely broken to pieces; and the words לְשׁוֹבֵב יַעֲקֹב אֵלָיו must of necessity show the destination to which this servant was appointed —In the words וְיִשְׂרָאֵל לֹא יֵאָסֵף, "but Israel was not gathered," the metaphor is taken from a scattered flock, which the faithful shepherd, after all his efforts, is unable to collect. The Masorites prefer to read לוֹ instead of לֹא. So also, among the ancient translators, Aquila and the Chaldee paraphrast, while Symm. Theod. and the Vulg express the negation. Most interpreters have followed the Masorites; among whom Gesenius and Rosenmuller suppose, that לֹא is only a different mode of writing for לוֹ. These interpreters translate: "that I should bring back Jacob to him, and that Israel should be gathered to him." But לֹא as a negation, stands here in its proper place. It had been said in the foregoing verse, that the Messiah had at first spent his strength in vain among the Jews, and this is given as the very reason why the gentiles in the following verse were promised to him as a possession. The reading לוֹ is not to be received, because its origin is easily explained by the carnal national pride of the Jews. They could not bear the idea, that a great part of Israel themselves should reject the Messiah, and be cast off by him; they therefore sought by all means to get rid of so unpleasant a truth. This was seen long ago by Jerome. He strikingly says "Satis miror, quomodo vulgata editio (the Latin translation before Jerome) fortissimum contra Judaeorum perfidiam testimonium alia interpretatione subvertit dicens; congregabor et glorificabor coram domino, cum Theodotio et Symmachus nostrae interpretationi congruant. De Aquila autem non miror, quod homo eruditissimus linguae Hebraicae et verbum de verbo exprimens, in hoc loco aut simularit imperitiam, aut Pharisaeorum perversa expositione deceptus sit, qui interpretari vult; et Israel ei congregabitur h. e deo, cum verbum Hebraicum in h. l. non scribatur per ל et ו, sed per ל et א." Other interpreters, setting out in like manner with the erroneous idea, that the words וְיִשְׂרָאֵל לֹא יֵאָסֵף must be synonymous and parallel with לְשׁוֹבֵב יַעֲקֹב אֵלָיו, and therefore cannot contain a prediction of the unbelief of the Jews, regard לֹא as indeed a negation, but seek to do away the reference to the unbelief of the Jews by forced interpretations. Thus after the example of Kimchi and De Dieu, Kocher supposes, that before לֹא the relative אֲשֶׁר is to be supplied: "ut reducam Jacobum ad ipsum et Israelem, qui non colligitur scil neglectus a suis pastoribus, salutisque ipse negligens." Others, after Luther, take the verb אָסַף in the sense *to carry away*: "that Israel be not carried away"—All these interpreters begin the parenthesis with the words וְאֶכָּבֵד, when it rather commences, as v d Palm has shown, with וְיִשְׂרָאֵל. The words: "God was my strength," are of the same import with: "I was esteemed in the eyes of Jehovah," as much as to say: he could not do otherwise than make me, his servant, great and honorable. Others erroneously "since he, my God, gave me greater power, than the conversion of the chosen Jews required," or, עז being taken in the sense *praise, honor*: "since my God will employ me for the signal glorification of his name." These words contain the reason of what follows: since Israel, to whom I was first sent will not be gathered, and as I nevertheless enjoy Jehovah's peculiar protection, and high esteem, far from depriving me of my just reward, he confers upon me the glory of being the Saviour, not of the Jews only, but of the gentiles also.

V. 6. "He, I say, said: it is too little, that thou shouldst be my servant to raise up the tribes of Jacob, and restore the preserved of Israel; I make thee for the light of the nations, to be my salvation to the ends of the earth." Sense: the conversion of the chosen Israelites alone would be a reward too small for thee. Thy destination is a higher one. As the sun disperses the natural darkness, so shalt thou dispel the spiritual darkness, the sin and error, of the heathen. נָקַל is praeter in Niphal as נָמַס Ps 22 15 (comp. Gesen. Lehrg. p. 367). It is used here impersonally. In the same sense, it is construed with מִן Ez. 8 17. הֲנָקֵל לְבֵית יְהוּדָה מֵעֲשׂוֹת, "is it too small a thing for the house of Judah, to do, etc." Comp. Ewald Gramm. p 599, 600. The verbs הָקִים and הָשִׁיב are to be understood in a spiritual sense. This appears from the synonymous expression שׁוֹבֵב אֶל יְהוָה in the foregoing verse, and from the nature of the blessing, which the Messiah should confer upon the heathen. If he is to be their light and salvation, then also his being sent to the Jews, cannot respect their temporal, but only their spiritual rebuilding and conversion. Rosenmüller here again chooses to separate לְהָקִים from עֶבֶד and refer it to Jehovah. We must not translate "ad erigendum," but: "erigendo, seu dum erigam, qui restituam tribus Jacobi et servatos Israelis reducendo." In opposition to this, see the remarks on v 5. Here this interpretation is the more objectionable, since it destroys the whole antithesis. For "it is too little for me, that thou shouldst be my servant" does not stand in opposition with: "I give thee for a light to the heathen," but it is precisely as servant of God, that the speaker shall enlighten the heathen. Moreover, Rosenmüller himself supposes, that לְ in the two last members of the verse points out the object, and the destination, but it is manifest, that it must then answer the same purpose in the foregoing also —נְצוּרֵי

ישְׂרָאֵל *the preserved of Israel*, those who have not perished in the divine judgments, but have been preserved by the mercy of God, see chap. 1. 3. 10. 21. Mic. 5. 6, 7, here especially, those, who should be converted and delivered by the Messiah, and consequently were preserved from the judgments which fell upon the rebellious. The marginal reading is נְצוּרֵי as participle Pa. from the verb נָצַר, the reading of the text נְצִירֵי as an adjective form, with a passive meaning. The prefix ו in וּנְתַתִּיךָ is to be translated, *on this account, therefore.* Several interpreters translate the last member: that I may extend my salvation to the ends of the earth; but it is better to make לִהְיוֹת dependant on נְתַתִּיךָ. As the Messiah in the foregoing member is called the light of the heathen, because he enlightens them, so here he is called the salvation of the heathen, because he brings them salvation. There is here, as Gesenius rightly remarks, as in other Messianic predictions, e. g. Ps. LXXII, an allusion to the promises made to the patriarchs, Gen. 12. 8. 22. 18. 26. 4. Through thee, says Jehovah, shall the ancient promises of a future extension of salvation to all the heathen nations be fulfilled.

V. 7. "Thus saith Jehovah, the Redeemer of Israel, his Holy One, to him whom all despise, to the servant of the rulers, kings shall see and rise up, princes shall see, and prostrate themselves before him, for Jehovah's sake, who is true, for the sake of the Holy One of Israel, who hath chosen thee." The form בְזֹה is commonly taken, either as Infin. in Kal, or as a noun from the verb בָּזָה *to despise. The despised*, or *contempt of the soul* will then import, he who is despised of all. Others, as Vitringa, take the form as an anomalous participle in Pa. after the form עָשׂוּ, Job 41:24, with this difference, that here we have Hholem, there Shureq. But it is most correct to regard it with Gesenius, as stat. constr. of an adjective form with a passive sense, בְזֹה as קָדוֹשׁ and גָּבוֹהַּ.—נֶפֶשׁ *soul*, here, for *every man.* The Part. Pi. מְתָעֵב according to most interpreters is here passive. Comp. Gesen. Lehrg. p. 242. But it is not necessary to apply this usage here, which, to say the least, is extremely rare. We may rather give to תעב the sense, which accords with Pi. to bring into contempt, *faciens abominari gentem* s. v. a. *qui genti est abominationi.* By גּוֹי is to be understood the Jewish people, who are here so called by way of contempt, as in chap. 1. 4. 10. 6. The appellation עֶבֶד מֹשְׁלִים *servant of the rulers*, stands on the one hand in opposition to עֶבֶד יְהוָֹה v. 3, and on the other to: "kings shall rise up, princes shall prostrate themselves," in the verse before us. The Messiah voluntarily subjects himself to human power, although by his nature, as servant of God, he is exalted above all the powers of the world, and after his glorification shall be acknowledged by them as such. Christ submitted himself to the earthly magistracy, and refrained from using his divine power. After יִרְאוּ *they shall see*, the object is not expressed. Some improperly supply *him;* the object is rather to be supplied from v. 6, they shall see the fulfilment of the divine promise, by which the Messiah was destined to be the Saviour of the heathen, or generally, the splendid condition to which he shall be exalted. To rise up, and to prostrate themselves, are both signs of humble subjection. The expression: on account of Jehovah, etc., is much the same as, this shall be brought to pass by Jehovah, who is faithful in the fulfilment of his promises, and will therefore fulfil those made to thee, his chosen. The ו in וַיִּבְחָרֶךָ stands for אֲשֶׁר.—The whole verse forms a compendium of what is more fully expressed, chap. 52. 13 etc. and chap. LIII.

V. 8. "Thus saith Jehovah: at a time of mercy have I heard thee, in the day of salvation helped thee; and I will preserve thee and give thee for a covenant of the people, that thou mayest succor the land, and distribute the heritages which have been laid waste." Henceforth the redemption and deliverance to be accomplished by the Messiah are described, but the deliverance from the Babylonish exile also, is still continually before the eye of the prophet, and he describes the spiritual deliverance by images taken from it. How far the prophet himself, when his *ecstasy* had ceased, was enabled to discriminate between the two deliverances, and determine the real import of the images presented to him in vision, it is not in our power to decide. He here transfers himself in the spirit to the time when the work of redemption by the Messiah had been completed. It is at this period, that the address of Jehovah is to be conceived of as having been made. Hence the use of the praeter עֲנִיתִיךָ and עֲזַרְתִּיךָ is explained.—Several interpreters take רָצוֹן in the sense of *inclination, pleasure;* at a time of pleasure, i. e. at a time when it pleased me, at a chosen time. Thus the LXX καιρῷ δεκτῷ, Vulgate *tempore placito.* But this is contradicted by the parallelism בְּיוֹם יְשׁוּעָה *in the day of salvation.* We must therefore, with others, take רָצוֹן in the sense of *grace.* The meaning will then be: when the time of imparting mercy and salvation to all men (v. 6) has arrived, I will hear thee, and help thee, I will exalt thee to glory, and cause that through thee my salvation shall be bestowed on mankind. Respecting בְּרִית עָם, *covenant of the people* for *Mediator of the covenant of the people*, see on chap. 42. 6. By עָם here the natural Israel cannot be meant; it was somewhat different in the passage referred to, where עָם and גּוֹיִם were placed in contrast. We are rather to understand by it, as appears from v. 6, 7, the better portion of the covenant people, the נְצִירֵי יִשְׂרָאֵל, who constitute the foundation of the theocracy upon which the gentiles were to be built. In the words לְהָקִים אֶרֶץ etc. the figure is taken from the resuscitation of ruined cities, and desolated lands, with distinct reference to the recultivation of the land of Judea after the Babylonish exile. As the Jews after the exile shall repossess their natural inheritance, which had been laid waste, so shall the Messiah renovate the renewed spiritual inheritance, and restore it to those, whom he shall have delivered from spiritual bondage. Calvin appropriately says: "huc pertinent prophetae verba, ut intelligamus, nihil praeter dissipationem et vastitatem in mundo esse. Mittitur enim Christus, ut quae prostrata sunt et diruta instauret.—Si integra essent omnia, frustra Christus ad nos mitteretur. Itaque diligenter consideranda est nostra conditio quoniam alieni deo, vita destituti atque ab omni spe salutis exclusi sumus: sed a Christo restituimur in integrum et patri coelesti reconciliamur."

V. 9. "In that thou sayest to the prisoners go forth, to those who are in darkness, come to the light." The first half only of v. 9 belongs to the prophecy of the Messiah as a person; with the second, commences a more general representation. The figures of the first part were explained on chap. 42. 6. הִגָּלֵה *be uncovered*, i. e. come out of the dark prison into the clear day-light.

Isaiah 50. 4—11.

The Messiah is again introduced as speaking. He declares that he has not come forward of his own will, but has received from Jehovah both his saving doctrine and the power to preach it, v. 4. He has willingly undertaken the work which Jehovah has committed to him, and endured all the sufferings and all the shame and ignominy connected with it, v. 5, 6. This fortitude resulted from his firm confidence in Jehovah, who, he well knew, would stand by him, and destroy his enemies, v. 7—9. He then directs his discourse to them who fear God, and exhorts them when they shall be led in the dark path of suffering, as he had been, to place their trust in Jehovah alone But to the ungodly, who rely upon themselves for help, instead of putting their trust in Jehovah and his servant, he declares, v 11, that they will bring upon themselves, by their inventions, destruction to be accomplished by him.

The Messianic interpretation is confirmed by the authority of the Saviour himself, Luke 18. 31, 32 It universally prevailed in the ancient Christian church, and Grotius, who refers the prophecy in a lower sense to Isaiah, and only in a higher one to Christ, met with general opposition Even Le Clerc rejected this interpretation. The reference to the Messiah has been strenuously maintained by Michaelis, and v d Palm among the recent interpreters.

On the other hand several (as Doderlein, Dathe, Koppe, Augusti, etc.) suppose the prophet himself, either Isaiah or some other one living in the exile, to be the subject of the portion. Jerome cites this interpretation, as the prevailing one among the Jews in his time. Rosenmuller also adopts it, though with singular inconsistency, since he explains all the parallel passages of the Jewish people. Gesenius also heré puts in the back ground the hypothesis which he adopts in the case of the other similar passages, which makes the collective body of the prophets the subject, and appears to regard the prophet himself as the only subject, although he so strongly insists that in chap XLII, XLIX, L, LIII, LXI, one and the same subject must necessarily be assumed. According to Paulus, it is not the prophet who speaks, but the better and pious portion of the people.

But against these interpreters, and in favor of the Messianic, there is 1. the testimony of the New Testament Compare the cited passage of Luke with Matt. 26. 27 2 All the characteristics of the servant of God — all that is said of his humiliation, as well as of his exaltation and the destruction of his enemies, entirely agrees with Jesus Christ; and the most minute lines of the picture are repeated in his history We know of nothing similar in the life of Isaiah V 11 even ascribes to the servant of God the judgment of the ungodly. 3 The parallel passages, to which we have referred, every other interpretation of which is liable to insurmountable difficulties.

Finally, this Messianic prophecy is distinguished from the two former, chap. XLII and XLIX, to which in other respects it bears a close resemblance, by the circumstance that it dwells rather upon the sufferings and uniform patience of the Messiah, while in them the glorification which followed his sufferings and the extension of his salvation to the heathen are exhibited. All these several features are combined in chap. LIII, where the sufferings and the exaltation of the Messiah are predicted with equal clearness.

V. 4 "The Lord Jehovah has given me an eloquent tongue, that I might know how to console the weary; every morning he wakeneth mine ear that I may hear as one instructed" Theodoret: ταῦτα ἀνθρωπίνως λέγει ὁ δεσπότης χριστός, πολλὰ δὲ τοιαῦτα καὶ ἐν τοῖς ἱεροῖς εὐαγγελίοις εὑρήσομεν· Ἰησοῦς γάρ φησι προέκοπτεν ἡλικίᾳ καὶ σοφίᾳ καὶ χάριτι παρὰ θεῷ τε καὶ ἀνθρώποις לשון למודים literally. a tongue of the instructor, such a tongue as they possess, an eloquent tongue. Similar is the expression, chap 49 2, "he made my mouth for a sharp sword," only there it is more the penetrating, and here the consoling, power of the Messiah's discourse, which is spoken of Others (after the LXX, who erroneously translate. λόγον παιδείας) a tongue of instruction, a tongue which shall be employed in the instruction of the people The word למודים never occurs in an abstract signification. Most interpreters regard the ἅπ᾽ λεγ עות as a denominative of עת time, a convenient time, and give it the meaning opportune, tempestive loqui But Rosenmuller and Gesenius have justly given up this interpretation, partly because עת would give a denominative עֲתַת, and partly because the construction with two accusatives would be unsuitable. The verb עות is rather to be explained by the Arabic, where the corresponding غاث in the 4th conjugation signifies to help, to sustain; it is then construed with a double accus rei et personae; verbally, to prop or that I may prop the weary a word, or with a word, i. e. sustain him by a word of consolation So Aquila ὑποστηρίσαι, and Vulg. sustentare Mistaking the construction, Rosenmuller supplies to דָבָר the preposition ב. Other similar verbs also are construed with two accus Thus e g סָמַךְ Gen. 27. 37, דָּגָן וְתִירוֹשׁ סְמַכְתִּיו, "with corn and new wine have I sustained him" רוּחַ נְדִיבָה תִסְמְכֵנִי, "give me a joyful heart" By יָעֵף the weary, v. d. Palm, after Michaelis, understands the literally weary. It is, they say, the highest power of eloquence to enchain those who are weary, and at the same time hungry and thirsty; but it is evident that this explanation is very insipid, and that the expression is to be understood figuratively, with the Chaldee paraphrast, Kimchi, and Jarchi. The figure is supplied by men who, wearied with bearing a heavy burden, and enervated by heat, are revived by water or wine. What these refreshments are to those who are weary in body, shall the discourse of the servant of God be to the weary in spirit. The weary then are those who, oppressed by suffering and sin, feel fatigued and burdened, κοπιῶντες καὶ πεφορτισμένοι, Matt 11: 28, the same who, chap 42· 3, had been represented under the figure of a bruised reed and smoking wick, the נִשְׁבְּרֵי לֵב in the parallel passage 61: 2. — The הֵעִיר אֹזֶן to awaken the ear, i. e. to prepare one to receive the revelation and instruction The expressions גָּלָה אֹזֶן to uncover the ear, and פָּתַח אֹזֶן to open the ear, and כָּרָה אֹזֶן to bore the ear, in the sense to reveal, are all related. The figure is taken from a teacher who, in the morning, before he commences his instruction, summons his pupils to him After Christ had assumed the form of a servant, he always spake and acted under the influence of the Holy Spirit Several interpreters translate כַּלִּמּוּדִים as disciples, i e like docile disciples. It is true that לִמּוּדִים often has this meaning; but it is not easy to suppose that the word should be used in two different senses in the very same verse It is better therefore to translate . like the learned or the practised, i. e attentive, and with complete insight into what is imparted.

V 5 "The Lord Jehovah opened mine ear, and I was not disobedient and drew not back." The phrase to open the ear is used as well of the imparting of instruction, as also of a commission, 1 Sam. 9. 15 Ruth 4. 4 , the latter is the meaning here. The Messiah receives from God a very difficult commission, the command to accomplish the redemption of mankind ; he willingly undertakes it, notwithstanding all the sufferings therewith connected The expressions are taken from a yoke of oxen, who go backward instead of forward, and will not suffer themselves to be guided

V. 6 "I gave my back to those who smite, and my cheeks to those who pluck ; I hid not my face before reproach and spittle " Although this was in part especially fulfilled in Christ, Matt. 26 67. Luke 18: 31, yet these particular traits, according to the custom of the Hebrew poets to particularize every thing, served in the first instance for the contemporaries of the prophet to express the thought that the Messiah would experience, and patiently endure, the most shameful and abusive treatment. But God so directed the event that even these special traits occurred again in the history of the Messiah, a remark which we have already made before, and shall yet have occasion many times to repeat. מֹרְטִים כְּחָיַים properly to pluck the jawbones, i. e to pluck out the beard. This is the greatest of all indignities in the East. 2 Sam. 10. 4 Lowth on chap. 7: 20. Harmer's

Observations II. p. 61. III. p. 434 seq. Among the Romans, mischievous boys were accustomed to pull out the long beard of the philosophers with tweezers, and the phrase *vellere barbam* was employed for *to insult, to abuse.* See the passages in Le Clerc ad h. l. "I have not hid my face before reproach and spittle." To spit, even in the presence of any one, in the East, is considered as an insult. See Herodotus and Xenophon in Lowth on the passage, Harmer's Observations III. p. 376, Niebuhr Beschreibung von Arabien § 26. But how much more to spit in one's face. See Num. 12:14. Deut. 25:9. Job 7:19. 30:10. Christ, Luke 18:31, refers this passage to himself. See Mark 14:65. 15:19.

V. 7. "But the Lord Jehovah helps me; therefore shall I not be brought into disgrace; therefore do I make my face as a flint and know, that I shall not be ashamed." The sense: I know that Jehovah will conduct me through suffering to glory, and in the view of the future, I endure with fortitude all that is inflicted upon me. The expressions: to harden the heart, the forehead, the face, were employed in a good and in a bad sense,—in a good sense for firmness in the discharge of duty and in enduring the sufferings connected with it, as here and in Ez. 3:8, it is said: "I make thy face hard against their face, and thy forehead hard against their forehead. I make thy forehead as hard as a diamond, which is harder than a rock. Therefore fear not before them." בוש *to be ashamed, deceived in his hope, to be disgraced.*

V. 8. "He is near, who justifies me, who will contend with me? Let us stand forth together; let him, who will be my adversary before the tribunal, come near to me." We must conceive this discourse of the servant of God as spoken in his humiliation; and during his sufferings. The image is here, as is frequently the case, taken from a judicial proceeding. God himself will soon stand forth at the same time as his powerful patron and his judge, and by deed declare him righteous and his enemies guilty. He has therefore so little occasion to dread his foes, and fear their power, that he can confidently challenge them to engage with him in the unequal conflict. The verb הצדיק *to justify, to declare righteous*, whether it is done by word or by deed, as the Messiah was declared righteous by his resurrection and glorification, and his enemies guilty by the destruction of Jerusalem. The verb עמד spoken of the appearing of the parties before a tribunal. בַּעַל מִשְׁפָּט *dominus litis*, the adversary. The Hebrews were obliged to endeavor to supply their deficiency in concrete nouns by the combination of words; for this end they employed especially the nouns בַּעַל and אִישׁ. See e. g Ez 24· 14. Isa. 41 1

V. 9. "Behold the Lord Jehovah will help me; who is he, that will condemn me? behold they shall all pass away as a garment. the moth shall consume them." הוּא stands in place of the verb substantive, the relative is to be supplied after it. So also chap 43 25 אָנֹכִי הוּא מֹחֶה פְשָׁעֶיךָ, "I am he, who blotteth out thy transgressions" The full expression is found, e. g. 1 Chron 21· 17, אֲנִי הוּא אֲשֶׁר חָטָאתִי, "I am he, who has sinned." See Gesen. Lehrg. p 739 With the same emphasis as הוּא here in other passages זֶה also is placed. See Gesen l. c. p. 751. In the last member the figure and reality are blended together. It is as much as to say: they shall pass away, as a garment which is devoured by moths

V. 10. The servant of God concludes with a twofold address, first, in this verse, to those who fear God, then in the following, to the ungodly.—"Who is among you, that fears Jehovah, and regards the voice of his servant, let him trust, if he walks through darkness in which no light shines upon him, on Jehovah, and stay himself on his God." The Messiah admonishes those, who fear God, when they find themselves in severe calamity, not to seek deliverance by their own power, but, in imitation of his example, to throw themselves entirely into the arms of the faithful God, who will then illuminate their night, as he had done his. Who is there among you, etc., is the same as if there is any one among you The interrogative מִי seems here in contrast with כֻּלְּכֶם v. 11, to express the small number of the pious. See chap. 53. 1. There is no necessity, however, on that account, to translate with Michaelis: who is among you, precisely by. how few may be among you. בָּכֶם *among you*, refers to the whole people. חֲשֵׁכִים Accus in answer to the question *where* Darkness without light, for suffering, from which there appears to be no escape and no deliverance.—"Let him trust in Jehovah, let him stay himself on his God," viz., as I have done or do. Then will the same divine assistance be granted him

V. 11. "Behold, all ye, who strike a fire, furnish yourselves with blazing torches, walk in the conflagration of your fire, in the glowing fire, which you have kindled. This shall ye receive at my hand; in sorrow shall ye lie down." The figure, commenced in the foregoing verse, is carried forward The pious walk patiently through the darkness, until Jehovah kindles for them a light The ungodly kindle a fire for themselves, but the fire, that should light and warm, consumes them. Without a figure every one, who, refusing to hear the servants of Jehovah, and put his trust in God, seeks deliverance by his own plans, shall perish, although he may for a time flatter himself with the agreeable expectation of a happy issue. Jerome, Le Clerc, Vitringa, Michaelis, Lowth, v. d. Palm, give too narrow a meaning to a general expression, which is still daily fulfilling, when they make it refer merely to the projects of the rebellious Jews after the time of Christ, who by their insurrection against the Romans, kindled a fire, which consumed their city and nation. This was indeed one remarkable instance of the fulfilment of the declaration. The verb קָדַח *to strike a fire*. Difficult is the ἀπ. λεγ זִיקוֹת, Schultens, Doderlein and Paulus render it *bands*; a meaning, which does not suit the connexion. Rosenmuller and Gesenius compare זִקִים Prov 26·18, which however comes from a radical זָקַק, and suppose, that the word means *burning arrows*, which, shot from a slackened bow, cause a fire where they fix themselves. But this is inadmissible, since it cannot be said: walk in burning arrows, which you have set on fire The explanation of Vitringa, Augusti and others, is less objectionable, who give to the word the meaning *faggots*. ye, who kindle a fire, and encompass yourselves or the same with faggots, in order to make a great conflagration. The Chaldee זְקתָא has the meaning *stick*. But "walk in the faggots, which ye have kindled," would still be somewhat stiff It is most in accordance with the connexion to translate it *torches* or *glowing fire*. Thus the LXX, φλόγα. Vulgate *flammas*. In the Syriac זיקא has the meaning *lightning*. To gird about torches or fire is the same as, to encompass or furnish themselves therewith. Before בְּאוּר the relative is to be supplied לְכוּ *walk*, i. e. ye will walk, nevertheless, with the accessory idea, that this result, as it is immediately after expressly said, proceeds from him, who makes the declaration. By the words· from my hand, etc., the Messiah appropriates to himself the judgment of the ungodly. The ל in לְמַעֲצֵבָה serves as a designation of the condition. LXX ἐν λύπῃ. Symm. ἐν ὀδύνῃ. The verb שָׁכַב *to lie down*, is spoken of those, who are lost without deliverance, here perhaps in continuation of the figure of the fire, of those, who are severely burned by it

Isaiah 52 12—Chap 53

We have now come to a portion which may be regarded, in many respects, as the most important of all the Scriptures of the Old Testament, and better adapted than any other to lead us to a right understanding of the whole. The clare-obscure, which usually attends the prophetic representation, seems here to have entirely vanished. The highest operation of the Spirit of God coincides with the most entire suppression of all conscious and voluntary agency on the part of the prophet. And thus, like a pure mirror, he has reflected upon us the sublime and divine truth which was given him; or rather, the Spirit of Christ in the prophet has employed him as an instrument to reveal the sufferings he should endure after his manifestation in the flesh, and the glory that should follow. 1 Pet. 1· 11.

We here give, in the first place,

A HISTORY OF THE INTERPRETATIONS OF THIS PASSAGE,

I. *By the Jews.*

1. There can be no doubt that the Messianic interpretation was universally received, at least among the better portion of the Jews, in those earlier times, when they still held more firmly to the traditions of their fathers, and before they had become so entirely carnal in their disposition, and their controversy with the Christians had made them so prejudiced in their exegesis. This is confessed even by those later interpreters who pervert the meaning of the prophecy, as Abenezra, Jarchi, Abarbanel, Moses Nachmanides. Even Gesenius asserts "the later Jews, no doubt, relinquished this interpretation, in consequence of their controversy with the Christians." We will here collect, from the existing Jewish writings, the principal passages in which it is found. The whole translation of the Chaldee paraphrast, Jonathan, refers the prediction to the Messiah, although, as we shall hereafter see, he allows himself in many perversions. He paraphrases the very first member הא יצלח עבדי משיחא (behold my servant, the Messiah, shall prosper.) In the Medrasch Tanchuma (an old commentary on the Pentateuch) on the words הִנֵּה יַשְׂכִּיל עַבְדִּי, ed Cracov f 53, c 3 1 7, it is remarked זה מלך המשיח ירום וגבה ונשא

ISAIAH 52.12—CHAP 53.   485

מאוד ורים מן אברהם ונשא ממשה וגבה מן מלאכי השרת (This is the king Messiah, who is high, and lifted up, and very exalted, higher than Abraham, exalted above Moses, higher than the ministering angels) This passage is also remarkable, because it contains the doctrine, which is contested by the later Jews, of the exaltation of the Messiah above all created beings, and even above the angels themselves, and consequently that of-his deity. Still more remarkable is a passage cited from the very old book Pesikta, in the tract Abkat Rokel (אבקת רוכל printed in a separate form at Venice, 1597, and copied in *Hulsii theologia Judaica*, where this passage occurs p. 309) כשברא הב"ה עולמו פשט ידו תחת כסא הכבוד והוציא נשמת המשיח אמר לו רוצה אתה להבריאות ולגאול את בני אחר ששת אלפים אמר לו הין אמר לו א"כ תסבול היסורין למרק עונם דהוא דכתיב אכן חליינו נשא אמר לו אסבול אותם בשמחה (When God created his world, he stretched out his hand under the throne of his glory, and brought forth the soul of the Messiah. He said to him wilt thou heal and redeem my sons after six thousand years ? He answered him : I will God said to him: wilt thou then also bear the punishments, in order to blot out their sins, as it stands written, *but he bore our diseases*, chap. 53: 4. He said to him : I will joyfully bear them) In this passage, as well as in several that follow, the doctrine of the vicarious sufferings of the Messiah, rejected by the later Jews, is contained, and derived from the LIII chap. of Isaiah Similar is the language of Rabbi Moses Haddarschan on Gen. 1 3 (in Latin in Galatinus *de arcanis Cath ver*. p. 329, in the original in Raymund Martini *pug. fid.* fol. 333. Comp. Wolf Bibl. Hebraica I. p 818). "Jehovah spake. Messiah, my righteous one, those who are concealed with thee, will be such that their sins will bring a heavy yoke upon thee. The Messiah answered Lord of the world, I cheerfully take upon myself those plagues and sorrows. Immediately therefore the Messiah, out of love, took upon himself all torments and sufferings, as it is written in Isaiah LIII "he was abused and oppressed" See another passage, where v 5 is referred to the Messiah. In the Talmud (Gemara, tract. Sanhedrin chap. 11) it is said of the Messiah he sits before the gates of the city of Rome among the sick, and the leprous, (literal understanding of v. 3). To the question, how is the Messiah named, it is replied : he is called חיוורא, *the leper*, and in proof v 4 is quoted, according to the false interpretation of נגוע by *leprosus*, which is also found in Jerome — In the book Rabboth (a commentary on the Pentateuch and the five Megilloth, though as to its essential parts very ancient, much interpolated at a later period, and, as the Jews declare, composed about the year A D 300, comp. Wolf l c II. p. 1423 seq) on Ruth chap 2 14 (p. 46, ed. Cracov.), the 14th verse is quoted and referred to the sufferings of the Messiah — In the Medrasch Tillin (an allegorical commentary on the Psalms, printed at Venice 1546), it is said on Ps 2 7. fol 4 "the things of the Messiah and his mysteries are announced in the law, the prophets, and the hagiographa. In the prophets, e. g in the passage Isaiah chap 12· 13 and 42 1. In the hagiographa, e. g. Ps. cx. and Dan. 7. 13." — In the book Chasidim (a collection of moral tales printed at Venice and Basel 1581) is the following account, p 60 "There was, among the Jews, a pious man, who in summer made his bed among fleas, but in winter set his feet in cold water, and when it froze his feet froze at the same time. When asked why he did this, he answered, that he also must make some expiation, since the Messiah bears the sins of Israel" (משיח סובל עונות ישראל) Among the later interpreters, Rabbi Alschech assents to the more ancient explanation (His commentary on Isaiah LIII is given entire in *Hulsii theologia Judaica*, p 321 seq. He says רז״ל פה אחד קיימו וקבלו כי על מלך המשיח ידבר ואחריהם נמשך כי להיות כי הוא דויד הוא משיח כנודע (Our ancient Rabbins, on the testimony of tradition, have ever unanimously admitted that the discourse is here concerning the king Messiah For the same reason, we also, following them, conclude that David, i. e. the Messiah, must be held as the subject of this prophecy, which is indeed manifest.) We shall, however, hereafter see that he follows the true interpretation only in the first three verses. — Passages are to be found in the cabbalistic book Sohar also, especially remarkable The age of this book is very uncertain, but it cannot be shown to have been composed under Christian influence. We here adduce only some of the principal passages (Sohar ed. Amstelod p. II. fol. 212. ed Solisbac. p II. f. 85 Sommeri theol. Sohar p. 94) בשעתא דאמרין ליה למשיחא צערא דישראל בגלותהון ואינון חייבין דבהון דלא מסתכלי למנדע למאריהון ארים קלא ובכא על אינון חייבין דבהון דהוא הוא דכתיב והוא מחולל מפשעינו מדוכא מעונותינו בגנתא דעדן אית היכלא חדא דאקרי היכלא דבני מרעין כדין משיח עאל בההוא היכלא וקארי לכל מרעין וכל כאבין כל יסוריהון דישראל דייתון עליה וכלהו אתיין עליה ואלמלא דאיהו אקיל מעלייהו דישראל ונטיל עליה לא הוי בר נש דיכיל למסבל יסוריהון דישראל על עונש דאוריתא הה״ד אכן חליינו הוא נשא וגו (When the Messiah was informed of the affliction of Israel in their captivity, and that they themselves were the guilty cause of it, since they had not cared for the knowledge of their Lord, he wept aloud over their sins Therefore it is said in the Scriptures, Isa 53: 5 : He was wounded for our sins, he was smitten for our transgressions.—In the garden of Eden there is an apartment, called the chamber of the sick The Messiah goes into this apartment, and calls all the diseases, all the pains, and all the chastisements of Israel to come upon him, and they all do so. And had he not taken them away from Israel, and laid them upon himself, no man could have borne the chastisements of Israel, which are sent upon him on account of the law, as it is said : but he hath taken our diseases upon himself, etc) In another passage (Sohar ed Amstelod. p. III f. 218 Solisbac. III f. 88. Sommeri theol Sohar p 89), it is said "When God wills to give to the world a means of healing, he smites one of the pious among them, and on his account gives healing to the whole world Where do we find this confirmed in the Scripture ? In Isa. 53.5, where it is said : He was wounded for our misdeeds, he was smitten for our sins."

What has been said is sufficient proof, that the older Jews, following tradition, referred the passage to the Messiah, and indeed, as appears from the majority of the passages quoted, to the *suffering* Messiah. But it would have been really a surprising phenomenon, had this interpretation continued to be predominant among the Jews. The cross of Christ, according to the declaration of the Apostle, is "to the Jews a stumbling-block, and to the Greeks foolishness" The idea of a suffering and atoning Messiah was repugnant to the carnally-minded Jews, since they were without that, which prepares the way for its reception, the knowledge of sin and the consciousness of the need of redemption , and since, ignorant of the holiness of God, and consequently of the import of the law, they believed that through their own strength, by works of the law, they might be justified before God. They desired only an outward deliverance from their misery, and their oppressors, not an inward redemption from sin They therefore looked exclusively at those passages of the Old Testament, explained in accordance with their carnal disposition, in which the Messiah in glory is predicted There were other reasons also, which must have rendered them averse to understand the passage of a suffering Messiah. As they could not compare the prophecy with the fulfilment, the deep humiliation of the Messiah here announced, the contempt he endures, his violent death, appeared to them irreconcilable with those passages, in which nothing of this kind is mentioned, and only the glorified Messiah is foretold. They had too little knowledge of the nature of the prophetic vision to enable them to perceive, that the prophecies consist only of separate fragments, which must be arranged together before a complete image of the object can be formed. They supposed, that the Messiah must appear at once in glory, because in many places, he is so exhibited to us, in consequence of his presenting himself in glory to the eye of the prophets, and finally they were led by their controversy with Christians to invent other interpretations. As long as they explained the passage of the suffering Messiah, they could not deny that there was the most striking agreement between this prophecy and the history of Christ. Now as the Christians in their controversy with the Jews, always commenced, and concluded with this prediction, which is fitly called by Hulsius a *carnificina Judaeorum*, and as the latter perceived, in numberless instances, the impression made by arguments grounded on the passage, so nothing could be more natural, than their endeavors to find a remedy for the evil. This task was rendered the more easy in proportion, as they were destitute of sensibility to truth in general, and especially of skill in exegesis, so that they would see no reason for rejecting an interpretation, on the ground of its being unnatural and forced.

In support of what has now been said, we here briefly present the arguments, with which Abarbanel opposes the explanation of the passage, which refers it to a divine Redeemer, who should suffer, and make expiation. He seeks in the first place to lessen the authority of tradition, so much relied on by the later Jewish interpreters in other cases where it harmonizes with their inclinations, by the absurd remark, that the ancient teachers designed to give an allegorical, and not a literal interpretation, and at the same time assert, what is shown to be erroneous by the passages we have quoted, that they referred only the first four verses to the Messiah. Then, after having combatted the doctrine of original sin, he proceeds thus " Suppose even that original sin exists, when God whose power is infinite, willed to pardon, was his hand too short to redeem (Isa 50 2), so that he was obliged on this account to assume flesh, and take chastisements upon himself?—And should I even grant that it was necessary that an individual of the human race should bear this punishment, in order to make satisfaction for all, it would at least have been more suitable, that one from the midst of us, a wise man, or a prophet, should have assumed the punishment, and not God himself. For admitting also, that he had taken flesh upon himself, he would still not have become as one of us.—It is altogether impossible and self-contradictory, that God should make himself corporeal. For God is the first cause, infinite and almighty. He cannot, therefore, assuming flesh, subsist as a finite being, and take the spiritual punishment of man upon himself, of which there is nothing contained in the Scripture.—If the prophecy relate to the Messiah, it must be either Ben Joseph, or Ben David, (see Gen Tr). The former will perish in the beginning of his wars, neither what is said of the exaltation, nor of the humiliation of the servant of God, happens to him. Much less can the latter be intended." (Then follows the quotation of several passages which treat of the exalted Messiah.) These are the *a priori* grounds on which Abarbanel, like every natural man, contests the doctrine of the vicarious satisfaction of a divine Redeemer, and justifies his rejection of the traditional interpretation of the passage before us.

That it was, nevertheless, difficult for the carnally minded among the Jews to reject this tradition, is shown by the paraphrase of Jonathan. This work takes the middle ground between the older interpretation, which was also retained by the better portion of the Jews in later times, and the more modern one. Jonathan (see his paraphrase in Lowth's Comm. by Koppe on the passage, in Hulsii theol. Jud. and elsewhere) reverences tradition, so far as to make the whole prophecy relate to the Messiah; but on the other hand, in order to satisfy his opposition to the doctrine of a suffering and atoning Messiah, he refers all that is here said of the state of humiliation to the state of glorification, by the most violent distortions, and arbitrary interpolations. One trace of the true interpretation, however, is perhaps found on v. 12, where, Jonathan says, that the Messiah will give his soul unto death, if he does not perhaps understand by it, merely the invincible courage with which the Messiah will expose himself to every danger in the conflict with the enemies of the covenant people.

This mode of proceeding, however, could satisfy but few. Further efforts were therefore made, and an entirely different subject of the prophecy was sought for. How uncertain they were, is evident from the example of Abarbanel, who explains it in two entirely different ways, viz, of the Jewish people, and of king Josiah, and then leaves his readers to take their choice. Truth alone is uniform and certain; error brings with it disagreement and uncertainty; a remark illustrated by the following enumeration of the various interpretations of this passage, which in later times have appeared among the Jews. (The most distinguished non-Messianic interpreters of the passage are found in the Rabb. Bibles; and also in Hulsius l. c. p. 339 in the original together with a translation) The interpreters to whom we refer may be divided into two principal classes. 1. Those, who understand by עֶבֶד יְהוָה a *collectivum,* and 2. those, who refer the prophecy to some single person. The first class may again be subdivided into those, a) who make the subject the whole Jewish people in opposition to the gentiles, and b) those, who make it the pious part of the Jews in opposition to the ungodly These views and their defenders we now proceed to examine more closely.

II. Among the non-Messianic interpreters the most widely diffused opinion is, that the Jewish people are the subject of the piece. This opinion existed at an early period, which need not surprise us, since the motive for departing from the Messianic interpretation existed equally early. When Origen makes use of this passage against some learned Jews, they answer ταῦτα πεπροφητεῦσθαι ὡς περὶ ἑνὸς τοῦ ὅλου λαοῦ καὶ γενομένου ἐν τῇ διασπορᾷ καὶ πληγέντος. (Origenes c. Cels ed. Spencer l. I. p. 42). This explanation is followed by R. Solomon Jarchi, Abenezra, Kimchi, Abarbanel, Lipmann (ספר נצחון fol 131). The principal features of this view are the following The prophecy describes the affliction of the people in their present exile; the firmness, with which they endure it for the honor of God, and resist every temptation to forsake his law and his worship; and the prosperity, honor, and glory, which they shall obtain in the time of their redemption. V. 1—10, the heathen are introduced as speaking, and make an humble and penitential confession, that they have hitherto mistaken the people of God, and unjustly despised them on account of their sufferings, since it now appears from their exaltation, that these sufferings have not been inflicted upon them by God for the punishment of their sins. When some of these interpreters, as Abenezra, and Rabbi Lipmann, understand by the עֶבֶד יְהוָה, only the pious part of the nation, who have remained faithful to Jehovah; this constitutes no material difference, since they also place עֶבֶד יהוָה in contrast with the heathen, and not like the interpreters of the following class, with the ungodly, or less righteous part of the nation.

III. Others take the appellation עֶבֶד יְהוָה as a collective designation of the pious, and find in the passage the idea of a kind of vicarious satisfaction, made by them for the ungodly. These interpreters approach nearer the truth, in so far as they do not, like those of the foregoing class, subvert the doctrine of the vicarious satisfaction either by a figurative explanation, or like Kimchi, by the absurd remark, that this doctrine is an error put into the mouths of the heathen, but they depart from it in as far as they generalize what belongs to a definite subject, and, agreeably to the pride of the natural heart, attribute to mere men what belongs only to the God-man. This view has been most definitely expressed by the commentator on the book עין ישראל or עין יעקב which has been often printed, and contains all sorts of tales from the Talmud. He says: "it is fit to suppose that the whole portion is a prophecy in respect to the righteous, who are tried by afflictions." He then makes of the righteous two classes, those who must endure in general much affliction and suffering, and those who are publicly put to death, as Rabbi Akiba and others. He supposes that the prophet shows the dignity of both these classes of the righteous, to whom the name servant of God justly belongs. In like manner R. Alschech. He refers, as we have already seen, chap. 52. 13—15 to the Messiah alone, and to his glory obtained by severe sufferings. Then the prophet speaks, as he supposes, in the name of all Israel, approves what God had said, and confesses that his explanation of the sufferings of the Messiah has enlightened them respecting the sufferings of the pious in general. They perceive it to be hasty and erroneous to infer guilt from suffering, and resolve that henceforth when they see a righteous man suffer, they will think of no other cause, than that he is bearing their diseases, and that his chastisements are for their welfare. The עֶבֶד יְהוָֹה is therefore a kind of personification of the righteous.—It is probable that a similar view lies at the foundation of those passages in the Talmud, where one part of this prophecy is referred to Moses, and another to Rabbi Akiba, whom the Jews revere as a martyr. It does not appear, that the prophecy was limited to Moses, or Akiba, but it was referred to them, only as belonging to that collective body which was supposed to constitute its subject.

IV. The view which makes an individual, other than the Messiah, the subject of the prophecy, has found among the Jews comparatively the fewest defenders. We have seen already, that Abarbanel, besides the interpretation which makes the Jewish people the subject, proposes still another, which refers it to king Josiah. Rabbi Saadias Haggaon explained the whole portion of Jeremiah.

Still, the Rabbins have not been able, with all their efforts, entirely to supplant the true interpretation, and thus to divest the passage of all that is dangerous to their views. Among the cabbalistic Jews it is still the prevailing one. In many instances, this very chapter has been, to proselytes from Judaism, the first ground of their conviction of the truth of Christianity. So says Jo. Isaac Levita in the treatise *Defensio veritatis Hebraicae S. Sc.* p. 82: "Ingenue profiteor illud ipsum caput ad fidem Christianam me perduxisse. Nam plus millies caput illud perlegi, contuli accurate cum multis translationibus. Deprehendi centies plus de Christo mysteria in textu Hebraeo contineri, quam ulla alia in versione reperiantur." Many similar instances occur in the reports of the missionaries among the Jews, especially those of the Callenberg Institute.

2. *History of the interpretation of the passage by Christians.*

Its course has been much the same among them as among the Jews. Like causes have, in both cases, produced like effects. The true exposition was relinquished by both, when the prevailing opinions became opposed to its results; and if we descend to particulars, we shall also find a great resemblance between the methods of interpretation proposed.

From *a priori* reasoning, no other conclusion could be drawn, than that the Christian church, so long as she possessed Christ at all, would find him here, where he is so clearly and plainly set before us; and that while she acknowledged in general his authority and that of his apostles, she must here also follow their distinct and manifold testimony. And such is indeed the fact. With the exception of a certain Silesian, by the name of Seidel, who, in total unbelief, asserted that the Messiah never had come, and never would come, (see Jac. Martini l. 3 *de tribus Elohim* p. 592) and Grotius, both of whom wished to make Jeremiah the subject, no man in the Christian church, during seventeen centuries, ventured to call in question the Messianic interpretation. On the contrary, this passage was always regarded as the plainest and most splendid of all the prophecies of the Messiah. We will now make a few citations from the great mass of testimonies. Augustine asserts, De civitate Dei, l. 18 c. 29 (t. II.

p. 194 ed. Tauchn.) "Jesaias inter illa, quae arguit iniqua et justa praecepit, et peccatori populo mala futura praedixit, etiam de Christo et ecclesia, h. e. de rege et ea, quam condidit civitate, multo plura, quam ceteri prophetavit: ita ut a quibusdam evangelista, quam propheta potius diceretur." He then cites this passage for proof, and concludes with the following words: "Verum ista sint satis: et in eis sunt exponenda nonnulla; sed sufficere arbitror, quae ita sunt aperta, ut etiam inimici intelligere cogantur inviti." He expresses himself in a similar manner, De consensu Evangelistarum l. 1. c. 31. (Opp. ed. Clerici, t. III. p. 2 p. 15). Theodoret remarks on the passage (Opp. ed. Hal. t. II. p. 358) ἐν τοῖς ἐξῆς τὴν ταπείνωσιν αὐτοῦ τὴν μέχρι θανάτου παριστᾷ· μεγίστη δὲ τοῦ πνεύματος ἁγίου ἡ ἐνέργεια· τὰ γὰρ μετὰ πολλὰς γενόμενα γενεὰς οὕτω τοῖς ἁγίοις προφήταις προέδειξεν, ὡς μὴ λέγειν ἐλεινοὺς ἠκούσαμεν, ἀλλ᾽ εἴδομεν. In like manner Justin, Irenaeus, Cyrill of Alexandria, and Jerome declare themselves. From the evangelical church we here adduce only the testimony of two of its founders. Zuingle says in Adn. ad h. 1. (Opp. t. III. Tur. 1544, fol. 292)· "Quae nunc sequuntur, adeo clarum Christo testimonium praebent, ut ipse nesciam an uspiam scripturarum quicquam aut constantius inveniatur, aut clarius dici quicquam posset. Frustra enim omnia pertentat Judaeorum pervicacia." Luther remarks on this passage (Opp. ed. Lips. t. VII. p. 352) "And surely there is no text nor prediction of the Old Testament, which speaks more plainly than this chapter, both of the sufferings and of the resurrection of Christ. Therefore it becomes all Christians to know it well, even by heart, in order to confirm and defend our faith, chiefly against the stiff-necked Jews, who deny this their only promised Christ, solely on account of the offence of his cross."

It was reserved for the last quarter of the 18th century to reject the Messianic interpretation. *It could no longer be retained.** For if this passage contains a prediction of the Messiah, it harmonizes so strikingly with the history of Christ, that its origin cannot possibly be accounted for upon natural principles. But then, at the same time, the whole fabric of our opponents falls to the ground, since it rests on

---

* The author of the article über die Mess. Zeiten in Eichhorn's Bibl. d. bibl. Litt. Bd. 6, candidly confesses p. 635, that the Messianic interpretation would soon find general approbation among biblical critics, had they not in recent times attained to the conviction, " that the prophets predict nothing of the future, except what they could know and anticipate without any special divine revelation."

the assumption, that every supernatural influence on the internal or external nature, including of course prophecies and miracles, is impossible, or at least incapable of proof. An expedient therefore was sought, and the more easily found, since worthy predecessors already existed in the Jews, whose explanations and objections had only to be appropriated, and invested with the semblance of solidity by the learning bestowed upon them

The non-Messianic interpretation among Christians, like those among the Jews, may be divided into two principal classes 1. Those, built upon the hypothesis, that the subject of the prophecy is a collective one. 2. Those, in which the servant of Jehovah is regarded as a single individual, though not the Messiah The first class is again susceptible of several subdivisions, a) the interpretation, which makes the subject the whole Jewish people; b) the abstract of the Jewish people; c) the pious part of the Jewish people, d) the priesthood; e) the prophetic order!!

II Comparatively the greatest number of non-Messianic interpreters make the whole Jewish people the subject. This hypothesis is adopted by Döderlein (in der Vorr. und den Anm zu der 3ten Ausg. des Jesaias) though he still fluctuates between it, and the Messianic interpretation, which he had before zealously defended; Schuster (in a separate treatise on this portion Gott. 1794), Telge, Stephani (in den Gedanken uber die Entstehung und Ausbildung der Idee von einem Messias, Nurnberg 1787), the author of the letters on Isaiah LIII in the 6th Vol of Eichhorn's Bibliothek, which are written in an improper tone, Eichhorn (in seiner Bearbeitung der Propheten), Rosenmuller (in der 2ten Ausg. seines Commentars), who has relinquished to others the interpretation, which makes the prophetic order the subject, and which he had been the first to recommend Besides these, there are many others In substance this hypothesis continues entirely the same as we have seen it among the Jews. The only difference is, that these interpreters understand by the sufferings of the servant of God, the sufferings of the Jewish people in the Babylonish exile, while the Jewish expositors understand by them their sufferings in their present exile They also suppose, that v 1—10, the heathen are introduced as speaking, and make the penitential confession, that they have mistaken Israel, and now perceive that his sufferings are not the punishment of *his* sins, but that he has suffered, as a substitute for *their* sins

III The hypothesis, which makes the subject the Jewish people in the abstract, in opposition to its individual members Of this it is impossible to form any distinct idea, since the whole consists merely of its parts, and therefore the people in the abstract cannot be innocent, when all the individuals are guilty; and still less can the former undergo vicarious sufferings for the latter This hypothesis has continued to be peculiar to its author (Eckermann theol. Beitrage Bd. 1 H. 1 p. 192 seq.); and has found as yet no other advocate. See in opposition die Briefe uber Jesaias LIII l. c. p 192 seq.

IV. The supposition, that the pious part of the Jewish people, as contrasted with the ungodly, is the subject, has been especially defended by Paulus (Memorabilien Bd. 3 p. 175—92 and Clavis zum Jesaia)* His fundamental view is the following: the pious part of the people were punished and carried into exile with the ungodly, not on account of their own sins, but the sins of the latter, who improved their temporal condition in the exile by their apostasy from the religion of Jehovah Hence the ungodly inferred that the hope of the pious, that Jehovah would help them, was in vain, but as the exile came to an end, and the pious returned, they saw that they had erred, and that this hope was well grounded. They deeply lament, therefore, that they have not long ago done penance.

V. The hypothesis, which makes the priesthood the subject, was defended by the author of " ausfuhrlichen Erklarung der sammtlichen Weissagungen des A T. 1801," but has since found no other followers.

VI. The hypothesis, that the subject was the prophets collectively, was just advanced by Rosenmuller in the articles (Leiden und Hoffnungen der Propheten Jehovahs, in Gablers neuestem theol Journal Vol. II p. 4. p. 333 seq)† Being afterwards abandoned by him it passed over to De Wette (de morte J. Chr expiatoria p. 28 seq.) and Gesenius.

VII. Among the interpretations, which refer the prediction to a single individual, though not the Messiah, scarcely one has found any other patron besides its author. We here barely refer to them, in order to show by an example, whither sagacity will wander, when it divests itself of the sense of truth Among the subjects proposed, are king Uzziah (by Augusti, who has probably relinquished it since in consequence of a change in his theological sentiments, and who declared, even at the time he brought it forward, that, with the ex-

* With him Ammon agrees, Christologie p 108 seq
† Also Gabler adopts this hypothesis l c p 365

ception of Uzziah, the prophecy could refer to no one but Jesus), king Hezekiah (by Konynenburg and Bahrdt), the prophet Isaiah himself (by Staudlin, in opposition to whom see Spohn in a Programm Wittemb 1794), an unknown prophet, who is supposed to have been slain by the Jews in the exile (by an anonymous writer in Henkes Magazin Bd. I H. 2), the royal race of David, who, though innocent, suffered, when the children of the unfortunate king Zedekiah were put to the sword by the command of Nebuchadnezzar (Bolten on Acts 8. 33), and lastly the Maccabees (by an anonymous author in the Theologischen Nachrichten J 1821 S. 79 seq.)

But still the true interpretation has found many able defenders, who did not suffer themselves to be carried away by the perverse spirit of the times. Among the recent commentators upon the whole of Isaiah, who have remained true to this interpretation are Cube, Dathe, Doderlein (who nevertheless hesitates in his last edition), Hensler, Hezel, Kocher, Koppe, Lowth, Michaelis, v. d. Palm, Rieger, Vaupel. Its principal defenders, besides, are the following :[*] Hess (in der Gesch. d Könige von Juda and in the treatise. vom Reiche Gottes), M F. Roos (Jesus der Erloser der Menschen Jes. LIII, Tub 1788. 8), Storr (dissertatio, qua insigne de Christo oraculum Jes LIII illustr Tub 1790 4), very thorough, but tiresome, on account of the useless accumulation of citations and exhibiting many forced interpretations. See his Erklarung des Briefes an die Hebraer S. 175 coq. Jo Imm Hansi (commentatio phil thool in vat. Jes. LIII, Lips 1791. 8), a diligently labored treatise. Martini (commentatio philologico-critica in locum Jesaiae c. LIII. Rostochii 1791. 8), in a philological respect, it belongs to the most distinguished writings on the Old Testament in general, but still the theological views of its author, who inclines to *neology*, have exercised an unfavorable influence on his interpretation. Thus e. g he denies that the doctrine of a vicarious satisfaction is found in this portion of Isaiah, which Gesenius himself cannot refrain from acknowledging Nova commentatio in locum Jes LIII, quam praeside Dresdio—C F. A. Werner. Witt. 1793. (not very important, and concedes too much), Spohn in the dissertation against Staudlin already referred to, an anonymous writer (Schleusner?) in the Gottingischen Biblio-

---

[*] Bertholdt also is, in some measure, to be reckoned among the defenders of the Messianic interpretation He supposes the passage treats of an ideal Messiah, who is represented as suffering and struggling with the severest afflictions. Comp his dissertatio de ortu theolog vet. Hebr 1 p 135 seq. Einl 4 p. 1383

thek für theologische Litteratur Bd. 1 S. 118 seq Disputatio polemico-theologica in cap. Jesaiae LIII, quam praes A. Hylander—auctor Olaus Sunden Lundae 1803, (not important—directed chiefly against the hypothesis of Paulus). Lindemann, in an article in Henkes Museum II, 4 An anonymous writer in der Bibliotheek van Theologische Litterkunde voor het Jaar 1805 p. 485—531 Kruiger, commentatio de verisillima orac. Jes LIII interpretandi ratione Lips. 1809 4. (contains many very good general remarks, especially respecting the natural causes of the rise of the idea of a suffering Messiah). Jahn, appendix ad Hermeneuticam fasc II p. 1—66. Zollich, das Orakel von Christo vom Geiste der Weissagung ausgesprochen durch den Propheten Jesaias cap LII, LIII, in Zimmermanns und Heidenreichs Monatsschrift für Predigerwissensch Bd 4 p 121 seq Keller, in an article in Bengels Neuem Archiv für die Theol Bd II p 151 seq und p 253 seq , (praiseworthy, though the author has been at too much pains to refute the perversions of Eckermann and Eichhorn, which refute themselves) Steudel, observationes ad Jes LIII in zwei Academischen Abhandl Tub 1825, 26, (an excellent tract, the mode of exhibition somewhat tedious).

We here take for granted the correctness of the Messianic interpretation, inasmuch as the refutation of the opposite theories cannot be given before the explanation of the portion To this explanation we shall proceed after some preparatory remarks in conclusion, and endeavor to show the correctness of the Messianic interpretation

We have already seen, in our general preparatory remarks, that the main subject of the second part of the prediction of Isaiah is the deliverance of the people of God ; and indeed a twofold deliverance from the Babylonish exile, and from sin and error The two are not accurately distinguished from each other It may however be remarked in general, that from the commencement until chap XLIX, the former, and in the remaining chapters, the latter, was predominant in the view of the prophet Each of these deliverances shall be accomplished by a servant and messenger of Jehovah, the first by Cyrus, the second by Christ. The prophet had already, in a preceding part of the book, so plainly described Cyrus, that no trait remained to be added Nor had he left the latter unnoticed: God's servant and chosen, him whom his soul loves—Israel, by whom he glorifies himself But the features which he had hitherto given, were not sufficient to form a perfect image He had described him as the divine teacher and messenger, who, endowed by God with rich gifts, humbled himself, and meek and lowly came to seek that which was lost, he had represented him as a glorious king, who should found a kingdom of peace and righteousness, continually enlarge its boundaries, receive into it all the heathen nations, richly bless its members, and severely punish the despisers of his name. But still one great feature in the portrait was wanting. He had announced, that Cyrus should accomplish the temporal deliverance by his military valor, and the victories which Jehovah should grant him, but the method in which the spiritual deliverance should be accomplished, was not yet communicated to him. True, he had spoken already of the deepest humiliation of the Messiah, he had predicted the severe sufferings, the scorn and contempt of the people, which should overtake the servant of God, chap L. But he had not said that these very sufferings should be the only efficient cause of our salvation. Here then, for the first time, he completes the picture, when he announces, that the Messiah, at the same time both priest and offering, shall expiate our sins by his blood, and present himself to God as a sacrifice for our transgressions, that he shall bear our infirmities, and by his wounds heal ours. Three offices were instituted by God under the theocracy, that of prophet, priest and king; in a higher and more complete sense the Messiah was to combine them all in his own person.

The contents of course of the prophecy are as follows. In v. 13—15 chap 52, Jehovah speaks. They contain a brief summary of what is enlarged upon in chap LIII. The deepest possible humiliation of the servant of God, shall be followed by his exaltation to the highest glory; the nations of the earth shall be redeemed by him, and their kings shall submit to him with reverence. In chap 53· 1—10, the prophet speaks. The first verse is not in connexion with the rest, and contains a sort of introduction, or exclamation of complaint. The prophet, speaking in the name of all who foretel the Messiah, and who preach him after his appearance, announces that many will not believe their report, many will not acknowledge, as such, this glorious manifestation of the omnipotence and mercy of God. He then, v 2, continues the discourse, with this difference only, that he henceforth considers himself as one of the people, or rather as one of the better part of the people, who misapprehended the Redeemer at first in his humiliation, but recognized him as their Saviour and benefactor after his glorification, and perceived that his sufferings had been endured by him only for our salvation. This is the substance of the discourse the servant of Jehovah will appear in lowliness and with no outward splendor Sufferings more severe than man ever endured will overtake him. Freely and patiently will he endure them Finally he will be taken away by a violent death The rage of his enemies, which is still unsatisfied, will endeavor, though in vain, even in death, to dishonor him, the righteous and the innocent, v 2, 3, 7—9 The people, beholding his sufferings and being ignorant of their cause, believed them to be the deserved punishment of his own misdeeds, but (as the speakers now perceive) erroneously. Not his transgressions but ours were punished in him. His sufferings were voluntarily undergone for the salvation of men, who were exposed to destruction without them God himself was pleased in this way to restore for communion with himself those, who, having departed from him, were wandering in their own ways, v. 4—6. Great glory is designed for him after Jehovah has been reconciled by the sacrifice of his life freely offered The knowledge and love of God will be established on earth through him, and a numerous church collected, v. 10. V. 11 and 12, Jehovah again appears as the speaker, and confirms what had been said by the prophet.

Isaiah 52:13

Jehovah speaks The interpreters are divided, inasmuch as some suppose this verse to be connected with the foregoing, others, that it begins a new portion, which has nothing in common with what preceded. The first opinion is undeniably the more correct. The prophet, it is true, in the foregoing section, chap 52. 1—12, had been chiefly concerned with the nearer deliverance from the Babylonish exile But at the same time, under the figure of the temporal deliverance, the spiritual was concealed As now, in the foregoing portion, the deliverance itself, so in this its author appears before the spiritual eye of the prophet. Rightly Calvin "Postquam Jesaias de restitutione ecclesiae locutus erat, transit ad Christum, in quo omnia colliguntur. Loquitur de prospero ecclesiae successu, qui cum minime appareret, eos revocat ad suum regem, a quo omnia restituenda sunt eumque exspectari jubet" "Behold my servant shall reign well, he shall be high and extolled, and very exalted." The prophets do not proceed in the manner of historians, who follow the order of time, but they conduct us at once in *medium rem*, and often begin with that, with which they should strictly end. An example of this we have in the case before us; the prophet commences with the glorification, instead of the humiliation. By הִנֵּה the prophet indicates that a new object is presented to his view. Jehovah points, as it were, to the Messiah, as if he were present, as appears from the following verse, where he is addressed. The point of time, taken by the prophet, in his internal vision, is the period between the humiliation and the glorification of the Messiah. The latter is here, and in the following verses, generally designated by the future tense, the former by the past. The verb הִשְׂכִּיל has a twofold meaning, *to act wisely*, and *to be prosperous;* in accordance with the opinion of the Hebrews, that wisdom, i. e. piety, was the cause of prosperity, but folly, i. e. ungodliness, of adversity. The old translators have nearly all adopted the former, (Alex. συνήσει. Aq Symm. ἐπιστημονισθήσεται. Vulg. *intelliget*. Syr. ܢܣܬܟܠ). They have been followed by several of the earlier interpreters, as e. g. Joh. H Michaelis in den bibl. Hal. The recent interpreters, on the contrary, after the Chaldee paraphrast, who translates יַצְלַח *prospere aget*, have for the most part chosen the second meaning appealing especially to the parallelism with the second member. But it is better to unite them both *he will reign well;* which indicates at the same time, the prosperous and the wise government of his kingdom by the glorified Messiah, who appears as usual under the image of a powerful king. In this sense the verb is undeniably used in reference to the Messiah, Jer. 23. 5. Comp besides 1 Kings 2. 3. In the second member, the prophet combines all the verbs of the Hebrew language, which signify elevation, and yet subjoins מְאֹד in order most emphatically to exhibit the glorious exaltation of the Messiah.

V. 14. As this verse is closely connected with the 15th, we here give the translation of both. "Like as many were shocked at my servant,—his countenance was so disfigured, that it was no more a human countenance; his form, that it was no longer a human form, so will he sprinkle many Gentile nations, kings will shut their mouths before him; for what has not been announced to them they see, and what they have not heard they perceive" V. 14 contains the protasis, v. 15 the apodosis. The sense as the humiliation of the Son of man was the greatest possible, as he was abhorred by all those who beheld him in that condition; so will his glorification also be equally remarkable, people and kings will submit to him with the deepest reverence. כֵּן *sic, adeo* does not designate the *apodosis*, which does not begin till v. 15, but refers to the foregoing member, the reason is given why many were shocked, and the words from כֵּן to the end of the verse are to be put in a parenthesis. Jehovah, in the protasis, addresses the Messiah, עָלֶיךָ, in the *apodosis* he speaks of him again in the third person, יָדְעוּ and עָלָיו. Such a sudden change of person is in general very common in the poetical and prophetic portions of Scripture, but here there is moreover a particular reason for it. In the intervening sentence, which gives the reason of the astonishment, and is not directed to the Messiah, the second person could not be employed. The verb שָׁמֵם with עַל *to be astonished at any one*; whether from admiration, or abhorrence, must be determined by the connexion. In the latter sense it occurs, e. g. in Jer. 18 16. 19: 8. The word מִשְׁחַת properly a noun, *corruptio*, from שׁהת *to corrupt*; but here it is the abstract for the concrete, *disfiguration* for *disfigured*. The form is properly as מִקְטָל with Qamets, (Ges. Lehrg p. 494), and מִשְׁחַת with Pattahh is the con stat. which stands before prepositions, as well as before the Genitive, and is here followed by מִן, as in Is. 23 23. Hos 7 5. and often elsewhere Ges Lehrg p. 679). מִן in מֵאִישׁ and מִבְּנֵי אָדָם may best be taken as negative or privative, the infinitive הֱיוֹת being omitted "His visage is disfigured from the visage of a man," i e so that it is no countenance of a man any more, and his form, so that it is no longer the human form. מִן is often to be translated *so that not*. So Jer. 23. 1 " he has rejected thee מִמֶּלֶךְ *from a king*," i. e that thou art not a king. Jer 2 25 " keep thy foot, מִיָּחֵף, that it be not naked " Is 7: 8 מֵעָם " so that it is no more a people " מֵעִיר " so that it is no more a city " (See Gesenius p 786 Storr, Observationes ad Analogiam et Syntaxin p 253 Ewald, Gramm. p. 599) The full expression would be כֵּן מִשְׁחַת מַרְאֵהוּ מֵהְיוֹת מַרְאֵה אִישׁ וְתֹאֲרוֹ מֵהְיוֹת תֹּאַר אָדָם. But it is the practice of the Hebrews in comparisons, when the same subject must be named twice, to omit it the second time. See e g Ps 18 34 and 110 3 and other examples quoted by Schnurrer, Dissertationes Philologicae, p 169, and by Lowth, De S Poesie Hebraeorum p. 207, ed. II. Gott. When any thing has become entirely degenerate and deformed, the Hebrews are accustomed to say, it is *not* what it is Entirely parallel with this passage e. g. is Ps. 22 2 " I am a worm and no man." See further Deut. 32 21 לֹא עָם " a people that deserves not the name of a people," *gens contemtissima.* Is. 52: 2 בֹּא לֶחֶם *panis vilis*, and lastly chap. 53. 3. Many interpreters take מִן comparatively, in the sense *prae, before.* They explain the sentence thus כֵּן מִשְׁחַת מַרְאֵהוּ מֵמַּרְאֶה אִישׁ וְתֹאֲרוֹ מִבְּנֵי אָדָם "His visage was more disfigured than that of a man" etc. But it is apparent, that the former interpretation gives a far stronger, and therefore more appropriate, sense. תֹּאֲרוֹ stands for the regular תָּאֳרוֹ as in Is. 1. 31 פָּעֳלוֹ for פָּעֳלוֹ (Ges. p. 571.)— Several interpreters, as Jahn e. g. find a climax and an antithesis in אִישׁ and בְּנֵי אָדָם. They suppose that אִישׁ signifies people of rank, and בְּנֵי אָדָם those of the lower class. But although this contrast sometimes undeniably occurs, yet it would here greatly weaken the sense, and we must therefore assume that both expressions, as is often the case, are here entirely synonymous. With respect now to the sense of the whole parenthesis, the interpreters justly observe, that the deformity of his visage and form does not refer merely to the person of the Messiah, but must also be understood in a metaphorical sense. According to v. d. Palm, the foundation of the figure is a sick person, who is entirely deformed by a severe disease. As his acquaintances are alarmed when they see him, so are beholders shocked at the appearance of the Messiah. Luther: "the prophet does not speak of the form of Christ in respect to his person; but of the political and regal form of a sovereign, who, though an earthly king, does not go forth in the form of a king, but as the meanest of all servants, so that a more despised person than he, was never seen in the world." But most interpreters err, in making the metaphorical expression refer solely to the mean and despised condition of the Messiah, and not to his sufferings likewise. Thus of old Jerome, t. IV. p. l. 612. ed. Vallarsi. t. V. ed. Francof. "non quo formae significet foeditatem, sed quo in humilitate venerit et paupertate," and Martini, whom the recent interpreters, as usual, follow: "sententia loci non proprio sensu ad vultus foeditatem, sed ad conditionem externam universam tenuem, vilem et abjectam referenda." But the expression is much too strong for this. Besides a *compendium* of what follows is here given, and we can see no reason why regard should be had merely to that which is of inferior importance. Fitly Calvin: "Sic prodiit in mundum, ut passim contemtibilis esset. Delituit ejus gloria sub humilitate carnis. Atque haec causa stuporis fuit, quod sine ullo splendore inter homines versaretur, nec redemtorem eo statu et habitu venturum Judaei existimarent. Cum ad crucem ventum esset, illic longe plus stuporis fuit." And v. d. Palm:

"these expressions cannot be fully explained by a reference to the obscure poverty and degradation of our Redeemer; we must represent him to ourselves in his sufferings, in the most dreadful contempt and misery; and then we may be able to justify the strong language of the prophet." The humiliation and the cross of Christ were to the Jews a stumbling block, 1 Cor. 1 3, and to many they continue to be so still

V 15 The verb יַזֶּה, in all the numerous places where it occurs, signifies *to sprinkle*. It is used in speaking of the act of the high priest, who was yearly to sprinkle blood towards the ark of the covenant, in order to obtain forgiveness for the people, Lev 4. 6. 16 18, 19; of the sprinkling of the cleansed leper, Lev 14 17 etc, and of the sprinkling of the unclean with consecrated water. The consequence of these sprinklings was restoration to external theocratical purity. Comp the passages quoted But it is very common in the Old Testament for spiritual and inward purifications, and sanctification, to be represented by images and expressions taken from the outward purifications and sanctifications; and this was the more natural, since the latter, besides their main design, had the secondary one, of symbolizing that, which was spiritual So e g. chap 36 5, Ezekiel alludes to the practice of sprinkling with consecrated water, those who were to be purified· "And I will sprinkle clean water upon you, and ye shall be clean From all your filthiness, and from all your idols will I cleanse you" David refers to the same practice, Ps. 51: 9 "Cleanse me with hyssop, (see the cited passage, Lev. xiv) that I may be clean" These parallel passages fully justify us in giving to the verb יַזֶּה here the meaning *to purify, to cleanse from sin* This interpretation is confirmed by what is said, v 3—10, concerning the expiation of the sins of others by the sufferings and death of the servant of God, but especially by the words, "when he shall have brought an offering for sin," v. 10, and by יַצְדִּיק, *he will justify*, or *free from sin*, v. 11, which exactly corresponds with יַזֶּה in the verse before us Among the ancient translations, the Syriac follows this interpretation, which has ܡܕܟܐ, and the Vulg *asperget* which Jerome explains. "ipse asperget gentes multas, mundans eas sanguine suo et in baptismate dei consecrans servituti," where he understands the expression in too special a sense This explanation is followed by the authors of the New Testament, when, with reference to this passage, they speak of a *ῥαντισμὸς τοῦ αἵματος* of Christ;

comp. 1 Pet. 1 2 Heb 12 24. It has been generally adopted by Christian expositors, as Luther, Vitringa, Dathe, Kocher, Jahn and others After the example of Schroder (observationes selectae ad origines Hebraeas cap. VIII, § 10) in recent times, Martini, Rosenmuller, Gesenius, and Winer have objected: 1. That the verb could not then be construed with the Acc., but, as in the other places, with עַל before the thing to be sprinkled But as in general, the greatest diversity in the construction of verbs prevails in Hebrew, (as e g even in v 1 of the following chapter, the verb גָּלָה is construed with עַל, though elsewhere always connected with לְ or אֶל), so it is especially common for a verb to be construed with a preposition, which in other instances takes the Acc and *vice versa*. We have a remarkable example even in chap. 53. 11, where the verb הִצְדִּיק which has the Acc., every where else, is construed with לְ. In the case of the verb נָזָה the construction with the Acc also is explained by a slight modification of the meaning. Construed with עַל the verb means *to sprinkle*; with the Acc *to be sprinkled* This variation, however, has in its favor the analogy of other languages. In the cognate Ethiopic dialect נזה, corresponding to the Hebrew נָזָה, is used to denote the besprinkling of things and persons, comp. Heb. 9. 19 11: 28. Ps. 51 9. In Latin we say *spargere aquam*, but also *spargere corpus aqua, aspergere quid alicui*, and further *re aliquem, conspergere, perspergere, respergere quem* Kocher remarks "Id cur non potius Hebraeis liceat quibus compositorum defectum per varios usus verba simplicia sarciunt". 2. They object to this interpretation, that the connexion is opposed to it. The antithesis with עַמִּים leads us to expect some corresponding word But this very interpretation furnishes the most suitable antithesis No man will be freed from sin by the Messiah unless he suffers himself to be sanctified by him But no one will do this, who does not place all his confidence in him, and acknowledge him as his King and Lord. The believing and humble confidence therefore, with which the heathen draw near to the glorified Messiah, is placed in opposition to the contempt and abhorrence with which the Jews wondered at him in his state of abasement There is also then the most suitable parallelism with the second member. "Kings shall shut their mouths before him." In a manner altogether similar, chap. 53 11, it is mentioned as a reward, which the glorified servant of God shall obtain, "that he shall make many righteous" 3 It is said "If *to sprinkle*, means the same as to *free from sin with blood*, the material used in the purification would not be omitted. Should it be said in reply, that the noun *blood* might be easily supplied from the customary use of the verb to signify *purifying with blood*, this answer would not be valid, because purification was not effected merely by blood, but also by water and oil." This objection by no means lies against our interpretation, but at most only against that, which regards יַזֶּה as relating especially to purification by *the blood* of Christ. If the verb be taken in its general acceptation, *to free from sin*, the image may be borrowed, at the same time, from the *besprinkling* with both blood and water, and it is not necessary that the material should be subjoined. See Ps. 51. 9, where in the expression, "cleanse me and I shall be clean," the material is not mentioned, any more than in the case before us. V. d. Palm well paraphrases the passage. *Yet he thereby becomes the priest of many nations*, and explains it: to sprinkle is a work of the priest, and Jesus is here the great high priest of the whole world, who purifies it, and makes expiation for it. See Ps. 110. 4.

The modern interpreters, leaving the Hebrew usage, have attempted to give several explanations from the Arabic. Martini, Rosenmuller, and Gesenius compare the Arabic نزا corresponding to נזה *to spring, to leap*. Martini, indeed, proposes this explanation with much hesitation and with a feeling of uncertainty: "Quae vero de sensu lectionis receptae יַזֶּה ipse jam, quamquam timide, in medium prolaturus sum, ea quantum absint ab interpretatione justa et certa ipse satis sentio." He excuses his attempt only on the ground, that the received interpretation, for the reasons given above, is untenable. According now to Rosenmuller and Gesenius: "he shall make many nations to leap," is the same as "he shall fill with joy." They allege, that the verb نزا in Golius, has among other meanings, that of *exultavit prae hilaritate;* which however has not hitherto been established by any passage from an Arabic writer. Martini goes still further. He appeals to the circumstance, that among the orientals, the verbs which signify one particular emotion of mind, are frequently transferred to all the others. Thus he supposes, that the verb may have been employed also to express the effects of terror, surprise, and wonder. He translates: "eos sacro quodam horrore percellet suique reverentiam animis eorum infiget," and therefore approximates, though by an erroneous method, to that meaning of the verb יַזֶּה which we have vindicated. He was manifestly induced to go beyond Gesenius, and Rosenmüller by the feeling, that the interpretation · "he will make them leap for joy," with which they stopped short, gives no suitable sense. Against these interpretations, we urge, besides the arguments already adduced in favor of the received one, that we should never, and least of all in the case of a word of such frequent occurrence, depart from the established Hebrew usage, without some urgent reason, (see Schelling von dem Gebrauche der Arab. Sprache p 71 seq). This is a principle which the latest defenders of this hypothesis themselves firmly hold in theory, and by the practical application of which in other cases, they have merited great praise for their solid and judicious interpretation of the Old Testament. An appeal has also been made to the Alexandrine version, which renders οὕτω θαυμάσονται ἔθνη πολλὰ ἐπ' αὐτῷ. But even Martini remarks "in loco obscuro per ingenii felicitatem sensum utcunque conjectando assequi studebant"

The phrase פֶה קָפַץ, to shut the mouth, as well as the related one. to lay the hand on the mouth, is a designation of humble, and reverential subjection. In presence of a more honorable person, one does not venture to speak. See Job 29. 9. Ps. 107. 47. Ez. 16: 63. Mic 7: 16 The ground of this humble submission, is given in the second part of the verse. The heathen (that they are the subject of discourse appears partly from the expression גוֹיִם and מְלָכִים, partly from the parallel passage 53. 11, 12) shall receive the intelligence of the wonderful exaltation of the great servant of God, and of the mystery of his redemption, which was never before made known to them, as it had been to the Jews. Theodoret (Opp t II, p. 357, ed. Hal):
Οἱ γὰρ τὰς προφητικὰς οὐ δεξάμενοι προῤῥήσεις, ἀλλὰ τοῖς εἰδώλοις δουλεύοντες, ὄψονται διὰ τῶν κηρύκων τῆς ἀληθείας τοῦ κηρυττομένου τὸ κράτος καὶ γνώσονται αὐτοῦ τὴν δύναμιν. Jerome "Principes seculi, qui non habuerunt legem et prophetas, et quibus de eo non fuerit nuntiatum, ipsi videbunt et intelligent. In quorum comparatione Judaeorum duritia reprehenditur, qui videntes et audientes Jesaiae in se vaticinium compleverunt Similarly Calvin: "Judaei aliquid audierant de Christo ex lege et prophetis, sed gentibus penitus ignotus erat Unde sequitur, haec verba proprie ad gentes pertinere" Of the two possible explanations. "those, to whom it had not been declared, have seen it, etc" and "that which had not been declared to them, they have seen," the latter, which was adopted by all the old translators, except the LXX, is clearly to be preferred The LXX, and after them Paul, Rom 15. 21 οἷς οὐκ

ἀνηγγέλη περὶ αὐτοῦ, ὄψονται, καὶ οἳ οὐκ ἀκηκόασι, συνήσουσι. The verb ראה *to see*, often means *to perceive, to experience in general*, whether by any other sense than that of the sight, or by the mind. Comp. e. g Jer. 24 "Hast thou not seen, what this people says." Eccl. 1· 16 . "My heart has seen much wisdom and knowledge"

Isaiah 53:1.

Before the prophet, in continuation of v. 13—15 of the foregoing chapter, begins the representation of the vicarious sufferings of the Messiah, he laments over the unbelief of a large portion of mankind, occasioned by his deep humiliation; and (as v. d Palm justly remarks) especially of the Jews, since the believing submission of a great part of the Gentiles had already been foretold in the preceding verse. Calvin happily exhibits the sense: "Propheta hic veluti in medio orationis cursu resistit. Si quidem cum antea nomen Christi ubique promulgandum atque ignotis gentibus patefaciendum esse diceret interea vero tam humile futurum, ut haec fabulosa videri possent, abrumpit sermonem suum, atque exclamat neminem ista crediturum. Simul dolorem suum exprimit, quod tam increduli sint homines, ut salutem suam rejiciant — — Nec tantum de se uno loquitur, sed veluti is, qui sustinet personam omnium doctorum — Neque sui temporis homines tantum comprehendit Jesaias, sed posteros omnes, usque ad finem mundi. nam quamdiu exstabit Christi regnum, hoc impleri necesse erit Quamobrem fideles adversus tale scandalum, hoc testimonio muniri debent" "Who believes our report, and the arm of Jehovah, to whom is it revealed?" The prophet is indeed the speaker, but he includes with himself all the heralds of the Messiah. It is not necessary to suppose with Jerome, v d Palm, and others, that he includes merely his fellow prophets, who had predicted the *future* Redeemer, since the prophet must easily foresee that the same causes would also hinder the general success of the message concerning the *manifested* Messiah, and he might therefore include those who should proclaim it The verse is referred to the latter, John 12 38. Rom 10 36. The question does not imply an entire negation, but only expresses astonishment at the small number of believers; or rather, the prophet, whose spiritual eye rests upon the great multitude of the unbelievers, overlooks, for the moment, the other side, and in his grief, expresses that as *general*, which is applicable only to a *large part*. The word שְׁמֻעָה properly as fem. part pass. *that which is heard*, and then as a noun: *the discourse*; so chap. 28: 19 and also the Greek ἀκοή Rom 10 16. Gal 3. 2 1 Thess 2 13 According to this interpretation, the suffix is to be taken actively. So the Chaldee מַן הֵימִן לִבְסוֹרְתָנָא "who believes our annunciation?" Several, as Martini, Jahn, and Rosenmuller take the suffix passively. "what we hear." Martini appealing to Num 24. 4. Is. 21 10 25. 22. Hab 3. 2, supposes it to mean: "that which is revealed to us from God" Jahn translates "quod a nobis auditur fere incredibile est" He proceeds upon the supposition, that the speakers in this verse must be the same as those in the following, and that there is no reason to suppose that in this verse the publishers of the message come forward, but in the following, those to whom it is announced. But this reason is not sufficient, since according to our interpretation also, there is no proper change of persons, but in both verses the prophet speaks; only with this difference, that in the first verse he reckons himself among those who announce the message, and in the second verse with that portion of the people who had learned from the glorification of the Messiah, the true import of his sufferings. The arm, as the seat of power, frequently signifies power itself Jer. 17: 5 Job 22. 8 2 Chron 32. 8 The arm of Jehovah is therefore, a designation of the divine omnipotence. Chap 59 16. Deut 4 34 5 15 26. 8 This then is the sense of the second member who rightly perceives the glorious manifestations of the omnipotence of God, which will be exhibited in the sending of the Messiah? Martini: "quae pro virtute sua omnipotenti, incomprehensibili illa, neque ingenio humano penetranda olim perfecturus est Jehovah, quis demum intelligat?" The omnipotence of God is manifest to him, who believes the message concerning the Messiah; for his mission itself, the miracles he wrought, his resurrection and glorification, are the greatest demonstrations of the divine omnipotence. On the contrary, unbelief in Christ proceeds from a doubt of the omnipotence of God, since the unbeliever will not admit the interposition of a supernatural cause It is somewhat differently explained by Jahn, with closer adherence to the figure, but with less strength: "Cui brachium operantis revelatur, is conspicit operantem et cognoscit, cujus sit opus. Sensus itaque est, quis perspicit esse opus Jehovae." That the verb גָּלָה which is always elsewhere connected with אֶל and לְ should here be joined with עַל seems not to be without reason. It appears thereby to be intimated, that the revelations must come *from above*. In order to show to what forced interpretations of particular parts, the non-Messianic interpreters are obliged to resort, we here introduce Rosenmuller's exposition of the whole verse. According to his hypothesis, that the Gentiles are here introduced as speaking, he paraphrases the first member thus: had we merely heard, and not seen it, no one of us would have believed it, and thus he supplies an ellipsis, of which there is not the slightest intimation in the text. After to whom is the arm of Jehovah revealed, he arbitrarily supplies כְּמוֹ עָלֵינוּ and paraphrases: "cui tale Jovanae potentiae documentum unquam innotuit, quale nos jam videmus in admiranda hac populi Hebraei vicissitudine?"

V. 2. According to v. d. Palm, the prophet, v. 1, censures the unbelief of the Jews. Then, v. 2 and 3, the Jews are introduced as speaking, and giving the reasons why they could not receive this Redeemer. In the first half of the 4th verse the prophet removes these doubts. The second half contains the answer of the Jews. From v. 5 the prophet continues to speak without interruption. But there is no sufficient ground in the text for the assumption of such a change of person. It is on the contrary manifest, that the persons, who say, v. 4, that the servant of Jehovah has borne their diseases and pains, are the same, who say they have esteemed him as one smitten of God. It is much more simple to assume that, v. 4, etc. the prophet speaks, including with himself the better portion of the people. These, having now attained to knowledge and faith, here give the cause of their former unbelief. They had expected a Redeemer to come in all outward splendor and glory, as a victorious king; and now instead of this they see him poor, afflicted, abased, suffering, abused. "He grew up before him as a shoot, as a root-sprout out of dry ground; he had no form nor beauty that we should look upon him, no comely appearance, that we should desire him." This verse refers to the humble condition of the Messiah before his sufferings. The words מֵאֶרֶץ צִיָּה in the second member must also be supplied in the first. The word יוֹנֵק properly *suckling*, then as also the fem. יוֹנֶקֶת metaphorically, *a sprout*: "qui succo radicis, quasi lacte alitur." Many interpreters refer the suffix in לְפָנָיו to the people. So J. H. Michaelis in den bibl. Hal.: "coram illo populo superbo et incredulo, opinione regni mundani, quod Messias erigere deberet, fascinati, ut brachium dei in Christo exertum, non videat nec agnoscat." But this is unnatural, since עַם does not precede. It must of necessity relate to the immediately foregoing יְהֹוָה. *Before Jehovah*, that is, observed by Jehovah · known to him although unknown to the world. The prophet thereby incidentally points to the cause of his humiliation. The word לִפְנֵי sometimes means *before*, with the accessory idea of provident care, comp Job 8 16, he is green before the sun shine, for *sole adjuvante*. So Martini. "praesente h. e moderante atque gubernante Jehovah, ἐνώπιον τοῦ Θεοῦ" The word שֹׁרֶשׁ, *root*, here designates, as in chap 11 10, by Synecdoche, the stem or shoot that springs from the root. A shoot that springs up in a dry soil is insignificant and puny This comparison appears to allude to the origin of the Messiah from a family, which had once resembled a lofty tree in height and glory, but was now sunk in abasement See chap. 11: 1, where the Messiah is called a sprout from the root of Jesse. As the Messiah is here, in reference to his state of humiliation, compared to a weak and insignificant sprout, so in Ez 17· 23, in reference to his state of glorification, he is compared to a lofty and splendid cedar, under which all the fowls of heaven shall dwell The Jews expected that he should thus appear even from the very first, and because they were disappointed, they despised him. תֹּאַר *form*, and מַרְאֶה *appearance*, for *beautiful form*, and *beautiful appearance*. Comp 1 Sam 16: 18 אִישׁ תֹּאַר *a man of form*, for a handsome man. The וְ before וּמַרְאֵהוּ and וְנֶחְמְדֵהוּ is in both instances to be translated, *that*. Appositely Symmachus: οὐκ εἶδος αὐτῷ οὐδὲ ἀξίωμα, ἵνα εἴδωμεν αὐτόν, οὐδὲ θεωρία, ἵνα ἐπιθυμηθῶμεν αὐτόν. Several interpreters, as J H. Michaelis, regard both members as interrogations, in which the Jews would justify themselves for rejecting the Messiah. "He had no form; and should we look upon him? no beauty, and should we desire him?" They appeal to passages like chap. 37: 1—11. 1 Sam. 35: 11, where likewise וְ is followed by a question. But as the speakers had already attained to faith in the Messiah, and were now only giving the reason of their *former* unbelief, such an impassioned question is unsuitable to their character. The verb רָאָה *to look upon, to regard as worthy of attention*. It is emphatic in like manner also in Arabic رأى, and in Syriac ܚܙܐ. The verb רָאָה has the sense *videre cum delectatione*, only when it is construed with בְּ. What is said of the form, and the beauty of the Messiah is not so much to be referred to his person, as to his whole appearance

ISAIAH 53·3.   511

in his state of abasement. Calvin: "Non solum de Christi persona haec intelligi debent, qui mundo contemptibilis et ignominiosae tandem morti adjudicatus est, sed de toto regno, cujus nulla in oculis hominum forma, nullus decor, nulla magnificentia fuit." The history of its founder is repeated in the history of the Church. As in the one case, so in the other, the way to glory and joy is through humiliation and suffering.

V. 3 "He was despised, and the most abject of all men, a man of sorrows and familiar with disease; he was as one one before whom a man covers the face; we despised him and esteemed him not." From the humble condition of the Messiah in general, the prophet proceeds to his sufferings. חֲדַל אִישִׁים is translated by some interpreters *forsaken of men*. They refer to Job 19 14. where the verb חָדַל is spoken of friends who forsake the unfortunate. But according to this interpretation חֲדַל must be passive, though it is elsewhere always active. But besides, Martini forcibly objects to this. "Sic vis sermonis, quae augeri debebat, imminueretur, contra morem Hebraeorum poetarum, qui ita verba synonyma conjungere amant, ut posterius priori paulo sit gravius." The weakness of the sense must also strike every one. According to Martini and several others, חָדֵל signifies *small, contemned, despised*. אִישִׁים belongs, they suppose, as well to נִבְזֶה as to חֲדַל, and thus serves to express the superlative, the despised and contemned of men, for the most despised and the most contemned among *all men*. Comp Ps 22 7 Prov 15: 20 Gesenius Lehrg. p. 692. b But חָדֵל never occurs in the alleged sense. It is safest to compare Ps 39 5, "Lord teach me to know the number of my days, let me know מֶה חָדֵל אָנִי when I shall cease," scil. to suffer and to live. חָדֵל, therefore, is one who ceases to do, or to be, any thing. חֲדַל אִישִׁים "he who ceases of men," i. e. who ceases to be a man, or to belong to the number of men, i. q. the most abject of all men; so that this interpretation, as to the sense, though not grammatically, corresponds with that of Martini. It is confirmed by chap 52 14 and the passages there quoted. It is also found in Abenezra, who paraphrases חדל להח ב עם אנשים "desiit hominibus accenseri," and in most of the ancient versions. Thus the Alex τὸ εἶδος αὐτοῦ ἄτιμον καὶ ἐκλεῖπον παρὰ τοὺς υἱοὺς τῶν ἀνθρώπων. Symm.: ἐλάχιστος ἀνδρῶν. The Vulgate: novissimus virorum. Syriac: ܘܢܓܒܐ ܣܒܐܒܕ ·— אִישׁ מַכְאֹבוֹת "the man of sorrows," he who has sorrows, as it were, for his possession. So Rev. 29: 1 אִישׁ תּוּכָחוֹת "a man of chastisements," one who is frequently chastised, who possesses, as it were, chastisements as his property. Symm ἀνὴρ ἐπίπονος. Most interpreters explain יְדוּעַ חֹלִי by *known, distinguished by disease,* for, afflicted by it in a remarkable manner. Martini. "exemplum sive monimentum insigne hominis ignominia injuriisque affecti." So among the old translators, Symm.: γνωστὸς νόσῳ. But there is another interpretation far more suitable, and more in accordance with the parallelism . *one known to disease,* i. q a confidant of disease—one who has formed, as it were, the bond of friendship with it , corresponding to "the man of sorrows." יָדוּעַ is then taken altogether in its usual acceptation (See Deut. 1 13—15, likewise the Part. Pu. Job 19 14.) Thus it is explained by the old translators, who have been erroneously supposed to have read the active instead of the passive participle. Alex.: εἰδὼς φέρειν μαλακίαν. Vulgate. sciens infirmitatem. Syriac : ܝܕܥ ܟܐܒܐ . They only resolve the personification of disease, which lies at the foundation. Since the Part. Pa. can here be taken in its proper meaning, there is no occasion to urge, that it is often used for the Part. Act. e. g. אֲחֻזֵי *tenentes* Cant. 3 8 בָּטוּחַ *confidens* Ps. 112. 7. זָכוּר *recordans* Ps 103 14. (See the examples in Michaelis, Lumina Syriaca § 26) The word חֹלִי, here on account of the accent with Hholem, otherwise חֳלִי, is spoken not merely of a disease, arising from the usual natural causes, but also of wounds. See 1 K. 22 34 Jer. 6 7 10: 19. It might therefore here also signify wounds. Comp. v 5. מְחֹלָל *pierced through* But it is better to suppose that disease, here and in the following verse, is a figurative designation of severe sufferings of body and of soul. Thus it often occurs, e g. Is 1 4—6 Ez. 33: 10 Ps 103 3. It is not without reason that Koppe and Ammon conjecture, that the image is taken particularly from the leprosy, which was not only one of the most terrible diseases, but was also, in a special manner, regarded as a divine punishment. Hence many expressions in the following verses are explained. The words וּכְמַסְתֵּר פָּנִים מִמֶּנּוּ are interpreted in different ways מַסְתֵּר is best taken as a substantive, formed from the Part in Hiphil (Ges. Lehrg. p 496) in the sense of *hiding, concealment*: "he was as a hiding of the face before it," i. e. as a thing or person before whom a man covers his face, because he cannot bear the disgusting sight. The suffix in מִמֶּנּוּ then refers not to the servant of God, but to the thing compared. Martini adopts this explanation, only he connects, at the same time, the clause with the following. "Sicuti rem, a qua faciem avertunt, ita cum fastidio eum sprevimus." Most interpreters take מַסְתֵּר as Part. in Hiph. for מַסְתִּיר. But in opposition to this it must be remarked, that this form with Tseri never occurs in the Sing. masc. though sometimes in the Sing. fem and often in the plural, a usage, however, mostly confined to the later idiom, which inclines to the Aramaean. See Gesen Lehr. § 94. 8. The words are then explained in various ways. 1. Some translate: "he was as one who hides his face before us," so that the suffix in מִמֶּנּוּ will not be the suff of the third Sing but of the first pers. Plur So the LXX, Vulgate, Chaldee, Aquila, Jarchi, v. d. Palm, Jahn. Those who adopt this explanation, find here an allusion either to the Mosaic law, which requires the lepers to cover their faces, Lev 3 45, or to the custom of covering the face in mourning, 2 Sam 15· 30. Ez. 14 17; or to the covering of the face for shame, Mic. 3 7. But this interpretation gives a feeble sense. Besides, the object of the whole passage is to show, not how the servant of God will demean himself, but how he will be regarded and treated by men 2. Others suppose that the expression is elliptical for כַּאֲשֶׁר מָמֶנּוּ מַסְתֵּר פָּנִים " as one before whom he is covering the face," i e. before whom a man covers the face So Gesenius But it would be difficult to justify this forced interpretation, on philological grounds. 3. Others: "he was as one causing to conceal the face," i e he induced others to cover up their faces before him; the view of his sufferings was so terrible, that those who saw him covered the face So among others Rosenmuller, who avails himself of the words of J. H Michaelis, only with the modification that he understands as neuter the alleged participle מַסְתֵּר · " quod facit, ut alii abscondant faciem = sicuti res tam foeda et abominanda, ut homines eam adspicere dedignati faciem tegant et avertant." This interpretation deserves indeed the preference among those which regard נִסְתָּר as a participle. But still it is inconsistent with the fact, that the verb סָתַר in Hiphil, never means *to cause to conceal*, but only *to conceal*, and that particularly the phrase הִסְתִּיר פָּנִים often occurs in the sense *to hide or cover the face*, but never otherwise נִבְזֶה can be taken either as a participle in Niphal, as in the beginning of the verse, so Aq Symm Theod · ἐξουδενωμένος, διὸ οὐκ ἐλογισάμεθα αὐτόν. LXX : ἠτιμάσθη, or as 1 Fut. Kal Thus the Syriac ܘܣܢܝܢܐ. The words לֹא חֲשַׁבְנֻהוּ can be translated either "we esteemed him not," or "we esteemed him as nothing." It is customary in the Hebrew to express the same thing first positively, and then again negatively, for the sake of greater energy.

V. 4. Those, who have attained to faith in the Messiah, confess in this verse, that they have greatly erred in despising the servant of God on account of his humiliation and suffering —"But he bare our sickness, and took our pains upon himself, and we esteemed him as one afflicted of God, smitten and tormented of God." The sense he, from whom we turned away with horror, because we inferred from his sufferings some great crime of his own, for the punishment of which they had been inflicted by God, bore the punishment not of his own sins, but of ours. The very thing which gave offence to us, not only belonged to the work which God had committed to him, but constituted its most important part. אָכֵן *particula adversativa: verum, ast.* In the words *he bore*, etc., the metaphor is taken from an appressive burden, which one removes from the shoulders of another, and places on his own. *Our sickness, our pains*, for the sickness which we should have suffered,—the pains which we should have endured. Diseases and pains are an image of the outward and inward sufferings, which the Messiah should undergo in our stead, and thereby deliver us from the punishment of our sins. חֳלָיֵנוּ is the plural of חֳלָיִים with the suff. and would properly be written *plene* חֳלָיֵינוּ.—נָשָׂא some would translate: *abstulit, removit*, but in opposition to the whole context, and the parallelism with סָבַל. The members are entirely synonymous, and only differ in words. Moreover, the verb נָשָׂא in connexion with sin, elsewhere means to bear it, or the punishment of it; see Ez. 18: 19 לֹא נָשָׂא הַבֵּן בַּעֲוֹן הָאָב, *the son shall not bear the sin of the father.* Num. 14: 33. Lev. 5: 1. 20: 17. Alex. φέρει Symm. ἀνέλαβε.—Matt. 8: 17 cites these words, after having related that Christ had delivered men from their bodily infirmities. Recent interpreters have hence erroneously concluded that Matthew has by no means referred the passage to the vicarious sufferings of Christ. But Matthew was certainly far from intending by this special reference, to set aside the principal one. Christ was sent for the general purpose of removing by the sacrifice of himself, the evil which sin had brought into the world. This work he commenced, when he cured bodily diseases. Thereby he pointed to his chief calling, to the spiritual evils of men to be removed by him, with the same power, through his vicarious satisfaction. Calvin: "Matthaeus hoc vaticinium citat, postquam retulit Christum varios morbos curasse, cum tamen certum sit, ipsum non curandis corporibus, sed animis potius destinatum esse. Nam de spiritualibus languoribus intelligit propheta. Sed in miraculis, quae sanandis corporibus edidit Christus, specimen praebuit salutis, quam animis nostris affert, ideoque Matthaeus ad symbolum transfert, quod ipsi rei et veritati conveniebat." That Matthew had no intention of denying the spiritual import of the passage, appears from chap. 20:28: ἦλθε δοῦναι τὴν ψυχὴν αὐτοῦ λύτρον ἀντὶ πολλῶν. Comp. v. 10. The word נָגוּעַ conveys of itself the subordinate idea, *to be smitten of God*, and there is no occasion to supply אֱלֹהִים from the following member. Ps. 73:14. Thus the leprosy which was regarded as a punishment from God, was called κατ' ἐξοχὴν נֶגַע. Several interpreters, as Jerome, would explain נָגוּעַ directly by *leprosus*. Such was the interpretation of the ancient Jews, who derived from this passage the opinion, that the Messiah would be afflicted with the leprosy. Comp. the Talmudic tract Sanhedrin chap. XI, and the book Jalkut on Isaiah, chap. LX. But there is no ground for this specific application. Theodoret aptly translates: μεμαστιγωμένος, *afflicted with severe sufferings*, the same as πληγεὶς θεοῦ μάστιγι by Aeschyl. in the Sept. adv. Thebas; comp. Sirach 30:14; 40:9. Luke 7:21, and examples in Martini on the passage, out of the Arabic writers, who, in like manner, regard sufferings as lashes inflicted by God. In the words מֻכֵּה אֱלֹהִים *one smitten of God*, the genitive designates, as it often does, the efficient cause. The form מֻכֵּה is the con. stat.; the absol. stat. is written מֻכֶּה. This is found in some manuscripts, and was formerly favored by several Roman Catholic critics (Bellarminus de Verb. d. l. II c. 2, Galatinus and others) from doctrinal views, because the passage would then afford a testimony to the deity of the Messiah, (a smitten God). The verb נָכָה is used in general of divine punishment, but especially of the infliction of diseases. Num. 14:12. Deut. 28:22. After all the three words we must supply on account of his own sins. For it was true, that the sufferings of the Messiah were inflicted by God; the mistake was only in reference to their design. To infer great guilt from great suffering was very customary with the Hebrews. It arose from a misconception of the theocratic doctrine of retribution. They erroneously extended the law of visible retribution, by which the fate of the covenant people was always determined, to individuals, not reflecting, that God according to his wise and holy purposes can inflict suffering on the pious, even without the previous commission of crime.

V. 5. "And he was pierced for our misdeeds and bruised for

our sins, the punishment was laid on him, that we might have peace, and by his wounds we are healed." The prophet here again includes himself, not merely by a rhetorical figure, but in the consciousness of his sinfulness and need of redemption. מְחֹלָל is a Partic. Po. from חָלַל *to wound, to pierce.* מִן signifies *on account of.* By the verb דָּכָא *to crush,* the most severe inward and outward sufferings are figuratively designated. Suitably the LXX μεμαλάκισται. Aq συνετρίβη. מוּסַר שְׁלוֹמֵנוּ properly *the punishment of our peace,* i. e. the punishment whereby peace, salvation, and happiness were procured for us—our reconciliation with God effected. The word מוּסָר stands also in other places for chastisement by *words,* but here the whole context, in which severe sufferings are the subject of discourse, as well as the parallelism, requires it to be understood of chastisement by *deed.* This also appears from עָלָיו which indicates that the punishment lay as an oppressive burden upon him who made atonement. The interpretation of a certain theological school, therefore, is wholly inadmissible, which, in order to remove from the passage, the doctrine of Christ's vicarious satisfaction, translates: "the instruction of our peace (how we can be again reconciled to God) is in him." Comp. Hasenkamp, Briefe über wichtige Wahrheiten der Rel. Duisburg 1794. 2ter Th. p. 161 seq. The word מוּסָר has moreover the subordinate idea of a punishment, which may serve as a warning to others. חַבֻּרָה *wound, stripe,* here stands collectively נִרְפָּא is the pret. Niph therefore properly: *it is healed to us,* or *healing has happened to us.* The construction arises from a certain modification of the idea conveyed by the verb רָפָא *to heal,* i. e. to impart healing. In a similar manner we may also explain the construction, v. 11, of הִצְדִּיק with לְ *to justify,* i. e. to impart righteousness. As the punishment of sin and suffering are often represented under the image of a disease, so is deliverance from them under that of healing.

V. 6. The cause is given which moved the Messiah to undergo such severe sufferings, viz the wretchedness of mankind who were alienated from God, but whom God would reconcile to himself by his sufferings. "We all were going astray like sheep, we turned every one to our own way; but Jehovah cast upon him the sin of us all." Calvin: "Ut melius infigat animis hominum beneficium mortis Christi, ostendit, quam necessaria sit ista sanatio, cujus prius mentionem fecit.—Est hic elegans antithesis. Nam in nobis dissipati sumus, in Christo collecti; aberramus natura atque in exitium praecipites agimur, in Christo viam reperimus, qua ad salutis portam ducamur, obruunt nos scelera nostra, at transferuntur in Christum, a quo exoneramur." Under the figure of sheep without a shepherd, who are exposed without defence to all dangers, the prophet represents the miserable state of mankind estranged from God, and sunk in sin and error. Theodoret Οὔτε γὰρ ἴσα πάντων τὰ πλημμελήματα, οὐδὲ εἷς ὁ τρόπος, ἄλλα γὰρ τὰ Αἰγυπτίων εἴδωλα καὶ ἄλλα τὰ Φοινίκων, καὶ τὰ Ἑλλήνων ἕτερα καὶ ἄλλα τῶν Σκυθῶν ἀλλ' ὅμως, εἰ καὶ διάφοροι τῆς πλάνης οἱ τρόποι, πάντες ὁμοίως τὸν ὄντα θεὸν καταλελοιπότες, ἐῴκειμεν προβάτοις πλανωμένοις καὶ προκειμένοις τοῖς λύκοις.—כַּצֹּאן (contracted from כהצאן) properly not: as *a* flock, but as *the* flock. The article is not here superfluous, as it might seem It is employed, among other uses, "when only individuals of a species are spoken of; but such individuals as are clearly understood by the hearer to be definite in that species, from the circumstances of the discourse and connexion of the words" Ewald Grammatik p 567 We were going astray like the flock, i. e. we wandered like the flock, e. g. a wandering flock, a flock which has no shepherd This import of the article, was observed even by Kimchi Comp 1 Pet. 2 25. ἦτε γὰρ ὡς πρόβατα πλανώμενα. In general the image of sheep without a shepherd is frequently employed to exhibit, at one time the moral debasement; at another, the wretchedness of men estranged from God. See Ez. 34 5 Matt 9 36. —" We turned every one, etc." As a lonely wanderer pursues his way in sadness, and exposed to manifold dangers, so were we proceeding through life alone, neither guided by God, nor united with brethren by his love Augusti says, Exeg. Handbuch: "each one acted and lived only for himself, not for a common object, there was no public spirit." His remarks are just, if taken in a deeper sense. It is only the common bond of union with God, which can unite all; without this there is only caprice, self-will and discord. The verb פָּגַע with בְּ imports, sometimes in general to strike against any one, to hit him; sometimes to thrust at any one in a hostile manner, to assault him According to Kimchi and others, the punishment is here represented as an assaulting enemy, they take the word in the latter sense, and translate *hostiliter in eum irruere jussit*. Still we may very well abide by the general meaning, *he caused to light on him.* The sense: Jehovah caused him alone to bear the sufferings, which we should have borne as a punishment for our sins. So Symm: κύριος δὲ καταντῆσαι ἐποίησεν εἰς αὐτὸν τὴν ἀνομίαν πάντων ἡμῶν. Vulg.: "posuit in eo iniquitatem omnium nostrum." The עָוֹן here, as it often does, includes also the punishment of sin. The view of the Hebrews respecting the close connexion of sin and punishment, virtue and prosperity, is plainly stamped on the language, and the two ideas are often expressed by the same words.

V. 7. The prophet had commenced, v. 2, the description of the sufferings of the Messiah, v. 4—6, he had digressed, in order to assign the causes of these severe sufferings. He now resumes the description, and sets before us in this verse the perfect meekness and patience of the great servant of God in his distress. "He was abused, but he suffered patiently and opened not his mouth; as a lamb which is brought to the slaughter, and as a sheep which becomes dumb before its shearers, he opened not his mouth." The words נִגַּשׂ וְהוּא נַעֲנֶה are variously explained. The verb נָגַשׂ has commonly the meaning *to push, to drive*, and is employed especially to denote the rigid prosecution of claims for debt. The former more general sense is adopted by v. d. Palm and the anonymous writer in Bibliothek v. Theol. Letterkunde. According to them the word נִגַּשׂ imports "he was demanded," and they translate: "they (the Jewish people) unanimously demanded his death, and behold he suffered!" But, in opposition to this, it is to be observed, that the verb נָגַשׂ never occurs precisely in the sense *to demand*, which is different from *to push, to drive*. Others suppose there is an allusion to the special use of the word to denote the exaction of a debt. God, who punishes the sins of men in the Messiah, appears as a creditor who exacts his debt. Thus Hensler: "God demands the debt, and he, the great and righteous one, suffers." Kuinol and Jahn: "ille exactionem sustinuit v. solutio iniquitatum ab eo exacta fuit." This interpretation has certainly much to recommend it, nor is the objection of Martini valid, that the metaphorical meaning of the verb cannot be justified; for the punishment of sin is very commonly represented under the image of an exaction of debt. (Comp. Ausl zu Matt 6 12 Luke 13: 4. Buxtorf, Lex Chald s v. חַיָּב and הוֹב.) But still another interpretation, adopted by Martini, Gesenius, and others, seems to deserve the preference, according to which the verb נָגַשׂ is taken in the sense *to abuse, to afflict*. The Part. נוֹגֵשׂ is frequently used to denote those who abuse and afflict others. Even the praeter in Niph occurs in a similar sense, 1 Sam 14 24 וְאִישׁ יִשְׂרָאֵל נִגַּשׂ בַּיּוֹם הַהוּא *Israëlitae afflicti erant illo die.*—The interpreters find a difficulty in וְהוּא. Gesenius translates: "he was abused, who was be-

ISAIAH 53 7, 8.   519

sides afflicted." וְהוּא then answers to the Latin *isque*; נַעֲנֶה will refer to the usual sorrowful condition, and נִגַּשׂ to the additional ill treatment · "Already afflicted by disease and suffering, men oppressed him still." But it is difficult to establish the supposed difference between עָנָה and נָגַשׂ. עָנָה also denotes great ill treatment. Comp e g Gen 16: 6. Exod 22. 22. Ps. 105 18. The sense is far more appropriate if we translate, with Jahn and Steudel, "idem tamen vexari se patiebatur." Symmachus gives this meaning. προσηνέχθη καὶ αὐτὸς ὑπήκουσε, as also the Vulgate · "oblatus est, quia ipse voluit." The verb עָנָה in Niphal has, in accordance with this, the accessory idea of *patient suffering*, which is found also in the adjectives עָנִי and עָנָו. Besides, the conjugation Niph in general has often a reflexive sense. Thus v. 12 נִמְנָה *to be numbered*, with the accessory idea of causing one's self to be numbered. Ewald (Gramm. p 191) regards the reflexive signification in Niph as the original one, but this may with reason be doubted. But what especially favors the interpretation is, that then the patience of the Messiah in this sentence, as well as the whole verse, is described. After כַּשֶּׂה the relative אֲשֶׁר is to be supplied. Comp. Jer 11 19, "I was as a lamb that is led to the slaughter."—The second member וְלֹא יִפְתַּח פִּיו Gesenius, after Luther, refers to the lamb. But this cannot well be done, since יִפְתַּח does not agree with the feminine רָחֵל, and must therefore be referred to the more distant שֶׂה. Such a repetition has moreover a peculiar charm, and frequently occurs. Thus Judg 5 16, the words בִּפְלַגּוֹת רְאוּבֵן גְּדוֹלִים חִקְרֵי לֵב are repeated, and indeed in such a manner as to give a certain emphasis to the discourse. With just such an emphasis the phrase יְצוּעִי עָלָה occurs in Gen 49 4. In the second part of Isaiah also, such repetitions many times occur. In general, repetition in Hebrew serves for emphasis, and to give prominence to a thought. (Comp Ewald l c. p 636.) The LXX also refer it to the servant of God · οὕτως οὐκ ἀνοίγει τὸ στόμα. With reference to this verse, John the Baptist calls Christ (John 1·29) the lamb of God Comp 1 Pet 1. 18, 19 Acts 8 32, 35. In harmony with it in sense is 1 Pet 2 23, ὃς λοιδορούμενος οὐκ ἀντελοιδόρει, πάσχων οὐκ ἠπείλει, παρεδίδου δὲ τῷ κρίνοντι δικαίως. Christ opened indeed his mouth, but not to threaten, not to revile, but only to promote the honor of God, to bear testimony to his love, to pray for his enemies

V 8 The sense: a violent death was the termination of the sufferings which he assumed on account of the sins of the people.—
"By oppression and a judicial sentence he was dragged to punish-

ment (but who can declare his posterity?) he was taken away out of the land of the living for the sin of my people, upon whom the punishment should have fallen." The word עֹצֶר properly *confinement*, then *violent oppression*. מִשְׁפָּט *judgment, judicial decision*, then rendered more definite by the connexion, sentence of punishment (Jer 1. 16. 2 Kings 25 6) and punishment itself. (Deut. 21 22. Ez. 5: 8 Jer 48. 1). The word has never the precise meaning *suffering*, attributed to it by Gesenius It is most correct with several interpreters (Doderlein, Kuinöl, etc.) to regard oppression and judgment here as a Hendiadys for, an oppressive, unrighteous, judicial proceeding So 1 Kings 19· 12, *silence and a voice*, for a low voice. Jer. 29 11, *futurity and hope*, for a hopeful futurity. Comp. Gesen Lehrg. p. 854 The verb לָקַח occurs of a violent leading away to punishment, 1 Kings 20 33 Prov. 24. 11, of a violent taking away in general, Ez 22 25. Similar words are also used in Arabic of a violent leading away to death or imprisonment Comp the examples in Martini p 79. לָקַח therefore means *he was dragged to punishment*. "Judicii violentia ad supplicium rapitur" Doderlein, Dathe But still with Rosenmuller and others we may translate: *he was taken away*; namely out of the land of the living, as it is said in the second hemistich. Comp. Ez 33: 4, 6. This interpretation is certainly more favored by the parallelism, than the former. The older interpreters for the most part refer these words to the glorification. They take מִן not as causative, but in the sense *out of*, and translate the verb לָקַח either by: *to rescue, to deliver*, or by *to take up, to take away*, namely to God. So the Vulg "de angustia et judicio sublatus est Jerome on the passage says: de tribulatione atque judicio ad patrem victor ascendit." Joh H Michaelis: "exemtus et ad dextram majestatis assumtus est" Entirely similar is the explanation of Gesenius: from his distress death finally delivered him; borrowed from Martini, who paraphrases: "exantlatis cruciatibus et diris animam efflavit" But this interpretation has the whole context against it. The words must then refer to the better condition of the Messiah, the description of which does not commence till v. 10. That they must signify a violent death is evident from v. 9, where it is said that the ungodly, not satisfied with his murder, attempted to abuse him even in death To this we are led also by the expression itself. For although the verb לָקַח is indeed in some passages used also of a merely natural death, yet on account of the parallelism: "he was taken away out of the land of the living;" it can

ISAIAH 53.8

here refer only to a violent death, or to a proceeding which had caused such a death. מן therefore as in the word מֵעֹצֶר and in several places in this portion, e g v. 5, must here denote the *causa efficiens*. The following words are of difficult interpretation וְאֶת דּוֹרוֹ מִי יְשׂוֹחֵחַ. The verb שׂוּחַ or שִׂיחַ has 1 the meaning *to reflect*, and 2 *to relate, announce* The most common interpretations are the following 1 Several (Luther, Calvin, Vitringa, etc) translate. " who will declare the length of his life ?" i. e. who is able to determine the duration of his future life ? To this we cannot object with several, that the prophet would here anticipate himself, since the prediction of the glorification commences at v 10. For according to every interpretation the words stand out of the connexion, and contain an incidental thought to be placed in a parenthesis. But more weight is due to the remark, that the word דּוֹר never occurs in the sense of *length of life* 2. After Storr, others (Doderlein, Dathe, Martini, Rosenmuller, Gesenius) translate " who of his contemporaries will consider it," or " considered it ?" The אֶת דּוֹרוֹ is taken as the accus. absol = to the nom absol " quod attinet ad aequales ei homines " But in opposition to this we observe: a) " That אֵת can never designate the subject which would be directly contrary to its origin and import The places adduced in favor of it, rather point out אֶת according to the sense of the writer as a sign of the object, and what is certain and correct should be well distinguished from the few real deviations." Ewald Gramm p. 596 But granting that this assertion is not in its whole extent correct, (for even Ewald himself must admit that the later and less exact writers sometimes used אֵת as a designation of the subject), yet so much at least must be conceded, that in most places where אֵת is usually taken as a designation of the subject, it is in fact a designation of the object, whence it follows that it should not be taken so readily and without any urgent necessity as a designation of the subject b) This interpretation supposes an unnatural ellipsis " who of his contemporaries considers," scil. the cause of his death ? Gesenius, it is true, after Martini, seeks to obviate this by connecting these words with what follows : " who of his contemporaries considered that he was taken out of the land of the living, on account of the sin of my people." " Hominum istius aetatis quis est, qui ad animum revocet mortem adeo ipsam virum illum non propter sua ipsius crimina, sed propter populi mei scelera subiisse " But then the manifest parallelism between לֻקָּח and נִגְזַר מֵאֶרֶץ חַיִּים disappears 3 Lowth, v d. Palm and others translate: "who of all his contemporaries spoke?"=there was no man among all his contemporaries, who uttered a single word in his vindication. But the first objection urged against the foregoing explanation applies also, as well as others, to this. 4 Le Clerc translates: "Vitae ejus in his terris praestantiam, quis est qui pro dignitate laudare possit." But דוֹר is never used to signify the conduct, or manner of life. 5 Others, and this appears to be the best interpretation, translate: "who can express his posterity, the number of his descendants?" Thus the LXX: τὴν γενεὰν αὐτοῦ τίς διηγήσεται In like manner Kimchi: "quis dicturus esset ejus generationem tam magnam fore?" The prophet, as it were anticipating himself, points by an incidental remark, from the lowest humiliation to the glorification of the Messiah דוֹר race, frequently stands for posterity, e. g Lev. 23 43. For the sense we must compare the expression יִרְאֶה זֶרַע v. 10. It has been objected, that the verb שׂוּחַ when used for reflection and speaking, is connected with בְּ; but this objection is not valid; (comp what has been remarked on chap. 52· 15), especially as verbs entirely similar are construed both with ב and with the Accus A synonyme of שׂוּחַ is e. g הָגָה which in Ps. 77· 13 and Ps 143 5 stands in parallelism with it, and besides has nearly all its significations in common with it. (Comp. Gesenius s v. הָגָה). This verb is commonly construed with ב, but in Ps. 2: 1 and Is. 33 18, it occurs with the Accus. The particle כִּי does not here assign the cause but merely points out the connexion with the foregoing This usage is not uncommon, e g. 1 Sam 2 21 כִּי פָקַד יְהוָה אֶת חַנָּה "and Jehovah visited Hannah" Ezra 10 1. כִּי בָכוּ הָעָם "and the people wept." Comp Noldii concordant partic. p 395 Nr. 6. The verb נִגְזַר properly *to be cut off, to be destroyed*, never occurs, (not even in the passages Ps 88 6 and Lam 3 54 cited in favor of such a meaning) of a peaceful and natural, but always of a violent and premature death The metaphorical expression seems here to be used with reference to the foregoing image of a shoot —In the last member, Paulus, after the example of several older translators, erroneously supposes, on account of the word עַמִּי that here Jehovah must again speak. Jehovah is first introduced again as speaking in the 11th verse: "on account of the sins of my people," is not different from, "on account of our sins." The speaker does not place himself in opposition to his people, but includes himself among them The לָמוֹ poetic form for לָהֶם is to be referred to the collective עַם. Before נֶגַע the relative אֲשֶׁר is to be supplied thus: "on account of the sins of my people, to whom the punishment," scil. was destined, or belonged. Many other interpreters take the suff. in לָמוֹ as sing. and translate: "On account of the sin of my people, the punishment has fallen upon him." On the contrary Gesenius and Rosenmuller, after Abenezra and Abarbanel, maintain that לָמוֹ can never stand as singular; they translate: "for the sin of my people punishment is to *them*," and hence infer that the subject of the portion cannot be an individual, but must be a collective. But Jahn justly remarks in opposition to this: "nimis abruptus esset sermo, si in praecedentibus et subsequentibus in singulari numero compellaret dei servum, nunc in hac unica intermedia sententia subito verteretur in pluralem." But granting the assertion in respect to לָמוֹ to be correct, still no objection to the Messianic interpretation could be drawn from this passage, since, as Gesenius himself is obliged to concede, nothing can be said against the correctness of the first mentioned explanation, in accordance with which לָמוֹ is taken as plural. Finally the assertion itself is by no means true. "Although מוֹ is properly plural, yet it has gradually lost its etymology and its meaning, and is used, though seldom, for the masc. sing. also. This *misuse* of the word cannot be denied; it is in all probability singular, Job 20: 23. 27: 23, as appears from the whole context of 10 or 20 verses in which the singular is constantly employed. But this usage is certain, Is. 53: 8, where throughout only the singular appears; 44: 15 where the plural does not at all suit the sense, and the writer himself explains לָמוֹ in the same connexion by לוֹ; Ps 11: 7 where *his face* can refer only to God. Habak. 3: 4 explains לָמוֹ Deut. 33. 2 by לָּוֹ." Ewald Grammatik p 365. In the Ethiopic also the suff מוֹ which usually expresses the plural, is used for the sing. likewise, e. g. Luke 2: 4. John 19: 27. Acts 1: 20. Comp. Ludov de Dieu oratio de convitiis in Judaeos—ad calcem observat. miscellan. Leovard. 1714 p 56. The LXX translate לָמוֹ by εἰς θάνατον, probably because they regarded it as an abbreviation for לָמוּת. They have been improperly followed by several interpreters.

V. 9. "They appointed him his grave with the wicked, (but he was with a rich man after his death); although he had done nothing unrighteous, and there was no guile in his mouth." The sense: not satisfied with his sufferings and his death, they sought to insult him, the innocent and the righteous one, even in death, since they wished to bury his corpse among criminals. It is then incidentally remarked, that this object was not accomplished. Christ was buried by Joseph of Arimathea, who is here called עָשִׁיר, as in Matt 27 57 ἄνθρωπος πλούσιος. This interpretation, after the example of Cappell, has been defended by many commentators, especially by Pfeiffer (honor divitis Christo cum impiis sepeliendo in morte obtingens. ad Es. 53. 9, Erl 1762), Dathe (on Glassii philologia sacra t. 1, p 180), Jahn and v. d. Palm. It requires the verb נָתַן here to be taken in the sense *to appoint*, which it frequently receives through the connexion. Comp e. g chap. 55. 4. Gen. 15: 18, where the verb נָתַן designates the determination and purpose. Verbs have frequently an inchoative sense * *to give* i q *to wish to give*.† Abenezra says: והכתוב אמר ויתן על מחשבתו: *textus dicit: Et dedit scil. in cogitatione sua*. The word ויתן either stands impersonally: *he gave*, for *one gave*, comp. Ps 72 15 Eccles 2 21, or the subject must be supplied from the foregoing עַמִּי, *my people appointed*. Others supply Jehovah as subject. וַיִּתֵּן *he appointed* i q *he seemed to give*. "Et dedit sepulchrum ejus cum maleficis (ut videbatur fore), at u. s. w." The sense one would naturally think, that he, who died as a criminal, would receive the burial of a criminal. But there is much to be objected to this interpretation The אֶת before רְשָׁעִים is not a sign of the Accus. but a preposition, *cum* The objection of Rosenmuller is of little weight, that after the verb נָתַן this particle always serves as a designation of the accusative For the verb נָתַן stands here on a level with all other active verbs; but that they often have את after them in the sense, *cum*, appears from passages, such as Gen. 43 32. 15: 18 and many others, comp Iken on the passage. Criminals, רְשָׁעִים, received among the Hebrews a disgraceful burial. So says Josephus, Antiq l. IV c VIII § 6: ὁ δὲ βλασφημήσας θεον καταλευσθεὶς κρεμάσθω δι᾽ ἡμέρας, καὶ ἀτίμως καὶ ἀφανῶς θαπτέσθω. Maimonides in Iken, l. c "Interfecti a domo judicii nequaquam sepeliuntur in sepulchris majorum suorum, sed duo sepulchreta a domo judicii ordinata sunt pro iisdem, unum pro lapidatis et combustis, alterum pro decollatis atque strangulatis" As now the prophet had said in the foregoing verse that the Messiah would die a violent death, like a malefactor, so he here subjoins; that they had

---

* See examples in Iken on the passage in der bibl Hagana II, 2, p 245 Glassius philol S 1 III tract 3 can 7, 8

† Yet we may also translate with Iken 'they prepared for him the grave' The verb נתן frequently implies *facere ut quid sit* Comp the examples in Iken l c p 247 seq

ISAIAH 53.9

also appointed, or according to Iken, prepared for him a common interment with executed criminals. "Videt—he says—propheta, spiritu agitatus, eos, quibus cura haec incumbebat omni nisu jam occupatos, ut cuncta pararent, mortuumque servatorem inhoneste sepelirent, et quod videt lectoribus suis enarraturus ait: Pararant cum maleficis sepulchrum ejus. Quam vive, quam perspicue!' The ו in וְאֵת is adversative: but with a rich man in his death, *he was*, is to be supplied. The plural מוֹתִים instead of the sing. as Ez 28.8, 10. The case is the same in many other words. Thus Job 21.32· "He will be carried to the graves," i. e. to a grave. This usage is especially frequent in poetry. Examples are given by Gesenius Lehrg. p. 665. Ewald Gramm. p 326. After the example of Abarbanel and R. Lipmann, Paulus, Gesenius and Rosenmüller would prove from this plural, that the subject of the prophecy must be a collective. But then indeed we should have the plural of the suff. not of the noun. בְּמוֹתָיו we translate *after his death*; a meaning already required by the parallelism with קִבְרוֹ. בְ is taken in the sense of *afterwards*, as in Isaiah 16.14 (in three years, for after three years), Lev. 11:31 (every one who touches them in their death, for after they are dead). See numerous other examples in Noldius (concord part p 157 Nr. 20) and in Rosenmüller on the passage. And thus the objection to this interpretation, that Jesus was with criminals in his death, and with a rich man in his grave falls to the ground. עַל has the signification, *although*. Comp Job 16.17. עַל לֹא חָמָס בְּכַפַּי, "quamvis non sit injuria in manibus meis." 10.7. 34.6. Jer. 2.34. It does not refer to the second member standing in a parenthesis, but to the first. The greater part of those who follow this interpretation, take עַל in the sense, *because*, and refer it to the second member. But to this there are the following objections. 1. The second member is here appropriate only when taken as a parenthesis, in like manner as וְאֶת דּוֹרוֹ מִי יְשׂוֹחֵחַ in the foregoing verse, in which the prophet, as it were, anticipates himself, since this verse belongs to the description of suffering; and the description of the reward does not commence till the following verse. 2. We have then a very feeble sense: the servant of God will be buried with a rich man, *because* he had been perfectly righteous.—*He had done nothing unrighteous*, etc., neither in word or deed had he transgressed, a poetic enumeration to designate entire innocence. In accordance with this passage, Peter (1 Pet 2. 22) says: ὃς ἁμαρτίαν οὐκ ἐποίησεν, οὐδὲ εὑρέθη δόλος ἐν τῷ στόματι αὐτοῦ. The objections, which after Iken (l. c. p. 272 seq.), Martini, Rosenmuller, and Gesenius have brought against the interpretation of the whole verse, have been already refuted in our defence of it, so far as they deserve notice. Objections like the following refute themselves; viz that הוּא or הָיָה after עָשִׁיר would not be wanting, though they are omitted in instances without number, (comp. Glassius III, 3 can 56); that: 'he was with a rich man after his death,' cannot be equivalent to: 'he was buried with a rich man,' for the prophetic poetry allows far bolder expressions, and the clearness of historical narration must not be required of prophecy; that *grave* and *death* are here antithetical and plainly distinguished from each other, for they rather stand in parallelism with one another, and there is no objection to translate בְּמוֹתָיו *after his death*, and then the *Hysteron-proteron* urged especially by Iken falls away; and lastly that so definite a prediction is against the analogy of the prophecies, which are not wont to relate to such particular circumstances; an assertion which has already been sufficiently refuted in the general Introduction.

Let us now direct our attention to the more recent explanations of this verse. After the example of several others, Gesenius interprets "they gave him his grave with the ungodly and with a wicked wretch in his death," scil. they gave him his grave. According to this interpretation the word עָשִׁיר signifies a *wicked man* * Several endeavor to establish this meaning by a comparison with the Arabic عاثِر *stumbling*. But that this word means *sinning*, as is supposed, is very doubtful. Castell has indeed this signification, but it is not confirmed by examples. What Rosenmuller (after Martini) alleges, is not conclusive. Besides in other derivatives of the verb عثر, the sense of wickedness does not occur. It is moreover, in violation of a fundamental rule in the comparison of the dialects, to give by this means a new meaning to a word of such frequent occurrence, and one not connected with the others which are certain. Gesenius himself remarks against this comparison: "I hesitate to apply this word, since according to etymology it is not elsewhere at all related to the Hebrew עָשַׁר." Several interpreters, as Luther, Calvin, and lastly Gesenius, would derive the meaning *ungodly* from the Hebrew usage itself. And it is indeed true, that the words which

---

* So of old R. Jona in Salomoh B. Melech on the passage. Calvin, Luther in the marginal gloss: "a rich man, one who gives himself to the pursuit of wealth, i. e. an ungodly man." Lakemacher obs. phil. VIII 5, 5.

Isaiah 53:9.

signify power and wealth, frequently have in Hebrew the accessory idea of proud arrogance and violence, while on the other hand, those which designate poverty and weakness, have the secondary sense of innocence. But that עָשִׁיר, *a rich man*, could stand, with entire rejection of the principal idea, for precisely an ungodly man is totally without proof, and in itself considered, improbable. Comp. in opposition Iken l. c. p. 267, etc. In the passage, Job 27. 19, which is appealed to, the associate idea of pride and wickedness is indicated with sufficient definiteness by the connexion, and the principal idea, that of wealth, remains. Here on the contrary the principal idea would so entirely vanish that we could by no means translate *a rich ungodly man*. Then the singular itself עָשִׁיר shows that the word is not to be taken as standing in the parallelism with רְשָׁעִים. But should any choose, notwithstanding these difficulties, to follow this interpretation, still the verse would contain nothing opposed to the reference of the prophecy to the Messiah. We need only translate: they appointed him his grave with the ungodly and with criminals, when he was dead.

Martini translates: "Pararunt illi sepulchrum cum scelestis, tumulum sepulchralem cum violentis, quamquam ille vim nemini intulerat et a fraude fuerat alienus." He regards ב in בְּמוֹתָיו as *radical* instead of *servile*. בָּמוֹת *hill* = sepulchral hill. This interpretation was suggested by Abenezra, and has been approved by Oecolampadius, Zuingle, Schindler, Drusius, Iken, Lowth, Kuinol, Ammon, and others. But to this it may be objected; 1. the first Qamets in בָּמָה is impure (as if from a verb בום) and can never be resolved into Sheva. Comp. Gesenius Lehrg. p. 594. With a suffix the form is בְּמוֹתֵימוֹ Deut. 32: 29, and in the stat. con. בָּמוֹת יַעַר Micah 3. 12. 2. Should we however, though certainly without any sufficient ground, determine upon a change of vowels after the example of three Mss. collated by De Rossi, there would still be the objection, that the noun בָּמוֹת which occurs as singular also, has never the meaning sepulchral hill. Besides this sense has little affinity to the usual one; for בָּמוֹת does not mean a mound of earth which it is customary to throw upon graves, but an eminence.

Rosenmuller translates: "he committed his interment to the ungodly and the criminals after he was dead." But this interpretation is liable to very strong objections. How does the expression, *he committed*, agree with *although he had done no unrighteous deed*, which last surely requires that in what precedes some injury inflicted should be the subject of discourse? How can it be said of a person who is already dead, that he commits his burial? How could the heathen, who are supposed in this verse still to speak, call themselves רְשָׁעִים? Then the noun קֶבֶר, never occurs of the *act*, but only of the place of interment. And finally the objections which have been brought against the first mentioned interpretation are of equal weight against this and the foregoing.

V. 10. In this verse the prediction of the glorification of the servant of God commences. The sense: all the suffering described has been inflicted by Jehovah upon his servant, and will end with his glorification and the establishment of the divine kingdom on earth — "But it pleased Jehovah to bruise him, he has subjected him to disease (laid upon him heavy sufferings). When he has brought a sin-offering, he shall behold a posterity, he shall prolong his days, and the purpose of Jehovah shall prosper through him." According to v. d. Palm, this verse is connected with what precedes. He was innocent; why then was he so tormented and afflicted? Because it was Jehovah's will, and not perhaps, because the Lord was too weak to rescue him out of the hands of his enemies. And what was the ground of this will? He should present a voluntary sin-offering, redeem mankind through his sufferings. דַּכְּאוֹ is the Infin. in Pi. The copula is wanting before הֶחֱלִי. The suff. is to be supplied from the foregoing דַּכְּאוֹ. The verb הֶחֱלָה as has been before shown, signifies not merely to make sick, but also "plaga letali aliquem afficere." Here however disease and bruising are only a figure of the severe suffering inflicted by Jehovah on the Messiah. Comp. v. 3 and 4. The form הֶחֱלִי stands for הֶחֱלָה. The less usual form in Hebrew (see Josh 14:8) is the common one in the Aramaean. Gesen. Lehrg. 432. The ground of this variation of form in Hebrew seems to lie in the not unfrequent interchange of the verbs לָה and לָא. (Gesenius l. c. p. 418 Nr 8) That this is the case with the verb חָלָה, in particular, is shown by the future וַיֶּחֱלָא 2 Chron. 16:12, and the derivative תַּחֲלוּאִים. The interpretation we have given of the first member is easy and natural. Not so that of others, (Gesenius after Martini) who translate: "it pleased Jehovah to make his wound ill," for to wound him severely. They assume that דַּכְּאוֹ stands for דַּכְּאוֹ with Dagesh euphonic. (Gesenius Lehrg p 86) or as *infin. nominascens* in Pi. The Praeter הֶחֱלִי is supposed to stand for the infin with לְ. It is true that this interpretation is rendered somewhat plausible by the passage, Micah 6:13, where: I make thy

ISAIAH 53. 10.

wound ill, stands for, 'I bring upon thee a deadly wound.' Comp. Nah. 3 19.—Before the second member Jahn supplies וַיֹּאמֶר, which is indeed often omitted, while he supposes that thenceforth Jehovah speaks. But as in the last member Jehovah is still spoken of in the third person (חֵפֶץ יְהוָה) it is better to suppose that the prophet still continues to speak, and that Jehovah is first introduced as speaking, v. 11 and 12, and confirms what the prophet had said —תָּשִׂים is to be taken as 3d fem. and joined with נַפְשׁוֹ. שׂוּם is often synonymous with נָתַן; see the Lexicons. נֶפֶשׁ often stands like the Arabic نَفْس, for the personal pronoun When his soul brings = when he brings. It is unnecessary, with some interpreters, to give to the verb שׂוּם the intransitive meaning, *to place one's self*, or with others to suppose an ellipsis אִם תָּשִׂים נַפְשׁוֹ אָשָׁם כָּמוּר = כָּמוּר תָּשִׂים אָשָׁם נַפְשׁוֹ (since it cannot be said of the soul, it brings the soul for a sin offering, although examples otherwise satisfactory may be adduced for the ellipsis of נֶפֶשׁ) or with others even to translate: 'when thou wilt have brought his soul as a sin offering,' as an address to Jehovah, who in this and the preceding verses is uniformly spoken of in the third person It is not indeed here expressly said that the Messiah will be not only the priest who brings the sin offering, but the sacrifice also; this however was not necessary, since it was sufficiently clear from what had preceded. The word אָשָׁם *guilt, transgression*, and then *sin-offering* (Comp. Jahn Archaologie Th. 3 § 100 and § 102). As in reference to the outward theocracy, purity was regained, and the transgression expiated through the typical sacrifices which the typical priests presented, while at the same time there was an allusion to the great future sacrifice, so the prophet here announces that through the antitypical offering which the antitypical and only true priest should bring (comp. chap. 53 15), purity as to the inward theocracy, and the forgiveness of sins should be procured. Here also according to the usual custom of the prophet, things of the New Testament are represented under images taken from those of the Old Testament. According to this passage Paul affirms, 2 Cor. 5 21, God has made Christ to be ἁμαρτία i. e. a sin-offering whereby we became righteous before God, as in Rom 8 3: God has sent Christ περὶ ἁμαρτίας as a sin-offering, and Christ is called ἱλασμός, ἱλαστήριον, a propitiatory sacrifice for all sins, Rom 3 25 1 John 2: 2. 4·10 Comp. Heb 9. 14: ὃς ἑαυτὸν προσήνεγκεν ἄμωμον τῷ θεῷ. Without a figure therefore the sense is: when he has freely given himself up to bitter suffering and a bloody death, in order, by the expiation of our sins, to procure for us forgiveness and righteousness. The particle אִם has here its usual meaning, *when*, not *postquam*, as Rosenmuller explains it. The passages to which he appeals, after the example of Noldius (concord. part. s. v. Nr. 11), are not to the point, either because the verb is not as here in the Fut. but in the Praet (Amos 7. 2) or because the meaning *postquam* rests only on an erroneous interpretation (Job 14. 14). In the description of the rewards which the servant of God will receive for accomplishing the work committed to him, the inferior must again serve as a figure to designate the higher. Long life and numerous descendants are regarded by the Hebrews as the highest prosperity, as a theocratic blessing and a reward of piety. In a higher and spiritual sense shall this reward be given to the Messiah. The LXX (ἡ ψυχὴ ὑμῶν ὄψεται σπέρμα μακρόβιον), the Vulgate (*posteritatem videbit longaevam*), and Lowth would connect the two members יַאֲרִיךְ יָמִים and יִרְאֶה זֶרַע with one another; but it is far better to take them separately. הַאֲרִיךְ יָמִים, *to make the days long*, for *to live long*; יִרְאֶה זֶרַע *he will see seed* for *he will enjoy a numerous posterity*. These descendants (דּוֹרוֹ) are none other than the many and mighty, whom God according to v. 12 has given to the Messiah for a possession, and who according to chap. 52. 15 were to be freed from sin, and v. 11 justified through him, the punishment of whose sins he has taken upon himself, v. 5, and for whom, v. 12, he intercedes with God. The natural relation between father and son is often transferred to spiritual subjects. The prophets bore the name of father, their disciples that of sons of the prophets 1 Kings 2. 25. In a higher sense, believers begotten of God in a spiritual manner and obedient to him, as dutiful children, and forming, as it were, his family, are called the posterity of God, or of the Messiah. Ps 22: 31: "The seed which shall serve him shall be reckoned to the Lord for a posterity," i. e. the descendants of the Messiah shall be considered as God's posterity, as his children. Ps. 110. 3. Gen 6. 2, where by בְּנֵי הָאֱלֹהִים the worshippers of God are designated. In the East, Christians are still called مسيحيون ال المسيح 'the posterity or the family of the Messiah,' comp. Schulz b. Paulus in der Sammlung der Reisen Th. 7 p. 49.—According to Martini יִצְלָח in the last member does not indicate the future, but the past. He translates: "Jehovae enim mandata felicissime executus est." But for this there is no ground. The prophet here describes the reward which the Messiah shall receive. This consisted in the fact, that the concerns, cause of God, i. e. religion should be promoted and extended through him, which in effect is synonymous with: 'he will see a posterity.'

V. 11. Jehovah is again introduced as speaking—"Because of the labor of his soul he beholds, satisfies himself, by his knowledge shall he, the righteous one, my servant, justify many and bear their sins." מִן in מֵעֲמַל shows the *causa efficiens*. Rightly the Vulg: *Pro eo, quod laboravit anima ejus*. Others free from the suffering of his soul, or *after* the suffering of his soul. But it is more suitable, that here, as in the foregoing verse the suffering should be given as the cause of the glorification. עָמָל expresses at the same time the idea of labor and suffering.—The object of the verb יִרְאֶה is wanting. Michaelis: 'from his severe labor he will again look up with joy.' But for this sense of the verb רָאָה there is no certain proof, besides יִשְׂבָּע would not then be exactly appropriate. In supplying the ellipsis interpreters differ; some propose טוֹב *good*; others זֶרַע; but it is best to supply, 'the fruits and rewards of his sufferings,' announced in the foregoing verse. The verbs יִרְאֶה and יִשְׂבָּע are connected in different ways. Some here apply the Hebrew usage, which places two verbs, where we apply but one with an adjective, or adverb = he will see himself satisfied. Rosenmuller supplies בַּאֲשֶׁר between the verbs, which however gives a false sense. The correct view becomes evident from the remark, overlooked by nearly all interpreters, that the figure of a husbandman lies at the foundation, who cultivates his land with labor and care, with pleasure first beholds the ripe fruit, then gathers in the harvest and satisfies himself; he has sown in tears and now reaps in joy. It hence appears that the two verbs must be separated, and that they form a sort of climax. Le Clerc: "hic latet comparatio: quemadmodum agricola collecta copiosa messe fructu laboris sui satiatur, sic Messias animum suum successu miro Evangelii, postquam in coelum ascenderit, pascet." Many interpreters however connect בְּדַעְתּוֹ with the first member. Among these Martini refers the suff in בְּדַעְתּוֹ to Jehovah. דַּעַת יְהוָֹה *piety, fear of God*. He then explains: "pietatis suae largissimos fructus percipiet." But there is this objection among others: that the suff must relate to the Messiah, as he only is spoken of in the third person, whereas Jehovah is introduced as speaking himself (עַבְדִּי). Jahn somewhat better takes the suff as passive: "saturabitur cognitione sui i. e. fruetur illa beatitudine abunde, ut permulti eum agnoscant celsissimum benefactorem." But this also is unnatural, and בְּדַעְתּוֹ is no doubt, in accordance with the accents, to be referred to what follows בְּדַעְתּוֹ is variously understood; דַּעַת is infin. of יָדַע. Participles and infinitives however in connexion with suffixes can be regarded either as parts of the verb, or as nouns; in the former case the pronoun designates the object, i. e. is in the accusative; in the latter the subject of the action, i e is in the genitive, (see examples in Ges. Lehrg p 299). Several interpreters understand the suff here as subjective. Thus Gesenius 'through his wisdom' But it is an objection to this, that not the wisdom, but the expiatory suffering of the Messiah, as we shall see in the explanation of הַצְדִּיק, was to be the efficient cause of the justification Others. ' through his religion' But only דַּעַת יְהוָֹה, and not דַּעַת alone, signifies *piety, religion*, and that only subjectively, which is unsuitable here. Others: ' through his doctrine,' namely the doctrine of his suffering, and the atonement thereby effected This interpretation does indeed allow the verb הַצְדִּיק to be taken in the true sense; but then דַּעַת as a noun has never the meaning *doctrine*, but always only that of *insight, wisdom, understanding* We are therefore obliged to take the suff objectively or passively. Through his knowledge i e through the knowledge of him. This is the condition on which any one appropriates to himself the righteousness procured by the Messiah Thus Joh. H. Michaelis in den bibl Hal. " per scientiam sui (Le Clerc cognitione sui), non qua ipse cognoscit, sed qua vera fide et fiducia ipse tanquam propitiator cognoscitur." John 17 3. Rom 3 22, 25 V. d. Palm. " by his knowledge, that is by the knowledge of him, by knowing him on the ground of his mission, and by virtue of his merits."— Gesenius would take the verb הַצְדִּיק, in comparison with Dan. 12: 4, in the sense *to conduct to true religion, to convert*. But יַצְדִּיק is explained by the following parallel member, *he will bear their sins.* It must therefore be translated *to justify*, and referred to the deliverance from sin effected by the suffering of the servant of God The *significatio forensis* is the prevailing one of the verb צָדַק in Niph Comp e g 5. 23. That justification in the proper sense, and not mere instruction, is here the subject of discourse, appears from the whole context; the Messiah throughout the whole portion, is certainly described, not as a teacher, but as a priest, who, in order to deliver us from sin, has presented himself as a voluntary sin-offering. This interpretation is further favored by the construction with לְ,

and lastly by the position of צַדִּיק. The construction of the verb with לְ is explained by a certain modification of the meaning of the verb, הִצְדִּיק, with the accus., *justificare*; with לְ, *justitiam afferre*. The verb הָרַג suffers a similar modification, 2 Sam. 3. 30, הָרְגוּ לְאַבְנֵר *mortem intulerunt Abnero.* In like manner הֵנִיחַ with the accus. *to cause to rest;* with לְ, *to grant rest;* הוֹשִׁיעַ *to deliver*, with לְ, *to grant deliverance.* Comp. Gesen. Lehrg. p. 817. צַדִּיק עַבְדִּי 'the righteous, my servant,' for 'my righteous servant.' The adjective in some instances stands before the noun, when an emphasis rests upon it. (Comp. Gesen. p. 705.) But this is not sufficient to explain the construction here, a circumstance which has been overlooked by the interpreters. צַדִּיק cannot be directly referred as an epithet to עַבְדִּי, because the former is *indefinite*, while the latter is rendered *definite* by the suffix. But whenever the substantive has the article, or is made definite by a suffix or a genitive, the adjective must have the article also. Comp. Gesen. p. 704. We must therefore conclude that צַדִּיק stands before, independently, as supplying the place of a noun. A similar construction is found in Jer. 3. 7, 10, בָּגוֹדָה אֲחוֹתָהּ יְהוּדָה 'the faithless, *her sister Judah*, converts not herself to me.' By giving prominency to צַדִּיק and connecting it immediately with הַצַּדִּיק, it is intended to show the close connexion between the righteousness of the servant of God, who, though perfectly innocent and sinless (comp. v. 9), nevertheless suffered the punishment of sin, and the justification to be imparted by him. These words therefore explain יַזֶּה chap. 52. 15; they also confirm what had been said v. 3—6, especially the declaration 'by his wounds we are healed.' v. 5. Martini translates: "servator legatus meus salvos praestabit multos i. e. felicitate augebit et ornabit." But this explanation accords as little with the context as it is capable of being justified by philology; צַדִּיק cannot mean *servator*, nor הִצְדִּיק *to bless.* — In the last words, as in v. 4, sin with its punishment is figuratively represented as a heavy burden. Lam. 5. 4. Among the Arabians وِزْر *burden*, is a common name for sin. Likewise أَصَار *onera*

Calvin: "Egregia nimirum est permutatio. Christus justificat homines dando ipsis justitiam suam et vicissim in se suscipit peccata ipsorum, ut ea expiet." Jerome: "Et iniquitates eorum ipse portabit, quas illi portare non poterant et quarum pondere opprimebantur." Several interpreters (Martini, Hensler, etc.) propose to translate the verb יִסְבֹּל in the Praeter. 'he bare, or took away, their sufferings." But Gesenius justly objects, that all the preceding and following futures refer to the state of exaltation.* And throughout the whole verse, the subject of discourse is not the procuring of righteousness, (this was done in the state of humiliation described in v. 2—9), but only the conferring of it, as the subjective condition of which, the knowledge of the servant of God had been mentioned in the preceding member. The Messiah takes upon himself the sins of every one who, after his exaltation, fulfils this condition, i. e. he causes his own vicarious obedience to be reckoned to him, and imparts to him forgiveness. "He will bear their sins," is the same, only under a different image, as "he will justify them." Gesenius explains it thus: "and he relieved the burden of their sins; namely, through his doctrine he will reform them, and thereby procure for them forgiveness." But he is here in opposition to himself, since he explains נְשׂוּא חֳלִי and סָבַל מַכְאֹבִים, v. 4, of the vicarious satisfaction, nor do the corresponding חֵטְא רַבִּים נָשָׂא and יַפְגִּיעַ, v. 12, admit of any other explanation. Besides, סָבַל עָוֹן does not signify 'to alleviate the burden of sin,' but 'to take it entirely upon one's self,' and that this can mean *to improve by instruction*, is neither philologically demonstrable, nor reconcilable with the whole context, comp. what has been said on יַצְדִּיק above.

V. 12. "Therefore will I give him the mighty for a portion, and he shall divide the strong as a spoil, for a reward; because he has given up his life to death, and suffered himself to be numbered with the transgressors. And he will take the sins of many upon himself, and make intercession for the transgressors." The verb חָלַק, Job 39. 17, has the sense: 'to give a portion, to allot.' So also here many interpreters rightly render the word, (Alex. διὰ τοῦτο αὐτὸς κληρονομήσει πολλούς. Vulg. *ideo dispertiam ei plurimos*. Chald., Martini, Rosenmuller.) Others: 'I give him his lot among the mighty,' equivalent either to: 'I will assign him his place among the mighty,' or, 'the mighty shall be a part of the spoil to be imparted to him.' On the contrary, Martini justly remarks *friget utrumque*; especially, according to the first rendering, this explanation by no means suits the remaining splendid expressions, wherewith the glorification of the servant of God is described. Gesenius offers in

* The expression עֲוֹנֹתָם הוּא יִסְבֹּל is plainly synonymous with יַצְדִּיק, and on account of the parallelism itself cannot well be taken as the Praeter. Alex. καὶ τὰς ἁμαρτίας αὐτῶν αὐτὸς ἀνοίσει. Symm. ὑπενέγκει.

favor of it, that the fourth member would then form a suitable contrast with it. He, who was placed on a level with criminals, now stands with the mighty and powerful. But the antithesis according to the former explanation is certainly far stronger and more beautiful, *with* transgressors, *over* many and powerful.—רַבִּים can be translated either *many*, or *powerful* and *great*. The latter is favored by the parallelism with עֲצוּמִים. In any case it is unnecessary with Rosenmuller to supply after רַבִּים and עֲצוּמִים either גּוֹיִם or עַמִּים. — Several (Gesenius and others) translate the second member: 'he will divide spoil with the strong.' But we obtain a far stronger and finer sense if we regard את not as a preposition, but as the sign of the accusative. 'He will divide the strong as spoil,' scil. among his companions, which imports nothing more than : he will have them in his power, and do with them as he pleases. Martini "victoris est de praeda parta disponere ejusque optima parte sibi vindicata, reliquae inter socios partitionem facere." Comp. Gen. 49. 27. Ex. 15. 9. Ps. 68. 13. Judg. 5. 30. After the example of Jewish interpreters (Abarbanel. *hoc in Christum non competit* כי לא עשה מלחמה ולא שלל) some late critics (Paulus, Gesenius, etc.) would draw from these words a proof against the reference of the prophecy to Christ, who certainly enjoyed no worldly triumph. But such a misapprehension of the figurative language can hardly be explained, except by attributing it to doctrinal prejudice. After the usual custom of the prophets to exhibit spiritual objects by sensible images, the spiritual victory of Christ over the nations who take his easy yoke upon themselves, is here described under the figure of a worldly victory. Martini. "Inest descriptio amplissimi et splendidissimi imperii expressa imaginibus ab imperatore humano, qui terra sub ditionem suam redacta regnum occupat, praedaque parta potitur repetita." That worldly triumphs are not here the subject of discourse, appears, 1. From the manner, pointed out in the preceding verses, in which the Messiah has attained to this exaltation. Such triumphs are not won by the deepest humiliation, by suffering and death, voluntarily endured for the salvation of mankind. 2. From what the Messiah in the state of exaltation, shall accomplish in behalf of those who betake themselves to him. He shall sprinkle them with his blood, chap. 52. 13, justify them and bear their sins, v. 11; and intercede for sinners, v. 12;— these are surely not designations of a worldly conqueror. The רַבִּים and עֲצוּמִים are none others, than the nations and kings, chap. 52. 15, and the generation and posterity of the Messiah, v. 8, 10. Similar figures are found, Ps 2 8, where Jehovah says to the Messiah: "Ask of me, and I will give thee the heathen for an inheritance, and the uttermost parts of the earth for thy possession." Comp Isa 11 10.—The merits of the servant of God are then once more repeated, as a reward for which God has granted him these great spiritual conquests. In the words הֶעֱרָה לַמָּוֶת נַפְשׁוֹ, properly, *he has poured out his life unto death*, or *in death*, the metaphor was taken from animals, which lost their life with their blood, on which account blood was regarded as the seat of the soul. Comp. Gen 9: 4. Lev. 17· 11. There is an allusion to the figure of an animal sacrifice, v 10. Comp. Ps. 141 8, and numerous examples of similar phraseology from the Arabic poets in Schultens *ad excerpta Hamasae p.* 452, and in Martini and Gesenius on the passage. The word נִמְנָה *he was numbered*, has here, as we have already seen v 7, the secondary meaning, *he suffered himself to be numbered*. This is demanded by the context, and the parallelism with . 'he has poured out his life' The ground of the Messiah's glorification was not that he was numbered, but that 'he *voluntarily* suffered himself to be numbered' with the transgressors The evangelist Mark adduces this passage, when he relates that Christ was fastened to the cross between two thieves, without intending by this special reference to exhaust the whole sense of the declaration —We must not, with many interpreters, after the example of the LXX, take יַפְגִּיעַ as referring to the state of humiliation. (So also Gesenius in direct contradiction to his remark on v 11, that all the futures in the preceding and following verses relate to the state of exaltation. If יַפְגִּיעַ here stands for the praeter, then surely יִסְבֹּל must there stand for it also) Rather is the Aorist נָשָׂא determined to be the *future* by the context, in which only the exaltation is the subject of discourse, and it corresponds with יִסְבֹּל. Compare what has been said on the foregoing verse. The verb פָּגַע has in Kal among other significations, the meaning *to meet*, in Hiph therefore *to cause to meet* To make something meet, or happen to any one, (whether petitions or actions must be determined by the context) stands then for *to intercede with him*. Most interpreters here erroneously understand הִפְגִּיעַ of mere prayer. Rightly Martini : " intelligendum est illud auxilium, quod miserias easque gravissimas et durissimas mortemque adeo ipsam subeundo Messias popularibus suis praestitit " Not by simple prayer, as plainly appears from the preceding context, will the servant of God intercede with him for sinners, but by presenting before him his vicarious suffering and his merits, as a ground of their obtaining mercy and forgiveness of their sins. Very happily Calvin: "Ut in veteri lege sacerdos, qui nunquam sine sanguine ingrediebatur, simul pro populo intercedebat, ita quod illic adumbratum fuit, in Christo impletum est. Primum enim sacrificium corporis sui obtulit et sanguinem fudit, ut poenam nobis debitam persolveret. Deinde ut valeret expiatio advocati officio functus est, atque intercessit pro omnibus, qui fide hoc sacrificium amplecterentur." Comp. Rom. 8. 34 (ὅς καὶ ἐντυγχάνει ὑπὲρ ἡμῶν), Heb. 9. 24 (Christ has gone into the holy place νῦν ἐμφανισθῆναι τῷ προσώπῳ τοῦ θεοῦ ὑπὲρ ἡμῶν), 1 John 2. 1 παράκλητον ἔχομεν πρὸς τὸν πατέρα Ἰησοῦν Χριστὸν δίκαιον. The word וְהוּא shows that the last two members are not to be viewed as depending on תַּחַת אֲשֶׁר

We have now *first*, to refute the objections to the Messianic interpretation; *secondly*, to bring forward the grounds on which it rests, and *lastly*, to show that the non-Messianic interpretation is untenable. We borrow the objections from Gesenius, who has collected every thing at all plausible which the earlier writers, and particularly the Jews, have alleged.*

1. "Though the similarity of the condition of this pious sufferer with that of Christ is so great, yet still there is much also which is unsuitable to him." All that Gesenius here adduces has been already refuted in the exposition, excepting only, that according to chap. 52: 15, kings should do homage in person to the servant of God. But this stands self-refuted; for this passage has no more a *personal import* than the parallel one chap. 49. 7. But without treating all history with contempt, who can deny that kings have bowed and do still bow their knees before the glorified Christ? The objection therefore is of as little force as the remark of Abarbanel on v. 10, whom Gesenius seems to have imitated. "The verb יִרְאֶה designates the seeing of a man, בחייו ובימיו, *dum adhuc vivit et superstes est.*"

2. "The name *servant of God* never occurs of the Messiah." Granting this assertion to be true, still it would prove nothing. The

---

* A refutation of the objections of Dr. Ammon (bibl. Theologie II, p. 40 seq.) which are surely now given up by the author himself, may be found in Jahn l. c. p. 63.

appellation *servant of God*, in the stricter sense, designates, as we have already seen, any one who is called to the execution of a divine purpose, and who stands to God in a relation similar to that sustained by the servants of a court (called עֲבָדִים by the Hebrews) to earthly kings. Moses was called servant of Jehovah, Num 12. 7, and Joshua, Judg. 2. 8. Every Israelitish king was servant of Jehovah; David was often thus called, e. g. Ps 89. 21. Eliakim bears this name, chap. 22. 20. The prophet calls himself so, chap. 20. 3. In so far as they were destined to preserve the knowledge and worship of the true God, the Jewish people also bear this name in several places. It is attributed to the angels, Job 4. 18, where עֲבָדָיו stands in the parallelism with מַלְאָכָיו 'his messengers.' Even Nebuchadnezzar, Jer. 25. 9. and 27. 6. is called a servant of Jehovah, in so far as he was an instrument in the hand of God, though without his own knowledge and will. It is merely accidental that Cyrus does not bear this title; all the attributes of a servant of God are ascribed to him. It is therefore, in every respect, inconceivable why the Messiah, the great messenger of God, (מַלְאָכִי Mal. 3. 1), he who, in the assumed form of a servant, was obedient to God even unto death, (Phil. 1. 7), who came not to do his own will, but the will of him who had sent him, (John 6. 38), could not receive this appellation, since he was strictly that which the name imports, which can by no means be regarded as a *nomen proprium* of one particular order, or individual, but was common to all the ministers and instruments of God. But in addition to this, the assertion is by no means correct. The Messiah bears the name in the passage Zech 3. 8, unanimously interpreted of him. "I will bring forth, saith God, my servant Branch," where the Chaldee explains, מְשִׁיחָא וְיִתְגְּלִי, *Messiam et revelabitur*. He receives it chap. 42: 1. (where the Chaldee interprets, הָא עַבְדִּי מְשִׁיחָא. Kimchi. זהו מלך המשיח) chap. 49. 3, 6. chap. 50. 10. consequently in nearly all the Messianic passages in the second part.

3. "The idea of a suffering and atoning Messiah is foreign from the Old Testament, and in contradiction to its prevailing representations, even admitting it to have been entertained by some about the age of Christ." This objection also has been borrowed from the Jews. What has been remarked in the general Introduction is sufficient for its refutation. It will have no weight so long as the authority of Christ is valid in the church, who himself affirmed that his whole suffering had been predicted in the Old Testament, and explained to his disciples the prophecies respecting it. But even if the

idea of a suffering and atoning Messiah occurred in no other passage of the Old Testament, still it would prove nothing. For we could not determine *a priori* that God might not enlighten one particular prophet, who showed himself susceptible of such a revelation, respecting a subject which he concealed from the rest. It is certainly true, that in the Messianic predictions, the prophetic and regal offices of Christ are represented more frequently than his sacerdotal, the great mass of the people, who were to be retained through these predictions in an adherence (though only an outward one) to Jehovah, could as little understand this doctrine as the apostles before the Spirit was given; while for the pious, whose minds were prepared for its reception, the intimations which were given, and which have been collected in the passage referred to, were sufficient. Besides chap. L, we here direct the attention to the passage chap. 11· 1, which even Gesenius interprets of the Messiah, and where his appearance in humiliation is indicated, as in chap 53 2, by the figure of a feeble shoot that springs up from the stem of Jesse, which had been cut down. But it is difficult to perceive wherein consists the contradiction between the doctrine of the suffering, and that of the glorified Messiah. Were there, however, an apparent contradiction, it would be done away by the history of Christ. Indeed the suffering appears, even in this prophecy, as the condition of the glorification, the glorification as its consequence and reward. The Messiah appears here also as a king, to whom all earthly kings with their people should be subject — The whole assertion proceeds from the erroneous opinion, that each individual Messianic prophecy must contain a full picture of the Messiah; whereas, on the contrary, they supply one another's deficiencies, and for the most part present us with only a partial view of Christ.

4. "The Messianic interpretation regards all as future; which the language does not allow. The suffering, contempt, and death of the servant of God are here represented throughout as past, since chap 53 1—10, all is expressed in the Praeter. Only the glorification appears as future and is expressed in the future tense. The writer therefore stands between the suffering and the glorification, and announces, that he, who has hitherto suffered, shall now be glorified. The latter only is still future." The answer to this has already been given on chap 52. 13. The prophet does not occupy a historical, but a prophetic point of view. The prophets described events as they followed each other in prophetic vision. That which formed the condition was expressed in the present or past, that

which was the consequence, in the future. Comp. the general preliminary remarks on the second part of Isaiah. As the prophet there takes his station in the Babylonish exile, and thence beholds the deliverance as future, so he here places himself between the suffering and the glorification of the Messiah, and the former appears to him as past, the latter as yet to come. Only in this way could he discriminate between the condition and its consequence, and place in their proper relation the suffering and exaltation of the Messiah.* *Besides, it is by no means true, that the prophet always represents the suffering as past, and speaks of it only in the Praeter.* In some instances he passes involuntarily from the prophetic to the historical point of view, and employs also the future, even where he speaks of the suffering. Thus v. 7 יִפְתַּח, v. 8 יְשׂוּחָה, v. 10 חָשִׂים, according to Gesenius also יַפְגִּיעַ, v. 12, while on the contrary, v. 12, he uses the Praeter נָשָׂא of the state of exaltation. (Comp יִסְבֹּל v. 11) †

5 "It is perfectly evident that this servant of God is the same person, who is the subject of discourse in the parallel passage. Chap. 42 1—7. 99· 1—9 50 4—11. 61 1—3 In these passages there is yet a great deal more which cannot apply to Christ" We here entirely agree with our opponents that the subject of both portions must be the same, and we must with them complain of the mischievous inconsistency of those interpreters who find the Messiah here, but another subject there. We believe however that on these passages we have sufficiently proved that what Gesenius adduces from them as irreconcilable with the Messianic interpretation, either rests on a false exegesis, which is too literal and overlooks the figurative character of the prophetic discourse, or if it were correct, would militate still more strongly against his own exposition. How, e. g. can the introduction of the Messiah as speaking in some of the passages referred to, be an objection with one, according to whose own interpretation a person in like manner, and indeed not an actual, but a fictitious person, the collective body of the prophets, comes forward as a speaker?

6. "In what precedes, as well as in what follows, the subject of

---

* The ancient translators also have not taken these Praeters as designating the real past; but have frequently rendered them by futures. So the Seventy v. 14 *ἐκστήσονται* -*ἀδοξήσει*. Aquila and Theodotion v 2 *ἀναβήσεται*.

† The same thing is found also in the parallel passage c 49 8 Gesenius himself there remarks "as the deliverance is still impending, the Praeters עֲזַרְתִּיךָ and יְצַרְתִּיךָ cannot be well understood otherwise than as futures"

discourse is the restoration of the State after the exile. It was consequently entirely impossible for those, who then read the oracle, to refer it to a Redeemer to be expected in future times." But this was not necessary. The only point of importance was, that the prophet and his hearers should become acquainted with the future suffering of the great servant of God, as the condition of their salvation, and embrace the coming Redeemer with the same love with which we ought to embrace him now he has appeared. The fact was sufficient, the *when* they needed not to know, as indeed the nature of the prophetic vision did not admit of their knowing it. Without detriment to the reality they might constantly suppose, the great event would ensue immediately after the deliverance from the Babylonish exile. Indeed, had they known the long distance of time, it would have enfeebled their desire and cooled their love. "It could little concern the reader of that day to know what was to happen after half a thousand years." He only can say this, who has no regard for what is most dear to others, and constitutes the central point of their whole life.

The further allegation of Gesenius, that this interpretation forcibly separates the portion from its connexion with the whole book; and that to understand it as a definite prediction is against the analogy of all biblical prophecies, which refer in vague anticipations to the immediate future, has been already sufficiently refuted and will here be left unnoticed. It only remains to remark a striking contradiction, which occurs on one and the same page (III. p. 164). It is first said, that all biblical prophecies relate only to the immediate future, and directly after, the author declares that the hope, which he also finds expressed in the passage, of a splendid triumph of the religion of Jehovah over the heathen at some future day, has been realized by the prevalence of Christianity, and he therefore does not hesitate, so far as this, to acknowledge in this portion a Messianic prophecy which has been fulfilled.

We now proceed to exhibit the grounds of the Messianic interpretation. All the arguments are here combined by which in general any passage can be proved upon the principles laid down in the Introduction, to relate to the Messiah.

1. This interpretation is confirmed by the testimony of tradition. The Jews, in more ancient times, unanimously referred this prophecy to the Messiah (Comp. the history of the exposition of this passage; further Joh. Heinr. Michaelis ad h. l. in den bibl. Hal., Huls.

theol Jud 1 c., Grabe, notae ad spicil. patr. t I p. 362; Hulsii nucleus prophetiae Lugd 1683 p 668 seq.; Danz in Meuschenii N. T. ex Talm. ill. p 836 and the authors there quoted Eisenmenger entd Jud. P. II, 758 Calov. bibl. ill. II p. 249 seq Raym Martini pugio fidei P. 2 c 9 11 12 u. a m a. St Hornbeck c. Jud p 249 536 u. v. a.) The authority of tradition, however, in this case, is so much the more weighty, in proportion as the Messianic interpretation conflicted with the disposition of the people, while the origin of the later non-Messianic interpretations can be satisfactorily explained by the prevailing mode of thinking

2 The citations of this prophecy in the New Testament serve not only to show, that the Messianic interpretation was the prevailing one in those times, (otherwise the writers would have justified it, as e. g in the case of the 16th Psalm, and in reference to the divine dignity of the Messiah, Ps. 110, the same thing is also evident from the declaration of John the Baptist taken from the passage before us, John 1 29 ἴδε ὁ ἀμνὸς τοῦ θεοῦ, ὁ αἴρων τὴν ἁμαρτίαν τοῦ κόσμου, comp chap 53. 4, 7, 11), but also to furnish us with infallible evidence of its correctness. That in John 12. 38 and Rom. 10 16, the first verse of the 53d chapter is cited to explain the unbelief of the greatest part of the people, and in the former passage, with the formula ἵνα πληρωθῇ, would not it is true of itself be sufficient for proof The passage, however, in Luke 22. 37 affords decisive evidence Christ himself there says, the prophecies relating to him are about to have an end, (so only can the expression τὰ περὶ ἐμοῦ τέλος ἔχει be understood; comp Matt 26. 54, where Christ says he must suffer and die in order that the Scripture may be fulfilled) and therefore the declaration also· "he was numbered with the transgressors," must be accomplished in him. Comp chap 53: 12 He therefore places the prophecy with those which treat of himself, and it is certainly so far Messianic as our Lord could know and desire to speak the truth The reply of Gesenius, that Mark does not attribute these words to Jesus, but adduces them on a later occasion (chap. 15 28) in his own person, can surely prove nothing Why should not Mark, in his own person, adduce a prophecy relating to Christ, which Christ himself had previously cited? And we make no groundless assumption, when we assert, that in those passages where Christ says he must suffer and die κατὰ τὰς γραφάς, he had this passage chiefly in view. (Comp. Gen. Introd.) For the opponents themselves confess, that if the doctrine of a suffering and atoning Messiah is contained

any where in the Old Testament, it is in this passage. Acts 8 28—35, Philip, in reply to the question of the treasurer from Ethiopia, as to the subject of the prophecy, explains it of Christ, and grounds upon it all his instructions concerning him. The passage Matt 8 17 has already been adduced in the exposition. After De Wette (de Morte Exp p. 94), Gesenius (l c p 163) lays peculiar stress upon the circumstance, that the passage was never referred to the atoning death of Christ, and maintains that the citation Matt 8 17 militates against this doctrine. In respect to the latter we refer to the exposition; the former is incorrect. The apostle Peter, (1 Pet 2 21—25), when speaking of the vicarious satisfaction of Christ, employs *verbatim* the principal passages of this prophecy. It was not because the apostles did not explain this prophecy of the expiatory death of Christ, that they so seldom cited it, when they speak on that subject, but because it was so familiar to them and to those to whom they wrote, that direct quotation was unnecessary, a bare allusion being sufficient. This appears from the numerous passages, in which we meet with allusions to the prophecy, or reminiscences of it. (Comp e g Mark 9 12. Rom 4 25. 1 Cor 15 3. 2 Cor 5 21. 1 John 3 5. 1 Pet 1 19.) This passage is, as it were, the theme, which lay at the foundation of the apostolic annunciation respecting the atoning death of Jesus. This Gesenius himself confesses in a passage, which stands in striking contradiction to that just quoted, l c p. 191 "Most Hebrew readers, who were now so familiar with the ideas of sacrifice and substitution, must however have necessarily so understood it, *and it is not to be doubted, that the apostolic representation of the expiatory death of Christ, rests preeminently on this ground*"

3 There can be no question, and the best interpreters (Gesenius, v d. Palm and others) acknowledge, that the subject of these prophecies can be no other than that of those in chap XLII, XLIX, L, LXI. Now if these can be referred only to the Messiah, all the arguments in favor of their Messianic character, and which we will not here repeat, are equally applicable to the prophecy before us, and *vice versa* In addition to this, the passage chap 11 1 וְיָצָא הֹטֶר מִגֵּזַע יִשָׁי וְנֵצֶר מִשָּׁרָשָׁיו יִפְרֶה, which is also explained of the Messiah by Gesenius, has so striking a resemblance to chap. 53 2, that both must be referred to the same subject.

4 To these external arguments we must subjoin the internal, derived from the characteristics attributed to the subject of the prediction. Though each particular feature can be shown to have been

fulfilled in Christ, yet we will here confine ourselves to that which belongs to him exclusively, and can be referred to no one else without entire caprice. We mention, first of all, the doctrine that through the vicarious sufferings of the great servant of God, the people are freed from the punishment of sin, reconciled to God, and made righteous. Several have attempted, and indeed in different ways, to remove this doctrine from the portion. Kimchi remarks: "we must not suppose that the thing is so in fact, that Israel in exile really bears the sins and diseases of the heathen, for this would militate against the justice of God, but that the heathen will pass such a judgment upon it, when they behold the splendid redemption of Israel." It is easy to see the weakness of this argument of Kimchi against the vicarious satisfaction. This doctrine would militate against the justice of God only where the sufferer (the opposite of this case, according to the passage) did *not* assume his sufferings *voluntarily;* and besides, such *a priori* and dogmatic objections are of no weight, since corrupt reason is not in a condition to sit in judgment on the doctrines of revelation. It is equally plain, that the method by which he proposes to get rid of the doctrine is extremely forced, and would leave nothing certain in all the Scriptures. Some more recent interpreters (Martini, ad h. l. De Wette, De Morte Expiatoria, p. 22 sq *) have chosen another way. They propose to take the expressions as only figurative, and that we should not seek in them for the doctrine of a vicarious satisfaction for our sins, provided by the righteousness of God through the Messiah. According to Martini (l c p. 60) all these expressions signify nothing more than: "calamitates illas gravissimas ministro isti divino perferendas popularibus ejus utiles futuras atque salutares." But it is decisive in favor of the literal interpretation, that the prophet speaks of this subject, not merely in one particular passage, but constantly returns to it, and always places the redemption and the suffering of the Messiah, in relation to each other, as cause and effect. Thus he says, chap. 52 15, "the Messiah will deliver many heathen from their sins," chap 53 4, "he has taken our diseases and pains upon himself," v 5, "he was pierced for our transgressions," etc. v 6, "Jehovah has cast upon him the sins of us all," v. 8, "he has borne the punishment which the people should have borne;" v. 10, "he has presented himself as a sin-offering to God," etc. To this it may still be added, that the expressions נשא

---

* In some measure, also, Umbreit Theol Studien u Crit 1, 2 p. 328. But he expresses himself very obscurely

in chap. 52: 15, and אָשָׁם in chap. 53: 10, are taken from sacrifices; and the suffering and death of the Messiah are represented as effecting an inward reconciliation with God, in the same manner as the death of the victim signified objectively that outward purity was thereby restored, as to the external theocracy. Indeed, substitution evidently took place in the sacrifices, in respect to external theocratic purity, though by no means in reference to inward sanctification; and this might well be done without prejudice to the divine institution of sacrifices. This much is certain, that had the prophet wished to deliver the doctrine of the vicarious satisfaction, he could not possibly have used stronger expressions. No passage of the New Testament on the expiatory death of Jesus is more definite in doctrine than this; and yet the vicarious satisfaction is there taught, even in the opinion of numerous rationalist interpreters of recent times, (comp. e. g. De Wette, Dogmatik § I. 293 sq. Bretschneider, Dogm § I. 154, 155), those only excepted who (as Paulus) are so strongly biased by doctrinal interest, that they entirely sacrifice exegesis to it. But upon these, time has already passed judgment. The arguments are so striking, that even Rosenmuller (Gabler's Journal II. § 365), Gesenius, and others, cannot avoid the confession that the passage contains the doctrine of a vicarious satisfaction, after Alschech among the Jews has done homage to the truth. — We now proceed to consider the arguments of De Wette (l. c.) against the literal meaning. 1. He appeals to two passages where the word כֹּפֶר *ransom* occurs in a figurative sense. The first is Is. 43: 3, where Jehovah says he has given Egypt, Ethiopia and Seba as a ransom for the Israelites. We must here entirely agree with De Wette, in opposition to Gesenius, who, l. c. p. 190, finds in this passage also, the doctrine of a vicarious satisfaction.* A satisfaction of this sort contradicts all the Old Testament ideas of the divine justice, and, as we shall hereafter see, has no analogy in its favor. De Wette justly says: "Ad amorem Jehovae erga populum suum demonstrandum comparat propheta Israelitarum sortem cum sorte aliorum populorum, qui dum illi captivitate liberarentur, in ditionem Persarum redacti sint, ita ut quasi dici posset hos populos in locum Israelitarum succedere et eorum libertatem sua redi-

---

* "The divine justice was not yet satisfied by the suffering of the people in exile, and therefore other nations are given up for them." What Gesenius remarks, p. 75 on the passage itself, is in contradiction to this. "Jehovah gives great, rich, and powerful nations, as Egypt, Ethiopia, and Seba, as a prize to the conqueror, instead of Israel, and, *as it were*, a ransom for them."

mere." The second is Prov. 21.18 כֹּפֶר לַצַּדִּיק רָשָׁע וְתַחַת יְשָׁרִים בּוֹגֵד 'the evil doer is a ransom for the righteous, and the ungodly for the pious.' This passage, as Gesenius himself acknowledges, (and thereby confirms the correctness of the figurative acceptation of Is. 43 3), means nothing more than this "the sufferings which the pious have long endured, are afterwards imposed upon the righteous in their stead; the latter must, *as it were*, redeem the former." But still both these passages fail to prove the point in question. For the existence of the doctrine of the vicarious satisfaction in this passage, does not depend on a single expression, which certainly might be interpreted figuratively, but on the perpetual recurrence of the same doctrine under the greatest diversity of expression. Besides in the passages referred to, the expression כֹּפֶר occurs, and not as in this instance אָשָׁם (comp יָדַע) which does not so easily admit of being understood figuratively. 2. "The prophet is so free from all superstition, that he almost rejects sacrifices, and the whole outward worship of God. Comp. chap 66 3. But it is impossible to perceive what difference there should be between an expiation of sin accomplished by animals, and one accomplished by a man." The prophet in the cited passage, like all prophets, zealously opposes the opinion that sacrifices, *ex opere operato*, procure the divine favor and forgiveness of sins, which would be entirely contrary to their original design and import. That he need not on this account have rejected the doctrine of the vicarious satisfaction, is very evident from the example of the writers of the New Testament, and indeed of the whole Christian church, who, with similar sentiments as to sacrifices, still taught this doctrine. When De Wette places expiation by animals upon a level with expiation by a man, he falsely assumes that, in view of the prophet, the servant of God was a mere man. Surely, what the prophet says of the glorified Messiah is unsuitable to a mere man; and that he was well acquainted with the divine nature of the Messiah, appears from other Messianic passages, in which divine names and properties are attributed to him. That a man should make satisfaction for men, as we shall see hereafter, would certainly be contrary to the doctrine of the Old Testament. The passage therefore is inappropriate here, which De Wette cites from Mic. 6 6—8, where the people inquiring how they should make atonement to Jehovah, and whether they should offer their own children as a sin-offering, are told that Jehovah does not require this, but righteousness, love, and humility. Only in virtue of his perfect innocence and righteousness, such as were never found in any man, could the servant of God deliver us from sin, and on this very circumstance peculiar stress is laid, comp. chap. 9. 11. When, 3) De Wette maintains that the prophet could not teach this doctrine, because it is subversive of piety, the promotion of which he had so much at heart, we might also with this *a priori* argument, which arises from want of experience, and, as it is to be hoped, no longer held valid by the author himself, prove that the whole Christian church, that a Luther, Arndt, Spener, have not held it. The doctrine of the vicarious satisfaction is then definitely and clearly contained in this passage. But now we find in the New Testament the same things said of Christ, as are here attributed to the subject of the prophecy. It is true that Christ, during his life, more seldom expressed himself definitely and clearly concerning the design of his death, and his vicarious satisfaction. See, however, Matt. 20. 28. 26. 28. John 3. 14. 6. 51—55. 12. 27. etc. Bretschneider l. c. § 154. The reason was, that the carnally minded disciples were not prepared, before Christ's death, and the giving of the Holy Spirit which depended upon it, to understand this doctrine in its true import; it preeminently, therefore, belongs to the "many things" which Christ had still to say to the disciples, but which they could not yet bear. But after his death he fully instructed his disciples concerning it (Luke 24. 27), and the complete information which they have given us, flowed partly from his instructions, and partly from the illumination promised immediately to them, and actually granted. Comp. Storr, Abhandlung uber den Versohnungstod Jesu, als Anhang seines Commentars zum Hebraerbrief.

There is besides, the specific trait given in v. 9, that the servant of God should be interred with a rich man (Joseph of Arimathea). It would be superfluous further to point out the coincidence between the prophecy and its fulfilment, since it must be self evident to every one acquainted with the evangelical history.

These positive arguments for the Messianic interpretation are likewise so many negative ones against every other. It would be an idle waste of time to refute the views, (approved of only by their authors) of those who would refer the prophecy to any individual subject besides Christ, from king Uzziah to the Maccabees. All these interpreters have been satisfied with seizing upon some single feature, which is found again in the history of some individual. The rest they have entirely overlooked, or sought to set aside by false and unnatural interpretations. By such a mode of proceeding, one might invent innumerable expositions of the prophecy, besides those already mentioned. The refutation would consequently be useless; since it is merely accidental, whether this or that person has not proposed some individual or other, to whom the prophecy no more refers, than to a hundred others. It is an objection to all these references to distinct individuals, that they make their appearance here, without exception, as a *deus ex machina*, no one can tell whence they come, and whither they go, or give any reason why the prophet abruptly brings them before us.

There are only three interpretations which are entitled to our attention, on account of their more general prevalence, and greater plausibility. The first regards as the subject the whole Jewish people, the second, the pious part of them; and the third, the collective body of the prophets. It is common to them all, that the subject is not an actual, but only an ideal person, a *collectivum* personified.

Against the first of these, we urge chiefly the following arguments.

1. It is true, that the Jewish people are sometimes personified as a unity, and called עֶבֶד יְהוָה. But such a personification, extended through a whole section, without the slightest intimation that the discourse does not relate to one individual, can be confirmed by no analogous example. In v. 3 the subject is termed אִישׁ; in v. 10 a soul is attributed to him, grave and death are used in reference to a subject of the singular number. Did the prophet wish to be understood, he must have given at least some hint as to his meaning. Martini well observes: "Vix exemplum afferri posse putaverim, quod prophetae continuata allegoria de populo universo tanquam de singulari persona, ita loquuti fuisse deprehendantur, ut argumenti non ad individuum quoddam, sed ad nationem ipsam referendi, nullum, ne levissimum quidem, vestigium eluceat." It is totally different in the other passages where the prophet designates the people of Israel by the name עֶבֶד יְהוָה. He there guards against all uncertainty by adding the name יַעֲקֹב and יִשְׂרָאֵל comp. chap. 41 8, 9. 44 1, 2, 21. 45 4. 48 20, moreover, in order to show that the עֶבֶד יְהוָה is a collective, he makes use of the plural along with the singular, when speaking of and to the Israelites. Comp. e. g. chap. 42 24, 25. 48 20, 21. 43 10—14. 44 8. But there is nothing like this in the case before us. In addition to these objections, such an extended allegory, which as we have already remarked is without an example in the Hebrew literature, would be very inappropriate and feeble. "Porro ipsius hujus oraculi argumentum gravius et sublimius illi senten-

tiae non favet. Sub tali enim imagine propheta vix depingere potuisset nationem totam Judaicam vel miserrimam et omnium gentium odio et contemtui expositam, quin oratio saepius tumidius atque frigidius justo videretur." Hansi.

2. The subject of the portion has undertaken his sufferings *voluntarily;* (according to v. 10 the servant of God presents himself as a sin-offering, v. 12 he is crowned with glory, because he has poured out his life in death, which the usage of the language permits us to understand only of a voluntary act of self-devotion,) *innocent* himself he bears the sins of others, (v. 4—6 and v. 9); his sufferings are the efficient *cause of the righteousness* of the people (v. 11); he suffers *quietly* and *patiently*, without allowing himself to be provoked to bitterness against the authors of his sufferings (v. 7) Of all these four marks not one belongs to the people of Israel a) They went not voluntarily into the Babylonish exile, but were carried away by violence b) They did not suffer innocently, but bore in the exile the punishment of their own sins As a theocratic judgment this had been predicted by Moses, Lev. 26: 14 Deut 28. 15. 29. 19. 32: 1 In this light it is represented by all the prophets. Jeremiah and Ezekiel perpetually inculcate anew, that this punishment will surely fall upon the people, on account of the prevalence of gross vice, and especially in consequence of idolatry. Isaiah himself, in the second part, admonishes the Jews that they would be driven into exile by the divine justice, and delivered from it only by the divine mercy Comp e g. 56—59, particularly the penitential confession of the people themselves in the last chapter. And when we look at the immediate occasion of the exile, what is said of the sufferer, v. 9, does not suit the Israelites: "he had done no unrighteous deed, and there was no guile in his mouth" The immediate occasion of the exile, complained of by Jeremiah, was the perjured alliance with Egypt against Nebuchadnezzar. Rosenmuller endeavors to remove this difficulty by the remark that the prophet does not speak in his own person, but in that of the heathen people who would conciliate the favor of the Israelites by this flattery "Aliter enim loqui necesse est, ubi suo ipsius nomine suos objurgat et redarguit, aliter ubi alias gentes, antea populo Hebraeo adversarias, sed nunc ad meliorem mentem redeuntes iisque sese associare cupientes de eo dicentes in medium producit" But this explanation is untenable, even if we leave out of view, that the prophet would not, without further remark, put into the mouth of others a discourse, the contents

of which he did not himself approve, since he could not fail to perceive that his approbation would be taken for granted by every one For the innocence of the subject is declared, not only in v. 1—10 of the 53d chap which Rosenmuller, after the example of the Jews, attributes to the heathen, but just as plainly also in the discourse of Jehovah, chap 52 13—15 and chap 53. 11, 12. Only when innocent himself could the sufferer deliver the heathen from sin, v 11 he is called distinctly the righteous; v. 12 it is spoken of as meritorious, that he suffers himself to be numbered with the transgressors. c) The suffering of the Jewish people cannot be represented as the efficient cause of the righteousness of the heathen, as vicarious in their behalf. This could not be the case, even because the Jewish people neither voluntarily assumed their sufferings, nor were they innocently involved in them; on the contrary, they suffered through their own fault and against their will. But, in general, there is, and from the nature of the case there could be, no example in the Old Testament of the sufferings of one man being regarded as vicarious for others. We have here De Wette in our favor, who l c p 22, justly observes that the doctrine of substitution by a man is not found, and, according to its prevailing system of doctrine, could not be found in the Old Testament, (Micah 6· 6—8 He afterwards, however, erroneously as has been shown, turns this argument for the Messianic interpretation, against it De Wette himself proves, that the Hebrews neither held, nor could hold the doctrine of a vicarious satisfaction made by men. As now it has been proved, that a vicarious satisfaction is taught in Isaiah, he cannot avoid referring the prophecy to the Messiah.—The first condition of such a satisfaction, and that which is so represented in the portion before us, is the entire innocence of the sufferer. Whoever is himself sinful cannot assume the punishment of the sins of another, but his suffering is either a punishment from the divine justice, or a corrective from the divine mercy. The doctrine of a vicarious human satisfaction, therefore, would be in direct contradiction to that of the Old Testament respecting the universal sinfulness of mankind. Comp. Gen. 6. 5 8 21 Job 15. 14—16. Ps. 14. 3. 51. 7. 53 4. Prov. 20 9. Even the prophets, the best and noblest part of the nation, often include themselves with the people when they speak of their sinfulness Isaiah (chap. vi) when he was favored with a view of the divine glory says: "woe is me, for I am of unclean lips, I dwell in the midst of a people of unclean lips" A substitution by man is most distinctly contradicted also in Micah 6. 6—8 Ps. 49 8—10: "No brother can redeem his brother, no man can give to God a ransom for another. So precious is the ransom of their souls, that he must wait forever, even though he should live forever and not see the grave." It is likewise contradicted by the passage, Ez 18 20: "the soul that sinneth it shall die; the son shall not bear the iniquity of the father, nor the father the iniquity of the son; but the righteousness of the righteous shall be upon him, and the unrighteousness of the unrighteous shall be upon him." Nor would it avail any thing here also, with Kimchi, to resort to the supposition, that the prophet only expresses the thoughts of the heathen, without giving them his approval. For the doctrine of the vicarious satisfaction is contained in the discourse of Jehovah no less, than in those verses in which the heathen are introduced as speaking.

We must however here enter into an examination of the passages, by which Gesenius l. c. p. 189 seq. endeavors to prove in opposition to De Wette, that the doctrine of a vicarious satisfaction by man is widely diffused elsewhere in the Old Testament, and deeply impressed on the Hebrew mode of thought. How little to the purpose, the passages are which he has cited has been thoroughly shown by Steudel l. c. I, p 37 seq. These passages are the following. "The guilt of the fathers is visited upon the children, Ex. 20 5." This however does not relate to substitution, for this does not consist in the circumstance, that another is punished at the same time with the guilty, but that he who has committed the sin is entirely freed from punishment, in consequence of its being assumed by another. This law however has a totally different object and import. It was intended to make the sensible impression of visible rewards and punishments yet deeper, by their extension to the descendants of the pious and the ungodly. All ancient legislators held it necessary to sustain their laws by the same means. On this subject Cicero says (ep. 12 ad Brutum ed. Ern 1774 t. III, p. 1155) "Nec vero me fugit, quam sit acerbum, parentium scelera filiorum poenis lui. Sed hoc praeclare legibus comparatum est, ut caritas liberorum amiciores parentes reipublicae redderet." Now as in other States the promulgation of this law was thought to be indispensably necessary for attaining the object of the State, we shall find it the more expedient in the theocracy, in proportion as its object was higher than that of all other States. "The punishment is inflicted on the posterity, when it had not taken place before, 2 Sam 21· 1—14."

Nearly the same holds good here also. The crime, which Saul had perpetrated upon the Gibeonites, had brought a plague upon the land of the Israelites, who had suffered it to remain unpunished. As the proper offender could no longer be punished, but the punishment must be inflicted in order to sustain the holiness of the law with the people, the descendants, who according to this law were also culpable, were punished, or the author of the crime was punished in them. It is sometimes unavoidable, that a part should suffer if the whole is to be preserved, which could be effected in the theocracy only by most strictly maintaining the sanctity of the law. There was here no substitution, even because it was not the author of the crime, but the people who had left it unpunished, who were freed from the penalty incurred. "David's sin in numbering the people, Jehovah caused to be expiated by a three days' pestilence, and the death of 7,000 people, 2 Sam. 24. 10—25." Here also there is nothing said of a vicarious satisfaction. The punishment was not voluntarily undergone, the people did not suffer innocently, for although in this particular instance, they had taken no part in the offence, still they could not complain of the punishment as unjust, because on account of their sinfulness in general in other respects, no punishment could be greater than they deserved. That David was not exempted from punishment through the punishment of the people is evident from his praying to God in deep distress, v. 17, rather to punish himself and his family. It was here also the object of the punishment inflicted on the people to promote the sacredness of the law and awaken reverence for the divine justice among a people, who, yet rude and carnal, must be led and kept in obedience by these outward chastisements, because they could not yet be influenced by love. " The sin of David with Bathsheba was expiated by the death of the child, 2 Sam. 12. 15—18." But this passage by no means proves the point. For Nathan had already announced forgiveness to David (comp. v. 13) before he foretold the death of the child; its death, therefore, cannot be regarded as vicarious, and indeed the loss of the child was so distressing to David (comp v. 22) that the suffering fell rather upon him, than the child. The reason why the child must die is given in the narrative itself, v. 14. Had David been entirely exempted from punishment, the enemies of the Lord would have accused God of partiality and taken occasion therefrom to blaspheme his name. The suffering of David also for the loss of the child, must aggravate his suffering for the cause of it, the sin he had committed. "Because Achan seized upon that which was consecrated, the whole army of Joshua was given up to the enemy, Josh 7 1." Here again we look in vain for substitution, for the transgressor himself was not saved from punishment, through the calamity, which was sent upon the people On the contrary, he was burnt with all his goods and his family. Comp. v. 15, 24 The punishment of the people was designed to make them zealous to extirpate from among them every crime and misdemeanor, the individual is strictly watched, when the whole body is made answerable for his actions. It was nothing more than a theocratic punishment, intended as a warning. "Even in Isaiah, chap. 65· 7, sinners are punished for the sins of their fathers, as well as their own." That there is here no substitution, which requires, along with a voluntary assumption, an entire freedom from guilt, is evident, even from what Jehovah says. "I will recompense your transgression and the transgression of your fathers together" The sense is no other than this · You, who are the more culpable for not having been led to repentance by the long-suffering of God, shall experience in full measure the punishment, which indeed your forefathers, whom you are in no respect behind in wickedness, have merited. "Still more to the one before us is the passage Dan 11 35, where the subject of discourse is the martyrdom of the pious in the religious persecutions, and it is said 'the pious will fall, in order to purify, cleanse, and sanctify those i. e the rest;' which can hardly be understood in any other way than as referring to their death as martyrs." But the sense of this passage is plainly no other, than that the example given by the pious, of self-denial, and a steadfastness in the faith of the fathers not to be shaken even by death, will exert a salutary influence upon the rest, and strengthen the wavering, a result confirmed by the history of all religious oppressions. "Among the Arabians also a very frequent proverbial expression is grounded upon this idea, فِدَاكَ نَفْسِى, *let my life be thy ransom;* and several similar sayings, show at least that the notion of a vicarious satisfaction was very familiar to the orientals, and hence passed over into the language itself" What these expressions have to do here, is hard to be conceived They plainly signify nothing further than "Thou art so dear to me, that I would willingly give up what I most love, my own life and the life of my father, if I could thereby rescue thee from impending danger."—This then is the result of our investigation: among all the passages cited by Gesenius, there is not one, which conveys the idea of a vicarious satisfaction effected by man for man. Besides, this idea is excluded by the doctrinal system of the Old Testament, and least of all can a vicarious satisfaction on the part of the people of Israel be the subject of discourse, since its essential requisites, their own innocence and the voluntary assumption of the suffering, were in their case entirely wanting.

d) The fourth characteristic also of the suffering subject, entire patience and devotedness to the will of God, belong not to the Israelitish people. How can it be said of the whole people that they have not opened their mouth to complain; when even the noblest and best of them poured out their sadness in complaints and imprecations? Comp Jer 20 7 seq 15. 10—21 Ps. 137 8, 9. Lam. 3 64—66. They must surely have been an entirely different people from the representations of the prophets, and particularly of Isaiah himself, if the prophet could give them this praise.

3 In this interpretation it is altogether arbitrarily assumed that v. 1—10 the heathen, or the foreign nations hitherto hostile to the Jews, are introduced as speaking. The heathen are never thus introduced without some intimation of it in what precedes and follows. And even were we not to hesitate on this account, how could they, or the prophet in their name, declare that it was the burden of their punishment, which oppressed the exiled Jews?

4. This hypothesis makes the groundless assumption, that the death and burial of the servant of God is to be referred only to the misfortunes and ruin of the same. It is indeed true, that (Ezek. xxxvii) the carrying away into the exile is represented under the figure of a death, and the deliverance from it under that of a resurrection (comp. also Isaiah 26 19); but there every thing shows that the discourse is to be understood only as figurative, while here there is not the slightest intimation of this.

5 It is contradicted by the parallel passages in which the servant of God is plainly distinguished from the people. Comp. chap 42 6 49 5, 6. 50 9

6 It renders a very unnatural interpretation of several verses necessary. Thus e. g chap 53 1 (comp the exposition), also v. 2, where, after Jarchi, Rosenmuller explains the words. "he grew up before him as a shoot and as a root out of a dry soil " 'priusquam ad hanc magnitudinem ascenderet, gens erat perquam humilis et ascendit e terra sicut surculus.' But this were an entirely unsuitable

figure, as the Israelites had certainly been prosperous in the beginning, and did not experience adversity till afterwards. Comp. Ps. 80: 9. Ez 19. 10—13 Jer. 2· 21

Compare the refutation of this hypothesis in Origen c. Celsum 1, 11 § 7 according to Mosheim. Hulsii nucleus prophetiae Lugd 1683, p. 672 seq. Jahn, app. Herm II, 40 seq Martini, Hansi, Steudel, Keller l. c., and others.

The interpretation, which makes the pious portion of the people the subject, need not detain us so long It has much resemblance to the one which refers the prophecy to the collective body of the prophets, and is liable to several of the objections immediately to be adduced against that hypothesis. Of the arguments which refute the interpretation that makes the whole people the subject, those under No. 1, 2, and 4, apply also, with some slight modifications, to the present exposition What may still be specially urged against it, is the following. The speakers, v. 1—9 represent themselves as entirely free from all suffering; they place themselves in contrast with that suffering servant of God, who has taken upon himself the suffering due to them. How could the godly portion of the people say this, when in the same captivity they participated in the unhappy lot of the ungodly? How could the suffering of the pious be vicarious for the ungodly, since they themselves suffered? That the ungodly enjoyed in the exile a comparatively better lot than the pious, is a groundless hypothesis It is contradicted by the example of a Daniel, of Esther and Mordecai, of Ezra, and the opulent Nehemiah, Neh 5· 14—19.

See in opposition to this exposition especially Jahn l. c and die Briefe uber Jes. LIII, in Vol. VI of Eichhorn's Bibl. In these last, another turn which has been given to the hypothesis, though properly deserving of no refutation, has been fully refuted. It supposes עֶבֶד יְהֹוָה to designate only the nobler part of the nation carried away by Nebuchadnezzar, who made expiation seventy years for the sins of their brethren and died, but afterwards returned in their posterity. On this occasion the author of the prophecy, one of the Jews left behind, presents and recommends them to his countrymen in Palestine, as their deliverers and sanctifiers. The principal arguments against this perfectly strange idea are the following.

1. That only the noblest and best of the people were carried away is contradicted by Ez. 20: 28, where it is said that the rebels and apostates from Jehovah should be separated and carried away,

and also by Jer. 39 9, 10, where it is said that only a mass of the lowest people were left behind. But it was precisely among the distinguished and great, as appears from the complaints of the prophets, that the corruption was peculiarly great, and hence the punishment fell, in an especial manner, upon them Comp 2 Chron 36 14 seq. 2 The Israelites who were left in Palestine fled to Egypt, Jer. chap. 43 4—8. 44. 1, 2. 2 Kings 25 56. Consequently no settled inhabitants remained in the country. Palestine became a wild land of Nomades. Nowhere is there an intimation, that the returning exiles found a part of the former inhabitants still in the land These arguments are so conclusive, that we scarcely need to call the attention further to the fact, that this hypothesis can be carried out only by many distortions of the text, by erroneously assuming that Isaiah was not the writer, etc.

We come now to the last hypothesis to be examined, the idea of those who regard the *collectivum* of the prophets as the object of the prophecy, and suppose it to contain a sort of *apotheosis* of the prophetic order The prophets, who even before the exile had much to suffer, were exposed during that period to still greater contempt and derision ; to which might be added, contempt and derision on the part of the heathen Hence may be explained, it is said, the apology of the prophetic order for themselves, as well as the origin of such splendid and enthusiastic hopes as we find here and in the parallel passages chap XLII etc. Against this hypothesis we offer the following remarks.

1 The supposition of such a personification of the prophetic order rests upon arguments which prove nothing. This will be evident from an examination of the passages to which its defenders appeal. The first of these is chap 44 26, where Jehovah says מֵקִים דְּבַר עַבְדּוֹ וַעֲצַת מַלְאָכָיו יַשְׁלִים "I am he who verifies the word of his servant, and fulfils the prophecy of his messengers" The parallel מַלְאָכָיו is supposed to indicate that עֶבֶד stands collectively. But there is absolutely no reason to think that there is here a synonymous, and not rather a synthetic parallelism. The latter is indeed indicated by the second member of the verse "who says of Jerusalem, she shall be inhabited, and of the cities of Judah, they shall be built again," where Jerusalem and the cities of Judah constitute in like manner not a synonymous but a synthetic parallelism (Moller, de Authentia or Jes c. 40—66 p 184) By 'the servant of Jehovah' Isaiah himself is to be understood, as in chap. 20 3. What he says

of himself in the first member, he says in the second in respect to all prophets of the true God. The second, adduced only by De Wette, and passed over by Gesenius as not affording proof, is chap. 59: 21: "And I make such a covenant with them, saith the Lord, my Spirit which is with thee, and my words which I have put in thy mouth, shall not depart from thy mouth, nor from the mouth of thy seed and thy seed's seed, saith the Lord, from henceforth to eternity." This is said to be equivalent to : "quae tu spiritus mei afflatu protulisti, ea ab omnibus seriorum temporum prophetis, qui sunt quasi filii illius prophetae, repetentur." Even granting this exposition to be correct, the passage would still fail of proving a personification of the prophetic order. But Rosenmuller has justly observed in opposition to it, after the example of the best interpreters: "Non prophetam, ut Hieronymus et alii existimarunt, alloquitur, sed populum Hebraeum, uti et verba praemissa et quae sequuntur clarissime ostendunt. Est autem hic personarum enallage, quum enim in tertia plur. persona (אתם) loqui coepisset vates, pergit in persona secunda singularis, oratione ad populum ipsum directa." Comp. 32: 2. All the promises which precede and follow relate to the whole community; and it were a singular leap, if the prophet first announced a covenant to be established with this community, and then, in assigning the object of it, should suddenly pass over to the mercies which would be conferred, not upon the people, but the prophetic order. — It is unnecessary to dwell on chap 53: 8, since the argument drawn from לָמוֹ has already been refuted. But this hypothesis is not only incapable of being proved, but altogether improbable. It rests on the entirely erroneous view that the prophets formed a corporation by themselves. The difference between them and the priests consisted precisely in this, that the latter formed an exclusive order which constantly supplied its own members, while the call to the prophetic office depended solely on the will of Jehovah, and the relation of every prophet was to him, and not to the remaining prophets. The objection, which has been adduced against the hypothesis of the Jewish people being the subject under No 1, applies therefore with still greater force in this case; the defenders of that hypothesis might appeal to passages where the Jews appear as an individual, but there are none where the prophets are so represented

2. But this opinion appears most untenable if we take the position of its defenders, and deny the genuineness of the second part. Immediately after the Babylonish exile the prophetic order ceased;

Jewish tradition is unanimous in giving Haggai, Zechariah, and Malachi as the last of the prophets, and prophecy as included among the things which were wanting to the second temple. The communication of the prophetic spirit anew is not expected till a future time. All Jewish chronologists make the cessation of the prophetic office a chronological epoch, and begin with it a new era, as is done even in 1 Macc 9 27, with which comp. 4· 46. 14 41 Numerous passages from the Talmud and other Jewish writings are collected in Knibbe, Historie der Propheten ubers. von Freytag. Bern 1709 p. 347 seq. und in Joh Smith's dissertatio de prophetia et prophetis c. 12, also reprinted at the end of the Comm. von Clericus zu den Propheten Amsterd 1731 fol. p XXVI. Now, even leaving entirely out of view the true idea of a prophet, it is difficult to conceive how the prophet could speak of a great corporation of the prophets, at a time when there were only a few of them still in existence, who, in respect to the power, the abundance and the purity of the spirit were far inferior to those of more ancient times It is difficult to imagine how the prophet could cherish the enthusiastic hope, that they, whose authority even before the exile was sunk so low among the people, would attain to such glory, spread the true religion over the whole earth, and even, as the defenders of this hypothesis maintain, live to enjoy a worldly triumph

3. Of the arguments which have been advanced against the explanation which makes the Jewish people the subject, those under No. 2 and 4 are applicable also to this Never do we find an example, where prophets freely submitted to suffering in the hope of thereby delivering others from sin. On the contrary, when sufferings are inflicted upon them, they always declare that heavy divine punishment should fall upon the authors of their distress. Comp. e. g. Jer. 20: 12 That they were very far from regarding themselves as entirely free from sin and guilt, we have already seen.

4. The servant of God can be no other than he who forms the object of the parallel prophecies, chap. XLII, etc. But in these still more occurs which can by no means belong to the prophetic order. Thus in chap 49 3, the servant of God is called Israel, a difficulty, which Gesenius knows of no other method to remove, than that of declaring the word spurious in opposition to the manuscripts and translations

5 The prophet regards himself, v 2, etc as a different person from the servant of God, and contrasts himself with him. He in-

cludes himself among the people. Now, how could the prophet say, that he took part in despising the prophetic order, that he endured his sufferings for himself, and regarded himself as one smitten of God, etc? Gesenius appeals l. c. p. 159 to chap 59 9—13, where the prophet numbers himself with the people and also calls their sins his own. So also, 42. 24. But this is certainly a different case. The prophet, like every other member of the people, had a real part in their sins. Comp. Dan. 9. 5, etc. But how could he take part in the contempt, etc of his own order? How could the vicarious sufferings, in which he himself participated, be borne for him?

6. The sufferings of the prophets in the exile were the same as those of the people. That the former were by no means chiefly oppressed by the heathen appears from the example of Jeremiah. After the capture of the city, Nebuchadnezzar showed him great respect, and gave him the choice of his place of residence. Comp. Jer. 39: 11, etc. How then could the people despise them, how believe them to be smitten of God?

7 The sufferings of the prophets could not be regarded as instead of the sufferings of the ungodly part of the people; for the latter suffered no less than the former.

8. According to this hypothesis, the prophets indulged the hope, that they should be the rulers of the restored and flourishing State, and celebrate worldly triumphs. To say nothing of the folly of this hope, it was entirely opposed to the destination of the prophetic order. The government, in the theocracy, was ever assigned to the posterity of David by divine appointment. Consequently, had the prophets laid claim to it, they would have rebelled against God, whose rights it was their duty to defend. The prophets were extraordinary messengers of God, the invisible head of the theocracy, called to teach, reprove, warn, and console, heralds of peace and righteousness to an apostate people. That they remained true to this destination, is proved by the whole history of the Israelites.

9. But should we, as indeed we are obliged to do, understand figuratively what is said of the servant of God, and find in the passage spiritual instead of worldly triumphs, still it would not be applicable to the prophetic order. It would be against the analogy of all other prophecies respecting the conversion of the heathen, if the prophets here attributed it to themselves. Nowhere do we find an example of the prophets mistaking their destination to operate only on the covenant people; nowhere the mention of an attempt on their part

to extend their agency to the heathen nations. Never do they look to themselves for the accomplishment of their high hopes in reference to the future, but always to the Messiah alone. They are so little influenced by prejudices in favor of their order, they give themselves up so entirely to the instructions of the Holy Spirit, that they even repeatedly announce, that in Messianic times the necessity for the prophetic order will entirely cease, since all will then be immediately taught of God. Comp e. g. Joel chap 3. Isaiah 54. 13. 59. 21. 4 3. 11: 9 Ez. 11: 19. 36 27. Jer 31. 33

10. It is an unnatural assumption of these interpreters, that the death and burial relates to one portion of the prophetic order, the glorification on the contrary to those who sinned, since it is one and the same subject, who suffers, dies and is glorified.

The interpretation, therefore, which rests on the infallible testimony of the New Testament, is here also demonstrated by internal and external arguments, to be the true one in opposition to all who reject this testimony. If now the ground which produced these devious interpretations be once removed, there will be as little necessity for a detailed refutation of them, as there is that the interpreter should still notice the perverse interpretations of the Socinians. We conclude with the words of Storr: "Rideant alii tantum regem, ridet ille majori jure homunciones, quos sibi, si et hoc vaticinium et alia multa veritatis argumenta serio meditari pertinaciter nolint, nihilo secius, at conterendos, datos esse novit (Ps 2). Utinam ii saltem, qui semen Christi salutari volunt, in rectam viam se reduci et peccato, quod cum summa patentia dudum Christus portavit, liberari paterentur, sicque justitiae vivere, vestigiis domini insistere et doctrinae ejus efficaciam, quam multi jam experti sunt, suo quoque exemplo docere discerent"

END.

ERRATA AND EMENDATA

Page.
28, line 15 from top, after he, insert, who was.
30, " 7 " bottom, for their, read, these
34, " 10 " " for Samuel, " the Sammael
38, " 1 " " dele is.
39, " 9 " top, for forms, read, terms
43, " 13 " bottom, for had, " was
49, " 7 " " for we, read, he
51, " 5 " top, " forced, " freed
53, " 15 " bottom, for this Messiah, read, the Messiah
56, " 8 " top, for upon, read from
56, " 4 " bottom, had, read, have
75, " 5 " " for descendants, read, descendant
79, " 7 " bottom, for preserve, read, receive
91, " 5 " " for interpreted, read, interrupted
93, " 12 " " dele and, before v 8.
100, " 18 " top, for Jarchi's remarks exemplify, read, Jarchi remarks expressly
102, " 3 " top, for at last, read, lastly
" " 23 " " for the sun, etc, " the sun burns the roots, so that all dries up
104, " 14 " top, for now, read, won.
106 " 14 " " after great, insert, king.
122, " 17 " bottom, for usual, read, unusual
" " 1 " " " this life, " his life
136, " 11 " top, for insufficient, " sufficient
138 " 16 " " " cut, read, cast.
143, " 2 " bottom, for words, read, events.
146, " 17 " top, for actually, read, surely
152, " 10 " " before a, insert, as
" " 11 " " for revelation, read, revelations
167, " 1 " " " opposers " oppressors
200, " 10 " " " bind it, read, bind it to God.
203, " 9 " bottom, dele the semicolon after Socinians, and insert it after Arminius.
205, " 13 " top, for ultimately, read, intimately.

Page
207, line 20 from top, for repeat, read, repeat.
210, " 17 " " after leprosy, insert, of the Messiah
215, " 3 " dele the, before atoning and insert, no
225, " 10 " bottom, for Jews, read, seers.
231, " 13 " " for verses, read, words
232, " 3 " " " redemption read representation.
233, " 11 " top, for with care read with ease
241, " 7 " " after do insert, not
246, " 15 " " for opposer, read, opposers
" " 16 " " " theories, " their theory
247, " 3 " bottom, for richness, read, sickness
253, " 13 " top, for assert, read, can scarcely conceive how he can represent,
254, " 3 " top, insert or, after prediction.
256, " 17 " " dele and, before since
301, " 15 " bottom, for this, read, the
317, " 5 " top, for produce, read, procure.
327, " 21 " " " this, read, his.
331, " 20 " " " insert " before If
" " 12 " bottom, for seems, read, serves
333, " 6 " " for his, read, this
" " 8 " " " then, " these
368, " 13 " " " successively, read necessarily
371, " 13 " top, for common, read, proper
384, " 10 " bottom, for a Jew, read, a few
388, " 17 " " for hope, read scope
396, " 20 " " dele nearer, and insert, the nearer, after beholds
404, " 11 " top, for thev, read, there
424, " 1 " bottom, insert of his people, after deliverance of
460, " 18 " top, for favorable, read, parallel

CPSIA information can be obtained at www.ICGtesting.com
Printed in the USA
LVOW03s1614030314

375862LV00008B/324/P